Risk in the Global Real Estate Market

Founded in 1807, John Wiley & Sons is the oldest independent publishing company in the United States. With offices in North America, Europe, Australia and Asia, Wiley is globally committed to developing and marketing print and electronic products and services for our customers' professional and personal knowledge and understanding.

The Wiley Finance series contains books written specifically for finance and investment professionals as well as sophisticated individual investors and their financial advisors. Book topics range from portfolio management to e-commerce, risk management, financial engineering, valuation and financial instrument analysis, as well as much more.

For a list of available titles, visit our web site at www.WileyFinance.com.

Risk in the Global Real Estate Market

International Risk Regulation, Mechanism Design, Foreclosures, Title Systems, and REITs

MICHAEL C. I. NWOGUGU

WILEY

John Wiley & Sons, Inc.

Published by John Wiley & Sons, Inc., Hoboken, New Jersey.
Published simultaneously in Canada.

Library of Congress Cataloging-in-Publication Data:

Nwogugu, Michael C. I.
Risk in the global real estate market : international risk regulation, mechanism design, foreclosures, title systems and REITs / Michael C.I. Nwogugu.
p. cm. – (Wiley finance)
Includes bibliographical references and index.
ISBN 978-1-118-01135-5 (cloth); ISBN 978-1-118-01135-5 (ebk);
ISBN 978-1-118-01135-5 (ebk); ISBN 978-1-118-01135-5 (ebk)
1. Real estate business. 2. Risk. 3. Mortgages. 4. Foreclosure. 5. Real estate investment trusts. I. Title.
HD1375.N96 2011
332.63′244–dc23

2011032162

Printed in the United States of America.

10 9 8 7 6 5 4 3 2 1

Risk in the Global Real Estate Market

This book is dedicated to my paternal grandparents,
Mr. and Mrs. Gabriel O. Nwogugu,
and my maternal grandparents,
Bishop and Mrs. L. M. Uzodike

Contents

Preface

The purpose of this book is to present a long overdue and multi-faceted critique of the main elements of global real estate markets and generally accepted risk management approaches within the context of constitutional economics, and to introduce new mortgage-alternatives products that solve some of the existing problems. Constitutional economics is almost entirely neglected in modern academic real estate analysis, fiscal policy, and monetary policy, even though it has substantial macroeconomic implications.

The global financial crisis has exposed many weaknesses in financial markets' (especially real estate and fixed income markets) monetary policy and regulation in many countries. More than 110 countries created new constitutions or substantially amended their constitutions between 1990 and 2010, with many of the new constitutions based on U.S.- and U.K.-style constitutions. It is now clear that the major distinguishing factors between countries that were affected by the global financial crisis of 2007–2011 and those that were relatively insulated included the size of their national mortgage markets, the existence of special constitutional courts, prevalence of special mortgage statutes (such as deficiency judgment statutes) and types of mortgage products, lack of culture of compliance, efficiency of legal processes (e.g., foreclosures), and underwriting quality. However, despite greater international coordination and new laws that were enacted during the past three years, global risk regulation remains highly ineffective as manifested by the recent failure of government stimulus programs and government-sponsored risk-reduction programs in many developed and third-world countries.

This book is unique because:

- It explains how constitutions affect risk regulation, fiscal policies, monetary policy, and the economics of real estate transactions.
- It introduces new theories of "takings"—in most common law and commonwealth countries, takings significantly affects land policy, urban development policy, property values, and tax revenues.
- It explains why mortgages, foreclosures, title systems, asset securitization, and REITs are unconstitutional.

- It explains how constitutions and risk regulations affect economic models and real estate transactions.
- It explains the effects of preemption and federalism on risk regulation, risk management, and real estate transactions.
- It introduces economic psychology theories that relate to risk and constitutional economics.
- It explains the institutional context within which real estate and risk management function.

WHO THIS BOOK IS FOR

The scope of this book is international, and the issues raised are especially relevant to countries that are developing their constitutions and/or real estate markets and capital markets.

This book is written for management consultants; investment professionals, research analysts, and portfolio managers; corporate governance professionals; central bankers; urban development professionals; economists and government regulators; real estate and banking professionals; lawyers; and senior-undergrad (fourth-year undergraduate), as well as PhD and master's degree students.

WHAT THIS BOOK COVERS

Chapter 1, Regulation and Constitutional Torts, explains the nature of constitutional torts within the context of the commonalities among constitutions of different countries. It is noteworthy that most commonwealth countries "borrowed" their constitutions from England, and during the past 20 years, more than 70 countries have either enacted new constitutions that are based on the U.S. Constitution or have amended their constitutions to be similar to the U.S. Constitution. The chapter also introduces federalism and preemption and associated regulatory arbitrage, which are subsequently shown to have significant economic and behavioral effects on parties to mortgages, foreclosures, titles systems, and asset securitization transactions, particularly in countries that have federal systems of government. The chapter explains the traditional tests for constitutionality (which are similar across most common law countries). The chapter introduces the *theory of substantial inducement* as an alternative to the state action requirement in constitutional law. "Quasi-constitutions" and social capital are also explained as important elements of regulation of transactions and enforcement of statutes.

Mechanism Design is a growing area of economics, which, unfortunately, has not been applied in a practical manner to many modern socioeconomic problems. Moreover, most of the research on mechanism design has been theoretical work, and not practical applications. Chapter 2, A Critique of Mechanism Design, surveys the literature and critiques of existing academic thought on mechanism design. Some of the criticism and issues discussed are relevant to the design of mortgage markets, alternatives to foreclosures, and mortgage-alternative products.

While traditional mortgages are very similar across most countries, the regulation and organization of mortgage markets has almost completely omitted the psychological effects and social problems caused by mortgages and foreclosures, which have become serious public health problems in many countries. Chapter 3, on public health, surveys recent empirical and theoretical research based on data/samples from various countries that conclusively show that mortgages and foreclosures cause long-term mental health problems for individuals and households (and employees of lenders); and that governments have not addressed these issues at all or sufficiently in terms of public health interventions and/or changes in mortgage/foreclosure regulations and the design of mortgage products. The consequences of these mental health problems are manifested in higher crime rates, divorces, personal bankruptcies, and individual productivity losses, all of which have adverse multiplier psychological effects on other individuals and groups. It is very likely that these mental health problems will continue because the same causal factors and choice patterns are very likely to continue in the future.

During 2003 to 2010 the global mortgage and housing markets experienced substantial structural changes and shocks. Chapter 4, on psychological factors inherent in housing demand and mortgage demand, analyzes key events during this period, and shows that some of the socioeconomic trends pertaining to mortgages and housing were associated with both psychological effects and causes. This chapter also introduces the testable hypothesis of psychological biases and effects that can explain changes in housing demand and mortgage demand. The implication is that all house-price forecasting models are inaccurate because they don't incorporate these trends or psychological biases/effects.

Chapter 5, Behavioral Biases in Property Taxation and Property Appraisal, introduces new theories and biases inherent in the property appraisal process and the property taxation process, which may affect mortgage market dynamics and demand for real estate. Again, the resulting implication is that property-price forecasting models are inaccurate because they don't incorporate these psychological biases/effects.

Foreclosures are quite common in most countries and the actual procedures are patterned after the British- and U.S.-type foreclosures. The detrimental effects of foreclosures have been extensively documented in many academic and practitioner journals and books—but there has been no detailed analysis of the constitutionality of foreclosures. Chapter 6 fills that gap, and shows why foreclosures are unconstitutional. New theories of takings are introduced. The chapter also shows how foreclosures reduce the effectiveness of central banks' monetary policies.

Preemption remains a major element of constitutional analysis—in most countries, federal laws (and or constitutions) often conflict with state statutes, which causes substantial macroeconomic and microeconomic problems for governments, societies, and households. In some countries (such as the United States), bankruptcy codes conflict with mortgage statutes. Although the U.S. Supreme Court has established some standards for preemption, these standards don't address many elements of modern commerce and complexity. Chapter 7, on the constitutionality of the bankruptcy codes' preemption of mortgage statutes, explains the economic ramifications of such preemption and the conditions under which it increases social welfare.

Chapter 8, Mortgages and Deeds of Trust, explains why elements of traditional mortgages (such as right of redemption, anti-deficiency statutes, anti-prepayment penalty statutes, and so on) are unconstitutional. This chapter also introduces new theories of takings and explains how mortgages drastically reduce the effectiveness of central banks' monetary policies and governments' quasi-fiscal policies, and also distorts (reduces low-cost matching) the marriage market and the job markets.

The subprime mortgage markets in most countries have similar characteristics in terms of the timing and magnitude of bubbles and shocks. Chapter 9, on subprime mortgages, explains why subprime mortgages are unconstitutional (equal protection, speech, and so on) and highly detrimental to social welfare.

Property Title systems are the backbone of property transactions, and are critical for perfection of security interests and verification. Unfortunately, the two main types of property title systems (the Torrens system and the recording system) are unconstitutional. Chapter 10 on title systems explains the economic ramifications of the unconstitutionality of title systems and introduces new theories of takings.

REITs have been introduced in many countries despite the many inherent problems in the REIT structure. Ernst & Young (2010), the European Public REIT Association (2010), and Allens Arthur Robinson (2009) provided a comparison of characteristics of REITs in various countries—which confirm that REITs in most countries are very similar to U.S. REITs. Nwogugu (2007, 2008a, 2008b) explained the corporate governance and securities law problems caused by the REIT format. Chapter 11 on REITs explains how REITs are unconstitutional.

Until the U.S. asset-backed securities (ABS) markets collapsed in 2008, asset securitization was a major source of financing for many companies in many countries. Although the literature on ABS and securitization is extensive, very few articles have addressed the legality and constitutionality of asset securitization. Nwogugu (2008c, 2008d, 2009) showed that asset securitization is unconstitutional and violates usury statutes, fraud statutes, antitrust laws, and civil RICO laws (U.S.). Chapter 12 on asset securitization extends Nwogugu (2009), and explains how securitization is not only unconstitutional, but also substantially reduces the effectiveness of central banks' monetary policies.

Chapters 13 through 15 on the CIS Region, the CEE (Central and Eastern Europe) Region, and China: (1) introduce the elements of a proposed new mortgage-alternatives market for China and CIS/CEE countries; (2) explain why asset liability management (ALM) is wrong and is an obstacle to lending in both developed and developing countries; and (3) introduce new mortgage-alternative products for the China and CIS/CEE markets that address many of the problems inherent in traditional mortgages, alternative mortgages, title systems, and foreclosures. While ALM has remained a staple of modern banking, modified duration and convexity are wrong, and perceived interest rate risk is often overestimated and can be a framing effect. Perceived interest rate risk ranks below the median among other risks that lenders face (such as liquidity risk, documentation/legal risk, etc.) in terms of severity.

There is a companion web site for this book that lists the supporting court cases and some other related articles. The web address is www.wiley.com.go/nwogugu.

Michael C. I. Nwogugu
July 2011

REFERENCES

Allens Arthur Robinson. 2009. Asia-Pacific REIT Survey. April 2009. Available at www.trust.com.au/Assets/Files/TA_REIT_Survey%202009.pdf.

Ernst & Young. 2010. Global Real Estate Investment Trust Report 2010: Against all odds. Available at: www.ernstandyoung.ch/Publication/vwLUAssets/Global_Real_Estate_Investment_Trust_Report_2010_Against_all_odds/$FILE/EY_Global_REIT_report_2010_Against_all_odds.pdf.

European Public REIT Association. September 2010. EPRA Global REIT Survey 2010.

Nwogugu, M. 2007. Some securities law problems inherent in REITs. *Journal of International Banking Law & Regulation* 22 (11): 594–602.

Nwogugu, M. 2008a. Some corporate governance problems pertaining to REITs—Part one. *Journal of International Banking Law & Regulation* 23 (2): 71–89.
Nwogugu, M. 2008b. Some corporate governance problems pertaining to REITs—Part two. *Journal of International Banking Law & Regulation* 23 (3): 142–162.
Nwogugu, M. 2008c. Securitization is illegal: Some antitrust, usury, RICO, and tax issues. *Journal of International Banking Law & Regulation.*
Nwogugu, M. 2008d. Illegality of securitization, bankruptcy issues and theories of securitization. *Journal of International Banking Law & Regulation.*
Nwogugu, M. 2009. Economic policy and the constitutionality of asset securitization. *International Company & Commercial Law Review* 20 (7): 245–254.

Risk in the Global Real Estate Market

CHAPTER 1

Regulation and Constitutional Torts

Constitutional torts are increasingly relevant in the analysis of mortgages/foreclosures, title systems, real estate investment trusts (REITs), and securitization because of the significant regulation of and increasing government intervention in capital markets and financial institutions—as manifested by the significant government intervention in global mortgage markets, the U.S. government's takeover of Fannie Mae and Freddie Mac (both account for more than 50 percent of residential mortgages in the United States), and government bailouts of banks and insurance companies in many countries in Europe and Asia. Also, increasing outsourcing of services by government agencies has created more grounds for constitutional tort claims.

In *Monroe v. Pape* (U.S. 1961) and in *Bivens v. Six Unknown Named Agents of the Federal Bureau of Narcotics* (U.S. 1971), the U.S. Supreme Court announced that federal officials can be sued personally for money damages for the alleged violation of constitutional rights that arise from official acts. These two cases have spawned a line of research on constitutional torts, which is well developed but does not cover constitutional law and socioeconomic problems inherent in mortgages, land titles, REITs, asset securitization, and foreclosure processes. The focus in this book is on the development of new constitutional tort theories and review of existing constitutional tort theories that are applicable to the economics and regulation of mortgages, land title systems, securitization, REITs, and foreclosures. Detailed analysis of some constitutional tort court cases are addressed in the books and journal articles cited herein. Constitutional tort theories have not changed significantly during the past 15 years, and most of the related litigation revolves around immunity of the government and government employees, special tort statutes (such as Section 1983 in the United States), and limitation of damages.

In the United States, mortgages, title systems, and foreclosures are regulated mostly by state laws, although there are a few federal regulations—this is somewhat similar to the European Union regulatory scheme and raises questions about federalism and inefficiency of statutes because many real estate transactions involve interstate commerce. The unconstitutionality of state mortgage/real estate laws is intricately intertwined with economic factors, all of which have substantial (multitrillion-dollar/euro) economic effects. However, it appears that economic implications were not major considerations when the federal or state constitutions of many countries were drafted or revised, and interpretations of constitutions by most courts also do not seem to consider socioeconomic consequences.

The existing literature on risk regulation for mortgages and foreclosures, REITs, title systems, and securitization is well developed but does not address the economic effects of constitutions or public health issues. The net result is that most of the economic models of mortgage default risk, housing tenure/demand, and securitization are misspecified because they do not incorporate the economic effects of constitutional torts on mortgage/foreclosure laws and title systems.

FEDERALISM, PREEMPTION, AND RISK

Federalism and preemption are established legal principles that have substantial impact on risk regulation, transaction costs and monitoring costs, and the efficiency of mortgages/foreclosures, title systems, REITs, and securitization in most countries. Modern banking is now almost inseparable from insurance, and many non-insurance entities now provide direct or indirect insurance products. Banks and nonbank entities that trade derivatives provide insurance (entities that provide third-party guarantees are essentially providing insurance). Furthermore, like the U.S. banking industry, the U.S. insurance industry has a dual regulatory regime because states regulate insurance companies. This raises the issues and problems of optimal federalism and preemption.

The following examples illustrate some of the consequences of federalism. Unlike the German *Grundgesetz* (constitution) and the *Canadian Constitution Act*, the U.S. Constitution does not explicitly grant the U.S. federal government powers over banking. However, the Commerce Clause and the Supremacy Clause of the U.S. Constitution implicitly grant the U.S. federal government the powers to regulate banking and to preempt state banking laws. In the United States, banks are regulated by both state governments and the U.S. federal government. The U.S. Constitution grants the federal government the power to "coin money" and "regulate the value thereof" (U.S. Const. art. I, § 8, cl. 5). Another major difference is that most western and eastern European countries have "federal constitutional courts" that do not exist in the United States. These constitutional courts have limited the scope of business transactions in Europe, and perhaps limited the extent of the damage from the global financial crisis of 2007 to 2010. Although most U.S. states have antideficiency judgment statutes, federal Canadian laws permit deficiency judgments in all Canadian states, and this has greatly reduced the occurrence of mortgage defaults and foreclosures in Canada (Canada had much less exposure to the global financial crisis of 2007 to 2009 than the United States and some western European countries). In the United States, insurance and reinsurance companies are formally regulated by the state governments (which establish capital requirements) and are also informally regulated by the National Association of Insurance Commissioner (NAIC; a private entity), unlike the European Union, where the insurance industry has been deregulated and insurance companies set their own capital requirement standards. Insurance companies were a major cause of the subprime crisis and the global financial crisis because they insured securities, assets, and loans; are major derivatives traders; and provided guarantees. AIG became insolvent and was taken over by the U.S. government. Most of the risks in the banking sector are transferred to the insurance sector through one of the following ways:

- Derivatives contracts.
- Insurance of loans and leases.
- Insurance of performance or projects.
- Insurance of assets.
- Loan trading.
- Portfolio securitization.
- Special securities, such as catastrophe bonds and currency-linked bonds.
- Reinsurance of captive insurance subsidiaries of banks.
- Insurance securitization.
- Purchase of debt and preferred stock of banks.

Banks differ from insurance companies in various ways (CEA, June 2010), and the following distinguishing factors can facilitate or hamper risk regulation:

- Funding and balance-sheet structure, types of investments and assets, sources of funding, duration of assets and liabilities.
- Type of ownership and shareholders.
- Liquidity risk.

- Risk ownership and transparency.
- Interconnectedness with other financial institutions.
- Ability to participate directly or indirectly in reinsurance (some may argue that loan trading is a form of reinsurance).
- Volatility of business operations.
- The nature of the entity's asset-liability management and investment management.
- Macroeconomic role.
- Risk exposure at the institutional level.
- Systemic risk exposure.

Federalism is a critical element of enforcement of risk regulations. The literature on federalism is extensive and addresses many issues, but does not analyze constitutional torts in detail within the context of mortgages and foreclosures. The adverse effects of sub-optimal federalism and the dual banking system in the United States are obvious. For example, from 2005 to 2009, more than 60 percent of subprime lenders were state-chartered local banks that operated in only one state. In the United States, mortgage brokers and real estate brokers are licensed and regulated at the state level and they perform quasi-banking functions even though they do not have capital to lend—they were and remain the primary borrower contact for mortgages, and they collect data from prospective borrowers, run credit checks, and advise borrowers about appropriate lenders, electronically send loan applications to lenders for fulfillment, and influence or participate in negotiating loan terms. During 2005 to 2009, most (at least 70 percent) of the mortgage brokers and real estate brokers in each state operated in only one state and were not subject to the same stringent banking regulations as banks. Hence, this "state-broker-intervention" was a major cause of the subprime problems in the United States.

Khalil (2007) compared federalism in the United States and German banking industries and described the effect of the German Constitution on banking. In the United States and Europe, the lack of fiscal federalism for matters pertaining to mortgages, foreclosures, title systems, and REITs exacerbates risk and increases transaction costs, monitoring costs, and enforcement costs in the following ways:

- It permits and facilitates costly regulatory arbitrage among the states (or countries).
- It reduces governments' abilities to monitor the true risks of transactions.
- It precludes "learning effects"—because best practices in any state can be implemented in only that state/jurisdiction, and ongoing

regulatory competition among states reduces the incentives to share ideas.

- Lack of "complete" or optimal federalism increases taxes because it substantially increases the cost of government and also creates costly uncertainty (all of which are funded by higher taxes).

On the other hand, the related issue of preemption of statutes also increases risk. In the United States and the European Union, preemption has been a major cause of the failure of banking regulations because there is a redundant and duplicitous dual regulatory structure—there are federal banking laws and each state has its own banking laws (the same dual regulatory scheme exists in the European Union, where various countries have their own banking laws and the European Union has a "federal" regulatory scheme). In the United States, the state banking laws govern mortgages, foreclosures, and title systems, while the federal banking laws do not cover these three areas in detail. Preemption and limited federalism of the type that exists in the United States and the European Union causes costly uncertainty and costly state verification because under the threat of preemption, parties incorporate litigation costs and additional transaction costs, which distorts decision-making processes and incentive systems. This type of preemption and limited federalism also causes regulatory arbitrage—many mortgage brokers, savings banks, and community banks in the United States operate in only a few states (two to four adjacent states) and can regularly shift operations and allocate resources among states in order to circumvent many state and federal banking regulations. Many mortgage brokers, real estate brokers, savings banks, and community banks in the United States operate in only one state and can effectively circumvent many federal banking regulations. Preemption and suboptimal federalism also cause harmful regulatory competition among states. Although lending processes in the United States and the European Union are automated, given that there is still substantial human input in the lending process (data collection, data verification, classification of data, etc.), the harmful effects of preemption and suboptimal federalism permeate the incentive/compensation systems of banks and financial institutions, which in turn increases the bankruptcy risk of these organizations.

Preemption is a by-product and result of "inadequate" or suboptimal federalism. Hence, in countries where there are heterogeneous populations or cultures that insist on some form of regional independence, there may be optimal levels of federalism that promote economic development and reduce risk in transactions. However, given the global financial crisis, it is likely that such limited federalism will not be beneficial in the realm of mortgages, foreclosures, REITs, and title systems. It is impossible to determine the accurate "optimal" amount federalism (other than full federalism) in a country like the United States or the European Union even with constitutional amendments, because (1) the nature of the U.S. Constitution and the European Union treaty grants subsidiary states certain rights; (2) even if there were constitutional amendments, regulatory competition among states will likely prevail—states will likely amend their own constitutions and/or enact mortgage/banking laws that will provide incentives for certain types of banking activities; and (3) the lending process involves other regulated entities (insurance companies, mortgage brokers, real estate brokers), and without federal statutes, states can always enact their own laws to encourage patterns of transactions.

THE RESTORING AMERICAN FINANCIAL STABILITY ACT OF 2010 (RAFSA)

In July 2010 the U.S. Congress enacted the Restoring American Financial Stability Act of 2010 (RAFSA), which consists of several individual distinct statutes and substantially changes the nature and effects of federalism and preemption in the United States—the RAFSA grants more powers to the federal government to regulate more financial services, but because the statute leaves critical details up to the U.S. SEC and the U.S. Federal Reserve system, sections of the RAFSA may be challenged in court on constitutional grounds as void for vagueness. Some researchers have questioned the criminal law provisions in the RAFSA, and the extent of regulations of both the size of banks and trading of derivatives (two critical issues that led to the global financial crisis).

Nwogugu provides a more detailed critique of RAFSA. The U.S. government has a duty to enact risk regulations and statutes that will reduce bankruptcy risk and contagion. Under the state-action and constitutional tort theories, the failure of RAFSA to enact the earlier mentioned regulations constitutes actionable constitutional torts. The RAFSA is notable because it is the first set of statutes anywhere that has attempted to address risk regulation comprehensively—the RAFSA is critiqued in more detail in *Constitutional Economics of Institutions in International Risk Regulation* (Michael Nwogugu, unpublished manuscript).

THE EXISTING "TESTS" FOR UNCONSTITUTIONALITY

The common trend among the court decisions and constitutional theories in the United States, Asia, Latin America, and the European Union is that none of them use or consider *"federal" risk-based tests* of unconstitutionality, and all of them follow the "traditional tests" for constitutionality, which are woefully inadequate to handle the complexities of modern interconnected international financial systems. The importance of an efficient financial system has become very clear—without it, sufficient basic services and necessities (e.g., hospitals/health care, schools, housing, transportation, food) will not be available or affordable.

Currently, traditional tests in constitutional analysis focus on the following core elements: the "balancing-of-interests" test, the "discriminatory classifications" tests, the "burden-on-interstate-commerce" test, the "economic harm" test, the "state-action" requirement, the Penn-Central three-pronged tests, and the "Agins" tests (whether specific statutes or conduct advances or impedes "special interests" or "government interests"). These tests do not consider elements of risk, and are insufficient in today's economy (many academicians have criticized Takings literature and methods of constitutional analysis).

Equal protection theories (and other constitutional law theories) are based on classifications of persons and/or transactions. However, in the United States, the advent of the Internet, continuing reduction of race-based economic disparitics in some spheres of life, increasing political participation of minorities, economic advancement of minorities, and the growth of commerce within and among a growing minority population have reduced the usefulness of such discrimination tests. In commerce among immigrants or minority persons, it is sometimes difficult to classify persons or transactions based on wealth, activity, or race, or location.

The volume of interstate and international communications and commerce in the United States and in many foreign countries, and the amount of coordinated activities and regulatory actions among states/countries have all increased exponentially during the past 15 years due to the Internet, improved and cheaper phone systems, cheaper transportation, increasing dispersion of locations of household members, and increasing mobility of households. Thus, the definition of *burden on interstate commerce* as currently construed by courts is overbroad and relatively vague and should be much more narrowly tailored to special circumstances.

Similarly, the growth of the Internet, innovations in electronics, and consumer marketing have changed the definitions of and expectations for privacy. Consumer data are collected, stored, and sold in many ways. Often, consumers do not have the resources to pursue lawsuits against offending parties, and governments also do not have sufficient resources to prosecute offenders, and the result has been an involuntary internalization of violations of privacy rights, and a change in norms and expectations. Given that the U.S. Constitution was written when society was much different, the interpretations and implementation of the right-to-privacy clause should be cognizant of modern-day lifestyles and possibilities. Like interstate commerce and privacy, the nature of modern contracting continues to evolve, and courts have often developed diverse and sometimes conflicting principles and objectives in the interpretation of contracts.

In the United States and some common law countries, the nature of application of the separation-of-powers doctrine changed drastically during the past twenty years—many federal agencies now routinely combine rule-making, adjudication, and enforcement functions. In *Executive Preemption*, Young states in part, "But as Justice White observed in *INS v. Chadha*, [f]or some time, the sheer amount of law . . . made by the [administrative] agencies has far outnumbered the lawmaking engaged in by Congress through the traditional process." Whether one views this development as a "bloodless constitutional revolution" or as a necessary "renovation" of the constitutional structure in response to the complexity of modern society, the advent of the administrative state has profound implications for the U.S. Constitution's core commitments to federalism and separation of powers in general and for preemption doctrine in particular. Specifically, preemption doctrine has yet to resolve the extent to which executive action should be treated differently from legislation, or to grapple with the considerable range of diverse governmental activities that march under the banner of executive agency action (federal administrative action is, in important ways, considerably more threatening to state autonomy than legislation is. As the constitutional limits on national action fade into history, the primary remaining safeguards for state autonomy are political, stemming from the representation of the states in Congress, and procedural, arising from the sheer difficulty of navigating the federal legislative process). Many new federal statutes (such as the Emergency Economic Stabilization Act of 2008 and the Restoring American Financial Stability Act of 2010 in the United States) contravene the separation-of-powers doctrine. This change in the interpretation of the U.S. Constitution (which has been implicitly supported by the U.S. Supreme Court in 2010 judgments) can be attributed to concerns about the size of government, and sheer inability or unwillingness to restructure the federal government. The volume of rule making by U.S. federal agencies has now surpassed that of the U.S. Congress.

Several articles have challenged the usefulness of the state-action requirement in constitutional law analysis. Although the U.S. Supreme Court has extended state action to include acts by private persons/entities that are encouraged, authorized, or supported by the government, in the context of modern-day life and commerce, the state-action requirement remains overbroad and vague, and should either be abolished or narrowly tailored to special circumstances. Many governments now outsource many functions to private companies that essentially function as quasi-governments. In other instances, governments enact statutes that give certain entities actual or perceived (as in Fannie Mae and Freddie Mac) government guarantees/support. Furthermore, there are many instances where individuals intentionally violate another person's constitutional rights, and such offenses cannot be adequately addressed by traditional tort law.

The Substantial Inducement Theory is introduced here as an alternative to the state-action requirement—and the Substantial Inducement Theory has two parts. In the first part, where the government, institution, or person, through specific acts or laws, causes (without requiring) a person to act in a way that results in a violation of constitutional rights, such inducement by the government/institution/person is effectively the equivalent of compulsion, and is a sufficient basis for constitutional law claims. Such inducement could be established with or without evidence of consideration/benefits/payments. Because there is no affirmative requirement of an act or acts, and it can be argued that the person could just walk away, the second part of this theory consists of a balancing test in which the government's interest is weighed against the person's property interests in conduct, privacy, speech, or property.

The Substantial Inducement Theory is relevant because there are many instances where the burden of proof (required to establish compulsion) is too high or too expensive to achieve. In such cases, the facts and/or reasonable inference should be adequate to establish a deprivation of constitutional rights. Furthermore, most perpetrators who want to deprive rights may know of the compulsion requirement and can easily tailor their actions to avoid evidence. Furthermore, in most developed capitalist societies, incentives (grants, tax credits, sweepstakes, gifts, promotions, etc.) are an established topic and are widely applied by private entities and government agencies in various aspects of life. The compulsion requirement does not incorporate the incentive phenomenon/trend, which grows and permeates more of daily life as time progresses.

Within the context of constitutional law, the term *property interests* has not been properly defined by the U.S. Supreme Court, and there continues to be diverse opinions among U.S. courts about the nature and scope of property interests. At least thirty-five U.S. states have enacted statutes that allow compensation for Takings that do not meet the generally accepted definitions of property interests or Takings, where there has been a diminution of property value.

The use of three types of scrutiny for analyzing constitutional law disputes in the United States (strict scrutiny, intermediate scrutiny, and rational scrutiny) is not justified. The implied classification of rights can result in unjustified prioritization of justice (when litigation costs, transaction costs, opportunity costs, and enforcement costs are considered); and it is not clear that: (1) the drafters of the Constitution intended there to be such classifications; or (2) such classifications are optimal for social welfare.

QUASI CONSTITUTIONS

Many jurisdictions like the United Kingdom and the European Union do not have formal constitutions but have formal agreements or rules that are generally accepted and have substantial permanence (not subject to costless change in the near future) and thus are "functional" constitutions but not formal constitutions. Similarly, in many common law jurisdictions, some statutes have the effect of constitutions because of their actual or perceived permanence and the implicit costly amendments. These two types of statutes are quasi constitutions. Hence, the state-action requirement (or Substantial Inducement requirement) should be expanded to include quasi constitutions as statutes that provide enabling constitutional law directives. Seven feasible criteria for quasi constitutions are as follows:

1. Permanence (actual and perceived)—Refers to the extent to which the statute or agreement is deemed to be a permanent element of daily life and/or transactions.
2. Costly amendment—Refers to the cost of amending the subject statute/agreement, which must be significant and excessively burden defined classes of persons or transactions in order for the statute/agreement to be deemed a quasi constitution.
3. Universal acceptance—Refers to the acceptance and common use of the statute/agreement by the general population.
4. Government action—The government must have enacted the statute or must be a party to the agreement or conduct.
5. Enforceability—The statute or agreement or conduct must be applicable to the general public, and must be enforceable in courts of law or other forums.
6. Statutory interpretation—The historical interpretation of the statute or the agreement by courts, other forums, or the government must be akin to that of constitutions in terms of scope, protection of rights, and remedies.
7. Legislative intent—The legislative intent of the statute or the agreement must be akin to that of constitutions in terms of scope, protection of rights, and remedies.

SOCIAL CAPITAL

Social capital is well defined in the economics, sociology, psychology, and public policy literature and has become major currency in human interactions. Social capital is sometimes linked to wealth and employment status. Indeed many of the transactions that raise issues of constitutional rights often involve social capital (such as Takings, constitutionality of statutes that affect a narrow class of persons, and so forth). The ability of some firms (and individuals) to participate in some markets (such as fixed income markets) depends on the magnitude and extent of their social capital. The effectiveness of the enforcement of statutes and government policies often depends on the social capital of government officers and agents who are charged with such enforcement—this has been manifested in the relative successes/failures of policy implementation by the Bush administration (e.g., the Iraq war, and the bank bailouts that have been criticized as unconstitutional) and the Obama administration (in the United States—the federal health-care overhaul bills), the Brown administration (U.K.), the Mugabe administration (Zimbabwe), the Putin administration (Russia), the "Lula" administration (Brazil), the Kim administration (North Korea), and the Mandela administration (South Africa). Social capital has been defined in many ways: (1) as individual relationships and networks, (2) as trust and norms, (3) as group relations, and (4) as the ability to effect change. McGreal (2008) defined social capital as the ability of a person or a group to use the government to increase its social capital—and thus, the analysis in McGreal (2008) is distinguishable from social capital discussed herein. The type of social capital referred to herein is private-sector relationships and social networks that are mostly outside the realm of government. Thus, laws/statutes and conduct that can substantially reduce or can reduce the social capital of any protected class for a material period of time and within certain contexts should be declared unconstitutional. Also, the extent to which social capital is an enforcement advantage or disadvantage, and the relative effects of social capital (of government-supported actors, unprotected classes) on protected classes and unprotected classes of persons can be for a test of unconstitutionality.

REFERENCES

Brentwood Academy v. Tennessee Secondary School Athletic Ass'n, 531 U.S. 288 (2001).

Burnham, W. 1989. Separating constitutional and common law torts: A critique and a proposed constitutional theory of duty. *Minnesota Law Review* 73: 515–525.

CEA (European Insurance and Reinsurance Federation), *Insurance: A Unique Sector-Why Insurers Differ From Banks*, June 2010, http://www.cea.eu/uploads/DocumentsLibrary/documents/1277383780_cea-report-insurance-a-unique-sector.pdf.

Currie, D. 1986. Positive and negative constitutional rights. *University of Chicago Law Review* 53: 864–890.

Ellman, S. 2001. Constitutional confluence: American "state action" law and the application of South Africa's socioeconomic rights guarantees to private actors. *New York Law School Law Review* 45: 21–75.

Gardbaum, S. 2006. Where the (state) action is. *International Journal of Constitutional Law* 4: 760–779.

Heinzerling, L. E. 1986. Actionable inaction: Section 1983 liability for failure to act. *University of Chicago Law Review* 53: 1048–1061.

Helfman, A. L. 1993. *State tort law: Determining the comparative level of local government immunity*. Ph.D. Dissertation, University of Delaware.

Jamison, F. 2008. State constitutional law—Freedom of speech—A tightening of the reins. *Rutgers Law Journal* 39: 969–979 (describing the history of the state action requirement; and comparing state and federal constitutions in the United States).

Kania R. 1983. A theory of negligence for constitutional torts. *Yale Law Journal* 92: 683–693.

Khalil, M. 2007. Impediments to financial development in the banking sector: A comparison of the impact of federalism in the United States and Germany. *Michigan Journal of International Law* 28: 431–441.

McGreal P. 2008. Social capital in constitutional law: the case of private norm enforcement through prayer at public occasions. *Arizona State Law Journal*, 40: 585–649.

Nwogugu, M. 2011. *International Risk Regulation, Mechanism Design and Constitutional Economics of Institutions* (unpublished manuscript).

Scott, D. 1979. Respondeat superior liability of municipalities for constitutional torts after "Monell": New remedies to pursue? *Missouri Law Review* 44: 514–551.

Shapiro, J. 1994. Snake pits and unseen actors: Constitutional liability for indirect harm. *University of Cincinnati Law Review* 62: 883–897.

Tulsa Professional Collection Services v. Pope, 485 U.S. 478 (1988).

Tushnet, M. 2003. The issue of state action/horizontal effect in comparative constitutional law. *International Journal of Constitutional Law* 1: 79–98.

CHAPTER 2

A Critique of Mechanism Design

Mechanism design theory (MDT) is the body of theory pertaining to economic mechanisms that are often defined by rules, norms, time, medium, and location. Mortgages (deeds of trust), title systems, real estate investment trusts (REITs), and foreclosure processes (for real estate and property taxes) are market mechanisms that are typically designed and implemented by legislatures (and governments of most common law countries) for the protection of investors, borrowers, and lenders, for enhanced social welfare, and for the improved coordination of transactions. These market mechanisms and the associated constitutional law and economic problems that they create are evidence that existing MDT is inaccurate and impractical. An analysis of MDT in this context is important because a well-developed MDT can vastly improve foreclosure processes and the efficiency of mortgages and title systems as instruments of security and transfers. The literature on MDT has some major gaps and inaccuracies, some of which are explained later.

MDT is based on the inaccurate assumption that all agents truthfully disclose their preferences, and that all agents disclose their preferences at the same rate and at the same time. MDT does not account for the value that the agent, principal, or participant gains by withholding information about their preferences. MDT erroneously assumes that each mechanism is fair and unbiased, but in reality, even completely automated mechanisms have biases that arise from programming errors, computer learning patterns, and/or customer usage patterns. Most mechanisms involve some human intervention and/or human processes, and existing MDT does not account for human biases and processes such as altruism, regret, aspirations, and so on, both in the participants and in the people who are involved as part of the mechanism.

Existing MDT does not account for varying levels of "confidentiality" of agents' information—rather, MDT erroneously assumes that a binary situation exists in which information is either publicly known or is completely private. Existing MDT does not incorporate the effects of government regulation on agents and on the mechanism; and does not account for the unconstitutionality/constitutionality of mechanisms. MDT erroneously assumes that all agents are rational and self-interested; but there can be many reasons for agents' irrationality and/or agents' propensity to act for the benefit of the society or for the benefit of an interest group. MDT erroneously assumes that there is always some minimum level of uniformity of agents' preferences; but on the contrary, agents' preferences vary widely.

MDT is based on the incorrect assumption that each mechanism is monolithic and static in time, space, and expense, and it does not account for differences in agents' information-processing capabilities. In reality and on the contrary, some mechanisms are dispersed in space (various locations) and time (requires participation, revisions of knowledge, and various disclosures at various times) and expenses (the costs of participation in the mechanism varies).

MDT is based on the mistaken assumption that in mechanisms, monitoring costs, compliance costs, switching costs, access costs, decision costs (the costs of contemplating a decision), and sanctions (for noncompliance with the mechanism) are minimal or nonexistent. In reality, these types of costs are monetary/physical and/or nonmonetary/psychological and can have significant effects on the efficiency of mechanisms.

MDT is erroneous in assuming that agents have quasi-linear utility functions and are risk-neutral; but in reality, agents' attitudes toward risk vary dramatically and depend on many factors. Furthermore, agents' utility functions are more likely to be nonlinear (and not linear) because the agent will react to the various dimensions of the mechanism (economically, psychologically, and socially); he or she will react to the prospect of there being other participants and also to perceived opportunity costs, in addition to his or her normal utility function.

MDT is based on the incorrect assumption that the social choice functions inherent in mechanism designs have linear "Benefit Effects"; where a benefit effect is defined as the economic gain or loss of social welfare across all agents and across the society/economy, as the mechanism functions during a specified time interval. Hence, the benefit effect is defined with respect to time and to the entire economy. Contrary to MDT, benefit effects are likely to be nonlinear because agents' characteristics vary in terms of wealth, utility functions, risk aversion, time horizon, preferences, and so on; the economy is not static and changes in various elements of the economy are not discrete; and finally, not all eligible agents or permitted agents or financially capable agents will participate in the mechanism.

MDT wrongly implies that the social choice functions inherent in mechanism designs have uniform and same "Impact Effects" across all agents, where an impact effect is the magnitude of the monetary and nonmonetary impact of the mechanism on all agents. MDT erroneously assumes that all social choice functions inherent in mechanisms have linear effects on agents' utilities and participation strategies.

MDT incorrectly assumes that all eligible, financially capable, and permitted agents will participate in the mechanism, and will participate at the same time. MDT erroneously defines the success/efficiency of mechanisms primarily in terms of utility, but this approach does not sufficiently incorporate other elements and results of mechanisms—such as psychological gains/losses, emotions, social capital, reputation effects, and so forth. Furthermore, as used in Mechanism Design Theory, utility is relatively static. McCauley (2002) states that there are several problems in the use of utility. Most MDT is based on equilibrium as a relevant state and as an objective; and the concept of equilibrium is static. In reality, true equilibrium does not exist, and cannot be achieved in mechanisms due to: (a) continuous changes in agents' preferences, information processing capabilities, time constraints, wealth, access to information, and so on; (b) transaction costs and opportunity costs; (c) mental states of agents; (d) government regulations and/or industry standards/practices; and (e) agents' varying reactions to incentives over time.

MDT is based on the incorrect assumption that each agent's and all agents' preferences are static over time, and that mechanisms are preference formation-independent (i.e., the mechanism does not affect the agents' processes of forming their preferences). In reality, most mechanisms are interactive, and the agent's preferences change over time as he or she interacts with both the mechanism and other agent-participants and nonparticipants.

In most MDTs, mechanisms are defined and designed only in terms of agents' preferences, public actions, and private actions. This approach does not incorporate the effects of agents' reactions to incentives, and values of hidden information to agents, and agents' information processing capabilities, the mechanism's information processing capabilities, regulation, and government enforcement.

Contrary to MDT, the set of all possible preferences of agents is not finite. Within this context of mechanisms and group action, the definition of "finite" should be based on achievability, and not on mathematical ranges.

MDT is based on the inaccurate assumption that the mechanism is removed from, and distinct from, the agents. On the contrary, the agents typically form a major part of the mechanism (as in auctions, online file sharing networks, and multiple listing systems).

MDT inaccurately implies that the mechanism's main role is either allocation or coordination. In reality, many mechanisms serve other economic and non-economic purposes (some of which are unintended) such as: (a) psychological re-assurance (e.g., voting, auctions, etc.), (b) information dissemination, (c) comparison—which increases social welfare by reducing overall agents' search costs, and (d) entertainment.

MDT erroneously assumes that mechanisms can be deliberation-proof (in equilibrium, all agents do not have any incentive to strategically deliberate). In most existing mechanisms, agents deliberate while using the mechanism (or immediately after using the mechanism, and in ways that can materially change the mechanism's allocations).

CONCLUSION

While MDT can be reformulated into a powerful analytical and design tool, current MDT is significantly flawed, to the point that its usefulness is severely limited. Groupthink about MDT has been very much prevalent among MDT researchers—many of their theories and theorems are quite similar and impractical, and it is sometimes difficult to discern what is truly new and innovative in MDT. In the chapter on new mortgage-alternative products, new elements of MDT are introduced and used for the design of new financial products.

REFERENCE

McCauley, J.L. 2002. Adam Smith's invisible hand is unstable: Physics and dynamics reasoning applied to economic theorizing. *Physica A: Statistical Mechanics and Its Applications* 314 (1–4): 722–727.

3

General Public Health and Social Psychology Issues in Global Housing Markets and Mortgage Markets

Although there have been significant attempts to develop new types of mortgages in various countries during the past 25 years, most efforts have ignored the adverse psychological effects of debt/mortgages and foreclosures on individuals, households, private institutions, and government regulators. The first section of this chapter delineates problems inherent in mortgages. The second part surveys empirical and theoretical research on substantial public health problems caused by mortgages and foreclosures in various countries.

Traditional mortgages refer to common instruments that are used to finance property purchases—such as adjustable-rate mortgages (ARMs), fixed-rate mortgages, mortgages without deed-in-lieu clauses, and so on. The traditional mortgage is an inefficient contract and the associated foreclosure proceedings are also inefficient and socially, economically, and psychologically costly.

The social, economic, and psychological costs of mortgages and foreclosures are staggering and both have become public health disasters in many countries. The side effects include hypertension and other illness; intra-household disputes, failed marriages, depression from loss of homes; litigation costs; declines in neighborhood home values due to foreclosures; lenders' administrative costs, governments' costs incurred to regulate and monitor mortgages/foreclosures; financial losses incurred by banks from their mortgage portfolios; brokerage fees; derogatory credit reports (which prevent the borrower from getting other loans and jobs); antisocial behavior; crime; abandonment of real estate; social stigma and depression (from perceived loss of a "huge" investment often measured in terms of the mortgage balance and value of the property, when in fact, the borrower's true interest in the property is typically less than 50 percent); and so on. The pressure to pay monthly mortgage P&I payments and insurance/taxes/utility bills, and the unrealized expectations associated with property values, mortgages, and foreclosures strain marriages, intra-household relationships, and work relationships and significantly distort individuals' perceptions, values/morals, rationality, and sensitivity to risk. The United States now has an obesity epidemic where more than 70 percent of the U.S. population is overweight and more than 30 percent of the population is obese. More than 60 million U.S. adults suffer from hypertension. These health conditions can be partly attributed to mortgages.

The global primary mortgage markets consist of: (1) financial institutions and nonfinancial institutions that are lenders; (2) borrowers; (3) attorneys; (4) real estate brokers; (5) mortgage brokers; (6) lawyers; (7) title companies; (8) appraisal companies; (9) servicing companies; (10) purchasers of mortgages; (11) mortgage insurance and property insurance companies; (12) loan servicing companies; (13) government agencies; and (14) securitization sponsors. The main products in the primary mortgage markets are mortgages (whole loans, participations) and mortgage insurance. The primary mortgage markets are also international because many foreign banks and financial companies lend and buy mortgages in foreign markets.

The global secondary mortgage markets consist of: (1) financial institutions and nonfinancial institutions that are either securitization sponsors or sellers of mortgages or purchasers of commercial mortgage-backed securities (CMBS)/residential mortgage-backed securities (RMBS); (2) other sellers of mortgages and guarantees; (3) attorneys; (4) securities brokers; (5) mortgage brokers; (6) lawyers; (7) appraisal companies; (8) accounting/auditing companies; (9) servicing companies; (10) purchasers of mortgages; (11) mortgage insurance companies; (12) loan servicing companies; (13) government agencies; and (14) securitization sponsors. The main products in the secondary mortgage markets are whole loans, CMBS, RMBS, and mortgage derivatives (interest-only securities; principal-only securities; mortgage options). Secondary mortgage markets are global because foreign investors often purchase CMBS/RMBS.

SURVEY OF PUBLIC HEALTH PROBLEMS CAUSED BY TRADITIONAL MORTGAGES AND FORECLOSURES

There is an existing body of theoretical and empirical research using data from various countries that confirm that debt and mortgages have adverse effects on individuals, households, private institutions, and government employees (O'Neill, Sorhaindo, Xiao, and Garman 2005; Mortgage Bankers Association 2008; Mohamed 2006; Kingsley, Smith, and Price 2009; Garvill, Garling, Lindberg, and Montgomery 1992; Díaz-Serrano 2004; Department of Trade and Industry 2004; Cooke, Barkham, Audin, Bradley, and Davy 2004; Cairney and Boyle 2004). Table 3.1 illustrates housing stress indicators for major U.S. cities as of October 2010.

The remainder of this chapter surveys research on the adverse public health and psychosocial consequences of mortgages, debt, and foreclosures. Note that many of the empirical studies that use regressions are subject to the usual problems inherent in regression analysis (e.g., sample selection biases; normality of data; fit of distributions, etc.).

Nettleton and Burrows (1998) explored the consequences of mortgage debt for both the health of indebted homeowners and their use of primary health-care services, using secondary analysis of data from the British Household Panel Survey. They found that mortgage indebtedness has an independent effect on people, and it increases the likelihood that men will consult their physicians. They suggest that policies that have encouraged the growth of homeownership are premised on the idea of individual responsibility, a notion that underpins other spheres of contemporary welfare policies. Thus, mortgage indebtedness is likely to have profound psychosocial consequences for those who experience it.

Nettleton and Burrows (2000) analyzed the health consequences of the experience of mortgage foreclosure and examined how the statistical relationship between the onset of mortgage indebtedness and health is generated among families that lost their mortgaged home. Nettleton and Burrows studied the narratives of 44 adults and 10 children from a sample of 30 households that experienced mortgage foreclosure and found that there is psychological stress, relative deprivation, and psychosocial injuries of "inequality structures."

Thomson, Petticrew, and Douglas (2003) reviewed observational data of housing-associated health risks to highlight the key impacts to consider when doing a housing HIA (health impact assessment) and developed a table of synthesized findings indicating the expected health effects of specific housing improvements.

Van Laere, De Wit, and Klazinga (2009) analyzed the public health problems that arise from evictions—they surveyed caseworkers of housing associations that deal with rent arrears, and case workers of nuisance control care networks, and compared evicted households with nonevicted households. They found that for households reporting rent arrears, social problems were reported in 71 percent and medical problems in 23 percent. The independent risk factors for eviction included being of Dutch origin

TABLE 3.1 Housing Stress Indicators for Major Cities in the United States (as of October 2010)

Metro Area	% Spending >30% of Income on Housing	% of Population without Health Insurance	% of Population Not Working	Housing-Stress Indicator
United States, average	37.5	15.1	33.1	85.7
Miami-Fort Lauderdale-Pompano Beach, FL	57.7	25.6	33.3	116.6
Riverside-San Bernardino-Ontario, CA	54.3	20.5	39.5	114.3
Los Angeles-Long Beach-Santa Ana, CA	54.3	21.5	33.5	109.3
San Diego-Carlsbad-San Marcos, CA	53.9	17.0	36.4	107.3
Las Vegas-Paradise, NV	49.6	22.3	32.2	104.1
Orlando-Kissimmee, FL	47.6	21.2	32.6	101.4
Tampa-St. Petersburg-Clearwater, FL	46.6	18.5	34.4	99.5
Sacramento–Arden-Arcade–Roseville, CA	48.4	12.6	35.4	96.4
San Jose-Sunnyvale-Santa Clara, CA	50.5	12.3	31.6	94.4
New York-Northern New Jersey-Long Island, NY-NJ-PA	48.8	12.9	32.2	93.9
Phoenix-Mesa-Scottsdale, AZ	41.3	17.9	33.5	92.7
San Francisco-Oakland-Fremont, CA	50.2	11.9	30.6	92.7
Detroit-Warren-Livonia, MI	39.0	12.9	39.1	91.0
New Orleans-Metairie-Kenner, LA	38.0	18.8	33.7	90.5
Jacksonville, FL	40.0	16.8	33.3	90.1
Chicago-Naperville-Joliet, IL-IN-WI	42.9	14.4	31.9	89.2
Virginia Beach-Norfolk-Newport News, VA-NC	42.1	11.7	34.6	88.4
Atlanta-Sandy Springs-Marietta, GA	36.5	19.2	32.4	88.1
Houston-Sugar Land-Baytown, TX	32.2	24.6	31.1	87.9
Memphis, TN-MS-AR	35.9	16.3	35.4	87.6
Portland-Vancouver-Beaverton, OR-WA	40.9	14.8	31.3	87.0
Dallas-Fort Worth-Arlington, TX	32.0	24.0	29.6	85.6
Seattle-Tacoma-Bellevue, WA	43.0	12.1	29.9	85.0
San Antonio, TX	30.1	20.0	34.4	84.5

TABLE 3.1 *(Continued)*

Metro Area	% Spending >30% of Income on Housing	% of Population without Health Insurance	% of Population Not Working	Housing-Stress Indicator
Providence-New Bedford-Fall River, RI-MA	42.9	9.0	29.9	81.8
Austin-Round Rock, TX	31.6	20.5	27.7	79.8
Cleveland-Elyria-Mentor, OH	35.2	11.5	32.7	79.4
Philadelphia-Camden-Wilmington, PA-NJ-DE-MD	37.4	10.0	31.7	79.1
Richmond, VA	34.1	12.8	31.5	78.4
Denver-Aurora-Broomfield, CO	35.0	15.3	27.3	77.6
Birmingham-Hoover, AL	31.0	12.3	34.2	77.5
Charlotte-Gastonia-Concord, NC-SC	31.7	15.7	30.1	77.5
Washington-Arlington-Alexandria, DC-VA-MD-WV	38.3	11.0	27.2	76.5
Baltimore-Towson, MD	36.8	10.1	29.4	76.3
Nashville-Davidson-Murfreesboro-Franklin, TN	32.4	13.3	30.5	76.2
Oklahoma City, OK	26.4	17.9	30.6	74.9
Milwaukee-Waukesha-West Allis, WI	35.3	9.9	28.6	73.8
Columbus, OH	30.6	12.7	30.1	73.4
Boston-Cambridge-Quincy, MA-NH	40.2	4.7	27.6	72.5
Indianapolis-Carmel, IN	28.2	13.6	29.9	71.7
Hartford-West Hartford-East Hartford, CT	35.5	7.6	28.4	71.5
Louisville-Jefferson County, KY-IN	27.5	12.4	31.6	71.5
Cincinnati-Middletown, OH-KY-IN	28.1	11.8	30.9	70.8
St. Louis, MO-IL	29.7	10.5	30.4	70.6
Rochester, NY	29.4	7.9	31.9	69.2
Kansas City, MO-KS	27.6	13.2	27.8	68.6
Minneapolis-St. Paul-Bloomington, MN-WI	34.7	9.1	24.7	68.5
Pittsburgh, PA	28.1	8.6	31.0	67.7
Buffalo-Niagara Falls, NY	27.8	7.9	31.2	66.9

Source: Izzo, P. "Which Cities Face Biggest Housing Risks?" October 5, 2010. Available at: http://finance.yahoo.com/real-estate/article/110907/which-cities-face-biggest-housing-risks?mod=realestate-buy.

(odds ratio {OR] 2.38 [1.30 to 4.36]) and having a drug-addiction problem (OR 3.58 [0.96 to 13.39]). For the nuisance households, social problems were reported in 46 percent and medical problems in 82 percent, while financial difficulties were a risk factor for eviction (OR 8.04 [1.05 to 61.7]). Because of the social and medical problems that were prevalent, prevention practice evictions should be considered both a socioeconomic and a public health problem.

Crossley (2004) analyzed the relationship between health status and debt using data from the Panel Study of Income Dynamics (PSID), in order to find out whether debt accumulation is associated with self-reported health levels, after controlling for income and education. Crossley found that debt burdens may be an important predictor of health beyond other measures of socioeconomic status including education and income.

Pevalin (2009) investigated whether repossessions/foreclosures and evictions increase the likelihood of common mental illness (using data from the core longitudinal panel of the British household panel survey). Regression models were used with weighted data; and common mental illness was measured by the 12-item General Health Questionnaire. Pevalin found that housing repossession/foreclosure is associated with an increased risk of common mental illness (adjusted OR 1.61, 95 percent confidence interval [CI] 1.10 to 2.36), whereas eviction from rented property shows no increased risk (0.97, 0.76 to 1.20); and that the pattern over time shows a clear increase in the years before repossession. Thus, repossession of owned property significantly increases the risk of common mental illness immediately after the event; however, eviction from rented property is a more common event but is not associated with an increased risk of common mental illness. Pevalin attributed this difference to losing the security of owned housing and the often transitory nature of the rented housing population. Between 1991 and 2008, there were more than half a million repossessions and more than 1 million eviction orders made on behalf of social and private landlords in the United Kingdom. The characteristics of housing repossession in the United Kingdom are distinct from other European nations due to the cost of housing, the high housing cost/income ratio, and the decline in the supply of social housing, all of which makes it more difficult to recover from a repossession and get another form of housing.

Van Laere, De Wit, and Klazinga (2009) evaluated the functioning of the signaling and referral system set up for households at risk of eviction in Amsterdam, using interviews and questionnaires completed by employees of 12 housing associations (for rent arrears) and by employees of 13 nuisance control care networks (for nuisance). For 275 households with rent arrears, housing associations reported social problems in 196 (71 percent), of whom 94 (48 percent) were in contact with social assistance; they also reported medical problems in 62 (23 percent), of whom 18 (29 percent) were in contact with medical assistance. House visits resulted in a much higher identification of problems, and were associated with a reduced eviction risk (relative risk 0.57 [95 percent CI: 0.43 to 0.75]). For 190 nuisance households, nuisance control care networks reported social problems in 103 (54 percent), of whom 13 (13 percent) were in contact with social assistance; they also found medical problems in 155 (82 percent), of whom 142 (92 percent) were in contact with medical assistance.

Taylor, Pevalin, and Todd (2007) studied the impact of unsustainable housing commitments on psychological well-being in the United Kingdom—the extended recession and stagnant housing market in the 1990s after the boom of the late 1980s resulted in more than half a million housing foreclosures. Taylor, Pevalin, and Todd's main hypothesis was that housing payment problems and residential mortgage debt have adverse impacts on heads of households' psychological well-being over and above those caused by financial hardship more generally. They used data from the British Household Panel Survey 1991–2003; the samples for analysis consisted of: (1) 5,651 male heads of households who provided 26,618 person-year observations, and (2) 2,534 female heads of households who provided 9,091 person-year observations. Summary statistics and multivariate, fixed effects regression models were used. Mental health was measured by the 12-item General Health Questionnaire. Taylor, Pevalin, and Todd found that for both female and male heads of households, housing payment problems and entering arrears have significant detrimental effects on mental well-being. The sizes of these effects are in addition to and larger in magnitude than those associated with financial hardship more generally. The net effects appear to be relatively stable over the time of the panel data. Thus, housing payment problems have independent psychological costs over and above those associated with general financial hardship.

Fitch et al. (2007) attempted to improve psychiatrists' knowledge and confidence in dealing with patients' debt, and they provided basic definitions of debt and problem debt; outlined the impact that debt can have on patients' health, social, and financial well-being; identified the stages and signs that a patient may be accruing problem debt; described how psychiatrists should respond; and reviewed the methods of assessing patients' mental capacity to make financial decisions. As of 2009, one in four people with mental health problems in Britain reported debt or arrears, which is nearly three times the rate among individuals without similar conditions. Some health professionals reported that they lack basic knowledge to effectively intervene and that patient debt is often not acted on until a crisis emerges. Government surveys indicate that 1 in 11 people in the U.K. report debt or arrears, but among individuals with mental health problems, this figure rises to 1 in 4, and to 1 in 3 among people with psychotic conditions. When applied to the nationally recommended caseload for community mental health nurses of 35 patients, these figures suggest that between 9 and 12 of these patients might be living with debt or arrears. Fitch et al. state that research suggests that health professionals are not addressing patients' debt because they feel insufficiently knowledgeable and confident. This could mean that a "debt crisis" has not been identified or managed, that the mental health of many individuals could worsen; and that such individual victims may have an even larger set of future problems pertaining to their careers, families, and the professionals who support them.

Balmer, Pleasence, and Buck (2006) examined social and demographic predictors of debt problems, whether debt problems tend to occur in combination with other problems, and which people tend to obtain long-term debt rather than short-term debt. Balmer, Pleasence, and Buck used data from a survey of 5,611 adults' experiences of civil justice problems throughout England and Wales and found that the best predictors of debt were receipt of benefits and long-term illness or disability, with long-term ill or disabled respondents also being more susceptible to long-term debt. Balmer, Pleasence, and Buck also discussed the usefulness of health interventions that recognize the relationships among civil justice problems and health, illness, or disability.

Capone and Metz (2003) examined the experience of the loss mitigation program at the U.S. Federal Housing Authority (FHA) in order to understand how postdefault loan workout tools are being used by loan servicers to lessen foreclosure rates and stabilize neighborhoods. Capone and Metz found that the chances of defaulted borrowers retaining their homes were substantially higher in 2002 to 2003 than they were during 1997 to 1998 simply due to maturity of the program. They also found that house price changes, property price class, and the borrower's race have measurable effects on the probability that any given borrower who cannot cure the default by himself/herself will succeed in keeping the home.

Acevedo-Garcia et al. (2004) summarized the empirical evidence for the effect of housing mobility policies on health outcomes and found that, excluding policies concerned with the physical characteristics of housing (e.g., exposure to lead), only housing mobility has been evaluated for its effects on health. Acevedo-Garcia et al. reviewed 13 articles covering five housing mobility studies and ranked them according to their methodological strength.

Smith, Searle, and Cook (2008) analyzed the value that home buyers attach to the financial returns on housing and the extent to which home equity is earmarked and used as a financial buffer. Although most debate on homeownership and risk has focused on the management of mortgage debt, there are other risks for home buyers in settings where housing dominates people's wealth portfolios; where the investment dimensions of property are at a premium; and where housing wealth is, de facto, an asset base for welfare. They used qualitative research with 150 U.K. mortgage holders to assess the character, extent, and possible mitigation of this wider risk regime. Smith et al. (2008) showed that elements of housing risk (i.e., overinvestment in a single asset, overdependence on housing wealth, and vulnerability to the underperformance of housing assets) are important social policy and public health issues that should be mitigated by governments. The United Kingdom is similar to a growing number of countries whose economic policies, household wealth, and welfare regimes revolve around home equity.

Smith et al. (2003) analyzed the relationships between housing and health inequalities by qualitative interviews in three British regions in order to establish the links between health capital, on the one hand, and the network of resources, environments, events, institutions, and social relations constituting the housing system, on the other. Smith et al. found that homeownership (which generally appears therapeutic) can have the opposite effect for people whose resilience is low or whose health is in decline.

Within the context of promotion of homeownership by the Hong Kong government, La Grange (2001) analyzed whether homeowners in Hong Kong have a higher sense of social belonging than renters and found that tenure status is a spurious independent variable in assessing respondents' sense of belonging to Hong Kong. They also found that the significance of tenure is greatly reduced when other variables such as age, identity, income, and foreign-abode right are controlled. In addition, they found that those who possess a comparatively high sense of social belonging were typically Hong Kong Chinese, older persons, have high incomes, and do not hold any foreign right of abode.

Lauster (2008) analyzed the relationship between aspects of the housing market influenced by housing policy and stability of marriages for cohabiting couples in Sweden, using data on 3,851 cohabiting couples that was obtained from the Swedish Family Survey of 1992. Lauster found that greater affordability of housing increases the stability of the relationship between couples, and that greater availability of detached housing significantly weakens couple stability. Lauster noted that although several articles have attempted to link housing policy to health and psychological well-being, few have measured how housing policy might actually strengthen or weaken families as units.

Rogers et al. (2008) studied the relationship between lay perceptions of locality, adversity, mental health, and social capital in an area undergoing urban regeneration. Rogers et al. found that perceptions of material and nonmaterial aspects of the locality and the way in which people vulnerable to mental health problems coped with living in adversity were identified as being more highly valued than intended or actual changes to structural elements such as the provision of housing or employment. Rogers et al. noted that residents' narrative accounts included concerns about the absence of social control in the locality, the reputation of the area, a lack of faith in local government agencies to make changes considered important to local residents, a reliance on personal coping strategies to manage adversity, and perceived threats to mental health, which reinforced a sense of social isolation.

Valins (2004), Ford (1999), Rust and Skillern (2008), Nettleton and Burrows (2000), Cairney and Boyle (2004), Green-Pimentel (2010), Nettleton (1998), Searle, Smith, and Cook (2009), Engelhardt, Eriksen, Gale, and Mills (2010), Taylor (2011), Brown, Taylor, and Price (2005), Burrows (2003), Alley, Pagan, Lipman, Soldo, Krasny, Shardell, Asch, and Cannuscio (2009), Macintyre, Ellaway, Der, Ford, and Hunt (1998), Smith, Easterlow, Munro, and Turner (2003), and Colic-Peisker and Johnson (2010) also found that mortgages, foreclosure risk, and homeownership cause stress and psychological problems, and are substantial public health risks.

Nettleton (2001) found that the mortgage foreclosure process disrupts the lives of, and has adverse effects on, the children. Mably and Jones (2007) found that debts have a detrimental effect on individuals' mental and physical health due to stress, stigma, and fewer associated life opportunities. Sharpe and Bostock (2002) found that debt is added stress on individuals and causes anxiety and depression and compounds emotional and physical health. In their study of credit card debt among 900 individuals in Ohio, Drentea and Lavrakas (2000) found that the debt/income ratio was significantly associated with worse physical health and self-reported health. In addition, having more debt-related stress was statistically associated with worse health. The Drentea and Lavrakas study relied upon self-reported health status rather than clinically diagnosed conditions.

Reading and Reynolds (2001) found that depression was strongly associated with financial adversity in a sample of 271 families with young children. In their study, anxiety about debt was the strongest independent socioeconomic predictor of the depression score at both initial and follow-up occasions of women in their study. Being in debt, by itself, also predicted maternal depression.

Kempson, McKay, and Willitts (2004) cited a U.K. survey of almost 8,500 individuals, which showed that 38 percent of those exhibiting moderate depression had not been paying their debts on time, as were 34 percent of those who had attempted suicide; 24 percent of those with mild alcohol dependence; and 49 percent of those with severe alcohol dependence. Among the total population, 13 percent of those aged 16 to 59 had been in arrears in the past year.

Grant (1995, 2000) stated that respondents with disabilities often ascribed the onset of mental health problems, such as depression and anxiety, to the process of dealing with debt. Moreover, some respondents had contemplated suicide, which was also identified in Edwards (2003), who reported on the stress of living on a very tight budget, such that almost two-thirds of respondents stated that they were not coping with their debts, with three in five of these people stating that they were not coping and feeling in crisis. Parker (1990) reported similar findings, with most respondents in her U.K. survey stating that their mental health, and to a lesser extent their physical health, was affected by their having debt.

In Edwards's (2003) survey of more than 900 over-indebted clients of Citizens Advice Bureau in the United Kingdom, 62 percent mentioned that they were suffering from stress, anxiety, or depression. Edwards stated that unmanageable debt can have devastating consequences and that the CAB experience can happen irrespective of the amount owed—thus, depression, ill health, relationship breakdown, arguments within families, doing without essentials including food, and facing homelessness can all result from a debt problem.

Kober (2005) interviewed 51 disabled people with debt problems, and surveyed 400 members of a disability campaign network, based on their experiences of having debt. Results from this work suggested that 35 percent had visited their primary care doctors about anxiety and depression linked to their debts and 12 percent stated that their situation had made them to contemplate suicide.

Dietz and Haurin (2003) reviewed the literature (economics, sociology, geography, political science, psychology, etc.) that describes the micro-level economic and social consequences of homeownership. Dietz and Haurin found substantial evidence that homeownership has important effects on some household behaviors and outcomes. Dietz and Haurin also found that much of the past academic literature on the consequences of homeownership is deficient (from a theoretical or econometric perspective).

The Apgar and Duda (2005) study found that foreclosure imposes substantial economic and social welfare costs on families and municipal governments.

The Pollack et al. (2009) study was based on a survey in Pollack and Lynch (2009) of 250 homeowners in Philadelphia (Pennsylvania, United States) who had sought credit counseling for home mortgage foreclosure. Pollack et al. also compared people undergoing foreclosure to members of the community at large using the Philadelphia Public Health Management Corporation's 2008 survey of a random sample of Philadelphia-area adults. Pollack et al. found physical and mental health problems among those facing foreclosure that were significantly more severe than among similarly vulnerable individuals in the general population, which implies that poor health may be either a cause or an effect of foreclosure. Pollack et al. found that: (1) more than one-third of study participants met screening criteria for major depression; (2) homeowners undergoing foreclosure reported significantly worse overall health than the community sample, but this difference was no longer significant after socioeconomic characteristics were taken into account; and after adjusting for demographic and financial factors, however, people undergoing foreclosure had significantly higher rates of hypertension and heart disease than others in the community; (3) compared to the community sample, those in foreclosure were more likely to be uninsured (22 percent compared to 8 percent). Nearly 60 percent reported that they had skipped or delayed meals because they could not afford food, and people undergoing foreclosure were also more likely to have forgone filling a prescription because of the expense during the preceding year (48 percent versus 15 percent); (4) about 9 percent of the study participants reported that a medical condition in their family was the primary reason they were undergoing foreclosure; and (5) more than one quarter of those in foreclosure said they owed money to medical creditors. In 2009, more than 2.8 million housing units in the United States received a foreclosure notice (this represents about 1 in every 45 properties and a 120 percent increase in the number of foreclosed properties since 2007).

Bhattacharya (2009) attempted to unify the *institutions view* and the *disease view* of development, and argues that overcoming diseases is of prime importance at an early stage of economic development, whereas institutions are more important at a later stage. Bhattacharya used the development history literature on Africa, India, China, and the Americas to support his hypothesis.

Pollack, Griffin, and Lynch (2010) analyzed the association between housing affordability and health, after controlling for perceptions of neighborhood quality, and determining whether this association differs by housing tenure (renting versus owning). Pollack, Griffin, and Lynch used data from the 2008 Southeastern Pennsylvania Household Health Survey (a telephone-based survey of 10,004 residents of Philadelphia and its four surrounding counties, were analyzed), and propensity score methods to compare individuals who reported living in unaffordable housing to similar individuals who lived in affordable homes. Overall, 48.4 percent of the sample reported difficulty paying housing costs. Individuals who lived in unaffordable housing had increased odds of poor self-rated health; hypertension; arthritis; cost-related health-care noncompliance; and cost-related prescription nonadherence. There were no significant associations between housing affordability and heart disease, diabetes, asthma, psychiatric conditions, being uninsured, emergency department visits in the past year, obesity, and being a current smoker. Renting rather than owning a home increased the association between unaffordable housing and self-rated health, and cost-related health-care noncompliance. This study provides further evidence that the financial strain of unaffordable housing is associated with trade-offs that may harm health.

Jenkins et al. (2008) tested the hypothesis that the association between low income and mental disorder is mediated by debt and its attendant financial hardship. Jenkins et al. used a cross-sectional, nationally representative survey of private households in England, Scotland, and Wales, which assessed 8,580 participants aged 16 to 74 years and living in households who were asked detailed questions about income, debt, and financial hardship. In the study, psychosis, neurosis, alcohol abuse, and drug abuse were identified by the Clinical Interview Schedule–Revised, the Schedule for Assessment in Neuropsychiatry (SCAN), the Alcohol Use Disorder Identification Test (AUDIT), and other measures. Jenkins et al. found that those with low income were more likely to have mental disorder (OR 2.09, 95 percent 1.68 to 2.59) but this relationship was attenuated after adjustment for debt (OR 1.58, 95 percent CI 1.25 to 1.97) and vanished when other socio-demographic variables were also controlled (OR 1.07, 95 percent CI 0.77 to 1.48). Of those with mental disorder, 23 percent were in debt (compared with 8 percent of those without mental disorder). The more debts the participants had, the more likely they were to have some form of mental disorder, even after adjustment for income and other socio-demographic variables. People with six or more separate debts had a six-fold increase in mental disorder after adjustment for income. This study adds to the literature by showing (without use of complicated or highly questionable statistical methods) that both low income and debt are associated with mental illness, but the effect of income appears to be mediated largely by debt.

Stuckler, Meissner, and King (2008) studied whether a banking system crisis increases short-term population cardiovascular mortality rates. Stuckler, Meissner, and King used an international, longitudinal multivariate regression analysis of cardiovascular disease mortality data from 1960 to 2002; and found that a system-wide banking crisis increases population heart disease mortality rates by 6.4 percent in high-income countries and by about 25 percent in low-income countries, after controlling for economic change, macroeconomic instability, population age, and social distribution.

Stuckler et al. (2009) analyzed the health effects (mortality, etc.) of economic crisis, particularly its effect on unemployment—they examined relationships between changes in employment and mortality, and how such relationships were modified by different types of government expenditure for 26 European Union (EU) countries between 1970 and 2007. Stuckler et al. used multivariate regression, which was adjusted for population-aging, past mortality and employment trends, and country-specific differences in health-care infrastructure. Stuckler et al. found that every 1 percent increase in unemployment was associated with a 0.79 percent rise in suicides at ages younger than 65 years, although the effect size was non-significant at all, and with a 0.79 percent rise in homicides; but road-traffic deaths decreased by 1.39 percent. A more than 3 percent increase in unemployment had a greater effect on suicides of people younger than 65, and on deaths from alcohol abuse. Stuckler et al. did not find any consistent evidence across the EU that all-cause mortality rates increased when unemployment rose, although populations varied substantially in how sensitive mortality was to economic crises, depending partly on differences in social protection. Stuckler et al. noted that every U.S. $10 per person increase in investment in active labor market programs reduced the effect of unemployment on suicides by 0.038 percent. Thus, this study indicates that increases in unemployment cause significant short-term increases in premature deaths from intentional violence, while reducing traffic fatalities; and active labor market programs that reintegrate workers in jobs could mitigate some adverse health effects of economic downturns. However, the findings of this study are subject to the usual limitations of regression analysis (and the underlying assumptions about data) and sample selection.

Jenkins et al. (2009) identified positive links between recession, debt, and health using the U.K. as a case study, and proposed solutions identified in workshops held during the U.K. Government's Foresight Review of Mental Capital and Wellbeing. Jenkins et al. also found that: (1) further longitudinal research is also needed to identify the relationship between debt and mental health; (2) there is a lack of coordinated activity across health, money advice, and creditor organizations—and a renewed emphasis on coordinated "debt care pathways" and better communication between local health and advice services is needed.

Bezruchka (2009) found that: (1) in rich countries, mortality rates decline faster during recessions than during periods of economic growth; (2) in countries with strong social safety nets, business cycles cause smaller changes in the health of the population; (3) in terms of business cycles, mortality is procyclical, increases with economic exapansions, declines with economic contractions, and is not countercyclical (the opposite), as expected; (4) while most nations enjoyed sustained declines in mortality during the past century, the pace of the decline has been slower during economic booms and greater during so-called *busts*; and (5) in contrast, for poor countries, shared economic growth appears to improve health by providing the means to meet essential needs such as food, clean water, and shelter, as well as access to basic health-care services; but after a country reaches a gross national product

(GNP) per capita (or gross domestic product [GDP] per capita) of $5,000 to $10,000, few health benefits arise from further economic growth.

Bennett, Scharoun-Lee, and Tucker-Seeley (2009) conjectured that foreclosure may be associated with a range of psychological and health behavior outcomes that, in turn, might increase chronic disease risk. Bennett, Scharoun-Lee, and Tucker-Seeley stated that from 1997 to 2006, home prices increased 124 percent in the United States, with even greater increases in Europe: 194 percent in Britain, 180 percent in Spain, and 253 percent in Ireland; and that between 2007 and 2010, more than 7.5 million U.S. homes were placed in foreclosure.

Lea, Webley, and Walker (1995) conducted a postal survey study of factors correlated with consumer debt and investigated several psychological variables that have been suggested as causes or effects of debt. Questionnaires were sent to three groups with different debt histories during the preceding two years: nondebtors (no debt to the company), mild debtors (late payment to the company), and serious debtors (sued for debt recovery by the company). Economic and demographic factors predicted debt category well, supporting previous results. Lea, Webley, and Walker found that: (1) further variance between groups was accounted for by people's money management skills and facilities, by measures of their time horizons, and by aspects of their consumer behavior; (2) nondebtors had more money management facilities (e.g., bank accounts) than debtors, and rated their abilities at money management more highly; (3) debtors had shorter time horizons than nondebtors; (4) debtors were more likely to buy cigarettes and Christmas presents for children than nondebtors; (5) no group differences were found for attitudes to debt or locus of control; and (6) there were significant group differences for measures of economic socialization, social comparisons, use of credit, and other aspects of consumer behavior, but these differences were not independently significant on multivariate analysis. Lea, Webley, and Walker stated that their findings must be qualified because of the sample size (low return rates), and that the results suggest that a complex of psychological and behavioral variables affect debt and are affected by it.

Ranyard and Craig (1995) analyzed the role of installment credit in personal budgeting, and the way people evaluate installment credit (especially in terms of mental accounts). Ranyard and Craig conjectured that consumers utilize a *dual representation* of installment credit based on *total accounts* and *recurrent budget period accounts*. Ranyard and Craig did a study wherein mature adults were presented with advertisements for in-store credit, which were aimed at eliciting spontaneous evaluations of installment credit. Ranyard and Craig illustrated some of the ways that consumers construe installment sales credit in terms of total and recurrent budget period accounts. Ranyard and Craig concluded that mental accounts are natural representations, which help consumers to control the balance between income and expenditure over indefinite time periods.

CONCLUSION

It is obvious from these empirical and theoretical studies that traditional mortgages and foreclosures cause acute psychological illnesses and are a significant public health risk. These psychological problems have "multiplier" effects because: (a) they are not generally recognized and treated; (b) the borrower-victims affect close third parties—such as their children, spouses, co-workers, and so forth; (c) these psychological and psychiatric problems can also affect employees of lenders and government employees; and (d) these psychological and psychiatric problems substantially reduce economic productivity and social welfare.

REFERENCES

Acevedo-Garcia, D., T. L. Osypuk, R. E. Werbel, E. Meara, D. M. Cutler, and L. F. Berkman. 2004. Does housing mobility policy improve health? *Housing Policy Debate*, 15 (1): 49–98.

Aldrich, J., and F. Nelson. 1984. Linear probability, logit, and probit models. Paper # 45 in the Sage Series on Quantitative Applications in the Social Sciences.

Alley, D. E., J. A. Pagan, T. H. Lipman, B. Soldo, S. Krasny, M. Shardell, D.A. Asch, and C.C. Cannuscio. 2009. Economic strain and poor health: Associations between housing foreclosure and health. Working paper.

Apgar, W., and M. Duda. 2005. Collateral damage: The municipal impact of today's mortgage foreclosure boom. A report prepared for the Homeownership Preservation Foundation, Minneapolis, Minnesota. www.hpfonline.org/content/pdf/Apgar_Duda_Study_Short_Version.pdf.

Balmer, N., P. Pleasence, and A. Buck. 2006. Worried sick: The experience of debt problems and their relationship with health, illness and disability. *Social Policy & Society* 5: 39–51.

Bennett, G., M. Scharoun-Lee, and R. Tucker-Seeley. 2009. Will the public's health fall victim to the home foreclosure epidemic? *PLoS Medicine* 6 (6): e1000087.

Bezruchka, S. 2009. The effect of economic recession on population health. 2009. *Canadian Medical Association Journal* 181 (5): 281–285.

Bhattacharya, S. 2009. Institutions, diseases, and economic progress: A unified framework. *Journal of Institutional Economics* 5: 65–87.

Brown, S., K. Taylor, and S. W. Price. 2005. Debt and distress: Evaluating the psychological cost of credit. *Journal of Economic Psychology* 26 (5): 642–663.

Burrows, R. 2003. How the other half lives: An exploratory analysis of the relationship between poverty and home-ownership in Britain. *Urban Studies* 40 (7): 1223–1242.

Cairney, J., and M. Boyle. 2004. Home ownership, mortgages and psychological distress. *Housing Studies* 19 (2): 161–174.

Capone, C., and A. Metz. 2003. Mortgage default and default resolutions: Their impact on communities. For presentation at the Federal Reserve Bank of Chicago, Conference on Sustainable Community Development, Washington, DC, March 27. www.federalreserve.gov/communityaffairs/national/CA_Conf_SusCommDev/pdf/caponecharles.pdf.

Colic-Peisker, V., and G. Johnson. 2010. Security and anxiety of homeownership: Perceptions of middle-class Australians at different stages of their housing careers. *Housing, Theory & Society* 27 (1): 1–21.

Cooke, R., M. Barkham, K. Audin, M. Bradley, and J. Davy. 2004. Student debt and its relationship with student mental health. *Journal of Further and Higher Education* 28 (1): 53–66.

Crossley, A. 2004. The health consequences of debt: Evidence from the panel study of income dynamics. Department of Sociology, University of Pennsylvania, Philadelphia, PA. http://paa2004.princeton.edu/download.asp?submissionId=40609.

De Bruin, A., and S. Flint-Hartle. 2003. A bounded rationality framework for property investment behavior. *Journal of Property Investment & Finance* 21 (3): 271–281.

Department of Trade and Industry. "Tackling Over-Indebtedness Action Plan, 2004," London, July 2004.

Díaz-Serrano, L. 2004. Income volatility and residential mortgage delinquency: Evidence from 12 EU countries. IZA Discussion Paper No. 1396, November. Available at SSRN: http://ssrn.com/abstract=621044.

Dietz, R. D., and D. R. Haurin. 2003. The social and private micro-level consequences of homeownership. *Journal of Urban Economics* 54 (3): 401–450.

Drentea, P., and P. Lavrakas. 2000. Over the limit: The association among health, race and debt. *Social Science and Medicine* 50 (4): 517–529.

Edwards, S. 2003. *In Too Deep: CAB Clients' Experience of Debt*, Citizens Advice Scotland, http://www.citizensadvice.org.uk/docks/In_too_deep.pdf.

Engelhardt, G. V., M. D. Eriksen, W. G. Gale, and G. B. Mills. 2010. What are the social benefits of homeownership? Experimental evidence for low-income households. *Journal of Urban Economics* 67 (3): 249–258.

Fitch, C., R. Chaplin, C. Trend, and S. Collard. 2007. Debt and mental health: The role of psychiatrists. *Advances in Psychiatric Treatment* 13: 194–202.

Ford, J. 1999. The costs of un-sustainable home ownership in Britain. *Journal of Social Policy* 28 (2): 305–330.

Garvill, J., T. Garling, E. Lindberg, and H. Montgomery. 1992. Economic and non-economic motives for residential preferences and choice. *Journal of Economic Psychology* 13 (1): 39–59.

Grant, L. 1995. Head above water, *Community Care* 16 (11): 26–27.

Grant, L. 2000. Disabled people, poverty and debt: Identity, strategy and policy. In J. Bradshaw, and R. Sainsbury, eds. *Experiencing Poverty* (Surrey, U.K.: Ashgate, Aldershot).

Green-Pimentel, L. 2010. The relationship between housing cost burden and health status in older adults in the United States. Proceedings of the 2010 Annual Conference of The Housing Education and Research Association. www.housingeducators.org/Conference_2010/2010_HERA_Conference_Proceedings_Portland_OR_100210[1][1].pdf#page=103.

Jenkins, R., D. Bhugra, P. Bebbington, et al. 2008. Debt, income and mental disorder in the general population. *Psychological Medicine* 38 (10): 1485–1493.

Jenkins R., C. Fitch, M. Hurlston, and F. Walker. 2009. Recession, debt and mental health: Challenges and solutions. *Mental Health in Family Medicine* 6 (2): 85–90.

Kempson, E., S. McKay, and M. Willitts. 2004. *Characteristics of families in debt and the nature of indebtedness* (DWP Research Report 211). Leeds: Corporate Document Services.

Kingsley, G., R. Smith, and D. Price. 2009. The impacts of foreclosures on families and communities. Working Paper. The Urban Institute.

Kober, C. 2005. *In the balance: Disabled people's experiences of debt.* (London: Leonard Cheshire).

La Grange, A. 2001. Social belonging, social capital and the promotion of home ownership: A case study of Hong Kong. *Housing Studies* 16 (3): 291–310.

Lauster, N. 2008. Better homes and families: Housing markets and young couple stability in Sweden. *Journal of Marriage and Family* 70 (4): 891–903.

Lea, S., P. Webley, and C. Walker. 1995. Psychological factors in consumer debt: Money management, economic socialization and credit use. *Journal of Economic Psychology* 16: 681–701.

Mably, S., and N. Jones. 2007. The links between over-indebtedness and health in Wales. Wales Centre for Health. www.wales.nhs.uk/sites3/Documents/568/over-indebt%20and%20health%20report.pdf.

Macintyre, S., A. Ellaway, G. Der, G. Ford, and K. Hunt. 1998. Do housing tenure and car access predict health because they are simply markers of income or self esteem? A Scottish study. *Journal of Epidemiology and Community Health* 52 (10): 657–664.

Mohamed, R. 2006. The psychology of residential developers: Lessons from behavioral economics and additional explanations for satisficing. *Journal of Planning Education and Research* 26 (1): 28–37.

Mortgage Bankers Association. 2008. National Delinquency Survey, Second Quarter.

Nettleton, S. 1998. Losing homes through mortgage possession: A "new" public health issue. *Critical Public Health* 8 (1): 47–58.

Nettleton, S. 2001. Losing a home through mortgage repossession: The views of children. *Children & Society* 15 (2): 82–94.

Nettleton, S., and R. Burrows. 1998. Mortgage debt, insecure home ownership and health: An exploratory analysis. *Sociology of Health and Illness* 20 (5): 735–757.

Nettleton, S., and R. Burrows. 2000. When a capital investment becomes an emotional loss: The health consequences of the experience of mortgage possession in England. *Housing Studies* 15 (3): 463–479.

O'Neill, B., B. Sorhaindo, J. J. Xiao, and E. T. Garman. 2005. Negative health effects of financial stress. *Consumer Interests Annual* 51.

Parker G. 1990. *Getting and Spending: Credit and Debt in Britain.* (Exeter, U.K.: Avebury).

Pevalin, D. J. 2009. Housing repossessions, evictions and common mental illness in the UK: Results from a household panel study. *Journal of Epidemiology & Community Health* 63 (11): 949–951.

Pollack, C. E., B. A. Griffin, and J. Lynch. 2010. Housing affordability and health among homeowners and renters. *American Journal of Preventive Medicine* 39 (6): 607–608.

Pollack, C., and J. Lynch. 2009. Health status of people undergoing foreclosure in the Philadelphia region. *American Journal of Public Health* 99 (10): 1833–1839.

Pollack C., J. Lynch, D. Alley, and C. C. Cannuscio. 2009. Foreclosure and health status. LDI Issue Brief.

Poterba, J. 1984. Tax subsidies to owner-occupied housing: An asset market approach. *Quarterly Journal of Economics* 99 (4): 729–752.

Ranyard, R., and G. Craig. 1995. Evaluating and budgeting with installment credit: An interview study. *Journal of Economic Psychology* 16 (3): 449–467.

Reading, R., and S. Reynolds. 2001. Debt, social disadvantage and maternal depression. *Social Science & Medicine* 53 (4): 441–453.

Rogers, A., P. Huxley, S. Evans, and C. Gately. 2008. More than jobs and houses: Mental health, quality of life and the perceptions of locality in an area undergoing urban regeneration. *Social Psychiatry & Psychiatric Epidemiology* 43 (5): 364–372.

Rust, A., and P. Skillern. 2008. Empty houses and broken dreams. The Community Reinvestment Association of North Carolina. Available at: http://archive.cra-nc.org/files/Download/ForeclosuresJuly2008.pdf.

Searle, B. A., S. J. Smith, and N. Cook. 2009. From housing wealth to well-being. *Sociology of Health & Illness* 31 (1): 112–127.

Sharpe, J., and J. Bostock. 2002. *Supporting People with Debt and Mental Health Problems.* Community Psychology: Northumberland Health Action Zone.

Smith, S. J., D. Easterlow, M. Munro, and K. Turner. 2003. Housing as health capital: How health trajectories and housing paths are linked. *Journal of Social Issues* 59 (3): 501–525.

Smith S. J., B. A. Searle, and N. Cook. 2008. Rethinking the risks of home ownership. *Journal of Social Policy* 38 (1): 83–102.

Stuckler, D., S. Basu, M. Suhrcke, A. Coutts, and M. McKee. 2009. The public health effect of economic crises and alternative policy responses in Europe: An empirical analysis. *Lancet* 374 (9686): 315–323.

Stuckler, D., C. M. Meissner, and L. P. King. 2008. Can a bank crisis break your heart? *Global Health* 4: 1.

Taylor M. 2011. Measuring financial capability and its determinants using survey data. *Social Indicators Research*, 102 (2): 297–314.

Taylor M. P., D. J. Pevalin, and J. Todd. 2007. The psychological costs of unsustainable housing commitments. *Psychological Medicine* 37 (7): 1027–1036.

Thomson H., M. Petticrew, and M. Douglas. 2003. Health impact assessment of housing improvements: Incorporating research evidence. *Journal of Epidemiology & Community Health* 57 (1): 11–16.

Valins, O. 2004. When debt becomes a problem: A literature study. Ministry of Social Development, Wellington, New Zealand. www.familybudgeting.org.nz/documents/when%20debt%20becomes%20a%20problem.pdf.

Van Laere I., M. De Wit, and N. Klazinga. 2009. Preventing evictions as a potential public health intervention: Characteristics and social medical risk factors of households at risk in Amsterdam. *Scandinavian Journal of Public Health* 37 (7): 697–705.

Van Laere, I., M. De Wit, and N. Klazinga. 2009. Evaluation of the signaling and referral system for households at risk of eviction in Amsterdam. *Health & Social Care in the Community* 17 (1): 1–8.

CHAPTER 4

Public Health Issues

Psychological Factors Inherent in Housing Demand, Mortgage Demand, and House Prices

This chapter: (1) identifies some of the major causes of rapid changes in housing prices and housing demand that occurred in the United States between 1995 and 2010; (2) shows that the main causes of these changes in housing prices were psychological factors and behavioral biases; (3) introduces new theories of psychological effects and behavioral biases in the global housing sector (inherent in the real estate purchase/sale process); and (4) shows that all existing housing demand models and housing price forecast models are grossly mis-specified primarily because they do not incorporate psychological factors and behavioral biases (and because real estate data do not fit the statistical distributions and assumptions underlying the regressions and prediction models used in empirical studies). These new hypotheses can be used to improve existing housing-demand and housing-price prediction models, and to develop policy alternatives; and the hypotheses can serve as the foundation for new housing models. The hypotheses introduced herein have public health ramifications because they pertain to the behaviors and biases of market participants, and can explain adverse psychological effects of transactions on individuals and groups. Events that occurred in the U.S. housing markets are used to illustrate issues—because the U.S. housing markets are probably the best developed in the world, are highly regulated, and have been the subject of significant change between 1993 and 2011. In most countries, housing demand is intricately intertwined with traditional-mortgage volumes because most home buyers finance their purchases with traditional mortgages. Surprisingly, traditional-mortgage statutes are similar across countries.

Psychological factors played an important role in many aspects of the U.S. housing sector between 1995 and 2010, but most of these issues have not been analyzed theoretically or empirically in the existing literature. Lane, Seiler, and Seiler (2011); Einio, Kaustia, and Puttonen (2008); El-Attar and Poschke (2011); Seiler, Seiler, and Lane (2011); Seiler and Seiler (2010); Seiler, Seiler, Traub, and Harrison (2008); Seiler (2011); Seiler, Madhavan, and Liechty (2011); Seiler, Lane, and Seiler (2011); Seiler, Seiler, Lane, and Harrison (2011); Seiler and Seiler (2011); Ackert, Church, and Jayaraman (2011); Hayunga and Lung (2011); Eldred (2002); and Simonsohn and Loewenstein (2006) describe some behavioral biases associated with housing/property demand. Diaz-Serrano (2009) found that the change from renting to homeownership provides incremental utility to the household, but there are issues of affordability, economic and psychological limitations imposed by homeownership, and the documented stress and mental health problems associated with homeownership. Between 2000 and 2005 the total value of residential property in developed countries increased by more than $30 trillion to more than $70 trillion, an increase equivalent to more than 100 percent of those countries' combined gross domestic products (GDPs). The apparently global boom in house prices was partly attributable to: (1) psychological biases; (2) historically low interest rates in many countries, which encouraged home buyers to borrow more money; and (3) loss of faith in stock markets after they declined in value substantially and thus made real estate look attractive (*The Economist*, June 2005; Mohamed 2006; Meen and Meen 2003; Massa and Simonov 2005; Manzano 2006; Malpezzi, Englund, Kim, and Turner 2004; Levy and Lee 2004; Antonides and Kroft 2005).

The structural changes and rapid price increases that occurred in the U.S. housing market between 1995 and 2007 created some important legal issues. The housing market contributed to propping up the economies of the United States, U.K., Japan, and many developed countries from 1995 to 2007, and declines in housing prices have had significant negative consequences in some of these countries. Between 2000 and 2005, U.S. consumer spending and residential construction accounted for 90 percent of the total growth in U.S. GDP. More than two-fifths of all private-sector jobs created in the United States between 2001 and 2005 were in housing-related sectors, such as construction, real estate, and mortgage brokerage. It is clear that the true state of the U.S. economy is masked by borrowing that is used to finance construction, acquisitions, and consumer spending. Without such credit availability, the U.S. economy, productivity, GDP, and GDP growth would have been declining from 1995 to 2003. This illusion is in contrast to the economies of many countries where credit is much scarcer.

Several factors have been proposed and analyzed empirically in the existing literature, as causes of the rapid and substantial increases in U.S. home prices, and corresponding increases in mortgages from 1995 to 2003 (Baffoe-Bonnie 1998; Case and Shiller 2003; Garvill, Garling, Lindberg, and Montgomery 1992; Smith 2006). In the United States and many other developed countries, psychological factors were a major causal factor in people's/households' propensity to purchase and propensity to borrow (mortgages) between 1995 and 2003. Existing housing models (i.e., models of housing prices, housing demand, taxation) have not incorporated these psychological phenomena (Massa and Simonov 2005; Black et al. 2003; Diaz 1999). Furthermore, the existing housing-demand models and house-price models suffer from omissions and deficiencies explained in the following articles: Davis (1997); Tu, Kellett, Clerehugh, and Gilthorpe (2002); Hosmer, Taber, and Lemeshow (1991); Moss, Wellman, and Cotsonis (2003); Reagan (1998); McWilliams and Siegel (1999); MacKinley (1997); Harrison, Oler, and Allen (2005).

It is difficult to empirically establish the impact of psychological factors on housing prices in the United States from 1995 to 2003, primarily because the changes in home prices varied substantially according to town/region, and the price series (or even the logarithms of the series) typically do not fit known distributions (Case and Shiller 2003; Glaeser and Gyourko 2005; Garvill, Garling, Lindberg, and Montgomery 1992; Berkowitz and Hynes 1999; Antonides and Kroft 2005; Case, Quigley, and Shiller 2005; Cocco and Campbell 2003; De Bruin and Flint-Hartle 2003; Díaz-Serrano 2004; Taylor 2011; Van Poucke and Buelens 2002; Moss, Wellman, and Cotsonis 2003; McWilliams and Siegel 1999; Hosmer, Taber, and Lemeshow 1991; Hendershott and Weicher 2002; Harrison, Oler, and Allen 2005). The only possibly accurate method of testing these hypotheses is surveys, but even survey results are likely to vary significantly by region, type of housing unit, price of housing unit, family structure, and household income, so that no meaningful conclusions or deductions will materialize. The trends discussed here indicate that psychological factors were a major causation of said substantial increases in home prices in the United States from 1995 to 2003.

Baffoe-Bonnie (1998) showed that the impact of interest rates on housing prices and housing demand varied by region in the United States, and that in some regions an increase in the mortgage rates will result in an increase in housing prices; and that economic factors alone cannot explain the extreme fluctuations in real estate prices in some regions in the United States. The formula for calculating the impact of interest rates on housing demand is described in Case and Shiller (2003, 348–350); however, this formula is problematic because it does not incorporate psychological/behavioral factors (the relationship between the two variables is inverse), monetary economics factors such as money supply/demand, savings rates, PPP, capital flows, availability of credit, and so on (Hu 2005; Humphrey 2003; Leamer 2007; Poterba, Venti and Wise 2000; Sunden and Surette 1998).

Between 1995 and 2005, U.S. interest rates and mortgage rates declined substantially; more credit became available, and this resulted in substantial refinancing and some increases in housing prices (due to availability of credit, lower cap rates, lower opportunity costs, increased subprime lending, and increased volumes of securitization). Between 1997 and 2003, housing prices increased dramatically, in some cases at annual compounded rates of more than 60 percent (Painter and Redfearn, 2002). The increased availability of credit reduced the issue of liquidity constraints, which in turn resulted in higher home prices from 1995 to 2007. Higher volumes of securitization resulted in increased money supply and availability of credit. Hence, home buyers were more willing to pay higher prices (particularly because the cost of ownership remained relatively constant, and even declined in some regions, due to declining interest rates).

The significantly non-uniform (in terms of timing and dollar amounts) changes in prices of various classes of residential property (single-family homes, co-ops, condos, two- to six-family homes, apartment complexes) and non-uniform structural changes in regions of the residential market (Northeast, Southwest, Midwest, Southeast) are evidence of substantial influence of psychological factors in the price setting process for homes in the United States between 1995 and 2007.

From 1995 to 2007, macroeconomic trends in the United States differed markedly from economic trends in past periods with similar conditions, which is substantial evidence that psychological factors affected mortgage volumes, housing prices, and housing demand. This is confirmed by the following facts:

- From the beginning of the recession in the United States in the second quarter of 2001 until the third quarter of 2002, values of U.S. homes increased at an annualized rate of 7 percent (the Office of Federal Housing Enterprise Oversight, OFHEO). However, in the comparable period during the U.S. recession in 1990 to 1991, U.S. housing prices increased at an annual rate of 2 percent.
- From 1995 to 2003, the number of personal bankruptcy filings in the United States grew substantially—to 1,577,651 in calendar year 2002, up 5.7 percent from 1,492,129 in calendar year 2001 (Administrative Office of the U.S. Courts; www.abiworld.org/stats).
- During the second quarter of 2002, loan delinquency rates were 3.04 percent for conventional mortgages, 11.2 percent for FHA/VA mortgages, and 1.4 percent for home-equity loans; 1.23 percent for

all mortgages and 4.0 percent for subprime loans (Mortgage Bankers Association).

- The rapid increases in U.S. housing prices between 1995 and 2003 differ sharply from changes during the late 1970s, when U.S. real estate prices increased sharply even though interest rates were rising. Although the prime lending rate in the United States increased substantially from 1976 to 1979 and rose to 19 percent in 1979, U.S. real estate prices increased substantially during the same period—by 1979, the value of individually owned homes was then approximately $1.3 trillion, which was twice the value of corporate common stock owned by individuals at that time.
- During the 1990 to 1992 recession in the United States, domestic interest rates were at historically low levels, but did not result in the same rapid substantial increases in home prices.
- The worst bear markets in the U.S. real estate sector occurred during 1974 to 1975, 1980, and 1990 to 1992, and in each of these periods, the prime lending rate was declining. Real estate prices typically have a positive correlation with commodities. Gold prices declined substantially during the worst real estate bear markets in the United States (1974 to 1975, 1980, and 1990 to 1992). However, during 1997 to 2000, the Bloomberg/REIT (real estate investment trust) Index rose by only 1.2 percent (versus 79.9 percent for the S&P 500), whereas gold prices declined from nearly $400 per ounce to $255 per ounce (gold prices have increased since the second half of 2001). Between 2000 and 2005, the Bloomberg/REIT Index rose by 19.1 percent annually while the S&P declined by 3.2 percent annually. Similarly, REIT share prices normally have a positive correlation with 10-year bond yields, but from 1995 to 2003, REIT prices increased while bond yields declined.
- Real estate prices declined in Japan throughout the 1990s and into the early 2000s despite declining interest rates. The Japanese economy is closely linked to the U.S. economy—as manifested by: (a) the balance of trade between the United States and Japan; (b) the volume of dollar-yen derivatives transactions (swaps, collars, etc.); (c) the volume of Japanese investment in the United States (in real estate, U.S. Treasury bonds, common stock, etc.); (d) intellectual property held by Japanese entities in the United States; and (e) the correlation of macroeconomic variables of both countries. Hence, the rapid increases in home prices that occurred in the United States from 1995 to 2006 would have been expected in the Japanese housing sector. Perhaps the differences between the two housing markets can be partly explained by: (1) absence of urban renewal activities in Japan, (2) differences in rationality and expectations, and (3) credit systems and availability of loans.

- During the period from 1995 to 2003, the probability or fear that the U.S. Federal Reserve may increase interest rates was not likely to reduce home-buying activity (and hence reduce rapid increases in home prices) during the same period, because most would-be home buyers still had fixed-rate mortgages, the majority of loans that were being offered were fixed-rate mortgages; long-term bond yields had remained unusually low; and expectations of continued increases in home prices did not wane.
- Between 2001 and 2005, residential investment in the United States was at a 40-year peak, while the number of households was growing at its slowest rate in 40 years. This mismatch cannot be attributed to lower liquidity constraints, or to higher actual demand for housing, and is more likely to have been caused by psychological factors.

Between 1995 and 2003, the divergence of U.S. home prices from major macroeconomic indicators such as gross national product (GNP), gross domestic product (GDP), unemployment, real disposable income, and corporate profits is evidence that psychological factors were major determinants of the price setting process in the residential real estate sector. Between 1999 and 2003, home prices in most parts of the United States remained high despite the general recession/downturn, "localized recessions" (e.g., in New York metro area and San Francisco), weak economic conditions, and high consumer debt. Changes in real (inflation-adjusted) home prices had a negative/inverse relationship with GDP growth during 1991 recession, but between 1999 and 2002, the relationship remained positive and stable. Also, between 1997 and 2001 rising housing prices contrasted vividly with the declines in the stock market. Between 1997 and 2002, many of the regions in the United States with the highest house price appreciation (e.g., San Francisco, San Diego, New York, Boston, Seattle) had large concentrations of high-tech firms, declining share prices, and job losses in the U.S. high-tech sector (all of which would seem to represent a large shock to housing demand). Although increases in home prices from 1995 to 2003 may be partly explained by low and declining mortgage interest rates, interest rates also declined during the 1991 to 1992 recession in 1991 to 1992, but such decline did not prevent real house prices from declining during that period.

From 1995 to 2003, valuation and comparison metrics in the United States were substantially different from long-run averages (and this confirms that psychological factors account for much of the changes in mortgage volume, housing demand, and housing prices). The relevant facts are:

- Historically high price-to-income ratios from 1995 to 2003—average was at least 35 percent higher than pre-1995 levels.

- Historically high price-to-value ratios from 1995 to 2003—average was at least 35 percent higher than pre-1995 levels.
- High annual rate of appreciation of value—in many cities, the average rate of increases in home prices was at least 25 percent higher than pre-1995 levels. The annual rates of appreciation of value varied dramatically by region, by town, and by subclass of housing unit (i.e., co-ops, condos, apartment rentals, single-family homes), although people in all areas of the United States were affected by the U.S. Fed's activities, and presumably had access to similar mortgage rates, and could get the same or similar information through the Internet. Between 2000 and 2005, housing prices rose 107 percent in the District of Columbia, versus a U.S. national average increase of 48 percent. During 1980 to 2004, home prices in Massachusetts increased by 566 percent compared to the U.S. national average of 234 percent.

Most of the increases in the volume of traditional residential mortgages and in U.S. home prices from 1995 to 2003 were highly correlated, but cannot be attributed to material changes in household income or household disposable income. Homeowners' cost of ownership did not change materially from 1995 to 2003. Obviously, mortgage lending standards have declined; but debt service on home mortgage debt was only 9.86 percent of U.S. average household disposable personal income in the third quarter of 2004, up from a low of 9.08 percent in the fourth quarter of 1998, but down from a high of 10.41 percent in the third quarter of 1991. From 1995 to 2003, household income did not increase at a much faster rate than inflation. Hence, much of the increase in U.S. home prices from 1995 to 2003 cannot be attributed to material changes in income or disposable income, but rather to changes in consumer psychology.

Globally, between 1997 and 2003 real changes in home prices appear to have been persistent (positive price changes tended to be followed by more positive price changes, and vice versa for negative price changes). Such persistence in house prices indicates that housing markets are inefficient because: (a) the market takes time to clear; (b) psychological factors (expectations, etc.) are major determinants of housing prices; (c) prices and expectations of future price changes were set in a backward-looking manner; (d) house prices were not directly linked to macroeconomic variables (such as job growth and changes in personal income), which may or may not be persistent.

From 1995 to 2003, U.S. housing market dynamics were substantially affected by environmental psychology factors, which apparently became more important decision criteria because of the following factors: (1) urban renewal programs in many U.S. cities; (2) concern and publicity about environmental issues (recycling, etc.); (3) public concern and publicity about health issues (obesity, hypertension, smoking, cancer, etc.); (4) influx of women into the workforce—more women made more financial and consumption decisions in households, and women are typically more conscious about environmental psychology issues); and (5) the growth of double-income households and changes in the intrahousehold balance of power.

The relevant environmental psychology factors are:

- Neighborhood quality, as measured by crime, sanitation, noise, vegetation, retailing activities, and so on.
- Affinity for certain areas/activities/groups.
- The changes in the aggregate volumes of physical structures.
- Aesthetics of the housing unit (interior and exterior).

The following are testable hypotheses pertaining to changes in traditional-mortgage volumes, home prices, and housing demand—these hypotheses were derived from events in and data from the U.S., European, and Japanese housing markets.

PROPOSITION 1: CREDIT BIAS

Some lenders analyze aggregate/overall credit scores in specific neighborhoods as part of the loan approval process and the appraisal review process (in addition to analyzing the loan applicant's credit records). This procedure is somewhat different from "redlining" because these lenders will lend to "outsiders" with good credit scores who want to purchase homes in the subject neighborhood. Hence, this approach tends to limit the increases of assessed property values in low-income neighborhoods. Where many residents in a neighborhood cannot obtain mortgages, they will not be able to refinance their mortgages based on higher home values, and consequently, home prices will not increase as quickly as in other areas. Similarly, where many residents of a neighborhood can easily get mortgages, home prices will tend to increase at above-average rates. These trends can account for the creation and rapid growth of the subprime mortgage market as lenders sought to: (a) serve low-income households, and (b) protect their existing risk exposures to low-income neighborhoods by providing additional loans to support increasing housing prices. Thus, the credit bias can account for the subprime mortgage problems in the U.S. housing markets.

PROPOSITION 2: THE S&L CRISIS EFFECT

The psychological impact of the savings and loan (S&L) crisis that occurred in the United States during the 1980s and 1990s and the resulting government oversight created a constraint on the supply of housing units in the United States. The increase in prices of housing units from 1995 to 2003 can be partly explained by the change in the volume of new construction beginning in the early 1990s. Before then, the time series of prices of housing units were relatively volatile, and after that period, they have been relatively smooth. This 1990 breakpoint may not be coincidental. After the S&L banking crisis that occurred in the United States, scrutiny from banking regulators and skepticism in the capital markets reduced availability of credit to developers, and also served as a check on the boom-and-bust dynamics that seemed to characterize housing development in prior periods. This accounts for the fact that overbuilding did not occur during the intermittent periods of "economic expansion" that occurred between 1995 and 2003. Such constrained housing supply combined with increasing housing demand (from increased immigration, new births, increased number of single-person households, etc.), partly explains why prices of housing units may have remained firm and increased between 1995 and 2003. Thus, the credit crunch that constrained housing development in the United States from 1990 to 2000 (and thereby, stabilized home prices) was the result of psychological effects of the S&L banking crisis.

PROPOSITION 3: TENURE BIAS

People's perceptions of rental-tenure versus ownership-tenure also contributed to changes in home prices and housing demand in the United States from 1995 to 2003—this is referred to as *tenure differential* (Malpezzi, Englund, Kim, and Turner 2004; Bennett, Peach, and Stavros 1998). In many instances, people tend to view rental tenure as more of a shorter term arrangement, involving less emotion and financial commitment to the housing unit; and conversely, view ownership tenure as a long-term arrangement (the activities of "flippers" are localized, and in many U.S. cities/town, they constitute a small percentage of the total volume of sale/purchase transactions). Such perceptions are incorporated into the individual's selection of an investment horizon, and are shaped by the neighborhood, type of landlord, type of housing unit, expectations about increases in home values, household income, expected future financial commitments, knowledge, family structure, and so on. The tenure-differential was manifested from 1995 to 2003 by the annual changes in the percentage of renters who choose to purchase homes (increased); and the annual changes in the percentage of homeowners who choose to sell homes, and then rent housing units (increased).

The volume of "flipping" of housing units increased in many U.S. states from 1995 to 2003; from 1995 in housing markets like Miami and Las

Vegas, many purchasers flipped housing units, often for substantial profits. This trend has continued to present day—according to the *Economist* (June 2005), in Miami (Florida), approximately half of the original buyers of new apartments resell the new apartments within a short period of time, solely for short-term gains. Such flipping indicates the substantial impact of market psychology and expectations.

Tenure cost differential effect refers to the difference between the monthly cost of ownership and the monthly cost of renting. The tenure cost differential is conjectured to vary drastically when calculated on a monthly and yearly basis. This is because of frequency/amount of income, disposable income, timing of required payments, applicable penalties for breach of lease or mortgage, and so on. Tenure cost differential is positive if it costs more to rent than to own, and vice versa. From 1995 to 2003, tenure cost differential was increasingly positive primarily because of low mortgage interest rates, availability of subprime mortgages, and tax deductibility of mortgage interest payments.

PROPOSITION 4: LOW WILLINGNESS TO ACCEPT LOSSES (WTAL)

In the United States (as well as the United Kingdom, Germany, and other developed countries), sellers' low willingness to accept losses (WTAL) also contributed to increases in housing prices from 1995 to 2004. Genesove and Mayer (2001) explained how loss aversion could result in increasing home prices. Nwogugu (2006) defined WTAL. In addition to loss aversion, elements described in Genesove and Mayer (2001) and seller's low WTAL, homeowner's expectations, their psychological tendencies (nervousness, procrastination, conservatism, thriftiness, sensitivity to any change, attachments, value of money, etc.), states of mind, and mental budgets (different from actual cash budgets) also affected housing prices. The main effects of WTAL are: (a) as a psychological effect that stabilizes prices at certain levels; (b) increasing prices where material changes occur in the market; (c) calculations and revisions of magnitude and transferability of actual and perceived "losses"; (d) the magnitude of seller inertia; and (e) perceived impact on current and expected standard of living.

PROPOSITION 5: INVESTMENT HORIZON EFFECT

From 1995 to 2003, U.S. housing market dynamics were substantially affected by the relative shortening of the possible investment horizons of individual investors in U.S. securities markets, and hence their shift to real estate (and housing units) as an alternative to longer-maturity securities. The change in investment horizons of U.S. investors during this time was characterized by:

- The volume available of long-term corporate bonds and preferred stock declined.
- The volume of available long-term U.S. Treasury bonds declined.
- Individual investors experienced substantial losses in U.S. stock markets between 2000 and 2004 (even for stocks that were considered long-term "holds"), which may have caused some of them to change their investment horizons.
- The number of annual corporate bankruptcies increased from 1995 to 2003.
- The volume of purchases of housing units and the volume of residential mortgages increased substantially.

Hence, a household's propensity to sell or propensity to buy a housing unit (and hence, propensity to seek mortgages) is sensitive to changes in its investment horizon.

PROPOSITION 6: THE DEFERRED-DISUTILITY/DEFERRED PAIN BIAS

In the United States from 1995 to 2004, the psychological appeal (and not the suitability or economic efficiency) of, and the "deferred pain" feature inherent in new forms of financing increased the availability of credit and enabled nontraditional borrowers and lenders to enter the U.S. housing market. These new forms of financing included floating rate mortgages, low-down payment mortgages, no-documentation mortgages and no-verification loans, interest-only mortgages, and "negative amortization loans"—these new types of mortgages were obviously much more risky than traditional mortgages and many prospective home buyers could be deemed capable of reasonably comprehending the basic differences in risk of these loan types. According to the National Association of Realtors (U.S.), in 2004, 42 percent of all first-time buyers and 25 percent of all buyers made no down payment for their home purchases. From 1995 to 2003, many home buyers could get 105 percent loan-to-value (LTV) loans to cover buying/closing costs. In California, more than 60 percent of all new residential mortgages in 2004 were interest-only or negative-amortization loans, up from 8 percent in 2002 (the 2004 national figure was 30 percent of all new residential mortgages).

These new types of mortgages were essentially implied bets that home prices will continue to rise rapidly, enabling the borrower to sell the home at a profit or to refinance before any principal repayment. Such loans are usually adjustable-rate mortgages (ARMs), which expose the borrower to higher interest rates. In 2003, the volume of ARMs grew to at least 35 percent all mortgages in those states that had the biggest increases in home prices. These new loans were presumably appealing to prospective homeowners because they provided some psychological comfort despite the much greater inherent risk: (a) the feeling of independence associated with homeownership; (b) the satisfaction gained from building "perceived home equity" (primarily from increases in home prices), instead of paying rent; (c) the psychological convenience of no-documentation and no-verification loans; (d) the psychological appeal of deferment of the mortgage payments during the first few months of the mortgage; and (e) the increased belief or hope that interest payments on floating rate loans will remain low, and/or that floating rate loans could be subsequently refinanced easily as the homeowner's home equity increases or as the homeowner's credit score improves.

These new loans were also psychologically appealing to lenders and mortgage brokers because the following conditions existed: (a) new markets and rapid increases in loan volume accompanied by increased profits; (b) the perceived ease of securitization of these new forms of riskier loans, and hence transfer of risk; (c) the perceived ease of obtaining third-party credit enhancement (such as guarantees, loan insurance); and (d) the built-in credit enhancement mechanism in securitization—the senior-junior structure was common in securitization transactions and the risk of the "junior" portion of the loan pool is often offset by paying lower interest rates on the securitized bonds.

PROPOSITION 7: THE LENDER-EXPERIENCE EFFECT

There can be substantial differences between the decision process of experienced and inexperienced lenders. Some of these differences are:

- Search costs will affect lending decisions—lenders' search costs can also vary with experience.
- Emphasis on borrower credit will vary with experience.
- Ability or willingness to revise risk estimates, third-party property valuations, and internalized property valuations in a timely manner vary with lender experience.
- Correlations between lender decisions and performance evaluation criteria will vary with lenders' experience.

Hence, the lender-experience effect can account for: (a) lenders' willingness to provide loans; (b) lenders' willingness to accept higher property valuations; (c) the subprime loan problems; and (d) mortgage fraud.

PROPOSITION 8: THE GOVERNMENT INTERVENTION EFFECT

In many countries, the state and federal governments intervene in real estate and mortgage markets in various ways—such as providing mortgage insurance; granting tax credits to developers; allowing deductibility of mortgage interest for tax purposes; buying/selling mortgages. These government intervention mechanisms substantially affect consumer psychology and reactions to mortgages and housing tenure choices.

Buyers' willingness to repay mortgages sometimes declines over time, where the mortgage is insured by government agencies, or government-sponsored agencies. Such behavior can be attributed to conscious or subconscious protest (against government policies and/or banks' policies), opinions about fairness, frustration, increased knowledge (improves abandonment decisions). In the United States, the Federal Housing Administration (FHA) and the Veteran's Administration (VA) provide mortgage insurance for a substantial percentage of residential mortgages. Historically, the delinquency rates of FHA and VA mortgages have almost always been much greater than delinquency rates of conventional mortgages, home-equity loans, subprime loans, and the average for the overall residential mortgage markets. Real estate developers who obtain tax credits for renovation or new development are sometimes more likely to: (a) seek more tax credits; (b) enter into development projects that are not truly beneficial, solely to obtain tax credits; and (c) falsify records and applications in order to obtain tax credits. Such behavior can be attributed to conscious or subconscious protest, opinions about fairness, greed, perceived lack of adequate controls/oversight, or opportunism. In some cases, the developers who get tax credits are more prone to file and execute unfeasible projects, and the result is that many units are rented to low-income households, property maintenance is inadequate, code violations are high, and eventually social problems and crime increase—all of which shift risk and liabilities to the government.

Hence, the government intervention effect can account for the following trends and behaviors: (1) the growth of the regular residential mortgage and subprime mortgage markets in the United States, (2) strategic defaults, (3) the behavior of developers who seek or obtain government benefits, and (4) the quality of housing units provided wholly or partially with government benefits.

PROPOSITION 9: THE MULTIPLE-LISTING-SERVICE (MLS) EFFECT

In many U.S. jurisdictions, Multiple Listing Service (MLS) systems were introduced and made mandatory for real estate sales transactions. MLS systems typically increase exposure of properties and hence, increase market transparency and frequency of transactions, and in most circumstances, MLS also causes greater-than-normal increases in house prices (especially when property prices are rising). Six possible resulting psychological effects on the sellers are:

1. *Price inertia.* A tendency for the seller of a housing unit to maintain a relatively stable offering price after listing the property in an MLS, in order to support beliefs about prices.
2. *Exposure expectations* (and upward price bias). Wherein the seller assumes that more exposure will result in more purchase offers, and better terms/prices.
3. *Reference dependence.* Wherein the seller relies more heavily on recent sales transactions data to make decisions about the offering price and time-on-the-market for selling the housing unit.
4. *Justification.* Wherein sellers are quick to justify price increases, and otherwise unreasonable prices.
5. *Comparison.* Wherein sellers constantly seek "appropriate" comparisons in order to determine the "fair" price for their homes.

The possible resulting psychological effects of the MLS on buyers include, but are not limited to, comparison price referencing; justification; loss aversion; and increased expectations of higher prices.

PROPOSITION 10: PSYCHOLOGICAL LIMITATIONS ON SUPPLY OF HOUSING UNITS

The rapid increases in home prices (and the corresponding increases in volumes of traditional mortgages) that occurred in the United States (and some European countries) from 1995 to 2004 can be partly attributed to several psychological and nonpsychological factors that limited supply of new housing units. The psychological factors that limit the supply of new housing units included:

- Increased community activism that blocked new construction, including (1) greater consumer concern about environmental pollution and congestion from construction of new housing units; and (2) increased activity of community-based nonprofit organizations, which entered the housing market, blocked proposed new construction by private developers but could not deliver the same or more new housing units that the developers could have delivered.

- Changes in consumer tastes and purchasing patterns.
- Perceived risk of mortgages, particularly new financial products such as ARMs and negative-amortization mortgages.
- Consumer perceptions and relative valuations of various forms of wealth; that is, cash versus home equity versus securities versus intangibles.
- Changes in the perceived fairness of prices of housing units, closing costs, and search costs.
- Changes in consumers' willingness to commute: (a) maximum psychological threshold distances for commuting; (b) the nature of the commuting experience; (c) commuting costs; and (d) psychological reactions to crowds.
- Consumer habits.
- Changes in household dynamics: (a) divorce or separation; (b) changes in prioritization processes; (c) changes in the number of adults that earn income; (d) changes in interpersonal relationships and "alliances"; and (e) changes in the decision-making processes and final arbiter of decisions.
- Changes in consumer leisure time, leisure expenses, and propensity to save.
- Changes in consumers' perceived importance of credit scores (FICO, etc.).
- Consumer attachment to a specific town, neighborhood, or property.
- The psychological comfort gained from occupying different forms of housing; that is, apartments versus townhouses versus single-family homes versus lofts, and suburbs versus downtown locations versus urban areas versus farms versus rural areas.
- Increasing consumer willingness to share housing units as prices increased.

The nonpsychological factors that limit supply of housing units include:

- Zoning laws and ordinances, which limit new construction.
- Increases in construction costs.
- Availability of financing.
- Demographics.
- Structure and stability of the household—households that remain relatively stable in terms of number of individuals or income, or leisure expenditures, tend to have less need to move to a new housing unit of a different size.

VALIDITY OF HOUSING DEMAND MODELS

In most traditional analyses of housing, household income and housing costs have been used as the primary indicators of housing demand, but this approach is grossly inaccurate and does not reflect the many social and psychological factors that affect housing demand, sale/purchase intent, and housing supply. The allocation of household income, lending, and the default process are subject to psychological influences, intra-household relationships, externalities (controllable and uncontrollable), prioritization, and impulses. Hence, to equate household income to housing demand is improper (Malpezzi 2002; Glaeser and Gyourko 2005; Sinai and Souleles 2005).

Similarly, housing costs (rent, maintenance, mortgage principal/interest, property taxes, insurance, capital expenditures) are subject to:

- *Psychological factors.* Needs, attachments, moods, group think, reaction to physical environment, peer pressure, and so on (Ioannides and Zabel 2003).
- *Chosen levels of comfort.* May not have a positive correlation or substantial correlation with wealth and income (Case and Shiller 2003).
- *Chosen levels of consumption.* May not have a positive correlation or substantial correlation with wealth and household income, and is also affected by peer pressure, risk aversion, regret, and other factors (Levy and Lee 2004; Iwarere and Williams 2003; Benjamin, Chinloy, and Jud 2002; Case and Shiller 2003). Research has shown that Americans do not have a fixed income-to-price ratio or income-to-rent ratio—these metrics vary by region and household.
- *Imposed levels of consumption and comfort.* May not have a positive correlation or substantial correlation with wealth and household income, and may arise from factors such as natural disasters, wage garnishment, emergency illness, unforeseen conditions, and so on.
- *Externalities.* Taxes, rent controls/rent stabilizations (which may make renting more attractive than ownership), transaction costs; crime; environmental psychology issues, and so on, all of which affect the household's allocation of income and choices.
- *Impulses.* Individual and group impulses may also account for changes in allocation of income/resources to housing.
- *Allocation of income and intra-household dynamics.* Who controls spending, and the influence of household members on housing choices (Levy and Lee 2004).

Hence, the cost of housing by itself is not an accurate indicator of housing demand. Within the context of the immediately preceding statements, all existing housing demand models and housing price forecasting models are inaccurate. A correlation analysis of changes in household income and changes in the volume of housing sales will show substantial differences in the correlation coefficients for the periods before 1995 and during 1997 to 2003 (Kauko 2004; Landis and Elmer 2002; Malpezzi 2002; Hendershott and Weicher 2002; Diaz 1999; Boyle and Kiel 2001; Black et al. 2003; Mishkin 2007). Thus, all existing housing demand models and all existing housing price models are inaccurate.

CONCLUSION

The implications of the foregoing analysis are that:

- Psychological factors were a major cause of the subprime mortgage-default problems, mortgage fraud, and the rapid increases in housing-unit prices that occurred in the United States from 1995 to 2003. Similar patterns were also observed in Europe.
- Most housing demand models and all housing price models were, and continue to be, inaccurate.
- Social psychology, environmental psychology, real estate laws, and intra-family relations are major determinants of housing demand, the propensity to sell and propensity to buy, and are critical elements of any market demand equilibrium model or housing price model.

REFERENCES

Ackert L., B. K. Church, and N. Jayaraman. 2011. Is there a link between money illusion and homeowners' expectations of housing prices? *Real Estate Economics*, 39 (2): 251–275.

Antonides, G., and M. Kroft. 2005. Fairness judgments in household decision-making. *Journal of Economic Psychology* 26 (6): 902–913.

Apgar, W., and M. Duda. 2005. Collateral damage: The municipal impact of today's mortgage foreclosure boom. A report prepared for the Homeownership Preservation Foundation Minneapolis, Minnesota. www.hpfonline.org/content/pdf/Apgar_Duda_Study_Short_Version.pdf.

Baffoe-Bonnie, J. 1998. The dynamic impact macroeconomic aggregates on housing prices and stock of houses: A national and regional analysis. *Journal of Real Estate Finance and Economics* 17 (2): 179–197.

Benjamin, J., P. Chinloy, and D. Jud. 2004. Why do households concentrate their wealth in housing? *Journal of Real Estate Research* 26 (4): 329–343.

Bennett, P., R. Peach, and P. Stavros. 1997. Structural change in the mortgage market and the propensity to refinance. Federal Reserve Board of New York. Research paper no. 9736.

Berkowitz, J., and R. Hynes. 1999. Bankruptcy exemptions and the market for mortgage loans. *Journal of Law and Economics* 42 (2): 809–830.

Black, R., M. Brown, J. Diaz III, K. M. Gibler, and T. V. Grissom. 2003. Behavioral research in real estate: A search for the boundaries. *Journal of Real Estate Practice and Education*, 6 (1): 85–112.

Bostic, R., K. Enge, P. McCoy, A. Pennington-Cross, and S. Wachter. 2008. State and local anti-predatory lending laws: The effect of legal enforcement mechanisms. *Journal of Economics and Business* 60 (1–2): 47–66.

Boyle, M., and K. Kiel. 2001. A survey of house price hedonic studies of the impact of environmental externalities. *Journal of Real Estate Literature* 9 (2): 117–144.

Bromiley, P., and C. Papenhausen. 2003. Assumptions of rationality and equilibrium in strategy research: The limits of traditional economic analysis. *Strategic Organization* 1 (4): 413–437.

Case, K., and R. Shiller. 2003. Is there a bubble in the housing market? *Brookings Papers on Economic Activity* 2: 299–362.

Case, C., J. Quigley, and R. Shiller. 2005. Comparing wealth effects: The stock market versus the housing market. *Advances in Macro-Economics* 5 (1): 1235–1245.

Cocco, J., and J. Campbell. 2003. Household risk management and optimal mortgage choice. *Quarterly Journal of Economics* 118 (4): 1449–1494.

Davis, G. 1997. The logic of testing structural change in meat demand: A methodological analysis and appraisal. *American Journal of Agricultural Economics* 79 (4): 1186–1192.

De Bruin, A., and S. Flint-Hartle. 2003. A bounded rationality framework for property investment behavior. *Journal of Property Investment and Finance* 21 (3): 271–281.

Diaz, J. 1999. The first decade of behavioral research in the discipline of property. *Journal of Property Investment and Finance* 17 (4): 326–332.

Díaz-Serrano, L. 2004. Income volatility and residential mortgage delinquency: Evidence from 12 EU countries. IZA Discussion Paper No. 1396, November. Available at SSRN: http://ssrn.com/abstract=621044.

Díaz-Serrano, L. 2009. Disentangling the housing satisfaction puzzle: Does homeownership really matter? *Journal of Economic Psychology* 30 (5): 745–755.

The Economist. 2005. In come the waves: the global housing boom. *The Economist*, June 16, 66–68.

Einio, M., M. Kaustia, and V. Puttonen. 2008. Price setting and the reluctance to realize losses in apartment markets. *Journal of Economic Psychology* 29 (1) 19–34.

El-Attar, M., and M. Poschke 2011. Trust and the choice between housing and financial assets: Evidence from Spanish households. *Review of Finance* (forthcoming).

Eldred, G. W. 2002. *The 106 Common Mistakes Homebuyers Make (And How to Avoid Them)*. (New York: John Wiley and Sons).

Garvill, J., T. Garling, E. Lindberg, and H. Montgomery. 1992. Economic and non-economic motives for residential preferences and choice. *Journal of Economic Psychology* 13 (1): 39–59.

Genesove, D., and C. Mayer. 2001. Loss aversion and seller behavior: Evidence from the housing market. *The Quarterly Journal of Economics* 116 (4): 1233–1260.

Glaeser, E. L., and J. Gyourko. 2005. Why is Manhattan so expensive? Regulation and the rise in house prices. *Journal of Law and Economics* 48 (2): 331–370.

Harrison, J. S., D. Oler, and M. R. Allen. 2005. Event studies and the importance of longer-term measures in assessing the performance outcomes of complex events. Working paper, University of Richmond.

Haurin, D. R., and H. L. Gill. 2002. The impact of transaction costs and the expected length of stay on homeownership. *Journal of Urban Economics* 51 (3): 563–584.

Hayunga D., and P. Lung. 2011. Explaining asset mispricing using the resale option and inflation illusion. *Real Estate Economics* 39 (2): 313–344.

Hendershott, P., and J. Weicher. 2002. Forecasting housing markets: Lessons learned. *Real Estate Economics* 30 (1): 1–11.

Hosmer, D., S. Taber, and S. Lemeshow. 1991. The importance of assessing the fit of logistic regression models. *American Journal of Public Health* 81 (12): 1630–1635.

Hu, X. 2005. Portfolio choice for home owners. *Journal of Urban Economics* 58 (1): 114–136.

Humphrey, S. J. 2003. Feedback-conditional regret theory and testing regret aversion in risky choice. *Journal of Economic Psychology* 25 (6): 839–857.

Ioannides, Y. M., and J. E. Zabel. 2003. Neighborhood effects and housing demand. *Journal of Applied Econometrics* 18 (5): 563–584.

Iwarere, J., and J. Williams. 2003. The effect of income, ethnicity/race and institutional factors on mortgage borrower behavior. *Journal of Real Estate Research* 25 (4): 509–528.

Kauko, T. 2004. Towards infusing institutions and agency into house price analysis. *Urban Studies*, 41 (8): 1507–1519.

Landis, J., and V. Elmer. 2002. New economy housing markets: Fast and furious—But different? *Housing Policy Debate* 13 (2): 233–274.

Lane, M. A., M. J. Seiler, and V. L. Seiler. 2011. Identifying behavioral explanations for a subset of the real estate shadow market. *Journal of Housing Research* (forthcoming).

Leamer, E. 2007. Housing is the business cycle. National Bureau of Economic Research Working Paper #13428.

Levy, D., and C. Lee. 2004. The influence of family members on housing purchase and decisions. *Journal of Property Investment and Finance* 22 (4–5): 320–338.

MacKinley, A. 1997. Event studies in economics and finance. *Journal of Economic Literature* 35 (10): 13–39.

Malpezzi, S. 2002. Hedonic pricing models: A selective and applied review. Prepared for: Housing economics: Essays in honor of Duncan Maclennan. Edited by Kenneth Gibb and Anthony O'Sullivan; April 10. www.bus.wisc.edu/realestate/pdf/pdf/Hedonic%20Pricing%20Models%20Survey%20for%20Maclennan.pdf.

Malpezzi, S., P. Englund, K. Kim, and B. Turner. 2004. Cross country models of housing tenure, rents and asset prices: The effects of regulations and institutions. Paper prepared for the ENHR Conference, University of Cambridge, July 2–6, Cambridge, UK.

Manzano, M. 2006. Structure of the Spanish housing market and sources of finance: An overview. Bank for International Settlements. www.bis.org/publ/wgpapers/cgfs26manzano.pdf.

Massa, M., and A. Simonov. 2005. Behavioral biases and investment. *Review of Finance* 9 (4): 483–507.

McWilliams, A., D. Siegel, and S. H. Teoh. 1999. Issues in the use of the event study methodology: A critical analysis of corporate social responsibility studies. *Organizational Research Methods* 2 (4): 340–365.

Meen, D., and G. Meen. 2003. Social behavior as a basis for modeling the urban housing market. *Urban Studies* 40 (5/6): 917–918.

Mishkin, F. 2007. Housing and the monetary transmission mechanism. Board of Governors of the Federal Reserve System—Finance and Economics Discussion Series: August; 2007–40. http://www.federalreserve.gov/pubs/feds/2007/200740/200740pap.pdf.

Mohamed, R. 2006. The psychology of residential developers: Lessons from behavioral economics and additional explanations for satisficing. *Journal of Planning Education and Research* 26 (1): 28–37.

Moss, M., A. Wellman, and G. Cotsonis. 2003. An appraisal of multivariable logistic models in the pulmonary and critical care literature. *CHEST* 123 (3): 923–927.

Nwogugu, M. 2006. Regret minimization and willingness-to-accept losses. *Applied Mathematics and Computation* 179 (2): 440–450.

Painter, G., and C. L. Redfearn. 2002. The role of interest rates in influencing long run home ownership rates. *Journal of Real Estate Finance and Economics* 25 (2–3): 243–267.

Poterba, J., S. Venti, and D. Wise. 2000. Saver behavior and 401K retirement wealth. *American Economic Review* 90 (2): 297–302.

Reagan, J. 1998. Building a set of standards for use of regression in the journal of broadcasting and electronic media. *Journal of Broadcasting and Electronic Media* 42 (4): 535–539.

Schein, A. 2002. Concern for fair prices in the Isreali housing market. *Journal of Economic Psychology* 23 (2): 213–223.

Seiler, M. J. 2011. Forward and falsely induced reverse information cascades. *Journal of Behavioral Finance* (forthcoming).

Seiler, M. J., M. A. Lane, and V. L. Seiler. 2011. The psychology behind why underwater investment properties are not listed for sale. *Advances in Behavioral Finance and Economics* 1: 2 (forthcoming).

Seiler, M. J., V. L. Seiler, and M. Lane. 2011. Mental accounting and false reference points in real estate investment decision making. *Journal of Behavioral Finance* (forthcoming).

Seiler, M. J., P. Madhavan, and M. Liechty. 2011. Toward an understanding of real estate homebuyer Internet search behavior: An application of ocular tracking technology. *Journal of Real Estate Research* (forthcoming).

Seiler, M. J., and V. L. Seiler. 2010. Mitigating investor risk-seeking behavior in a down real estate market. *Journal of Behavioral Finance* 11 (3): 161–167.

Seiler, M. J., V. L. Seiler, M. A. Lane, and D. M. Harrison. 2011. Familiarity bias and perceived future home price movements. *Journal of Behavioral Finance* (forthcoming).

Seiler, M. J., V. L. Seiler, S. Traub, and D. M. Harrison. 2008. Regret aversion and false reference points in residential real estate. *Journal of Real Estate Research* 30 (4): 461–474.

Seko, M., and K. Sumita. 2007. Effects of government policies on residential mobility in Japan: Income tax deduction system and the Rental Act. *Journal of Housing Economics* 16 (2): 167–188.

Simonsohn, U., and Loewenstein, G. 2006. Mistake #37: The effect of previously encountered prices on current housing demand. *The Economic Journal* 116 (508): 175–199.

Sinai T., and N. S. Souleles. 2005. Owner-occupied housing as a hedge against rent risk. *The Quarterly Journal of Economics* 120 (2): 763–789.

Smith, S. J. 2006. Home ownership: Managing a risky business? In J. Doling and M. Elsinga Eds. *Home ownership: Getting in, getting from, getting out; part II.* Delft, IOS Press.

Sunden, A. E., and B. J. Surette. 1998. Gender differences in the allocation of assets in retirement savings plans. *American Economic Review* 88 (2): 207–211.

Taylor, M. 2011. Measuring financial capability and its determinants using survey data. *Social Indicator Research*, 102 (2), 297–314.

Tu, Y., M. Kellett, V. Clerehugh, and M. Gilthorpe. 2002. Problems of correlations between explanatory variables in multiple regression analysis in the dental literature. *British Dentistry Journal* 199 (7): 457–461.

UNC Charlotte Urban Institute and Metropolitan Studies and Extended Academic Programs. 2010. A Comprehensive Affordable-Housing Market Study for Mecklenburg County. The University of North Carolina at Charlotte; September. http://ftpcontent.worldnow.com/wbtv/housingstudy.pdf.

Van Poucke, D., and M. Buelens. 2002. Predicting the outcome of a two party price negotiation: Contribution of reservation price, aspiration price and opening offer. *Journal of Economic Psychology* 23 (1): 67–76.

CHAPTER 5

Behavioral Biases in Property Taxation and Property Appraisal

This chapter introduces psychology theories and behavioral biases pertaining to property taxation and property appraisals that can explain legal and economic problems such as *tax evasion*, *mortgage fraud*, *tax fraud*, and *appraisal fraud* (tax assessments for all types of real estate are often based on appraisals conducted on behalf of local/municipal governments). These new hypotheses can be used to improve existing housing demand and housing price prediction models, develop public health policies and mental health policies, and serve as the foundation for new housing models.

Although psychological factors affected many aspects of the housing sector in the United States and many countries during 1995 to 2010, and many researchers have documented various types of biases in investments and real estate, the existing literature on housing demand and housing price models does not cover many relevant psychological biases in property appraisal and property taxation. Property appraisal, particularly in debt-financed transactions, can have substantial effects on sellers, buyers, lenders, and tax administration staff at local/municipal governments. Mooya (2009; 2011) suggested that the traditional appraisal model was outmoded, and compared it with automated appraisals. Yiu, Tang, Chiang, and Choy (2006) and Nakamura (2010) differentiated between random bias and systematic bias in appraisals, and summarized the then-existing literature on appraisal bias; they also summarized three hypotheses for systematic bias—behavior contention, options-value, and different-base-of-valuation. Random bias includes appraisal smoothing (valuation timing), behavioral contention (anchoring to previous estimates), overreaction, and purely random bias. Systematic bias includes behavioral contention (anchoring bias and survival bias), options value hypothesis, and different base-of-valuation hypothesis. Also see Ackert, Church, and Jayaraman (2011); Hayunga and Lung (2011);

Biais and Weber (2009); Blank, von Collani, Fischer, and Nestler (2010); El-Attar and Poschke (2011); Chapman and Polkoynichenko (2011); Cao, Han, Hirshleifer, and Zhang (2011); Gilad and Kliger (2008); Mayer and Sinai (2007); Seiler, Seiler, and Lane (2010); Einio, Kaustia, and Puttonen (2008); Seiler and Seiler (2010); Shapira and Venezia (2001); Crane and Hartzell (2008); Seiler, Lane, and Seiler (2011); Seiler, Seiler, Lane, and Harrison (2011); Lane, Seiler, and Seiler (2011); Dempsey, Harrison, Luchtenberg, and Seiler (2010); Seiler, Seiler, Traub, and Harrison (2008); Seiler, Madhavan, and Liechty (2011); Nwogugu (2006); Nwogugu (2008a; 2008b); Lacour-Little and Malpezzi (2003); Loebs (2005); Quan and Quigley (1991).

BIASES IN PROPERTY TAXATION

This section develops testable hypotheses and theories of the psychological issues/effects and behavioral issues inherent in property taxation. State, local, and federal taxation tends to affect real estate ownership, values, and transactions, and hence, utility from participation in real estate and mortgage markets (Cornia and Slade 2005; Levy and Schack 1999; Riddiough 1997; Rosen 1979; Poterba 1984; Rubinfeld and Polinsky 1978; Gervais 2003). Existing housing models (i.e., models of housing prices, housing taxation) have not incorporated these psychological phenomena (Massa and Simonov 2005; Black et al. 2003; Shiller 2003; Cheng 1976; Shiller 2011; Dye and McMillen 2007; Haveman and Sexton 2008; Lutz 2008; Sexton 2003; Youngman 2007). Yiu, Tang, Chiang, and Choy (2006), Shiller (2011), and Nakamura (2010) explained the property tax assessment process. Swinney (2011) analyzed consumer perceptions of valuation uncertainty pertaining to products and found that the value of quick response is generally lower with strategic (forward-looking) customers than with nonstrategic (myopic) customers. Swinney (2011) also noted that a quick response strategy can increase firm profit when prices are increasing or when dissatisfied consumers can return the product at a cost to the firm, and quick response may decrease profit when prices are constant or when consumer returns are not allowed. The Swinney (2011) findings are also potentially applicable to: (a) lenders' appraisal-based loan-origination decisions; (b) real estate developers' appraisal-based decisions to build properties; and (c) real estate funds' appraisal-based buy/sell decisions. Kremer, Moritz, and Siemsen (2011) analyzed forecasting behavior and found that forecasters overreact to forecast errors in relatively stable environments, but underreact to errors in relatively unstable environments, and that the performance loss that is caused by these systematic judgment biases is larger in stable environments than in unstable environments (many government tax assessors use time series methods to derive assessed values and property tax rates for properties).

Furthermore, existing property demand/price forecasting models suffer from omissions and deficiencies explained in the following articles: Davis (1997); Tu, Kellett, Clerehugh, and Gilthorpe (2005); Hosmer, Taber, and Lemeshow (1991); Moss, Wellman, and Cotsonis (2003); Reagan (1998); McWilliams and Siegel (1999); MacKinley (1997); Harrison, Oler, and Allen (2005); Garvill, Garling, Lindberg, and Montgomery (1992); Militino, Ugarte, and Garcia-Reinaldos (2004); Kauko (2004); Watkins (1998).

Between 2005 and 2011 several U.S. state legislatures were considering new laws on property taxes and the proposals including the following:

- New bills to limit property taxes, and to increase the "homestead exemption."
- A reduction in property taxes, and more emphasis on (replacement with) sales taxes (the state legislature had capped the annual increase in property tax assessments at 3 percent per year until a home is sold or improved).
- New laws (amending the state constitution) to cap annual increases in property taxes to 3 percent per annum.
- Protesters in a state were gathering signatures for a citizen initiative that would require the state to refund tax payments to tax payers if state revenues rise faster than the annual inflation rate; the protesters also wanted to cap the growth in property tax bills at 1 percent per year.
- The state ordered cities and towns that had sharp increases in property taxes to calibrate disputed assessments to "comparable" properties, based on records of recent sales.

There are certain tax-related psychological biases inherent in proposed and actual real estate transactions, some of which are explained next.

Proposition 1: Tax Anticipation Bias

Individuals and households tend to choose and purchase properties where they believe there is lower likelihood of new property taxes or higher property taxes. The tax anticipation bias can be confirmed by comparing the absolute volume of and monthly changes in new home sales in states/towns that have historically high property tax rates (such as New Jersey, United States) and states/towns that have historically low property tax rates. The tax anticipation bias is much more pronounced in residential real estate markets (buildings that contain one to four residential units) than in commercial real estate markets, partly because: (1) in commercial properties, the landlord can pass property tax expenses to tenants; (2) in commercial properties, property taxes account for a much lower percentage of the total costs of ownership; and (3) in commercial real estate markets, the perceived and actual monetary impact of property taxes is dampened by current income from the commercial property (unlike most residential properties that do not generate income). In many U.S. cities/towns, property taxes became a more contentious issue between 1995 and 2003 with significant political ramifications as exemplified by economic and political changes in New Jersey during the period. Hence, although real estate taxes were relatively small expenses, the fear of possible tax increases (due to economic conditions and state/local politics) became a major valuation attribute that was more psychological than real (see www.njvoterinfo.org/ib/proptax.htm). According to a (New Jersey) *Star-Ledger*/Eagleton Rutgers Poll released in February 2003, about 68 percent of New Jersey residents stated that local property taxes were too high (50 percent stated that taxes were "much too high"). However, only 32 percent of respondents said that their state income taxes were too high and only 21 percent stated that the sales tax was too high. A December 2002 poll by Quinnipiac University found that 54 percent of respondents (New Jersey residents) named the local property tax as the tax that they disliked the most, followed by the federal income tax (17 percent), the federal Social Security tax (9 percent), the state sales tax (8 percent), and the state income tax (7 percent).

Proposition 2: Tax/Value Differential Bias

Individuals and households tend to value properties and make choices based on differentials between the assessed values and market values of the property. In many markets, the assessed values are often not updated because of budget constraints.

During 1995 to 2003, the often substantial divergence between market values of housing units and their "assessed values" (for real estate tax purposes) was sufficient to create psychological incentives or disincentives to purchase or sell real estate (and to obtain mortgages), and so was also a major determinant of housing demand and volatility of housing prices. This can be confirmed by comparing the ratio of assessed value to sale price for all listed properties on one hand, and for properties that were actually sold in any jurisdiction, on the other hand. Furthermore, the magnitude of the divergence between market values and "assessed values for tax" can become the basis for constitutional tort claims. This is because the government has the primary responsibility of establishing processes for imposing property taxes and for specific tax rates, and because said price differential carries vital information about appraisal procedures, internal controls, tax-determination procedures, rights of tax payers (appeals, hearings, etc.), and so forth.

Proposition 3: Tax Fixation Effect

Individuals and households are often fixated on property tax rates and tax-assessment processes, even though actual cash property tax liabilities are relatively small and are much less than other property operating expenses (where both are expressed as percentages of the property value). The tax fixation effect is different from "anchoring" because the tax fixation is on processes, appeals, comparisons, and ranges of values (as opposed to one amount, as is typical of anchoring). The tax fixation effect is more pronounced in residential real estate markets than in commercial real estate markets—this can be partly attributed to promises by politicians to change taxes, and the perceived effect of property taxes on municipal financing. Many surveys/polls (between 2003 and 2010) have shown that the high level of property taxes in New Jersey was the leading issue of voter concern in most elections that were held after 2002. Furthermore, there has been some inconsistency in assessing property values, and this resulted in inequitable disparities in the tax burden among municipalities and income groups.

Proposition 4: The Tax Foreclosure Bias

Taxation of real estate provides another level/class of perceived risk for lenders, prospective buyers, and property owners because the government can foreclose on properties for tax delinquencies. Hence, the willingness of lenders, prospective buyers, and property owners to participate in real estate markets will be affected by their perceptions of the likelihood of tax foreclosure and/or increases/reductions in assessed property taxes. The tax foreclosure bias is more prevalent in residential real estate markets than commercial real estate markets because (1) most residential properties are primary residences that do not generate income, and (2) most commercial properties are owned by relatively well-capitalized companies that have sufficient cash reserves (unlike typical homeowners, who live from paycheck to paycheck). In most U.S. states, real estate taxes are the primary source of revenue for most local governments; this has created an excessively regressive tax system that is not related to income and the ability to pay, and that imposes significant financial burdens on those with fixed incomes, such as senior citizens and people with disabilities.

Proposition 5: Tax Consequences Bias

There are substantial and very different tax consequences from debt-financed property ownership, equity-financed property ownership, and rental of commercial or residential real property. These differences create various incentives and disincentives for buyers, sellers, brokers, and banks to participate in real estate transactions, to commit funds to real estate, and to do transactions at specific times. Hence, the individual's or group's propensity to sell/buy real estate partly depends on his or her cognition and perception of tax consequences of the proposed transaction. The tax consequences bias may be similar in both residential property markets and commercial property markets. The tax consequences bias can be confirmed by comparing the volumes of property sales/purchases in jurisdictions that have few taxes with jurisdictions that have many and complex taxes—and the comparison factors should include knowledge of different market participants, perceived and actual complexity of tax laws, perceived tax benefits from transactions, and so on.

PSYCHOLOGICAL EFFECTS AND BIASES INHERENT IN PROPERTY APPRAISAL

Most banks/lenders perform property appraisals before lending decisions are made. Similarly, tax administration staff at local/municipal governments perform or supervise property appraisals. These appraisals are regarded as major elements of internal controls and corporate governance (Capozza, Isrealsen, and Thomson 2005; Joslin 2005). The literature contains some empirical analysis of only two main types of psychological influences pertaining to real estate appraisals—namely anchoring and risk aversion. Yiu, Tang, Chiang, and Choy (2006), Cornia and Slade (2005), Rosen (1996), Hansz (2004), and Gwin and Maxam (2002) list various studies that analyze behavioral biases including anchoring and risk aversion. Joslin (2005), Muller and Riedl (2002), Pereira, Lins, and Novaes (2005), and Crosby (2000) list and analyze articles that discuss the effect of risk version, clients, and the institutional environment on the appraisal process. These articles note the importance of various factors on the appraisal process, such as the existence and terms of mortgages, existence of purchase/sales contract, client relationships, prior work by the same appraiser, prior appraisal by another appraiser, and familiarity with the region (Hilber 2005; Rosen

1979; Henderson and Ionnides 1989; Antonides and Kroft 2005; Massa and Simonov 2005; Black et al. 2003; Shiller 2003).

The appraisal has substantial psychological impact on sellers' propensity to sell, and buyers' propensity to purchase, and the key elements are such effects as: (1) perceived fairness of prices and valuation estimates; (2) perceived risk; (3) regret; (4) perceived achievement by consummating transaction; (5) utility of transaction; (6) price/liquidity relationships; (7) expectations; (8) feasibility of down payment; and (9) acceptable levels of losses. Some psychological biases that either have not been analyzed theoretically or empirically in the literature or have not been analyzed fully are introduced as testable hypotheses.

The property appraisal has become a major element in the sale/purchase decision process. Most property sales/purchases are financed with mortgage debt. To comply with corporate governance standards, banks/lenders must appraise properties in order to provide the mortgage—these appraisals are performed in-house or are outsourced. Hence, the lender's lending officer can influence the bank's appraisal, but seeks the third-party appraisal in order to obtain some level of certainty about property values.

Tax assessments by tax administration staff at local/municipal governments are major indices of property values—such appraisals are done in-house (by government staff) or are outsourced. Similarly, tax administration staff at local/municipal governments can influence the property appraisal process—their appraisals provide some positive or negative certainty effect to market participants.

Proposition 1: Time Bias

The user time bias refers to the changes in the period of time for which users of an appraisal report believe that the appraisal report is valid. The user time bias is conjectured to increase as the number of comparable transactions increases and as the dates of comparable transactions are more recent, as the perceived difficulty of obtaining comparable transactions increases, as the estimated future liquidity of properties in the market increases, and as the difference between the appraisal date and the signed date decreases, and vice versa. The appraiser time bias refers to the changes in the period of time for which the appraiser believes that his/her appraisal report is valid. The appraiser time bias is conjectured to increase (the period of validity increases) as the number of comparable transactions increases, as the dates of comparable transactions are more recent, as the estimated future liquidity of properties in the market increases, as the perceived difficulty of obtaining comparable transactions declines, as the difference between the appraisal date and the signed date decreases, and vice versa. Appraisals create a time bias because most users (banks and lenders) (1) believe that the appraisal is valid as of the signed date and for a few months after the transaction (however, the appraiser's signed date is sometimes different from the appraisal date, and the appraisal is only an opinion as of a specific point in time and can be rendered useless by a few new transactions); (2) believe the appraisal is based on perfectly comparable sales; (3) believe that the appraisal is not based on the appraiser's ability to gather and synthesize information about recent sales and elements of cap rates—where such information is not readily available, the appraiser may resort to interpolation and assumptions; and (4) are sometimes not aware of data smoothing effects and methods used by appraisers (Joslin 2005; Adair and Hutchinson 2005; Geltner, MacGregor, and Schwann 2003).

Proposition 2: Inaccuracy Apprehension Effects

The lender's/bank's property appraisal is typically done by an external appraiser who is retained by the bank or by internal staff appraisers (Pereira, Lins, and Novaes 2005; Gwin and Maxam 2002). The influence of lenders (and other appraisal clients) on the appraisal process is discussed in Levy and Schack (1999) and in Gwin and Maxam (2002). Crosby (2000) attempted to define valuation accuracy. Hence, there are traditional agency and "anchoring" problems. The appraisal industry is highly fragmented. Most appraisal companies are usually very small companies that have local operations and depend on personal relationships, word-of-mouth, and repeat business. Hence, for most appraisal companies, the cost of client rejection is substantial (i.e., the client's refusal to provide repeat business or references). In some instances, because third-party appraisal reports are usually submitted in stages, the appraisal evolves into a quasi-negotiation between the appraiser and the client. Jap, Robertson, and Hamilton (2011) studied the effects of rapport among negotiators, and the resulting agent misbehavior in face-to-face and online interactions; they found that as rapport increases, the propensity of negotiators to misbehave also increases. Thus, the typical appraiser is conjectured to harbor a fear of the perception of inaccuracy of his/her appraisal, which is typically submitted in stages. This apprehension of inaccuracy often results in excessive documentation in appraisal reports, quasi-negotiation of appraisal values with clients, appraised values that are equal to or very close to the agreed-upon transaction price, unwillingness to extrapolate from available comparable transactions, emphasis on one or two appraisal methods, substantial reduction or widening of the differences between the appraised values derived using different appraisal methods, recursive appraisals (wherein an appraised value in one period is very likely to be based on appraised values in prior periods), and other biases.

Proposition 3: Perceived Liquidity Constraint Effect

Appraisals affect buyers', lenders', and sellers' perceptions of market liquidity. Unfortunately, the typical lender appraisal may or may not incorporate liquidity considerations, and in most cases, does not. This is because:

- By the time the lender hires the appraiser (or has the appraisal performed by in-house staff), there is an apparently ready seller and an apparently ready buyer.
- The appraiser has a strong incentive to appraise the property at, or very near, the agreed-on sale/purchase price in order to facilitate the lending transaction, and to generate future business. This trend is related to the compensation structure for third-party appraisers, true independence of appraisers, and the state banking laws (if the state banking laws were to limit the number of appraisals that can be performed by any one appraiser for any specific lender, within any 6-month or 12-month period, the incentive structure and adverse agency problems inherent in the appraisal process and risk-management processes would change dramatically).

Hence, the "market" defined by the buyer and seller at the time of appraisal is typically different from the true market, and an "independently determined" market price for that type of property.

It is conjectured that where the lender's appraisal differs substantially from the agreed-on price, and the buyer cannot obtain a sufficient loan to finance the purchase, the lender's, buyer's, and seller's perceptions of market liquidity change substantially; such perceptions are dissipated throughout the local/regional market, and the following may occur: (a) the real estate broker's perceptions and value estimates are revised; (b) the lender's perceptions, risk tolerance, and value estimates are revised substantially; and (c) the seller's reservation price may change.

Property appraisals affect and determine the magnitude of the perceived liquidity constraint facing the buyer. Part of the seller's and the broker's decision process is conjectured to include a conscious and subconscious evaluation of the prospective buyer's ability to gather enough funds (debt or equity) to complete the purchase. Appraisals are a major determinant and basis for (1) the 100 percent to 105 percent loan-to-value (LTV) loans, adjustable rate mortgages (ARMs), and reverse mortgages that became hugely popular after 1999, and have enabled many more participants to enter the housing market, and (2) home-equity loans.

Proposition 4: Knowledge Bias

Knowledge bias refers to the likelihood that an appraiser will tend to consider or focus on only those valuation factors and property elements that he/she is most knowledgeable about. Also, given a specific purpose for the appraisal, an appraiser will likely focus excessively on property elements that are related to the stated purpose of the appraisal. This definition is different from the common investors' familiarity bias, which has been described in the literature. Most appraisals involve some type of comparisons among properties deemed to be similar. This process can be subjective, because there are no generally accepted methods for selecting comparable properties, and the appraiser has to use his or her judgment and experience in making adjustments for comparability.

Proposition 5: Time-Based Exaggeration Bias

Appraisers sometimes exaggerate or focus on elements of properties and appraisal factors that they encountered in recent appraisal assignments. This bias is conjectured to increase where the appraiser specializes in one or a few types of properties and when the time period between appraisal projects declines. The time-based exaggeration bias can be attributed to: (a) an appraisal process that includes excessive documentation; (b) expertise in appraising one or two types of properties; (c) the appraiser's managing a series of appraisals of technically complex mixed-use properties; (d) the combination of performing appraisals for clients that focus on technical aspects of appraisals and having relatively few appraisal clients; (e) appraising properties that have similar technical features (for different appraisal clients); and (f) portfolio appraisal projects where the client(s) have emphasized specific valuation factors.

Proposition 6: Extrapolation Bias

Where the appraiser is new to the area, or is not familiar with the property type or the neighborhood, the appraiser will tend to overextrapolate from available information. Similarly, when the appraiser is very familiar with the area or property type, the appraiser will tend to rely on his or her personal knowledge and underextrapolate from available data. Extrapolation bias can also result in reluctance to collect and analyze market data, overemphasis on one appraisal method, and inability to isolate critical appraisal factors.

The extrapolation bias can be confirmed by comparing the magnitude of appraisers' knowledge of the area and property types with the magnitude of extrapolation in appraisal reports during specific blocks of time.

Proposition 7: Diffused Cognition Bias

The diffused cognition bias refers to a state wherein the licensed appraiser, who functions normally in all other aspects of life and also functions normally in the usual appraisal project, is not able to adequately isolate and analyze the impact of various factors on the values of a specific property or a property portfolio (such as size, time, location, amenities, traffic/noise, flood plains, rent controls, and so on). That is, the appraiser's cognition is weakened or diffused only during the appraisal of a specific asset or portfolio. Hence, this effect is different from the typical cognition deficit, which applies to all aspects of the individual's life. There are several degrees of this bias. In the first stage, there isn't a lot of comparable information. In the more advanced stages, there is substantial market data and the appraiser is experienced in valuing the type of property, but still experiences diffused cognition. The diffused cognition bias can be attributed to: (a) overconfidence or lack of confidence; (b) emotions that are aroused by specific features of a property or portfolio and are not often controllable by the appraiser; (c) uncertainty about elements of the project; (d) anticipation of post-appraisal events; (e) the type of compensation to be paid to the appraiser; (f) concerns about fairness of the appraiser's compensation; (g) the effects of internalization of limitations or rules associated with the subject property or portfolio; and (h) the subconscious reactions to processes, rules or restrictions, and changes or expectations associated with the subject property or portfolio.

Proposition 8: Time-on-the-Market Bias

The time-on-the-market bias refers to a state where the licensed appraiser's estimates of value may be biased upward or downward primarily because of the period of time that the subject property (and in some cases, comparable properties) has been on the market, regardless of other indications of market liquidity and market value. Time-on-the-market bias can be confirmed by (a) the cross-sectional correlation between appraised values and time on the market for the properties; (b) comparison of deviations of appraised values from mean/median values on one hand, and on the other hand, time on the market; (c) the longitudinal correlations between appraised values (using two to three appraisal methods) and time on the market; or (d) the correlation between changes in appraised values of properties (i.e., quarterly or semiannual appraisals) and time on the market for both sold and unsold properties.

Proposition 9: Inertia Effect

Property appraisals can create inertia on the part of the lender (lender's staff), due to overreliance on the appraisal, reluctance to incur monitoring costs, compensation systems, performance evaluation systems, and the need for justification. The inertia effect can be substantial because appraisals are only opinions as of one specific point in time, and can be rendered completely useless by new information, such as announcements of new property developments, demolitions, major changes in local employment (plant closings, or company relocations, discovery of environmental problems, natural disasters, urban renewal programs, etc.). Most lenders appraise properties in their portfolio on a quarterly, semi-annual, or annual basis. Most lenders do not receive monthly property operating statements for their portfolio properties.

Proposition 10: Overreliance Effects

Overreliance effects are where the lender or appraiser or passive property owner heavily relies on reports and third-party documents to make decisions about a subject property. Overreliance effects are prevalent in modern real estate because of the nature of information gathering and analysis, the automation of the lending and servicing processes, and because many parties (lenders, owners) don't want to spend capital on monitoring costs. Thus, the recent subprime mortgage crisis in the United States (and other countries) can be explained by overreliance effects. The lender may become overly reliant on the property appraisal report, the property tax report, credit histories of borrowers, and other reports, which is inappropriate because the property appraisal and the other documents represent opinions as of a specific point in time. These documents often don't distinguish (and cannot help the lender distinguish) among the borrower's ability to pay, willingness to pay, regret, and willingness to accept losses. The appraiser may also become overreliant on specific sources of information and data (other than acquisition price, mortgage amount, or prior valuations). This may occur when the appraiser is not familiar with the area or property type, or is under time pressure, or seeks to cut appraisal costs.

Proposition 11: Information-Gap Effect

Most lenders do not receive monthly property operating statements for their portfolio properties. Also, most lenders don't inspect portfolio properties on a regular basis, but sometimes rely on annual or semiannual (or to a lesser extent, quarterly) appraisals. This creates an information gap that is not filled adequately by quarterly property appraisals (the most frequent appraisal period used by most lenders). This information gap affects the lenders' perceptions of risk and the need to intervene before a subject property deteriorates. Unfortunately, most mortgage/loan documents don't address this information in terms of requesting regular operating reports or granting the lender special powers in the event of financial distress. This information gap affects not only the current loan portfolio, but also the lender's loan evaluation processes for prospective loans.

Proposition 12: Conformism Effect

Appraisals sometimes can cause the following types of conformism among the lender's staff:

- Conformism in interpretation of the appraisal.
- Conformism in applying elements of the appraisal, such as cap rates and discount rates and comparables.
- Conformism in terms of determination of LTVs.
- Conformism in determination of net realizable values.

Conformism is conjectured to be more probable in larger and more structured environments, in companies that use in-house automated loan-processing systems, and in companies where the performance evaluation system and compensation system stress or are based on compliance with standards.

The appraisal process also involves some elements of conformism. The appraiser typically uses a limited and generally accepted set of methods to value properties. Some of these methods are inaccurate in instances where there are not enough data, there are no recent sales, or there are no truly comparable data. In such cases, the appraiser has to make "adjustments" and interpolate, which is more of an art. Furthermore, the nature of the appraisal business provides substantial incentives for overconformism: (1) there are appraisal standards that the appraiser must comply with; (2) the appraiser's prospects of obtaining future business are highly dependent on third-party perceptions of appraiser compliance with appraisal standards; (3) the appraisal business has substantial reputation effects and is a local business—most appraisers work on properties in their town/city/region; and (4) the appraiser's career-switching costs are high—the universe of appraisal jobs is limited.

Proposition 13: Environmental Psychology Deficit Effects

It is conjectured that most lenders' property appraisals do not sufficiently capture the elements of environmental psychology that significantly affect property values. This is because:

- Appraisers are trained to use a limited set of tools, appraisal methods, and valuation formulas. Most appraisal training programs and examinations don't contain any meaningful material about the effect of environmental psychology on property values, demand for property, and mortgages.
- Appraisers tend to focus on replacement costs, land values, income, and comparable sales.
- Appraisers may tend to consider the justification processes and internal control processes of the most relevant "end user" of the appraisal (which is the lender). Most of these processes are based on income, land values, and net realizable values from distress sales, within the context of default.
- Appraisers may not be cognizant of values attached to specific elements of neighborhoods, the property, or the town—this may be the result of the appraiser's education, social circles, family background, preferences, moods, or other factors.
- The values attached to specific elements of neighborhoods, the property, or the town is likely to vary significantly depending on the buyer and seller and the location.

Proposition 14: Risk-Shifting Effect

Many lenders typically sell residential mortgage loans in the secondary market. During 1996 to 2007, more than 40 percent of all residential mortgage loans (single-family and multifamily loans) in the United States were either purchased by Federal National Mortgage Association (FNMA) or Freddie Mac; or were insured by the Federal Housing Administration (FHA). These institutions typically perform their own property appraisals and have in-house appraisal standards. However, this trend may affect the primary lender's appraisal and appraisal-review process, because it provides incentives for primary lenders to lower appraisal and lending standards in order to complete more transactions in less time (most loans are sold shortly after origination) and, in effect, shift risk to secondary-market purchasers. In these instances, there is a quasi principal–agent relationship between the primary lender and FNMA/Freddie Mac or FHA. If the mortgage loans were to become statutorily marketable only after a specific "seasoning" period of one to two years, then the incentives, psychological motivations, and actual/implicit penalties for primary lenders and appraisers will change dramatically for the better. Whether the secondary-market loan purchaser is adequately compensated for this risk of lower appraisal standards has not be studied extensively in the literature. *The knowledge that banks can sell mortgages in the secondary markets can create a psychological laxness in the loan-approval process, even though much of the process is now automated.*

The laxness occurs when the borrower and the loan agent collude to falsify loan applications to fit underwriting standards, with the knowledge that the loans will be eventually sold off in the secondary market, and securitized, and that any losses from that particular mortgage will be offset by cash flow from other loans in the mortgage pool. Hence, securitization or residential mortgages are conjectured to increase the propensity to commit fraud in the loan application process. The second type of laxness can occur with the output of the loan approval process data: (1) because most types of loan approval processes are automated, government-sponsored enterprises (GSEs) that want to buy loans may become over-reliant on such automated systems and associated output, and (2) although real estate prices and rents varied dramatically by region/city, recent research has shown that loan purchases in the secondary market were done without regard to locality and local economic conditions.

The third type of laxness is caused by over-reliance on mortgage insurance by the borrower, primary lender, and loan purchaser. FHA provides mortgage insurance for a substantial percentage of residential loans. This affects the quality of underwriting standards programmed into automated underwriting systems and manual processes—generally reducing underwriting quality and shifting risk to FHA.

Proposition 15: The Default Effect

The primary lender tends to influence property appraisals. In the worst-case scenario (default by the borrower), the primary lender that decides to hold the mortgage loan will foreclose and obtain title to a property that will have to be sold for any recovery. Hence, there is an inherent and substantial incentive for appraisers to: (1) establish property values at or close to net-realizable values of the subject property (which factors in transaction costs, post-default holding periods, property price appreciation/depreciation, and realizable values); and (2) to incorporate or discount future price appreciation in stated values. Similarly, when the lender gets the appraisal, the lender's final estimate of value is likely to be biased toward the net realizable value and to incorporate distress sale conditions.

Proposition 16: Deferred Utility/Disutility Effect

Appraisals can result in "deferred utility/disutility" for the buyer and seller. Such deferred utility/disutility increases as the magnitude of substantial disagreement about the value of the property grows, and as the borrower has fewer pre-transaction financing alternatives. Such utility/disutility arises due to the buyer's negotiating position in the purchase process—the seller typically has a reservation price and also may have conscious or subconscious price floors or price comparables; and the lender is typically guided by property appraisals, over which it has some degree of influence (through the threat of termination of the appraiser's contract or prospects of future appraisal assignments). As the buyer reflects over the ownership costs, environmental psychology issues, and is also affected by comparison, said utility/disutility sets in. Similarly, the seller experiences such disutility/utility over time, as home prices increase or decrease. The said utility/disutility is deferred primarily because: (1) there is some euphoria immediately after a transaction; (2) the seller, buyer, and lender "settle in" to the realities and consequences of the transaction; (3) the seller, buyer, and lender wait for a while to confirm their expectations and judgments about the property, market, neighborhood, and so on; or (4) issues raised by the changes in the seller's and buyer's lifestyle immediately after the transaction take a while to resolve.

Proposition 17: The Deferred Conflict Effect

Appraisals by the lender (on which most loans are based) can result in deferred conflict, in which the lender's "authoritative appraisal" essentially defers intra-group conflicts among members of certain coalitions (e.g., the lender's staff, the buyer's household/staff, and the seller's household/staff). The duration and quality (number of times that the issue is raised/discussed after the sale/purchase transaction) of such conflict deferral varies:

- *Among members of the buyer's staff/household.* Depends on assumed and expected opportunity costs: timing, bargaining positions, sources of income, prioritization, degree of authority over group members, cognition, knowledge, availability of advice, coping, and so on.
- *Among members of the seller's staff/household.* Depends on assumed and expected opportunity costs: timing, bargaining positions, sources of income, prioritization, composition/structure of household, degree of authority over group members, cognition, knowledge, availability of advice, coping, and so on.

- *Among lender's staff*. Such conflicts are a function of opportunity costs, knowledge about risk and capital requirements, risk management processes, performance evaluation standards for staff, incentive programs, corporate governance concerns, internal controls, and so on.

Proposition 18: Value Dichotomy Effect

Value dichotomy effect refers to a situation wherein a property appraisal or group of appraisals (portfolio appraisals) has different values to the seller, buyer, lender, and other stakeholders (i.e., economic value, psychological value, confirmation value). The economic and psychological values of the property appraisal to the bank/lender, the borrower, and the seller can differ substantially and largely depend on their cognition and perception, knowledge of the regional markets, analytical capabilities, purpose of the transaction, search costs, and willingness to execute the transaction. Also, appraisals may contain, and appraised value may be subject to, caveats, qualifications, disclaimers, and notations, which can create substantial differences in actual and perceived property values and the value-confirmation relevance of appraisals.

The property appraisal has become a justification tool for lending officers and tax administration staff in local/municipal governments. Justification is a major psychological characteristic in the lending process and tax assessment process because: (a) at lending entities, most performance evaluation systems are based on compliance with specific standards; (b) loan sales in the secondary markets have now become a major financing tool for banks, and such loan sales are based on appraised values; (c) risk management systems are partly based on property appraisals; and (d) tax administration staff in local/municipal governments realize that their assessments have significant psychological, political, and public policy effects, as illustrated by the political upheavals caused by increases in property taxes in New Jersey within the past 15 years. *Conflict/bargaining reduction effect* means that the appraisal has become a major tool and a major causal factor in the bargaining process between the borrower and the lender, and a major tool in resolving internal lender conflicts about capital commitments and risk.

The value dichotomy effect is conjectured to be a major determinant of the probability of occurrence of the subject transaction (e.g., sale or mortgage financing).

Proposition 19: Qualifications Bias

Appraisals may contain, and appraised value may be subject to, caveats, qualifications, disclaimers, and notations that can create substantial differences in actual and perceived property values and the value-confirmation relevance of appraisals. *User qualifications bias* refers to situations where, for a given property or portfolio, many users of the appraisal will tend to focus on the value estimate and often overlook the caveats, qualifications, disclaimers, and notations that typically define and limit the applications of the appraised value. User qualifications bias is conjectured to increase as the complexity of the subject property increases; as the number of properties in a transaction increases (e.g., bulk sales); and as the perceived difficulty of obtaining comparables increases; and vice versa. The *appraiser qualifications bias* refers to situations where, for a given property or portfolio, the appraiser is more likely than not to include qualifications, limitations, and caveats in his or her appraisal report. The appraiser qualifications bias is conjectured to increase with the complexity of the property (e.g., mixed-use properties, unusual design of property, unusual HVAC, etc.); as the time difference between the appraisal date and the transaction date decreases; as the duration of the relationship between the appraiser and the lender decreases; and as the appraisal fees increase. Furthermore, the appraiser's choice of sales comparables and discount rates (for discounted cash flow or income capitalization approaches) is critical, and has been shown (in empirical research) to vary dramatically depending on the appraiser's experience.

CONCLUSION

The foregoing biases are prevalent in both developed countries and developing countries (banking/lending procedures and appraisal procedures are similar across countries), and also apply to commercial real estate. Also, although specific tax rates differ among countries, the process of setting tax policy and determining tax rates is similar across countries. The omission of these psychological biases from economic models (for the prediction of property demand, property prices, housing tenure, strategic default, and traditional mortgage default) renders those models inaccurate and ineffective.

Among lenders and institutional investors (and even government agencies that own or oversee property portfolios), traditional and automated appraisals have also become a major tool of performance measurement, compensation, and risk management. The increasing occurrence of appraisal fraud, tax fraud, and mortgage fraud in developed and developing countries occurred despite massive automation of lending/appraisal processes (especially in most developed countries). Such criminal misconduct, lending processes, and risk management processes can be better managed by understanding the underlying biases and their possible effects on institutions, groups, temporary coalitions, individuals, and the effectiveness of regulations and processes.

REFERENCES

Ackert, L., B. K. Church, and N. Jayaraman. 2011. Is there a link between money illusion and homeowners' expectations of housing prices? *Real Estate Economics* 39 (2): 251–275.

Adair, A., and N. Hutchinson. 2005. The reporting of risk in real estate appraisal property risk scoring. *Journal of Property Investment & Finance* 23 (3): 254–268.

Antonides, G., and M. Kroft. 2005. Fairness judgments in household decision-making. *Journal of Economic Psychology* 26 (2): 902–913.

Biais, B., and M. Weber. 2009. Hindsight bias, risk perception and investment performance. *Management Science* 55 (6): 1018–1029.

Black, R., M. Brown, J. Diaz, K. Gibler, and T. Grissom. 2003. Behavioral research in real estate: A search for the boundaries. *Journal of Real Estate Practice & Education* 6 (1): 85–112.

Blank, H., G. von Collani, V. Fischer, and S. Nestler. 2010. How many hindsight biases are there? *Cognition* 106 (3): 1408–1440.

Cao, H., B. Han, D. Hirshleifer, and H. Zhang. 2011. Fear of the unknown: Familiarity and economic decisions. *Review of Finance* 15 (1): 173–206.

Capozza, D., R. Isrealsen, and T. Thomson. 2005. Appraisal, agency and atypicality: Evidence from manufactured homes. *Real Estate Economics* 33 (3): 509–537.

Chapman, D., and V. Polkovnichenko. 2011. Risk attitudes toward small and large bets in the presence of background risk. *Review of Finance* 15 (4): 909–927.

Cheng, P. 1976. Bias and error detection in property tax administration. *Management Science* 22 (11): 1251–1257.

Cornia, G., and B. Slade. 2005. Property taxation of multifamily housing: An empirical analysis of vertical and horizontal equity. *Journal of Real Estate Research* 27 (1): 17–46.

Crane, A., and J. Hartzell. 2008. Is there a disposition effect in corporate investment decisions? Evidence from real estate investment trusts. Working paper, McCombs School of Business, University of Texas at Austin, April.

Crosby, N. 2000. Valuation accuracy, variation and bias in the context of standards and expectations. *Journal of Property Investment & Financing* 18 (2): 130–161.

Davis, G. 1997. The logic of testing structural change in meat demand: A methodological analysis and appraisal. *American Journal of Agricultural Economics* 79 (4): 1186–1192.

Dempsey, S. J., D. Harrison, K. Luchtenberg, and M. J. Seiler. 2010. Contingent choice behavioral models in the presence of information uncertainty. *Journal of Real Estate Portfolio Management* 16 (3): 289–399.

Dye, R., and D. McMillen. 2007. Surprise! An unintended consequence of assessment limitations. *Land Lines* (July), 8–13.

Einio, M., M. Kaustia, and V. Puttonen. 2008. Price setting and the reluctance to realize losses in apartment markets. *Journal of Economic Psychology* 29 (1): 19–34.

El-Attar, M., and M. Poschke. 2011. Trust and the choice between housing and financial assets: Evidence from Spanish households. *Review of Finance* 15 (4): 727–756.

Geltner, D., B. MacGregor, and G. Schwann. 2003. Appraisal smoothing and price discovery in real estate markets. *Urban Studies* 40 (5/6): 1047–1064.

Gervais, M. 2003. Housing taxation and capital accumulation. *Journal of Monetary Economics* 49 (7): 1461–1489.

Gilad, D., and Kliger D. 2008. Priming the risk attitudes of of professionals in financial decision making. *Review of Finance* 12 (3): 567–586.

Gwin, C., and C. Maxam. 2002. Why do real estate appraisals nearly always equal the offer price? A theoretical justification. *Journal of Property Investment & Finance* 20 (3): 242–254.

Hansz, J. A. 2004. The use of a pending mortgage reference point in valuation judgment. *Journal of Property Investment & Finance* 22 (3): 259–268.

Harrison, J., D. Oler, and M. Allen. 2005. Event studies and the importance of longer-term measures in assessing the performance outcomes of complex events. Working paper, February.

Haveman, M., and T. Sexton. 2008. Property tax assessment limits: Lessons from thirty years of experience. Policy Focus Report, Lincoln Institute of Land Policy.

Hayunga, D., and P. Lung. 2011. Explaining asset mispricing using the resale option and inflation illusion. *Real Estate Economics* 39 (2): 313–344.

Hilber, Christian A. L. 2005. Neighborhood externality risk and the homeownership status of properties. *Journal of Urban Economics* 57 (2): 213–241.

Hosmer, D., S. Taber, and S. Lemeshow. 1991. The importance of assessing the fit of logistic regression models. *American Journal of Public Health* 81 (12): 1630–1635.

Jap, S., D. Robertson, and F. Hamilton 2011. The dark side of rapport: Agent misbehavior face-to-face and online. *Management Science*, forthcoming.

Joslin, A. 2005. An investigation into the expression of uncertainty in property valuations. *Journal of Property Investment & Finance* 23 (3): 269–285.

Kauko, T. 2004. Towards infusing institutions and agency into house price analysis. *Urban Studies* 41 (8): 1507–1519.

Kremer, M., B. Moritz, and E. Siemsen. 2011. Demand forecasting behavior: System neglect and change detection. *Management Science* 57 (10): 1827–1843.

Lacour-Little, M., and S. Malpezzi. 2003. Appraisal quality and residential mortgage default: Evidence from Alaska. *Journal of Real Estate Finance and Economics* 27 (2): 211–233.

Lane, M. A., M. J. Seiler, and V. L. Seiler. 2011. Identifying behavioral explanations for a subset of the real estate shadow market. *Journal of Housing Research*, forthcoming.

Levy, D., and E. Schack. 1999. The influence of clients on valuation. *Journal of Property Investment & Financing* 17 (24): 380–400.

Loebs, T. 2005. *Systemic risks in residential property valuations: Perceptions and reality*. Collateral Assessment and Technologies Committee, June 2005, available at http://catcommittee.org/catc/index.php.

Lutz, B. F. 2008. The connection between house price appreciation and property tax revenues. *National Tax Journal* (September), 555–572.

Massa, M., and A. Simonov. 2005. Behavioral biases and investment. *Review of Finance* 9 (4): 483–507.

Mayer, C., and T. Sinai. 2007. Housing and behavioral finance. http://real.wharton.upenn.edu/~sinai/papers/Housing-Behavioral-Boston-Fed-v9.pdf.

McWilliams, A., D. Siegel, and S. H. Teoh. 1999. Issues in the use of the event study methodology: A critical analysis of corporate social responsibility studies. *Organizational Research Methods* 2 (4): 340–365.

Mishkin, F. 2007. Housing and the monetary transmission mechanism. Board of Governors of the Federal Reserve System—Finance and Economics Discussion Series, August, 2007–40. www.federalreserve.gov/pubs/feds/2007/200740/200740pap.pdf.

Mohamed, R. 2006. The psychology of residential developers: Lessons from behavioral economics and additional explanations for satisficing. *Journal of Planning Education and Research* 26 (1): 28–37.

Mooya, M. 2009. Market value without a market: Perspectives from transaction cost theory. *Urban Studies* 46 (3): 687–701.

Mooya, M. 2011. Of mice and men: Automated valuation models and the valuation profession. *Urban Studies* 48 (11): 2265–2281.

Moss, M., A. Wellman, and G. Cotsonis. 2003. An appraisal of multivariable logistic models in the pulmonary and critical care literature. *Chest* 123 (3): 923–927.

Muller, K., and E. Riedl. 2002. External monitoring of property appraisal estimates and information asymmetry. *Journal of Accounting Research* 40 (3): 865–881.

Nakamura, L. 2010. How much is that home really worth? Appraisal bias and house-price uncertainty. *Federal Reserve Bank of Philadelphia Business Review* (First Quarter), 11–22.

Nwogugu, M. 2006. Regret minimization and willingness-to-accept losses. *Applied Mathematics & Computation* 179 (2): 440–450.

Nwogugu M. (2008a). Prospective home-buyer propensity-to-buy in the housing industry. *Chaos & Complexity Letters* 3 (2): 169–190.

Nwogugu, M. (2008b). On the choice between renting and buying in the U.S. housing industry. *Chaos & Complexity Letters* 3 (2): 191–208.

Pereira, M., E. Lins, and L. Novaes. 2005. Real estate appraisal: A double perspective data envelopment analysis approach. *Annals of Operations Research* 138 (1): 79–96.

Poterba, J. 1984. Tax subsidies to owner-occupied housing: An asset market approach. *Quarterly Journal of Economics* (November), 729–752.

Quan, D. C., and J. Quigley. 1991. Price formation and the appraisal function in real estate markets. *Journal of Real Estate Finance and Economics* 4 (2): 127–146.

Reagan, J. 1998. Building a set of standards for use of regression in the journal of broadcasting & electronic media. *Journal of Broadcasting & Electronic Media* 42 (4): 535–540.

Riddiough, T. 1997. The economic consequences of regulatory taking risk on land value and development activity. *Journal of Urban Economics* 41 (1): 56–77.

Rosen, H. 1979. Housing decisions and the U.S. income tax. *Journal of Public Economics* 11 (1): 1–23.

Rubinfeld, D., and M. Polinsky. 1978. The long-run effects of a residential property tax and local public services. *Journal of Urban Economics*, April, 241–262.

Schiller, T. 2011. What's it worth? Property taxes and assessment practices. *Federal Reserve Bank of Philadelphia Business Review*, Q3, 21–24. www.philadelphiafed.org/research-and-data/publications/business-review/2011/q3/brq311_property-taxes-and-assessment-practices.pdf.

Seiler, M. J. 2011. Forward and falsely induced reverse information cascades. *Journal of Behavioral Finance*, forthcoming.

Seiler, M. J., M. A. Lane, and V. L. Seiler. 2011. The psychology behind why underwater investment properties are not listed for sale. *Advances in Behavioral Finance & Economics* 1 (2), forthcoming.

Seiler, M. J., P. Madhavan, and M. Liechty. 2011. Toward an understanding of real estate homebuyer Internet search behavior: An application of ocular tracking technology. *Journal of Real Estate Research*, forthcoming.

Seiler, M., and V. Seiler. 2010. Mitigating investor risk seeking behavior in a down real estate market. *Journal of Behavioral Finance* 11 (3): 161–167.

Seiler, M. J., V. Seiler, and M. Lane. 2010. Mental accounting and false reference points in real estate investment decision-making. *Journal of Behavioral Finance*, forthcoming.

Seiler, M., V. Seiler, M. Lane, and D. Harrison. 2011. Familiarity bias and perceived future home price movements. *Journal of Behavioral Finance*, forthcoming.

Seiler, M., V. Seiler, S. Traub, and D. Harrison. 2008. Regret aversion and false reference points in residential real estate. *Journal of Real Estate Research* 30 (4): 461–474.

Seko, M., and K. Sumita. 2007. Effects of government policies on residential mobility in Japan: Income tax deduction system and the Rental Act. *Journal of Housing Economics* 16 (2): 167–188.

Sexton, T. A. 2003. *Property tax systems in the United States: The tax base, exemptions, incentives, and relief.* Center for State and Local Taxes, University of California–Davis.

Shapira, Z., and I. Venezia. 2001. Patterns of behavior of professionally managed and independent investors. *Journal of Banking and Finance* 25 (8): 1573–1587.

Shiller, R. 2003. Is there a bubble in the housing market? *Brookings Papers on Economic Activity* 2: 299–362.

Smith, S. J. 2006. Home ownership: Managing a risky business? In J. Doling and M. Elsinga (Eds.). *Home ownership: Getting in, getting from, getting out; part II.* Delft, IOS Press.

Swinney, R. 2011. Selling to strategic consumers when product value is uncertain: The value of matching supply and demand. *Management Science* 57 (10): 1737–1751.

Tu, Y., M. Kellett, V. Clerehugh, and M. Gilthorpe. 2005. Problems of correlations between explanatory variables in multiple regression analysis in the dental literature. *British Dentistry Journal* 199 (7): 457–461.

Watkins, C. 1998. Property valuation and the structure of urban housing markets. *Journal of Property Investment & Financing* 17 (2): 157–175.

Yiu, C., B. Tang, Y. Chiang, and L. Choy. 2006. Alternative theories of appraisal bias. *Journal of Real Estate Literature* 14 (3): 321–331.

Youngman, J. M. 2007. The variety of property tax limits: Goals, consequences, and alternatives. *State Tax Notes* (November 19), 541–557.

CHAPTER 6

Foreclosure Statutes and Processes

Foreclosures are a major element of real estate markets in most countries, and remain the primary remedy for mortgage defaults. Some states have enacted deed-in-lieu statutes (wherein the borrower relinquishes the property upon mortgage default that is not cured)—but this remedy is not common. Foreclosure processes are similar across countries. Many theoretical and empirical studies have confirmed that foreclosures are economically, socially, and psychologically inefficient (for example, see the studies cited in Chapter 4 on public health). This chapter explains how various elements of foreclosures are unconstitutional; although U.S. law is used herein, the principles are applicable in most common law jurisdictions and commonwealth countries.

Many authors have noted the problems inherent in foreclosure processes; see, for example, Ambrose and Capone (1996); Capone (1996); Hatcher (2006); Pence (2003); Cox (2008); Stark (1997); Johnson (1993); Jacoby (2010); Tatom (2008); Center for Responsible Lending (2008); Blair and Piette (2006); Davies (2008); Kiff & Klyuev (2009); Brescia (2008); Myers (2008); Good and Hammond (2006); Shanker (2003); Riddiough and Wyatt (1994); Randolph (1996); Merrill and Smith (2000); Whitman and Nelson (2004); Whitman (2005); Todd and Grover (2008); Bernstein (2008); Painter (2006); Giantomasi (2004); Ackermann (2008). (Also see this book's web site for other citations.)

FORECLOSURES REDUCE THE EFFICIENCY OF MONETARY POLICIES AND FISCAL POLICIES

Foreclosures dampen and reduce the efficiency of both monetary and fiscal policies. First, foreclosures substantially reduce banks' incentives to provide business loans and/or mortgages to borrowers in neighborhoods that have experienced relatively high rates of foreclosures—this was partly why the U.S. government's troubled asset relief program (TARP) failed (the banks that received TARP funds from the U.S. government refused to provide business loans and mortgages partly due to concern about perceived high foreclosure rates in some cities/towns). This trend often reduces economic activity in such neighborhoods (housing construction, renovations, home improvement, retail sales, new business formation, expansion of small businesses, etc.).

Foreclosures dampen central banks' monetary policies—specifically, the changes of benchmark interest rates and purchases/sales of government securities, primarily because foreclosures reduce the effect of interest rates on changes in real estate prices, which in turn is a barometer that triggers disinvestment, or inaction of investment. Foreclosures dampen the effects of the central banks' changes of capital reserve requirements for banks, primarily because foreclosures reduce the incentive for banks to provide mortgages or to lend regardless of capital reserve requirements.

Similarly, foreclosures dampen fiscal policies, as was manifested in the United States during 2007 to 2010; during this period, despite tax breaks and new tax credits, the U.S. economy did not improve (unemployment remained high, etc.). More importantly, in many countries, foreclosures cause fiscal/financial stress for local governments for whom property taxes account for more than 60 percent of their annual revenues.

SOME ADVERSE CONTAGION EFFECTS OF FORECLOSURES

Foreclosure causes: (a) information contagion—wherein news of foreclosure affects the volume of sales of real property and general consumption; (b) credit contagion—wherein lenders tend to reduce lending to geographic areas that are deemed to be prone to foreclosures; and (c) inertia contagion—wherein residents of neighborhoods that have known high foreclosure rates (information that is often publicly disclosed) tend to lose faith in their ability to overcome foreclosure and "underwater mortgages" (where the mortgage value exceeds the value of the underlying property), reallocate their resources to other expenses, and do not make extra efforts to prepare for or solve foreclosures.

These contagion effects of foreclosure: (a) compel prospective entrepreneurs to wait and delay their plans; (b) compel households that face foreclosure to shirk and consider strategic default; and (c) compel banks to reduce lending. For families facing foreclosure, information contagion, and/or high income-to-mortgage ratios (i.e., high costs of ownership), new tax credits, and reduction of income tax rates are almost meaningless, and cannot stimulate the economy.

THE STATUTORY BAN OF WAIVER OF JUDICIAL FORECLOSURE IN CONVEYANCING DOCUMENTS AND THE OMISSION OF NONJUDICIAL FORECLOSURE FROM STATES' LAWS ARE UNCONSTITUTIONAL

In most western U.S. states and in some common law countries, the deed of trust (mortgage) contains clauses that waive or expressly prohibit judicial foreclosures; such clauses can reduce transaction costs and are particularly relevant in the subprime mortgage market where borrowers cannot afford most legal proceedings, and defaults and foreclosures have significant information effects and cause negative externalities. Borrower defaults and judicial foreclosures reduce the market values of surrounding properties, and reduce the perceived credit ratings of borrowers in the same area, and also affect the perceived credit ratings of lenders that provide loans in the same area, and affect the perceived direction/trend of property prices. Judicial foreclosures typically last for 6 to 36 months and can be very expensive—sometimes the foreclosure transaction costs are as much as the value of the subject property. On the contrary, in the eastern U.S. states, mortgages do not usually contain such foreclosure waiver clauses; and some state laws expressly prohibit such waiver clauses.

Different western U.S. states have different laws/statutes for the deed of trust (DOT) and the waivability of judicial foreclosures. Given that real estate is increasingly an interstate phenomenon, there are substantial incentives to standardize laws that govern waivers/prohibitions of judicial foreclosure or nonjudicial foreclosures in various states. These incentives include the reduction of transaction costs, reduction of litigation costs, the general advancement of real estate laws, increasing the quality and effectiveness of regulation, reduction of search costs, and reduction of insurance costs and insurance losses.

The lack of specific state-law legislation that expressly addresses the inclusion/prohibition/waiver of judicial foreclosure proceedings clauses in the DOT is a major omission that is a state action for purposes of constitutional law analysis, because the state has an affirmative duty to enact laws that enhance the efficiency of transactions. The state legislature is one of three entities that can do so (others being the federal government and the local government; but if uniformity of laws is the main objective, the federal government is best positioned to enact such laws), and the action is by the state; the action affects the legal rights and property interests of market participants and nonmarket participants. Similarly, and for the same reasons, the omission of nonjudicial foreclosure in foreclosure statutes is a "state action."

Procedural and Substantive Due Process

With regard to due process, there are two distinct issues: The first is the lack of specific government legislation that requires the inclusion of nonjudicial foreclosure proceedings clauses in the DOT or mortgage; the second issue is the lack of specific government legislation that governs the issue of the inclusion/prohibition/waiver of judicial foreclosure proceedings clauses in the DOT or mortgage.

Under the Fifth and Fourteenth Amendments of the U.S. Constitution, the lack of specific legislation that requires the inclusion of summary or full judicial foreclosure proceedings clauses in the DOT *does not* constitute a violation of the lender's and borrower's procedural and substantive due process rights. This is because the elimination of judicial foreclosure proceedings can significantly reduce transaction costs, negative externalities, information asymmetry, and adverse information/price effects. In such circumstances, the state's legitimate interest in enacting and implementing laws for efficient transfers of interests in real property and for credit transactions, and the borrower's right to due process, are far outweighed by the increased efficiency of nonjudicial foreclosure; and the fact that the borrower will have typically agreed in writing to the nonjudicial foreclosure (and thus has waived notice prior to deprivation of property) and that the borrower's right to an opportunity to remedy the default do not guarantee future satisfaction of the mortgage.

On the contrary, the lack of specific state-law legislation that governs the issue of the inclusion/prohibition/waiver of judicial foreclosure proceedings clauses in the DOT or mortgage is an adverse "state action" and constitutes a violation of the lender's and borrower's procedural and substantive due process rights under the Fifth and Fourteenth Amendments of the U.S. Constitution. This omission unfairly discriminates between sophisticated and knowledgeable lenders who can draft appropriate DOT/mortgage documents to protect their rights and lenders who do not have access to such knowledge, and also unfairly discriminates between borrowers who can draft (or have access to lawyers who can draft) appropriate DOT/mortgage documents to protect their rights and borrowers who do not have such knowledge or access to such knowledge. The omission also unfairly discriminates between borrowers who can afford the economic, social, and psychological costs of judicial foreclosures and borrowers who cannot afford such monetary and nonmonetary costs. These (intentional or unintentional) classifications do not serve any purpose and do not advance the government's interests in providing adequate legal infrastructure for efficient transactions. Each borrower has a constitutionally guaranteed property interest in notice of any adverse claims on the property, and also has property interests in fair adversarial procedures for adjudicating claims on owned property, even if such procedures are summary proceedings or nonjudicial foreclosure proceedings. These property interests arise from state constitutional law, expectations, and norms. Similarly, under the Fifth Amendment and the Fourteenth Amendment, each lender has a constitutionally guaranteed property interest in notice of any adverse claims on the property used as collateral for the loan, and in fair adversarial procedures for adjudicating claims on property, even if such procedures are summary proceedings. These property interests arise from state constitutional law, expectations, and norms.

Equal Protection

The lack of specific state legislation that addresses the waiver/inclusion/prohibition of judicial foreclosure proceedings clauses in DOTs or mortgages is a major omission and a state action that constitutes a violation of the lender's and borrowers' constitutionally guaranteed right to equal protection of the law. The state or federal government has an affirmative duty to enact laws that protect entities and persons that do business within its jurisdiction.

In most common law jurisdictions, where mortgages or DOTs are used, the lender typically has the most senior interest in the underlying real property. The lender has constitutionally guaranteed property interests in fair procedures that pertain to claims on the collateral/property, in the protection of its interests in property, in remedy/repair of damages to the collateral property, and in information about any actions that impair the collateral and any applicable remedies. These property interests arise from state property laws, municipal property laws, expectations, usage of trade, norms, and the state constitutional law.

In addition to the discriminatory classifications mentioned earlier, the state omission (not enacting legislation that clarifies foreclosure proceedings clauses in mortgages or DOTs) results in discriminatory classifications that unfairly discriminate between lenders that use real estate as collateral and lenders that use other types of assets as collateral; unfairly discriminate between lenders/borrowers that have the knowledge about foreclosure clauses, and those that don't; and unfairly discriminate between lenders that perfect security interest through the land registry, and lenders that perfect security interests through other methods (e.g., Uniform Commercial Code, security agreements). Furthermore, said classifications unfairly discriminate between in-state and out-of-state borrowers/lenders; and unfairly discriminate between parties that purchase/sell different sizes of properties—the economic value of any statutory/mandatory foreclosure clause varies directly with the value of the subject property.

The foregoing challenged classifications do not serve any compelling government interest, and the classifications are not substantially related to serving any legitimate government interest.

Right to Contract

The lack of specific state-law legislation that governs the issue of the inclusion/prohibition/waiver of judicial foreclosure proceedings clauses in the DOT or mortgage is an adverse state action that constitutes violations of the borrower's and the lender's right to contract. Similarly, the lack of state laws that address the inclusion/prohibition/waiver of judicial foreclosure clauses in DOTs/mortgages constitutes a violation of the borrower's and the lender's right to contract. The borrower and the lender have constitutionally guaranteed property interests in entering into contracts as they see fit, so long as such contracts do not have a negative effect on third parties—such property interests arise from state constitutional law, state contract laws, state/municipal property laws, expectations, and norms. The lack of statutes that govern the inclusion/prohibition of foreclosure proceedings clauses in mortgages or deed of trust substantially impairs the contractual rights of lenders and borrowers in a mortgage. The lender and borrower have constitutionally guaranteed rights to state contractual procedures for managing default of the mortgage (which may include foreclosure). These rights arise from state constitutional law, norms, and expectations. Although traditional foreclosure processes can be costly and time-consuming, nonjudicial foreclosures, "expedited foreclosures," and "arbitrated foreclosures" are feasible substitutes for traditional foreclosure proceedings. The statutory ban on foreclosure-proceedings clauses in DOTs/mortgages or omission of relevant foreclosure statutes is not a reasonable and narrowly tailored means of promoting the government's interest in ensuring that foreclosure costs are minimized—the ban is overbroad, and is not geared to any affected or identified class of borrowers or lenders (such as subprime borrowers or small banks).

The resulting discriminatory classifications discussed earlier do not serve any useful purposes and do not advance any government interest (interest in implementing cost-effective and efficient loan default procedures). The government does not gain from foreclosure proceedings that are expensive to both taxpayers and borrowers. The said failure of the government to enact comprehensive foreclosure statutes can be circumvented by transacting with an out-of-state lender/borrower such that the more favorable laws of other states will apply to the loan; or by including forum selection clauses in the mortgage documents and deeds of trust. Even with such circumvention, there can be adverse effects on in-state residents in the form of higher transaction costs, negative information effects, borrowers' migration to out-of-state lenders (and hence, loss of taxes for the state government and interest revenues for local banks), increases in the cost of title insurance, and declines in property values and negative perceptions of market prices by buyers and sellers—that is, lower property values due to absence of statutory foreclosure proceedings and associated "unfairness."

The government's legitimate interest in reducing transaction costs in real estate transactions and promoting efficient capital markets is far outweighed by the impairment of the lender's and borrower's contractual rights that result from the statutory ban on foreclosure proceedings clauses.

The Takings Clause

The lack of specific state-law legislation that requires or prohibits the inclusion of judicial foreclosure (or nonjudicial foreclosure) proceedings in deeds of trust is a major omission and constitutes a violation of the Takings Clause of the U.S. Constitution. The relevant state action is the failure of the government to enact legislation that mandates the inclusion/exclusion of judicial foreclosure proceedings in mortgages/deeds of trust. *Goldberg v. Kelly*, *Board of Regents v. Roth*, and *Perry v. Sindermann* define property interests; and where as in this instance, the government is the only party that can provide recognizable rights (statutory inclusion/exclusion of judicial foreclosure clauses), a failure of the government to act is as much a deprivation of constitutional rights as a traditional Taking; and such failure to act results in a reduction of residents' ability to profit and harms residents of the state. By failing to enact laws that govern the inclusion or prohibition of judicial foreclosure clauses in mortgage-type agreements, the state is essentially regulating such clauses (DOTs/mortgages) in a manner that unduly diminishes residents' property values.

The standard tests for Takings cases include: the "reduction-of-value" test (ability to profit before and after Takings) is evaluated and there must be impairment; the "cause-of-harm" test (show that one person's use causes harm to another's property, and there is state action); the Government Invasion Theory (show that government takes possession of property); and the "noxious-use" test. Government regulation of private property constitutes a Taking if it does not substantially advance a legitimate government interest, and if the regulation is imposed on persons and/or groups without the government paying adequate compensation to the property owners for any resulting economic losses.

Bell and Parchomovsky (2001a) attempted to introduce the concept of "Derivative Takings," which had been discussed in prior literature and pertains to negative externalities caused by physical Takings or regulatory Takings; derivative Takings is not entirely distinguishable from, and overlaps with physical Takings and Regulatory Takings. Bell and Parchomovsky cited *United States v. Causby*, 328 U.S. 256 (1946) as an example. Bell and Parchomovsky stated in part: "In *Causby*, the plaintiffs-respondents claimed that the establishment of an air route above their houses worked a taking on their property. Writing for the Court, Justice William O. Douglas ruled that the establishment of the air routes created an easement on the property owners' air rights. However, he ruled that only those property owners whose houses lay *directly below* the air routes had a right to compensation under the Fifth Amendment. Justice Douglas denied compensation to the other property owners, who incurred essentially the same harm as a result of the same government action, on the grounds that their property had not suffered a 'physical invasion.'... The result in *Causby* is neither fair nor efficient. The outcome is unfair because, from the point of view of the equally harmed property owners, the location of the lots relative to the flight routes is irrelevant and arbitrary. Harm to the property directly overflown—the physical Taking—is fully compensated, while the same harm to the neighboring lot that lies one inch from the line of the air route—the derivative Taking—remains fully uncompensated. The outcome is inefficient because it permits the government to externalize on private property owners a substantial part of the cost of a decision or policy that is acknowledged to be a taking, leading to inaccurate assessments of the cost effectiveness and desirability of government policies...."

However, derivative Takings is a highly subjective and speculative concept because there will always be disagreements about the extent of damages caused by Takings. As a matter of fiscal, economic, and urban policy, one municipal government may decide to compensate property owners whose properties are within five meters of the condemned property while another municipal government may use 10 meters as the cutoff point, whereas in both instances and in most instances, properties within 30 meters will be affected positively (better access, increased traffic for shops, etc.) and negatively (loss of property, excessive traffic, etc.). The key issue is that the physical demarcation for purposes of compensation is a function of many factors, some of which are subjectively decided and include the short-term financial resources of the local government. Furthermore, the concept of "Derivative Takings" has been analyzed extensively in prior literature.

In *Lingle v. Chevron USA*, 544 U.S. 528 (2005), the U.S. Supreme Court held that the "substantially advances" formula that was previously applied in Takings cases is actually a due process question that should not be considered in Takings decisions; and the Court defined four classes of takings claims, which are: a "physical taking"; a "Lucas-type total regulatory taking"; a "Penn-Central Type" Taking; and a "land-use exaction violating the *Nollan* and *Dolan* standards."

There has not been any U.S. Supreme Court case that has directly addressed the issue of the lack of specific state-law legislation mandating inclusion of judicial foreclosure proceedings in deeds of trust. In *Kelo v. City of New London*, the U.S. Supreme Court reversed much of the existing Takings case law and ruled that eminent domain can be used to obtain property for what can reasonably be deemed "private" use—this ruling effectively eliminates the "public use" requirement in eminent domain and Takings cases. Furthermore, the issue of definition of "public use" and "private use" within the context of Takings remains somewhat unresolved. Some courts have held that the Takings Clause is most naturally construed to authorize Takings for public use only if the public or government actually uses the Taken property. Furthermore, any interpretation of public use and private use in Takings cases must recognize that most Takings cases are adjudicated by state courts, and state court judges are not as independent as federal judges, because they are sometimes elected, and are often influenced by elected officials who typically like redevelopment projects. The language of the Takings Clause, the inferable legislative intent of the Takings Clause, the historical application of the Takings Clause by most U.S. courts, and the nature of judges in Takings cases support this point of view.

The Takings elements are explained as follows. The lender has constitutionally guaranteed property interests in protecting its economic interest as capital markets change and when default occurs—in this instance the economic interest consists of the opportunity cost incurred by the lender, loss of interest payments, monitoring costs, and transaction costs. These property interests arise from state contract laws, state property laws, state constitutional laws, norms, and expectations. The losses incurred by the lender include increased transaction costs (due diligence costs, risk management costs, and legal costs); increased costs of foreclosure; and increased public perception that the lender is a riskier entity. These losses include: the differences between actual interest rate paid and the stated interest rate (in the loan documents); any losses that arise from increased monitoring costs; and the cost of reassessing the impact of interest rate changes on the borrower's credit and on the borrower's propensity to refinance the loan. These losses constitute psychological losses and economic losses, and thus a Taking. The monetary amount involved (loss incurred by lenders) is transferred to public use in various forms, such as lower effective interest rates for borrowers; the ability of borrowers to use the foreclosure process to frustrate lenders; and borrowers' economic and psychological gains from defaulting on loans. The public includes all people and companies that borrow in the capital markets. The lender is not compensated for said Taking, because the lender does not receive any special benefit and/or compensation for losses. The government has some interest in promoting and enhancing orderly and efficient capital markets and real estate in which individuals and companies can borrow at reasonable rates. However, the Takings do not advance the government interests in any way.

The Takings implicit in the government's omission of foreclosure statutes do not conform to any of the above-mentioned types of Takings because there is no physical occupation, there is no total regulatory Taking, there are no exactions that violate the *Nollan* and *Dolan* standards, and there is no Penn-Central Type Taking. Also, there are no Derivative Takings. This new type of Takings is referred to as *Omissions Takings* and is defined in a later section in this chapter.

Interference with Interstate Commerce

Where the lender or borrower resides outside the state where the property is located, the lack of specific state-law legislation mandating inclusion of judicial foreclosure proceedings in DOTs constitutes an illegal and unconstitutional interference with interstate commerce, and burdens interstate commerce. This is because the omission by the government unfairly discriminates between in-state and out-of-state lenders and borrowers, and it imposes additional costs on out-of-state lenders and borrowers (those located in states that use mortgages that contain such judicial-foreclosure clauses), such as increased transaction costs, monitoring costs, and opportunity costs. The omission by the government unfairly discriminates between lenders and borrowers who have adequate knowledge about judicial foreclosure clauses or can afford to hire knowledgeable lawyers, and those who do not have the knowledge or cannot afford to hire lawyers.

The absence of specific state-law legislation mandating inclusion of judicial foreclosure proceedings in DOTs does not serve any meaningful economic purpose because the omission reduces lenders' incentives to provide loans in jurisdictions where such laws and clauses are not used. The omission reduces overall social welfare by causing banks/lenders to increase the interest rates they charge to borrowers, and by causing increases of lenders' and borrowers' mortgage insurance rates (because of increased transaction costs).

The lack of specific state-law legislation that mandates the inclusion of judicial foreclosure proceedings in DOTs does not advance any legitimate government interest, but rather, the omission reduces governments' tax revenues because, if implemented, lenders will probably pay lower income taxes due to increased costs and operating losses; property tax revenues will probably decline because property prices are more likely to decline where judicial foreclosure is not the norm. Furthermore, the lack of specific state-law legislation mandating inclusion of judicial foreclosure proceedings in DOTs merely prolongs judicial processes unnecessarily and imposes additional costs on the government.

The Privileges and Immunities Clause

The primary purpose of the Privileges and Immunities Clause is to preclude the enactment of state laws that discriminate against nonresidents for economic reasons. The lack of specific state-law legislation that requires the inclusion of judicial foreclosure proceedings in DOTs is a major omission and a state action that constitutes a violation of the lenders' and borrowers' constitutionally guaranteed rights under the Privileges and Immunities Clause. Hirsch (1990) and several U.S. Supreme Court cases explain the standards for testing for violations of the Privileges and Immunities Clause. The state has an affirmative duty to enact laws that protect entities and persons that do business in its jurisdiction. The government/state is one of two entities that have the authority to codify judicial foreclosures (the other being the legislature).

In most common law jurisdictions, the lender typically has the most senior interest in the underlying real property. The lender has property interests in fair procedures that pertain to claims on the collateral/property, in the protection of its interests in property, in remedy/repair of damages to the collateral property, and in information about any actions that impair the collateral and any applicable remedies. These property interests arise from contract law, expectations, norms, and the state constitutions.

The state omission (not specifying foreclosure proceedings) results in classifications that unfairly discriminate between in-state and out-of-state borrowers and lenders.

The foregoing challenged classifications do not serve any compelling government interest, and the classifications are not substantially related to serving any legitimate government interest.

THE BORROWER'S POST-FORECLOSURE RIGHT OF REDEMPTION IS UNCONSTITUTIONAL

Under state laws in most eastern U.S. jurisdictions and statutes in some common law countries, the borrower retains the right to a post-foreclosure redemption of the property, if the borrower pays the amount/price agreed to, at auction of the property. The state action involved is both the right of redemption statutes and the courts' common law rulings that permit the borrower's right to post-foreclosure redemption of the property. This borrower's post-foreclosure right of redemption is typically granted by state-law statute or by case law, and constitutes a violation of the lender's constitutionally guaranteed rights to substantive and procedural due process and equal protection. The subprime mortgage borrower can use the right of redemption to frustrate the lender.

Due Process Rights

In most jurisdictions/countries, the foreclosure process is expensive and typically takes 6 to 36 months. During the foreclosure process, the lender has to pay for carrying costs such as insurance, property taxes, and utilities. In most cases, prior to foreclosure, the lender was probably owed interest and principal payments for the prior 4 to 24 months. The statutory or common law borrower right of redemption introduces costly uncertainty for both lenders and borrowers, reduces property values because of the stigma of foreclosure proceedings, and greatly reduces the lender's ability to sell the foreclosed property. The foreclosure process is supposed to conclusively and effectively determine the rights of both parties, and hence, once the borrower's default has been established, it is inequitable to grant the borrower any right of redemption, because by then, the borrower would have had adequate opportunities to repay the loan. Furthermore, it is conceivable and highly probable that the borrower who redeems the property after foreclosure is likely to default again.

Under present regulations in most common law countries, borrowers can use the right of redemption to frustrate the landlord and to effectively get the landlord to finance their rents. The lender has constitutionally protected property rights in fair, nonrepetitive, cost-effective, and efficient judicial proceedings to clear title and take possession where the borrower has defaulted on the mortgage. These property rights arise from expectations, social norms, state contract law, state tort laws, and state constitutional laws. The government does not have any valid interest in having an adjudged delinquent borrower reclaim a property after foreclosure sale, particularly where said borrower does not pay all of the lender's carrying costs and transaction costs incurred during the default period, and during and after the foreclosure period. Most borrowers who have enough funds to request post-foreclosure right of redemption can easily obtain other accommodation, and hence face insignificant disruption costs. In the rare instances where such borrowers cannot find accommodation, the government's expense on housing assistance (in the case of residential property foreclosures) is far outweighed by the degree of deprivation of lenders' rights, and the magnitude of lenders' carrying costs and transaction costs.

Right to Contract

The borrower's statutory post-foreclosure right of redemption constitutes a violation of the lender's constitutional right to contract for several reasons. The state action is the state's grant of a statutory post-foreclosure right of redemption to the borrower. The mortgage typically states the terms of default, and the associated remedies, and is a binding contract between the borrower and the lender. Hence, the borrower's statutory post-foreclosure right of redemption impairs and restricts the borrower's and lender's ability to contract, and thus is unconstitutional. These agreed-upon remedies stated in the mortgage should be enforced without any opportunity for the borrower to take back the property. By the time the foreclosure process reaches the sale of the asset, the lender has typically incurred substantial cash expenses, loss of time, and opportunity costs in the foreclosure process. The foreclosure process also typically devalues the property. More importantly, the borrower's right of redemption provides a ready method for nasty borrowers to frustrate lenders by forcing them to incur substantial cash losses and loss of time, and then repurchase the property.

Furthermore, the borrower's right of redemption was created in English law more than 200 years ago, when social, political, and economic conditions were very different from what exists today. The lender has constitutionally protected property rights in enforcement of contracts, and noninterference in contractual relations by third parties. These property interests arise from state contract laws, state constitutional laws, and so on. The government's interest, if any, in providing the borrower with a second opportunity to acquire the property, is far outweighed by (a) the need to maintain/enforce contractual relations that form the foundations for modern business, and (b) protection of lenders' rights and provision of adequate incentives to encourage financial institutions to lend.

Interference with Interstate Commerce

The relevant state action is the common law or statutory post-foreclosure right of redemption. The borrower's statutory post-foreclosure right of redemption constitutes an illegal and unconstitutional interference with interstate commerce, and burdens interstate commerce where the lender or borrower resides outside the state where the property and the foreclosure proceedings are located. This is because the borrower's right of redemption significantly and unnecessarily prolongs foreclosure proceedings, and hence, increases out-of-state borrowers' and lenders' transactions costs and monitoring costs more than it does for in-state lenders/borrowers.

Granting borrowers the statutory or common law right of redemption does not serve any meaningful economic purpose because: (a) the right-of-redemption statutes merely increase transaction costs and monitoring costs of borrowers and lenders; (b) right-of-redemption laws impose significant costs on lenders—monitoring costs, transaction costs, compliance costs, holding costs, default costs, negative externalities, changes in market values of properties; (c) right-of-redemption laws reduce lenders' incentives to provide loans in jurisdictions where such laws are applied; and (d) right-of-redemption laws reduce overall social welfare by increasing borrowers' interest rates and increasing lenders' and borrowers' mortgage insurance rates. It is unlikely that a borrower who has defaulted on a mortgage, and failed to perform during the default cure period, will have sufficient means to reacquire the property, without any substantial risk of future default on any new mortgage loan.

Granting the borrowers statutory or common law right of redemption does not advance any legitimate government interest. The application of such states reduces governments' tax revenues in the following ways: (1) lower income taxes from lenders, and (2) lower property taxes—because property prices are likely to decline on application of right-of-redemption statutes (due to the stigma of foreclosure and greater probability of borrower default); and overall property prices are likely to be lower in towns/cities/states that have borrower right-of-redemption laws (than in otherwise comparable areas). Right-of-redemption statutes merely prolong judicial processes unnecessarily and hence impose additional costs on the government. Borrowers and third-party speculators can repeatedly exercise the right of redemption in order to frustrate lenders. This can reduce property values in addition to causing substantial losses for the lender.

Equal Protection Rights

The borrower's statutory post-foreclosure right of redemption violates the Equal Protection Clause of the U.S. Constitution because it unfairly and illegally results in very different judicial treatment of mortgages and similar financial instruments such as traditional business loans, leases, and contracts, and it unfairly and illegally discriminates between persons who have security interests in real estate and persons who have security interests in other forms of properties. The borrowers' post-foreclosure right of redemption unfairly discriminates between people who choose to perfect security interests through the mortgage recording system (municipal land registry) and those who perfect security interests using alternative methods (such as Uniform Commercial Code filings, security agreements, possession of collateral), and also unfairly discriminates between lenders who are sophisticated and knowledgeable enough to expressly obtain a waiver of the right of redemption, and lenders who do not have the knowledge. The borrowers' right of redemption unfairly discriminates between lenders that have the resources to pay for carrying costs and transaction costs during and after the foreclosure process, and lenders who do not have such resources. The relevant state action is the enactment of the statutory or common law post-foreclosure right of redemption for grant of the borrower's post-foreclosure right of redemption.

The foregoing classifications are used directly or indirectly by the courts in foreclosure proceedings—rulings are based on such classifications. The challenged classifications do not serve any compelling state interest and the classifications are not substantially related to serving any government interest. As explained in preceding sections, the borrower's statutory post-foreclosure right of redemption reduces the incentive to lend, and increases lender's transaction costs and monitoring costs, while reducing the government's tax revenues.

Restriction of Free Speech Rights

The borrower's statutory post-foreclosure right of redemption constitutes a violation of the lender's free speech rights. The mortgage contract, DOT, and title/deed and title insurance are forms of protected free speech for several reasons. The mortgage/DOT, the associated promissory note, and deed are forms of communication to capital markets, regulators, real estate market participants, and investors. Empirical finance studies have identified information content in mortgage filings and foreclosure processes particularly for large commercial real estate. The mortgage/DOT, the deed/title, and title insurance represent expressions of the lender's and borrower's financial condition and prospects, and such expressions typically do not violate any civil or criminal laws. Such speech is not offensive and does not directly deprive others of their rights. The foreclosure process grants the lender certain rights: (1) to state certain facts about recovery of title through foreclosure, and so on, and to make information requests from the borrower; and (2) to take title to the foreclosed property. The foreclosure and the outcomes of the foreclosure process are all forms of protected speech by the lender and include: (a) application for foreclosure judgment; (b) the entry of foreclosure judgment; (c) the recording of the foreclosure judgment at the county clerk's office; and (d) the lender's takeover of title to the foreclosed property. Such processes, expressions, and information represent expressions of the lender's and borrower's condition and prospects, and such expressions typically do not violate any civil or criminal laws, and are not offensive and are required to address the rights of an aggrieved party.

The borrower's right-of-redemption statute typically does not apply to other forms of obligations, such as business loans and leases. The lender has a protected property interest in the foreclosure process, and in property that it gains from the foreclosure process—this right arises from state constitutional law, expectations, and norms. The borrower's statutory post-foreclosure right of redemption unnecessarily increases the lender's transaction costs and monitoring costs, complicates the lender's credit analysis and monitoring efforts, imposes financial burdens on the lenders, and increases the bankruptcy risk of lenders by increasing the probability of uncompensated loss.

The borrower's statutory post-foreclosure right of redemption does not serve any legitimate purpose because it increases the government's expenses—continued litigation costs; it reduces the government's tax revenues—lenders incur losses due to higher recovery costs and transaction/monitoring costs; and it increases the probability of "inefficient continuance," where an otherwise insolvent borrower or a borrower who cannot maintain mortgage payments uses this post-foreclosure right of redemption to continually frustrate lenders.

THE UNCONSTITUTIONALITY OF PREEMPTIVE FORECLOSURE RULES

In some U.S. states and common law countries, some sections of foreclosure statutes (the "*Preemptive Foreclosure Rules*") preempt contractual post-default nonjudicial remedies and terms outlined in mortgage agreements.

Due Process Rights

The Preemptive Foreclosure Rules in the United States (and some common law countries) constitute a violation of the procedural and substantive due process rights of mortgagees and auction winners (winners in judicial auctions to purchase foreclosed properties) because such rules impose substantial monetary and nonmonetary costs on mortgagees such as: interest/principal payments (due before and during the foreclosure proceedings); the opportunity costs of mortgagee's funds diverted to pay for principal/interest; the mortgagee's attorney's fees; the value of mortgagee's time spent in foreclosure procedures; and the mortgagee's eviction costs. In most common law countries, the Preemptive Foreclosure Rules impose substantial monetary and nonmonetary costs on lenders such as: interest/principal payments (due during the foreclosure proceedings); the lender's attorney's fees; the lender's internal administrative costs for the foreclosure procedures; and the lender's costs for evicting the borrower.

The government has an affirmative duty to enact and enforce efficient foreclosure laws that minimize the transaction costs of borrowers, lenders, and the court system, while enhancing the price discovery processes in property markets. The government's omission of this duty constitutes a state-action for purposes of constitutional law analysis. Nonjudicial foreclosure and short sales are examples of more efficient processes for handling default. The Preemptive Foreclosure Rules burden interstate commerce and increase transaction costs of not only lenders and borrower, but also courts that have to contend with increased litigation to resolve issues that could have been defined in contracts. Given that most borrowers retain lawyers for mortgage-related transactions, the government interest in protecting borrowers and lenders is far outweighed by adverse effects and costs of Preemptive Foreclosure Rules. Hence, the Preemptive Foreclosure Rules in some U.S. states and most common law countries are unconstitutional.

The Right to Contract, and Right of Association

In some U.S. states and common law countries, some sections of foreclosure statutes (the Preemptive Foreclosure Rules) preempt contractual postdefault nonjudicial remedies and terms outlined in mortgage agreements. This constitutes a violation of the mortgagees' and lenders' constitutionally guaranteed right to contract, and right of association for several reasons. Such Preemptive Foreclosure Rules are discriminatory because they are not applicable to similar obligations such as business loans and leases; and they are not applicable in other circumstances. These Preemptive Foreclosure Rules do not serve any meaningful economic purpose and increase lenders' and borrowers' transaction costs, and adversely affect distinct investment-backed expectations of lenders and the expectations of borrowers. The Preemptive Foreclosure Rules completely change the economic viability of mortgages (from the perspectives of lenders, borrowers, Fannie Mae, Freddie Mac and the U.S. Federal Deposit Insurance Corporation [FDIC]) and are relatively oppressive. The Preemptive Foreclosure Rules discourage persons and banks/lenders from entering into potentially profitable contracts/debt. In this instance, the government interest in protecting borrowers and lenders is far outweighed by the profitability of the transactions that are otherwise precluded by these Preemptive Forcclosure Clauses; by the existence of federal and state common law (covering fraud, securities, corporations, and any concerns, such as state debtor/creditor laws), and the substantially negative effects of such Preemptive Foreclosure Clauses on the propensity of lenders to provide mortgages; and by the increase in post-default transaction costs and monitoring costs created by such Preemptive Foreclosure Rules.

Equal Protection

The Preemptive Foreclosure Rules constitute violations of the Equal Protection Clause of the U.S. Constitution. The state action involved is the enactment of, and the required mandatory compliance with, Preemptive Foreclosure Rules. The Preemptive Foreclosure Rules unfairly discriminate between various (intentional and unintentional) classes of persons such as: (1) entities that register or have their principal places of business in different states; (2) in-state and out-of-state persons; (3) holders of large and small mortgages—the economic effects of the Preemptive Foreclosure Rules are much more pronounced in large mortgages; and (4) borrowers/lenders who have the resources to litigate and those who do not—one of the effects of the Preemptive Foreclosure Rules is that it increases litigation, which is necessary to decide issues that would otherwise be specified in the mortgage agreement. The Preemptive Foreclosure Rules typically do not apply to other types of loans and obligations, such as traditional business loans (secured by accounts receivables, inventory, and long-term leases, and increase transaction costs, monitoring costs, and compliance costs of both lenders and borrowers. The Preemptive Foreclosure Rules unfairly discriminate between various classes of persons—foreclosure discriminates between borrowers who use mortgages and borrowers who use simple promissory notes; between large banks/lenders that can afford the staff and infrastructure to handle multiple foreclosures and small lenders who cannot afford the administrative costs of multiple foreclosures; between borrowers who have in-depth knowledge about foreclosure processes and borrowers who do not know much about the costs of foreclosure processes; and between neighborhoods that have many financially distressed mortgagors and properties in foreclosure and neighborhoods that do not. The Preemptive Foreclosure Rules increase the actual and perceived illiquidity of mortgages and thus prevent or make it much more difficult to create and maintain critical secondary mortgage markets. The Preemptive Foreclosure Rules increase the all-in cost of mortgages to lenders because they must incur costs where they do not have contractual remedies to deal with defaults and other problems. This often causes lenders to increase mortgage interest rates.

Hence, application of Preemptive Foreclosure Rules causes significant differences in the magnitude of legal liability, and the magnitude and quality of protection provided by foreclosure processes to individuals with different wealth and for different classes of real estate; the magnitude and quality of protection provided to lenders with different amounts of capital at risk, and different loan documents/contracts; and the magnitude of protection provided to lenders and borrowers with different amounts of mortgage insurance. Also, the enforcement of the Preemptive Foreclosure Rules causes significant and discriminatory differences in the magnitude of transaction costs and monitoring costs depending on the judicial procedures of the specific court (state court, federal court, municipal court, etc.); discriminatory differences in the magnitude of financial disclosure by the lender and borrower (that typically have information effects); and discriminatory differences in the borrower's subsequent cost of capital and ability to obtain loans. These discriminatory classifications arise solely because of enforcement of the Preemptive Foreclosure Rules. These (intentional or unintentional) discriminatory classifications do not advance or support the government's interest in creating and implementing laws that enhance the efficiency of transactions. The above-mentioned classifications (on which the unfair discriminating conduct is based) do not serve any compelling state interest; the classifications are not substantially related to serving any state interest and thus constitute violations of the Equal Protection Clause of the U.S. Constitution.

Violation of the Takings Clause

Application of the Preemptive Foreclosure Rules constitutes a violation of the Takings Clause of the U.S. Constitution because the rules do not apply to other loans and obligations, and result in substantial transaction costs, monitoring costs, and compliance costs for both lenders and borrower. The state action is the enactment of the Preemptive Foreclosure Rules. Takings occur outside the real property industry—the doctrine applies to all types of property, whether tangible or intangible. The Takings Clause also covers implied restrictions and temporary restrictions on use by the government—this is in contrast to the more typical express and compensated taking of property by the government.

Furthermore, lenders' and borrowers' property interests in effective dispute resolution procedures and fair treatment, and their property interests in freedom-to-contract as they see fit (these property interests have monetary/economic value), far outweigh the government's interest in protecting lenders and borrowers by enacting and implementing the Preemptive Foreclosure Rules.

The Preemptive Foreclosure Rules constitute a Taking for several reasons. Lenders and borrowers have constitutionally protected property interests in fair and effective laws that reduce their transaction costs, financing costs, and operating costs (such property interests arise from expectations, norms, state constitutional laws, and contracts). The Preemptive Foreclosure Rules do not provide any meaningful protection for borrowers.

Second, the Preemptive Foreclosure Rules do not apply to other forms of loans and obligations (such as business loans and long-term leases). Third, the Preemptive Foreclosure Rules do not serve any meaningful economic purpose; the same or similar objectives can be achieved through other more efficient means such as more uniform federal or state debtor/creditor laws. It is not clear that the Preemptive Foreclosure Rules are economically efficient and always decrease the incidence of crime and misconduct. Fourth, the lender and borrower have a property interest in determining appropriate dispute resolution terms and ownership policies—this is a property expectancy that also implicates the right to association. The lender and borrower have property interests in fair treatment and due process. The Preemptive Foreclosure Rules deprive both parties of these property interests. Fifth, the Preemptive Foreclosure Rules state actions effectively deprive lenders and borrower of said property interests in the right to equal protection of the law—these property interests arise from state contract laws, state property laws, state constitutional laws, norms, and expectations. Sixth, the general public benefits indirectly from said Takings, because where the Preemptive Foreclosure Rules are enforced, borrowers can use the foreclosure process to delay and frustrate lenders unnecessarily. Seventh, the lenders and borrowers do not receive any just compensation from the (state) government for these Takings. The lender and the borrower actually lose money/value due to increased processing costs, financing costs, and transaction costs. In essence, any benefits received by the lender and borrower as a result of compliance with Preemptive Foreclosure Rules are far outweighed by the sum of the increase in the lender's and borrower's perceived and actual bankruptcy risk (foreclosures are reported to bank regulators and to credit rating agencies), and the reduced flexibility of the lender's management team. Eighth, the Takings "public use" in this instance is the government's creation of "perceived protection" for lenders and borrowers by enactment of the Preemptive Foreclosure Rules.

The U.S. Supreme court decisions on Takings have not directly addressed the Preemptive Foreclosure Rules. In *Kelo v. City of New London*, the U.S. Supreme Court effectively reversed much of the existing Takings case law and ruled that eminent domain can be used to obtain property for what can reasonably be deemed private use—this ruling effectively eliminates the public use requirement in eminent domain and takings cases. In *Lingle v. Chevron USA*, 544 U.S. 528 (2005), the U.S. Supreme Court held that the "substantially advances" formula that was previously applied in Takings cases is actually a due process question that should not be considered in Takings decisions; and the Court defined four classes of takings claims, which are: a "physical taking"; a "Lucas-type total regulatory taking"; a "Penn-Central Type" Taking; and a "land-use exaction violating the *Nollan* and *Dolan* standards."

The Takings implicit in Preemptive Foreclosure Rules in U.S. states (and some common law jurisdictions) do not conform to any of the above-mentioned types of Takings because there is no physical occupation; there is no *Total Regulatory Taking*; there are no "exactions that violate the *Nollan* and *Dolan* standards"; and there is no "Penn-Central Type" Taking. Also, there is no "Derivative Takings." This condition gives rise to a new type of Takings that is henceforth referred to as *Subordination Takings* and is characterized in a subsequent section of this chapter.

ENFORCEMENT OF CORE FORECLOSURE PROCESSES AND THE FAILURE TO ENACT UNIFORM FEDERAL FORECLOSURE AND MORTGAGE STATUTES CONSTITUTE VIOLATIONS OF THE U.S. CONSTITUTION

In the United States, foreclosures are governed primarily by state laws. Foreclosure processes in the United States differ among states; however, they have somewhat common elements in terms of procedure—few U.S. state foreclosure laws have any nonjudicial foreclosure provisions (nonjudicial foreclosures are much more efficient and socially beneficial than traditional judicial foreclosures). The "Core Foreclosure Processes" in the U.S. states include statutory specifications about the filing of claims, the required standards of proof, use of juries, the entry of the foreclosure judgment, the public disclosure of the foreclosure judgment by the Court, the rights of tenants in judicial foreclosures, and the remedies available to the Court.

It is conjectured here that because all the Core Foreclosure Processes often increase transaction costs, opportunity costs, and information costs of lenders, borrowers, and courts, housing prices do not incorporate foreclosure risk quickly, and credit measures do not incorporate foreclosure risk adequately. Consequently, in the United States, from 1995 to 2010, lenders' reluctance to enter into foreclosure proceedings provided artificial price supports in housing markets and helped inflate housing prices; and in the United States, from 1995 to 2008, the mortgagee's/auction winner's losses in the foreclosure processes provided incentives and justification for them to raises housing prices substantially and rapidly, and such losses were not reflected in overall pricing in housing markets.

The net effect is that existing Core Foreclosure Processes in most U.S. states increase the information content of pending and announced foreclosure proceedings; and also have substantial and adverse information effects on lenders and borrowers that reduce overall social welfare in the following ways. The Core Foreclosure Processes cause the lender to choose voluntary misinformation and inertia instead of exercising its property rights. Misinformation takes the form of false disclosures to regulators and investors (e.g., not recognizing loan losses; refusing to recognize impairment of collateral) and selective implementation of loan review policies and communications to borrowers. The Core Foreclosure Processes provide substantial disincentive for lenders and borrowers to invest in monitoring. Core Foreclosure Processes provide substantial incentives for borrower/mortgagors to shirk—they have the best information about the condition of the collateral/property, the probability of borrower post-foreclosure redemption, and the borrower's circumstances. Foreclosure laws create substantial time-consuming procedures that increase the lender's transaction costs and benefit the borrower. Lenders' reactions to Core Foreclosure Processes can be partly attributed to the fact that the quality of information that lenders have about the average borrower's propensity to repay is affected by psychological factors, time, and so on; and because there typically is no direct information exchange among lenders about any specific borrower except publicly available credit reports (provided by third parties), there is substantial information asymmetry among lenders about characteristics of specific borrowers, and even specific proposed real estate projects (or other capital investments).

A substantial and growing percentage of mortgage transactions in the United States (and in many common law countries) involve interjurisdictional or interstate transactions, and the existence of differences among state foreclosure laws often increases transaction costs and opportunity costs of borrowers, lenders, and courts. Furthermore, non-uniformity of foreclosure statutes causes moral hazard and substantial information asymmetry among lenders and borrowers. Lenders have the resources to retain lawyers who can select the jurisdictions with the most favorable foreclosure processes. Most borrowers retain local lawyers whose practices are limited to one state or jurisdiction—lenders have perhaps an unfair information advantage. The Internet and the continuing growth of interstate commerce has reduced differences in cultures and expectations among states in the United States. Hence, the failure of the U.S. federal government to enact uniform federal mortgage and foreclosure laws is a significant omission and a "state action" for purposes of constitutional law analysis. The federal government is the only entity that can create uniform foreclosure statutes in the United States.

Some U.S. Supreme Court cases have erroneously held that foreclosure laws are not property rights, but these cases fail to consider: (a) the significant transaction-cost and monitoring-cost impacts of foreclosure laws; (b) the significantly negative information effects of a regime in which foreclosure laws are not property rights; (c) the economic value of specialized processes such as foreclosures; and (d) the value of the public auction in foreclosures, as opposed to a private appraisal. Furthermore, the government has a duty to enact efficient foreclosure laws that enhance the efficiency of capital markets. Without adequate laws for the resolution of default, lenders will not have much incentive to lend, or will lend at very high interest rates—this is clearly evident in many developing countries that do not have foreclosure/mortgage laws. State residents also have an expectancy interest in foreclosure laws and such interests are essentially property interests. The sociocultural and psychological contexts in which foreclosure processes are implemented are complex and make foreclosures property rights.

Due Process Rights

Existing non-uniform foreclosure laws and processes in the United States (and some common law countries) constitute a violation of the procedural and substantive due process rights of mortgagees and auction winners (winners in judicial auctions to purchase foreclosed properties). In most countries, the procedural and substantive due process statutes (e.g., the due process clause of the U.S. Constitution) prohibit judicial/adjudicatory processes that are overly expensive and/or impose substantial burdens on any party in the proceeding. In the United States, the Core Foreclosure Processes impose substantial monetary and nonmonetary costs on mortgagees such as: information costs (disclosure of foreclosure actions; effect on credit ratings); the adverse effect of foreclosure news on property values (judicial foreclosures are conjectured to have more information content than nonjudicial foreclosures), and the opportunity costs of mortgagees' funds diverted to pay for principal/interest; mortgagees' attorney's fees; and the value of mortgagees' time spent in foreclosure procedures.

In the United States, the non-uniformity of foreclosure processes imposes substantial monetary and nonmonetary costs on mortgagees such as: the opportunity costs of mortgagees' time; the attorney's fees; the cost of uncertainty; and the information cost (disclosure of foreclosures). In some jurisdictions, even after foreclosure sale, the mortgagor/debtor still has the right (usually up until one year) to pay the debt and take back the property (the right of redemption is addressed earlier in this chapter). Under existing Core Foreclosure Processes, the mortgagor has substantial incentives and various methods to delay and complicate foreclosure proceedings (during which the mortgagor typically does not pay interest/principal or maintenance expenses). In most common law countries, the foreclosure processes impose substantial monetary and nonmonetary costs on lenders such as: interest/principal payments (due during the foreclosure proceedings); the lender's attorney's fees; the lender's internal administrative costs for the foreclosure procedures; the lender's costs for evicting the borrower.

The government has an affirmative duty to enact and enforce efficient foreclosure laws that minimize the transaction costs of borrowers, lenders, and the court system, while enhancing the price discovery processes in property markets. The government's omission of this duty constitutes a state-action for purposes of constitutional law analysis. Nonjudicial foreclosure and short sales are examples of more efficient processes for handling default.

The government interest in protecting borrowers and lenders is far outweighed by adverse effects and costs of foreclosure statutes and processes. Hence, foreclosure statutes in some U.S. states and most common law countries are unconstitutional.

Equal Protection

The discriminatory results of non-uniformity (at least 50 different state foreclosure laws) and the discriminatory effects of the Core Foreclosure Processes in U.S. states trigger the Equal Protection Clause of the U.S. Constitution. The government's failure to create uniform foreclosure and mortgage laws is an omission and a state action because the U.S. Congress is the only and the best positioned entity to enact such uniform foreclosure laws; Congress has a duty to enact laws that reduce transaction costs and compliance costs, and provide the same magnitude of legal protection to all similarly situated parties. Furthermore, U.S. states have different debtor-creditor laws that result in different defenses to claims pertaining to financial distress of borrowers.

Hence, both the application of the Core Foreclosure Processes in some states and the non-uniformity of foreclosure statutes in various states cause significant differentials in: the magnitude of legal liability, and the quality of protection provided by foreclosure processes to individuals with different wealth and for different classes of real estate; the magnitude and quality of protection provided to lenders with different amounts of capital at risk, and different loan documents/contracts; the magnitude of protection provided to lenders and borrowers with different amounts of mortgage insurance; and the magnitude of transaction costs and monitoring costs depending on the specific court (state, federal, municipal, etc.) and judicial procedures. The Core Foreclosure Processes in some states and the non-uniformity of foreclosure statutes in various states cause significant differentials in the magnitude of financial disclosure by the lender and borrower (that typically have information effects), and in the borrower's subsequent cost of capital and ability to obtain loans. These discriminatory classifications arise solely because of differences in state laws and/or because of the inefficiency of Core Foreclosure Processes.

Existing Core Foreclosure Processes in some U.S. states and the non-uniformity of foreclosure statutes in the U.S. states and some common law countries (that do not have statutory nonjudicial foreclosures or short sales) unfairly discriminate between various classes of persons. Foreclosure discriminates between borrowers who use mortgages and borrowers who use simple promissory notes; discriminates between large banks/lenders that can afford the staff and infrastructure to handle multiple foreclosures and small lenders who cannot afford the administrative costs of multiple foreclosures; discriminates between borrowers who have in-depth knowledge about foreclosure processes and borrowers who do not know much about the costs of foreclosure processes; and discriminates between neighborhoods that have many financially distressed mortgagors and properties in foreclosure and neighborhoods that do not. These foregoing (intentional or unintentional) classifications do not serve any meaningful purpose for the government and are detrimental to social welfare. The above-mentioned classifications (on which the unfair discriminating conduct is based) do not serve any compelling state interest and the classifications are not substantially related to serving any state interest.

Violation of the Takings Clause

Takings occur outside the real property industry—the doctrine applies to all types of property, whether tangible or intangible, and the Takings Clause also covers implied restrictions and temporary restrictions on use by the government. The Core Foreclosure Processes and the non-uniformity of state foreclosure statutes constitute violations of the Takings Clause of the U.S. Constitution because the rules do not apply to other loans and obligations; they result in substantial transaction costs, monitoring costs, and compliance costs, and they deprive lenders and borrowers of their economic rights.

Furthermore, lenders' and borrowers' property interests in effective dispute resolution procedures and fair treatment, and their property interests in freedom-to-contract as they see fit (these property interests have monetary/economic value), far outweigh the government's interest in protecting lenders and borrowers by enacting and implementing foreclosure laws.

The Core Foreclosure Processes and non-uniformity constitute a Takings for the following reasons. First, lenders and borrowers have constitutionally protected property interests in fair and effective laws that reduce their transaction costs, financing costs, and operating costs (such property interests arise from expectations, norms, state constitutional laws, and contracts). Second, the Core Foreclosure Processes and non-uniformity impose additional costs on borrowers and lenders.

Third, the Core Foreclosure Processes do not serve any meaningful economic purpose; the same or similar objectives can be achieved through other more efficient means, such as state debtor/creditor laws that apply to all types of collateral. It is not clear that the Core Foreclosure Processes are economically efficient and always decrease the incidence of crime and misconduct. Fourth, the lender and borrower have a property interest in efficient and nondiscriminatory dispute resolution ownership policies (this is a property expectancy that also implicates the right to association) and in fair treatment and due process, and the Core Foreclosure Processes and non-uniformity deprive both parties of these property interests, which arise from state contract laws, state property laws, state constitutional laws, norms, and expectations. Fifth, the general public benefits indirectly from said Takings, because pre-foreclosure borrowers can use the threat of foreclosure to influence lenders. Pre-foreclosure lenders can exploit differences in state foreclosure laws to their advantage. Pre-foreclosure lenders can use the threat of foreclosure to influence pre-foreclosure borrowers. The lenders and borrowers do not receive any just compensation from the government for these Takings. The lender and the borrower actually loses money/value due to increased processing costs, financing costs, and transaction costs. In essence, the benefits received by the lender and borrower as a result of compliance with foreclosure laws are far outweighed by the sum of the following factors: (1) the increase in the lender's and borrowers' perceived and actual bankruptcy risk (foreclosures are reported to bank regulators and to credit ratings agencies), and (2) lenders' management's reduced flexibility.

With regard to Core Foreclosure Processes, the Takings "public use" is the creation of perceived legal protection for lenders and borrowers by the enactment and use of Core Foreclosure Processes. The Takings public use inherent in non-uniformity in this instance is the exploitation of non-uniformity by lenders and borrowers and their attorneys for their own benefit.

The U.S. Supreme Court decisions on the Takings issue has not directly addressed the Core Foreclosure Processes or non-uniformity of state foreclosure statutes. The holdings in *Kelo v. City of New London* are relevant. In *Lingle v. Chevron USA*, 544 U.S. 528 (2005), the U.S. Supreme Court held that the "substantially advances" formula that was previously applied in Takings cases is actually a due process question that should not be considered in Takings decisions. The Court defined four classes of takings claims, which are as follows: a "Physical Taking"; a "Lucas-type Total Regulatory Taking"; a "Penn-Central Type" Taking; and a "land-use exaction violating the *Nollan* and *Dolan* standards."

The Takings implicit in the Core Foreclosure Processes in U.S. states (and some common law jurisdictions) and in non-uniformity do not conform to any of the above-mentioned types of Takings because there is no physical occupation; there is no Total Regulatory Taking; there are no "exactions that violate the *Nollan* and *Dolan* standards"; and there is no Penn-Central Type Taking. There is no Derivative Takings as defined in Bell and Parchomovsky (2001a, 2001b, 2005). This condition creates two new types of Takings, hereafter referred to as *Non-uniformity Takings* and *Core Takings*, which are characterized in a later section of this chapter.

ALTERNATIVE FORECLOSURE SYSTEMS

Whitman and Nelson (2004) provide some detailed explanations of inherent weaknesses of the present foreclosure laws in the United States, and also outline a new foreclosure system that is supposedly more efficient in terms of cost, time, and clarity of property interests. As explained in the chapter on new mortgage-alternatives products, most existing mortgages are very inefficient, and the best property financing instruments are those that completely avoid foreclosure and/or drastically reduce the cost of foreclosures. Many such products tend to resemble installment sales contracts.

In the United States, during the period from 2008 to 2010, both the Bush administration and the Obama administration introduced various programs for borrowers who faced foreclosure, or were in the foreclosure process. Most of these programs included loan modifications or short sales. However, as of June 2010, it was reported that borrowers were exiting many of these programs, and that such programs were not functioning well.

The key issues are: (a) that almost all types of foreclosures impose substantial transaction costs, opportunity costs, compliance costs, and information costs on market participants (mortgagees, mortgagors, neighbors, lenders, etc.); and (b) unlike many industries, the nature of the loan/mortgage product has a substantial effect on the viability of mortgage markets and housing markets. Thus, the optimal loan completely eliminates foreclosure or substantially reduces the processes and duration of foreclosure.

NEW THEORIES OF TAKINGS

This section defines various new theories of Takings, which were mentioned in earlier sections of this chapter.

Omissions Takings

Omissions Takings are a new type of takings and their elements are as follows:

- The Takings arise from the government's omission of a critical controlling statute, or from the government's omission of a critical clause in its contract with an agent.
- The omitted statute or contract clause creates economic utility/disutility or regret.
- The effects of the omitted statute(s) or contract clause prevail even without a specific transaction (such as a foreclosure).
- For any borrower-lender pair, the effect of the Takings varies with the size of the transaction (foreclosure or mortgage) and the knowledge of the parties (lender, borrower).
- The government is not a direct beneficiary of the omission of the statute or the contract clause.
- The affected parties may or may not have suffered economic harm.
- The omitted statute or contract clause causes substantial asymmetrical preference matching among the parties to the transaction.
- The omitted statute or contract clause causes: (1) asymmetrical coordination and (2) increased coordination between the affected parties and third parties.

Subordination Takings

Subordination Takings are characterized as follows:

- The statute precludes certain terms and conduct for any two parties to a specific type of transaction.
- The prohibited conduct has substantial information content.
- The prohibited conduct involves specific terms in agreements.
- The parties cannot improve their position within the jurisdiction.
- The prohibited or limited conduct has substantial economic value to both parties in the transaction.
- The parties cannot circumvent the statutory prohibition without changing the form (legal classification) of the transaction or agreement.
- The government is not a direct beneficiary of the Takings.

Non-Uniformity Takings

Non-uniformity Takings have the following characteristics:

- The deprivation of rights arises solely from the adverse effects of non-uniformity of laws among jurisdictions in one country.

- The federal government is the only entity that can create the desirable uniformity of laws.
- The Takings can exist even without a transaction (e.g., without a foreclosure).
- The non-uniformity of laws pertains to both substantive laws and procedural laws.
- The economic losses caused by procedural non-uniformity are greater than the economic losses caused by substantive non-uniformity.
- There is substantial information asymmetry among the parties (i.e., lender, borrower, court, owners of adjacent properties).
- The magnitude of the Takings (and thus, the effectiveness of balancing-of-interests tests) is a function of the borrower's commitment to the property interest, which in turn is a function of his or her current knowledge, wealth, and ability to substitute assets or transfer utility.
- The economic losses caused by non-uniformity are wholly or partially reversible—by contracting (contractually eliminating choice-of-law statutes/rules), by judicial intervention, or by inaction by one party (lender or borrower).
- For any transaction, there is symmetrical constitutional tort liability for two or more parties—for example, in a foreclosure, there is liability to both the lender and borrower.
- The demand for the associated public use is directly proportional to the volume of transactions.
- The subject assets/collateral cannot be easily substituted with other assets.

Core Takings

Core Takings are characterized as follows:

- The deprivation of rights arises because a "core statute/proceeding" (part of a larger set of statutes/procedures) is applied to a specific set of facts that pertain to two or more parties in a specified type of transaction.
- The deprivation of property interests affects only a portion of the rights of all the parties simultaneously.
- The core substantive law/statute cannot be circumvented by contracting or by judicial intervention. The parties cannot improve their positions within the jurisdiction.
- The core procedural laws are not discretionary—compliance is mandatory.

- The core procedural laws create more economic harm than the associated core substantive laws.
- The Takings exist without a transaction (i.e., without a foreclosure).
- The magnitude of the Takings (and thus, the effectiveness of balancing-of-interests tests) is a function of the borrower's commitment to the property interest, which in turn is a function of his or her current knowledge, wealth, and ability to substitute assets or transfer utility and asymmetrical commitment to the property interest (e.g., lender and borrower have different levels of commitment to the foreclosure mechanism).
- The economic losses caused by asymmetrical commitment (to the property interest and to the subject asset) are partly reversible—only by judicial intervention or by inaction by one party (lender or borrower).
- For any transaction, there is symmetrical constitutional tort liability for two or more parties—for example, in a foreclosure, there is liability to both the lender and borrower.
- The demand for the associated public use is directly proportional to the volume of transactions.
- The subject assets/collateral cannot be substituted with other assets.

CONCLUSION

The major elements of foreclosure processes and results are clearly unconstitutional in the United States (and perhaps in most common law countries). Furthermore, the existing literature documents many other socioeconomic problems inherent in various foreclosure processes. In addition, foreclosures dampen monetary transmission and implementation of fiscal policies. There remains a divide and lack of congruence between the nature/structure of existing mortgages and foreclosure statutes, which amplifies the negative effects of foreclosure statutes. Thus, foreclosure statutes in most common law countries should be substantially revised to reduce inherent transaction costs and adverse socioeconomic effects on property owners and municipal governments (which often rely heavily on property taxes).

REFERENCES

Ackermann, J. 2008. The sub-prime crisis and its consequences. *Journal of Financial Stability* 4 (4): 329–337.

Ambrose, B. W., and C. A. Capone. 1996. Cost-benefit analysis of single-family foreclosure alternatives. *Journal of Real Estate Finance and Economics* 13 (2): 105–120.

Bell, A., and G. Parchomovsky. 2001a. Takings re-assessed. *Virginia Law Review* 87: 277–287.

Bell, A., and G. Parchomovsky. 2001b. Givings. *Yale Law Journal* 111: 547–557.

Bell, A., and G. Parchomovsky. 2005. A theory of property. *Cornell Law Review* 90: 531–541.

Bernstein, D. 2008. *Bankruptcy code modifications and mortgage markets.* Available at: http://papers.ssrn.com/sol3/papers.cfm?abstract_id=1292336.

Blair, R. D., and C. A. Piette. 2006. Antitrust injury and standing in foreclosure cases (The antitrust enterprise: Principle and execution). *Journal of Corporation Law* 31 (Winter): 401–411.

Brescia, R. H. 2008. Capital in chaos: The subprime mortgage crisis and the social capital response. *Cleveland State Law Review* 56: 271–285.

Capone, C. 1996. *Providing alternatives to mortgage foreclosure: A report to Congress.* Washington, DC: U.S. Department of Housing and Urban Development.

Center for Responsible Lending. 2008. *Voluntary loan modifications fall far short: Foreclosure crisis will continue unabated without court-supervised modifications.* Available at: www.responsiblelending.org/pdfs/paulson-brief-final.pdf.

Cox, P. 2008. Foreclosure reform amid mortgage lending turmoil: A public purpose approach. *Houston Law Review* 45 (3): 684–694.

Davies, Z. E. 2008. Rescuing the rescued: Stemming the tide of foreclosure rescue scams in Washington. *Seattle University Law Review* 31 (Winter): 353–363.

Giantomasi, G. 2004. A balancing act: The foreclosure power of homeowners' associations. *Fordham Law Review* 72 (May): 2503–2513. Available at: http://law.fordham.edu/publications/articles/500flspub11002.pdf.

Good, S., and C. M. Hammond. 2006. Real estate auctions—legal concerns for an increasingly preferred method of selling real property. *Real Property, Probate & Trust Journal* 40: 766–776.

Hatcher, D. 2006. Foreclosure alternatives: A case for preserving homeownership. *Profitwise News and Views* (February): 1–4.

Hirsch, W. 1990. State residency laws: Their constitutionality under the privileges and immunities clause. Working paper, UCLA Department of Economics.

Jacoby, M. 2010. The value(s) of foreclosure law reform. *Pepperdine Law Review* 38: 101–116.

Johnson, A. M. 1993. Critiquing the foreclosure process: An economic approach based on the paradigmatic norms of bankruptcy. *Virginia Law Review* 79: 959–962.

Kelo v. City of New London, 545 U.S. 469 (2005); *Lingle v. Chevron*, 544 US 528 (2005); *SWIDA v. National City Environmental*, 768 N.E.2d 1 (Sup. Ct., Illinois, 2002).

Kiff, J., and V. Klyuev. 2009. *Foreclosure mitigation efforts in the United States: Approaches and challenges.* IMF Staff Position Note No. 09/02. Washington: International Monetary Fund.

Merrill, T., and H. Smith. 2000. Optimal standardization in the law of property: The numerus clausus principle. *Yale Law Journal* 111 (1): 1–70.

Myers, R. T. 2008. Foreclosing on the subprime loan crisis: Why current regulations are flawed and what is needed to stop another crisis from occurring. *Oregon Law Review* 87: 311–316.

Painter, S. 2006. Subprime lending, suboptimal bankruptcy: A proposal to amend §§ 522(f)(1)(B) and 548(a)(1)(B) of the Bankruptcy Code to protect subprime mortgage borrowers and their unsecured creditors. *Loyola Chicago University Law Journal* 38: 81–91. Available at: www.luc.edu/law/activities/publications/lljdocs/vol38_no1/painter.pdf.

Pence, K. M. 2003. *Foreclosing on opportunity: State laws and mortgage credit.* Washington, DC: Board of Governors of the Federal Reserve System.

Randolph, P. A. 1996. The future of American real estate law: Uniform foreclosure bills and the Uniform Land Security Interest Act. *Nova Law Review*, 20: 1109–1120.

Riddiough, T. J., and S. Wyatt. 1994. Strategic default, workout and commercial mortgage valuation. *Journal of Real Estate Finance & Economics* 9 (1): 5–22.

Shanker, M. 2003. Will mortgage law survive? *Case Western Law Review* 54: 69–102.

Stark, D. 1997. Facing the facts: An empirical study of the fairness and efficiency of foreclosures and a proposal for reform. *University of Michigan Journal of Law Reform* 30: 639–648.

Tatom, J. A. 2008. *The US foreclosure crisis: A two-pronged assault on the US economy.* University of Munich, July. http://mpra.ub.uni-muenchen.de/9787/1/2008-WP-10_Tatom.pdf.

Todd, R., and M. Grover. 2008. Targeting foreclosure interventions: An analysis of neighborhood characteristics associated with high foreclosure rates in two Minnesota counties. *Journal of Economics and Business* 60 (1–2): 91–109.

Whitman, D. 2005. New directions in mortgage law: Restatements and uniform laws. *New York Real Property Law Journal* 33: 14–24.

Whitman, D., and G. Nelson. 2004. Reforming foreclosure: The uniform nonjudicial foreclosure act. *Duke Law Journal* 53: 1399–1410.

CHAPTER 7

Unconstitutionality of U.S. Bankruptcy Code, Preemption of State-Law Mortgage Foreclosure Statutes, and Related Economic Effects

Bankruptcy codes exist in most countries, and surprisingly there are often conflicts between the provisions of bankruptcy codes and those of mortgage statutes (and/or debtor-creditor statutes) in most countries. This situation exists partly because of the following factors: (1) the process of creation of bankruptcy codes and mortgage statutes (in the United States, bankruptcy codes and federal statutes, while most mortgage statutes are state statutes; (2) many countries have different statutes/systems/procedures for the perfection of security interests in real estate and in personal property; and (3) in some countries, bankruptcy courts are distinct from ordinary civil courts (e.g., United States), and are sometimes distinct from constitutional courts (European countries).

The preemption of mortgage statutes by bankruptcy codes has or can have substantial economic and psychological effects both in corporate bankruptcy and personal bankruptcy cases, because it has direct impact on rights, divisibility of rights, probability of recovery, lenders' incentives to provide loans, propensity to breach loan agreements; transmission of monetary policies, and the magnitude/types of remedies that can be implemented by courts (e.g., punitive damages for fraud/misconduct) because bankruptcy courts often have specialized but limited powers. Preemption was defined in an earlier chapter in this book.

EXISTING LITERATURE

The existing literature on bankruptcy law preemption of foreclosure laws is relatively scant, and consists mostly of journal articles that were written after the *Sherwood v. Lycos* (U.S. Court of Appeals for the Ninth Circuit) decision in 2005. Indeed the U.S. Supreme Court and the highest courts of most states have not ruled directly on this preemption issue.

In *Sherwood Partners Inc. v. Lycos Inc.,* the U.S. Court of Appeals for the Ninth Circuit held that the bankruptcy code preempted the provisions of the California Assignment for the Benefit of Creditors (ABC) law relating to preference claims—this was a major development in the bankruptcy, real estate law, and commercial law fields. In *Ready Fixtures Co. v. Stevens Cabinets* (June 2007), the United States District Court for the Western District of Wisconsin refused to follow the Ninth Circuit's decision in *Sherwood Partners Inc. v. Lycos Inc.,* and held that the bankruptcy code does not preempt the preference provisions of Wisconsin's ABC statute. In *Haberbush v. Charles & Dorothy Cummins Family LP* (United States), the California Appellate court also declined to follow *Sherwood Partners Inc. v. Lycos Inc.* There have been other conflicting court decisions in different jurisdictions. Nathan and Cargill (2007), Feld (2006), Johnson (2007), Luo (2008), Morrison (2009), Berman and Vance (2008), and Johnston (2007) explain some of the issues. Also see: Ahern (2001); Bellia (2001); Bergl and Rosenthal (2003); Eidenmuller (2005); Hetland and Hansen (1987); Longhofer and Peters (2004); Hetland and Hansen (1987); Eidenmuller (2005); Merrill and Smith (2000, 2001).

In *Butner v. United States*, the U.S. Supreme Court held that state law should control the issue of mortgage holder's right to rents. In *Butner v. U.S.*, the Court noted that "[p]roperty interests are created and defined by state law. Unless some federal interest requires a different result, there is no reason why such interests should be analyzed differently simply because an interested party is involved in a bankruptcy proceeding" (Id. at 55). Adler (2007) critiqued the "Butner Principle" and noted that it is founded on the faulty premise that if bankruptcy law provides its own entitlements, the result will be destructive forum shopping. Adler argues that the Butner Principle should be discarded and that courts or Congress should adopt a sensible federal priority regime that includes super-priority for tort victims.

U.S. courts have ruled on federal bankruptcy law preemption of other state laws (not pertaining to foreclosures/mortgages). In all these cases, the courts' framing of the issues and post-judgment academic analysis of the courts' decisions focused on only whether the state law was preempted. This line of reasoning is somewhat unfortunate because given statutory construction, legislative intent of the U.S. Congress and state congresses, practicality considerations, transaction costs, monitoring costs, information asymmetry costs, and efficiency of legal processes, there are instances where the federal statute can incorporate the state statute (both can function simultaneously) and vice versa. For example, California's Uniform Commercial Code (UCC) and real estate statutes function simultaneously; and many U.S. federal bankruptcy courts apply state real estate statutes when determining issues pertaining to creation of property rights.

According to Weinberg (2006), the U.S. Supreme Court has held that state preference statutes similar to California Code of Civil Procedure Section 1800 are not preempted by federal bankruptcy law. See *Stellwagen v. Clum*, 245 U.S. 605 (1918) (The Supreme Court upheld an Ohio preference statute against a claim that the state statute was preempted by the Bankruptcy Act of 1898); *Pobreslo v. Joseph M. Boyd Co.*, 287 U.S. 518 (1933). The Supreme Court upheld a Wisconsin statute that regulated general assignments that contained a preference provision); *Mayer v. Hellman*, 91 U.S. 496 (1875). An Ohio statute that provided for general assignments and avoidance of preferences was upheld. Furthermore, the decisions of lower federal courts (courts other than the U.S. Supreme Court) on federal questions are not binding on state courts. See *Walker v. Kiousis*, 93 Cal. App. 4th 1432, 1441 (2001). Decisions of the lower federal courts on federal questions are not binding on state courts.

There have been some articles that have analyzed foreclosure sales within the context of standard fraudulent conveyance literature (Ehrlich 1985; Washburn 1980). Some court cases have also analyzed foreclosure sales within the context of standard fraudulent conveyance literature. See, for example, *In re Ehring*, 900 F.2d 184 (CA9 1990); *United Savings Assn. of Texas v. Timbers of Inwood Forest Associates, Ltd.*, 484 U.S. 365, 374 -75 (1988). See *Dewsnup v. Timm*, 502 U.S. 410 (1992) (slip op., at 7) (Scalia, J., dissenting). These cases and articles have shown that there has been significant lack of consistency among U.S. bankruptcy courts—some bankruptcy courts have voided foreclosures as fraudulent conveyances, while others have declined to void foreclosures.

Luo (2008) described a "Constitutional Preemption Doctrine" wherein any intent by federal legislation to preempt state law must be clear in the wording of the federal statute. Luo also states in part, "With respect to bankruptcy, the Court has determined that the preemption doctrine invalidates laws providing for debtor discharge but does not extend to ABC statutes that give the assignee the rights of creditors generally. The general principle is that "only state laws which conflict with the bankruptcy laws of Congress . . . are suspended; those which are in aid of the Bankruptcy Act can stand."

The existing law on federal preemption is somewhat unclear. U.S. courts have identified three types of preemption, but they have not been consistent in applying the classifications. In *Bibbo v. Dean Witter Reynolds, Inc.*, the

Court described the three different types of preemption of state law by federal law under the Supremacy Clause, (U.S. Constitution, Article VI), which are: (1) *express preemption*, which occurs when Congress expresses an intent to preempt state law in the language of the statute; (2) *field preemption*, where Congress intends fully to occupy a field of regulation; and (3) *conflict preemption*, where it is impossible to comply with both federal and state law, or where state law stands as an obstacle to the accomplishment and execution of the full purposes and objectives of Congress. Fortunately, it is not necessary to specify any class of preemption in order to resolve the constitutionality of the U.S. Bankruptcy Code's preemption of state-law real property foreclosure laws.

SURVEY OF MACROECONOMIC EFFECTS OF BANKRUPTCY CODES

Several articles on the economics of bankruptcy codes are worth noting. Li and Sarte (2006) analyzed the macroeconomic effects of Chapter 7 and Chapter 13 bankruptcies, which are two ways of filing for personal or corporate bankruptcy in the United States. Feld (2006) analyzed the limits of the bankruptcy preemption of various state laws (pertaining to reorganizations, foreclosures, and debtor/creditor relationships). Luo (2008) supports the anti-preemption position (i.e., supports the decisions of state courts to bar preemption and apply state debtor/creditor statutes) for four main reasons: (1) there can be no conflict when no bankruptcy petition has been filed; (2) the weight of authority, including Supreme Court precedent and subsequent state and federal decisions, favors upholding the state law; (3) California's ABC statute does not interfere with the operation of the federal bankruptcy code but furthers the goals of insolvency legislation; and (4) statutes, such as Section 1800, make good policy.

A debtor can file Chapter 13 bankruptcy as often as every six months, but the debtor cannot incur additional debt without the bankruptcy trustee's approval while he or she is in Chapter 13 proceedings. A Chapter 13 debtor can keep all of his or her assets but must propose a repayment plan based on future earnings, usually for three to five years. The repayment plan must satisfy the "full payment" or "disposable income" tests (debtor is required to pay all of his disposable income to the Chapter 13 plan for up to five years, unless debtor proposes to pay all of his or her debts). The amount of debt the debtor should schedule for repayment must be greater than the value of nonexempt assets the debtor would have lost under Chapter 7. The debtor's declared income must include income from a secondary job and spousal income, and changes in current and future income. At the end of the repayment period, any remaining unpaid debt is discharged. The main complaint against Chapter 13 is that it reduces workers' willingness to work, or causes them to stop working because they are required to use all of their disposable income to pay debts.

In the United States, a Chapter 7 debtor can file under that chapter only once in six years; usually the bankruptcy appears in his or her credit report for up to 10 years. Under Chapter 7, a debtor must turn over all of his assets exceeding some exemption level to a bankruptcy trustee. The bankruptcy court will then discharge many types of unsecured debt including credit card debt, installment loans, and medical bills; and the trustee uses the proceeds of liquidation of all of the debtor's nonexempt assets to repay his or her debts.

Li and Sarte (2006) analyzed the implications of U.S. personal bankruptcy rules for resource allocation and welfare, and found that: (1) general equilibrium considerations, the choice of bankruptcy chapter and production are relevant determinants of the effects of policy reform; (2) contrary to prior published research, completely eliminating bankruptcy provisions causes significant declines in overall economic output and social welfare by reducing capital formation and labor input; (3) subjecting Chapter 7 filers to means testing (i.e., aimed at restricting Chapter 7 to only the neediest households) will not improve current bankruptcy provisions and, at best, will not change aggregate filings, output, and social welfare (but may lead not to just greater debt repayment but also more Chapter 13 bankruptcies); (4) an alternative tightening of provisions of Chapter 7, in the form of lower asset exemptions, can increase economic efficiency; (5) Chapter 13 allows debtors to keep their assets, but enter a partial repayment plan that functions as a wage tax that discourages labor effort, and affects production and welfare, while the discharge of all unsecured debt net of exemptions in Chapter 7 affects risk premia, overall volume of debt, and capital accumulation; and (6) lowering asset exemptions for Chapter 7 bankruptcy can increase economic efficiency, because it will increase the volume of Chapter 7 filings, reduce the incentive to save (because of greater confiscation of assets in bankruptcy), and thus increase probability of default, which reduces volumes of consumer debt and frees up capital for corporate expansion, which helps increase output and welfare.

In contrast to the existing literature, Li and Sarte (2006) attempted to show that the analysis of consumer bankruptcy requires: (1) a general equilibrium framework with endogenous factor supply, risk premia, and wages; and (2) both bankruptcy chapters currently available to debtors (Chapters 7 and 13), each of which has its own incentive effects on labor supply and capital formation. The problems inherent in the Li and Sarte (2006) study are as follows:

- The relationship between changes in risk premiums for individuals and output is not as strong as Li and Sarte (2006) postulate.

- The Li and Sarte (2006) emphasis on production and labor is somewhat excessive and unwarranted because: (1) automation is increasingly prevalent in many services and production industries; (2) jobs are outsourced to foreign countries and many finished products are imported into the United States; (3) the effects of Chapters 7 and 13 on leisure were not fully analyzed by Li and Sarte, and vary drastically depending on the type of bankruptcy chosen, household wealth, social capital, education/knowledge, profession, family structure, individual and household aspirations, age, and so on; and (4) creation of intellectual capital is often not proportional to the amount of labor input, and the intellectual capital accounts for more than 40 percent of the wealth and output in the United States and most developed economies.
- The perceived stigma and loss of social capital caused by a personal bankruptcy filing are moderated by the existence of mortgage companies, auto finance companies, and other lenders that will provide credit to persons that filed for Chapter 7 or Chapter 13 bankruptcy, and the existence of the "no-income no-verification" loans.
- The stock of capital available for production is often distinct from the capital that is available for lending to individuals.
- Often, the people who file for personal bankruptcy are not entrepreneurs or even decision makers in small companies that can hire people—and hence, the effect of personal bankruptcy on capital formation is limited and has not been analyzed properly. That is, the capital formation question is mooted by the fact that such financially distressed persons do not pursue job-creating activities that require capital.
- Housing and associated tenure choices (e.g., renting versus ownership) are just as important as capital and production in the analysis/comparison of different types of bankruptcy.
- Li and Sarte (2006) did not do a thorough analysis of the behavioral issues associated with personal bankruptcy—it is just not enough to assume or conclude that filing for personal bankruptcy automatically reduces the productivity of the individual.
- Li and Sarte (2006) reasoned that creditors collect more effectively on their loans under Chapter 7 provisions, which lowers the lending rate, which then leads to greater consumer debt, which in turn reduces the available supply of capital and, given the reduction in labor input, output and welfare fall. This argument is not entirely correct because the cash capital that is available for production is often distinct from cash capital that is available for consumer lending; and increasing importation of goods and outsourcing typically reduces or eliminates the need for growth capital.

Levitin (2009) analyzed the usefulness of the proposed amendments to the U.S. Bankruptcy Code, which were to permit write-downs of mortgages by bankruptcy courts. Levitin also empirically tested whether protecting lenders from losses in bankruptcy court proceedings encourages them to lend more and at lower rates, and thus encourages homeownership (which has been the economic rationale for the policy against bankruptcy modification of home-mortgage debt), and found that this assumption is wrong and that permitting mortgage modification/reduction in bankruptcy will have little or no effect on the cost of mortgage credit or on mortgage availability. Levitin also found that: (1) mortgage markets are indifferent to bankruptcy-modification risk; and (2) lenders face smaller losses from bankruptcy court modification of mortgages than from foreclosure, and the market is unlikely to price against bankruptcy court modification of mortgages. Levitin argues that given market neutrality toward bankruptcy-court modification of mortgages, such modification/strip-down presents the best solution to the foreclosure crisis; and unlike other proposed solutions, bankruptcy modification offers immediate relief, solves securitization-related problems, addresses both problems of payment-reset shock (from resetting adjustable rate mortgages, ARMs) and negative equity (from declining property values), eliminates speculators, spreads burdens between borrowers and lenders, avoids the costs and moral hazard of a government bailout, and is the least invasive method of stabilizing the housing market.

Levitin (2009) noted that lenders prefer a smaller loss from modification to a larger loss from foreclosure; but voluntary modification has not been happening on a large scale due to contractual impediments, agency costs, practical impediments, and other transaction costs. Although government refinancing or insurance plans would take months to implement, during which time foreclosures would continue, bankruptcy modification can preclude moral hazard for lenders and borrowers of a bailout. Levitin also argued that based on data on the relative losses that lenders incur in modification and foreclosure, as long as lenders face larger losses in foreclosure than modification, the mortgage market will not price and ration credit based on bankruptcy-modification risk; and thus, the bankruptcy code should be amended to permit debtors to modify all mortgages. Levitin erroneously argues that the U.S. bankruptcy system cannot handle the current home-foreclosure crisis since the U.S. Bankruptcy Code supposedly forbids any modification of mortgage loans secured solely by the debtor's principal residence—that is, defaults on such mortgage loans must be cured and the loans then paid off according to their original terms, including all fees that have been levied since default, or else the bankruptcy stay on collection actions will be lifted, and the mortgagee will be permitted to foreclose on the property. This argument is flawed because: (1) in the United States, mortgages secured by two-family, three-family, and four-family houses that are not primary homes constitute a substantial percentage of outstanding "residential mortgages"; and (2) as explained in this chapter, under certain circumstances (e.g., "Reasonably Equivalent Value Doctrine"; "Equitable Subordination"; the application of the *Bankruptcy Abuse Prevention and Consumer Protection Act of 2005*), the bankruptcy stay preempts all proposed and ongoing foreclosure proceedings, including those for primary residences.

The Levitin (2009) study: (a) does not state whether lender's indifference/sensitivity to a bankruptcy court's modification/reduction of mortgages will vary if other related bankruptcy statutes are changed, or if the structure of mortgages changes, or if the overall volume of mortgages declines or increases substantially; (b) does not analyze the lenders' costs of funds (e.g., discount window; traditional bank depositors; bond market investors; interbank market), which is a determinant of the lender's reaction to the proposed change in legislation; (c) did not analyze the possible effects of lenders' accounting treatment of such losses that may be incurred in bankruptcy court (such losses can be immediately realized, recognized, and expensed in the income statement, or can be unrealized, capitalized, and deferred)—the accounting treatment will affect the lenders' capital reserve calculations, which will probably affect lenders' incentives to provide mortgages; (d) did not analyze the issue of the bankruptcy court's discretion when applying the proposed amendments—the bankruptcy judge may order that the lender may recover the strip-down amount if after the bankruptcy proceedings, the property value increases and exceeds the mortgage balance at the beginning of the bankruptcy proceedings; and (e) did not analyze the issue of the implicit U.S. Bankruptcy Code's preemption of state law deficiency judgment statutes and foreclosure statutes, and the possible reactions by terminal state courts (it may take two to four years to resolve such conflicts of law).

Scarberry (2011) stated that the proposed amendments to the U.S. Bankruptcy Code, which will permit the reduction of underwater home mortgages (i.e., where the outstanding mortgage balance exceeds the property value) to the court-determined value of the homes, and other modifications of home mortgages in Chapter 13 will substantially change the risk characteristics of home mortgages, and future availability of mortgages, and will be detrimental to social welfare. Scarberry conjectured that: (a) the proposed amendments will expose mortgage holders to all of the future downside risk in the real property market without the benefit of future appreciation; and (b) the proposed bankruptcy code amendments will treat home mortgages less favorably than other secured debt in Chapter 13 bankruptcy (home mortgages will be the only secured debts that could be stripped down and paid off at a court-determined interest rate, with monthly payments lower than those required by the credit contract, over a period of up to nearly 40 years, rather than the no-more-than-five year period that would still apply to other secured debts). The Scarberry critiques of Levitin (2009) appear reasonable and are as follows: (1) the Levitin empirical studies rely on an incorrect understanding of current and past bankruptcy law and of the proposed bankruptcy modification legislation, and the Levitin empirical studies erroneously compare the effects of the strip-down in the proposed legislation, with the effects of the very different kinds of strip-down that, in limited circumstances, are currently available or were at one time available under the U.S. Bankruptcy Code; (2) Levitin does not consider the different incentives that the proposed legislation will create in terms of encouraging debtors with large negative equity to file Chapter 13 bankruptcy petitions and encouraging Chapter 13 debtors to argue that their homes/properties have a low value for their homes rather than to report an inflated value; (3) the proposed amendments to the bankruptcy code can cause somewhat perverse results because homeowners who made the lowest down payments, and/or who paid the most inflated prices for their homes, and then did a cash-out refinancing of their mortgages to take equity out of their homes for purposes of consumption, will benefit the most from the proposed statutes, while homeowners who made large down payments, and were careful not to pay inflated prices, and did not use their home equity to finance consumption, will get the fewest benefits from the proposed legislation; and (4) in the long run, the resulting resentment caused by the proposed legislation may undermine public support for the primary function of consumer bankruptcy laws, which is "to grant a fresh start to the honest but unfortunate debtor."

However, Scarberry (2011) notes that under current laws in the United States (and also in some European countries), homeowners with substantial negative equity may have little incentive to continue to make mortgage payments. However, the foreclosures that occur due to negative equity have an indirect effect on the wealth of homeowners who have not defaulted on their mortgages—which is a downward price pressure wherein the existence of negative equity causes high foreclosure levels in the immediate neighborhoods, which causes home prices to drop, which in turn creates additional negative equity, which then causes foreclosure levels to remain high, which causes home prices to drop further, and so on. Thus, any steps taken to reduce the levels of negative equity, including the strip-down of home mortgages, can help stop the downward price pressure, help stabilize home values, and also help reduce high foreclosure rates. To achieve this, Scarberry suggests: (a) any legislation that permits strip-down of mortgages should include clauses for the mortgage holder's recapture of a substantial portion of any future increase in the value of the home; (b) any such legislation should have clear eligibility criteria that are designed to minimize the negative effects; (c) consideration should be given to the kind of strip-down that the current legislative proposals permit, because the Obama and Bush administrations' programs for modification of home mortgages have failed; and (d) any such legislation should limit home mortgage modification to mortgages originated prior to January 1, 2008, by which time it had become very clear that the United States and other countries had entered a period of serious mortgage crisis.

Chen and Corbae (2011) attempted to find the optimal length of public disclosure of bankruptcy filings. In the United States, the Fair Credit Reporting Act (FCRA) requires that any public disclosure of bankruptcy filing must be removed from an individual's credit record after 10 years. Contrary to Chen and Corbae, FCRA does not necessarily weaken incentives not to default, because: (a) there are "irrational lenders" who provide loans to people who have filed for bankruptcy; (b) the public disclosure of bankruptcy is a strong incentive not to default; and (c) Chen and Corbae developed a model to assess the welfare consequences of changing the amount of time that adverse events can appear on an individual's credit record—they calibrated the model to U.S. data where the exclusion/disclosure parameter was set to be 10 years on average, and then tried to find the time period that maximizes *ex post* economy-wide welfare using a consumption equivalent measure. Their model predicts that agents prefer to remove the bankruptcy flag after one year, though the gains are small.

Aysun and Honig (2010) notes that countries with intermediate levels of quality of institutions experience larger output contractions after sudden stops of capital inflows than less-developed nations; but this effect is not common in countries with strong institutions. Aysun and Honig analyzed this hypothesis by using a calibrated dynamic stochastic general equilibrium (DSGE) model that is based on the financial accelerator framework developed in Bernanke, Gertler, and Gilchrist (1999). Aysun and Honig defined financial market institutional quality in terms of creditors' abilities to recover assets from bankrupt firms—which in part depends on preemption of state debtor-creditor statutes, and the perceived efficiency of bankruptcy statutes. Aysun and Honig found that bankruptcy costs directly affect vulnerability to sudden stops of capital flows, but also has an indirect impact by affecting the extent of liability dollarization. Aysun and Honig simulations showed an inverted U-shaped relationship between bankruptcy costs and the output loss after sudden stops of capital flows.

Battiston et al. (2007) attempted to address the potential domino effects of trade credit, which links many firms from different industries. At least two other types of credit chains also exist in mortgage markets: (1) financial companies and mortgage funds (that provide mortgages to borrowers) obtain lines of credit from banks, which borrow in the capital markets or from central banks to finance such credit lines; and (2) second mortgages on properties and home-equity lines of credit are often the source of equity for the purchase of other properties. However, the three important omissions in the Battiston et al. study are as follows:

1. In these circumstances and credit networks, the transmission of monetary policy is substantially dampened by the incentive/disincentive effects of different types of bankruptcy, the preemption of state debtor/creditor statutes by bankruptcy codes, the perceived efficiency and information effects of bankruptcy courts, the perceived efficiency of state-law alternatives to bankruptcy (such as "assignments for benefit of creditors"), information effects (of bankruptcy or state-law alternatives), and so on.
2. The magnitude of reputational effects on the propensity to default varies drastically by industry, and after a certain level of financial distress a firm's internal concerns for reputation can dissipate; external providers of trade credit will become much more reluctant to lend.
3. The extent to which industry executives are inbred (companies recruit mid-level and senior-level managers from each other) has a substantial effect on the consequences of default (i.e., reorganization, bankruptcy, or prepackaged bankruptcy).

Hausch and Ramachandran (2009) developed a market-based approach to resolution of financial distress in bankruptcy that is appropriate if claimants are severely cash-constrained and there is merit in having existing owners-managers remain in control. Their approach is different from auctions in foreclosures (which have been shown to be inefficient). Their approach was developed in response to the 1997 Asian Crisis, where the large numbers of financially distressed firms, creditors with poor incentives, and inexperienced courts obstructed the usual negotiated resolution that is prevalent in bankruptcy courts around the world. In the Hausch and Ramachandran scheme, creditors bid for their position in a queue (and within the relevant classes of claims in order to honor any absolute priority or hierarchy of claims, if any), which is serviced in sequence from the firm's operating cash flows; and creditors that accept a greater proportionate reduction in the face value of their claims are placed ahead of the others. No one in the queue (including owners who are last) is paid anything until the first in line are fully paid using the firm's operating cash surpluses. Hausch and Ramachandran attempted to show that in equilibrium, their scheme reduces the aggregate debts of the firm sufficiently to provide a positive expected residual return to the owner-managers, and can result in an outcome that is superior to other bankruptcy procedures. The key issue is that while the bankruptcy codes in most jurisdictions allow various mechanisms for resolution of financial distress, the foreclosure process allows only an auction process, which is often inefficient in most countries.

In summary, given the foregoing, the bankruptcy code's preemption of state debtor-creditor laws and/or mortgage statutes has substantial macroeconomic ramifications, which have not been analyzed in the literature.

THE FINANCIAL ACCELERATOR THEORY IS INACCURATE

Bernanke, Gertler, and Gilchrist (1999) introduced the financial accelerator concept, which is inaccurate for the following 11 reasons:

1. The cause-effect relationship between the credit markets and the macroeconomy are symbiotic and evolving; that is, they both affect each other in ways that change over time.
2. As was illustrated during the 2005 to 2009 boom in subprime mortgages in the United States and Europe, borrower net worth has not been a major factor in credit markets. Also, in credit card markets and auto-loan markets, borrower net worth is not a major factor, and lenders routinely lend to people with minimal assets. Similarly, many entrepreneurs have minimal assets and net worth, and the successful ones tend to start businesses that require low upfront capital. Even when an entrepreneur's company is operating (but before the initial public offering [IPO]), lenders do not typically rely on the equity value of the shares, but focus on liquidation values of specific assets such as accounts receivables, inventory, equipment, and real estate.
3. The financial accelerator concept completely omits the issues of borrower psychology, borrowers' biases and lenders' biases.
4. The financial accelerator concept does not consider the incentive systems of lenders and compensation of bankers (which were major causes of both the subprime mortgage crisis and the subsequent global credit crunch of 2008 to 2011). Incentive systems of lenders and the compensation of bankers are major dampeners of both government monetary policy and quasi-governmental monetary policy (which is defined as the internal monetary policies of large international banks such as Citigroup, Barclays, UBS, and Standard Chartered).
5. The financial accelerator concept completely omits the preemption of state debtor/creditor statutes and similar statutes (e.g., foreclosure statutes, assignment for benefit of creditors), which are major determinants of the incentive effects of bankruptcy laws and are also major dampeners of monetary policy.
6. Given that many loans are based on the borrower's income, truth telling and disclosure become critical, and these issues were omitted from the development of the financial accelerator concept. However, costly state

verification is relevant only when the loan agreement does not contain summary recovery provisions, sufficient disclosure clauses, or nonjudicial foreclosure clauses; when bankruptcy is expensive; or when the borrower can frustrate recovery efforts (e.g., there is a borrower's right of redemption in a foreclosure), and so on.

7. The external finance premium described as a major element of the financial accelerator is not relevant because the differences in lending rates charged to borrowers have been based mostly on reported consumer credit scores and bond ratings, and not on borrower wealth or borrower contributions to financed projects (e.g., the 103 percent loan-to-value [LTV] mortgages or 100 percent auto financing).
8. The magnitude and timing of information asymmetry between borrowers and lenders varies drastically depending on the type of asset/collateral (e.g., housing versus cars versus household durables versus major capital projects) and the location of the borrower and collateral, in addition to other factors.
9. The financial accelerator concept completely omits the substantial effects of asset securitization (which changes lenders' and borrowers' incentives and opportunity costs) and the use of derivatives (e.g., swaps and options, which change lenders' expectations, borrowers' expectations and opportunity set, the value of time to borrowers, cost of funds, opportunity costs, and targeted borrowers).
10. Loan risk is often not diversifiable—swaps and options may be used to hedge interest rate risk, but other risks (credit risk, legal risk, documentation risk, etc.) are often transaction-specific and/or firm-specific.
11. The extent to which the parties to a financial contract react to monetary policy and credit supply is also determined by their cognition, willingness to accept losses (WTAL), the value of losses to each party (and hence, their absolute tax position), propensity to procrastinate, perceptions of the efficiency of the legal system, and litigation resources (having funds to litigate breaches of the contract), all of which are monetary policy dampeners, but were omitted in the development of the financial accelerator concept.

CRITERIA FOR PREEMPTION: EQUITABLE SUBORDINATION, FRAUDULENT TRANSFERS (THE "REASONABLY EQUIVALENT VALUE" DOCTRINE), THE *DEPRIZIO CONTROVERSY*, AND THE BANKRUPTCY ABUSE PREVENTION AND CONSUMER PROTECTION ACT OF 2005

In the United States, the U.S. Bankruptcy Code and bankruptcy common law are implicated in real estate transactions when there is financial distress or there are bankruptcy filings. In most instances, state/local real estate laws and debtor/creditor laws govern the relationship between lender and borrower. The issue of U.S. Bankruptcy Code preemption of state mortgage foreclosure laws has several implications for the subprime mortgage markets. Most subprime borrowers are low-income persons with derogatory credit histories and are more likely to file for bankruptcy than regular borrowers. These subprime borrowers can use state mortgage foreclosure laws to frustrate lenders by extending the judicial foreclosure process, and by bidding on the foreclosed property at post-judgment auctions (using the borrower's post-judgment right-of-redemption statutes or clauses to purchase foreclosed properties). Similarly, subprime borrowers can use Chapter 13 and Chapter 7 (U.S. Bankruptcy Code) filings to stop foreclosure proceedings and delay mortgage payments. Permitting preemption by the U.S. Bankruptcy Code will probably provide a forum that is better able to handle subprime borrowers' debts (real estate and non–real estate debt/obligations).

The U.S. Bankruptcy Code preempts U.S. state foreclosure laws and state debtor-creditor statutes in at least four ways, which are summarized as:

1. *Section 362(a)* of the U.S. Bankruptcy Code creates an "automatic stay," which precludes the creditor from seeking to obtain property of the estate or from assessing or collecting on a prepetition claim against the debtor. See: 11 U.S.C. § 362(a)(3) & (6).[1] Debtors can remedy a "willful violation" of the automatic stay through § 362(h), which Congress enacted in 1984.
2. The U.S. Bankruptcy Code's (11 U.S.C. §§ 548, 544 & 547) *fraudulent conveyance statutes* can be used to invalidate completed or ongoing state-law real property foreclosure proceedings in civil courts.
3. The doctrine of *equitable subordination* can be applied in the U.S. Bankruptcy Court to preempt ongoing and completed state-law foreclosure proceedings.
4. The *DePrizio Controversy*—The Section 550 fraudulent conveyance statutes in the U.S. Bankruptcy Code can also be used to invalidate completed or ongoing state-law real property foreclosure proceedings.

An equitable subordination claim, under Section-510(c) of the U.S. Bankruptcy Code, has been deemed under some circumstances to be a "core" proceeding under the bankruptcy code, and may preempt a pending state foreclosure proceeding. Although state-court foreclosure proceedings are generally deemed *non-core*, a related equitable subordination claim may not be remanded to state court where the foreclosure action is based on the same facts as the debtor's equitable subordination claim. The courts' rationale is that if the automatic stay in bankruptcy was terminated and foreclosure proceeded, the trustee (or debtor in possession) would be deprived of the equitable-subordination defense, which is available solely as the result of federal bankruptcy law (i.e., Section 510[c] of the Code).

Under the Fraudulent Transfer statutes of the U.S. Bankruptcy Code (the "Reasonably Equivalent Value" Doctrine; 11 U.S.C. §§ 548, 544 & 547), the bankruptcy court can preempt and/or void a state-court foreclosure proceeding (the foreclosure is deemed and analyzed as a "transfer"). Upon the bankruptcy court's avoidance of the transfer, the property is then transferred back to the bankruptcy estate, subject to a lien for the price paid for the asset. The issue of inadequate consideration will not apply to sales at the market price that would generally benefit creditors and are not voidable. A transfer is deemed to be constructively fraudulent under Section 548(a)(1)(B) of the Code and may be set aside if all of the following five conditions exist:

1. The transfer was made within one year prior to the filing of the bankruptcy petition.
2. In the transfer, the creditor received "less than reasonably equivalent value" in a transaction.
3. The transferor was insolvent at the time of the transfer or was rendered insolvent as the result of the transfer (insolvency test).
4. The transferor was undercapitalized at the time of the transfer or became undercapitalized as the result of the transfer (capitalization test).
5. The transferor was unable or rendered unable by the transfer to pay its debts as they became due (cash-flow test).

In *BFP v. Resolution Trust Corp.* (BFP), the U.S. Supreme Court held that in a mortgage foreclosure "Reasonably Equivalent Value" is the price received at a regularly conducted, noncollusive foreclosure sale of the property, where all the requirements of the state's foreclosure laws have been complied with. However, the Court stated that its opinion applied only to real-estate mortgage foreclosures—and does not apply to nonjudicial foreclosures, deeds in lieu of foreclosure, or tax foreclosure sales unless there are certain due-process and procedural safeguards. The term *Reasonably Equivalent Value* is not defined or explained by the U.S. Bankruptcy Code, and has been construed differently by both federal and state courts and on a case-by-case basis (and there has not been uniformity among the courts about the interpretation of the term and its definition). The factors considered by the courts include: (1) the good faith of the parties; (2) the difference between the amount paid and the fair market value; (3) the percentage of the fair market value paid; (4) whether the transaction was arm's length; and (5) the timing of the transaction. Some recent court opinions have applied the

BFP holding, to uphold other forced sales, such as judicial tax sales, upon a finding that the procedural and substantive rights of the debtor had been adequately protected. However, at least one court has ruled that a tax foreclosure sale, although conducted in accordance with state law, was invalid and constituted a fraudulent transfer (see: *Sherman v. Rose* [CA10, 1998]).

Scarberry et al. (2006) noted that in some instances, bankruptcy courts allow debtors who are natural persons to avoid liens that will impair their bankruptcy exemptions, even though such liens might be valid under nonbankruptcy law (see § 522[f]). Scarberry et al. also noted that unperfected Article 9 security interests and unrecorded mortgages also can be avoided in bankruptcy court, even though they might be effective under nonbankruptcy law against the other creditors who might not qualify as the persons entitled under nonbankruptcy law to defeat such unperfected or unrecorded interests. See 11 U.S.C. § 544(a)(1) & (3) (2006).

In limited circumstances, the DePrizio Doctrine can be used for preemption of state-law foreclosures. Section 101(32, 31) of the U.S. Bankruptcy Code defines *insider*. If a transfer is made to or benefits an insider, and (1) the debtor was insolvent at the time of the transfer, (2) the transfer gives the creditor more than the creditor would obtain in a Chapter 7 liquidation absent the transfer, and (3) the transfer occurred within one year prior to the bankruptcy filing; then the debtor may set aside the transfer under § 547 of the Code, on which the debtor and the creditor are placed in the position that they were before the rescinded transfer. Section 202 of the Bankruptcy Reform Act of 1994 (1994 Reform Act) amended § 550 of the Code. Section 202 of the 1994 Reform Act expressly intended to overrule *DePrizio* by stating that payments to a noninsider lender may only be recovered if made during the 90-day period following such payments. Section 202 added the following subsection (c) to § 550 of the Bankruptcy Code: "*If a transfer made between 90 days and one year before the filing of the petition—is avoided under Section 547(b) of this title; and was made for the benefit of a creditor that at the time of such transfer was an insider; the trustee may not recover under subsection (a) from a transferee that is not an insider.*"

The relevant legislative history of Section 202 states that: "This section overrules the *DePrizio* line of cases and clarifies that non-insider transferees should not be subject to the preference provisions of the Bankruptcy Code beyond the 90-day statutory period" (140 Cong. Rec. H10767, daily edition October 4, 1994). Section 550 provides that the bankruptcy trustee may recover transferred property for the benefit of the estate from the initial transferee or the entity for whose benefit the transfer was made, or any intermediate or immediate transferee of the initial transferee, unless certain exceptions apply. The amendment to § 550 was intended to effectively overrule *Levit v. Ingersoll Rand Finance Corp.* (*In re V.N. DePrizio Constr.*

Co.) and its progeny. *DePrizio* effectively extended the preference avoidance period from 90 days to one year for "noninsider" creditors when the transfers benefited an "insider." *DePrizio* permitted a bankruptcy trustee to recover preferential payments (consisting of debt payments made to noninsider lenders during this extended one-year preference period) under §§ 547 & 550 of the Code, when the debt was guaranteed by insiders (in this case, the controlling shareholders) of the debtor.

In *O'Neill v. Orix Credit Alliance, Inc.* (*In re Northeastern Contracting, Inc.*), 233 B.R. 15 (U.S.; D.Conn, 1999), the Connecticut bankruptcy court held that the DePrizio Doctrine would be applied in the Second Circuit, in a case that was originally filed before the passage of the 1994 Reform Act, to the extent that the debtor's payments to a noninsider creditor benefited an insider-guarantor. The court also stated that the DePrizio Doctrine was effectively overruled by the 1994 congressional amendments to the Bankruptcy Act—all of the federal circuit court cases upholding the DePrizio Doctrine were decided prior to the passage of the 1994 Reform Act.

The Bankruptcy Abuse Prevention and Consumer Protection Act of 2005 (Public Law No. 109–8, 119 Stat. 23, April 20, 2005; USA) (the Reform Act) was enacted in 2005. The Reform Act has not addressed the problems inherent in the federal bankruptcy law preemption of state real property laws. The Reform Act places tighter restrictions and requirements on the process of filing for bankruptcy and seeking discharge or reorganization of debts. The Reform Act can be used to preempt foreclosure proceedings.

Thus, the foregoing describes the different basis for federal bankruptcy foreclosure laws as property rights.

Foreclosure statutes are not merely procedural, but are also substantive, and can be sufficient to completely address default. Foreclosure rules are relevant in bankruptcy, and the question of incorporation of foreclosure rules into bankruptcy proceedings is relevant. Furthermore, state foreclosure laws and federal foreclosure statutes are essentially property rights, which should be upheld in bankruptcy proceedings—deprivation of such rights is unconstitutional. The property rights elements arise as follows. The state foreclosure laws can provide a needed and complete remedy for claimants, and state foreclosure laws are necessary to protect the constitutional rights of market participants' (lenders, borrowers, insurance companies, etc.) right to contract, due process, and equal protection. State foreclosure laws are in line with expectations and norms in modern commerce and society—expectations of orderly procedures for adjudicating disputes about real property. The federal bankruptcy code and associated proceedings recognize some other state laws as property interests—and there are no major distinctions between such laws and foreclosures laws, in terms of importance, purpose, transaction cost effects, and monitoring cost effects. The Butner Principle (discussed earlier) mandates that U.S. Bankruptcy Courts should use state mortgage/property laws when determining issues pertaining to the creation of property rights.

However, some U.S. Supreme Court cases have held that foreclosure laws are not property rights. See: *United Savings Assn. of Texas v. Timbers of Inwood Forest Associates, Ltd.; Owen v. Owen; United States v. Whiting Pools, Inc.; Gelfert v. National City Bank of N.Y.; BFP v. Resolution Trust Corp.* These cases fail to consider: (a) the transaction-cost and monitoring-cost impacts of foreclosure laws; and (b) the significantly negative information effects of a regime in which foreclosure laws are not property rights. Foreclosures have significant economic value and are an incentive for lenders to provide loans. Without adequate laws for the resolution of default, lenders will not have much incentive to lend, or will lend at very high interest rates—this is clearly evident in many developing countries that do not have foreclosure/mortgage laws. The public auction in foreclosures (as opposed to a private appraisal) also has significant value to both lenders and borrower, particularly in states/jurisdictions where the lender has post-foreclosure recourse to the borrower's other assets. The government has a duty to enact efficient foreclosure laws that enhance the efficiency of capital markets. State residents also have an expectancy interest in foreclosure laws and such interests are essentially property interests. The sociocultural and psychological context in which foreclosure processes are implemented are complex and make foreclosures property rights.

THE U.S. SUPREME COURT'S STANDARDS FOR PREEMPTION CASES

In order to preempt traditional state regulation, the federal statutory purpose must be "clear and manifest," and otherwise, the U.S. Bankruptcy Code will be construed to adopt, rather than to displace, preexisting state law. The U.S. Supreme Court has established seven standards and criteria for analyzing preemption cases:

1. Whether the U.S. Congress has set forth a comprehensive regulatory scheme:

   In this instance, the U.S. bankruptcy laws are not a comprehensive scheme. Unlike state foreclosure laws, the U.S. bankruptcy laws do not set forth any specific procedural steps for adjudicating claims pertaining to real property. Despite the significant differences (temporal, physical, monetary, value, ownership, etc.) between real property and other types of assets, the U.S. Bankruptcy Code treats real property the same as other assets. Supposedly, several provisions of the U.S. Bankruptcy Code provide mortgagees distinct and presumably adequate protections for their interests. See 11 U.S.C. 101, 548(c), 550(d)(1), 362 & 362(d). However, these statutes provide the mortgagee with the same protection as state foreclosure laws—in the U.S. Bankruptcy Courts, the mortgagee's claims are subject to negotiation and the judge's discretion, unlike in foreclosure proceedings. The U.S. bankruptcy laws do not provide mortgages with efficient procedures for settling their claims: (a) bankruptcy involves negotiations among creditors and submission of a plan of reorganization or a cram-down, all of which takes time; (b) bankruptcy involves approval of the plan of reorganization; and (c) the debtor loses principal and interest payments during bankruptcy procedures.

2. Whether the subject matter is technical and whether the relevant history and background are complex and extensive:

   Real property typically has much longer history and expected life (depreciation period) than other assets. Unlike most other assets, real property would have typically changed ownership and have been mortgaged, and capital expenditure would have been incurred over time—a relatively more complex background. Real property is also relatively less liquid and incurs high transaction costs in sales. Real property is also relatively more technical than other assets—real property involves more compliance with more laws/regulations and knowledge about building operations.

3. Whether application of state law will undermine legal efficiency and predictability:

   In the case of real property, application of state foreclosure laws will increase efficiency and predictability (compared to federal bankruptcy laws). The outcomes of bankruptcy processes are highly negotiated, more expensive, have less to do with the underlying lien/liability, and involve more reorganization of the capital structure than foreclosure processes. The outcome of the foreclosure process is not negotiated or left to the discretion of the judge—in the foreclosure process, the validity of the lien and the alleged default are ascertained and there is an auction and then distribution of proceeds. The public auction process adds transparency and reality to the allocation of values, unlike the bankruptcy process. Foreclosure processes do not have the often tedious negotiations that exist in bankruptcy proceedings. The judge in the foreclosure proceedings has much less discretion than bankruptcy judges. Although they are charged with critical business and strategic decisions, most bankruptcy judges do not have any formal training in business and have not worked in business. Because of the creditor negotiation, the comingling of assets and subsequent changes in capital structure, the required approval of the plan of reorganization by a judge, and the significant discretion granted to bankruptcy judges, the foreclosure process is much more predictable than the bankruptcy process. Hence, in the case of real property, the application of state law will be more advantageous and efficient than the application of federal bankruptcy laws.

4. Whether the U.S. Congress has delegated the authority to implement the statute to an agency, and if so, whether that federal agency's degree of authority and discretion suggest a Congressional intent to limit judicial interference with the agency's work:

   The U.S. Congress has not delegated the implementation of the federal bankruptcy statutes to any government agency. The U.S. bankruptcy court system is a part of the U.S. federal court system and is not a distinct agency. The federal bankruptcy statutes can be used/implemented in the U.S. District Court, the U.S. Court of Appeals, and the U.S. Supreme Court. That the U.S. Congress did not delegate the authority to implement the bankruptcy code to any agency is an indication of the intent of the U.S. Congress.

5. Whether the federal law provides recourse for the affected private party:

   The U.S. Bankruptcy Code does not provide sufficient recourse for the affected party. Almost all complaints about issues arising from bankruptcy proceedings have to be adjudicated in the same bankruptcy court or in the Bankruptcy Appellate Courts. As mentioned, while the U.S. Bankruptcy Code treats real property the same as personal property, there are certain differences between both—in terms of time (real property typically involves longer term issues/commitments, leverage; real property often involves mortgages), ownership (real property has ownership regimes that are different from those of personal property), mobility (real property is typically fixed while personal property is mobile).

6. Whether the state law interferes with the methods by which the federal statute was designed to reach its goal:

   The federal bankruptcy code achieves its goal by negotiations among the parties, judicial decisions, third-party asset appraisals, and issuance of orders by the bankruptcy judge. The state foreclosure laws do not substantially interfere with the operational methods of the U.S. Bankruptcy Courts. The state foreclosure laws are implemented by state and federal courts and associated judges. As is normal with almost all types of disputes that are being adjudicated in more than one forum, judges may issue orders to consolidate cases in the U.S. Bankruptcy Court. Where a person/entity in foreclosure proceedings files for bankruptcy, or is involuntarily placed in bankruptcy, as presently construed and applied in most states, the foreclosure laws can be applied simultaneously with the federal bankruptcy rules. This is because: (a) most debt bankruptcy proceedings are about assets other than real estate; (b) the systems for perfecting security interests in real estate differs from the perfection system for other types of assets; (c) the state foreclosure laws do not require negotiation or the same magnitude of judicial discretion as in federal bankruptcy laws; (d) transactions that involved the use of mixed collateral are not very common; (e) within the bankruptcy proceeding, the creditors secured by real property can be easily separated from other creditors, and their claims resolved efficiently using state foreclosure laws.

7. The nature of statutory construction of the federal statute:

   The statutory construction of the U.S. Bankruptcy Code is too general, whereas real property disputes require more specific rules.

The foregoing summary application of existing U.S. Supreme Court standards for preemption indicates that the U.S. Bankruptcy Code should preempt state foreclosure statutes. However, these U.S. Supreme Court preemption standards are obviously not sufficient, given the increasingly complex nature of modern-day real estate transactions that involve derivatives/swaps, complex ownership (joint ventures, estates-for-years, etc.), and other issues. The next section introduces new preemption standards.

NEW STANDARDS FOR PREEMPTION CASES

Apart from the foregoing standards established by the U.S. Supreme Court, the following are nine new preemption standards that are also applicable.

1. The extent to which one party can use the federal statute to illegally or unfairly frustrate the other party, incur unnecessary incremental costs for the other party, or otherwise avoid liens:

   Many debtors unscrupulously use the U.S. Bankruptcy Code stay provisions to delay or to avoid real estate foreclosure, and to delay/void other liens, and hence to incur unnecessary costs for the lenders/assignees. However, the specific circumstances where bankruptcy court proceedings have been used to prevent foreclosure and were subsequently deemed to have been in good faith are described in various cases and are easily distinguishable. Fed. R. Bankr. P. 9011 (a rule equivalent to Rule 11 of the Rules of Civil Procedure) has been used by bankruptcy judges to impose sanctions in hundreds of cases in which various conduct and pleadings were deemed to violate the rule's prohibition against filing frivolous or baseless pleadings. With respect to Chapter 13 cases in bankruptcy, in many instances, Fed. R. Bankr. P. 9011 was invoked because of the improper use of bankruptcy laws to delay or avoid foreclosure of the debtor's property.

2. The extent to which an exception to preemption is implied in the federal statute:

   Since the systems of credit, title in property, and security interests are important state interests, the U.S. Bankruptcy Code must be presumed to contain an implicit foreclosure exception (which the U.S. Congress must override expressly or not at all)—more than mere plain language is required to indicate preemption of state law foreclosure proceedings. In *Owen v. Owen*, 500 U.S. 305, 313 (1991), the U.S. Supreme Court held that the state "opt-out" policy embodied in Section 522(b)(3) did not require immunity from avoidance under Section 522(f) for a lien binding under Florida's exemption rules; and emphasized that there was nothing in the text of Section 522(f) that remotely justified treating the state and federal exemptions differently. In *Johnson v. Home State Bank*, 501 U.S. 78 (1991), the U.S. Supreme Court relied on plain code language to allow a debtor who had "stripped" himself of personal mortgage liability under Chapter 7 to reschedule the remaining indebtedness under Chapter 13, even though a plausible contrary argument based on code structure was feasible and there a complete dearth of precedent for the maneuver under state law and prior bankruptcy practice.

3. The extent to which the state government is better positioned to protect relevant property interest of parties involved:

   The security of the titles to real estate is a legitimate and compelling state interest, and is also a property interest of both lenders and borrowers. The power to ensure that security of title to real estate is implicit in, and more suited to, the very nature of state government. The state government is closer to the daily activities of citizens and interacts more frequently with citizens than the federal government. Given the frequency and complexity of real property transactions, it will be much cheaper for the state government to implement related regulations than for the federal government to do so. Allowing the state to regulate real property foreclosures and liens appropriately recognizes differences in culture among states.

4. The extent to which preemption will cause significant economic losses for any party in the dispute:

   Preemption of state foreclosure laws results in significant economic losses for creditors secured by real property because: (a) creditors secured by real estate are automatically transformed into unsecured creditors in bankruptcy proceedings; (b) values of claims held by real estate creditors declines because the allocation of claims is no longer based on their security interests, but on negotiations among creditors, the debtor's plan of reorganization, and the bankruptcy judge's discretion; (c) the bankruptcy proceedings are typically much longer, and the creditors lose more money in such proceedings.

5. The extent to which a federal law's information effects will disrupt markets and prices, and increase transaction costs and monitoring costs:

   A state lien and state-law foreclosure process has different information effects compared to federally created lien and foreclosure processes—the differences are: (a) a state-created lien and foreclosure process is less likely to disrupt national property price patterns; and (b) a federally created foreclosure process will require a national database that would have to be updated in real time to be effective; and will have greater and more negative effect on property prices in more regions. As explained in Efrat (2006) and Sutton and Callahan (1987), bankruptcy has significant stigma effects. Furthermore, stock markets and bond markets tend to react more to bankruptcy processes than to foreclosure processes.
6. The constitutionality of the federal regulatory scheme:

   The constitutionality of the subject federal regulations is a major decision factor. For example, Finley (1980) and some other authors have shown that the U.S. Bankruptcy Courts are unconstitutional.
7. The relative/comparative constitutionality of the state regulatory scheme:

   The adequacy of constitutional protections embedded in existing state-law foreclosure proceedings, relative to the magnitude and adequacy of such protections in the U.S. Bankruptcy Code, is also a major consideration. Some court opinions have applied the BFP holding (*BFP v. Resolution Trust Corp.*, 511 U.S. 531, 114 S.Ct. 1757 [1994]) to similar forced-sale situations such as state-law judicial tax sales, and have upheld such sales upon a finding that the procedural and substantive rights of the debtor had been duly protected.
8. The efficiency and accuracy of the federal regulatory scheme:

   Fisher and Martel (2004), Davydenko and Franks (2006), Chemerinsky (2005), Trujillo (2006), and other studies have proved and illustrated the inaccuracy and inefficiency of the U.S. Bankruptcy Court processes. In the United States, during the past 20 years, a statistically significant number of companies that emerged from bankruptcy-court-supervised reorganization subsequently failed. However, the key issues are that the bankruptcy code can be improved, more experienced bankruptcy trustees can be selected, and better reorganization plans can be developed.
9. The nature of transaction costs, moral hazard, and agency problems in the state and federal regulatory systems:

A state lien and state-law foreclosure process has different transaction cost effects compared to a federally created lien and foreclosure process: (a) a state-created lien and foreclosure process is more likely to disrupt local/regional property price patterns (a federal system expands markets and increased comparability can reduce price volatility), will reduce information diffusion, and will create inefficient "local/regional" markets; (b) a federally created foreclosure process will require a national database that will have to be updated in real time to be effective, create more transparency, increase competition among service providers, and enhance comparability across regional markets; (c) a federally created lien and foreclosure system is more likely to increase standardization, and thus, reduce transaction costs, due diligence costs and compliance costs; and (d) a state-created lien and foreclosure process for real property is more likely to create agency problems between the real estate broker and the owner, whereas federal foreclosure processes will provide more incentives for real estate brokers to make interstate transactions and expand the potential markets for foreclosed properties and distressed properties (and in the United States, the subprime crisis of 2006 to 2010 and the subsequent government-sponsored mortgage modification programs which failed and resulted in mass post-modification foreclosures have confirmed that state foreclosure processes are inefficient and are not suitable for interstate transactions).

Given the foregoing, the U.S. Bankruptcy Code preemption of state mortgage laws is most probably a better alternative, if: (a) the U.S. Bankruptcy Code can be continually amended as mentioned; (b) there continue to be substantial differences among state mortgage laws; (c) transaction costs remain relatively high (compared to costs involved in buying/selling other assets such as stocks, bonds, commodities); (d) continued localization of real estate transactions breeds criminal activities and reduces transparency; (e) there continue to be substantial differences among penalty systems of different states; or (f) there continue to be substantial differences in the perfection of security interests in personal property and real property among different states.

Issue Preclusion and Applicability of the Full Faith and Credit Clause

The doctrine of issue preclusion applies where the federal statute attempts to invalidate a state court ruling. In this instance, the doctrine of issue preclusion applies to the bankruptcy court invalidation of any completed state court foreclosure proceeding, or invalidation of key court rulings in a state foreclosure proceeding. Issue preclusion generally binds a litigant to a previous and final determination of fact or law where certain requirements exist.

Under the Full Faith and Credit Clause, the analysis of issue preclusion begins with applicable state law on the matter. With respect to the question of issue preclusion, in *In Re Jones*, the U.S. Court of Appeals for the Seventh Circuit stated that, as a federal court, it "must give to a state court judgment the same preclusive effect that as would be given that judgment under the law of the State in which the judgment was rendered" (*In re Jones*, 226 F.3d at 920). In *In Re Jones*, the court also stated that, under Ohio law, "the doctrine of issue preclusion 'precludes further action on an identical issue that has been actually litigated and determined by a valid and final judgment as part of a prior action among the same parties or those in privity with those parties.'" The U.S. Seventh Circuit noted that the parties had stipulated that, under Ohio law, the only issue relevant to whether the issue-preclusion doctrine applied in this case was whether the parties challenging the prior judgment were in privity with the parties to that action. The U.S. Seventh Circuit Court found that because the bankruptcy trustee represents the interests of all the creditors of the bankruptcy estate, and because the debtors' creditors were not the real parties in interest in the foreclosure action, the trustee was not in privity with the debtors.

CONSTITUTIONAL LAW ISSUES

The lender's right to foreclose on a defaulted mortgage or to enforce a deficiency judgment may be precluded or delayed under the U.S. federal bankruptcy laws. Under the U.S. Bankruptcy Act of 1978, and similar/related state laws, all deficiency judgment and foreclosure proceedings are automatically suspended once the borrower files a bankruptcy petition. This bankruptcy stay of these two types of proceedings constitute an unresolved conflict of laws and a violation of the lender's procedural and substantive due process rights, the lender's equal protection laws, a violation of the separation of powers doctrine, and a violation of the Takings Clause. For purposes of constitutional law analysis, the "state actions" involved are: (a) the granting of stay of foreclosure proceedings by the bankruptcy judge; or (b) the voiding of completed or ongoing foreclosure proceedings by the application of fraudulent conveyance provisions of the federal bankruptcy code.

DUE PROCESS RIGHTS

The foreclosure proceeding is supposed to provide a complete, fair, and efficient process for resolving default. The foreclosure process has the same objective as federal bankruptcy proceedings, which is the orderly resolution of creditors' claims. However, the foreclosure process is more complicated because the lender typically pays the carrying costs in addition to the transaction costs. The intervention of the bankruptcy court (by issuing a stay) represents an unwarranted duplication of the foreclosure process. Because the bankruptcy process will typically involve more claimants, and more issues, it is typically longer and more expensive than foreclosures. The lender and the borrower both have constitutionally protected property interests in fair and cost-effective court proceedings that do not impose undue complexity and hardship on them.

The primary issue is that mortgages are typically secured by real estate while other debts can be secured by other assets such as accounts receivables, inventory, and securities. That is, although the mortgage and associated security agreement may claim security interests in non–real-estate assets, the mortgagee relies primarily on the underlying real estate for fulfillment of its claims. This asset/collateral stratification is critical because: (a) it forms the basis for the existing systems of perfecting security interests—mortgages and mortgage recording are used for real estate collateral while Uniform Commercial Code is used for business loans; and (b) it also forms the basis of determining the source of payment of obligations—mortgages typically get paid from real estate income/sales, while interest/principal for business loans are paid from business income. Furthermore, although the company's business may be bankrupt and business assets serve as collateral for business loans, the real estate owned by the same entity, which serves as collateral for a mortgage (and presumably rented to other entities) may be performing well—in such situations, it is inequitable to tie up the "performing" real estate in bankruptcy court with "nonperforming assets," particularly where incorporating the real estate and mortgage into bankruptcy proceedings will substantially reduce the value of such real estate; or the real estate can serve as a source of new capital for the distressed company if it is not part of the bankruptcy estate. Thus, the bankruptcy stay represents somewhat of an unwarranted and inefficient mixture of well-established processes and norms for security interests and payments and can be deemed to constitute a violation of the lender's substantive due process rights.

The bankruptcy stay of foreclosure proceedings or deficiency judgment proceedings constitutes a violation of the lenders' procedural due process rights because of the substantial costs inherent in foreclosure proceedings;

because bankruptcy and foreclosure processes seek similar objectives (resolution of claims/priorities of security interests); because of the typically greater costs inherent in bankruptcy proceedings; and because of the unfairly and disproportionately detrimental effect of bankruptcy proceedings on real estate values, compared to values of other assets in bankruptcy.

Equal Protection

In the absence of uniform comprehensive federal foreclosure statutes, the bankruptcy stay of foreclosure proceedings constitutes a deprivation of the lender's constitutionally guaranteed right to equal protection of the law. The state action involved is the enactment of the bankruptcy stay statute, and the actual judicial order granting the stay of foreclosure by the bankruptcy judge.

The bankruptcy stay unfairly discriminates between the lender and other creditors with similar rights, and it unfairly discriminates between borrowers and lenders who choose to remain in foreclosure proceedings and those borrowers/lenders who decide to switch venue from foreclosure proceedings to bankruptcy court—ideally, the choice of venue should not result in such drastic differences in final outcome. The bankruptcy stay unfairly discriminates between borrowers and lenders who select real estate as collateral, and borrowers and lenders who select other types of assets as collateral. The bankruptcy stay also unfairly discriminates between borrowers and lenders who choose to leave the foreclosure process at different times—that is, the bankruptcy stay is granted regardless of the stage of foreclosure proceedings. The bankruptcy stay unfairly discriminates between borrowers and lenders who have different levels of knowledge about legal proceedings and the choice/advantages/timing of obtaining a bankruptcy stay, and those borrowers/lenders who do not have such knowledge. The bankruptcy stay also unfairly discriminates between the foreclosing lender who decides to file for involuntary bankruptcy of the defaulting borrower, and the lender who chooses to continue in foreclosure proceedings. The challenged classifications do not serve any compelling state interest and the classifications are not substantially related to serving any state interest. The government's interest in promulgating laws for efficient bankruptcy and foreclosure is far outweighed by: (1) the inefficiency and losses that arise from non-uniformity of state foreclosure laws (in terms of transaction costs, compliance costs, penalty systems, etc.); and (2) the somewhat unique nature of mortgages and associated methods for perfection of security interests (the substantial differences between the UCC regime and mortgage recording systems).

The Bankruptcy Stay of Foreclosure Proceedings Constitutes a Violation of the Takings Clause

The bankruptcy stay of foreclosure (and/or deficiency judgment processes) constitutes a Taking that deprives lenders of their constitutional rights. Under the accepted interpretation of the U.S. Constitution, government regulation of private property constitutes a Taking if: (1) it does not substantially advance a legitimate state interest, and (2) the regulation is not imposed with adequate compensation for the property owners for any resulting economic losses. Under U.S. Supreme Court case law, the standard tests for Takings cases include: the "reduction-of-value" test (ability to profit before and after takings, is evaluated and there must be impairment); and the "cause-of-harm" test (show that one person's use causes harm to another's property, and there is state action); and the Government-Invasion Theory (show that government takes possession of property); and the "noxious-use" test.

There have been several key U.S. Supreme court decisions on the Takings issue, although none directly addresses the federal preemption of foreclosure issue. In *Kelo v. City of New London*, the U.S. Supreme Court effectively reversed much of the existing Takings case law and ruled that eminent domain can be used to obtain property for what can reasonably be deemed *private* use—this ruling effectively eliminates the public use requirement in eminent domain and Takings cases. Furthermore, the issue of definition of public use and private use within the context of Takings remains somewhat unresolved. Some courts have held that Takings clause is most naturally construed to authorize takings for public use only if the public or government actually uses the taken property. In *Lingle v. Chevron USA*, 544 US 528 (2005), the U.S. Supreme Court defined four classes of Takings claims, which are: a "physical taking"; a "Lucas-type total regulatory" Taking; a "Penn-Central Type" Taking; and a "Land-use exaction violating the *Nollan* and *Dolan* standards."

The net effects of *Kelo v. City of New London* and *Lingle v. Chevron* are: (a) reduction of property rights of and constitutional protections for property owners; (b) elimination of the "substantially advances" requirement from Takings cases, thereby increasing transaction costs, litigation costs, and the burden of proof on homeowners in Takings cases.

The bankruptcy stay of state-law foreclosure proceedings or the bankruptcy court's application of fraudulent conveyance statutes to void foreclosures constitutes a Takings. First, lenders have constitutionally protected property interests in fair and effective judicial/adjudicative proceedings (such property interests arise from expectations, norms, state constitutional laws, and contracts)—the issue of whether foreclosure laws/processes are property interests was addressed in preceding sections. Second, the state actions described herein effectively deprive the lender of said property interests in effective adjudicative procedures, and right to equal protection of the law. Third, the lenders incur losses because of greater transaction costs and monitoring costs—historically, in the United States, bankruptcy court proceedings are longer and more expensive than foreclosure proceedings, and the real estate lender's probability/magnitude of recovery is lower in bankruptcy proceedings. Fourth, the associated public use is that the general public benefits indirectly from said Takings, because there are presumably more assets for the bankruptcy estate, more claimants have a better chance at recovery in the bankruptcy process, and the bankruptcy estate is bigger. Fifth, the lender is not compensated for this Takings in any way, and actually loses money/value due to increased processing costs in bankruptcy, and lower probability of recovery in bankruptcy (primarily due to more claimants in bankruptcy proceedings). Sixth, although the government has a legitimate interest in consolidating apparently related adversarial proceedings, and preemption apparently advances the government interests to some extent, the foreclosure process is more efficient, more fair, and more precise than bankruptcy proceedings, and bankruptcy proceedings impose significant information costs, monitoring costs, and adverse selection costs on the participants, compared to foreclosure proceedings. The bankruptcy code preemption of foreclosure laws effectively converts a secured lender into a general unsecured creditor, with resultant loss.

The Takings implicit in the federal preemption of foreclosure laws is a government intervention that has substantial economic multiplier effects that sometimes affect neighboring towns and properties. Bankruptcy cases are primary case law in more courts nationwide, and hence the information effects of any bankruptcy case are greater than that of state law adjudication of foreclosure proceedings. Corporate bankruptcy cases tend to have negative effects on the share prices of other companies in the same sector or industry—this effect has been confirmed in empirical studies. Converting a foreclosure case into a bankruptcy case connotes the commencement of a more advanced form of financial distress—this information is internalized by market researchers, appraisers, and brokers in their assessments of the condition of the local economy, and thus real property prices. Insurance companies base their estimates of insurance premiums on local and regional economies, which are based on the number of foreclosures and bankruptcies—bankruptcies tend to increase payouts by insurance companies, and, hence, increasing the number of bankruptcies relative to the number of foreclosures generally increases the costs of various types of insurance products. Preemption has information asymmetry costs—many real estate brokers and appraisers understand foreclosure process and how they affect property prices, but few understand the bankruptcy process and the inherent and sometimes drastic changes in property values—thus, bankruptcy code preemption drastically increases information asymmetry in real estate markets. Hence, the government's interest in achieving efficiency by preemption is far outweighed by the collective property interests of the local property owners in efficient and cost-effective foreclosure proceedings with minimal negative effects on overall social welfare.

The Takings implicit in U.S. Bankruptcy Code preemption of state-law foreclosure proceedings do not conform to any of the above-mentioned types of Takings because: there is no physical occupation, there is no total regulatory Taking; there are no exactions that violate the Nollan and Dolan standards; there is no Penn-Central Type Taking; and there are no derivative Takings as defined by Bell and Parchomovsky (2001a, 2001b, 2005).

Thus, these conditions create a new type of Takings henceforth referred to as *Stay Takings,* which is characterized in a later section of this chapter.

THE SEPARATION-OF-POWERS DOCTRINE

The bankruptcy stay of state-law foreclosure proceedings constitutes a violation of the Separation-of-Powers Doctrine because the U.S. Bankruptcy Court performs both rule making (creates the discretionary case law necessary to preempt state foreclosure laws, and to initiate a case in bankruptcy court) and adjudicatory functions—*the U.S. federal bankruptcy code does not contain any provisions that expressly preempt state foreclosure laws*, and express preemption is a major requirement in this instance. The U.S. Bankruptcy Court adjudicates the bankruptcy dispute after the bankruptcy stay is issued (and the foreclosure is effectively converted into bankruptcy proceedings). Furthermore, in some instances, the bankruptcy judge's order constitutes a perfection of security interests in assets—but this is a function that is traditionally relegated to the executive branch of government, and its performance by the bankruptcy judge constitutes a violation of the Separation-of-Powers Doctrine.

These combinations of rule making and adjudication by the U.S. Bankruptcy Court is a state action and a clear violation of the Separation-of-Powers Doctrine.

A NEW THEORY OF TAKINGS

The following are definitions of a new theory of Takings, which was introduced in an earlier section of this chapter.

Stay Takings

Stay Takings are characterized as follows:

- The Takings arise solely because of (state or federal) preemption or a judicially ordered stay of acts or proceedings.
- The property interests in the stayed or precluded acts/proceedings have economic value to the parties (i.e., lender and borrower). The stayed proceedings are special proceedings.
- There is asymmetrical commitment by the parties to the property interest (e.g., right-to-foreclosure processes) or to the subject asset (the collateral property); that is, the lender is more interested in foreclosure than the borrower who typically wants to negotiate extensions or short sales.
- There is substantial information asymmetry among the parties (e.g., lender, borrower, court).
- The transaction costs that may be incurred by the parties (i.e., lenders, borrower, and court) in the stayed/precluded proceedings/lawsuit (T_s) may or may not be greater than the transaction costs inherent in the alternate prevailing proceedings, if any (T_a). The magnitude of the Takings increases as the difference between T_s and T_a increases.
- For any qualifying transaction, there is asymmetrical liability by third-party tortfeasors to the parties (i.e., lender and borrower); that is, the harm caused by any third party to the stayed proceedings/act causes unequal harm to both the lender(s) and the borrower.
- For any qualifying transaction, there is asymmetrical liability allocation to the lender(s) and borrower(s); that is, for any type of offense, the offending borrower often does not bear the same magnitude of liability/penalties as an offending lender.

CONCLUSION

The key issues are the legislative intent of the U.S. Bankruptcy Code as regards foreclosure proceedings, the interpretation of the U.S. Bankruptcy Code with regard to state law foreclosure proceedings, and the practical effectiveness of preemption. It can be reasonably inferred from the legislative materials on the U.S. Bankruptcy Code that it was not meant to preempt state law foreclosure proceedings. Unlike similar statutes, the U.S. Bankruptcy Code does not expressly preempt state law foreclosure proceedings. Given the importance of this preemption issue (in terms of transaction costs, market efficiency, etc.), any intent by the U.S. Congress to use the U.S. Bankruptcy Court to preempt foreclosures would have been expressly stated. With regard to the interpretation of the U.S. Bankruptcy Code, none of its sections expressly states or infers that it can preempt the state foreclosure proceedings. Furthermore, the U.S. Supreme Court has not addressed the issue of U.S. Bankruptcy Code preemption of state foreclosure laws. The U.S. Bankruptcy Code grants bankruptcy judges substantial discretion as to what matters should be adjudicated under bankruptcy stays. Finally, the practical effectiveness of U.S. Bankruptcy Code preemption of state law foreclosure proceedings can be high or low in some circumstances, depending on the magnitude and severity of the factors mentioned—in addition, the economic costs (transaction costs, monitoring costs, opportunity costs, etc.) of preemption vary drastically with the value of the underlying property and the investment opportunities available to the lender and borrower. Hence, imposing a rigid rule (preemption or no preemption of foreclosure) without reference to the magnitude of property value and other factors is probably not economically or psychologically efficient or optimal. Whether foreclosure proceedings are shorter than bankruptcy proceedings depends on the popularity and suitability of prepackaged bankruptcy and the willingness of the parties to agree on a plan of reorganization in bankruptcy court—in contrast, foreclosure proceedings often require lengthy processes that often end in auctions (which can be rendered meaningless by the exercise of the borrower's right of redemption). Hence, preemption can substantially reduce the transaction costs of the lender and the borrower. Furthermore, the real estate lender is increasingly more likely to have the same set of priorities with other lenders whose loans are secured by other types of assets owned by the same distressed company/person. This is because the mortgagee's security interest is increasingly mixed or connected with other assets (although the security perfection regimes for real estate differ from those of most other types of assets) and the lender/mortgagee depends on the same or connected accounts receivables; the mortgagee often seeks other collateral (e.g., the borrower's bank accounts, the borrower's other assets, and an assignment of rents). Hence, preemption is likely to shorten negotiations among creditors/lenders (that have different collateral owned by the same entity in bankruptcy) and increase the probability that lenders will file a reasonable plan of timely reorganization.

NOTE

1. *Javens v. City of Hazel Park*, 107 F.3d 359, 363 (6th Cir. 1997) (The stay provision "gives the debtor a breathing spell" and "stops all collection efforts, all harassment") and H.R. Rep. No. 95–595, at 340 (1978) (on the legislative intent of bankruptcy laws).

REFERENCES

Adler, B. 2007. The questionable axiom of *Butner V. United States*. New York University Law and Economics Research Paper No. 07–01; January. Available at SSRN: http://ssrn.com/abstract=954153.

Ahern, L. 2001. "Workouts" under revised Article Nine: A review of changes and proposal for study. *American Bankruptcy Institute Law Review* 9 (Spring): 115–125.

Aysun, U., and A. Honig. 2010. Bankruptcy costs, liability dollarization, and vulnerability to sudden stops. *Journal of Development Economics* 95 (2): 201–211.

Battiston, S., D. Delli Gatti, M. Gallegati, G. Greenwald, and J. Stiglitz. 2007. Credit chains and bankruptcy propagation in production networks. *Journal of Economic Dynamics and Control* 31 (6): 2061–2084.

Bell, A., and G. Parchomovsky. 2001a. Takings re-assessed. *Virginia Law Review* 87: 277–287.

Bell, A., and G. Parchomovsky. 2001b. Givings. *Yale Law Journal* 111: 547–557.

Bell, A., and G. Parchomovsky. 2005. A theory of property. *Cornell Law Review* 90: 531–541.

Bellia, A. 2001. Federal regulation of state court procedures. *Yale Law Journal* 110: 947–957.

Bergl, E., and H. Rosenthal. 2003. *The Political Origin of Finance: The Case of Federal Bankruptcy Law in the US*. Working paper, SITE, and Princeton University. March.

Berman, G. L., and C. E. Vance. 2008. State law preference actions: Still alive after *Sherwood Partners v. Lycos*. *American Bankruptcy Institute Journal*.

Bernanke, B., M. Gertler, and S. Gilchrist. 1999. The financial accelerator in a quantitative business cycle framework. Chapter 21 in *Handbook of Macroeconomics*. http://faculty.wcas.northwestern.edu/~lchrist/course/Czech/BGG%201999%20 Handbook%20chapter.pdf.

BFP v. Resolution Trust Corp., 511 U.S. 531, 537; 114 S.Ct. 1757 (1994).

Bibbo v. Dean Witter Reynolds, Inc., 151 F.3d 559 (6th Cir. 1998).

Butner v. United States, 440 U.S. 48 (1979).

Chemerinsky, E. 2005. Constitutional issues posed in the Bankruptcy Abuse Prevention and Consumer Protection Act of 2005. *American Bankruptcy Law Journal* 79: 571–602.

Chen, D., and D. Corbae. 2011. On the welfare implications of restricting bankruptcy information. *Journal of Macroeconomics* 33 (1): 4–13.

Davydenko, S., and J. Franks. 2006. Do bankruptcy costs matter? A study of Defaults in France, Germany and the UK. Working paper, September.

Eidenmuller, H. 2005. Free choice in international company insolvency law in Europe. *European Business Organization Law* 6: 423–447.

Efrat, R. 2006. The evolution of bankruptcy stigma. *Theoretical Inquiries in Law* 7, no. 2 (July): 365–375.

Ehrlich, S. B. 1985. Avoidance of foreclosure sales as fraudulent conveyances: Accommodating state and federal objectives. *Virginia Law Review* 71: 933–962.

Feld, A. 2006. The limits of bankruptcy code preemption: Debt dischard and voidable preferences re-considered in light of *Sherwood Partners*. *Cardozo Law Review* 28: 1447–1457.

Finley, L. 1980. Article III limits on Article I courts: The constitutionality of the bankruptcy courts and the 1979 Magistrate Act. *Columbia Law Review* 80 (3): 560–596.

Fisher, T., and J. Martel. 2004. Empirical estimates of filtering failure in court-supervised reorganization. *Journal of Empirical Legal Studies* 1 (1): 143–164.

Haberbush v. Charles and Dorothy Cummins Family Limited Partnership, 139 Cal. App. 4th 1630, 43 Cal. Rptr. 3d 814 (2nd Dist. 2006).

Hall, S. 2002. Note, preemption analysis after *Geier v. American Honda Motor Co.*, 90 *Ky. L. J.* 251.

Hausch, D., and S. Ramachandran. 2009. Systemic financial distress and auction-based bankruptcy reorganization. *International Review of Economics & Finance* 18 (3): 366–380.

Hetland, J., and C. Hansen. 1987. The "mixed collateral" amendments to California's Commercial Code—covert repeal of California's real property foreclosure and anti-deficiency provisions or exercise in futility? *California Law Review* 75 (1): 185–216.

In re V.N. DePrizio Constr. Co., 874 F.2d 1186 (7th Cir. 1989) and *English v. General Electric Co.*, 496 U.S. 72, 78–79 (1990).

Javens v. City of Hazel Park, 107 F.3d 359, 363 (6th Cir. 1997) and H.R. Rep. No. 95–595, at 340 (1978).

Johnson v. Home State Bank, 501 U.S. 78 (1991).

Johnson, O. 2007. The Bankruptcy Code as complete preemption: The ultimate trump. *American Bankruptcy Law Journal* 81: 31–41.

Johnston, S. 2007. Federal preemption of state preference statute in *Sherwood Partners v. Lycos*—An unduly restrictive standard? *Norton Annual Review of Bankruptcy Law*, 288–299. www.cov.com/files/Publication/a12e2cf7-7e80-4cc1-82dd-2c1a70edfd13/Presentation/PublicationAttachment/04606baf-1200-4827-8190-354f45ad0a8d/ Federal%20Preemption%20of%20State%20 Preference%20Statute%20in%20Sherwood%20Partners%20V.%20Lycos .pdf.

Levitin, A. 2009. Resolving the foreclosure crisis: Modification of mortgages in bankruptcy. *Wisconsin Law Review* 566–627.

Li, W., and P. Sarte. 2006. U.S. consumer bankruptcy choice: The importance of general equilibrium effects. *Journal of Monetary Economics* 53: 613–631.

Longhofer S., and S. Peters. 2004. Protection for whom? Creditor conflict and bankruptcy. *American Law & Economics Review* 6 (2): 249–259.

Luo, V. 2008. A preference for states? The woes of preempting state preference statutes. *Emory Bankruptcy Developments Journal* 24: 513–522.

Merrill, T., and H. Smith. 2000. The property/contract interface. *Columbia Law Review* 101 (4): 773–852.

Merrill, T., and H. Smith. 2001. What happened to property in law and economics? *Yale Law Journal* 111 (2): 357–398.

Moringiello, J. 2001. A tale of two codes: Examining Section 522(F) of the Bankruptcy Code and Section 9-103 of the Uniform Commercial Code and the proper role of state law in bankruptcy. *Washington University Law Quarterly* 79: 863–873.

Morrison, E. R. 2009. Bargaining around bankruptcy: Small business workouts and state law. *Journal of Legal Studies* 38.

Nathan, B., and S. Cargill. 2007. Are state preference laws preempted by the United States Bankruptcy Code? Not necessarily! *Credit and Financial Management Review, A Journal for Credit and Financial Administrators* 13 (4).

O'Neill v. Orix Credit Alliance, Inc. (*In re Northeastern Contracting, Inc.*), 233 B.R. 15 (D.Conn, 1999).

Owen v. Owen, 500 U.S. 305, 313 (1991).

Povel, P. 1999. Optimal "soft" or "tough" bankruptcy procedures. *Journal of Law, Economics & Organization* 15 (3): 659–669.

Rasmussen, R., and D. Skeel. 1995. The economic analysis of corporate bankruptcy laws. *American Bankruptcy Law Institute Review* 3: 85–115.

Roost v. Associates Home Equity Services, Inc. (*In re Williams*), 234 B.R. 801 (Bankr. D.Or. 1999).

Scarberry, M. 2011. A critique of congressional proposals to permit modification of home mortgages in Chapter 13. *Pepperdine Law Review*. Forthcoming.

Scarberry M., K. Klee, G. Newton, and S. H. Nickles. 2006. Business reorganization in bankruptcy: Cases and materials. 381–85, 438 (3d ed. 2006).

Sherman v. Rose (*In re Sherman*), 223 B.R 555, 559 (10th Cir. B.A.P. 1998).

Sutton, R., and A. Callahan. 1987. The stigma of bankruptcy: Spoiled organizational image and its management. *Academy of Management Journal* 30 (3): 405–438.

Trujillo, B. 2006. Regulating bankruptcy abuse: An empirical study of consumer exemption cases. *Journal of Empirical Legal Studies* 3 (3): 561–609.

Washburn, R. M. 1980. The judicial and legislative response to price inadequacy in mortgage foreclosure sales. *South California Law Review* 53: 843–851.

Weaver, K., and Y. Shen (Deutsche Bank). 2009. *Drowning in debt: A look at "underwater" homeowners*. Available at www.sacbee.com/static/weblogs/real_estate/Deutsche%20research%20on%20underwater%20mortgages%208-5-09.pdf.

Weinberg, J. B. 2006. California general assignments: New developments. www.usisg.com/docs/ca_gen_assignments.pdf.

Wright v. Union Central Life Ins. Co., 311 U.S. 273, 278–279 (1940).

CHAPTER 8
Mortgages and Deeds of Trust

Mortgages and deeds of trust remain the primary modes of documenting debt/lending in real estate transactions in many countries, including all the commonwealth countries. Surprisingly, mortgages in most countries are very similar and are based on, or derived from, U.S./U.K.–type mortgages. Many empirical and theoretical studies have confirmed that mortgages and deeds of trust are inefficient (Ambrose and Buttimer 2009; Bar-Gill 2009; Miles 2005; Tiwari and Moriizumi 2003; Ambrose and Capone 1996; Quigley and Van Order 1990; Scarberry 2009; Shiller 2009; Peterson 2009; Mayer, Pence, and Sherlund 2009; Ben-Shahar, Leung, and Ong 2009; Green and Wachter 2005; Whitman 1993).

Traditional mortgages refer to common instruments that are used to finance property purchases such as adjustable rate mortgages (ARMs), fixed rate mortgages, and mortgages without deed-in-lieu clauses. The traditional mortgage is an inefficient contract and the associated foreclosure proceedings are also inefficient and socially, economically, and psychologically costly (Ackermann 2008; Ambrose and Buttimer 2009; Bar-Gill 2009; Tiwari and Moriizumi 2003; Ambrose and Capone 1996; Shiller 2009; Malloy 2009; Painter 2006; Black 2008; Zhu 2006; Bedi 2009; Bottelier 2010; Shanker 2003; Whitman and Nelson 2004; Whitman 2005; Todd and Grover 2008; Eggert 2007; Engel and McCoy 2007; Wolf 2010; Good and Hammond 2006; Myers 2008; Davies 2008; Kiff and Klyuev 2009; Blair and Piette 2006; Center for Responsible Lending 2008; Tatom 2008; Jacoby 2010; Johnson 1993; Stark 1997; Cox 2008; Hatcher 2006; Alberts 2007; Bernstein 2008; Ghent and Kudlyak 2009; Kosareva and Tumanov 2008; Merrill and Rabenhorst 2003; Rabenhorst and Ignatova 2009; Hancock and Passmore 2009; White 2010).

Pento (2011) (also see U.S. Department of the Treasury 2011) states in part:

> *To counter the increasing demands that government reduce its micro-management of the economy, last week, the Obama Administration offered a fig leaf in the form of a white paper entitled "Reforming America's Housing Finance Market." In addition to marking the official end of the Bush era "ownership society," where increasing the level of home ownership was a national priority, the document contains a recommended regulatory overhaul of the Federal Housing Authority (FHA) as well as Fannie Mae and Freddie Mac (together known as Government Sponsored Enterprises [GSEs]), that intends to bring the share of government owned home loans from the current 95% to 40% over the next 5–7 years.... In the report, the Obama Administration makes the important admission that government interference in housing had dangerously distorted the market.... Thus, this plan will insure that government's role in the mortgage market will likely expand in the years ahead.... When interest rates are set by a few people behind closed doors, as they are by the Federal Reserve, massive distortions can occur in the supply demand metric. ... The GSEs now provide financing for nine out of ten mortgages. Therefore, the real estate market today is virtually 100% distorted and manipulated by government forces.... The government has already clearly shown that its erstwhile implicit guarantee is now in fact explicit for GSE debt. Therefore, in typical government fashion, the proposed reforms are merely a repackaging of the previous sham.*

IMPROPER COUPLING/COMBINATIONS OF MORTGAGE MARKETS, RENTAL MARKETS, SAVINGS/INVESTMENT MARKETS, AND PROPERTY-VALUE MARKETS

One of the biggest problems in the global mortgage markets (in all countries) has been the improper coupling/combinations of mortgage markets, rental markets, savings/investment markets, and property-value markets, which has been a key result of enactment/adoption of real estate laws that were based in whole or part on English laws and are prevalent in the United States, commonwealth countries, and more recently, the Commonwealth of Independent States (CIS), China, and Brazil. These real estate laws have erroneously imposed mortgages as a solution in property-value markets and rental markets, have imposed property-value price discovery as a solution in mortgage markets, and have imposed mortgages as a solution to rental contracts. These improper combinations are done in ways that produce inefficient price discovery processes, increase transaction costs and monitoring costs, facilitate cheap noncompliance, increase information asymmetry, and reduce transparency in a system that is both complex and critical. Research has shown that most consumers cannot value or comprehend mortgages and yet the purchase of a house is the largest investment of more than 60 percent of all households in most developed countries. Ironically and unfortunately, governments have exacerbated this inefficient-combination problem by actively encouraging mortgage-financed home purchases as an element of household savings. The savings/investment markets should either be detached from mortgage, rental, and property-value markets, or the combination should be drastically reformulated.

MORTGAGES CAUSE FRAUD AND MISALLOCATION OF RISK

Traditional mortgages do not allocate risk and liability efficiently—lenders are typically not compensated adequately for the risk that they are taking. Liability for defaults and nonperformance of mortgage contracts are often allocated almost entirely to borrowers when in fact lenders contribute substantially to such defaults, for example, by weak underwriting standards, by not explaining mortgage terms to borrowers (most borrowers cannot price, and do not understand mortgages), and so on.

Mortgages cause rampant mortgage fraud (which occurred in the United States during 1995 to 2009), nonmortgage fraud, and crime committed by household members who are under pressure to pay mortgages.

The introduction and implementation of mortgages in the CEE region and CIS region and in most emerging market countries have caused many problems and fraud. The CIS mortgage markets are still nascent. The Chinese, Japanese, and Canadian mortgage markets are much more developed than the CIS-region mortgage markets, but are all based on U.S.-style and U.K.-style regulations and statutes (Zavisca 2008, 2010; Mashkina, Heliste, and Kosonen 2007; Guseva 2009; Freshfields Bruckhaus Deringer LLP, January 2009; Kopeikin 2010; Guseva 2009; Ma 2009; Chen 2006; Deng, Zheng, and Ling 2005; Hong and Chen 2009; Nemoto 2005; Ozeki 2007; Courchane and Giles 2002; Ambrose and Capone 1996). China has experienced the same types of fraudulent activities that exist in the U.S. mortgage markets (Bottelier 2010; Bedi 2009; Ben-Shahar, Leung, and Ong 2009; Hancock and Passmore 2009). Although homeownership rates in Canada and the United States are similar (64 percent to 70 percent), there are substantial differences in terms of policy, financial systems, regulation, and outcomes. Mortgage default risk is often not correlated with the borrower's ability to pay or willingness to repay, and this creates distortions in pricing mortgages.

Mortgage prepayment risk is often not driven by rational behavior and is difficult to model accurately—in the United States, strategic defaults by borrowers during 2006 to 2010 contributed to the subprime mortgage mess. Prepayment risk is often correlated with speculation and sentiment, whereas prepayment risk is often and erroneously perceived to be related to changes in interest rates.

Foreclosures can be used to frustrate lenders—the increase in "strategic defaults" in the United States is another prime example of the inefficiency of mortgages and foreclosures.

TRADITIONAL AND ALTERNATIVE MORTGAGES ARE INEFFICIENT AND CREATE WRONG INCENTIVES

Many problems in mortgage markets can be attributed to suboptimal incentive systems of market participants, detrimental government intervention, ineffective penalty systems, and the structure of mortgage products (which exacerbate moral hazard, information asymmetry, strategic defaults, "cheap noncompliance," and value inflation).

The social and psychological costs of mortgage default adversely affect social welfare and create wrong incentives. There are many temporary borrower-specific and neighborhood-specific psychological factors that affect housing tenure and default decisions and prepayment decisions, which has not been (or cannot be) captured by many of the econometric models developed for the mortgage industry. Traditional mortgages incur substantial and unnecessary transaction costs and monitoring costs for both the borrower and the lender.

Mortgages and the dream of home equity and the tax/interest deductions associated with homeownership foster home-price inflation and provide a powerful incentive for consumers not to save money (by investing in securities and other types of assets); and compel households to spend substantially more than 33 percent of their total income on housing, which results in high stress, intra-household conflicts, and associated illnesses. In the United States, the recent massive erosion of home equity has left many households without any retirement savings. The reality is that homeownership is not suitable for every household, and increasing homeownership should not be a long-term policy objective of any government because of the inherent problems it breeds. The key issues are:

- Who has the best skills to manage debt in order to maximize social welfare? The consumer, a finance company, or a real estate development company?

- Who is best positioned to obtain cheap debt and/or hedge debt in order to maximize social welfare? The consumer or a finance company or a real estate development company?
- Who is best positioned to bear the risk associated with price fluctuations? Consumers or institutions?
- Who will minimize price inflation, transaction costs, speculation, and fraud? History has shown that larger institutional investors are better at doing so than individuals.

Clearly, many existing macroeconomic theories and much of what has been written about monetary transmission during the past 50 years have been proven wrong by: (1) the events of 2005 to 2010 and the global financial crisis; (2) the continuing growth of the Internet and the resulting information diffusion, knowledge aggregation, and social-network effects; (3) the pension crisis and low household savings rates in many countries; (4) increasing ineffectiveness of monetary policy; (5) increase in competition among lenders; (6) the increasing use of swaps/derivatives; (7) increasing financial integration.

MORTGAGES REDUCE THE EFFICIENCY OF MONETARY TRANSMISSION

One of the major problems is that traditional Western mortgages (now prevalent in China, Latin America, Africa, CEE, and CIS countries) reduce the efficiency of governments' monetary policies and fiscal policies in several ways, some of which are described next.

Most traditional mortgages are fixed rate mortgages. Thus, for there to be any "pass-through" effects of changes in interest rates or sales/purchases of government securities by central banks, borrowers must refinance their mortgages, which then triggers several adverse effects and other costs: (a) borrowers incur new fixed rate mortgages; and (b) borrowers incur substantial hidden and disclosed transaction costs (such as appraisals, mortgage broker fees, bank fees, legal fees, and prepayment penalties) such that often the borrower's post-refinancing cost of funds may exceed or be the same as the cost of his or her prior mortgage.

When the central bank reduces benchmark interest rates (typically to increase economic activity), the increased affordability of mortgages causes inflation of housing prices, which in turn increases the volume of home-equity loans and discretionary consumption (that does not necessarily increase useful economic output—partly due to importation and outsourcing), and often reduces loan quality. As was illustrated from 2005 to 2009 in the United

States, the result is often higher mortgage default rates and foreclosures, all of which dampens monetary policy transmission. Reducing benchmark interest rates increases the attractiveness of the rates paid on deposits at financial/depository institutions because changes in these rates tend to lag changes in market rates; the public tends to purchase the assets included in the money stock, and money growth increases.

When the central bank reduces benchmark interest rates, there is less impact on mortgage-heavy banks (compared to the average bank) for the following reasons: (a) the effect depends on the extent to which the rate change affects long-term interest rates; (b) any increase in the value of the mortgages can be offset by the sum of the bank's derivatives/swaps positions; (c) the mortgage-heavy bank is likely to have fulfilled its quota of mortgages (asset allocation effect); (d) in most cases, the mortgage-heavy bank's incentives to provide business loans and consumer loans will decline due to lower loan margins, and because such banks can make more profits from originating and selling mortgages; and (e) mortgage-lending processes are highly automated and incur fewer transaction costs than the average business loan, and thus, mortgage-heavy banks will be much less likely to allocate capital and resources to business lending.

When the central bank increases money supply by buying government bonds and/or agency securities (interest rates typically decline), households that have traditional mortgages are much less likely to be affected—they often cannot obtain new loans or second mortgages; if they increase their credit card debt, their risk profiles will be more likely to worsen, and they typically cannot start new businesses because of the mortgage burden and the possibility of disclosure of mortgage defaults or late payments to consumer credit reporting companies. History has shown that the proceeds of most home-equity mortgages are not used for activities that directly increase economic output or productivity. When money supply is increased, banks that own above-average holdings of mortgages (mortgage-heavy banks) will experience fewer shocks than ordinary banks because: (a) they typically can sell the mortgages in secondary markets and the liquidity of whole-loan mortgage markets in many countries has been relatively independent from monetary policies partly due to securitization; (b) many mortgages have mortgage insurance and have shorter payment frequencies than regular business loans, and so mortgage-heavy banks are less likely to provide more business loans; and (c) the resulting lower interest rates provide disincentives for mortgage-heavy banks to grant business loans and/or consumer loans.

When the central bank reduces money supply by issuing new government bonds, interest rates usually increase, but there is much less effect on the household that has a traditional mortgage. This is because a substantial portion of the household's income is used to pay for relatively fixed/constant housing costs, the leveraged household has much less borrowing capacity, and the leveraged household has much lower incentive to refinance. Also, mortgage-heavy banks and insurance companies experience fewer shocks from such contractionary policies (compared to banks with low mortgage holdings) because declines in the values of their loan portfolios will be wholly or partially offset by declines in the values of their liabilities (deposits, discount window loans, issued bonds, and such) and increases in the whole-loan market values of the mortgages (lending volumes will decline); and mortgage-heavy banks can use securitization and whole-loan mortgage market sales to monetize their mortgage holdings (securitization often provides ABS that are AAA or AA rated but have higher yields than government securities).

When the central banks tighten/increase capital reserve requirements, money supply generally declines, but there is less effect on households that have mortgages (compared to those without mortgages) because they can obtain home-equity loans; and they can refinance their mortgage (including cash-out refinance), and in such environments, refinance loans are usually deemed less risky than new mortgages. An increase in banks' capital reserve requirements will have a disproportionately lower effect on banks for which mortgages account for an above-average percentage of assets for the following reasons: (1) mortgages pay monthly cash (unlike bonds, preferred stock, and common stock that pay quarterly or semiannually), and given reinvestment and compounding, mortgage-heavy banks will have relatively more cash to lend; (2) unlike traditional business loans, many mortgages are usually insured, and this provides some psychological assurance to mortgage-heavy lenders and becomes a basis for providing business loans and more mortgages, whereas the central bank intended to have the opposite effect; and (3) in most developed countries (and in countries that have active securitization markets), the whole-loan market for residential and commercial mortgages is relatively much more liquid than the whole-loan market for business loans—thus mortgage-heavy banks will experience fewer effects.

When central banks loosen/reduce capital reserve requirements, the money supply generally increases (and the central bank's intent is to boost economic activity), but there is less effect on households that have mortgages (compared to those without mortgages) because: (a) they can obtain home-equity loans in almost all economic scenarios; (b) they may be able to refinance their mortgage depending on the magnitude of prevailing interest rates; (c) the change in capital reserve is a "quiet policy," which is not publicly disclosed outside the bank management community, unlike changes in interest rates; and (d) in such environments, refinance loans are usually deemed less risky than new mortgages. An increase in banks' capital reserve requirements will have a disproportionately lower effect on banks for whom mortgages account for an above-average percentage of assets for the following reasons: (1) mortgages pay monthly cash (unlike bonds, preferred stock, and common stock that pay quarterly or semiannually), and given reinvestment and compounding, mortgage-heavy banks will have relatively more cash to lend; (2) unlike traditional business loans, many mortgages are insured, and this provides some psychological assurance to lenders and becomes a basis for providing business loans and more mortgages, whereas the central bank intended to have the opposite effect; and (3) mortgage-heavy banks will likely sell their mortgages in the whole-loan mortgage market in order to fund new mortgages (rather than providing business loans and/or personal loans that may facilitate the intended economic expansion)—because these banks can generate more profits from originating and selling mortgages than from originating and holding business loans and/or personal loans.

Some monetary policies are "quiet policies" (e.g., changes in capital reserves, sales/purchases of government securities, changes in taxation of financial instruments and/or transactions) because they are typically not widely disclosed, and are watched by mostly the banking/finance management community. Other monetary policies are "noisy policies" (e.g., changes in benchmark interest rates) because they are widely disclosed and are watched by consumers and the general public. The dampening effect of mortgages on monetary transmission is conjectured to be greater for quiet policies than for noisy policies.

When the central banks reduce benchmark interest rates, interest rates charged for loans may not always decline, and any change in interest rates will depend on the distribution of outstanding corporate debt and consumer debt along the yield curve, and the distribution of credit quality of corporate and individual borrowers across credit scores. Hence, because greater mortgage volumes cause increased lender focus on consumer credit scores and corporate credit ratings (compared to business loans), which in turn reduces the lenders' sensitivity to changes in capital reserve requirements and benchmark interest rates, mortgage loans dampen monetary transmission.

Kiss and Vadas (2007) used different econometric techniques such as time series, panel, and pooled-mean-group (PMG) estimators to analyze the link between macroeconomic variables and house prices in Hungary, and the effect of monetary policy on housing investment and consumption.

Den Haan, Sumner, and Yamashiro (2009) found that in Canada, bank mortgage loans and nonmortgage loans to consumers decrease after a monetary policy tightening, but on the contrary, business loans increase following a monetary tightening. The unusual response of increasing business loans cannot be explained by an increase in the demand for funds due to a reduction in real activity; these results are consistent with a change in bank portfolio behavior in favor of business loans in response to a monetary tightening. This behavior is perhaps motivated by compensation/incentives of bank officers, risk-management concerns, expected behavior of depositors, relationship-management issues (not to lose long-term corporate clients), and so on.

Den Haan, Sumner, and Yamashiro (2010) found that the impulse response function (IRF) of an aggregate variable is time-varying if the IRFs of its components are different from each other and the relative magnitudes of the components are not constant. Den Haan, Sumner, and Yamashiro analyzed the behavior of loan components and found that the induced time variation for total loans is substantial, which may explain why studies describing total loans do not often find a robust response of total bank loans to a monetary tightening.

Safaei and Cameron (2003) analyzed financial factors as propagation mechanisms for the disturbances originating in the real economy—and specifically, the origination of disturbances from bank credit and allows for the propagation of disturbances within a relatively simple macrodynamic system that utilizes the structural vector autoregression approach. The Safaei and Cameron results for the Canadian economy support the "credit view" of the monetary policy transmission mechanism. Safaei and Cameron also showed that bank credit to individuals affects real output in the short run, whereas bank credit to businesses does not (consumers but not the business firms appear to be credit-constrained).

Brady (2010) showed that the consumer loan-supply effect has diminished over time; and contrary to assumptions for the lending channel theory, after the mid-1980s, households are not constrained in accessing nonrevolving or revolving bank loans in response to a monetary shock. Brady noted that the increase in revolving loans from commercial banks following a policy shock may indicate that the balance sheet channel of the transmission mechanism is stronger; that is, for households willing to take on more expensive revolving debt, an increase in the federal funds rate may have more effect on the household balance sheet than before the growth in credit card use. Brady also noted that the data also suggest that nonbank forms of finance decrease at the same time that commercial bank loans increase after a contractionary policy shock. Although households do not appear constrained in obtaining bank credit (as assumed in the lending channel), liquidity constraints in credit markets may still help explain a decline in nonbank loans. Brady stated that the impulse response functions they documented suggest that households are not constrained in accessing credit from commercial banks; increases in consumer loans from banks after a policy shock imply that households can access credit (and smooth consumption) after a policy shock; and that the disappearance of the loan-supply effect after 1984 suggests that monetary policy has little real effect on consumers through the lending channel. Brady concluded that given the growth of nonbank consumer credit in the past decade, this finding suggests that a new aspect of the transmission mechanism may have emerged as the traditional lending channel has diminished.

THE MORTGAGE WEALTH ILLUSION: INEFFICIENT HOUSEHOLD ALLOCATIONS AND REDUCTION OF THE MARGINAL PROPENSITY TO SAVE

Mortgages provide a false sense of wealth and security to borrowers (the *mortgage wealth illusion*)—although the borrower appears to own the home, the reality is that the mortgagee's interest is very much present and is senior to the borrower's ownership interest (which typically does not exceed the down payment, if any, and is subject to fluctuations in local home prices and positive/negative speculation). This is critical because the home mortgage is usually the biggest financial transaction of most households. For the typical homeowner, home equity accounts for more than 60 percent of his or her total wealth, and one popular way to grow rich quick is to directly or indirectly inflate home prices. Borrowers' anchoring on home values and extreme dependence and belief in home equity as a savings mechanism foster housing bubbles, fraudulent appraisals, speculation, and, eventually, financial catastrophe and ruin. If homeowners are made more aware of the realities and risks of home equity, they will have more incentives to develop other savings/retirement schemes. The mortgage wealth illusion has been a substantial disincentive to save money (by making more liquid investments)—the loss of liquid savings/investment that is attributable to the mortgage wealth illusion is significant (the household savings rate in the United States is less than 5 percent compared to more than 8 percent in Japan, and is lower than that of many developing countries that have much lower Mortgage/GDP ratios).

Traditional mortgages change and complicate household resource allocation decisions in ways that are detrimental to both the household members and social welfare. Mortgages cause inefficient household allocation decisions—such as underallocation to liquid savings/investments; underallocation to work and productivity (mortgage stress can substantially reduce productivity); the mortgage wealth illusion; mortgage fraud; overallocation of resources to mortgage-related payments; inadequate retirement planning due to reliance on home equity and anchoring on home values.

Traditional mortgages reduce households' marginal propensity to save (MPS). The typical monthly mortgage payments for homes constitute 33 to 45 percent of the monthly income of most households in developed countries, while income taxes constitute about 25 to 40 percent of monthly income. This means that most of these borrower-households have minimal savings and disposable income. This often creates several effects: (1) there is upward pressure on house prices that is often not supported by economic fundamentals and evolves into bubbles that later crash; (2) these borrower-households view their homes and the anticipated increases in property values as an investment and a source of emergency cash; and (3) borrower-households are not very concerned about the potential adverse impact of illiquidity of houses, or such concerns are outweighed by expected increases in home prices.

The traditional macroeconomic view has been that changes in earnings are the main determinant of consumer spending—this theory has been proven wrong by the subprime crisis, wherein the following factors have combined to distort and render consumer spending virtually unpredictable: (1) the ease of obtaining home-equity loans; (2) property flipping fostered by the use of mortgages; (3) rampant inflation of home prices; (4) fraudulent mortgages; (5) "cash-out" refinancing; and (6) appraisal fraud.

TRADITIONAL AND ALTERNATIVE WESTERN MORTGAGES REDUCE SOCIOECONOMIC FLEXIBILITY THAT SUBSTANTIALLY AFFECTS PSYCHOLOGICAL WELL-BEING

Mortgages substantially reduce the decision flexibility of adults and households, which often translates to: (1) suboptimal choices about jobs, marriage, relocation, socialization, friendships, and so on; (2) pressure on individuals to behave in certain ways because of their mortgage burdens; and (3) perceived loss of control of many aspects of life.

Many couples who have mortgages often find that they are subject to the quadruple burden that substantially reduces their ability to make choices and rational decisions: (1) a mortgage—which often means less leisure time and holding a job regardless of the conditions and circumstances at the workplace; (2) children—which requires regular income and less leisure time (and to some couples, requires a "home," which in turn necessitates mortgage-financed purchase of a housing unit); (3) a job—which requires commitment to a location, coping with unpleasant situations at work, and, often, inability to switch jobs; and (4) a fixed environment (neighbors, schools, amenities, municipal tax rates, etc.)—which the couple must interact with for long periods of time regardless of whether they like the environment (partly because of the high cost of switching homes).

TRADITIONAL AND ALTERNATIVE MORTGAGES DISTORT THE MARRIAGE MARKET

Mortgages have substantial adverse effects on, and reduce matching in, the marriage market (Clark 2006). Most lenders' mortgage origination decisions are based on consumer credit scores or corporate credit ratings. In many countries, prospective marriage partners often check each other's consumer credit scores and perceived ability to obtain credit before they make marriage decisions (such data are now easily available on the Internet). Disagreements between married couples about mortgage payments and/or about selling mortgage-financed homes often evolve into separations and divorces.

In some countries, divorce rates are highest among households that own mortgage-financed single-family homes.

Lauster (2008) analyzed the relationship between housing policy and couple outcomes/stability for cohabiting couples in Sweden, using data on 3,851 cohabiting couples, and found that greater affordability increases couple stability and greater availability of detached housing significantly weakens couple stability.

Dew (2008) analyzed how debt changes relate to changes in marital satisfaction, using data on 1,078 couples, and found that: (a) changes in consumer debt predicted recently married couples' marital satisfaction; (b) changes in variables associated with couples achieving their marital expectations (e.g., spending time together, arguing about finances) partially explained these findings; and (c) changes in consumer debt negatively predicted couples' time together and positively predicted arguments over money, which in turn were both associated with declines in marital satisfaction.

Rainer and Smith (2010) studied the relationship between unanticipated house price shocks and marital dissolution in the UK, using individual household data from the British Household Panel Survey and county-level house price data from the Halifax house price index. They found that: (a) positive and negative house price shocks have asymmetric effects on the probability of partnership dissolution; and (b) negative house price shocks significantly increase the risk of partnership dissolution, whereas positive house price shocks do not have a significant effect (and the destabilizing effect of negative house price shocks is greater for couples who have dependent children, low family income, and high mortgage debt).

Mortgages also affect the probability of remarriages, because remarriage candidates often consider each other's financial position (and are more likely to enter into prenuptial agreements) before making remarriage decisions (and are likely to have divorced partly because of financial issues). The percentage of remarried persons has been rising very quickly in many developed countries (partly due to high divorce rates and increasing social acceptance of divorce). Hence, the existence of traditional mortgage debt substantially reduces the probability of remarriage, and vice versa.

Burgoyne and Morison (1997) investigated money matters in remarried couples; they noted that the number of remarried couples was increasing, and their financial affairs were likely to be more complex than for first-married couples. They used data from 38 interviews of 20 couples in the UK (ages of respondents ranged from 28 to 83, with the majority in the 30–55 range, and only half still had dependent children). Burgoyne and Morison (1997) found that there was some separateness in financial arrangements that conflicts with earlier research, and about half of the couples were using an independent management system to manage their finances, compared with less than 2 percent of couples in the general sample. This separateness is prime evidence that financial concerns (and thus debt burdens of each couple) are the prime determinants of the success of many remarriages.

Between 2000 and 2009, the number of recognized marriages in China declined by as much as 5.1 percent annually (2005), and has risen by as much as 14.8 percent annually (2006); the average growth has been about 3.4 percent annually. The number of marriages in China increased in 2009 despite the economic turmoil. According to a report in the China Popin web site (quoting the *Beijing Morning Post*), 12.1 million people got married in 2009 (an increase of 10.4 percent over 2008). In China, divorces increased by 25.2 percent during the housing boom of 2004, but increased by 8.8 percent in 2009 to 2.5 million. In a different 2011 survey of the Chinese population, more than 70 percent of single women respondents said that they would marry only a prospective husband who owned a home, and 50 percent of Chinese women respondents said that financial considerations ranked above all else, while good morals and personality were not in the top three requirements. Fifty-four percent of single male respondents ranked beauty first, according to the report, which surveyed 32,000 people and was jointly issued by the Chinese Research Association of Marriage and another organization.[1] According to the report, as many as 24 million men in China may become perpetual bachelors by 2020. In China, each household is limited to only one mortgage, and most households cannot afford to buy homes without traditional mortgages. Thus, it is clear that in China (and in many countries), mortgage-financed home purchases affect the propensity to marry.

TRADITIONAL WESTERN MORTGAGES AND ALTERNATIVE MORTGAGES DISTORT THE JOB MARKET

Traditional mortgages distort and increase mismatching in the job market. In many instances, unemployed or underemployed mortgagors are restricted to looking for jobs within their state or within commuting distances solely because of their mortgage burden and the adverse consequences of mortgage default. In order to get jobs in other states or distant locations, they have to simultaneously sell their current home, buy a new home in the new location, and bear all the associated economic and psychological costs. Many people who are not happy in their current jobs often cannot resign or look for new jobs because of their mortgage burdens; this results in reduced productivity and depression, which has multiplier effects because it affects the worker's relationships with their immediate coworkers and household members. Furthermore, in most developed countries, when the mortgage-financed housing market is deemed by the central bank to be overheated, these central banks often react by increasing benchmark interest rates and reducing money supply (by issuing government bonds, reducing discount-window lending, or increasing capital reserve requirements), and these measures are usually publicly announced. Such central bank actions: (a) increase the perceived and actual cost of capital of many companies, (b) compel companies to reduce or defer their expansion plans or lay off staff in anticipation of economic contraction and reduced consumer and corporate consumption, and (c) reduce the volume of new construction, which results in job losses. On the contrary, *mortgage alternatives* are much less likely to cause the same adverse economic effects as traditional mortgages because mortgage alternatives: (1) substantially reduce speculation in housing markets; (2) link homeowners' expectations and investments to securities markets, which are much more liquid and transparent; (3) provide homeowners with more flexibility in terms of location, portfolio reallocation, and obtaining new jobs; and (4) provide banks/lenders with more liquidity compared to traditional mortgages.

The social and psychological costs of mortgage default are far greater than that of rental-lease default—this condition adversely affects social welfare and creates the wrong incentives. Mortgage defaults drastically reduce consumer confidence and consumer spending, which in turn reduces overall economic activity and increases the probability of economic recessions and mass layoffs at companies. Mortgage defaults cause banks/lenders to incur losses and to increase lending rates not just for real estate, but also for business loans (in order to recover losses and to compensate for greater overall perceived risk in the economy), which then increases companies' cost of capital and causes them to either postpone hiring or to lay off workers. Mortgage default is often a major distraction and usually causes the individual borrower to be less productive at work, which may result in economic losses for the employer or layoffs. Among married couples, mortgage default affects not only both spouses, but also their extended family (e.g., parents, cousins, etc.), who may be wholly or partially dependent on the couple.

Henley (2004) studied whether workers adjust their hours of work in response to capital gains and losses (specifically, financial windfalls and real housing wealth gains). Using British panel data on individual employees from 1992 to 2001, Henley found that both male and female workers reduced their work hours significantly in response, in particular, to housing gains; and that men increased their work hours in response to real housing losses, whereas women reduced their work hours in response to real housing gains. Henley noted that observed adjustments in work-hours seem to be only partial responses.

Some common terms of mortgages and deeds-of-trust statutes are unconstitutional (e.g., ban of prepayment penalties; borrowers' right of redemption). The remainder of this chapter explains the socioeconomic rationale for such unconstitutionality and some of the economic consequences.

THE STATUTORY OR COMMON LAW PROHIBITION OF PREPAYMENT PENALTY/YIELD MAINTENANCE OR LIMITATIONS ON PREPAYMENT PENALTY ON DEFAULT ARE UNCONSTITUTIONAL

In some U.S. states, prepayment/yield-maintenance provisions in mortgage/loan documents are unenforceable because state statutes and/or state common law expressly or implicitly prohibit such provisions. Hence, these statutory and common law prohibitions of prepayment penalties or limitations on the amount of prepayment penalties qualify as a "state action." As is explained in this chapter, these limitations are unconstitutional.

Anti-prepayment-penalty statutes have had and continue to have significant economic implications for the subprime mortgage market because more than 50 percent of outstanding subprime mortgages were floating rate loans, some of which reset at higher interest rates.

Many courts have ruled on the applicability of anti-prepayment-penalty statutes and common law, but no U.S. appellate court has ruled on the constitutionality of anti-prepayment-penalty laws, which should naturally be evaluated within the context of banking regulations and economic considerations. The legislative intent of most anti-prepayment-penalty statutes has been to protect the average borrower who presumably may not understand the economic ramifications of prepayment penalties—the reasons advanced are similar to those for the enactment of usury laws, but are unjustified in this instance.

First, many borrowers retain attorneys and brokers who understand and can explain prepayment penalty terms (attorney's fees are typically included in closing costs, which are financed); many prepayment clauses in loan documents are not complicated and more borrowers are increasingly sophisticated and pay attention to details of loan terms. Second, the lender has constitutionally protected property interests in fair terms of contracts to protect its economic interests, which in this case consist of the difference between the stated interest rate and market interest rates and other associated transaction costs—these property rights arise from state constitutional law, state contract laws, state property laws, expectations, and norms. Third, the advent of the Internet has made information more accessible and borrowers have instant and ready access to a wide variety of information about loan terms. Fourth, prepayment penalties are justified because economic conditions change increasingly more rapidly, risk management incurs transaction costs, and the lenders have contractual and fiduciary duties to their depositor-clients and other sources of funds. Fifth, public policy mandates that prepayment penalties be upheld (most lenders obtain funds for lending from individuals who deposit money in bank accounts) because yield maintenance provisions ensure that lenders meet their contractual obligations to these depositors; otherwise, there could be "bank runs" with attendant contagion, and financial distress of banks, which will force the federal government to spend substantial amounts of money to bail out troubled banks. Last, prepayment penalties can greatly reduce agency problems, adverse selection, and moral hazard problems inherent in the lending process and in customer-relationship management.

Hence, prohibiting prepayment penalties increases the probability that subprime mortgage interest rates will be greater, that subprime mortgage lenders in other states will eliminate prepayment options and other subprime lenders will seek additional down payments, or additional collateral, and that subprime borrowers will not be able to refinance their mortgages in order to obtain lower interest rates.

The Right to Contract

The state law ban/restrictions on prepayment penalties in mortgages/deeds of trust constitutes violations of the borrowers' and the lenders' constitutionally guaranteed right to contract for the following reasons. First, the borrower and lender both have constitutionally guaranteed property interests in entering into contracts on their own terms—such property interests arise from state constitutional law, state contract law, state property law, expectations, and norms. Second, the terms of the prepayment penalty typically do not contravene any prevalent government interest. Third, the prepayment penalties are necessary to protect the lender's economic interests, to provide necessary incentives to the lender to advance credit (the credit crunch that occurred between 2007 and 2010 is an example of consequences of inadequate incentives for lenders), and to prevent government intervention in the banking system (as evidenced in the recent bank bailouts from 2008 to 2011 by the U.S., U.K., and European governments, and other countries). Finally, prepayment penalties are necessary to provide relevant incentives (flexibility to refinance) to the borrower to borrow capital and to actively manage his or her debt.

The elimination or restriction of prepayment penalties does not serve any useful government interest, but rather increases the bankruptcy risk of banks/lenders/finance companies, reduces the interest payable to depositors at banks, and reduces the pool of capital available for lending. As mentioned, the government's interest in protecting the individual borrower is far outweighed by the economic parameters of, and economic justification of, lending operations, and by the bank disintermediation process and the economic benefits of prepayment clauses in mortgages. Since prepayment penalties are typically associated with fixed-rate loans, and lenders have a viable alternative to prepayment penalties (issue only floating rate loans), and borrowers have a viable alternative to prepayment penalties (obtain only floating-rate loans or obtain fixed-rate loans combined with swaps), there is absolutely no need for statutory or common law prohibitions or limitations of prepayment penalties. In these circumstances, the overall economic cost of this government intervention in financial markets (higher transaction costs, higher bankruptcy risks of lenders, more litigation, and the like) far exceeds any benefits that borrowers will gain from such intervention.

Prepayment penalties are different from usury laws, hence the same limitations should not apply. Usury laws serve a relevant consumer protection purpose. Prepayment penalties are justified by the fact that the lender incurs expenses to issue a loan and monitor the loan, and incurs a sometimes significant opportunity cost when the loan is prepaid, at which time, the market conditions may have changed substantially.

Equal Protection

The anti-prepayment-penalty statutes and common law constitute violations of the Equal Protection Clause of the U.S. Constitution. The state action is the enactment of the anti-prepayment-penalty statute, and/or the controlling common law court judgment. The statutory or common law elimination, limitation, or reduction of prepayment penalties unfairly discriminates between borrowers who claim to have the knowledge and sophistication to understand contract terms and those who claim not to—regardless of whether such claims are unverifiable; and also unfairly discriminates between parties who sign loan contracts in one state that permits prepayment penalties, and parties that sign loan contracts with similar terms in another state that does not. The anti-prepayment-penalty statutes or common law unfairly discriminates between lenders who make loans of different sizes and different maturities (the value of the prepayment penalty varies drastically by the size of the loan and the maturity/term of the loan). The statutory elimination, limitation, or reduction of prepayment penalties unfairly discriminates between any two borrowers with substantially different credit ratings—the borrower with a better credit rating is less likely to be hampered by prepayment penalties, and more likely to easily refinance loans regardless of applicability of prepayment penalties, whereas the borrower with a lower credit rating is more likely to be hampered by applicability of prepayment penalties; the mere existence of prepayment penalties will have a disproportionately greater negative effect on this borrower's refinancing terms. The anti-prepayment-penalty statutes or common law unfairly discriminates between borrowers who have good credit ratings and subprime borrowers (who often need to refinance their mortgages), because such elimination/reduction reduces the volume of credit that is available to subprime borrowers. The anti-prepayment-penalty statutes or common law unfairly discriminates between lenders that choose to provide fixed-rate loans and lenders that choose to provide floating-rate loans (because prepayment penalties are most valuable if the loans are fixed-rate loans, and/or longer-maturity loans); it also unfairly discriminates between lenders that use derivative products to hedge their interest-rate exposures and lenders that do not use derivative products; and unfairly discriminates between lenders that have acquired/developed/contracted substantial knowledge about risk management techniques and those lenders that have not done so. Lenders that know how to hedge their risk exposures are more likely to provide loans without any prepayment penalties, and hence are more likely to gain greater market share. The anti-prepayment-penalty statutes or common law unfairly discriminates between borrower-companies that operate in industries that are sensitive to changes in interest rates and inflation (e.g., financial services, real estate, retailing) and borrower-companies that operate in industries that are not sensitive to interest rates, because such limitations significantly reduces banks' willingness to lend to companies that are sensitive to interest rates.

Anti-prepayment-penalty statutes/laws unfairly discriminate between various classes of persons—between lenders who provide mortgages and lenders who provide other types of loans; between lenders who have the knowledge and infrastructure to seek out alternative investments/loans after borrower prepayment and lenders who do not have such knowledge; between large lenders who can afford to absorb the losses that arise from reinvestment risk (reinvestment in other assets at lower rates-of-return after prepayment by the borrower) and lenders who cannot afford to do so; and between borrowers who are knowledgeable about prepayment laws (and may repeatedly refinance loans) and borrowers who are not familiar with prepayment laws. The foregoing (intentional or unintentional) classifications do not serve any economic or regulatory purpose and do not enhance social welfare or the government's regulatory objectives. The discriminatory classifications described above are applied in the implementation of the anti-prepayment-penalty statutes.

The anti-prepayment-penalty-statutes are overbroad, and are not narrowly tailored to any class of persons or entities deemed to be at risk (such as subprime mortgage borrowers, or individual borrowers), or persons deemed to not need prepayment penalties (such as large, stable banks that have developed expertise in risk management). Hence the anti-prepayment statutes may be deemed to be void for vagueness.

Anti-prepayment-penalty statutes do not serve any meaningful economic purpose and the reasons are: (a) in most instances, any prepayment penalties that are due on refinance are included in the principal amount of the new replacement loan, and have minimal immediate impact on refinancing borrowers; (b) anti-prepayment-penalty statutes reduce the government's tax revenues (the statutes discourage refinancing and new lending, which reduces transactions and capital gains taxes); and (c) anti-prepayment-penalty statutes can substantially reduce the volume of refinancing, and hence reduces the liquidity of real estate markets.

The government's interest in protecting borrowers and ensuring effective capital markets is far outweighed by (a) the significant economic losses that banks incur on the application of anti-prepayment-penalty statutes, (b) the disincentive effect of anti-prepayment-penalty statutes on banks (reduces propensity to lend, and increases banks' search costs and monitoring costs), and (c) the negative effect of these statutes on the liquidity of real estate markets.

Due Process Rights

The anti-prepayment-penalty statutes and common law constitute violations of the Due Process Clause of the U.S. Constitution because lenders and borrowers have property interests in their constitutionally protected right to contract, and they cannot be deprived of this right without notice, or hearing, or compensation. Anti-prepayment-penalty statutes/laws impose substantial costs on lenders (such as reinvestment costs; monitoring costs; portfolio rebalancing costs). Lenders have a constitutional right to legally protect their economic interests—in this instance, the economic interest consists of the opportunity costs incurred by the lender when capital market conditions and interest rates change, and borrowers refinance their mortgages at lower interest rates and thereby compel the lender to issue new replacement mortgages that are less valuable. The profitability and stability of banks/lenders are sensitive to the "Interest Margin," which is sensitive to prepayments. Thus without yield maintenance, the lender is more likely to issue new mortgages/loans at lower interest rates while incurring additional costs. Second, lenders have a right to effective and efficient laws that regulate their activities—but as described in this chapter, the anti-prepayment-penalty regulations can be economically inefficient. As mentioned in preceding sections, anti-prepayment-penalty statutes/laws unfairly discriminate between various classes of persons.

A borrower who has some knowledge of anti-prepayment-penalty laws can repeatedly refinance a mortgage during one to two years believing that he or she is reducing his or her costs, but because many lenders agree to finance transaction costs, his or her all-in costs may actually be greater than the cost of the original loan. Furthermore, the total cost of such discretionary refinancing to social welfare can be substantial (increase in overall consumer debt, systemic risk); and such refinancings distort economic indicators (each of the banks/lenders will record an increase in "new loan volume").

The government's legitimate interest in promulgating efficient laws that protect borrowers and improve lending processes is far outweighed by the significant opportunity costs of anti-prepayment-penalty laws (operating losses incurred by financial institutions; reduced lending activity and systemic risk in capital markets), the resulting increased transaction costs, the economic loss to bank depositors (lower rates), and economic loss to borrowers—less funds available for lending, and higher interest rates.

The Takings Clause

The statutes and common law that limit or preclude prepayment penalties constitute violations of the Takings Clause of the U.S. Constitution. The state action involved is the enactment and/or implementation of these anti-prepayment-penalty laws. There have been several key U.S. Supreme Court decisions on the Takings issue, although none directly addresses the prepayment-penalty/yield-maintenance issue or the constitutionality of anti-prepayment-penalty statutes. Furthermore, the issue of definition of "public use" and "private use" within the context of Takings remains somewhat unresolved in U.S. law. The language of the Takings Clause, the inferable legislative intent of the Takings Clause, the historical application of the Takings Clause by most U.S. courts, and the nature of judges in takings cases support this point of view.

Under the accepted interpretation of the U.S. Constitution, government regulation of private property constitutes a Taking if it does not substantially advance a legitimate government interest, and the regulation is not imposed with simultaneous payment of adequate compensation for the property owners for any resulting economic losses.

In this context, the elements of Takings are described as follows. The lender has constitutionally guaranteed property interests in protecting its economic interest as capital markets change—in this instance the economic interest is the opportunity cost incurred by the lender when the spread between the stated interest rates and market interest rates becomes negative/unfavorable. These property interests arise from state contract laws, state property laws, state constitutional laws, norms, and expectations. The losses incurred by the lender in the process constitute economic losses, and thus a Taking. These losses include: the present value of the periodic differences between market interest rates and stated interest rate (in the loan documents); or losses arising from increased monitoring costs; or cost of reassessing the impact of changes in interest rate on the borrower's credit and on the borrower's propensity to refinance the loan. The monetary amount of the losses incurred by lenders is transferred to public use in the form of a lower effective interest rate for the borrower; and a "market value effect" in which the then prevailing lower effective interest rates slow the rate and magnitude of changes in overall interest rates. Said Taking can be construed as being for public use because the property taken is for public use—the general public and borrowers benefit from lower average interest rates. The public includes not only all people and companies that borrow in the capital markets, but also persons who hold assets that are sensitive to interest rates. The lender is not compensated for said Taking. The government has some interest in, and a duty to promote and enhance orderly and efficient capital markets in which individuals and companies can borrow at reasonable rates. Thus, the said Takings advances the government's interests to some extent.

The Takings implicit in the prohibition/limitation of prepayment penalties do not conform to any of the above-mentioned types of Takings because there is no "physical occupation"; and there is no "Total Regulatory Taking"; and there are no "exactions that violate the *Nollan* and *Dolan* standards"; and there is no "Penn-Central Type" Taking. Furthermore, the above-mentioned type of Takings do not conform to derivative Takings.

Thus, a new type of Takings called *Prohibitory Takings* is introduced here and is defined in a subsequent section of this chapter.

Interstate Commerce Clause

The statutory or common law prohibition of prepayment penalties constitutes an illegal and unconstitutional interference with interstate commerce, and burdens interstate commerce where either the lender or borrower resides outside the state where the property is located. This is because the prohibition of prepayment penalties increases transaction costs and monitoring costs for out-of-state lenders more than it does for in-state lenders/borrowers.

The statutory or common law prohibition of prepayment penalties does not serve any meaningful economic purpose because such laws reduce lenders' propensity to lend, and their propensity to lend to out-of-state borrowers; such statutes compel lenders to increase their base lending interest rates—in order to incorporate the cost of potential prepayment. The statutory or common law prohibition of prepayment penalties imposes significant costs on lenders—such as the cost of making new loans, monitoring costs, transaction costs, compliance costs, holding costs, negative externalities, and changes in market values of properties. The statutory or common law prohibition of prepayment penalties reduces overall social welfare by increasing lenders' and borrowers' mortgage insurance rates.

The prohibition or limitation of prepayment penalties does not advance any legitimate or meaningful government interest. The application of such statutes reduces governments' tax revenues because as a result lenders will probably earn less income and pay lower income taxes; and property owners will be liable for lower property taxes than in otherwise comparable areas because the prohibition of prepayment penalties will probably reduce overall volume of sale/purchase transactions, and reduce property prices in towns/cities/states that have such prohibitions.

THE LACK OF DEFINITION OF THE "FUTURE ADVANCES" CLAUSE IN MORTGAGES CONSTITUTES A VIOLATION OF THE U.S. CONSTITUTION

The extent to which the Future Advances Clauses in mortgages (or deeds of trust) protect the lender is not statutorily defined in some U.S. state laws. This constitutes a major omission and for purposes of constitutional law analysis also constitutes a state action because the state has a duty and a legitimate interest in enacting and enforcing laws for efficient property transactions. Typically, the priority of the lender's advance of additional cash depends on whether it was an obligatory advance or an optional advance. Obligatory advances usually entitle the lender to the same priority/security as the original mortgage. The optional advance does not guarantee the lender any priority, particularly where the lender has or should have had knowledge of intervening liens and junior mortgages.

Substantive Due Process

The optional advance does not guarantee the lender any priority (of security interests), particularly where the lender has or should have had knowledge of intervening liens and junior mortgages. This situation substantially increases lenders' transaction costs and also increases uncertainty about title and property values. Such uncertain costs include lower property values, increases in title insurance costs, and increases in lending rates. The government's failure to enact regulations that expressly define the legal status of optional advances and obligatory advances increases the occurrence of negative externalities because it causes costly uncertainty, contributes to substantial information asymmetry, increases perceived risk, and clouds titles. State governments know, or should know, of the use of future advances, and the resulting complications pertaining to the priority of security interests. Lenders have protected property interests in efficient laws for perfecting their security interests. These lenders' constitutional property interests arise from expectations, norms, state constitutional laws, and state contract laws. The failure to enact these statutes increases lenders' transaction costs and increases information asymmetry between lenders and borrowers.

Equal Protection

Similarly, the omission of passage of these laws constitutes a violation of lenders' constitutionally guaranteed equal protection rights because it unfairly discriminates between lenders that use real estate as collateral and lenders that use other types of assets as collateral; it also discriminates between lenders that perfect security interests through the land registry and lenders that perfect security interests through other methods (such as Uniform Commercial Code filings in the United States; security agreements, perfection-by-possession). The said omission of enactment/codification of these laws results in unfair discrimination between loans of different sizes and discriminates between lenders that have in-depth knowledge of security perfection processes and security interests and those that do not; it discriminates between lenders that use future advances clauses and those that do not and it also discriminates between lenders that choose foreclosure and lenders that choose loan renegotiation after financial distress.

The above-mentioned challenged discriminatory classifications do not serve any compelling state interest, and the classifications are not substantially related to serving any legitimate state interest.

THE GOVERNMENT'S FAILURE TO ENACT STATUTES THAT DEFINE THE QUALIFICATIONS/CHARACTERISTICS OF A FIRST MORTGAGEE

In most U.S. states, the first mortgagee's right to a first lien position is not established by statute, but is established only contractually and by case law.

This constitutes a major detrimental omission by state legislatures, which subsequently results in increased transaction costs, increased information asymmetry, and increased litigation risk. This omission by the government is a state action for purposes of constitutional law analysis, because the government has a duty to pass and implement statutes that improve the efficiency of transactions and reduce transaction costs; more specifically, given the practical importance of credit and security interests in modern commerce, the government has a duty to enact statutes that define the characteristics of a first mortgage (in many U.S. states, lien laws are distinct from mortgage laws even where security interests for liens and mortgages are perfected in the same way). Lenders and borrowers have property interests in efficient laws that facilitate transactions, and these property interests arise from expectation, custom, and state constitutional laws.

Equal Protection Clause

The noncodification and nonmandatory nature of the lender's first mortgagee position constitutes a violation of lenders' constitutionally guaranteed right to equal protection of the law. Only the federal, state, or municipal governments can enact and implement such laws.

In most common law jurisdictions, the secured lender (and some unsecured lenders) typically has the most senior interest in the underlying real property. The secured lender has constitutionally protected property interests in fair and transparent processes/procedures that pertain to third-party claims on the collateral/property, and also has interests in the protection of its interests in property. The lender has constitutionally protected property interests in remedy/repair of damages to the collateral/ property, and in information about any actions that impair the collateral (impairment of title or physical structure) and any applicable remedies. These property interests arise from state contract law, expectations, norms, and the state constitutional laws.

The lack of statutory definition of the nature of the lender's first mortgagee position unfairly discriminates between lenders that use real estate as collateral and lenders that use other types of assets as collateral. It unfairly discriminates between lenders that perfect security interest through the land registry (municipal government office) and those that perfect security interests through other methods (e.g., Uniform Commercial Code, security agreements, possession). The lack of statutory definition of the nature of the lender's first mortgagee position unfairly discriminates between lenders that retain different lawyers with different skill levels and seniority, and between properties that have different market values (the economic consequences vary drastically depending on the value of the property); it also unfairly discriminates between borrowers/purchasers that use different amounts of debt/loans to finance their purchases. The lack of statutory definition of the nature of the lender's first mortgagee position unfairly discriminates between title insurance companies that have different levels of risk aversion and different amounts of assets, and also unfairly discriminates between title insurance companies that employ staff with different skill levels. The lack of statutory definition of the nature of the lender's first mortgagee position unfairly discriminates between title insurance companies that have different exceptions for title coverage pertaining to definitions of first liens, and validity/elimination of liens in general.

Most of the above-mentioned discriminatory classifications are evident in court decisions, and in recording of liens and interests. The challenged discriminatory classifications do not serve any compelling government interest and the classifications are not substantially related to serving any government interest.

Substantive Due Process

The noncodification and nonmandatory nature of the lender's first mortgage position constitutes a violation of current and prospective lenders' constitutionally guaranteed substantive due process rights, because the resulting lack of clarity increases the lender's transaction costs, clouds title, and also increases the probability that lawsuits will be filed in order to establish the priority of security interests. The state action is the government's failure to draft relevant regulations that state the properties of first mortgages. Furthermore, the procedures established by most state governments (and governments of some common law countries) to adjudicate any resulting disputes are time-consuming and expensive, because they are typically lengthy court proceedings with jury trials and substantial discovery processes. Most states do not have summary judicial proceedings for determining the chain of title or the priority of security interests. Lenders have constitutionally protected property interests in fair adjudication procedures that pertain to claims on collateral/property, and they also have property interests in the protection of their interests in property, and property interests in information about any actions that impair the collateral and any applicable remedies. These property interests arise from contract law, expectations, norms, and the state constitutions.

The Free Speech Clause

The lack of statutory definition of the requirements/characteristics of the first-lien position is an omission by the government, which is a state action—the state action arises because the government has an affirmative duty to enact laws that govern such transactions in order to protect citizens, ensure efficiency of commerce, reduce transaction costs, and improve overall social welfare. The first-lien position typically grants to the lender certain rights such as the right to announce the terms of or changes to the loan covenants, the right to seek certain information from the borrower from time to time, and the right to file information in the land registry regarding its claims on the property. The first-lien position also grants to the lender the right to investigate and comment on filings by other parties in the land registry pertaining to their claims on the property and the right to file actions in court to protect its interests in the property. These lenders' rights constitute forms of free speech, which are protected by the U.S. Constitution because such speech is not offensive, is not criminal, and does not directly deprive others of their rights. These free-speech rights arise from state constitutional laws, the U.S. Constitution, expectations, and norms. The government has an affirmative duty to enact laws that protect people's right to free speech; and only three entities can enact such required laws—the federal, state, and municipal governments.

THE LENDER'S RIGHT TO RECEIVE PROCEEDS OF INSURANCE AND CONDEMNATION (ARISING FROM REAL ESTATE) IS NOT CODIFIED

In all U.S. jurisdictions the lender's right to receive the proceeds of insurance (fire, arson, casualty insurance) and condemnation (by the government) is subject to negotiation and is not codified in any state or federal laws. This is a major omission because it creates substantial information asymmetry, increases transaction costs, substantially increases the lenders' risk (and hence interest rates that lenders charge to borrowers), and encourages otherwise invalid third-party claims on title. Furthermore, this omission is a state action for purposes of constitutional law analysis, because the state has a duty to promulgate such laws and to enact laws that protect entities and persons that do business in its jurisdiction; and the state is one of two entities that has the authority to pass laws to codify the lender's right to receive proceeds of insurance and condemnation (the other entity is the federal government).

In some instances, the lender's right to receive proceeds of condemnation and insurance is contractually waived and the borrower is allowed to use such proceeds to repair the property or for other property-related expenses—but these are functions that can be easily performed by the lender or its agents.

The Equal Protection Clause

The noncodification and nonmandatory nature of the lender's right to receive proceeds of insurance and condemnation constitutes a violation of the lenders' constitutionally guaranteed equal protection rights.

The noncodification and nonmandatory nature of the lender's right to receive proceeds of insurance and condemnation arising from real estate: (a) discriminates between lenders that use real estate as collateral, and those that use other types of assets; and (b) unfairly discriminates between lenders that perfect security interest through the land registry, and those that perfect security interests through other methods (e.g., Uniform Commercial Code, security agreements). The challenged classifications do not serve any compelling state interest, and the classifications are not substantially related to serving any legitimate state interest.

In most common law jurisdictions, the lender typically has the most senior interest in the underlying real property. The lender has property interests in fair procedures that pertain to claims on the collateral; in the protection of its interests in property; in remedy/repair of damages to the collateral property; and in information about any actions that impair the collateral and any applicable remedies. These property interests arise from contract law, expectations, norms, and the states' constitutions.

The stated omission does not serve any economic purpose because it increases borrowers' cost of capital, and it increases lenders' bankruptcy risk.

Substantive Due Process

The noncodification and nonmandatory nature of the lender's right to receive proceeds of insurance and condemnation constitutes a violation of the lenders' constitutionally guaranteed substantive due process rights, because insured events are those that are foreseeable and are likely to occur; and the state's omission is clear—not drafting relevant regulations. Furthermore, there are no established effective procedures to adjudicate any resulting disputes (lawsuits are costly), and the lack of effective procedures imposes or can impose substantial additional costs on the lender.

The lender has property interests in fair procedures that pertain to claims on the collateral/property; in the protection of its interests in property; in remedy/repair of damages to the collateral property; and in information about any actions that impair the collateral and any applicable remedies. These property interests arise from contract law, expectations, norms, and the states' constitutions. The subprime mortgage market illustrates the problems inherent in such a lack of statutory definitions of lenders' rights. If the lenders' right to proceeds of title insurance, mortgage insurance, or other insurance is not codified (is negotiable), lenders will probably increase their interest rates and will probably incur more transaction costs, compliance costs, and monitoring costs.

The Takings Clause

The noncodification and nonmandatory nature of the lender's right to receive proceeds of insurance and condemnation constitutes a violation of the Takings Clause. The state action has been defined in preceding paragraphs. The standard tests for takings cases include the "reduction-of-value" test (ability to profit before and after takings, is evaluated, and there must be impairment; the "cause-of-harm" test (show that one person's use causes harm to another's property, and there is state action); the "government-invasion theory" (show that government takes possession of property); and the "noxious-use" test. Government regulation of private property constitutes a Taking if it does not substantially advance a legitimate state interest, and the regulation is not imposed with adequate compensation for the property owners for any resulting economic losses. In this circumstance, the elements of the Takings are as follows. The lender has constitutionally guaranteed property interests in protecting its economic interest as capital markets change—in this instance the economic interest is the proceeds of insurance and condemnation. These property interests arise from state contract laws, state property laws, state constitutional laws, norms, and expectations. The losses incurred by the lender constitute an economic loss, and thus a Taking. These losses include: (1) differences between market interest rate and stated interest rate (in the loan documents); (2) losses arising from increased monitoring costs; and (3) cost of reassessing the impact of interest rate changes on the borrower's credit and on the borrower's propensity to refinance the loan. The monetary amount involved (loss incurred by lenders) is transferred to "public use" in various forms: lower effective interest rate for the borrower, and a "market value effect," in which lower effective interest rate slows the rate and magnitude of changes in overall interest rates.

The said Taking can be construed as being for public use because the property taken is for public use—the general public benefits from lower average interest rates. The public includes not only all people and companies that borrow in the capital markets. The lender is not compensated for said Taking, because the lender does not receive any special benefit and/or compensation. The government has some interest protecting borrowers, and in promoting and enhancing orderly and efficient capital markets and real estate markets in which individuals and companies can borrow at reasonable rates; and the Takings do not advance the government interests to some extent.

The U.S. Supreme Court has not directly addressed the issue of lack of statutory definition of, and the nonmandatory nature of, the lender's right to receive proceeds of insurance and condemnation.

The Takings implicit in the lack of statutory definition of, and nonmandatory (discretionary) nature of, the lender's right to receive proceeds of insurance and condemnation do not conform to any of the above-mentioned types of Takings because there is no *physical occupation*, there is no Total Regulatory Taking, there are no "exactions that violate the *Nollan* and *Dolan* standards," and there is no "Penn-Central Type" Taking.

The Right to Contract

The noncodification and nonmandatory nature of the lender's right to receive proceeds of insurance and condemnation constitutes violations of the borrowers' and the lenders' constitutionally guaranteed right to contract because this omission is significant, and increases borrowers and lenders' transaction costs, monitoring costs, and risk. The borrower and lender have constitutionally guaranteed property interests in entering into contracts—such property interests arise from state constitutional law, state contract law, state property law, expectations, and norms; and the codification of the lender's right to receive proceeds of insurance and condemnation does not contravene any prevalent government interest. The codification of the lender's right to receive proceeds of insurance and condemnation is necessary to protect the lender's economic interests, prevent government intervention in the banking system, and provide relevant incentives to lenders and borrowers.

The noncodification and nonmandatory nature of the lender's right to receive proceeds of insurance and condemnation increases the bankruptcy risk for banks/lenders/finance companies, reduces the interest payable to depositors, and reduces the pool of capital available for lending. As mentioned, the government's interest in protecting the individual borrower is far outweighed by the economic parameters of lending operations, and the bank disintermediation process and economic benefits of the codification of, and permitting the lender's right to receive proceeds of insurance and condemnation.

Interference with Interstate Commerce

The noncodification and nonmandatory nature of the lender's right to receive proceeds of insurance and condemnation constitutes an illegal and unconstitutional interference with interstate commerce, and burdens interstate commerce where either the lender or borrower resides outside the state where the property and condemnation proceedings are located, and one state does not codify or permit the lender's right to receive proceeds of insurance and condemnation. This is because such differences in statutes: (a) unfairly discriminate against out-of-state lenders or borrowers; (b) increase the lenders' bankruptcy risk and transaction/monitoring costs of out-of-state lenders in states that do not codify or permit the lender's right to receive proceeds of insurance and condemnation; and (c) result in significant losses for lenders.

The noncodification and nonmandatory nature of the lender's right to receive proceeds of insurance and condemnation does not serve any meaningful economic purpose and does not advance any legitimate government interest for the following reasons. First, the lender has an economic interest in the property—in many instances, the monetary value of the lender's interest in the property is greater than that of the borrower's interest in the property. Second, it merely increases transaction costs and monitoring costs of borrowers and lenders. Third, it imposes significant costs on, and unfairly discriminates against, out-of-state lenders (compared to in-state lenders)—monitoring costs, transaction costs, compliance costs, holding costs, default costs, negative externalities, and changes in market values of properties. Fourth, it reduces lenders' incentives to provide loans in jurisdictions where such laws are applied. Fifth, it reduces overall social welfare by increasing borrowers' interest rates and increasing lenders' and borrowers' mortgage insurance rates. Sixth, the application of such statutes reduces governments' tax revenues: (1) lower income taxes from lenders and (2) lower property taxes than in otherwise comparable areas—because property prices are likely to decline upon application of right-of-redemption statutes; and overall property prices are likely to be lower in towns/cities/states that have borrower right-of-redemption laws.

ANTI-DEFICIENCY STATUTES ARE UNCONSTITUTIONAL AND THE LENDER'S RIGHT TO DEFICIENCY JUDGMENT MUST REMAIN ENFORCEABLE

In the United States, as of June 2009, there were at least $11 trillion worth of mortgages outstanding and at least $10 trillion worth of business loans outstanding. In the United States (and some common law jurisdictions), certain state real estate anti-deficiency-judgment statutes are unconstitutional. These violations of constitutional law create increased information asymmetry, increased transaction costs and compliance costs, negative externalities, inefficiency in real estate transactions, and increased agency problems.

Hence, anti-deficiency-judgment statutes affect housing prices and demand for housing, and all housing price/demand models are misspecified.

Anti-deficiency-judgment statutes typically apply to both mortgages and business loans, and are enacted by state legislatures. The existing literature on constitutionality of anti-deficiency-judgment statutes and real estate laws is scant—most articles address the issue tangentially. The constitutionality of state mortgage/real-estate laws is intricately intertwined with economic factors.

Some U.S. states statutorily prohibit deficiency judgments in foreclosures and after business loan defaults, even where the borrower has contractually consented to additional collateral (other assets) and/or other express deficiency judgment proceedings. Such anti-deficiency-judgment legislation may preclude deficiency judgments before or after foreclosure, or after judgment upon default of a business loan—and thus, these statutes affect "strategic defaults."

Sapienza and Zingales (2009) found that:

- People under the age of 35 years and over the age of 65 years were less likely to say it was morally wrong to default compared to middle-aged respondents.
- People with a higher education (8 percentage points) and African-Americans (14 percentage points) are less likely to think it is morally wrong to default, whereas respondents with a higher income are more likely to think it is morally wrong.
- Default is considered less morally wrong in the U.S. Northeast (6 percentage points) and West (8.5 percentage points).
- There was little difference in the moral view of strategic default among Republicans and Democrats, but Independents were less likely to say defaulting is immoral.
- Respondents who supported government intervention to help homeowners were 12 percentage points less likely to say strategic default is immoral.

Also see Stevenson (2010), White (2010), and Ghent, Kudlyak, and Slivinski (2009), which states, in part, "The recent surge in residential foreclosures has spurred interest in the factors that influence whether a borrower will default on his mortgage. The existing academic literature on the subject usually assumes that default is mainly a result of a borrower finding himself with a 'negative equity stake' in his home. Yet the lender may not be legally able to fully collect the outstanding debt in such cases. Whether a state allows lenders to pursue 'recourse'—that is, allows them to seize assets other than the home to recover the debt owed to them—is lost in much of the popular discussion of the current conditions in the mortgage market. Some states do allow lenders to cast a wider net when it comes to recouping their losses from a defaulted mortgage. Other states, such as California and Arizona, for instance, severely restrict the ability of lenders to pursue recourse."

The obvious state action involved is the enactment and implementation of the state-law statute or case law that prohibits deficiency judgment.[2] In some states, lenders are only permitted a single lawsuit to collect mortgage debt. The following states have some type of "one action" statute: California, Idaho, Montana, Nevada, New York, and Utah. Deficiency-judgment statutes are substantive laws and are essentially part of state foreclosure laws. Given the economic and public policy implications of anti-deficiency-judgment statutes, their constitutionality substantially depends on and should be analyzed within the context of banking regulations and economic factors (Bianco, Jappelli, and Pagano 2003; Alexander et al. 2002; Zazzaro 2005).

Several courts have ruled that anti-deficiency statutes are unenforceable. Several courts have ruled that similar laws *that permit deficiency-type judgments are valid and constitutional.* In *In re Route One West Windsor Limited Partnership*, 225 B.R. 76 (Bankr. D.N.J. 1998), the Court (applying New York law) held that: (a) a provision in the debtor's mortgage-loan agreement with an oversecured creditor to pay interest following default at the postdefault rate of 15.125 percent was not an unenforceable penalty and must be paid by the debtor; (b) the increased default rate of interest was justifiable and reasonable because it merely compensated the mortgagee for the increased risk and expense of collection; (c) the allowance of default interest on a claim in bankruptcy is determined by federal law, but noted that state law would be relevant because if the amount exceeded the allowable legal rate, then the bankruptcy court would not permit the mortgagee to recover such a windfall amount in a bankruptcy proceeding; (d) the principal of the debtor was a sophisticated businessman who had knowingly and freely allowed the debtor partnership to contract for the postdefault interest rate; (e) no other noninsider creditors of the debtor would bear the adverse effects of the increased rate of interest paid to the mortgagee; (f) under New York law, default interest rates as high as 25 percent had been consistently found to be reasonable; and (g) the mortgagee would not be permitted to receive both interest at the postdefault rate and late charges. The court therefore upheld the enforceability of the default-interest provision but not the provision for the payment of late charges by the debtor.

In a similar decision in *In re Dixon*, 228 B.R. 166 (Bankr. W.D. Va. 1998), the court held that it would accept the creditor's representation (without requiring testimony or evidence) that the relatively high default rate (36 percent) was proportionate to the reasonably anticipated damage from default and was not a penalty; and that the court did not have the "power to alter commercial contracts or to substitute [its] judgment for that of the parties" where the transaction was lawful, no other creditors were harmed, the default rate did not violate state usury laws, and there was no threat to the reorganization of the debtor by imposition of the default rate. The Court also stated that default interest rates are also necessarily higher than basic interest rates in order to compensate creditors for both the predictable and unpredictable costs of monitoring the value of collateral in default situations.

The legislative intent of anti-deficiency statutes has been debated in many cases. The standard anti-deficiency statute should be interpreted broadly in order to properly implement its legislative intent. In construing the meaning of the anti-deficiency statutes, a reasonable interpretation is that the manifest intentions of the Legislature were: (a) to limit the creditor's remedies to the property conveyed when the note and mortgage or deed of trust was executed to the seller/lender, and the securing instruments state that they are for the purpose of securing the balance of the purchase price; (b) to prevent an action for personal judgment on the note/mortgage/deed-of-trust against the defaulting borrower—who presumably will have to incur more transaction costs and legal fees to defend such actions; (c) to prevent the possibility of wholesale foreclosures followed by executions on deficiency judgments, which would leave a potentially large number of purchasers without their land/buildings, and without the assets necessary for subsistence; and (d) to protect less knowledgeable borrowers who may not fully comprehend the implications of deficiency judgment clauses in notes/mortgages.

However, the world and the global economy have changed significantly since most anti-deficiency statutes were enacted by U.S. state governments (most of the anti-deficiency judgment statutes were enacted during or just after the Great Depression in the United States—1930s—when it was critical to provide specific protections to a large number of poor and middle class people, and information and knowledge were more restricted).

The following key trends confirm the reduced usefulness of anti-deficiency statutes. First, borrowers are more aware of, and knowledgeable about, loan terms—since attorneys' fees are typically included in the financed closing costs, more borrowers can afford attorneys in the loan-closing process, and hence can get good advice about the implications of deficiency clauses. Second, the advent of the Internet has made more information accessible and comparability of loan terms is easier—borrowers have choices and hence, anti-deficiency statutes are an unwarranted government intervention in financial markets. Third, public policy requires that deficiency judgments apply where agreed on, because the lenders obtain funds from individual depositors, and hence have contractual and fiduciary duties to pay stated interest on these deposits—otherwise the federal government will have to spend substantial amounts of money to bail out troubled banks that cannot recover sufficient collateral. Fourth, anti-deficiency statutes increase overall borrowing costs for borrowers, because such statutes cause lenders to increase interest rates on loans in order to compensate for riskier collateral and for the lower probability of recovery. Fifth, lending processes have become more automated but also more complicated, and much of the lender's subjectivity has been eliminated from the lending process—there is now more emphasis on collateral quality and recoverability. Sixth, it is conjectured that deficiency judgment statutes tend to increase the volume of capital available for loans in the subject jurisdiction, because lenders are more comfortable about recovery rates. Seventh, the lender's cost of hedging risk on loans is partly based on recoverability of collateral in the event of default—and hence anti-deficiency statutes increase lending interest rates. Eighth, the deficiency judgment statute is justified because in the event of financial distress or default, the lender incurs additional transaction costs and monitoring costs. Ninth, since the early 1980s, mortgage borrowers have had a wider variety of alternatives in financing their loans, being able to choose between fixed (FRM) and various adjustable rate mortgages (ARMs)—the market share of the ARMs declined from more than 60 percent in 1984 to about 30 percent of all mortgage loans in the United States in 2006. Finally, despite a number of empirical and theoretical analyses, it is still unresolved under what conditions borrowers prefer the different mortgage instruments.

Deficiency-judgment clauses provide powerful economic and psychological incentives for borrowers to be careful about obtaining loans and about complying with loan terms.

In this instance, the economic usefulness of the deficiency-judgment statute is closely intertwined with and determines the legal validity of the statute—this can be attributed to several reasons. First, the deficiency-judgment clause or statute has immediate and long-term economic effects on the behaviors of both the borrower and the lender. Second, the deficiency-judgment clause or statute affects the determination of the key terms of the loan agreements, the lender's remedies. Third, the deficiency-judgment clause or statute affects the lender's overall transaction costs, and yield. Fourth, the deficiency-judgment clause or statute generally reduces agency problems, adverse-selection problems, moral hazard problems, and information-asymmetry problems inherent in the lending process and among lenders' staff. This is primarily because staff decisions are easier to justify, and so collateral recovery is extended. Fifth, deficiency-judgment statutes also reduces principal-agent problems between the lender and its staff.

The use of deficiency judgments is effective only to the extent that prospective and existing borrowers have adequate extra collateral—if not, the lenders will incur substantial monitoring costs and transaction costs in pursuing additional collateral, and the already financially distressed borrowers will incur additional transaction costs in defending deficiency-judgment lawsuits. The foregoing analysis implies that the economic usefulness and hence the legal validity of deficiency judgment statutes varies significantly with the wealth of borrowers, and hence the deficiency judgment statutes should apply only to certain classes of borrowers (e.g., borrowers whose wealth or income exceeds a minimum threshold). The events that occurred in the U.S. housing market between 1995 and 2003 tend to support this conjecture. The subprime loan market grew substantially and improper loans were granted to inappropriate/unqualified borrowers; the resulting defaults could have been avoided by using deficiency-judgment clauses. In most instances, the combination of limited collateral and the use of high loan-to-value loans and lack of deficiency clauses increased loan volume and access to capital, but reduced borrower incentives/motivation to repay loans. Where deficiency-judgment clauses and statutes exist, lenders are less likely to lend to poor borrowers than they are in jurisdictions without deficiency-judgment statutes.

The Equal Protection Clause

Statutory or common law prohibition of deficiency judgments in foreclosures even where the borrower has consented to additional collateral (other assets) and other express deficiency-judgment procedures/processes constitutes unconstitutional deprivation of the lender's right to equal protection of the law because these laws unfairly and illegally discriminate between lenders that have perfected/unperfected security interests in real estate on one hand, and on the other hand, lenders that have perfected/unperfected security interests in other types of assets; these laws also unfairly and illegally discriminate between borrowers who use real estate as collateral and other borrowers who use other types of assets as collateral. Anti-deficiency-judgment statutes unfairly discriminate between lenders/borrowers who perfect security interests using the mortgage recording systems, and those who use other perfection methods; the statutes unfairly discriminate between borrowers with different amounts of wealth—the anti-deficiency-judgment statutes favor borrowers with relatively greater assets. Lenders are more likely to pursue deficiency judgments against borrowers with greater assets than borrowers with few or no assets. Anti-deficiency-judgment statutes (a) unfairly discriminate between borrowers with different types of assets—the anti-deficiency-judgment statutes favor borrowers with more marketable assets (lenders are more likely to pursue deficiency judgment actions against borrowers with marketable assets than borrowers with illiquid or unmarketable or intangible assets); (b) unfairly discriminate between borrowers who can present procedural issues as defenses in deficiency judgment proceedings and borrowers who cannot present such defenses; and (c) unfairly discriminate between junior mortgagees secured by assets with stable market values and junior (second, third mortgagees) mortgagees secured by assets with highly volatile market values.

The earlier mentioned classifications are used by courts in adjudicating disputes. The challenged classifications do not serve any compelling government interest and the classifications are not substantially related to serving any government interest.

Anti-deficiency-judgment statutes do not serve any meaningful economic purpose because: (a) such statutes merely increase transaction costs and monitoring costs of borrowers—higher interest rates, greater lender propensity to sue or pursue foreclosure for any perceived breach by the borrower; (b) such statutes impose significant costs on lenders—monitoring costs, transaction costs, loss from changes in property values, holding costs, default costs, negative externalities, and changes in market values of properties; (c) such statutes reduce lenders' incentives to provide loans; and (d) such statutes create substantial negative externalities and reduce overall social welfare by increasing borrowers' interest rates and increasing lenders' and borrowers' mortgage insurance rates. Anti-deficiency-statutes increase moral hazard among borrowers.

Anti-deficiency-judgment statutes do not advance any legitimate major government interest. The application of such statutes reduces governments' tax revenues: (a) lower income taxes from lenders; (b) lower property taxes than in otherwise comparable areas—because property prices are likely to decline upon application of anti-deficiency-judgment statutes, and overall property prices are likely to be lower in towns/cities/states that have anti-deficiency-judgment statutes. The application of anti-deficiency-judgment statutes increases the risk that the government will have to bail out banks that have defaulted loans—this factor is relevant given the increasing sophistication of borrowers in hiding their assets, the advent of the Internet, globalization, and the growth of nontraditional mortgages and subprime mortgages.

The Due Process Clause

Anti-deficiency statutes are violations of lenders'/borrowers' substantive and procedural due process rights to fair and efficient processes. These anti-deficiency-judgment statutes are economically ineffective because they reduce the values of properties (lenders and prospective buyers factor in anti-deficiency-judgment and deficiency probabilities in their valuations of the property), increase transaction costs (lender charges higher interest rates on loans; loan insurance becomes more expensive), and increase uncertainty and litigation risk in real estate markets. Lenders/borrowers have constitutionally protected property interests in rights to fair and efficient processes, and in initiating and maintaining contractual relations with each other, in their privacy, and in the expectations of conformance to normal business relations. These property rights arise from state contract law, state constitutional law, expectations, and norms.

Deficiency involves a deprivation of the lender's economic interest—the lender incurs an economic loss of property; and under the U.S. Constitution, the lender must have adequate means of adjudicating/resolving such deprivation and access to an adversarial proceeding.

The government's interest in protecting borrowers from unfair terms and deceptive practices is far outweighed by: (a) the need for enforcing valid contracts, which is the foundation of modern commerce; (b) the need for fair adversarial processes to address deprivation of property; (c) the need for enforcing security interests where properly perfected and where the borrower has directly or indirectly assented to such security interests; (d) the potential for bank failure cause by anti-deficiency statutes, and subsequent government bailout expenditure—the recent events in the U.S. subprime mortgage market in 2006–2007 are an example; and (e) the negative externalities cause by anti-deficiency-judgment statutes.

Illegal Restriction on Interstate Commerce

Anti-deficiency-judgment statutes constitute illegal restrictions on interstate commerce for several reasons. The anti-deficiency-judgment statutes make it harder for out-of-state lenders to recover collateral and hence discourage lenders from interstate transactions; the in-state deficiency statute may not be applicable to an out-of-state lender that resides in a state that has an anti-deficiency statute—this situation unfairly and unconstitutionally restricts interstate lending transactions. The anti-deficiency-judgment statutes discourage out-of-state lenders from lending within the subject state, because such lenders will have lower recovery rates. Also, out-of-state title insurance and mortgage insurance companies are less likely to provide coverage (or will provide coverage at higher premium rates) in jurisdictions where there are anti-deficiency statutes. The anti-deficiency-judgment statutes increase the transaction costs of borrowers that seek to do business with out-of-state lenders and insurance companies.

As described in preceding sections, anti-deficiency-judgment statutes do not serve any meaningful economic purpose and do not advance any major government interest.

The Contract Clause

Anti-deficiency-judgment statutes are illegal and unconstitutional restrictions on the lender's and borrower's constitutionally protected right to contract. The deficiency clause in mortgages and deeds of trust is typically contractually agreed on at closing of the transaction.

Lenders/borrowers have constitutionally protected property interests in initiating and maintaining contractual relations with each other, in their privacy, and in the expectations of conformance to normal business relations. These property rights arise from state contract law, state constitutional law, expectations, and norms.

The government has a legitimate interest in protecting borrowers from unfair terms and deceptive practices. The government's interest in protecting borrowers from unfair terms and deceptive practices is far outweighed by: (a) the necessity to enforce valid contracts and security interests, which are the foundations of modern commerce; (b) the increased transaction costs (e.g., higher interest rates for mortgages, increased upfront due diligence expenses, increased mortgage insurance costs, etc.) and loss of social welfare (e.g., foreclosures, declines in property values, etc.) caused by anti-deficiency-judgment statutes—the fact that the subprime crisis did not occur in Canada can be attributed to the existence and use of deficiency judgment clauses in mortgages in Canada; and (c) the need to reduce lenders' actual loan losses and potential loan losses (potential loan losses can substantially increase lenders' perceived risk and systemic risk).

The Free Speech Clause

The anti-deficiency-judgment statutes constitute violations of the lenders' free speech rights. The Deficiency Clause and the deficiency judgment process grants the lender certain rights to state certain facts in some circumstances, and to make information requests from the borrower. Such expressions and information requests are constitutionally protected free speech because they represent expressions of the lender's and borrower's condition and prospects, and such expressions typically do not violate any civil or criminal laws, and are not offensive and do not directly deprive others of their rights.

The mortgage contract and deed of trust (DOT) are forms of protected free speech for several reasons. The mortgage and DOT are forms of communication to capital markets, regulators, real estate market participants, and investors. Empirical finance studies have identified information content in mortgage filings, particularly for large real estate. The mortgage/DOT represents expressions of the lender's and borrower's condition and prospects, and such expressions typically do not violate any civil or criminal laws. Such speech is not offensive and does not directly deprive others of their rights.

Hence the anti-deficiency-judgment statutes violate the right to free speech because the statutes typically do not apply to other forms of obligations—business loans, liens, and so on. The lender and borrower have a protected property interest in determining appropriate terms for contracting and financing. The anti-deficiency-judgment statute rule complicates the lender's credit analysis and monitoring efforts, and imposes financial burdens on the lenders. The anti-deficiency-judgment statutes increase the bankruptcy risk of lenders by increasing the probability of uncompensated loss.

The Takings Clause

The anti-deficiency-judgment statutes and common law constitute violations of the Takings Clause. The state action involved is enactment or implementation of these laws. There have been several key U.S. Supreme Court decisions on the Takings issue, although none has directly addressed the anti-deficiency-judgment statutes or related common law.

The Takings elements are as follows. First, the lender has constitutionally guaranteed property interests in protecting its economic interest as capital markets change—in this instance the economic interest is the opportunity cost and actual loss of money that is incurred by the lender, when contractual deficiency clauses in loan agreements are breached. These property interests arise from state contract laws, state property laws, state constitutional laws, norms, and expectations. Second, the losses incurred by the lender constitute an economic loss, and thus a Taking. These losses include: any differences between market interest rate and stated interest rate (in the loan documents); any losses arising from increased monitoring costs; the cost of reassessing the impact of interest rate changes on the borrower's credit and on the borrower's propensity to refinance the loan; the loss of loan principal amount; and the transaction costs. The monetary amount involved (loss incurred by lenders) is transferred to "public use" in various forms such as: (1) elimination of loan deficiencies owed by borrowers and (2) reduced transaction costs for borrowers. The lender is not compensated for said Taking, because the lender does not receive any special benefit or compensation. The government has some interest promoting and enhancing orderly and efficient capital markets in which individuals and companies can borrow at reasonable rates; and the Takings advance the government interests to some extent.

The Takings implicit in anti-deficiency statutes do not conform to any of the types of Takings defined in *Lingle* because: there is no physical occupation, there is no "Total Regulatory Taking," there are no "exactions that violate the Nollan and Dolan standards," and there is no "Penn-Central Type" Taking. There are no "Derivative Takings."

Thus, this gives rise to a new type of Takings referred to as *Supplemental Takings,* which is defined in more detail in the next section of this chapter.

NEW THEORIES OF TAKINGS

Prohibitory Takings

Prohibitory Takings were introduced in an earlier section of this chapter and are defined as follows:

- The Takings arise solely from the statutory prohibition or governmental limitation of contract terms, and pertain to substantive laws only (not to procedural issues).
- The Takings occur when there is a transaction (i.e., mortgage).
- The parties have property rights in the limited/prohibited conduct or contractual term, and such property rights have economic value to one or more parties to the transaction.
- There is uniformity of commitment by both parties (lender and borrower) to the property interests involved (i.e., right to contractual prepayment penalty).
- Fairness is a major criterion in judicial orders and in the legislative intent of statutes that authorize such Takings.
- The Takings are unquestionably intentional—the prohibiting statute, government order, or government action clearly intends to limit or preclude the specific acts or contractual terms.
- The parties (lender and borrower) can always improve their position without judicial intervention—by contracting (e.g., without the prepayment penalty, the lender will increase lending interest rates and the borrower will either not borrow, or seek only floating-rate mortgages and perhaps purchase interest caps).
- The transfer of utility by any of the parties (e.g., lender or borrower), if any, depends on the size and sophistication of that party. For example, a large institutional borrower that borrows a floating- (fixed-) rate loan with a face value of $50 million without a prepayment clause can also purchase a series of "caps" ("floors") such that whenever interest rates rise (decline), the borrower will earn profits from the caps (floors) (caps are interest rate call options; floors are interest rate put options). Similarly, the lender for a floating- (fixed-) rate loan without any prepayment penalty can purchase a series of floors (or sell some floors) such

that when rates decline (increase) the lender will earn some profits. This is relevant because the extent of the tortfeasor's liability for damages partly depends on whether the parties had other alternatives.

Supplemental Takings

Supplemental Takings are characterized as follows:

- The Takings arise wholly or partly because one or more parties in a transaction has to be made whole.
- The Takings exist only if there are one or more transactions between or among the parties.
- There must be cooperation and some measure of coordination among the parties in order for the property interest to exist.
- There is asymmetrical commitment by both parties to both the property interest and the subject property.
- The property interest that is destroyed or damaged has substantial economic value, and the affected party cannot improve its absolute position or relative position without judicial intervention or change of venue.
- There is transfer of utility/disutility from one party to the other, such that one party's loss is the other party's gain.
- The social capital of a class of affected persons (e.g., lenders) has been substantially damaged by the offending/challenged statute or common law (in jurisdictions that have anti-deficiency-judgment statutes, borrowers are more likely to falsify loan application documents, to shirk or default, and to interfere with the appraisal process).
- One or more of the parties have investment expectations; the damaged property interest supplements adjacent/adjunct property interests (e.g., the right to deficiency judgment supplements the lender's property interests in foreclosure proceedings and related property interests). The property interest arises primarily from custom and expectations, and not necessarily for statutes.
- The government does not gain directly from the challenged deprivation of property rights.

CONCLUSION

Some mortgage statutes (e.g., anti-prepayment-penalty statutes and anti-deficiency-judgment laws) are unconstitutional, create rights of action for constitutional tort claims, and affect market psychology and the behavior of market participants. Thus, the propensity to sell, the propensity to buy, holdouts, shirking, contract performance, adverse selection, risk aversion, willingness to accept losses, and agency problems are influenced by legal factors. These factors have not been reflected in most housing-demand and housing-price forecast models.

Traditional "Western" mortgages substantially reduce the efficiency of monetary transmission in both developed countries and developing countries—this phenomenon may partly account for the global financial crisis of 2007 to 2011, and for the subprime mortgage crisis that occurred in the United States during 2007 to 2009, during which most traditional monetary policies failed to stimulate the economies of many countries.

NOTES

1. Andrew Jacobs, "For many Chinese men, no deed means no dates," *New York Times*, April 14 2011, www.nytimes.com/2011/04/15/world/asia/15bachelors.html?pagewanted=2&_r=1&partner=rssnyt&emc=rss.
2. See also "Anti-deficiency laws and our mortgage crisis," a blog post from April 3, 2008 (http://jaydiatribe.blogspot.com/2008/04/anti-deficiency-laws-and-our-mortgage.html), and the list of non-recourse mortgage states and anti-deficiency statutes (available at www.helocbasics.com/list-ofnon-recourse-mortgage-states-and-anti-deficiency-statutes). Anti-deficiency/nonrecourse states include Alaska, Arizona, California, Connecticut, Florida, Idaho, Minnesota, North Carolina, North Dakota, Texas, Utah, and Washington.

REFERENCES

Ackermann, J. 2008. The sub-prime crisis and its consequences. *Journal of Financial Stability* 4 (4): 329–337.

Ambrose, B. W., and C. A. Capone. 1996. Cost-benefit analysis of single-family foreclosure alternatives. *Journal of Real Estate Finance and Economics* 13: 105–120.

Ambrose, B. and R. Buttimer. 2009. *The Adjustable Balance Mortgage: Reducing the Value of the Put*. The Pennsylvania State University, University Park, PA. www.business.uconn.edu/finance/seminars/papers/Ambrose_Buttimer_New_Mortgage_UConn.pdf.

Bar-Gill, O. 2009. The law, economics and psychology of sub-prime mortgage contracts. *Cornell Law Review* 94: 1073–1093.

Bedi, R. 2009. *Laundering the proceeds of mortgage loan fraud*. Saw Centre for Financial Studies, NUS, Singapore.

Ben-Shahar, D., C. Leung, and S. Ong. 2009. *Mortgage Markets Worldwide*. Adobe E-Book. Hoboken, NJ: Wiley-Blackwell.

Blair, R. D., and C. A. Piette. 2006. Antitrust injury and standing in foreclosure cases. (The antitrust enterprise: principle and execution). *Journal of Corporation Law* 31 (2): 401–419.

Bottelier, P. 2010. Beijing's new challenge: China's post-crisis housing bubble. *Carnegie Endowment for International Peace—Policy Outlook* (July).

Brady, R. 2010. Consumer credit, liquidity, and the transmissions mechanism of monetary policy. *Economic Inquiry* 49 (1): 246–263.

Burgoyne, C., and V. Morison. 1997. Money in remarriage: Keeping things simple—and separate. *Sociological Review* 45 (3): 363–395.

Center for Responsible Lending. 2008. *Voluntary Loan Modifications Fall Far Short: Foreclosure Crisis Will Continue Unabated Without Court-Supervised Modifications*. CRL Issue Brief, Janaury 30, 2008. www.responsiblelending.org/mortgage-lending/research-analysis/updated-analysis-of-paulson-plan.html

Chen, W. 2006. Legal implications of a rising China: WTO: time's Up for Chinese Banks—China's Banking Reform and Non-Performing Loan Disposal. *Chinese Journal of International Law* 7: 239–242.

Clark, S. 2006. The uniqueness of stable matchings. *Contributions to Theoretical Economics* 6 (1).

Courchane, M., and J. Giles. 2002. *A Comparison of U.S. and Canadian Residential Mortgage Markets*. Working Paper EWP0201, University of Victoria (Canada).

Cox, P. 2008. Foreclosure reform amid Mortgage Lending Turmoil: a public purpose approach. *Houston Law Review* 45 (3): 684–694.

Davies, Z. E. 2008. Rescuing the rescued: stemming the tide of foreclosure rescue scams in Washington. *Seattle University Law Review*, 31: 353–363.

Den Haan, W., S. Sumner, and G. M. Yamashiro. 2009. Bank loan portfolios and the Canadian monetary transmission mechanism. *Canadian Journal of Economics* 42 (3): 1150–1175.

Den Haan, W., S. Sumner, and G. M. Yamashiro. 2010. Bank loan components and the time-varying effects of monetary policy shocks. *Economica* 78 (312): 593–617.

Deng, Y., D. Zheng, and C. Ling. 2005. An early assessment of residential mortgage performance in China. *The Journal of Real Estate Finance and Economics* 31 (2): 117–136.

Dew, J. 2008. Debt change and marital satisfaction change in recently married couples. *Family Relations* 57 (1): 60–71.

Ghent A. C., M. Kudlyak, and S. Slivinski. 2009. *Deterring default: Why some state laws decrease the probability of mortgage foreclosures*. Economic Brief EB09-09, Federal Reserve Bank of Richmond (September).

Ghent, A. C., and M. Kudlyak. 2009. *Recourse and residential mortgage default: Theory and evidence from U.S. states*. Working Paper 09-10, Federal Reserve Bank of Richmond, Working Paper 09-10 (July).

Good, S. and C. M. Hammond. 2006. Real estate auctions – legal concerns for an increasingly preferred method of selling real property. *Real Property, Probate and Trust Journal*, 40: 766–776.

Guseva, Y. 2009. Russian mortgage finance and legal reforms in times of financial crises: Transplanting American law models. *Columbia Journal of East European Law* 3 (10): 75–144.

Hancock, D., and W. Passmore. 2009. Three initiatives enhancing the mortgage market and promoting financial stability. *B.E. Journal of Economic Analysis & Policy* 9 (3) (Symposium): Article 16.

Hatcher, D. 2006. Foreclosure alternatives: a case for preserving homeownership. *Profitwise News and Views* (February 2006), 1–5.

Henley, A. 2004. House price shocks, windfall gains and hours of work: British evidence. *Oxford Bulletin of Economics and Statistics* 66 (4): 439–456.

Jacoby, M. 2010. The value(s) of foreclosure law reform. *Pepperdine Law Review*, UNC Legal Studies Research Paper No. 1550842.

Johnson, A. M. 1993. Critiquing the foreclosure process: an economic approach based on the paradigmatic norms of bankruptcy. *Virginia Law Review*, 79: 959–962.

Kiff, J. and V. Klyuev. 2009. *Foreclosure Mitigation Efforts in the United States: Approaches and Challenges*. IMF Staff Position Note No. 09/02.

Kiss, G., and G. Vadas. 2007. The role of housing market in monetary transmission—Evidence from Hungary. *International Journal of Housing Policy* 7 (3): 299–317.

Kopeikin, A. B. 2010. *Housing Reform in Russia: Affordable Housing Market Making*. Institute for Urban Economics (Russia).

Kosareva, N., and A. Tumanov. 2008. Assessing housing affordability in Russia. *Problems of Economic Transition* 50 (10): 6–29.

Lauster, N. T. 2008. Better homes and families: Housing markets and young couple stability in Sweden. *Journal of Marriage and Family* 70 (4): 891–903.

Ma, Y. 2009. A discussion on development of China's housing mortgage-backed securitization and American experiences. *Asian Social Sciences* 4 (4): 98–102.

Malloy, R. 2009. Mortgage market reform and the fallacy of self-correcting markets. *Pace Law Review* 30: 79–89.

Mashkina, O., P. Heliste, and R. Kosonen. 2007. The emerging mortgage market in Russia. An overview with local and foreign perspectives. Working paper, Helsinki School of Economics, Finland.

Merrill, S., and C. Rabenhorst. 2003. Developing secondary mortgage markets in southeast Europe—Assessments of the mortgage markets in Bulgaria, Croatia and Romania. Available at: http://pdf.usaid.gov/pdf_docs/PNADF362.pdf.

Myers, R. T. 2008. Foreclosing on the subprime loan crisis: why current regulations are flawed and what is needed to stop another crisis from occurring. *Oregon Law Review* 87: 311–316.

Nemoto, N. 2005. The battle over Japan's mortgage markets raises default risks. Standard & Poor's—Global Fixed Income Research.

Ozeki, K. 2007. Japan credit perspectives: Overview of Japan's residential mortgage market. Fixed Income Research, PIMCO (March).

Painter, S. 2006. Subprime lending, suboptimal bankruptcy: a proposal to amend §§ 522(f)(1)(B) and 548(a)(1)(B) of the Bankruptcy Code to protect subprime mortgage borrowers and their unsecured creditors. *Loyola Chicago University Law Journal* 38: 81–91.

Pence, K. M. 2003. Foreclosing on opportunity: state laws and mortgage credit. FEDS Working Paper No. 2003-16.

Pento, M. 2011. Geithner's failed makeover. (February 21). Available at: www.europacmetals.com/commentaries/newsid416/41/geithners-failed-makeover/default.aspx.

Rabenhorst, C., and S. Ignatova. 2009. Condominium housing and mortgage lending in emerging markets—Constraints and opportunities. IDG Working Paper No. 2009-04, July. Available at: www.urban.org/uploadedpdf/411921_condominium_housing.pdf.

Rainer, H., and I. Smith. 2010. Staying together for the sake of the home? House price shocks and partnership dissolution in the UK. *Journal of the Royal Statistical Society: Series A (Statistics in Society)* 173 (3): 557–574.

Safaei, J., and N. E. Cameron. 2003. Credit channel and credit shocks in Canadian macrodynamics—A structural VAR approach. *Applied Financial Economics* 13 (4): 267–277.

Shanker, M. 2003. Will mortgage law survive? *Case Western Law Review*, 54: 69–102.

Shiller, R.J. 2009. Policies to deal with the implosion in the mortgage market. *The B.E. Journal of Economic Analysis and Policy* 9 (3): Article 4.

Stark, D. 1997. Facing the facts: an empirical study of the fairness and efficiency of foreclosures and a proposal for reform. *University of Michigan Journal of Law Reform*, 30: 639–648.

Stevenson, Paul. 2010. Strategic mortgage default system. www.strategicloandefault.com/contact.

Tatom, J. A. 2008. The U.S. *Foreclosure Crisis: A Two-Pronged Assault on the U.S. Economy*. 2008-WP-10 July 2008; University of Munich. http://mpra.ub.uni-muenchen.de/9787/1/2008-WP-10_Tatom.pdf.

Tiwari, P. and Y. Moriizumi. 2003. Efficiency in housing finance: a comparative study of mortgage instruments in Japan. *International Journal of Housing Policy* 3 (3): 267–288.

Todd, R., and M. Grover. 2008. Targeting foreclosure interventions: an analysis of neighborhood characteristics associated with high foreclosure rates in two Minnesota counties. *Journal of Economics and Business* 60 (1–2): 91–109.

U.S. Department of the Treasury and US HUD. 2011. *Reforming America's housing finance market: A report to Congress* (February). Available at: www.treasury.gov/initiatives/Documents/Reforming%20America%27s%20Housing%20Finance%20Market.pdf.

White, B. T. 2010. Underwater and not walking away: Shame, fear and the social management of the housing crisis. Ariz. L. Studies Discussion Paper No. 09-35, October.

Whitman, D. 1993. Mortgage prepayment clauses: An economic and legal analysis. *UCLA Law Review* 40: 851–861.

Whitman, D. 2005. New directions in mortgage law: Restatements and uniform laws. *New York Real Property Law Journal* 33: 14–24.

Whitman, D., and G. Nelson. 2004. Reforming foreclosure: the uniform non-judicial foreclosure act. *Duke Law Journal* 53: 1399–1410.

Zavisca, J. 2008. Property without markets: Housing policy and politics in post-Soviet Russia, 1992–2007. *Comparative European Politics* 6 (3): 365–387.

Zavisca, J. 2010. To owe is not to own: Why Russians reject mortgages (and why Americans accept them). Working Paper, NCEER, University oF Washington.

Zhu, H. 2006. The structure of housing finance markets and house prices in Asia. *BIS Quarterly Review* (December): 55–60.

CHAPTER 9

Subprime Lending Is Unconstitutional

A substantial portion of the increases in annual volume of home purchases/sales (about 30 percent of total transaction volume) in the United States from 1995 to 2009 was financed with subprime mortgages (Cutts and Merrill 2008; Foote, Gerardi, Goette, and Willen 2008; Glaeser, Gyourko, and Saks 2005; Hendershott and Weicher 2002; Lax, Manti, Raca, and Zorn 2004; Leamer 2007; Mian and Sufi 2008; Missal 2008; Mortgage Bankers Association 2008; Pence 2006; Pafenberg 2005). The U.S. subprime mortgage crisis (2004 to 2011) illustrates some of the problems inherent in subprime mortgages. Between 2005 and 2010, there were more than $2 trillion of outstanding subprime mortgages in the United States alone (about three million subprime mortgages worth more than $1 trillion were originated in 2006 alone in the United States). According to the Center for Responsible Lending (U.S.), as of November 27, 2007, and in the United States alone, there were 7.2 million outstanding subprime mortgages that had an estimated value of $1.3 trillion.

Subprime lending is also rampant in the business loan sector, although such lending has attracted much less controversy. Most home buyers who used subprime mortgages were first-time homeowners, and hence, (a) their homes had more "Emotional Value" compared to other types of buyers; (b) more of subprime homeowners' net worth was in the form of home equity; and (c) such "subprime" homeowners were more willing to inflate housing prices. Lenders provided various rationales for continued subprime lending, despite the known inherent risks. The primary justifications were that annual default rates on subprime mortgages had historically been less than 7.5 percent, and that subprime mortgages expand homeownership, which "stabilizes" neighborhoods.

Bar-Gill (2009); Demyanyk and Van Hemert (2011); Fritts (2007); Ferrell, Bethel, and Hu (2009); Zywicki and Adamson (2009); Bethel,

Ferrell, and Hu (2008); Fitch Ratings (2007); Crews and Van Order (2005); and Schloemer, Li, Ernst, and Keest (2006)[1] explained some of the legal, behavioral, and economic issues pertaining to subprime lending.

The Ho and Pennington-Cross (2007) study concluded that state predatory lending laws do not have any consistent effect on the volume of subprime loans. Thus, it is fair to say that U.S. states have not fulfilled their duty to promulgate laws that protect subprime borrowers.

THE STATE-ACTION REQUIREMENT: THE SUBSTITUTION THEORY AND FAILURE-TO-ACT AS STATE ACTION

Subprime lending processes, loan agreements, and documents implicate, and are based on, various state laws/statutes pertaining to disclosure, processes/procedures, usury, debtor-creditor relations, anti-predatory lending, and so on; such state laws are stated in, and expressly made part of, subprime loan agreements/documents, such that use of such subprime loans/documents instantly triggers the Due Process Clause and violations of constitutional rights. Hence, the "state action" requirements for constitutional analysis exist in the form of (a) the incorporation of state statutes into subprime loan agreements, and (b) the use and incorporation of such state statutes into subprime loan agreements. This is henceforth referred to as the "Substitution Theory" of state action. The lenders are effectively acting in the position of the government and can be deemed to be "encouraged" by the government, which has an affirmative duty to enact laws that protect low-income and otherwise unqualified persons from predatory lending. Furthermore, the failure of federal regulators (such as the Office of Thrift Supervision, the Federal Deposit Insurance Corporation, the Federal Reserve Board, the Office of the Comptroller of the Currency, the National Credit Union Administration and the Conference of State Bank Supervisors; see www.encyclopedia.com/doc/1G1–159632244.html), to provide sufficient guidance and to enact laws that clarify underwriting standards and liability standards for subprime mortgages, is an omission that constitutes state action for purposes of constitutional analysis.

SUBPRIME LENDING IS UNCONSTITUTIONAL

Right to Privacy

Subprime lending constitutes a violation of the borrower's constitutionally protected right to privacy because the subprime borrower is typically required to make socially/economically detrimental disclosures that are, or may become, publicly available—such disclosures foreclose future economic opportunities for the subprime borrower and reduce the borrower's access to credit/capital. Also, such disclosures are required by state and federal banking/finance laws, anti-fraud laws, and consumer protection laws; such disclosures have lasting socially negative effects on the borrower and reduce the borrower's property interests in future economic wealth because prospective economic opportunities may be denied or reduced due to knowledge of information provided in such disclosures.

The subprime borrower has constitutionally protected property interests in access to credit and future economic opportunities—such interests arise under state contract law, state constitutional law, and expectations. The government's interest in ensuring adequate borrower disclosure for the benefit of lenders is far outweighed by the negative externalities caused by subprime borrower disclosures and by the direct economic, social, and psychological impact of such mandatory public disclosures on subprime borrowers and values of properties in their neighborhoods.

Subprime lending often reduces the social capital of subprime borrowers, who in these circumstances can be considered to be a disadvantaged and protected class of persons. This reduction of group social capital is near permanent because it has lasting adverse effects on neighborhoods and on individual subprime borrowers. Thus, subprime lending constitutes a violation of borrowers' constitutional rights.

The Equal Protection Clause

Subprime lending is a violation of the Equal Protection Clause of the U.S. Constitution because subprime lending results in substantial differences between the levels of statutory protection provided to subprime borrowers and regular "prime" borrowers; it also results in unfair discrimination between subprime borrowers who have financial and legal knowledge and subprime borrowers who do not have such knowledge. Subprime lending results in unfair discrimination between subprime borrowers who do not have access to capital and other borrowers who have access to capital; and in unfair discrimination between subprime borrowers who have cash to afford the postclosing transaction costs, monitoring costs, and refinancing costs that arise from subprime loans and subprime borrowers who cannot afford such costs. Subprime lending results in unfair discrimination between lenders who provide subprime mortgages and lenders who provide prime mortgages. Subprime lenders who are arguably taking more risk than traditional lenders are typically not provided with sufficient underwriting standards and liability standards by regulators such as the Office of Thrift Supervision, the Federal

Deposit Insurance Corporation, the Federal Reserve Board, the Office of the Comptroller of the Currency, the National Credit Union Administration, and the Conference of State Bank Supervisors (e.g., inadequate clarification for 2/28 and 3/27 exploding-ARMs).

The government's interest in regulating lending activities in the mortgage sector is far outweighed by: (a) subprime borrowers' property interests in fair laws that protect them from financial distress—these property interests arise from state constitutions and rational expectations; (b) the significant negative externalities, transaction costs, and default costs caused by inadequate regulation and ongoing regulatory guidance for subprime loans; and (c) subprime lenders' constitutionally protected property interests in clarity of regulations/laws, and enactment of laws that protect them from financial distress—these property interests arise from state laws and rational expectations.

Due Process

Subprime lending constitutes a violation of the borrower's procedural and substantive due process rights for several reasons. As mentioned, subprime lending documents/agreements incorporate state lending statutes that expressly require subprime borrowers to follow specific procedures for disclosure, reporting of unfair lender practices, default, and so on. These statutes and procedures have been shown to be inefficient (Pavlov and Wachter 2008; Mian and Sufi 2008; Center for Responsible Lending, 2009; Schloemer et al. 2006; Shroder 2007; Agarwal et al. 2006; Quercia, Stegman, and Davis 2007; Bethel, Ferrell, and Hu 2008; Adams, Einav and Levin 2007; White 2008; Zywicki and Adamson 2009; DiMartino and Duca 2007; Valiante 2010; Fitch Ratings 2007; U.S. Securities and Exchange Commission 2008).

Subprime lending involves and results in a deprivation of the borrower's constitutionally protected property interests in future wealth, because subprime lending increases the borrower's risk of bankruptcy, reduces the borrower's available cash and borrowing capacity, and compels the borrower to make suboptimal and biased economic decisions (such as savings, spending, preferences, and investments). Such property interests arise from state constitutional law, state contract law, and expectations.

The procedures and processes described in said incorporated state statutes are often burdensome and expensive, sometimes are not affordable, and unfairly discriminate between borrowers who have knowledge and those who do not; they unfairly discriminate between subprime borrowers who have access to legal counsel and those who do not have such access.

Furthermore, the lack of sufficient regulation and government guidance by federal agencies constitutes a deprivation of the substantive and procedural due process rights of subprime lenders. Subprime lenders have constitutionally guaranteed property interests in clarity of mortgage/banking laws, and in adequacy of laws that will protect them from financial distress. These property interests arise from state constitutions and expectations.

The Interstate Commerce Clause

The subprime mortgage constitutes an illegal and unconstitutional interference with interstate commerce, and burdens interstate commerce where either the lender or borrower resides outside the state where the property (and/or any subsequent foreclosure proceedings) is located. This is because subprime mortgages are inherently much riskier than traditional mortgages, and thus cause substantial increases in monitoring costs, compliance costs, and foreclosure/recovery costs for out-of-state lenders and borrowers (compared to similar costs for in-state borrowers or lenders). The relevant state-action was described in the foregoing sections.

CONCLUSION

Subprime lending causes substantial economic, psychological, and social capital losses to borrowers (who typically have low income and/or derogatory credit histories) and also causes often inefficient re-allocation of household income, which in turn creates stress and reduces "work" time, all of which reduce productivity and human capital in the economy. Subprime lending requires certain types of disclosures by the borrower, which have lasting socially negative effects (adverse effects on both the borrower and the borrower's neighborhood); the practice requires lender disclosures to regulators (often publicly available), which have negative information effects and negative externalities (perceived credit risk of borrowers in the neighborhood, perceived credit risk of banks that lend to borrowers in the neighborhood, interest rates for loans to borrowers, etc.). It's unlikely that modification of terms of subprime mortgages will solve the many inherent constitutional law problems.

NOTE

1. Based on a data set that includes loans originated between 1998 and 2006 on owner-occupied homes, estimated that 2.2 million households will lose their homes to foreclosure, and they will lose a total of $164 billion, which translates into approximately $75,000 per borrower.

REFERENCES

Adams, W., L. Einav, and J. Levin. 2007. Liquidity constraints and imperfect information in subprime lending. NBER Working Paper No. 13067.

Agarwal, S., S. Chomsisengphet, C. Liu, and N. S. Souleles. 2006. Do consumers choose the right credit contracts? Federal Reserve Bank of Chicago, USA; Working Paper No. 2006-11.

Agarwal, S. B., B. Ambrose, S. Chomsisengphet, and A. Sanders. 2008. Subprime lending and default: The impact of loan concentration. Unpublished working paper.

Bethel, J., A. Ferrell, and G. Hu. 2008. Law and economics issues in subprime litigation. The Harvard John M. Olin Discussion Paper Series.

Bar-Gill, O. 2009. The law, economics and psychology of subprime mortgage contracts. *Cornell Law Review* 94: 1073–1093.

Center for Responsible Lending. 2009. CRL State Legislative Scorecard: Predatory Mortgage Lending. Available at: www.responsiblelending.org/issues/mortgage/statelaws.html.

Crews, A., and R. Van Order. 2005. On the economics of subprime lending. *Journal of Real Estate Finance and Economics* 30 (2): 167–196.

Cutts, A., and W. A. Merrill. 2008. Interventions in mortgage default: Policies and practices to prevent home loss and lower costs. Freddie Mac Working Paper 08-01.

Demyanyk, Y., and O. Van Hemert. 2011. Understanding the subprime mortgage crisis. *Review of Financial Studies* 24 (6): 1848–1880.

DiMartino, D., and J. Duca. 2007. The rise and fall of subprime mortgages. Economic Letter, Federal Reserve Bank of Dallas, 2 (11). Available at: http://www.dallasfed.org/research/eclett/2007/el0711.html.

Ferrell, A., J. Bethel, and G. Hu. 2009. Legal and Economic Issues in Litigation Arising from the 2007-2008 Credit Crisis. In *Prudent Lending Restored: Securitization After the Mortgage Meltdown*, ed. F. Yasuyuki F., R. Herring, and R. Litan, 163–235. Brookings Institution Press, Washington DC.

Fitch Ratings. 2007. The impact of poor underwriting practices and fraud in subprime RMBS performance. Available at: www.americansecuritization.com/uploadedFiles/Fitch_Originators_1128.pdf.

Foote, C. L., K. Gerardi, L. Goette, and P. Willen. 2008. Subprime facts: What (we think) we know about the subprime crisis and what we don't. Federal Reserve Bank of Boston Public Policy Discussion Papers, #08-2.

Fritts, H. 2007. The subprime lending industry: An industry in crisis. *The Banking Law Journal* (May 2007).

Glaeser, E., J. Gyourko, and R. Saks. 2005. Why have housing prices gone up? *American Economic Association Papers and Proceedings* 95 (2): 329–333.

Hendershott, P., and J. C. Weicher. 2002. Forecasting housing markets: Lessons learned. *Real Estate Economics* 30 (1): 1–11.

Ho, G., and A. Pennington-Cross. 2007. The varying effects of predatory lending laws on high-cost mortgage applications. *Federal Reserve Bank of St. Louis Review* January/February, 39–59.

Lax, H., M. Manti, P. Raca, and P. Zorn. 2004. Subprime lending: An investigation of economic efficiency. *Housing Policy Debate* 15 (3): 533–571.

Leamer, E. 2007. Housing is the business cycle. National Bureau of Economic Research Working Paper 13428.

Mian, A., and A. Sufi. 2008. The consequences of mortgage credit expansion: Evidence from the 2007 mortgage default crisis. NBER Working Paper No. W13936.

Missal, M. 2008. Final Report of Michael J. Missal Bankruptcy Court Examiner. United States Bankruptcy Court for the District Delaware. *In re: New Century TRS Holdings, Inc. A Delaware Corporation, et al, Debtors.*

Mortgage Bankers Association. 2008. National Delinquency Survey, Second Quarter.

Pafenberg, F. 2005. Single-family mortgages originated and outstanding: 1990–2004. OFHEO staff research paper.

Painter, S. 2008. Subprime lending, suboptimal bankruptcy: A proposal to amend §§ 522(f)(1)(B) and 548(a)(1)(B) of the Bankruptcy Code to protect subprime mortgage borrowers and their unsecured creditors. *Loyola University Chicago Law Journal* 38: 81–92.

Pavlov, A., and S. Wachter. 2008. Subprime lending and house price volatility. University of Pennsylvania Law School Institute for Law and Economics, Research Paper No. 08-33, 2008. Available at: http://ssrn.com/abstract=1316891.

Pence, K. M. 2006. Foreclosing on opportunity: State laws and mortgage credit. *Review of Economics and Statistics* 88 (1): 177–182.

Quercia, R., M. A. Stegman, and W. Davis. 2007. The impact of predatory loan terms on subprime foreclosures: The special case of prepayment penalties and balloon payments. *Housing Policy Debate* 18 (2): 311–337.

Reiss, D. 2006. Subprime standardization: How rating agencies allow predatory lending to flourish in the secondary mortgage market. *Florida State University Law Review* 33: 985–1000. http://www.law.fsu.edu/journals/lawreview/downloads/334/reiss.pdf.

Schloemer, E., W. Li, K. Ernst, and K. Keest. 2006. Losing ground: Foreclosures in the subprime market and their cost to homeowners. *Center for Responsible Lending.* Available at: http://www.responsiblelending.org/pdfs/foreclosure-paper-report-2-17.pdf.

Shroder, M. D. 2007. The value of the sunshine cure: The efficacy of the real estate settlement procedures act disclosure strategy. *CITYSCAPE: Journal of Policy Development and Research* 9 (1): 73–84.

U.S. Congress Joint Economic Committee. 2007. *The Subprime Lending Crisis: The Economic Impact on Wealth, Property Values and Tax Revenues, and How We Got Here.*

U.S. Securities and Exchange Commission. 2008. Summary Report of Issues Identified in the Commission Staff's Examination of Select Credit Rating Agencies. pp. 34–35. Available at www.sec.gov/news/studies/2008/craexamination070808.pdf.

Valiante, D. 2010. 1. The market for subprime lending: A law and economics analysis of market failures and policy responses. 2. Legal and economic approach to tying and other potentially unfair and anticompetitive commercial practices: focus on financial services. 3. Shaping reforms and business models for OTC derivatives markets: Quo vadis? Ph.D. thesis. Available at: http://eprints.luiss.it/647/1/valiante-20100224_1-2.pdf.

White, A. 2008. The case for banning subprime mortgages. *University of Cincinnati Law Review* 77: 617–637.

Zywicki, T., and J. Adamson. 2009. The law and economics of subprime lending. *University of Colorado Law Review* 80 (1): 1–86.

CHAPTER 10

Constitutionality of Real Property Title Systems

The Recording System and the Registration/Torrens System of land titles are the most popular types of title systems around the world, and both can have significant effects on the efficiency of mortgages and foreclosure processes.

THE RECORDING SYSTEM AND THE REGISTRATION/TORRENS SYSTEM ARE UNCONSTITUTIONAL

Under U.S. laws, the Recording System and the Registration/Torrens System are unconstitutional (and given principles of commonality and the legislative histories of some common law countries, these title systems may also be unconstitutional in some common law countries). The use of real property title systems raises several critical constitutional law issues, most of which are not addressed in the literature. The relevant research consists of somewhat tangential materials. Land and property transactions typically invoke property rights, state statutes, and procedural issues that invoke constitutional protections (most of the reference articles and books are listed on this book's web site). The following sections analyze the various constitutional law problems inherent in real property title systems.

Right to Privacy

Real property title systems (Recording and Registration systems) effectively constitute violations of the right to privacy of the property owner and the prospective property purchaser, primarily because these title systems make publicly available details about land values, transactions, and other facts that the landowner may otherwise seek to keep private and away from the public domain. The state action is the mandatory use of the Registration System or the Recording System for real property transactions, and the inherent mandatory disclosure of property-related data to the general public. The property owner has a constitutionally protected property interest in the privacy and confidentiality of information about his or her property where such information may create liabilities, ill-will, envy, and unwarranted claims, if made public. The government can obtain and use property data (e.g., for tax purposes) without making them publicly available. Although the government has an interest in the efficient functioning of real estate markets, and government's disclosure of information about property values is useful for efficient functioning of property markets, such disclosure through titling systems is less relevant today than in the past because: (1) there are more ways to get information about property values other than government records—Internet sites, realtors, newspaper advertisements, trade journals, and so on; (2) in many jurisdictions, there are often substantial differences between market values and assessed-values of properties; and (3) disclosure of property data through titling systems may serve to erroneously reinforce inflated/inaccurate property values. Hence, the government's interest in providing conditions for efficient functioning of real estate markets is far outweighed by the landowner's privacy interests, the possible increase in overall average transaction costs due to such public disclosure, and other possible negative psychological effects that can be caused by public disclosure through government-sponsored titling systems. The concept of "Negative Privacy" is introduced here, and is defined as the requirement that information about a person be disclosed to the public in a certain manner. This contrasts with "Positive Privacy" (or traditional privacy) wherein individuals and information about them should not be portrayed in a certain manner without the consent of the affected individual. Privacy in this instance is positive privacy (the right not to have misleading information about an individual's property rights published and available to the public) and negative privacy (the requirement that the government disclose that the correct person is the title holder).

Free Speech

Filing a property record (deed, mortgage, or lien) under a property titling system is a form of speech because it is a form of personal expression; it is permitted by law; and it is a manifestation of an economic state. Such speech is not constitutionally protected because it is potentially offensive, the costs to correct the consequences are relatively substantial, and it can deprive property owners and others of their free-speech rights. Filing of false or misleading liens can damage a property owner's economic prospects; and filings of property data that divulge certain types of information may also damage the property owner's business prospects. Thus, the key issues are (1) the determination of the amount and timing of mandatory public disclosure pertaining to each property; and (2) the amount of disclosure that should be voluntary under the Recording System and the Registration System. The state action is the mandatory use of the property titling systems. The government's interest in promoting transparency and efficiency of property transactions can be far outweighed by the adverse economic and psychological impacts of disclosure inherent in title systems. Such mandatory disclosure can actually work against the government's interest where disclosure increases divergence of opinions in the market (e.g., where assessed values differ substantially from market values of properties); where mandatory disclosure causes downward drifts in property prices or supply-demand imbalance (where the basis/methods for calculating property taxes are complex and misunderstood); where mandatory disclosure reduces lenders' willingness to provide loans (e.g., where local ordinances are complex and include many complicated taxes, which cause many tax liens); or where mandatory disclosure reduces competition among real estate brokers (e.g., substantial differences in knowledge/perception among brokers).

Right to Contract (Contracts Clause of Article One, § 10)

In right-to-contract issues, *Energy Reserves Group v. Kansas Power & Light* established various tests. In this instance, the state action is the mandatory use of the Recording System or the Registration System for property transactions.

To the extent that the Recording System mandates filing of transactions/documents for recognition/validity of property rights, and the government registry/office implicitly or explicitly supports fraud/misconduct by accepting fraudulent claimants' documents for filing, then the Recording System interferes with the true landowner's right to contract, and hence, the Recording System is unconstitutional. The existence of the government's investigation process under the Registration System is further evidence of the unconstitutionality of the Recording System. In almost all situations (typical property transactions), the state does not have any overriding reasons or public policy considerations for such interference in contractual relations by sponsoring the Recording System. The state's interest in providing an orderly forum for recording of property transactions and efficient functioning of real estate markets is far outweighed by property owners' and property-purchasers' rights to contract.

Due Process Rights

Title systems affect real property values, primarily because of the differences in uncertainty and compensation created by choice of real property registration. The property owner and property claimant have constitutionally protected property interests in: (a) fair land title systems and processes that minimize their transactions costs, and (b) information about them in land registers. These property interests arise from state constitutional law, expectations, and freedom-of-information rights. The insufficient due process arises because the Recording System results in suboptimal accuracy and increased confusion about land/property rights, and typically, the only appeal is a lawsuit in a court of law, which is expensive and time-consuming (even special proceedings like quiet-title lawsuits). Therefore, by allowing the use of the Recording system, which is an inefficient process that actually impairs said property interests, the government deprives landowners and property claimants of their property interests in efficient and informative processes, without adequate due process. The government's recognizable interest in providing an efficient land transfer system is far outweighed by: (a) the increased transaction costs borne by property buyers and sellers; (b) the post-recording uncertainty about title (typically solved by purchasing title insurance); and (c) the resulting negative impact on property values.

The effect of the government's valuation of the property on a successful claim under the Registration System has not been analyzed in the literature. Such valuations are typically not subject to appeal, and in some jurisdictions there may be statutory bans against litigating the government's valuation. The property owner has constitutionally protected property interests in fair and accurate valuation processes; in fair and accurate allocation of property values to land, improvements, and fixtures; in an efficient appeal system to contest government's property valuations; and in an efficient appeal system to contest the government's determination of title. Hence, the quality and accuracy of such valuations (and the associated statutes that specify how and when the valuations are performed) may constitute a violation of the property owner's procedural and substantive due process rights. The insufficient means of appeal constitute a violation of the due process rights of the property owner, claimant, other property owners, and prospective property owners in the area/city.

The Takings Clause

The use of the Registration System or the Recording System for titling constitutes an uncompensated Taking, and hence a violation of the Takings Clause of the U.S. Constitution for several reasons. The property owner, mortgagee, and other claimants have constitutionally protected property interests in the efficiency of the title/recording method and the information disclosed about them. Under the accepted interpretation of the U.S. Constitution, government regulation of private property constitutes a Taking if: (1) it does not substantially advance a legitimate state interest, and (2) the regulation is not imposed with adequate compensation for the property owners for any resulting economic losses. The key U.S. Supreme Court decisions on the Takings issue have not directly addressed the unconstitutionality of title systems.

The elements of the Takings are as follows: The state takes and/or reduces the values of these property interests by sponsoring and using the Registration System (inefficient system; mandatory disclosure of property information) or the Recording System (inefficient system; mandatory disclosure of property information). The state action involved is one of the following: (1) the government's sponsoring and use of the Registration System or the Recording System for titles; (2) the assessed property value under the Registration System is relatively low (by comparison to similar towns/properties, etc.); (3) the property owner does not have any right of appeal to complain about the assessed property value (Registration System); (4) the assessment of real property values is based not entirely on property values, but on local municipal needs; or (5) the government does not have any fair procedures for assessing the value of the property. Although the "public use" element is not necessary, the public use requirement is satisfied because any benefits (fulfillment of municipal needs, excess tax revenues, etc.) are used by the local government for public purposes.

The general public benefits from the appropriation by the state because: (1) uncertainty created by the title system reduces the value of the property to its owner and to prospective buyers who then pay lower purchase prices; and (2) the universe of potential claimants (those who can claim ownership of the subject property) increases under the Recording System.

The affected property owners incur economic, psychological, and social losses and thus, there is a Taking. These losses include: (1) differences between market value and assessed value of properties; (2) losses arising from delays in reassessment of the property; (3) higher transaction costs and monitoring costs; and (4) decrease in property value due to uncertainties about validity of titles. The monetary amount involved (loss incurred by property owners) is transferred to public use in various forms such as: (1) municipal expenditures and (2) a "market value effect." The said Taking can be construed as being for public use because the property taken is for public use—the general public benefits. The public includes not only all people and households that qualify for rent control and rent stabilization, but also all renters and homeowners who are affected by changes in municipal services.

The property owner does not receive any form of compensation or even adequate compensation by the Taking (the use of the Registration System or the Recording System): (1) there is no increased security of title; (2) use of the Recording System or the Registration System does not guarantee more stable property prices; and (3) the property owner is not compensated for said Taking where he or she does not receive any special benefit and/or compensation such as tax credits.

The government has some interest in enacting and enforcing title systems, and the Takings advance the government interests to some extent—but facilitation of such benefits and interests is limited by the number of property units in the jurisdiction and the fairness of the title systems. However, the government has other ways to solve the titling problem. The Takings inherent in the use of title systems are a government intervention that has substantial economic multiplier effects that may even affect neighboring towns. There is substantial evidence that home equity accounts for 65 percent to 80 percent of the net worth of 60 percent to 80 percent of households in most developed countries. Hence, the government's interest in enforcing title systems is far outweighed by the collective property interests of the town's property owners in fair and cost-effective title systems.

The Takings implicit in title systems do not conform to any of the *Lingle* types of Takings because: there is no "physical occupation," there is no "Total Regulatory Taking," there are no "exactions that violate the *Nollan* and *Dolan* standards," and there is no "Penn-Central Type" Taking.

The Interstate Commerce Clause

The relevant state action is the mandatory use of the Registration System or the Recording System for real property transactions. The laws and regulations governing land title systems are typically established at the state level and implemented at the local/municipal level–town/city level. However, real estate/property transactions are increasingly interstate transactions. Hence, the Recording System and the Registration System for real property titles are unconstitutional and constitute violations of the Interstate Commerce Clause of the U.S. Constitution, because property transactions often involve interstate contacts, and hence should be regulated by federal laws.

Where the registration fee is relatively high (for both in-state and out-of-state parties), or is statutorily higher for out-of-state parties, then the Registration System constitutes a burden on interstate commerce and trade, and is essentially unconstitutional. Similarly, under the Registration System, where an out-of-state party incurs significantly higher costs in order to challenge a government-sanctioned appraisal, the Registration System constitutes an undue burden on interstate commerce, and is unconstitutional.

The Registration System unfairly discriminates against out-of-state potential title claimants, because they are less likely to be located in any government sponsored title search.

The foregoing challenged classifications do not serve any compelling state interest, and the classifications are not substantially related to serving any legitimate state interest.

The Registration System and the Recording System constitute illegal restrictions of trade (under the U.S. Constitution) and prevent potentially profit-maximizing transactions for several reasons. The U.S. Supreme Court has not issued any direct ruling on the constitutionality of real property titling systems. First, the Recording System can result in inaccurate recording of property transactions, which will result in significant transaction costs and information costs—such inaccurate recording can prevent the rightful property owner from consummating transactions, and thus constitutes an illegal restriction of trade. Second, where the fees for the Registration System are relatively substantial, the Registration System constitutes an illegal restraint on trade because it unfairly discriminates against, and imposes a financial burden on, parties whose inability to afford the registration fee deprives them of security provided by an accurate title system; and thus constitutes an illegal restraint on trade and interstate commerce.

The Equal Protection Clause

The Recording System is unconstitutional because it unfairly discriminates between those who know that timing of filing is critical and parties who do not have such knowledge; unfairly discriminates between those who can afford the recording fees and associated transaction costs and those who cannot; and unfairly discriminates between those who are using the Recording System to process purchases/sales of small properties and those who are using the Recording System for large properties—in essence the level of legal protection provided by the Recording System varies drastically and unfairly, with the size of the property. The Recording System unfairly discriminates between those who choose to perfect their security interests using the Uniform Commercial Code (UCC) and those who choose to perfect using the Recording System—in most states, the UCC expressly defers to the state-law mortgage systems, but UCC can be used to perfect security interests in real property. The Recording System unfairly discriminates between people who are buying/selling different types of properties—the level of legal protection provided by the Recording System varies drastically and unfairly according to the type of property involved—properties that are sensitive to interest rates (e.g., triple-net leased properties), or have only one tenant, or have many small tenants with short term leases, will tend to receive less legal protection than properties with the opposite characteristics. The Recording System unfairly discriminates between borrower-purchasers whose lenders are out-of-state and those whose lenders are in-state lenders, who typically charge higher interest rates and closing costs (i.e., title search, title insurance) for out-of-state loans than for in-state loans.

The Recording System unfairly discriminates based on the skill sets of the attorneys that advise the parties (seller, purchaser, lender, insurance company) to the sale/purchase transaction—higher skilled attorneys will produce more accurate work with lower long-term costs, while lower-skilled attorneys will produce more errors and at higher costs. The Recording System unfairly discriminates based on the degree of coordination among the lawyers for the different parties in the transaction. The Recording System unfairly discriminates based on the quality of the mortgage documents—the Recording System does not provide minimum standards/terms that govern the mortgage agreement, and all terms are contractual. The Recording System unfairly discriminates based on the type of transaction; that is, purchase/sale versus recording of a lease versus recording of an easement versus recording of a second mortgage versus recording of a deed all represent the notation of interests in the underlying property, but the transaction costs and the level of legal protection for each one vary drastically under the Recording System.

The Registration System is unconstitutional because it unfairly discriminates between those who know that timing of filing is critical and parties who do not have such knowledge; it also unfairly discriminates between persons who can afford the registration fees and associated transaction costs and those who cannot. The Registration System unfairly discriminates between those who are using the Registration System to process purchases/sales of small properties, and those who are using the Registration System for large properties, because in essence the level of legal protection provided by the Registration System varies drastically and unfairly, with the size of the property: (1) appraisal risk increases exponentially for large properties; (2) title risk increases exponentially for larger properties; and (3) challenges to title of small properties cost almost the same as challenges to title of large properties. The Registration System unfairly discriminates between those who choose to perfect their security interests using the Uniform Commercial Code and those who choose to perfect using the Registration System—in most states, the UCC expressly defers to the state-law mortgage systems, but UCC can be used to perfect security interests in real property.

The Registration System unfairly discriminates between people who are buying/selling different types of properties—the level of legal protection provided by the Registration System varies drastically and unfairly according to the type of property involved—properties that are sensitive to interest rates (e.g., NNN-leased properties), or have only one tenant, or have many small tenants with short-term leases, will tend to receive less legal protection under the Registration System than properties with the opposite characteristics. The Registration System unfairly discriminates between borrower-purchasers whose lenders are out-of-state, and those whose lenders are in-state lenders, who typically charge higher interest rates and closing costs (i.e., title search, title insurance) for out-of-state loans than for in-state loans. The Registration System unfairly discriminates based on the quality of the mortgage documents—unlike the Registration System, the Recording System does not provide minimum standards/terms that govern the mortgage agreement, and all terms are contractual. The Registration System unfairly discriminates based on the type of transaction; that is, purchase/sale versus recording of a lease versus the recording of an easement versus recording of a second mortgage versus recording of a deed all represent the notation of interests in the underlying property, but the transaction costs and the level of legal protection for each one vary drastically under the Recording System.

Hence, the Recording System and the Registration System create unnecessary and discriminatory classifications. The foregoing challenged classifications do not serve any compelling government interest, and the classifications are not substantially related to serving any legitimate and/or compelling government interest.

THE UNIFORM COMMERCIAL CODE (UCC), TITLE SYSTEMS, AND CONFLICT OF LAWS

The Registration System and the Recording System of property titles are used in many common law countries. In the United States, the Registration System and the Recording System can be completely preempted by the Uniform Commercial Code system, although as applied in most states, the UCC expressly defers to state mortgage and real property laws on all matters pertaining to perfection of security interests in real property. In the United States (and some developed countries), UCC laws are typically enacted and enforced at the state level; but traditional title systems are enacted and enforced at the local/municipal level. UCC systems are increasingly being used as title systems for land and buildings—UCC has traditionally been used as the primary title system for equipment and personal property.

U.S. law on preemption remains somewhat unsettled and most of the existing case law pertains to preemption of state laws by federal laws (and not preemption of local/municipal laws by state laws). Some courts have identified three types of preemption. In *Bibbo v. Dean Witter Reynolds, Inc.*, the Court described the three different types of preemption under the

Supremacy Clause (U.S. Constitution, Article VI), which are: (1) *express preemption*, which occurs when Congress expresses an intent to preempt state law in the language of the statute; (2) *field preemption*, where Congress intends fully to occupy a field of regulation; and (3) *conflict preemption*, where it is impossible to comply with both federal and state law, or where state law stands as an obstacle to the accomplishment and execution of the full purposes and objectives of Congress.

The preemption inherent in the UCC's express deferral to state-law real property statutes is somewhat inefficient: (a) loans with mixed collateral (land, buildings, fixtures, improvements) will require filing and processing under two separate systems of perfection (the UCC and the land titling system), thus incurring much higher transaction costs, monitoring costs, and information asymmetry costs; and (b) where the mortgage is used as collateral, perfection of security interests will require filing and processing under two separate systems of perfection (the UCC and the real property titling system) because in most states, while the underlying real property is perfected under real property statutes, security interests in the mortgage are typically perfected using the UCC system—this incurs much greater transaction costs, information asymmetry costs, and monitoring costs.

Some states, such as California, have developed mixed systems in which the UCC coexists with the real property statutes, but as explained in Hetland and Hansen (1987), there are several problems inherent in such combinations.

Furthermore, the controversy illustrated in Shaw (1979) by the holdings in *Rucker v. State Exchange Bank*, and *In Re Bristol Associates Inc.*, on one hand and *In Re Staff Mortgage and Investment Corporation*, *Groves v. United States*, and *Black v. Sullivan*, on the other hand is moot, primarily because the note and mortgage are economically the equivalent of the deed/title. In most common law jurisdictions that use the Recording or Registration Systems of land titles, the mortgage represents an ownership interest in the underlying property, which is typically the most senior interest. The mortgagee is economically in the position of the owner until the mortgage is paid in full. The mortgage and note are recorded in the land registry just like deeds, and the same perfection rules apply to both mortgages and deeds. Hence, the mortgage represents a notice that is equivalent to the deed. Similarly, the note secured by the mortgage represents a derivative ownership interest in the property that is senior to the deed/title. The note holder is economically in the position of property owner until the note and mortgage are paid. Hence, the mortgage represents a notice that is the informational equivalent of the deed; and it is more efficient and transparent to use only one method of perfection of security interests for the deed/title, mortgage, and note as collateral.

To the extent that UCC laws can serve as complete title systems for land, improvements, and other types of real property (without use of any land title system), the Registration System and Recording System are unconstitutional for several reasons.

Due Process

Given the foregoing, the use of different systems for the perfection of security interests for land/building, mortgages, and notes constitutes a violation of the procedural and substantive due process rights. The state action consists of: (a) the mandatory use of the Recording System or Registration System for perfection of security interests; and (b) the mandatory use of two different systems for perfecting security interests in land/buildings and in notes/mortgages.

First, the Registration System and the Recording System conflict with the UCC system. The UCC and real property statutes require different documentation, filing, and perfection processes, which are typically done at different offices. Second, disputes about priority of interests are adjudicated using different sets of statutes and case laws, and this creates negative externalities. Third, for purposes of perfection of security interests in real property, the UCC preempts the Registration System and the Recording System, because the UCC operates at the state level and is made effective by state-enacted laws whereas the Registration and Recording Systems are typically local/municipal ordinances; and although the UCC expressly defers to real property statutes on the issue of perfection of security interests in real property, the inferable legislative intent of the state legislatures that created the UCCs is that the UCC would cover various types of property—and by extension, can conceivably cover perfection of security interests in land, improvements, fixtures, and buildings. Any reasonable statutory interpretation of the UCC will yield a conclusion that the UCC is sufficient for perfection of security interests in land/buildings. Fourth, where there is mixed collateral, the use of two types of perfection processes/methods significantly increases the transaction costs, monitoring costs, and information asymmetry costs of the lender and the property owner.

The Equal Protection Clause

Given that the note, deed, and mortgage are economically similar in terms of information content, purpose, and nature of interests, the use of the Recording System and Registration System of land titles unfairly discriminates between persons who hold economically similar interests (note, deed, mortgage) in the same property; and unfairly discriminates between parties who can afford the costs of the two-pronged perfection requirements and those who cannot afford the costs.

The state action consists of the government's sponsorship of, and requirement of mandatory use of, the Recording System or Registration System for real property transactions (perfection of security interests); and the government's required use of two different systems for perfecting security interests in land/buildings and in notes/mortgages. The government has legitimate property interests in enacting and implementing efficient and effective systems for property transfers and perfection of security interests. The classifications created by such discrimination do not relate to or advance the government's interest.

The Registration System constitutes a violation of the Equal Protection Clause of the U.S. Constitution, because it unfairly and illegally discriminates between various classes of persons, some of whom can be considered disadvantaged. The Registration System discriminates between parties who can afford the costs of the registration fee and those who cannot—the registration fee is typically relatively high. The Registration System discriminates between parties who can afford to litigate the government-sanctioned appraisal (upon successful challenge to title) and those who cannot; and unfairly discriminates between parties who have different amounts of knowledge about land title systems. The Registration System discriminates between the level of knowledge of government-paid lawyers and the knowledge of private lawyers; it unfairly discriminates between parties who have different amounts of knowledge about land title systems. The Registration System of land titles unfairly discriminates between parties who have access to information about the financial condition of the special restitution fund (that makes reimbursements if there is a successful challenge to title) and those parties who do not have such access to information—access to such information affects the selection of disputes, the probability of litigation, and the probability of settlement of disputes. The Registration System of land titles unfairly discriminates between two parties who are negotiating over a low-price property, and separate pairs of persons who are negotiating about a high-price property—in essence, the magnitude and quality of the legal protection provided by the Registration System vary inversely with the value/price of the property.

The Recording System constitutes a violation of the Equal Protection Clause of the U.S. Constitution because it unfairly discriminates between those who can afford the costs of recording and those who cannot; it also unfairly discriminates between those who can afford highly paid lawyers and title agents and those parties who cannot afford to hire skilled agents and lawyers to conduct title due diligence. The Recording System unfairly discriminates between those parties who can afford title insurance and those who cannot; it also discriminates between parties who have the knowledge to file relevant documents as soon as possible and those who do not have the requisite knowledge to file in a timely manner. The Recording System unfairly discriminates between owners of different types of assets—the Recording System apparently provides different levels of protection for different types of property and property owners because those who own fixtures (security interests traditionally perfected by UCC filing or the Recording System) obtain different level of protection than those that own land/buildings.

The state has valid interests in promulgating and implementing efficient system for property transfers and for perfection of security interests. However, the foregoing discriminatory classifications are not related to, and do not advance, the state's interests.

The Interstate Commerce Clause

The mandatory use of the Recording/Registration Systems for perfection of security interests in real property constitutes an omission by the state (because the UCC is more efficient than state real property statutes, and using the UCC unifies/standardizes perfection of security interest for both land/buildings and personal property), and hence a state action. The economic, psychological, statutory-construction, and implementation differences between the UCC codes of any two states in the United States are much less than the differences between the real property laws of the same states. The said state action directly burdens interstate commerce because it unfairly discriminates against out-of-state residents who have to comply with two sets of "foreign" laws, and hence, incur higher transaction costs and monitoring costs.

CONCLUSION

Title systems remain a fundamental element of real property transactions in both developed and developing systems. The Recording System and Registration System are the basic classes of title systems—other second-tier systems (such as fee simple, ownership-by-lease, leasehold interests) operate within the Recording or Registration System frameworks. The unconstitutionality of the Recording Systems and the Registration System has substantial adverse effects on the efficiency of real estate markets, most of which have not been addressed sufficiently.

REFERENCES

Hetland, J., and C. Hansen. 1987. The "mixed collateral" amendments to California's commercial code – Covert repeal of California's real property foreclosure and anti-deficiency provisions or exercise in futility? *California Law Review* 75 (1): 185–216.

Shaw, G. M. 1979. Security interests in notes and mortgages: Determining the applicable law. *Columbia Law Review* 79 (7): 1414–1433.

CHAPTER 11

Constitutionality of Real Estate Investment Trusts

Despite significant evolution of real estate investment trusts (REITs), real estate markets, and associated state laws during the past 40 years, under U.S. laws, REITs are unconstitutional. The number and market values of REITs in the United States has grown dramatically during the past 20 years. The economic consequences of this REIT evolution are manifested in institutional investors' portfolio allocations and corporate governance efforts, real estate prices, interest rates, household economics, and other factors. Unfortunately, despite the many legal and economic problems inherent in REITs, some countries (e.g., Australia, China/Hong Kong, Canada, Japan, etc.) have enacted REIT statutes that are very similar to U.S. REIT laws (in terms of securities regulation and tax consequences), despite the many legal and economic problems inherent in U.S. REITs (see this book's web site for relevant articles and books). Many countries are considering introducing U.S.-style REITs laws.

Under U.S. laws, the REIT is a tax overlay that is defined in Sections 856–860 of the U.S. Internal Revenue Code (the IRC), the REIT Modernization Act of 1999 (the RMA), and the American Job Creation Act of 2004 (the AJCA). Japanese REITs are created pursuant to amendments to the Investment Trust Law (the Law Concerning Investment Trusts and Investment Corporations of Japan, Law No. 198 of June 4, 1951, as amended) and the listing rules of the Tokyo Stock Exchange. Under the Investment Trust Law, Japanese REITs (J REITs) can be established either as an investment corporation or as an investment trust. J REITs can either be open-ended or closed-ended. Closed-end J REITs are eligible for listing on the Tokyo Stock Exchange (the first two J REITs were listed on the Tokyo Stock Exchange in September 10, 2001). J REITs that are investment corporations can deduct dividends as expenses for tax purposes and also benefit from reduced real property acquisition tax and registration and license tax on their real estate acquisitions. The tax treatment for individuals who invest in J REITs is the same as for ordinary shares.

Korean REITs (K REITs) are created pursuant to the Real Estate Investment Company Act of July 2001, and the listing rules of the Korea Stock Exchange. Two forms of REIT are permitted—K REITs and corporate restructuring REITs (CR-REITs). CR-REITs have greater tax advantages and so are more attractive to investors. Both K REITs and CR-REITs must be established with a corporate structure. CR-REITs have finite lives (typically five years), while K REITs have unlimited lives. K REITs must have at least 50 billion won of capital. K REITs must be listed on a stock exchange, unlike CR-REITs, which are required to list as soon as they meet the eligibility requirements for listing on the Korea Stock Exchange or the Korea Securities Dealers Automated Quotation. CR-REITs must invest at least 70 percent of their assets in real estate assets being sold by companies undergoing restructuring due to insolvency or reorganization, or by companies that intend to use the proceeds of sale to retire debt obligations. K REITs are granted a 50 percent exemption on acquisition tax and registration tax. Neither K REITs nor investors in K REITs receive any tax benefits relating to dividend payments from K REITs. CR-REITs are fully exempt from acquisition tax and registration tax and can deduct dividends for tax purposes if they comply with the 90 percent dividend payout rule.

Singapore's REIT rules are set out in the *Securities and Futures Act of 2001*, the Monetary Authority of Singapore's *Code on Collective Investment Schemes* and the guidelines relating to property funds set out in Appendix 2 of the Code. Singapore REITs (S REITs) can be established either as a corporate or as a trust structure. S REITs are subject to prohibitions on engaging in property development activities, investing in unlisted property development companies, vacant land, and mortgages. Only an S REIT established as a unit trust can apply to the Inland Revenue Authority of Singapore to pass on to investors any tax paid by the S REIT as a tax credit, so that tax is paid at one level only. There are no other tax exemptions for S REITs.

Hong Kong REIT laws are codified in the Hong Kong Securities and Futures Commission's (SFC) *Code on Real Estate Investment Trusts* (HK-REITs Code). H REITs must be established as Hong Kong domiciled unit trusts. Corporate structures are not permitted. H REITs can either be listed on the stock exchange of Hong Kong Limited or unlisted. If unlisted, an H REIT must offer an annual redemption facility for up to 10 percent of its units in issue. There are no tax benefits for the H REIT itself, for investors in the H REIT, or for persons transferring investments to the H REIT.

Canadian REIT laws are codified in Chapter 21 (Bill C-70), and An Act to Amend the Income Tax Act, the Income Tax Application Rules and related Acts (Part V – Amendments Relating to Real Estate Investment Trusts) (1995). Canadian REIT rules are similar to U.S. REIT rules.

The European Public REIT Association (2010), Allens (2009), The Trust Company and Baker & McKenzie (2011), and Ernst & Young (2010) provide more detailed descriptions of the REIT statutes and characteristics of REITs in many countries. The following are theories and hypotheses of some of the problems inherent in the formation and use of REITs.

REITs were initially introduced in the United States to: (a) make commercial real estate more accessible to individual investors, and (b) increase liquidity in the real estate sector. The operations and performance of REITs have since diverged from this primary purpose. REITs have evolved significantly in the United States and abroad as noted in various articles and the legislative history of new REIT statutes/laws—in terms of REIT-qualification rules, REIT operations, financing, and disclosure rules. However, there have been many problems inherent in the use of the REIT format. The U.S. Securities and Exchange Commission (SEC) has investigated or prosecuted many companies for illegal conduct pertaining to REITs, such as (a) sales of nonregistered private REITs and (b) misleading statements about the nature of REIT dividends. See "Recovering REIT Losses" (Stoltmann and Burke 2011), which states in part:

> *The SEC's recent settlement with W.P. Carey is illustrative. The SEC settled a non-traded REIT kickback scheme with W.P. Carey. According to the settlement, W.P. Carey paid nearly $10 million in undisclosed compensation to a broker-dealer that sold shares of W.P. Carey's non-traded REITs to the public.*

Published by the law firm Stoltmann Law Offices, "Recovering REIT Losses" goes on to say:

> *According to our investigation, U.S. investors were defrauded out of over $6.2 billion through the purchase and sale of non listed REITs in the last four years alone. Non-listed REITs, including Inland American Real Estate Trust Inc., Piedmont/Wells, Inland, Behringer Harvard, Cole, Desert Capital, Dividend Capital, Grubb & Ellis, Whitestone, and KBS, were high risk, expensive and illiquid investments not suitable or appropriate for many retail investors, especially those who were elderly or retired.* ***1) Massive Sales Commissions and Expenses:*** *Driving the sales of approximately $12 billion a year in private REITs last year are massive sales commissions and fees, often running as high as 15%. REITs are not bought but*

rather sold by commission hungry financial advisors. 2) ***A Conservative Pitch:*** *Financial advisors across the country sold non-traded REITs like Inland American Real Estate Trust as an investment appropriate for elderly or retired clients who were looking for conservative investments. Clients were told by financial advisors (and the marketing material associated with the REITs) they could expect a stable value investment that would spin off a conservative 5% to 7% a year. What makes the commission and fee payout even worse is that many of these charges are hidden from the investors. The SEC's recent settlement with W.P. Carey is illustrative. Ameriprise Financial Services also got caught with its hand in the cookie jar. The firm agreed in 2009 to pay $17.3 million to settle charges by the SEC that it received undisclosed payments to sell REITs to customers. 3)* ***Artificially Stable Share Price:*** *A major problem in 2008 and 2009 for the holders on private REITs like Inland American Real Estate Trust Inc. is the inaccurate valuations of these investments. Due to the concentration in highly illiquid investments and the magic of fair value accounting, the share price of non-traded REITs almost always stays at the magical $10 a share level. It is extraordinarily rare to see the share price change in any material way during the holding period... shares of privately traded REITs with little or no market are priced by the same REIT managers and operators who selected properties for inclusion in the REIT portfolio. In essence, they are giving themselves their own report cards and this creates a significant conflict of interest. As of September 2009, after one of the worst real estate crashes in U.S. history, REIT operators and brokerage firms have finally started marking down the investments on customer statements. Unfortunately, the markdowns still do not come close to valuing these investments at their true value. The losses are much more severe. 4)* ***Undisclosed Returns of Principal:*** *The dividend structure of non-traded REITs helped lull investors into a false sense of security that everything was fine with their investment. With non-traded REITs, the dividend is often greater than the operating cash flow generated from the real estate. Yet what is distributed is still called a dividend. If the real estate cannot generate cash from operations sufficient to meet the represented dividend then other cash sources are used including loans, cash reserves, and proceeds from the sale of new securities and/or assets. Cash received from all of these sources is a return of capital, not a dividend. 5)* ***Complete Absence of Liquidity:*** *One of the biggest problems for retail investors with non-listed REITs is the lack of* *liquidity. FINRA has warned brokerage firms on multiple occasions that the liquidity of an investment is something that must be taken into consideration before making a recommendations (See NASD to Members 03–71: "The type of due diligence investigation that is appropriate will vary from product to product. However, there are some common features that members must understand about products.... The features include, but are not limited to: the liquidity of the product.")* ***Conclusion.*** *Financial advisors at firms like LPL Linsco Private Ledger, Merrill Lynch, Citigroup Smith Barney, Raymond James, ING and Morgan Stanley sold REITs and non traded REITs to retail investors. Many times, the true risks were not made clear to investors. Often, the investments were grossly unsuitable for the clients based on the investor's age, investment objectives and financial resources. Often, the large commissions blinded financial advisors to the true risks of these investments and caused brokerage firms to look the other way. Fortunately, some or all of the losses might be recoverable through FINRA arbitration claims or lawsuits.*

During 2009, the U.S. REIT market nearly crashed but the imminent crash was avoided by a surge of equity offerings by U.S. REITs at deeply discounted prices. Table 11.1 lists a sample of secondary equity offerings by U.S. REITs (listed by their stock symbols) during two months in winter/spring 2009. The table shows the extent of dilution of REITs' equity, in their quest to reduce their heavy debt burdens (amounts raised were in millions of U.S. dollars).

Table 11.2 shows the debt maturity schedules and credit ratings for some U.S. REITs (denoted by their stock symbols; the amounts are in billions of U.S. dollars).

The significant dilution that resulted from the REITs' equity offerings and the credit ratings of these REITs indicate that the credit quality of many U.S. REITs was below investment grade.

Similarly, during 2009, the Japanese REIT market crashed. Figure 11.1 shows the price trends for J-REITs. For more information, see the May 27, 2009, article "J-REITs to Get JPY1 Trillion Bail-Out, But Investors Aren't Buying Just Yet" (Whitten 2009), which states in part:

J-REITs remain under pressure because banks will renew existing loans but not provide new loans, and as J-REIT sponsors themselves fail, this seriously hinders the J-REITs ability to get refinancing and rollover maturing bond issues as property appraisers have sharply

TABLE 11.1 Secondary Offerings of Some U.S. REITs

				Price/Consensus FFO	
	Lead Underwriter	Amount Raised	% Dilution	Before Announce	Current
SPG	GS	1,150	8%	8.2x	8.5x
OEH	DB	149	56%	91.1x	99.7x
WRE	Wachovia	123	11%	10.5x	10.0x
REG	Wachovia	325	14%	11.3x	10.0x
DDR	N/A	105	25%	1.0x	2.0x
EQY	MS	107	10%	13.0x	11.5x
HCP	ML	**440**	8%	9.7x	**9.9x**
CLI	ML	**228**	14%	7.9x	7.2x
VNO	ML	**618**	8%	8.4x	10.0x
WRI	ML	**459**	37%	6.0x	6.5x
DRE	ML	575	47%	3.8x	4.8x
DRH	ML	86	20%	6.0x	8.2x
AKR	ML	69	17%	10.7x	12.5x
PLD	ML	1,154	66%	4.4x	5.3x
VTR	ML	350	10%	9.9x	10.9x
KIM	ML	748	39%	4.2x	7.8x
OFC	ML	73	5%	9.2x	12.1x
AMB	ML	577	47%	7.4x	35.1x
SPG	ML	543	6%	5.5x	8.5x
ARE	ML	308	25%	6.5x	6.4x
Total/Average			24%	11.7x	14.4x
REIT Average				8.4x	9.6x

GS = Goldman Sachs; ML = Merrill Lynch; DB = Deutsche Bank; MS = Morgan Stanley. Stock symbols of REITs are in the first column.
Source: http://static.seekingalpha.com/uploads/2009/5/13/saupload_dilution_1.jpg.

lowered appraised values particularly on residential properties due to falling residential property prices. Fund raising alternatives, such as issuing preferred shares, are not an option for J-REITs. As a result, there were only 92 property acquisitions by J-REITs in FY08 versus 501 in FY07, and the market for J-REITs and private real estate funds declined by 1% in second-half 2008 to around $217 billion. While talking about it since March, the Japanese government (specifically, the Financial Services Agency and the Land Ministry)

TABLE 11.2 Debt Maturity Schedules and Credit Ratings of Some U.S. REITs

	Retail REITs				Office REITs			
	SPG A3/A–	KIM Baa1/BBB+	WRI Baa2/BBB	REG Baa2/BBB+	BXP Baa2/A–	VNO Baa2/BBB	CLI Baa2/BBB	HIW Ba1/BBB–
Unsecured Debt Maturities, 2009	0.9	0.2	0.1	0.1	0.0	0.2	0.2	0.1
Unsecured Debt Maturities, 2010	1.1	0.2	0.1	0.2	0.0	0.2	0.2	0.2
Unsecured Debt Maturities, 2011	2.5	0.4	1.3	0.5	0.1	1.3	0.3	0.1
Unsecured Debt Maturities, 2009–2010	**2.0**	**0.4**	**0.2**	**0.3**	**0.0**	**0.4**	**0.4**	**0.3**
Unsecured Debt Maturities, 2009–2011	**4.5**	**0.8**	**1.5**	**0.8**	**0.1**	**1.7**	**0.7**	**0.4**

	Multifamily REITs				Industrial REITs			
	EQR Baal/BBB+	AVB Baa1/BBB+	BRE Baa2/BBB	UDR Baa2/BBB	PLD Baa2/BBB–	AMB Baa1/BBB	FR Baa2/BBB–	Total
Unsecured Debt Maturities, 2009	0.1	0.2	0.2	0.2	0.3	0.1	0.1	
Unsecured Debt Maturities, 2010	0.0	0.2	0.2	0.3	3.4	0.6	0.0	
Unsecured Debt Maturities, 2011	0.7	0.5	0.3	0.4	0.5	0.7	0.2	
Unsecured Debt Maturities, 2009–2010	**0.1**	**0.4**	**0.4**	**0.5**	**3.7**	**0.7**	**0.1**	**9.9**
Unsecured Debt Maturities, 2009–2011	**0.8**	**0.9**	**0.7**	**0.9**	**4.2**	**1.4**	**0.3**	**19.7**

Source: http://static.seekingalpha.com/uploads/2009/5/13/saupload_reit_maturities.jpg.

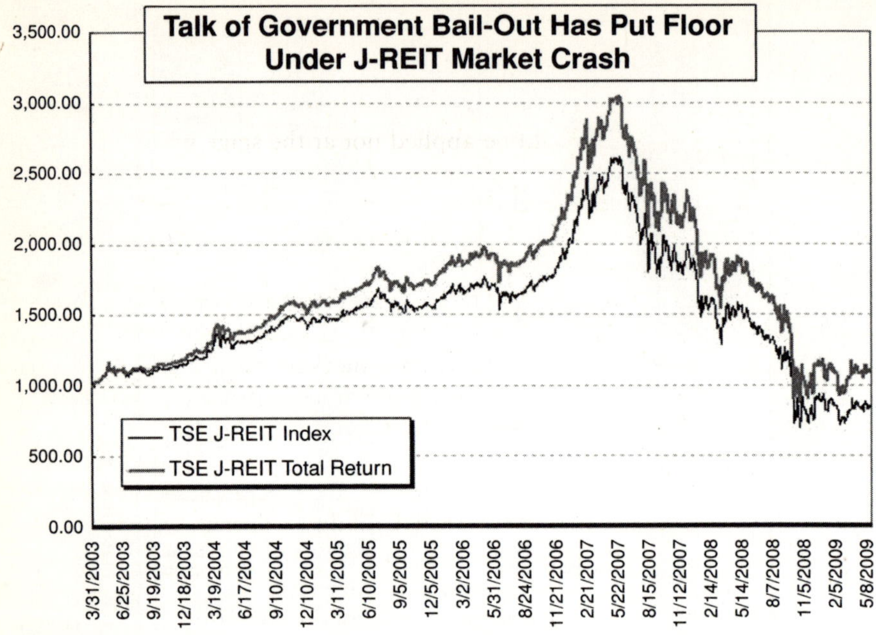

FIGURE 11.1 Japanese REIT Data
Source: www.istockanalyst.com/article/viewarticle/articleid/3245416.

> *appears to be in the final stages of pumping over $10 billion into the J-REIT market and removing impediments to consolidation in the industry. The J-REIT survivors will probably include, a) Japan Real Estate (8952.T), b) Global One Real Estate (8958.T), c) Mori Trust Sogo REIT (8961.T), d) Orix Jreit (8954.T) and e) Fukuoka Reit (8968.T).*

In the case of the U.S. REITs, the state action is the U.S. IRS's requirement that REITs comply with the asset tests, the income tests, and minimum dividend payouts in order to maintain REIT status. Similarly, in other countries that have REIT statutes, such statutes require compliance with the asset test, the income tests, and minimum dividend payouts in order to maintain REIT status. The obvious counterargument is that the corporate entity does not have to choose the REIT format. The elective and "voluntary" nature of the choice of REIT status does not preclude the viability of the state action—the state-action element applies because once the entity has elected to become a REIT, the REIT statutes then apply to current and future holders of the REIT Beneficial Interests. It is not the elective nature that determines whether the REIT statutes trigger a state action, but it is the enactment of the REIT statutes and the required compliance for those that elect REIT status. This raises the issue of the scope and timing of the state action test. The test for compulsion should be applied not at the stage where the entity is choosing the appropriate type of corporate form, but rather, when it has chosen the REIT format. Hence, the state-action test should be applied only when there is any type of statutory, implied, or express requirement for performance of any act.

The Substantial Inducement Theory was introduced in a prior chapter and applies to REITs. With regard to REITs, the government's interest in fair taxation and need to make the capital markets more accessible to individual investors can be achieved using much less intrusive means, and is far outweighed by the REIT's: (a) protected property interests (privacy and expectations interests) in its ability to make uninfluenced crucial financial decisions (i.e., dividend policy)—this interest arises from state corporation laws; (b) property interests in its financial flexibility—this interest arises from expectations, norm, and state constitutional laws and corporation laws; (c) property interests in absence of restrictions that limit the types of investors it can attract (i.e., REIT ownership restriction rules)—this interest arises from state constitutional laws, corporation laws, and custom; and (d) property interests in its ability to operate its business with minimally intrusive restrictions.

The Substantial Inducement Theory is relevant because there are many instances where the burden of proof required to establish compulsion is too high, or very expensive to achieve. In such cases the facts and/or reasonable inference should be adequate to establish a deprivation of constitutional rights. Furthermore, most perpetrators who want to deprive rights may know of the compulsion requirement and can easily tailor their actions to avoid evidence. Furthermore, in most developed capitalist societies, incentives (grants, tax credits, sweepstakes, gifts, promotions, etc.) are an established topic and are widely applied by private entities and government agencies in various aspects of life. The compulsion requirement does not incorporate the incentive phenomenon/trend, which grows and permeates more of daily life as time progresses.

THE REIT OWNERSHIP-CONCENTRATION RULES ARE UNCONSTITUTIONAL

REIT ownership concentration rules are prevalent in most countries—see Ernst & Young (2010), Allens (2009), The Trust Company and Baker &

McKenzie (2011), and European Public REIT Association (2010). These clauses in REIT statutes typically restrict or prevent what may be deemed majority ownership stakes in REITs.

The REIT Ownership Rules Constitute Violations of the Equal Protection Clause

IRC, RMA, and AJCA REIT-qualification ownership concentration restrictions are onerous, constitute violations of the Equal Protection Clause (under the U.S. Constitution), and prevent potentially shareholder-maximizing transactions such as strategic alliances, joint ventures, and executive compensation. Under these rules, REIT equity must be owned by at least 100 different people/entities, and one person/entity cannot own more than 9 percent of the REIT's equity.

The state action involved is the enactment of, and the required mandatory compliance with, REIT ownership concentration rules. The REIT ownership-restriction rules unfairly discriminate between: (a) investors who invest in REITs and investors who invest in other types of real estate entities such as LLPs, LLCs, Trusts, and C-Corporations; (b) REITs that seek to consummate certain corporate transactions (e.g., minority investments, joint ventures) and REITs that do not; (c) investors whose investment purposes include large equity stakes and control, and those that do not seek such purposes; (d) REITs whose bonus and incentive compensation plans/systems focus on or emphasize equity grants, and REITs whose bonus/incentive systems emphasize cash payments; (e) REITs that have some type of employee stock ownership plan and REITs that do not have such plans; and (f) REITs that are financially stable and do not seek capital, and REITs that seek to raise equity capital—by implication, also discriminates between REITs that have high credit ratings and REITs that have low credit ratings because the low-rated REITs are more likely to seek equity funding and will be restricted by these rules.

Furthermore, the REIT ownership rules do not serve any meaningful economic purpose and do not substantially advance any legitimate government interest because: (a) even with more than 100 shareholders, there can still be concentration of ownership (e.g., fund families); and (b) the 9 percent restriction can be easily overcome by using shareholder agreements, proxies, and derivative securities.

The above-mentioned classifications (on which the unfair discriminating conduct is based) do not serve any compelling state interest and the classifications are not substantially related to serving any state interest.

The REIT Ownership-Concentration Rules Constitute Illegal Restrictions of Trade and Interstate Commerce

IRC, RMA, and AJCA REIT-qualification ownership restrictions (concentration) are onerous, constitute illegal restrictions of trade and interstate commerce (under the U.S. Constitution), and prevent potentially shareholder-maximizing transactions such as strategic alliances, joint ventures, and executive compensation. These rules include: (a) the 100-or-more persons rule, (b) the five-or-fewer rule, and (c) the 9 percent-or-lower rule. The rules were stated in IRC Section 856 and modified by the RMA and the AJCA. Under these rules, a REIT's equity must be owned by at least 100 different people/entities, and one person/entity cannot own more than 9 percent of the REIT's equity.

The IRC, RMA, and AJCA REIT-qualification ownership concentration rules constitute illegal restrictions of trade and interstate commerce for several reasons. First, REITs and real estate companies have protected property interests in the ability to execute transactions without undue and unreasonable limitations—this property right arises from state corporation laws, customs, and expectations. The statutory REIT ownership rules constitute a direct violation of these constitutional rights.

The IRC, RMA, and AJCA REIT-qualification rules prevent or make it more costly or sometimes impossible to consummate many types of normal corporate transactions that can enhance REIT shareholder value and are typically interstate commerce—such as acquisition of minority/majority stakes in REITs, private placements of REIT securities, joint ventures by REITs, and REIT purchase of real estate using equity (Campbell 2002). REITs have to spend more resources to devise ways of circumventing these rules—often at significant costs (advisory fees, etc.). Hence, these rules create significant and real opportunity costs for the REIT and its shareholders. The results are that: (a) the REIT is much more constrained financially, operationally, and psychologically, and has much less financial flexibility; (b) agency problems are more pronounced; (c) REITs' managers are more prone to adverse selection problems in their choices of projects and transactions; and (d) these constraints are reinforced in the compensation and incentive systems of REITs.

The IRC/RMA/AJCA REIT-ownership restrictions do not serve any meaningful economic purpose because: (a) even with more than 100 shareholders, there can still be concentration of ownership (e.g., a family of funds that are managed by one investment management company can purchase more than 20 percent of a REIT's equity); (b) the 9 percent restriction can be easily overcome by using shareholder agreements, proxies, and derivative securities; and (c) the rules can be circumvented—as in where a large company (with many subsidiaries) acts as a "person," and its subsidiaries can then purchase more than the statutory permitted percentage of a REIT's equity.

The REIT ownership-restriction rules do not advance any legitimate government purpose. Individual investors do not necessarily get more protection by restricting the ownership of REITs' equity. As mentioned, the rules can be easily circumvented. These REIT ownership-restriction rules create and increase transaction costs, monitoring costs, and compliance costs—all of which burden interstate commerce.

The IRC/RMA/AJCA REIT ownership-restriction rules unfairly discriminate between personal properties that are located in different states that have different personal property laws, and different laws about the transfer of personal property and real property.

The IRC/RMA/AJCA REIT-ownership-restriction rules unfairly discriminate between REITs located in different states that have different corporation laws. The REIT's underlying corporate entity can be a partnership, LLC, C-Corporation, Trust, which are governed by different state laws. Hence, the classification of what an "equity interest" is varies dramatically depending on the state (where the REIT is located or where it was incorporated) and the type of entity (C-Corporation versus LLC versus Trust).

The REIT Ownership-Concentration Rules Constitute Violations of the "Right of Association" and "Right to Contract" Clauses of the U.S. Constitution

The ownership-concentration rules for REIT qualification under the IRS Tax Code constitute a violation of individuals' constitutional right of association and their right to contract freely for several reasons. Such rules directly impinge on people's constitutionally guaranteed right to associate with whomever they want, in manners they choose, and in accordance with the laws. The rules are not mandatory for similar tax rules and for corporate entities (such as C-Corps, LLPs, and LLCs).

The rules do not serve any meaningful economic purpose. The rules substantially affect distinct investment-backed expectations of investors. The rules completely change the economic viability of REITs, because it limits their activities and potential profitability. The rules are unduly and relatively oppressive. The rule prevents REITs from entering into potentially profitable contracts including strategic alliances, acquisitions of properties with equity interests, and executive compensation.

On their face, the rules do not necessarily decrease the incidence of crime and misconduct. Furthermore, the rules are not effective and can be easily circumvented, as follows:

1. The 100-or-more shareholders rule
   - One company can form 100 subsidiaries, each of which can then buy all shares of the REIT.
   - Owners of REIT equity interests can use proxies and shareholder agreements to circumvent this rule.
   - Having more than 100 owners of equity interest does not guarantee elimination of ownership concentration.
   - OTC derivative securities transactions can be used to obtain the economic equivalent of ownership concentration.
   - The rule does not provide any clear protection to investors. The federal government's interest in protecting indigenes and citizens is clearly outweighed by (a) the profitability of the transactions otherwise blocked by this rule and (b) the existence of federal and state securities laws and corporations laws.
2. The 9 percent-or-less ownership test
   - One person/company can use 10 or more controlled entities/companies to acquire the REIT's equity.
   - One person/company can use proxies and shareholder agreements to control more than 9 percent of voting power in the REIT.
   - The rule impedes potentially profitable transactions such as equity-financed property acquisitions, joint ventures, strategic alliances, employee pension plans, and executive compensation.
   - The rule does not necessarily decrease the incidence of crime or misconduct.
   - The rule is discriminatory because similar rules do not apply to similar tax codes and corporate entities (such as C-Corporations, LLPs, and LLCs).
   - The rule does not provide any clear protection to investors. The federal government's interest in protecting indigenes and citizens is clearly outweighed by (a) the profitability of the transactions otherwise blocked by this rule and (b) the existence of federal and state securities laws and corporation laws.

The REIT Ownership-Concentration Rules Violate the Takings Clause of the U.S. Constitution

The ownership-concentration rules for REIT qualification under the IRS Tax Code, the RMA, and the AJCA constitute a violation of the Takings Clause of the U.S. Constitution because the rules do not apply to other tax codes or forms of corporate entities, are not commonly accepted business methods, and result in substantial monitoring costs and compliance costs. These rules include: (a) the 100-or-more persons rule, (b) the five-or-fewer rule, and (c) the 9 percent-or-lower rule. The rules were stated in IRC Section 856 and modified by the RMA and the AJCA. It is important to note that: (1) Takings occur outside the real property industry—the doctrine applies to all types of property, whether tangible or intangible; and (2) Takings also cover implied restrictions and temporary restrictions on use by the government—this is in contrast to the more typical express and compensated taking of property by the government.

Furthermore, the REIT's and its shareholders' property interests in fair treatment, property interests in freedom-to-contract as they see fit, and property interest in voluntary dividend policies (these property interests have monetary/economic value) far outweigh the government's interest in protecting investors.

The U.S. Supreme Court decisions on the takings issue has not directly addressed the REIT-qualification statutes.

The REIT ownership-restriction rules constitute a Takings because of the following reasons. First, REITs have constitutionally protected property interests in fair and effective laws that reduce their transaction costs, financing costs, and operating costs (such property interests arise from expectations, norms, state constitutional laws, and contracts). The ownership-restriction rule does not provide any meaningful protection for investors—and can be circumvented. Second, the ownership-restriction rules do not apply to other entities—such as partnerships and S-Corporations. Third, the REIT entity has a property interest in determining appropriate ownership policies—this is a property expectancy that also implicates the right to association. The REIT and its shareholders have property interests in fair treatment and due process. The ownership-restriction rules deprive the REIT and its shareholders of these property interests. Fourth, the state action effectively deprives the REIT of said property interests in the right to equal protection of the law—these property interests arises from state contract laws, state property laws, state constitutional laws, norms, and expectations. Fifth, the general public benefits indirectly from said Takings because the REITs pay dividends to holders of their equity interests, and REIT dividends buoy stock markets. Empirical studies have shown that there is significant information content in REIT dividends—REIT dividends are generally good news that affects volatility and the propensity of other corporate entities to pay dividends. Sixth, the REIT and the holders of beneficiary interests in the REITs do not receive any just compensation from the U.S. government for these Takings. The REIT actually loses money/value due to increased processing costs, financing costs, and transaction costs. In essence, the tax benefits received by the REIT as a result of compliance with the ownership concentration rule are far outweighed by the sum of the following factors: (1) the increase in the REIT's bankruptcy risk, and (2) management's reduced flexibility. Seventh, the Takings "public use" in this instance is the creation of a tax status (REIT). The REIT-qualification rules do not serve any meaningful economic purpose. The same or similar objectives (of increased participation in public real estate markets by individual investors) can be achieved through other more efficient means. The REIT-qualification rules have increased the incidence of crime and misconduct in the United States.

The Takings implicit in the REIT ownership-restriction rules do not conform to any of the above-mentioned types of Takings because there is no physical occupation; there is no "Total Regulatory Taking"; there are no "exactions that violate the *Nollan* and *Dolan* standards"; and there is no "Penn-Central Type" Taking.

THE REGULATION OF REITs BY U.S. STATES CONSTITUTES VIOLATIONS OF THE U.S. CONSTITUTION

Most U.S. states have enacted various types of laws that affect the formation and operations of REITs such as the following: (a) corporations statutes—different states permit the incorporation of different types of companies and partnerships, and most of these corporate entities can elect REIT status; (b) different states have enacted different tax laws that apply to REITs; and (c) the trust statutes of some states also affect REITs.

The Commerce Clause of the U.S. Constitution

The regulation of REITs by U.S. states constitutes violations of the Commerce Clause of the U.S. Constitution. Some U.S. states regulate REITs in various ways, some of which are described as follows. Some states require that REITs comply with certain state tax codes in order to avoid corporate taxation—this discriminates against, and hinders interstate commerce to the extent that other states do not require similar compliance with their state tax laws. Some states require that REITs comply with state trust laws—this discriminates against, and hinders interstate commerce to the extent that other states do not require similar compliance with their state laws pertaining to trusts. Some states tax REITs (e.g., sales taxes, franchise taxes, property taxes). For any given state, such taxes discriminate against and hinder interstate commerce to the extent that other states do not require similar taxes, or other states have lower franchise taxes and/or sales taxes. Some states require compliance with state securities laws (blue sky laws, etc.)—this discriminates against, and hinders interstate commerce to the extent that other states do not require similar compliance with any state securities laws.

The state governments' interest in protecting its indigenes and earning tax revenues is far outweighed by the following factors: (1) the redundancy created by some of the parallel state laws—there are additional monetary costs and psychological costs incurred by companies who must comply with both overlapping federal and state laws that regulate the same activity; (2) a substantial portion (in most cases, the majority) of the transactions of most REITs are interstate commerce, and hence REITs should be regulated primarily by federal laws; (3) the applicable and applied state laws may conflict with IRS REIT tax rules; and (4) the states can earn revenues from other taxes—franchise taxes, property taxes, and taxes on dividends paid to investors that live in the state.

Hence, REIT-qualification statutes contravene the Commerce Clause of the U.S. Constitution. The U.S. Congress enacted the National Securities Market Improvement Act of 1996 (NSMIA), which significantly preempts state laws that require registration or place conditions on the registration of many types of securities. Notwithstanding the enactment of the NSMIA, states remain active players in the regulation of securities, and any prospective offeror must comply with state blue-sky laws.

Hence, in order to conform with the U.S. Constitution, new federal laws are required for REITs in order to define roles and obligations pertaining to the form of corporate entity, rights of equity owners, fiduciary duties, and so on.

The Equal Protection Clause

The regulation of REITs by U.S. state laws constitutes violations of the Equal Protection Clause of the U.S. Constitution. IRC Section 856, the RMA, and the AJCA define REITs as a *Trust*, but do not describe any specific trust laws. Thus, the most reasonable interpretation of IRC Section 856 is that state trust laws will govern such trusts—that is, the laws of the state where the original underlying entity (LLP, LP, C-Corp, trust) was registered or the state where it has its principal office. However, state trust laws and corporations' laws differ, sometimes significantly. Hence, IRC Section 856 and the RMA/AJCA REIT-qualification laws unfairly discriminate between any two REIT entities that register or have their principal places of business in different states. The state action involved is the enactments of, and the required mandatory compliance with REIT-qualification laws. The key issue is that the REIT entity is unique and Section 856/RMA/AJCA REIT rules are pervasive and affect all aspects of the REIT's operations; hence, implicitly appending different state laws to Section 856/RMA/AJCA (based on the location of the REIT's principal offices or state of registration) eliminates constitutionally required uniformity of laws. Furthermore, state trust laws are not specialized or dominant, and do not require special processes—state-law trusts can be formed orally, and the terms of trusts are flexible. Hence, the U.S. Congress's failure to enact accompanying federal trust law in the REIT-qualification laws is a major omission and a state action that constitutes a violation of the equal protection clause, because if there is no uniformity (at least 50 different state trust and corporate laws for each of three possible forms of entities—C-Corporation, Trust, and association) in treatment of REITs nationwide, then the Equal Protection Clause of the U.S. Constitution is triggered. The omission is a state action because the U.S. Congress is the only and the best positioned entity to enact such uniform trust laws, and Congress has a duty to enact laws that reduce transaction costs and compliance costs, and provide the same magnitude of legal protection to all similarly situated parties.

Under present U.S. rules, the original pre-REIT and post-REIT-qualification entity can be a C-Corp, taxable association, or Trust, and since the REIT-qualification rules are essentially an overlay, there can be substantial divergences in capital structure among REITs and reduced comparability of financial statements of REITs. Furthermore, U.S. states have different debtor-creditor laws that result in different defenses to claims pertaining to financial distress of the REIT. Hence, application of IRC Sections 856–860, the RMA, or AJCA causes significant differentials in: (1) legal liability; (2) financial disclosure of the entity; (3) capital structure; (4) cost of capital; (5) the state-law fiduciary duties required from boards of directors (C-Corporations), Trustees (state law trusts), and board of managers (associations); all of which constitutes violations of the Equal Protection Clause of the U.S. Constitution.

The above-mentioned classifications (on which the unfair discriminating conduct is based) do not serve any compelling state interest, and the classifications are not substantially related to serving any state interest.

THE ENTIRE REIT-QUALIFICATION STATUTES (IRC SECTION-856, RMA, AND AJCA REIT-QUALIFICATION RULES) ARE UNCONSTITUTIONAL

The REIT-qualification rules are statutes that define REITs; they typically include asset tests, dividend tests, ownership tests, activity tests, and income tests. In the United States, the REIT-qualification rules are IRC Sections 856–860, the RMA, and the AJCA.

The REIT-qualification rules in many countries are similar to the U.S. REIT-qualification rules, which violate the Equal Protection Clause, the Due Process Clause (substantive due process), the Takings Clause, the Free Speech Clause, and the Right-to-Contract Clause. In most common law countries there are limitations on the enforcement powers of the legislature in terms of preemption of state/municipal statutes. In the United States, the Congress's enforcement power under the fifth section of the Fourteenth Amendment is limited, and sometimes results in conflicts of laws—as in the enactment of the REIT statutes. Also, the regulation of REITs by U.S. states constitutes violations of the Equal Protection Clause.

The Spending Clause of the U.S. Constitution

Generally, the U.S. Congress is deemed to exceed its powers under the Spending Clause only when it aims to suppress ideas. The U.S. REIT-qualification rules (IRC, RMA, and AJCA) constitute a tax subsidy because they eliminate taxes at the corporate level; hence, they are an element of the federal government's fiscal planning and are covered by the Spending Clause of the U.S. Constitution.

The REIT-qualification rules effectively suppress ideas by substantially reducing REIT management's flexibility to implement strategies where the said ideas pertain to creative dividend policy, investor relations, operations strategies, capital-raising strategies, and restructuring ideas. Hence, the REIT-qualification rules violate the Spending Clause of the U.S. Constitution.

The REIT-Qualification Asset Tests and Income Tests Constitute Illegal Restrictions of Trade and Violations of the Interstate Commerce Clause

Under these rules, at least 75 percent of the REIT's assets should be in the form of certain assets (asset test), and the REIT must earn at least 75 percent of its income from certain sources (the income test). IRC, RMA, and AJCA REIT-qualification asset tests and income tests are onerous, constitute illegal restrictions of trade and interstate commerce (under the U.S. Constitution), and prevent potential shareholder-maximizing transactions such as investments, strategic alliances, joint ventures, and executive compensation. The reasons follow.

First, in some cases, compliance with the asset test and the income test is complicated, and constitutes effective restrictions on investment in certain types of securities. These assets and sources of income include publicly traded securities. Thus, there are issues of measurement dates, timing, and purpose of investment (available-for-sale, trading, held-to-maturity, etc.). Hence, the REIT has substantial leeway to manipulate earnings by misclassifying securities and assets. These rules effectively force REITs to make choices of investment that minimize their probability of noncompliance—which may eliminate investment in certain types of securities.

Second, REITs and real estate companies have protected property interests in the ability to execute transactions without undue and unreasonable limitations—this property right arises from state corporations laws, customs, and expectations.

Third, the IRC/RMA/AJCA REIT-qualification rules prevent, or make it more costly for, the REIT to consummate many types of normal corporate transactions that can enhance REIT shareholder value and are typically interstate commerce—such as the REIT's acquisition of minority/majority stakes in other companies, joint ventures by REITs, purchase of certain loans and debt obligations by REITs, and REIT purchase of real estate using equity (Campbell 2002). The results are that the REIT is much more constrained financially, operationally, and psychologically, and has much less financial flexibility; its agency problems are more pronounced; the REIT's managers are more prone to adverse-selection problems in their choices of projects and transactions; and these constraints are reinforced in the compensation and incentive systems of REITs.

The IRC/RMA/AJCA REIT asset tests and income tests unfairly discriminate between real properties that are located in any two different U.S. states that have different real property laws and mortgage laws and different laws about the transfer of real property. State law determines what can be classified as real property, and the nature of liens on real property.

The IRC/RMA/AJCA REIT asset tests and income tests unfairly discriminate between any two REITs that are located in two different states that have different personal property laws, and different laws about the transfer of personal property and real property. In the United States, state law determines what is classified as real property and personal property. Furthermore, certain jurisdictions may classify what is really real property (such as estate-for-years interests; options on real estate; real estate swaps; equity in a company that owns real estate) as personal property. Hence the IRC/RMA/AJCA REIT asset tests and income tests effectively increase REITs' transaction costs and search costs, because the out-of-state REITs have to ensure compliance with state laws, and that state law definitions of real property are suitable.

The IRC/RMA/AJCA REIT asset tests and income tests unfairly discriminate between any two REITs that are located in two different U.S. states that have different corporation laws. The REIT's underlying corporate entity can be a partnership, LLC, C-Corporation, or trust, which are governed by different state laws. Hence, the classification of what an "Asset" or "Income" is varies dramatically depending on the state (where the REIT is located or where it was incorporated) and the type of entity (LLC versus C-corporation versus trust).

U.S. Congress Exceeded Its Powers over States by Enacting IRC REIT-Qualification Rules (IRC Section-856, RMA, and AJCA REIT-Qualification Rules)

Under the principles explained in *City of Boerne v. Flores*, the U.S. Congress exceeded its powers over U.S. states by enacting the IRC, RMA, and AJCA REIT-qualification rules. The REIT-qualification laws effectively preclude (or almost preclude the impact or application of) any state regulations pertaining to corporate form of REITs, governance of REITs, formation of REITs, REIT dividend policy, and REIT dissolution. This is in contrast to all other forms of corporate entities such as C-Corporations, S-Corporations, partnerships, and LLCs. The U.S. Constitution expressly recognizes the power of states to regulate certain conduct and transactions. Hence, the U.S. Congress exceeded its powers by enacting the REIT-qualification statutes.

The Equal Protection Clause

The state action involved is the enactment of, and required compliance with, REIT-qualification laws (IRC, RMA, and AJCA). The IRC Section 856, RMA, and AJCA REIT-qualification statutes unfairly discriminate between parties that can afford the transaction costs of the specialized processes inherent in REIT formation and those that cannot afford them—the initial costs and ongoing costs of REIT qualification can be burdensome and are much greater than those of all other types of corporate entities. The REIT-qualification statutes unfairly discriminate between parties who have the knowledge and resources needed to qualify for REIT status and those who do not—the complexity and cost of the REIT-qualification statutes make it inaccessible to most people, and it is mostly sophisticated investors and companies with resources that can take advantage of these laws. The REIT-qualification statutes unfairly discriminate between parties who can pay for REIT shares and those who cannot—the formation of REITs under IRC Section 856/RMA/AJCA is conditioned on the REIT beneficiary's ability to pay for REIT shares. The REIT-qualification statutes unfairly discriminate between REITs that choose different corporate entities as their underlying corporate entity (i.e., partnership versus LLP versus C-Corporation); that is, in civil and criminal lawsuits, the defenses (to legal claims) available to the different types of underlying corporate entities supporting the REIT format (C-Corporation, Trust, association) vary dramatically under state law, and hence, it is unfair to allow different types of entities to be able to metamorphose into one form for tax purposes only, and yet be able to develop radically different defenses to any one legal claim.

The above-mentioned discriminatory classifications do not serve any compelling state interest and the classifications are not substantially related to serving any state interest.

The Due Process Clause of the U.S. Constitution

The IRC/RMA/AJCA REIT-qualification statutes violate the Due Process Clause of the U.S. Constitution. Entities can qualify for the REIT status by filing quarterly reports at the U.S. IRS. The IRS then makes a determination as to whether the entity complied with the asset tests, the income test, and other requirements for REIT status. The relevant state actions are the enactment of the REIT-qualification statutes and the government requirement that entities should comply with specific statutes in order to qualify as REITs. The REIT-qualifications process (as defined in IRC Section 856–860, the REIT Modernization Act of 1999, and the AJCA of 2004) constitute violations of the substantive and procedural due-process rights of the REIT entity and its trustees and shareholders, for the following reasons.

The IRC Sections 856–860, RMA, and AJCA REIT-qualification rules are not clear, and some inconsistencies/problems are:

- The income test includes publicly traded securities for which prices change daily. The IRC Codes do not specify any time horizons for measurement of assets. The income test does not require special appraisals.
- The assets test also affects publicly traded securities for which IRC Sections 856–860 and the REIT Modernization Act and the AJCA do not specify any time horizons or special procedures for measurement of assets. The assets test does not require special appraisals.
- IRC Section 856, the RMA, and the AJCA define a REIT but do not state the requirements for, and process for formation of, the associated trust. Trusts are flexible entities, can be formed orally or in writing, and hence require very specific terms in order to be efficient.
- The definitions of a *person* in IRS Tax Codes for REITs (IRC Sections 856–860), the RMA, and the AJCA remain ambiguous, if nonexistent.

> Institutional investors have been able to circumvent REIT-ownership concentration rules by claiming that their funds (or shareholders) are really the owners of each REIT equity interest, such that the institutional investors can own as many REIT shares as they want. Although this trend and custom are helpful in terms of increasing participation by institutional investors, they are illegal for the following reasons. The typical institutional investor functions as one entity with centralized decision making; the institutional investor's preferences and decision-making processes are not always the same as those of its shareholders. The major issue is the definition of the legal person in U.S. corporations' law. The key elements of a *person* are: (1) centralized decision making; (2) established by law (corporations, associations) or by human birth (natural person); and (3) nondivisibility as to claims on ownership interest—each owner of an interest cannot claim an ownership interest in a purchased interest such as a REIT equity interest.

Given the foregoing, the IRC REIT rules, the RMA, and the AJCA are void because of their vagueness and overbroadness under the Due Process Clause of the U.S. Constitution.

The IRS has complete jurisdiction and is the sole arbiter of compliance with REIT-qualification rules. There are no appeals and hence, any affected REITs do not have sufficient means of addressing issues. Since the REIT results in loss of tax revenues for the government, and government policies change with politics, the IRS has incentives to disallow REIT status as it deems necessary. The Article-14 Right-to-Fair-Trial is implicated.

The de-REITing costs incurred by the REIT (administrative costs, loss of investors, possibly an end to operations), by its shareholders (loss of tax status, loss of high dividends, increased volatility, declines in price of REIT interests, search costs, transaction costs, costs of reallocating assets, etc.), and by the capital markets in general (increased volatility, declining stock prices, cost of reallocating assets, transaction costs, search costs, etc.) are substantial and onerous (and constitute deprivations of procedural Due Process Rights).

Under U.S. laws, after de-REITing, a former REIT cannot obtain REIT status for the next five years. This penalty for noncompliance is excessive and constitutes a denial of procedural due process because after loss of REIT status, the entity is likely to wind down, lose substantial market value, and become incapable of raising enough money to file lawsuits, or pursue other legal alternatives in order to obtain remedies. The REIT status is the main attraction for investors without which there will probably not be any viable market for the entity's securities.

The IRC/RMA/AJCA REIT-qualification laws do not include any meaningful warning periods or grace periods. Given the severity of the penalties for noncompliance, such omission constitutes a significant due process deficiency.

Right to Contract

IRC Section 856, the RMA, and the AJCA violate the Contracts Clause of the U.S. Constitution. IRC Section 856, the RMA, and the AJCA specifically designate the entity resulting from compliance (with REIT-qualification statutes) as a Real Estate Investment Trust. This mandatory and statutory designation of a REIT/Trust as the preferred entity for actualization of a tax status constitutes a state action for purposes of constitutional analysis and deprives holders of REIT beneficial interest of the constitutional right to contract and to organize their business as they like. The right to contract arises from expectations, norms, and state constitutional law.

Furthermore, the REIT designation effectively changes the contractual relationships among the (former) owners of the underlying corporate entity (i.e., C-Corporation, LLC, LLP) that was converted to a REIT. The IRC/RMA/AJCA REIT-qualification rules change REIT corporate governance and the rights of the holders of REIT beneficial interests (equity owners). The IRC Section 856 and the RMA state that the original (pre-REIT) entity can be a Trust, C-Corporation, or association.

The government's interest in ensuring that individual investors can participate in commercial real estate markets is far outweighed by the sum of: (a) the magnitude of the changes of, and limitations on, the pre-REIT contractual rights of owners of the underlying entity; and (b) the magnitude and economic effects of the economic/legal/psychological restrictions imposed on REITs by the IRC/RMA/AJCA REIT-qualification rules, given that most REITs execute transactions. There are other ways to structure "synthetic REITs" without all the securities law problems and complexity inherent in REITs. The REIT format is not a reasonable and narrowly tailored means of promoting a public interest.

The Separation-of-Powers Doctrine

The IRC, RMA, and AJCA constitute violations of the Separation-of-Powers Clause. Under the IRC/RMA/AJCA REIT rules, the U.S. IRS retains jurisdiction on all matters pertaining to REIT qualification. The IRS is an agency of the U.S. executive branch. The IRS enforces the U.S. tax codes using various mechanisms. The IRS agency court administers disputes and complaints pertaining to REIT laws and REIT qualification. The IRS also issues opinions and quasi-rules pertaining to the details of compliance with the REIT-qualification statutes—these documents clarify the IRS positions on complex issues. This constitutes a violation of the Separation-of-Powers Doctrine because the IRS is responsible for both the adjudication and the enforcement/compliance aspects of the REIT-qualification rules (and for quasi rule making). There is no indication that when drafting the U.S. REIT-qualification rules the U.S. Congress made any exceptions to the Separation-of-Powers Doctrine.

The government does not have any legitimate property interest in combining the adjudicative and enforcement functions (and quasi rule-making functions) pertaining to the REIT-qualification statutes. The government's interest in reducing the costs of enforcing laws is far outweighed by the specialized nature of the REIT-qualification statutes, and the potentially significant transaction costs associated with REIT status. The combination of the enforcement and adjudicative functions pertaining to REIT-qualification laws does not advance any specific government policies.

THE MANDATORY REIT DIVIDEND PAYOUT RULE VIOLATES THE U.S. CONSTITUTION

In all countries that permit REITs, REIT statutes include mandatory minimum dividend payout rules, which are unconstitutional under U.S. laws (and laws of many common law countries).

The Takings Clause of the U.S. Constitution

The IRC Section 856 and the REIT Modernization Act of 1999 and the AJCA specify minimum dividend payout rates for REIT qualification (the 90 percent mandatory dividend payout rule). This constitutes relevant state action for purposes of constitutional law analysis. The U.S. Supreme Court decisions on Takings has not directly addressed the minimum-dividends rules for REITs. The U.S. Supreme Court standards for Takings have been discussed in prior chapters (i.e., the "reduction-of-value" test; the "cause-of-harm" test; the "government-invasion" theory; and the "noxious-use" test).

The minimum-dividends rules constitute a Takings because of the following reasons. First, REITs have constitutionally protected property interests in fair and effective laws that reduce their transaction costs, financing costs, and operating costs (such property interests arise from expectations, norms, state constitutional laws, and contracts). The minimum-dividend payout rules do not provide any meaningful protection for investors—mandatory payment of dividends drastically reduces the REIT's financial flexibility, and increases its bankruptcy risk, and forces the REIT to seek financing on potentially unfavorable terms. Second, the minimum-dividend payout rules do not apply to other forms of corporate entities (and tax status)—such as partnerships, S-Corporations, LLCs, and C-Corporations. Third, the REIT entity has a property interest in determining its appropriate dividend policies, which apply solely to its assets and operations—this is a property expectancy that also implicates the right to association. Fourth, the state actions effectively deprive the REIT of said property interests, and the right to equal protection of the law. These property interests arise from state contract laws, state property laws, and state constitutional laws, norms, and expectations. Fifth, the general public benefits indirectly from said Takings, because the holders of the REIT beneficial interests are paid the minimum dividends required by law regardless of the financial condition of the REIT and its future capital need. Empirical studies have shown that there is significant information content in REIT dividends—REIT dividends are generally good news that affects market volatility and the propensity of other corporate entities to pay dividends. Sixth, the REIT is not compensated for this Taking in any way, and actually loses money/value due to increased processing costs, financing costs, and transaction costs.

In essence, the tax benefits received by the REIT as a result of compliance with the minimum-dividend payout rule, if any, are far outweighed by the sum of the following factors: (1) the increase in the REIT's bankruptcy risk, (2) the REIT management's inability to formulate appropriate dividend policies to suit changing market conditions, and (3) the high dividend expectations of investors, which are created and encouraged by the 90 percent minimum dividend payout rule, and which result in a significant cash drain (most REITs pay out more than 110 percent of their "Funds from Operations"). Last, the Takings public use is the creation and use of a REIT tax status.

The minimum-dividend payout rules drastically increase information asymmetry in stock markets and also increase agency problems because the rules cause a "dividend competition" among REITs, which often have to continually borrow both to sustain dividends and to fund their normal operations. The minimum-dividend payout rules obfuscate the real capital needs of the REIT, and the resulting dividend policy is not based on the REIT's financial stability or performance. REIT Wrecks (2009) states in part:

> *In terms of the other key selling point, reliable income, non-traded REITs are not so reliable. Many, like Cornerstone Core Properties REIT, are busy funding their dividends from borrowings and returns of capital. Grubb & Ellis Healthcare REIT is a great (but not isolated) example of the lengths to which non-traded REITs will go*

to maintain their dividends. For the three months ended March 31, 2009, Grubb & Ellis paid distributions of $14,247,000, as compared to cash flow from operations of $5,895,000. In many cases, distributions paid in excess of cash flow are paid using proceeds from new investors. Slowly but surely, these fictitious dividends are starting to be cut.

The minimum-dividends rules reduce management's ability to convey signals about the REIT's future economic prospects (which is usually achieved by increasing or reducing the dividend payout rate and or the absolute amount of dividends) and they obfuscate dividend policy—changes in dividend payout rates are less likely to be related to REIT performance or capital markets conditions. Hence, the government's interest in achieving efficiency and protecting investors by regulating dividend policy is far outweighed by the collective property interests of the REIT shareholders and stock market participants in transparency and noncoercive dividend policies.

The Takings implicit in the REIT minimum-dividends rules do not conform to any of the above-mentioned types of takings because there is no "physical occupation"; and there is no "total regulatory taking"; there are no "exactions that violate the *Nollan* and *Dolan* standards"; and there is no "Penn-Central Type" Taking.

Thus, there is a new type of Takings that are henceforth referred to as *Reversible Two-Way Takings* (defined later in this chapter).

The Free Speech Clause

The sections of the IRC/RMA/ACJA that specify mandatory minimum-dividend payout rates for REIT qualifications constitute relevant state action and amount to a violation of the REIT entity's right to freedom of speech. Although the REIT-qualification statutes are vague about the definition of *person*, the REIT entity is considered a person for purposes of the U.S. Constitution and state constitutions.

REIT dividend policy is effectively a form of constitutionally protected speech for several reasons. Dividend policy is a form of communication to capital markets and investors. Numerous empirical finance studies have identified information content in dividend policy. Dividend policy involves recurring decisions and announcements. Dividend policy represents an expression of the entity's condition and prospects, which typically does not violate any civil or criminal laws.

Hence the 90 percent dividend-payout rule constitutes a violation of the REIT's right to free speech for several reasons. The rule does not apply to other forms of tax status, for example, partnerships, S-Corporations,

C-Corporations, and LLCs. The REIT entity has a constitutionally protected property interest in determining its own dividend policies. This property interest arises from state constitutional law, state contract law, state property laws, expectations, and norms. Independently determined dividend policy constitutes free speech. The government does not have any legitimate interest in imposing mandatory discriminatory dividend policies on a specific class of investors. The 90 percent dividend-payout rule complicates the REIT's capital budgeting and imposes financial burdens on the REIT entity—the REIT will have to raise capital from external sources in order to finance its growth. This is critical because real estate is a capital-intensive business. The 90 percent dividend-payout rule significantly increases the bankruptcy risk of REITs. This is more relevant where the REIT owns older properties that have low or no depreciation.

THE GOVERNMENT'S FAILURE TO REGULATE MANAGEMENT AGREEMENTS OF REITs CONSTITUTES A VIOLATION OF THE EQUAL PROTECTION CLAUSE OF THE U.S. CONSTITUTION

REITs' managers are provided certain protections and legal defenses for liabilities that arise while acting in their capacities as officers of the REIT. On the contrary, third-party property managers, whose relationship with the REIT is typically defined by a management agreement, and who subsequently perform the same functions that the owner-REIT would have done, are exposed to litigation risk and cannot use said legal defenses. This is because property managers are not considered REIT officers, and no statutory and common law privileges of REIT officers have been extended to contracted property managers. Similarly, these property managers can take certain actions without incurring liability, while REIT managers will incur liability by doing the same acts. The government's failure to regulate (enact specific regulations for management agreements) these agreements is a major omission and constitutes state action for purposes of constitutional law analysis because: (a) the government is the only party that can effectively regulate management agreements; (b) management agreements have significant economic, legal, operational, psychological, and risk implications for REITs and their shareholders; and (c) most REITs do not manage their properties, but subcontract day-to-day management to third parties via management agreements. These trends amount to violations of the Equal Protection Clause of the U.S. Constitution because the third-party property manager performs functions that are economically and physically what the owner would have done. Furthermore, the management agreement between the REIT and the property manager effectively confers the duties of REIT officers on the property managers, who should get the same legal protections and privileges.

The government's failure to regulate property management agreements used by REITs unfairly discriminates between: (a) REITs and property management companies that have the knowledge and resources to draft effective and favorable management agreements, and those who do not; (b) REITs that manage their properties using in-house staff, and those that use third-party management agreements; (c) property management companies and REITs that can afford the initial contracting costs, transaction costs, and monitoring costs inherent in management agreements and those that cannot; and (d) parties that choose different levels of compliance with terms of the management agreement.

The above-mentioned classifications (on which the unfair discriminating conduct is based) do not serve any compelling state interest, and the classifications are not substantially related to serving any state interest. The state actions involved are the enactments of, and the required mandatory compliance with, REIT-qualification laws.

REITs ARE UNCONSTITUTIONAL BECAUSE THEY RESULT IN ILLEGAL MISCONDUCT

As explained in Nwogugu (2007, 2008a, 2008b), the formation and operation of REITs is illegal and hence, REITs are unconstitutional.

A NEW THEORY OF TAKINGS

Reversible Two-Way Takings

Reversible Two-Way Takings were introduced in an earlier section of this chapter, and have the following characteristics:

- The Takings arise solely because a party voluntarily elects to comply with a statute in order to gain specific benefits (tax credits, tax abatements, etc.)—the statute is not mandatory.
- Such compliance with a statute automatically deprives the party of specific constitutionally guaranteed property interests, without further action by the government.
- The statute has exactly or almost the same tax effect on all entities that elect to use it.

- The statute partially transforms the nature of the corporate entity—in the United States the REIT is a tax overlay (the underlying corporate entity can be one of several types of corporate entities).
- The Takings can be reversed and eliminated when the party elects to stop using the statute, and hence the party can improve its position within the jurisdiction without any judicial intervention or action by the government. The cost of reversibility is relatively low—the cost to file IRS forms to de-REIT.
- The statute is an indivisible mechanism—the use value of the statute remains the same regardless of how many companies elect to use it.
- The subject statute does not preclude any critical action but merely requires affirmative compliance.
- The affected class-member derives a tax benefit upon full compliance.
- The costs of noncompliance can be substantial.

The Takings are "Two-Way" Takings because the party using the mechanism gains (e.g., gets tax benefits) but simultaneously loses some property rights (automatic deprivation of some property interests).

CONCLUSION

The REIT format as used in the United States (and in most common law countries) and the associated federal laws violate various clauses of constitutions, such as the right to contract, equal protection, commerce, regulation of interstate commerce, and free speech. New laws are required to define rights and obligations of all parties involved in the formation and operation of REITs. Alternatively, given the inherent securities law and corporate governance problems inherent in REITs, the REIT format should be eliminated.

REFERENCES

Allens Arthur Robinson. 2009. ASIA-PACIFIC REIT SURVEY April 2009. Available at: www.trust.com.au/Assets/Files/TA_REIT_Survey%202009.pdf.

Campbell, R.D. 2002. Shareholder wealth effects in equity REIT restructuring transactions: Sell-offs, mergers, and joint ventures. *Journal of Real Estate Literature* 10 (2): 205–222.

Ernst & Young. 2010. *Global Real Estate Investment Trust Report 2010: Against All Odds*. Available at: www.ernstandyoung.ch/Publication/vwLUAssets/Global_Real_Estate_Investment_Trust_Report_2010_-_Against_all_odds/$FILE/EY_Global_REIT_report_2010_-_Against_all_odds.pdf.

European Public REIT Association. 2010. EPRA Global REIT Survey 2010. September.

Nwogugu, M. 2007. Some securities law problems inherent in REITs. *Journal of International Banking Law & Regulation* 22 (11): 603–613.

Nwogugu, M. 2008a. Some corporate governance problems pertaining to REITs—Part One. *Journal of International Banking Law & Regulation* 23 (2): 71–89.

Nwogugu, M. 2008b. Some corporate governance problems pertaining to REITs—Part Two. *Journal of International Banking Law & Regulation* 23 (3): 142–152.

REIT Wrecks. 2009. Non-traded REITs are designed to be sold, not bought. Available at: http://reitwrecks.com/2009/05/non-traded-reits-are-designed-to-be.html.

Stoltmann, A., and Burke, J. 2011. Recovering REIT losses. Stoltmann Law Offices. Available at: www.reitfraudrecovery.com/index.html.

The Trust Company and Baker & McKenzie. 2011. Asia Pacific REIT Survey, April 2011. Available at: http://www.trust.com.au/documents/TRUST_REITS_2011.pdf.

Whitten, D. 2009. J-REITs to get JPY1 trillion bail-out but Investors aren't buying just yet. Available at: www.istockanalyst.com/article/viewarticle/articleid/3245416.

CHAPTER 12

Asset Securitization Is Unconstitutional and Should Be Banned

Under U.S. laws, all forms of asset securitization are unconstitutional. Securitization of many types of assets (loans, credit cards, auto receivables, intellectual property, etc.) was prevalent from 1990 to 2008, particularly for financially distressed companies and companies with low- or mid-tier credit ratings. Although the analysis in this chapter is based on the U.S. Constitution, the principles and theories developed here are applicable in most common law countries. The securitization processes and laws/regulations in many countries are based on, and are similar to, U.S. securitization procedures and associated statutes/regulations. Nwogugu (2008a, 2008b) shows that asset securitization violates usury statutes, fraud statutes, antitrust statutes, civil RICO statutes, and the U.S. Bankruptcy Code. Other authors have also explained the problems inherent in securitization; this chapter, however, focuses on Constitutional Law issues. The existing literature on legal and corporate governance issues pertaining to securitization is substantial, but has several gaps that have not been addressed sufficiently:

- The effect of economic and behavioral factors on the constitutionality of securitization, and vice versa.
- The economic consequences of the unconstitutionality of securitization.
- The effects of declaring securitization to be illegal/unconstitutional; and the necessary elements of new securitization laws.

The author published an earlier version of this chapter as an article in *International Company & Commercial Law Review* in 2009.

In analyzing the legality of securitization, the following criteria are relevant:

- Origins and history of asset securitization—legislative history, evolution of securitization processes, and current practices. Carlson (1998) traces the origins and history of securitization to direct and specific efforts/collaborations to avoid the effects of U.S. bankruptcy laws.
- Types of contracts used in securitization, and the key criteria for enforceability.
- The purposes, wording, and scope of applicable laws—state contract laws, state trust laws, state corporation laws, the U.S. Bankruptcy Code, and state/federal securities laws.
- How the relevant laws are applied in securitization processes—by market participants, regulators, and lawyers who represent investors.
- The people, markets, and entities/organizations that are affected by securitization.
- The usefulness of existing (if any), possible and proposed (if any) deterrence measures that are designed to reduce fraud/crime/misconduct.
- Transaction costs, compliance costs, and monitoring costs.

Clearly, securitization has reduces the effectiveness of transmission of monetary policies and has substantial effects, on lenders' incentives to provide loans, and on borrowers' propensity to breach loan contracts.

SECURITIZATION DAMPENS MONETARY TRANSMISSION AND PROVIDES WRONG INCENTIVES FOR BANKS AND SPONSORS

Aysun and Hepp (2011) attempted to show that the balance sheet channel of monetary transmission is stronger for U.S. banks that securitize their assets than for those that do not securitize assets—this hypothesis contradicts the widely confirmed negative relationship between financial development (e.g., existence of securitization) and the strength of the lending channel of monetary transmission. That is, the high rate of financial innovation that occurred after 1970 has reduced the effectiveness of the U.S. Federal Reserve Bank's policy tools (more commonly referred to as the monetary transmission mechanism). The Aysun and Hepp study focused on the balance sheet channel, using bank-level observations, and found that banks that did securitizations were more sensitive (than banks that did not do securitizations) to changes in borrowers' balance sheets and that monetary policy has a greater impact on (amplified) this sensitivity for securitizing banks than for nonsecuritizing banks. Aysun and Hepp developed optimality conditions, which they claim indicate that the positive effects of securitization on policy effectiveness may be attributable to the high sensitivity of security prices to policy rates. Aysun and Hepp arrived at these unusual empirical results, and their findings are wrong for the following 13 reasons:

1. Aysun and Hepp (2011) did not test for effects of compensation of, and incentives for, bank lending officers in large banks and small/midsize banks. Such effects may cause minimal or exaggerated reactions to monetary policies. Aysun and Hepp (2011) also did not distinguish between "voluntary" and "involuntary" monetary transmission. Involuntary monetary transmission is largely a function of the bank's portfolio of assets and liabilities. Voluntary monetary transmission refers to affirmative decisions made by bank executives (and tempered by incentives, executive compensation, bank supervision, customer relationships, knowledge/cognition) to comply with the intended effects of government monetary policies.
2. The Aysun and Hepp (2011) study covered only the periods after 2001, which in hindsight was a unique period with many economic phenomena never seen before—whereas a more realistic study would have covered a much longer period.
3. The postulated positive effects of securitization on the effectiveness of monetary transmission can be attributed to other causes such as: (1) "true sale" securitizations may create such effects/relationships, but not "assignment" securitizations; (2) increasing the volume of securitization provides more cash for the bank, and if such cash is invested in long-term loans, the Aysun and Hepp (2011) observed relationships are less likely, whereas if such cash is invested in short-term securities and cash equivalents, then the observed relationships are more probable; and (3) the global credit crunch began around 2006, and even then, large banks' loan-to-asset ratios were declining, and thus large banks were not lending as much as before, but were investing more cash in short-term liquid securities, which made them more sensitive to monetary policies.
4. The Aysun and Hepp (2011) sample of "small banks" consisted of banks that make relatively short-term and medium-term loans.
5. Aysun and Hepp (2011) did not use ordinary loan data for small banks—rather, they used proxies of relationships between small banks and local economies and local business—in part by using bank-holding-company level data (this may be misleading if subsidiary banks make

their own decisions about securitization, which is often the case). However, for large banks, they used Federal Reserve loan data (Federal Reserve's Call Report of Condition and Income). This is a key difference that affected the empirical results.

6. As acknowledged by Aysun and Hepp (2011), banks that securitize their loans are most often much larger banks, and given that the banking industry in most countries in concentrated (the top 10 banks account for more than 60 percent of total banking assets), the results of the Aysun and Hepp study cannot be generalized. Without securitization, these larger banks are more likely to respond to monetary policy than small/midsize banks simply because: (1) central banks scrutinize larger banks more; (2) a larger percentage of their senior officers are recruited from the central bank (compared to officers of midsize and small banks); (3) larger banks are more sensitive to credit ratings because they hold many more assets than the average midsize or small banks, their values and perceived risk (e.g., to credit rating agencies) are more sensitive to changes in monetary policy, and thus these banks are more likely to react to and reflect monetary policy than midsize or small banks; and (4) most traditional monetary policy tools affect the short end of the debt markets, and because larger banks have more assets and proportionally greater short-term liabilities than midsize/small banks, all else held constant, large banks will transmit monetary policies more than midsize/small banks.

   Mishkin (2007) states in part:

   > *. . . by raising or lowering short term interest rates, monetary policy affects the housing market and in turn, the overall economy, directly or indirectly through at least six channels: through the direct effects of interest rates on: (a) the user cost of capital, (b) expectations of future hours-price movements, (c) housing supply, and indirectly through (d) standard wealth effects from house prices, (e) balance sheet, credit channel effects on consumer spending, (f) balance sheet, credit channel effects on housing demand.*

7. Aysun and Hepp (2011) did not distinguish between "true sale" securitizations and "assignment" securitizations, and the differences have substantial effects on monetary transmission.
8. Aysun and Hepp (2011) studied only one side of the "equation" (the "Sellers")—the other side of the "equation" consists of the investors who purchase asset-backed securities (ABS) (many of whom are small and midsize banks), and the "servicers" who collect payments, substitute collateral, determine when a default has occurred, and initiate

foreclosures (the "Buyers"). Liquidity for the securitizing bank means simultaneous illiquidity for the ABS investors, and since the bank and the investors often function in the same financial ecosystem, on a system-wide basis there may be either no change or even a decrease in overall monetary transmission (particularly where investors and their portfolios are more sensitive to monetary policy than securitizing banks). When the investors purchase the ABS for cash, they become less able to transmit monetary policy—the ABS markets have relatively and historically low liquidity.

9. The finding of Keys, Mukherjee, Seru, and Vig (2009) that banks that are more regulated originate lower quality loans may also explain why monetary transmission is more likely in large banks than in smaller banks.
10. Aysun and Hepp (2011) did not distinguish among the objectives of bank securitization, such as getting rid of low-quality loans, raising capital, and reducing exposure to a specific segment of the bond market (e.g., short-term bonds versus medium-term bonds). Aysun and Hepp expressly stated that the lack of loan-level data makes it impossible to ascertain whether, and the extent to which banks' decisions to increase/decrease the amount of lending are caused by banks' liquidity positions or actual/perceived quality of their customer-borrowers' balance sheets; and that this same issue also makes it difficult to choose accurate proxies for measurement of the importance of balance sheets in loan transactions.
11. The Aysun and Hepp (2011) study did not consider that small/midsize banks often purchase ABS and mortgage-backed securities (MBS) (ABS/MBS and mortgage/housing related financial products constitute a much larger percentage of small banks' total assets, than for large banks), whereas most securitizing/sponsor banks are large banks. Such activity on the "buyer" and "seller" sides of securitizations affects banks' monetary transmission capabilities. The differences in the types of banks' assets can have substantial effects on monetary transmission. The Qualified Thrift Lender Test requires that at least 65 percent of S&L assets be mortgages and consumer products.
12. The assumption put forth by Aysun and Hepp (2011) that several banks affiliated with the same bank holding company have access to similar internal capital markets is a major assumption that is not entirely true for the following reasons: (1) the executive compensation systems of the subsidiary banks often differ; (2) the cost centers and cost structures of the subsidiary banks differ; and (3) the subsidiary banks often have different target combinations and actual combinations of liabilities (deposits, discount-window loans, interbank loans, swaps/derivatives,

bonds, etc.). In the United States, the 2010 revisions of the Bank Holding Company Act moves the supervision of BHCs to the U.S. Federal Reserve, and requires consolidated capital requirements for BHCs, and some other changes.

Estrella (2002) found that increasing securitization weakened the effectiveness of monetary policy actions on real output (GDP) in the mortgage markets. Estrella attributed the decline in monetary transmission not to the Federal Reserve's control over interest rates, but to noninterest-rate effects, such as liquidity in the markets and/or the supply of credit.

Furthermore, the global credit crunch of 2007 to 2010, which occurred in an environment of historically low interest rates and above-average money supply in many countries, and active securitization markets in many countries (except the United States where the ABS market collapsed in 2009), is significant evidence that securitization reduces the efficiency of monetary transmission.

Uhde and Michalak (2010) found that credit risk securitization has a positive impact on the increase of European banks' systematic risk. Uhde and Michalak used a unique dataset of 592 cash and synthetic securitizations issued by 54 banks from the EU-15 plus Switzerland over the period from 1997 to 2007. Uhde and Michalak also found that: (a) the increase in systematic risk is more relevant for larger banks that repeatedly engage in securitization; (b) securitization is more important for small and medium financial institutions; (c) banks have a higher incentive to retain the larger part of credit risk as a quality signal at the beginning of the securitization business in Europe; and (d) the overall risk-shifting effect due to securitization is more distinct when the pre-event systematic risk is low. The Uhde and Michalak study is inaccurate for four reasons:

1. The study did not distinguish between "true sale" securitizations and "assignment" securitizations.
2. The study did not consider the differences in the quality of loans/assets securitized (in terms of default risk, documentation risk, accounting risk, etc.).
3. The study did not differentiate between the average lives of the securitized assets.
4. As was amply illustrated from 2008 to 2010, the "risk transfer" supposedly inherent in securitization is an illusion because the investors who purchase risky investments reduce market liquidity when they incur ABS losses, and these same investors also have other financial contracts with securitization sponsors (e.g., they are swap counterparties) such that there is effectively no risk transfer.

Loutskina (2011) analyzed the role of securitization in bank management. Loutskina developed a new index of "bank loan portfolio liquidity," which was used to attempt to show that by allowing banks to convert illiquid loans into liquid funds, securitization reduces banks' holdings of liquid securities and increases their lending ability. Loutskina also found that securitization provides banks with an additional source of funding and makes bank lending less sensitive to cost-of-fund shocks. However, this finding is not entirely correct because the same cost-of-fund shocks affect most of banks' sources of funds (e.g., customer deposits, discount window loans, issuance of bonds). Loutskina also found that securitization weakens the ability of the the government authority to affect banks' lending activity but makes banks more susceptible to liquidity and funding crisis when the securitization market is shut down. Thus, Loutskina contradicts Aysun and Hepp (2011) and Uhde and Michalak (2010).

Gorton and Metrick (2011) developed a link between securitization and repo finance on one hand, and the problems in the U.S. subprime mortgage markets and housing markets on the other hand; and they suggested that the global financial crisis that began in 2007 originated in the repo market (which is a large, short-term market that provides financing for a wide range of securitization transactions and financial institutions—repo transactions are often collateralized ABS). Gorton and Metrick's (2010) data set included credit spreads for ABS backed by bonds; they found that changes in the LIB-OIS spread (a proxy for counterparty risk) were strongly correlated with changes in credit spreads and repo rates for securitized bonds. These changes implied that there was greater uncertainty about the solvency of banks and that values of repo collateral were lower (which resulted in increases in required collateral for any given transaction).

Keys et al. (2009) analyzed the effects of regulations on the quality of mortgage loan originations in the originate-to-distribute (OTD) market. They used the ease of securitization as the source of variation and noted that information asymmetries in the OTD market can lead to moral hazard problems within lending companies. Keys et al. found that the quality of loan origination varies inversely with the amount of regulation, which is somewhat counterfactual. Keys et al. interpreted this result as possible evidence that the fragility of lightly regulated originators' capital structure can mitigate moral hazard and increase lender due diligence. However, other possible causes of this phenomenon that were not discussed in Keys et al. are: (a) lightly regulated lenders spend less on due diligence; (b) lightly regulated lenders can act faster and close loans faster and thus, attract higher quality borrowers (lower quality borrowers are less sensitive to time because of their situation); (c) lightly regulated lenders are more likely to offer more customized loans that will attract higher quality borrowers; (d) heavily regulated lenders are more likely to offer government-sponsored lending programs for first-time property buyers, and for low-income buyers, all of whom are higher risk borrowers; and (e) there may be a contagion effect wherein lower quality borrowers learn (by word-of-mouth or social networks) about lenders that offer loans to low-quality borrowers, and then they congregate at such lenders (such contagion effects are likely to be prevalent in low-income neighborhoods, in low-income professions, or among workers in industries that employ many low-wage workers.

Keys et al. also found that incentives that require mortgage brokers to have "skin in the game" in addition to stronger risk management departments inside the bank partially alleviate the moral hazard problem in this setting. Keys et al. found that having more lenders provide loans for a mortgage pool is more likely to result in their tendering higher quality loans, which indicates that relative performance evaluation due to more competition among contributing lenders can also mitigate the moral hazard problem. Keys et al. concluded that their evidence suggests that market forces rather than regulation may have been more effective in mitigating moral hazard in the OTD market; which in turn means that governments should not enact policies that impose stricter lender regulations that fail to align lenders' incentives with objectives/incentives of ABS/MBS investors.

Piskorski, Seru, and Vig (2010) studied whether securitization affects the renegotiation decisions of loan servicers, and found that securitization causes a foreclosure bias (securitization increases the servicer's propensity to foreclose on a delinquent securitized mortgage). For seriously delinquent loans, Piskorski, Seru, and Vig found that bank-held loans had a significantly lower foreclosure rate than similar securitized loans (i.e., across various specifications and origination vintages, the foreclosure rate of delinquent bank-held loans was 3 percent to 7 percent lower in absolute terms and 13 percent to 32 percent lower in relative terms, compared to securitized loans). Piskorski, Seru, and Vig also found that there is a substantial heterogeneity in these effects with large effects among borrowers with better credit quality and small effects among lower quality borrowers. The results of Piskorski, Seru, and Vig can also be attributed to the following additional reasons that were not discussed in detail in the study: (a) the provisions of ABS indenture agreements may contain more stringent terms than the acceptance criteria for "portfolio loans"; (b) ABS servicers face breach of fiduciary duty claims from ABS investors, which may provide more incentives for such servicers to pursue foreclosure (bank lending officers often don't face such explicit breach of fiduciary duty claims); (c) the compensation of ABS servicers may account for this phenomenon; (d) unlike bank lending officers, the servicers' compensation, professional reputations, and social capital are often not affected by foreclosure costs, and servicers are sometimes praised for promptly identifying troubled loans and initiating recovery/foreclosure; and (e) the Asset substitution clauses in ABS indenture agreements provide incentives for servicers to quickly foreclose distressed loans.

Jones (2000) confirmed that securitization and other financial innovations have provided unprecedented opportunities for banks to reduce their regulatory capital requirements with little or no corresponding reduction in their overall economic risk. Jones also discussed various "Regulatory Arbitrage" methods and the resulting problems for bank supervisors. Blundell-Wignall and Atkinson (2010) explained some of the weaknesses in the Basel-3 proposals. Gyntelberg and Remolona (2006) stated that securitization has tended to increase liquidity rather than reallocate risk.

SECURITIZATION INCREASES TRANSACTION COSTS, SYSTEMIC RISK, INFLATION, AND HEDGING COSTS

Securitization is inefficient in the following ways. Many market professionals and risk managers clearly do not know how to value or hedge CMBS and RMBS. This trend had disastrous consequences from 2007 to 2010, and caused the collapse of the U.S. ABS market.

Securitization imposes at least two additional layers of unnecessary costs and uncertainty on an industry that is already heavily burdened with extremely high transaction costs. The reality is that by buying CMBS/RMBS, investors have implicitly paid for the services of third-party appraisers, servicing companies, accounting firms, and lawyers. The extra transaction costs do not provide any meaningful additional benefits for any party and are substantially detrimental to social welfare.

There is a substantial disconnect between the primary mortgage markets and ABS/CMBS/RMBS, such that the ABS/CMBS/RMBS prices often do not reflect the dynamics and prices in either real estate markets or the primary mortgage markets—this trend defeats the very purpose of securitization. Because of the heavy use of derivatives, the CMBS/RMBS markets are more closely linked with interest rate derivative markets and government bond markets than the underlying real estate markets.

Given that most investors in the secondary markets are institutional investors, the claimed but illusory benefits of securitization can be obtained by: (1) purchasing a portfolio of mortgages and recruiting a servicing company to manage daily operations, or building an in-house servicing department, (2) entering into swaps (principal risk and interest rate risk) for portfolios of mortgages, or (3) buying bonds or preferred stock of real estate companies that own rental properties.

Securitization drastically and substantially expands money supply in ways that make it difficult, if not impossible, for central banks to control the economy, or for international groups like the G7/G20 to coordinate their financial stability efforts—this was clearly illustrated during the global financial crisis of 2007 to 2010. Mortgages and securitization breed: (1) unpredictable home-equity loans, which breed unpredictable new consumer spending; (2) unpredictable unwarranted inflation of property values, which causes unpredictable consumer investment/spending/savings patterns and unpredictable corporate spending/investment; and (3) unpredictable transaction costs, which cause unpredictable spending and investment (e.g., the total annual real estate brokerage commissions in the United States have exceeded $50 billion during 2006 to 2009; and lawyers' fees and mortgage brokers' commissions are also substantial). In different countries, the results have been almost uniform, and include inflation of property values, substantial transaction costs, substantial information asymmetry costs, "flipping," mortgage fraud, declining mortgage underwriting standards, and increasing foreclosure rates.

Historically, the CMBS/RMBS and ABS markets have been, and remain, relatively very illiquid, highly specialized (relatively few participants), speculative (trading is often not based on the fundamentals of underlying mortgages), and opaque.

The reality is that the mortgage markets and market participants are very interconnected; and the much-touted "risk transfer" in securitization has been disastrous. The bulk of the risk transfer is between two classes of institutional investors (banks on one hand, and on the other hand, pension funds, other banks, private funds, and insurance companies) that are substantially mutually dependent and exist in the same financial ecosystem, such that the touted risk transfer is meaningless because of the mutual dependency. Thus, the same transferred risk comes back to harm and haunt the securitization sponsors and investment banks when the investors lose invested capital, which triggers a series of adverse connected/correlated events that substantially increase systemic risk: (1) liquidity and trading volume in markets immediately decline; (2) rating agencies generally reduce ratings of corporate securities and ABS, which cause price declines, which in turn prevent the same investors from buying/trading new issues and other securities; (3) investment banks and rating agencies lose revenues; (4) insurance companies lose profits due to payouts, and premiums increase, which causes credit-default swap rates to rise, which in turn reduces trading volume and prices; and (5) investors mark down the carrying value of their portfolios. For example, Bank A does a securitization and sells $50 million of ABS to each of Bank B, Bank C, and Bank D. However, Bank A has swap agreements with each bank with the following notional values: (1) $60 million swap with Bank B; (2) $100 million swap agreement with Bank C; and (3) $80 million swap agreement with Bank D. Banks A, B, C, and D have also borrowed from each other in the interbank lending markets. The Bank A ABS defaults because the underlying mortgages were bad. Bank B records a write-off of the ABS losses, its credit rating is reduced, and the credit default swap premium that Bank A pays for the swap rises substantially and vice versa. Bank C also records a write-off of the ABS losses, its credit rating is reduced and it cannot perform the swap agreement; and the credit default premiums that Bank A and Bank C have to pay rise substantially. Similarly, Bank D records a write-off of the ABS losses, its credit rating is reduced, and it cannot perform the swap agreement; and the credit default premiums that Bank A and Bank D have to pay rise substantially. Bank A also has to record losses for the swaps contract with Bank D. As a result of the defaults, Bank B, Bank C, and Bank D will refuse to purchase other ABS and corporate bond offerings being sold by other banks/sponsors and traditional companies. Bank A's, Bank B's, Bank C's, and Bank D's cost of capital will rise substantially as a result of the losses and write-offs from both the ABSs and the swaps contracts. Bank A, Bank B, Bank C, and Bank D all purchase bond insurance from one of five "national" bond insurance companies. Now assume that around the same time, exactly the same thing happens among another set of four banks in the same country (Banks E, F, G, and H) and also that each of Banks B, C, D, F, G, and H also sold their ABS to at least three other banks, and their ABS defaulted due to the low quality of the underlying mortgages. Banks A, B, C, D, E, F, G, and H and most other banks in the country all purchase bond insurance from one of the five "national" bond insurance companies. These banks also hire each other's staff, pay their staff based on similar compensation systems, and use the same or similar risk models. The result is that the cost of capital (in both the interbank markets and the general capital markets) of all eight banks and other banks will rise sharply, their lending volumes will likely decline, and their credit default swap costs (cost to hedge their debt obligations) and insurance costs will rise sharply. These banks that issued the ABS will all incur substantial mortgage workout and ABS-resolution expenses (i.e., negotiating with ABS trustees and the trust's lawyers). Thus, in most instances, securitization does not provide any true transfer of risk because the financial institutions shuffle assets among themselves and they are all essentially subsidiaries of one "shadow virtual company," and the potential and actual systemic risks of securitization are not justifiable under any circumstances.

Securitization causes declining underwriting standards and declining loan quality—this was illustrated during 2004 to 2009 in the United States when the ease with which lenders could sell mortgages into the secondary market provided substantial incentives for them to focus on loan volume at the expense of loan quality.

The remainder of this chapter explains how asset securitization violates several clauses of constitutions.

SECURITIZATION CONSTITUTES A VIOLATION OF THE COMMERCE CLAUSE OF THE U.S. CONSTITUTION

For purposes of constitutional law analysis, the relevant state action consists of any of the following. Given the significant magnitude of securitization transactions in the United States, and its pervasive effect on the overall U.S. economy, the U.S. Congress's failure to create a uniform set of federal laws (trusts, contracts, corporations, debtor/creditor laws, etc.) for securitization and associated collateral constitutes a state action. The government has an affirmative duty to create and enforce laws that govern interstate activities that have significant economic, legal, and psychological effects on its citizens and institutions. Second, the sponsor's selection of collateral for securitization is a consumer-protection type governmental regulatory role (the sponsor is a private actor that is performing the regulatory role of the government by selecting collateral that supposedly conforms to certain minimum standards of quality). As illustrated by the global financial crisis of 2008 to 2011 and the responses of governments of various countries, the government has a significant interest in assuring that investors are provided adequate minimum protection by controlling/regulating the quality of collateral in securitization transactions.

In the United States, securitization transactions are typically governed by a combination of state laws (trust laws, corporations laws, securities laws, and contract laws) and federal securities laws. Securitization involves interstate commerce where the collateral, the investors, the trustees/board members, and servicing agent are located in different states/provinces.

Securitization imposes substantial burdens on interstate commerce in several ways. First, in securitization, due diligence costs, transaction costs, compliance costs, and processing costs are generally greater for out-of-state collateral than for in-state collateral (primarily because of differences in state laws that govern securitization and debtor/creditor relationships), and hence, current/historical securitization processes/laws implicitly or directly discourage the use of geographically dispersed assets as collateral; and securitization constitutes a burden on interstate commerce.

Second, the geographical location of the servicer significantly affects the profitability of the securitization process (primarily because of the differences among state laws that govern securitization), and hence securitization encourages specific geographical preferences and burdens interstate commerce.

Third, under the present legal regime, securitization introduces conflicts of law problems that arise from non-uniform state laws, and this burdens interstate commerce.

SECURITIZATION CONSTITUTES A VIOLATION OF THE FREE SPEECH CLAUSE

Securitization constitutes violations of the Free Speech Clause of the U.S. Constitution.

The relevant state action consists of: the U.S. Congress's failure to create a uniform set of federal laws for securitization given the historically significant magnitude of securitization transactions in the United States, and its pervasive effect on the overall U.S. economy. The sponsor's selection of collateral for securitization is also a state action because the sponsor is acting in the role of the government, and the government has an interest in facilitating and assuring investor protection by implementing minimum standards of quality for collateral.

Typically, the sponsor of the securitization transaction and the trustees (or members of the board of directors) of the Special Purpose Vehicle (SPV) negotiate and determine the applicable dividend rates (where the trust issues preferred securities or other equity securities) and interest rates (on bonds issued by the SPV) prior to the offering, and the established terms are not changed during the life of the ABS. The sponsor and the intermediary bank typically appoint the SPV's trustees. The SPV's dividend policy and debt policy are established by the sponsor and the intermediary investment bank; and the SPV is typically organized as a state-law trust, LLP, LLC, or C-Corporation. However, the SPV should establish its own debt policy and dividend policy, which may change over time, depending on the performance of the underlying collateral.

These conditions constitute violations of the free speech rights of the SPV (and the SPV trustees), and holders of the SPV's beneficial interests, for several reasons.

First, corporate dividend policy and debt policy are constitutionally protected free speech and hence cannot be dictated by third parties—the SPV has protected property interests in determining and implementing its dividend policy and debt policy. The property interests arise from custom, state corporations/trusts laws, state contract laws, state constitutional laws, and expectations. Corporate dividend policy and debt policy are forms of speech and communication to capital markets and investors. Numerous empirical finance studies have identified information content in dividend policy. Dividend policy and debt policy involve recurring decisions and announcements. Dividend policy and debt policy represent expressions of the SPV's/entity's condition and prospects, and typically do not violate any civil or criminal laws, and do not harm other parties.

There is the required "compulsion" by the sponsor and the intermediary bank—they elect/select the trustees, the trustees do not get any compensation, and the securitization transaction will not be executed unless the trustees agree with the sponsor and the intermediary bank. There is actual and implied compulsion because the sponsor retains substantial and almost complete control of the SPV *before the securities offering*, during which the sponsor effectively compels the SPV to adopt specific dividend policies and debt policies.

SECURITIZATION CONSTITUTES A VIOLATION OF THE RIGHT-TO-CONTRACT CLAUSE OF THE U.S. CONSTITUTION AND IS ILLEGAL

For purposes of constitutional law analysis, the relevant state action consists of any of the following. The U.S. Congress's failure to create a uniform set of laws for securitization (given securitization's profound effects on the U.S. economy) constitutes a state action.

The sponsor's selection of collateral for securitization is essentially a governmental regulatory role, and hence constitutes a state action. The adverse events in the subprime mortgage markets and ABS markets in the United States during 2007 and 2008 confirm that the government has a significant interest in controlling and regulating the quality of collateral in securitization transactions.

The sponsor's act of specifying/controlling the terms of the ABS offering constitutes a state action, because by doing so, the sponsor is essentially acting in the regulatory capacity of the government.

The failure (omission) of certain industry participants such as the National Association of Securities Dealers, some securities exchanges and the U.S. Securities and Exchange Commission to enact specific laws that govern the ABS terms constitutes a state action. These entities are the government or are acting in the same regulatory role as the government. Securitization constitutes a deprivation of the SPV's, and the SPV shareholders' and the SPV trustees' constitutionally protected right to contract for several reasons. First, the sponsor has almost complete control of the SPV in the pre-offering period, and determines terms of the ABS issuance/offering. Second, the

SPV shareholders/bondholders and the SPV trustees cannot change the terms of the ABS, and typically cannot change elements of the post-offering operations of the SPV. Third, the state actions described above result in significant limitations/restrictions on the preexisting contractual rights of the SPV's shareholders and trustees—that is, their rights before the SPV purchases (true-sale) or accepts (assignment) collateral from the sponsor.

The SPV shareholders, bondholders, and trustees have constitutionally protected property interests in negotiating and entering into contracts (about the SPV's operations) that are not unconscionable, void, illegal, or otherwise offensive to others. These property rights arise from state constitutional law, state contract law, state property laws, expectations, and norms.

With regard to the right-to-contract issues in securitization, in some circumstances, there are no public policy concerns that justify upholding the sponsor's and intermediary bank's property interests in efficiently structuring and distributing asset-backed securities, which are far outweighed by the property interests of the SPV's bondholders and/or equity holders. The contracts at issue have far-reaching effects on other parties and significant economic effects on the parties.

SECURITIZATION CONSTITUTES A VIOLATION OF THE EQUAL PROTECTION CLAUSE

For purposes of constitutional law analysis, the relevant state action consists of the U.S. Congress's failure to create a uniform set of federal laws for securitization given the significant magnitude of securitization transactions in the United States (and its pervasive effect on the overall U.S. economy). Furthermore, the securitization sponsor's selection of collateral for securitization can be construed as a state action because it is essentially akin to a governmental regulatory role—the government has a substantial interest in controlling the quality of assets that are securitized in order to minimize disruptions caused by default of ABS.

Under the U.S. Constitution, securitization violates the Equal Protection Doctrine because the "specific combination of application of different laws/rules and circumvention of requirements of laws/rules" unfairly discriminates between those who have the knowledge to structure bankruptcy-remote entities/transactions and those who do not have the knowledge; unfairly discriminates between parties who can afford to hire skilled lawyers and accountants to circumvent relevant bankruptcy law statutes and those who cannot afford to hire skilled advisors; and unfairly discriminates between different securitization transactions that are effected using various combinations of state corporation laws, federal bankruptcy laws, state mortgage laws, and state Uniform Commercial Code (UCC) laws (in such circumstances, the final result is the same but the legal protections/remedies provided to various parties differ significantly). In securitizations, the "specific combination of application of different laws/rules and circumvention of requirements of laws/rules" unfairly discriminates between SPVs that are different entities (i.e., trusts versus LLPs versus LLC versus C-Corporations); it also unfairly discriminates between investors who have good knowledge of bankruptcy laws, securities laws, corporation laws, and collateral analysis and investors who do not have such knowledge.

In securitization transactions, the magnitude of legal protection provided by the legal documents (agreements, statutory protection, etc.) for the mortgagee/borrower and the investors differs significantly, and depends on the nature of the ABS tranche and the associated protections.

The foregoing challenged classifications do not serve any compelling government interest, and the classifications are not substantially related to serving any legitimate government interest.

SECURITIZATION CONSTITUTES A VIOLATION OF THE SEPARATION OF POWERS DOCTRINE

The Separation-of-Powers Doctrine is relevant to asset securitization, because several institutions simultaneously create and enforce laws that affect securitization. In securitization, the main disputes are about default, replacement/substitution of collateral, and trustees' duties. For purposes of constitutional law analysis, the relevant state action consists of the U.S. Congress's failure to create a uniform set of federal laws for securitization transactions given the substantial volume of securitization transactions in the United States. As discussed above, the sponsor's selection of collateral for securitization is also essentially a state action in which the sponsor is effectively performing a regulatory role in place of the federal government. This is because the federal government is statutorily and morally obligated to regulate the quality of collateral used in securitization transactions in order to reduce or eliminate disruptions that may arise from defaults of asset-backed securities. The federal government has effectively shifted part of this regulatory burden to the rating agencies, which control the quality of collateral used in securities—the ratings produced by rating agencies determine which ABS can be purchased and held by financial institutions, government agencies, certain institutional investors, and individual investors. The recent turmoil in the global securitization markets illustrates the importance of the role of selection of collateral for securitization.

When there are problems with securitization transactions in which SPVs are used, the three usual venues for resolution of disputes are the U.S.

Bankruptcy Court, the U.S. Securities and Exchange Commission (SEC), and the U.S. Internal Revenue Service (IRS). However, the bankruptcy laws that govern aspects of securitizations (and SPVs) consist of both federal bankruptcy statutes and bankruptcy judge-made law (such as stays). The judge-made law arises partly from the significant discretion granted to bankruptcy judges pursuant to bankruptcy statutes, and the substantial flexibility in subsequent interpretations of such judge-made laws. Hence, under the U.S. Constitution, the U.S. Bankruptcy Court's combined role of enactment and enforcement of laws pertaining to SPVs in securitization constitutes violations of the Separation-of-Powers Doctrine.

The U.S. SEC adjudicates disputes related to disclosure by SPVs, sponsors, rating agencies, and investors. The SEC enacts and implements (performs an adjudicatory function) its own rules pertaining to disclosure, which the SPV, sponsors, and rating agencies must comply with. Hence, the SEC's combined role of enactment of laws, adjudication of violations/disputes, and enforcement of laws pertaining to SPVs in securitization constitutes violations of the Separation-of-Powers Doctrine.

The U.S. IRS adjudicates disputes and noncompliance related to taxation of SPVs, sponsors, rating agencies, and investors; it also enforces the U.S. Internal Revenue Code. The U.S. IRS also creates man-made regulations, its own statutes, and case law (in its adjudicative proceedings). The IRS implements both its own rules and the U.S. Internal Revenue Code, which the SPV must comply with. Hence, under the U.S. Constitution, the IRS's combined role of enactment of regulations, adjudication, and enforcement of laws pertaining to Securitization SPVs constitutes violations of the Separation-of-Powers Doctrine.

THE ELEMENTS OF REQUIRED NEW REGULATIONS

It is conjectured here that the adverse effects of securitization vary drastically depending on the nature of collateral and its relationship with capital markets, and thus loan securitization can have much greater adverse effects on social welfare and monetary policy than the securitization of patents/trademarks. Hence, governments should ban the securitization of financial instruments.

If some form of asset securitization has to be continued, then there is a significant need for new federal securitization statutes in most common law countries. Ideally, these new federal laws will consist of securities laws, contract law, commercial law, corporation law (with emphasis on SPVs, special trusts, and traditional corporate entities that are used in securitization), and civil procedures. These statutes can be new comprehensive statutes and/or statutes that modify or clarify existing federal and state statutes that govern securitization in whole or in part. Given the constitutional problems discussed herein, the proposed federal statutes should achieve the following objectives:

- *Preempt state laws (contracts, corporations, debtor/creditor laws, and the like) that apply to the securitization process*—and there should be comprehensive preemption standards. The proposed federal statutes should provide more guidance and standards for corporate entities (such as C-Corporations, LLCs, LPs, trusts, and S-Corporations) that are used as SPVs in securitization transactions; particularly for rights of holders of equity interests, rights of holders of rights to payment, default by the SPV, proxy rights, representation in bankruptcy proceedings, corporate power, and so on.
- *Create and enforce civil and criminal sanctions that will be applicable only to securitization processes; and provide adequate civil and criminal penalties for conspiracy and for noncompliance.* Ideally, such penalties will be proportional to the perpetrators' total household wealth, future household wealth, propensity to commit crimes and the magnitude and scope of misconduct; existing civil and criminal sanctions that are applicable to securities law violations will still remain applicable to securitization processes.
- *Address the constitutional problems inherent in the securitization process, which are discussed in this chapter.* The proposed federal statutes should address some of the state-action problems discussed above, and should also govern the standards for the selection of collateral (amount, type, rating, duration, monitoring, third-party verification, over-collateralization, types of guarantees/insurance, servicing, etc.), and disclosure requirements for collateral used in securitization should be designed to improve transparency and help fulfill the government's regulatory obligations.
- *Address the true-sale/assignment controversy, the perfection of security interests in collateral, and the substantive consolidation controversy.* There should be a single body of federal law to govern these issues, and there should be clear filing requirements, evidentiary standards, and defined course-of-conduct or usage of trade (that will reduce transaction costs). The key considerations when developing these statutes should be to increase transparency and reduce transaction costs, information asymmetry, shirking, propensity for fraud, agency problems, and any perceived unfairness of legal requirements.
- *Respond to the findings and recommendations in Nolan (2005a, b) and the 2007 report of the European Financial Markets Lawyers Group (May 2007).*
- *Resolve the occasional conflicts between the UCC and state debtor-creditor statutes; and between the U.S. Bankruptcy Code and local/state mortgage laws.*

- *Provide specific disclosure requirements and standards for the entire securitization process*—such as for terms-sheets, written communications, press releases, computation materials, offering memoranda, and conference calls.
- *Resolve the inconsistencies between securities statutes (e.g., the 1940 Act in the United States) and securitization processes.* The provisions of the 1940 Act include limitations on transactions with affiliates, leverage, volume of senior securities, and the amount of unsecured borrowing, in addition to registration/compliance requirements and corporate governance requirements.
- *Ensure or facilitate some uniformity of tax consequences for the various types of corporate entities that are used as SPVs in securitization.* This may require the amendment of the tax code or the enactment of new tax laws that apply only to corporate entities that are designated as SPVs in securitizations.
- *Provide for summary court proceedings for various levels of offenses (based on culpability and expected magnitude of discovery) committed in the securitization process and subsequent sales of ABS.* The summary proceedings will include nonjury trials, special hearings for summary judgments, subpoenas, and search warrants. There should be limitations on motion practice, and limitations on the timing and extent of discovery. The proposed federal statutes should provide for standards of proof that will minimize investigation costs and enforcement costs while allowing for fairness and minimum standards of culpability.

THE IMPLICATIONS OF CHANGE

The asset-backed securities market is large and global, but in most countries, securitization principles were copied from, and are similar to, U.S. securitization laws and processes.

The key issue is whether U.S. state or federal appellate courts (or courts in other countries) will declare securitization to be unconstitutional and/or illegal, given the large scale of securitization. In the United States, the direct effects of any such "adverse" judicial decision will initially be limited to one state or federal appellate jurisdiction (any such decision will be considered as secondary opinions in other court jurisdictions in the United States), until other appellate jurisdictions follow or until the U.S. Supreme Court renders judgment on the issue.

During 2008, the U.S. Congress enacted new financial regulations, and partly implemented the U.S. Government's federal bailout scheme. In February 2009, U.S. President Barack Obama pledged $275 billion to a program that will reduce mortgage payments for as many as nine million financially distressed homeowners, and expand the role of Fannie Mae and Freddie Mac in reducing foreclosures. In July 2010, the U.S. Congress enacted the Restoring American Financial Stability Act. From 2009 to 2011, many countries enacted new financial regulations to deal with the global financial crisis and problems in mortgage markets and ABS markets. These trends are clear indications that deteriorating economic conditions may eventually compel the U.S. Congress (and/or foreign governments) to completely overhaul the legal framework for securitizations.

The global securitization market can reasonably be construed to expect further regulatory changes and new laws for securitization, given the scope and obvious ineffectiveness of the new laws enacted by the various countries from 2008 to 2010, the continuing increase in default rates of ABS worldwide, and drastic reduction of liquidity in many ABS markets around the world. Such expectations may already be priced into current ABS prices, and may also have resulted in the downward trends in the prices of ABS and some underlying collateral such as mortgages, bonds, and business loans.

The benefits of declaring securitization to be unconstitutional can outweigh any gains from continuing the current inefficient "composite" regulatory scheme for securitization that exists in most countries. The same conditions that precipitated the historic new financial regulations enacted by the U.S. Congress in 2008 to 2010 may continue to exist in whole or in part for the next few years. According to a U.S. research company, there are ongoing permanent changes in the standard of living in many countries, as manifested by increasing unemployment, increasing consumer and corporate bankruptcies, an $8 trillion negative wealth effect from declining home values in the United States, a $10 trillion negative wealth effect from declining and weakened capital markets (in the United States), and $14 trillion worth of consumer debt in the United States. As of December 2008, there was at least $890 billion of issued ABS in the United States, and the default rate for ABS increased during 2008 and 2007.

One approach will be to temporarily halt all new-issue securitization transactions while the U.S. Congress enacts new legislation (between July 2008 and May 2009, there was a significant decline in the volume of new-issue ABS globally). The other approach will be to simply maintain the status quo and gradually introduce new federal securitization legislation.

If some countries continue to approve and allow securitization transactions while appellate courts in the United States or a few other countries declare securitization to be unconstitutional, the economic consequences to the U.S. economy may not be significant for several reasons. First, a substantial volume of securitizations can be temporarily or permanently shifted to SPVs that are registered in "off-shore" jurisdictions (which typically offer tax benefits) or in other major financial centers such as London, Tokyo, and

Dubai. Most of the major investment banks (that control more than 50 percent of the global new-issues securitization market) have offices in all the major financial centers, and they manage their ABS risks on a global basis; thus the issue of choice of law and jurisdiction is somewhat less relevant. Second, it is probable that participants in the U.S. ABS market will create new securitization processes that may solve some of the constitutional problems enumerated in this chapter. Similarly, the financial services committees in the U.S. Congress are also likely to develop new laws that address the constitutional problems inherent in the current securitization processes in the United States (the events and new federal statutes that are associated with the subprime loan problems in the United States are an example of how the U.S. Congress can react to major legal problems in financial markets.

Third, most ABS are short-term or medium-term securities (they have terms of 0.5 to 5 years). Hence, declaring securitization unconstitutional in the United States will affect only a segment of the bond market, but any impact will probably be muted by the new laws that were enacted by the the U. S. Congress and government agencies in various countries during the period from 2008 to 2011, and by prior market expectations.

Fourth, if securitization is declared unconstitutional, the effects may not be overly detrimental but will result in an increase in servicing costs. In one scenario, where the collateral consists of income-producing assets, the ABS bondholders will take title to the collateral, and perhaps eliminate all equity interests and continue to receive the income and other cash proceeds from the collateral. Alternatively, the issuer/sponsor may be required to refund the outstanding balance of the issued ABS to investors—this scenario is most likely in a securitization that involves an assignment of collateral. Hence, any judgment that declares securitization to be unconstitutional must also include summary liquidation procedures or summary partition procedures, which will preclude formal bankruptcy proceedings. Bankruptcy proceedings are notably time-consuming and expensive, and the large number of bondholders or shareholders of securitization SPVs is likely to extend and complicate any bankruptcy process.

CONCLUSION

Under U.S. laws (and perhaps in most common law and commonwealth countries), securitization is clearly unconstitutional. The detrimental effects of loan securitization and its interference with government monetary policies warrant a government ban of securitization. Alternatively, governments should substantially reform securitization and enact comprehensive special federal securitization statutes.

REFERENCES

Aysun, U. and R. Hepp. 2011. Securitization and the balance sheet channel of monetary transmission. *Journal of Banking & Finance* 35 (8): 2111–2122.

Blundell-Wignall, A., and P. Atkinson. 2010. Thinking beyond Basel-3: Necessary solutions for capital and liquidity. *OECD Journal* 2010 (1): 1–23.

Carlson, D. G. 1998. The rotten foundations of securitization. *William & Mary Law Review* 39 (4): 1055–1119.

Estrella, A. 2002. Securitization and the efficacy of monetary policy. *Federal Reserve Bank of New York Economic Policy Review* 8 (1): 243–255.

European Financial Markets Lawyers Group. 2007. Legal obstacles to cross-border securitization in the EU. Working paper. Available at: www.efmlg.org/Docs/EFMLG_report%20on%20legal%20obstacles%20to%20cross-border%20securitisations%20in%20the%20EU_adopted%207%20May%202007.pdf.

Gorton, G., and A. Metrick. 2011. Securitized banking and the run on repo. *Journal of Financial Economics* (forthcoming).

Gyntelberg, J., and E. Remolona. 2006. Securitisation in Asia and the Pacific: Implications for liquidity and credit risks. *BIS Quarterly Review* June: 65–75.

Jones, D. 2000. Emerging problems with the Basel Capital Accord: Regulatory capital arbitrage and related issues. *Journal of Banking & Finance* 24 (1–2): 35–58.

Keys, B., T. Mukherjee, A. Seru, and V. Vig. 2009. Financial regulation and securitization: Evidence from subprime loans. *Journal of Monetary Economics* 56 (5): 700–720.

Klee, K., and B. Butler. 2002. Asset-backed securitization, special purpose vehicles and other securitization issues. *Uniform Commercial Code Law Journal* 35 (2): 5, 23–67.

Loutskina, E. 2011. The role of securitization in bank liquidity and funding management. *Journal of Financial Economics* 100 (3): 663–684.

Mishkin, F. 2007. Housing and the monetary transmission mechanism. Presented at the U.S. Federal Reserve Bank of Kansas. Available at: www.kansascityfed.org/Publicat/Sympos/2007/PDF/Mishkin_0415.pdf.

Nolan, A. 2005a. The securitization legal and regulatory framework. (Goodwin & Procter). ASF Securitization Institute, February 29, 2005.

Nolan, A. 2005b. Sweet Basel II: The regulatory capital treatment of securitization and credit derivatives activities of banking institutions. Goodwin Procter LLP.

Nwogugu, M. 2008a. Some corporate governance problems pertaining to REITs—Part One. *Journal of International Banking Law & Regulation* 23 (2): 71–89.

Nwogugu, M. 2008b. Some corporate governance problems pertaining to REITs—Part Two. *Journal of International Banking Law & Regulation* 23 (3): 142–152.

Schwarcz, S. 1999. Rethinking freedom of contract: A bankruptcy paradigm. *Texas Law Review* 77 (3): 515–599.

Uhde, A., and T. C. Michalak. 2010. Securitization and systematic risk in European banking: Empirical evidence. *Journal of Banking & Finance* 34 (12): 3061–3077.

CHAPTER 13

Recommendations for the Development of a Mortgage and Mortgage-Alternatives Market in the CIS Region, the CEE (Central and Eastern Europe) Region, and China

This chapter introduces an outline of the steps for, and elements of, a new mortgage-alternatives market for CIS (Commonwealth of Independent States) countries, CEE (Central and Eastern Europe) countries, and China. Although these countries now have mortgage markets in various stages of development, they have not developed mortgage-alternatives markets; the proposed mortgage-alternatives market will function simultaneously with existing mortgage markets in these regions. Most of the existing real-estate/mortgage statutes and land laws in the CIS/CEE countries and in China are derivations of English/U.K. and U.S. mortgage and real estate laws. The real danger is that many of the "pioneers" in the CIS/CEE/China real estate markets trained at U.S., Australian, and western European banks and financial institutions, and thus, are likely to transfer "Western" market practices, theories, and laws to the CIS/CEE and China mortgage markets.

As explained in preceding chapters, many elements of mortgages and foreclosure are unconstitutional, costly, and inefficient. In many countries, mortgage and foreclosure laws often conflict with other types of law such as bankruptcy statutes, commercial laws, and securities laws. The constitutional law issues mentioned in other chapters should obviously also be considered when developing mortgage-alternatives markets.

There is evidence of substantial demand for housing and mortgage products in the CIS and CEE regions and China, which raises the issue of the creation/expansion and regulation of primary and secondary markets for mortgages and mortgage alternatives in these countries (collectively, the "Regions"). Traditional mortgages refer to common instruments that are used to finance property purchases—ARMs, fixed-rate mortgages, mortgages without Deed-In-Lieu Clauses, and so on. In most countries, the traditional definition of alternative mortgages has been limited to only adjustable rate mortgages (ARMs), 100 percent loan-to-value (LTV) mortgages, and no-documentation or low-documentation mortgages. Mortgage alternatives are financial products that are alternatives to traditional mortgages and are used for the purchase/financing of real property, and include rent-to-own programs; installment sales contracts; leasehold mortgages; income-market loans; phased purchase contracts; full-recourse loans with wage garnishment clauses; and similar financial products. Mortgage alternatives differ from traditional mortgages and "alternative mortgages" in terms of allocation of risk, payoffs (of lender and borrower), allocation of ownership rights, effect on foreclosure processes, implicit savings mechanism, contribution to overall social welfare, liquidity, tax consequences, monitoring costs, and transaction costs.

The traditional mortgage and alternative mortgages are inefficient contracts, and the associated foreclosure proceedings are also inefficient and socially, economically, and psychologically costly (Ambrose and Buttimer 2009; Bar-Gill 2009; Miles 2005; Tiwari and Moriizumi 2003; Ambrose and Capone 1996; Quigley and Van Order 1990; Scarberry 2009; Shiller 2009; Peterson 2009; Mayer, Pence, Sherlund 2009; Essene and Apgar 2007; Ben-Shahar, Leung, and Ong 2009; Green and Wachter 2005; Levitin and Goodman 2008). Most of the problems in the global mortgage markets can be attributed to (1) suboptimal incentive systems of institutions and resulting effects on market participants; (2) inefficient long-term coupling of savings markets, rental markets, and property-values markets; (3) detrimental government intervention; (4) ineffective penalty systems; and (5) the structure of mortgage products and foreclosure processes (which exacerbate moral hazard, information asymmetry, strategic defaults, cheap noncompliance, and value inflation).

The inefficient coupling/combinations of mortgage markets, rental markets, savings/investment markets, retirement/expectations markets, and property-value markets has been a major result of U.K./U.S. real estate and mortgage laws that are prevalent in the United States, commonwealth countries, and more recently, the CIS/CEE countries, China, and Brazil. These real estate laws have erroneously and indirectly: (a) imposed mortgages as a solution in property-value submarkets and rental-contracts submarkets and leasehold submarkets (there is often a disconnect between market rents and values of leasehold interests); (b) imposed property-value price discovery and expectations as solutions in mortgage markets; (c) imposed mortgages as solutions in retirement markets; (d) imposed foreclosure processes as solutions in savings/investment markets; and (e) imposed inefficient auctions in submarkets that are often characterized by incomplete contracts, noncompliance contagion (where noncompliance spreads rapidly among market participants—for example, mortgage fraud; foreclosure fraud), strategic default, and substantial information asymmetry.

These *Inefficient Combinations* are done in ways that produce inefficient price discovery processes; increase transaction costs and monitoring costs; facilitate cheap noncompliance; reduce the rate of *Efficient Non-Binding Matching* in rental markets and borrower-mortgage markets; and increase information asymmetry and reduce transparency in a system that is typically complex, critical, and highly regulated with substantial government intervention. Recent research has shown that in many countries, most consumers cannot value or fully comprehend mortgages and yet the purchase of a house is the largest investment of more than 60 percent of all households in most developed countries. Ironically and unfortunately, central/federal governments in many countries have exacerbated the inefficient-combination and noncompliance contagion problems by actively encouraging home purchases financed with traditional mortgages as a major element of household savings. The savings/investment markets should be detached from and properly combined with mortgage, rental, and property-value markets (Ben-Shahar, Leung, and Ong 2009).

Klyuev and Mills (2007) found that changes in home-equity withdrawals (HEW) did not have a significant impact on U.S. savings in the short or long run, and thus housing wealth was not an "ATM." However, the Klyuev and Mills study is not accurate because it does not consider: (1) the upward pressure on home prices caused by consumer expectations and consumers' heavy dependence on home equity as a form of retirement wealth; (2) collusion between homeowners (who want to get home-equity loans) and property appraisers to inflate home prices (property appraisal is a local business and most appraisers grew up in the same towns that they work in or in nearby towns, whereas most lenders are out-of-state lenders); (3) the incremental propensity to consume that is caused by HEW exceeds the incremental propensity to save caused by HEW and incremental income; (4) the incremental debt burden caused by HEWs (which reduces savings rates); (5) consumers' expectations of continued increases in home equity creates excessive spending that substantially reduces savings rates; (6) the inflation rate in many developed countries is understated (and is very high in some sectors like residential real estate), and rapid increases in home prices (and thus, increases in home equity) typically cause uneven price inflation in the economy, which reduces real savings rates; (7) Klyuev and Mills (2007) used measures of savings that may not be deemed as standard "savings"; and (8) the sample was limited in terms of geography/locations, types of households, household wealth (households with different amounts of wealth behave differently), household disposable income, and so on.

Another major problem in the mortgage markets is that mortgages and foreclosures cannot handle the *Selective Credit Fulfillment* problem—wherein when faced with budget constraints, wide variety of choices, peer pressures of modern life, and their knowledge of the consumer credit-scoring system, individuals and/or households selectively fulfill their credit obligations in terms of the amounts and timing of payments they make to different creditors. The major results are that: (a) ability to pay is not proportional to, and may not be related to the willingness to pay, and can vary drastically over different time intervals; and (b) the traditional consumer credit scoring systems are inaccurate.

Mortgages and the dream of home equity and the tax/interest deductions associated with homeownership foster home price inflation and provide a powerful incentive for consumers not to save money by other means, for example, investing in securities, commodities, alternative investments, and other types of assets. In the United States, the recent massive erosion of home equity has left many households without any retirement savings. The reality is that homeownership is not suitable for every household; and increasing homeownership should not be a long-term policy objective of any government because of the inherent problems it breeds. The relevant issues are:

- Who has the best skills to manage debt in order to maximize social welfare? The consumer, a finance company, or a real estate development company?
- Who is best positioned to obtain cheap debt and/or hedge debt in order to maximize social welfare? The consumer household, a finance company, or a real estate development company?
- Who is best positioned to bear and manage the risk associated with price fluctuations? Consumers or institutions?
- Who is best positioned to manage the psychological and social burdens associated with debt?
- Who is best positioned to manage the changing differences in the relative valuations of housing wealth and other forms of wealth (such as cash savings and securities)?
- Who is best positioned to respond to changes in governments' monetary policies and fiscal policies, and to labor market fluctuations? Consumer

households (many of whom cannot understand their mortgages) or institutional investors and banks?

- Who is best positioned to minimize price inflation, transaction costs, speculation, and fraud in the housing and real estate industries? In many countries, history has shown that larger institutional investors are better at doing so than individuals.

The global primary mortgage market consists of: (1) financial institutions and nonfinancial institutions that are lenders; (2) borrowers; (3) attorneys; (4) real estate brokers; (5) mortgage brokers; (6) lawyers; (7) title companies; (8) appraisal companies; (9) servicing companies; (10) purchasers of mortgages; (11) mortgage insurance and property insurance companies; (12) loan-servicing companies; (13) government agencies; and (14) securitization sponsors. The main products in the primary mortgage markets are mortgages and mortgage insurance. The primary mortgage markets are also international, because many foreign banks and financial companies lend and buy mortgages in foreign markets. The global secondary mortgage markets consists of: (1) financial institutions and nonfinancial institutions that are securitization sponsors or sellers of mortgages or purchasers of CMBS/RMBS; (2) other sellers of mortgages and guarantees; (3) attorneys; (4) securities brokers; (5) mortgage brokers; (6) lawyers; (7) appraisal companies; (8) accounting/auditing companies; (9) servicing companies; (10) purchasers of mortgages; (11) mortgage insurance companies; (12) loan-servicing companies; (13) government agencies; and (14) securitization sponsors. The main products in the secondary mortgage markets are whole loans, CMBS, RMBS, and mortgage derivatives (interest-only securities; principal-only securities; mortgage options). Secondary mortgage markets are global because foreign investors often purchase CMBS/RMBS.

The CIS and CEE mortgage markets are nascent (Mashkina, Heliste, and Kosonen 2007; Black, Jaszczolt, and Lee 2002; Freshfields Bruckhaus Deringer LLP 2009; Kopeikin 2010; Segre 2010; European Central Bank 2009; Guseva 2009; Andersen and Hilz-Ward 2006; Radulovic 2006; Barisitz 2005; Klesta 2009; Kosareva and Struyk 1993; Palacin and Shelburne 2005; Rabenhorst and Mihalache 2006; Renaud 2004). The Chinese (Ma 2009; Deng, Zheng, and Ling 2005; Hong and Chen 2009; Cooke 2007; Deshpande 2007; Tang, Liu, and Wong 2006; Deininger and Songqing 2002; Kramer 2006; Ben-Shahar, Leung, and Ong 2009; Chiquier 2006; Berger, Hasen, and Zhou 2007), Japanese (see Nemoto 2005; Ozeki 2007; Konishi 2002; FRBSF 2006; Kramer 2006; Lea 2010), and Canadian (see Courchane and Giles 2002; Dunning 2009; Kiff 2009; CAAMP 2010a; CAAMP 2010b; Min 2010a, 2010b; Mortgage Architects Allen 2009; Standard & Poor 2010; McGee 2009; Traclet 2005; Wolf and Kwan

2008; Londerville 2005; DBRS 2007; Desjardin 2009; Londerville 2005; McGee 2009; Traclet 2005) mortgage markets are much more developed, but are all based on U.S.-style and U.K.-style regulations and statutes. China's mortgage market has experienced the same types of fraudulent activities that exist in the U.S. mortgage markets (Bedi 2009; Chen 2006). Although homeownership rates in Canada and the United States are similar (64 percent to 70 percent), and most home purchases are financed with mortgages in both countries, there are substantial differences in terms of government policies, financial systems, types of mortgages, availability of deficiency-judgment statutes, regulation and outcomes.

The proposals in this chapter clearly contradict most of the findings and recommendations in the three white papers written by Capitas Group International (Capitas Group International 2008, 2010a, 2010b; available at www.capitasgroupintl.com/whitepapers.html).

The key principles and objectives for the development of mortgage-alternatives markets for the CIS/CEE countries and China are:

- Transparency and adequate disclosure.
- Accountability and effective penalty systems.
- Stimulating liquidity—for example, through taxation, incentives, creation of liquidity centers, penalty systems.
- Efficient price discovery.
- Statutory efficiency refers to minimal regulations; minimization of conflicts of laws among agencies and across jurisdictions; maximization of social welfare; and achievement of the objectives and legislative intent of statutes.
- Minimization of regulatory friction.
- Minimization of transaction costs and low monitoring costs.
- Absence of *Enforcement Premia,* that is, a "state" where procedural rules and evidentiary rules ensure that investigation costs and enforcement costs are always lower than the sum of both awarded and realized penalties/fines.
- Facilitation of innovation and rapid adoption of best practices.
- Adequate consumer protection and efficient enforcement of consumer protection statutes.
- Maximization of social welfare.
- Counter-cyclical liquidity.
- Risk reduction.
- Stability of markets.
- Affordability of housing (both rental and purchase).

The following sections are the elements of viable primary and secondary markets for mortgages and mortgage alternatives in the CIS/CEE region and China: (1) the data collection; (2) analysis; (3) principles and policies; (4) coordination among institutions; (5) legal infrastructure; (6) penalty systems for misconduct; (7) compensation and incentive systems; (8) market definition; (9) disclosure and information effects; (10) prohibition of securitization; and (11) price discovery. New primary mortgage products and asset-liability matching are addressed in the next two subchapters.

SURVEYS AND NEEDS ASSESSMENT

Relatively complex real estate transactions and securitization transactions have been completed in the CIS/CEE countries and China. The purpose of the proposed survey and assessment is to evaluate the efficiency of what exists in each country (CIS; CEE; China) in terms of statutes and processes; analyze how new and proposed laws will function; identify gaps (regulatory, human, economic, social, psychological), and determine how best to proceed. The data that will be helpful for policy analysis are:

- Demographics.
- The state of real estate and mortgage markets.
- The scope of current mortgage, leasing, and real estate statutes/regulations in CIS/CEE/China—and the basis, if any, for harmonization of regulations among CIS/CEE countries and China.
- The scope of activities of, and rule making by, various trade associations in the mortgage and banking industries.
- Property values—extent of standardization of methods and data, evolution of values; academics (valuation courses for students and professionals).
- Adequacy of security-perfection systems and title systems—in terms of transparency; quality of disclosures; extent of computerization; conflicts of laws; quality/efficiency of court procedures.
- The nature and extent of integration of existing regional mortgage markets into global real estate and mortgage markets—although most mortgage and real estate statutes in CIS/CEE/China are based on U.K./U.S. statutes, there has not been mobility of capital and international investors have not been active in CIS/CEE/China real estate markets.
- Characteristics of existing real estate securities and mortgage securities markets.
- Household economics and savings patterns—household wealth; avoiding mistakes made by households and subprime consumers in the U.S. residential markets; standardization of lending criteria and

documentation for residential property; household savings and investment; liquidity of wealth, and so on.
- Land wealth and the nature of land markets.
- Agriculture.

COORDINATION AMONG INSTITUTIONS IN CIS/CEE COUNTRIES AND CHINA

In each CIS/CEE country and in China, there are institutions that are substantially or tangentially involved in the marketing, origination, sale, hedging, and servicing of mortgages. These institutions include:

- Mortgage finance agencies of national governments.
- Government tax agencies (state, municipal/local, and federal).
- The central banks.
- The credit ratings agencies—there should be at least two credit ratings agencies, preferably owned by a consortium of governments and companies in the regions.
- Trade associations for mortgage brokers.
- The main trade associations for real estate brokers and insurance companies.
- The constitutional courts in each country.
- The regular courts in each country.
- The ministry of finance.
- The securities regulation agencies.
- The stock exchanges and debt markets.
- Consumer protection agencies.
- Trade associations such as the ISDA, insurance trade associations, and accounting standards organizations (e.g., IASB).
- Law firms in CIS/CEE countries and China—many Western law firms now have offices in the region.

In this context, "*Coordination*" means:

- Uniformity of laws (statutes, procedures, and case laws) within the CIS/CEE region and China (to reduce transaction costs and eliminate regulatory arbitrage).
- Minimization of the number of statutes for each policy objective.
- Standardization of processes, documentation, and measures.
- Efficient allocation of rule making and adjudication among administrative agencies and courts (separation of powers).

- Where feasible, enactment of regional (CIS/CEE/China) statutes and establishment of regional (CIS/CEE/China) agencies for investigation and enforcement.
- Elimination of duplication of statutes; conflict of laws; and interagency jurisdictional conflicts, for example, conflict-of-regulations of government entities and private entities.
- Limitations on the rule-making powers of trade associations and private entities (e.g., stock exchange rules; ISDA; rules of private accounting standards organizations).
- Elimination of cross-jurisdictional regulatory lag—that is, beneficial regulatory innovation in one region should be immediately applied in other regions.

ESTABLISHMENT OF MORTGAGE AND REAL ESTATE RESEARCH NETWORKS (INSTITUTES)

The following inquiries and activities are designed to create knowledge networks in CIS/CEE/China in order to develop and promulgate best practices and foster constructive evolution in the real estate industry:

- Gathering of information about current CIS/CEE and Chinese research institutes that can expand their activities to include research on real estate and mortgage markets—and help develop more mortgage-alternatives products.
- Planning for new regional research institutes. The governments and universities should provide the initial research grants for the establishment of these research institutes. Eventually, trade associations and large companies in the industry will be expected to also contribute funds and human capital to these research institutes.
- Establishment of Internet-based research networks in the CIS/CEE/China. Such research networks will typically be based at major research universities, government agencies, trade associations, and policy institutes and will host online conferences and develop online educational materials for industry professionals.
- The creation of free (or low-cost) training materials for the "conversion" of:
  - Industry professionals—brokerage firms, investment banks, commercial banks, law firms, accounting firms, and so on.
  - Students—finance, accounting, math, statistics, economics, law, urban planning, and real estate students.

- Regulators—central banks and government agencies that regulate antitrust, securities, real estate, planning, housing, consumer protection, and tax issues.

THE MORTGAGE-ALTERNATIVES FUNDS

The objective is to reduce government intervention in mortgage markets, but simultaneously introduce catalysts that will create and stimulate liquidity and transparency in mortgage-alternatives markets. In many countries, the traditional method for increasing liquidity in mortgage markets has been the creation of government-sponsored "liquidity centers," which are entities that either buy mortgages in the secondary markets, or extend secured loans to banks and non-bank entities who then originate mortgages. These liquidity centers have been ineffective and in some instances have failed, and the results across most countries have been adverse and almost uniform, and have included: (a) lowering of underwriting standards, which resulted in increased default rates of residential mortgages, predatory lending, and blighted neighborhoods; (b) increasing the volumes of securitization, which simply added more transaction costs and distributed the risks to other parties in the same or related financial ecosystems (including insurance companies and pension funds), and hence, substantially/exponentially increased systemic risk; (c) increasing and excessive government intervention in housing and mortgage markets (e.g., capital infusions in banks, provision of mortgage insurance, all of which contributed to further distortions and losses); (d) elimination of households' home equity (and thus, their retirement savings) when markets crashed and housing bubbles burst; and (e) artificial supports for home prices based on consumer fears of loss of home equity and associated consumer propensity to preserve savings component of home equity, and consumer "debt burden," hence, the price discovery process became highly distorted. The specific principles and guidelines are:

- Establishment of three to five private mortgage alternatives and mortgage funds for which the seed capital will be provided by CIS/CEE governments and the Chinese government. Each fund will operate across all CIS/CEE countries and China. These funds will be for-profit entities with minimal government control. The funds will eventually be listed on securities exchanges as closed-end or open-ended funds.
- The funds will be funded with: (1) seed capital from governments; (2) issuance of bonds in Euro markets; (3) fees from mortgage and mortgage-alternatives servicing contracts; (4) equity and preferred

equity investments by private investors; (5) internally generated capital (interest income, sales proceeds, etc.); and (6) short-term loans from private entities.

- The funds will: (1) purchase/sell mortgage-alternative products and traditional mortgages; (2) originate mortgage-alternative products; (3) enter into swaps for portfolios of mortgage alternatives; (4) provide seed capital for other mortgage-alternative funds; and (5) provide third-party servicing for banks and nonbank lenders.
- Avoid problems that affected Fannie Mae and Freddie Mac in the United States, such as:
  - Deceptive AAA ratings based on the false impression that Fannie Mae and Freddie Mac were affiliated with or guaranteed by the U.S. government.
  - Excessive leverage and very low equity capital.
  - Increasingly weak/inaccurate mortgage underwriting criteria.
  - Provision of loan guarantees and mortgage insurance.
  - High volumes of subprime mortgages.
  - Excessive use of derivatives for speculation and/or hedging.
  - Nonrecourse purchases of RMBS and CMBS.
  - Nonrecourse purchases of mortgages.
  - Excessive securitization. (As of September 2010, the estimated costs of rescuing Fannie Mae and Freddie Mac in the United States exceeded $154 billion!)
- Each fund will provide real-time online public disclosure of all of its holdings of mortgage alternatives, mortgages, and financial products.
- Any purchases of mortgages and/or mortgage alternatives by any of the funds must be on a full-recourse basis.
- Each fund will not provide mortgage insurance or guarantees. In the best-case scenario, each fund will provide only second-loss mortgage insurance for any losses above 65 percent to 80 percent of the principal/interest of the mortgage alternatives or mortgages.
- Each mortgage-alternative fund cannot sell or buy any mortgage alternatives or financial products to any of the other mortgage-alternative fund or from any CIS/CEE or Chinese government.

LEGAL INFRASTRUCTURE

It is critical to develop and implement adaptive legal infrastructure. In the United States, the Financial Stability Act that was recently enacted (July 2010) is inadequate and does not solve many of the existing problems, but illustrates an approach to financial regulation. The key elements of the legal infrastructure are:

- There should only be national or regional (CIS/CEE/China) regulations/laws (no or minimal state laws), and uniform mortgage-alternatives statutes in CIS/CEE/China. Uniformity is necessary to reduce transaction costs; avoid regulatory arbitrage; reduce constitutional law frictions; encourage mobility of capital and knowledge across national borders; and unify markets. In the United States, the substantial and sometimes perplexing differences among the mortgage and real estate laws of different states/municipalities contributed to the economic crisis of 2007 to 2010—and results include fractionalization and isolation of markets, high transaction costs and search costs, and lower "matching" of buyers and sellers.
- Use of a mix of Common Law and Civil Codes—the law evolves to suit advances in finance, technology, market interactions, and title systems.
- Minimization or elimination of foreclosures by design of statutes and/or design of mortgage-alternative products.
- Deficiency judgment procedures (no anti-deficiency judgment statutes).
- Licensing—financial institutions and very few nonfinancial institutions should be licensed to provide mortgages and mortgage alternatives.
- Transparency and accountability.
- Mortgages and mortgage alternatives should be classified as securities and integrated into securities law framework.
- The conflicts among securities laws, real-estate/mortgage law, and commercial laws should be eliminated. Most of the conflicts pertain to perfection of security interests, title, transfers of title, and the regulations of sales.
- Expedited special court proceedings, such as:
  - Expedited special foreclosure and auction proceedings.
  - Expedited title-determination proceedings.
  - Expedited eviction proceedings.
  - Expedited proceedings for determination of validity of security interests and ownership interests.

Real Estate Auctions

The summary principles and objectives are:

- The main remedy for borrower/buyer default should be deed in lieu of foreclosure or other contract-related remedies that do not involve foreclosures and/or the auction/sale of the underlying property. Foreclosure has extremely high social, economic, and psychological costs and has caused the blight of many neighborhoods in many countries.

- Expedited court proceedings for auctions.
- There should be a statutory ban on borrower's right of post-foreclosure redemption.
- There should be auction insurance in addition to mortgage-alternatives insurance. Auction insurance will help guarantee minimum values of assets.
- Borrowers/buyers should be encouraged to purchase mortgage-alternatives insurance for mortgage-alternatives products—either by the tax system or other means.
- No absolute auctions.
- There should be one government-managed web site for listings of all foreclosure-based auctions.
- There should be a capital gains tax on proceeds of foreclosure auctions in order to discourage foreclosure auctions.

Regulation of Nonbank Lenders

Nonbank institutional lenders in mortgage-alternatives markets should be subject to most of the regulations that apply to banks for mortgages:

- These lenders include finance companies; insurance companies; Internet-based lenders; insurance companies, pension funds; and foundations.
- There should be stringent limits on the number and type of nonbank lenders that can provide mortgages and mortgage alternatives, all of which must comply with ongoing and real-time asset, liquidity, quality, risk management, public disclosure, and experience requirements.
- There should be stringent limits on the volume of mortgages and mortgage alternatives provided by each nonbank lender, and by the group of nonbank lenders as a whole.
- All lenders must publicly disclose (on a real-time basis online) their holdings of mortgages and mortgage alternatives, and their cost-basis for such assets.
- There will not be any government bailouts of failed nonbank lenders—financially distressed lenders will be forced to restructure their obligations preferably without formal bankruptcy proceedings, by first converting financial instruments into equity in order of increasing seniority (i.e., preferred stock, then junior debt, and then senior debt).
- The government will not provide any third-party insurance for mortgages and mortgage alternatives originated by nonbank lenders.

- Uniformity and standardization of risk measures, with a system of introducing and adopting risk management innovations by individual banks.
- Uniformity and standardization of processes, instruments, permits, and licenses.
- Certification of mortgage officers.
- Portfolio limits for nonbank lenders—mortgages and mortgage alternatives should account for less than a specific low percentage (e.g., 30 percent) of nonbank lenders' portfolios.
- Internet-based loan processing and quality control standards.
- Dynamic continuous real-time government auditing irregular and impromptu auditing of nonbank lenders.
- Limits on compensation of top-level and mid-level bank executives.
- Amendment of civil and criminal penalties for misconduct by nonbank lenders, so that their officers will bear some personal liability.
- Monitoring of job changes of senior and mid-level officers—certain positions at large nonbank lenders must be subject to the approval of the central bank.
- Monitoring of the content and quality of training programs at financial institutions.
- All sales of mortgages and mortgage alternatives must be full-recourse sales or a minimum of 80 percent-recourse sales.
- Nonbank lenders should not have access to discount window loans.

Regulation of Banks

The following are general regulatory principles for banks:

- Licensing—banks must be licensed in order to sell or buy mortgages or mortgage alternatives.
- There should be limitations on provision of mortgages and mortgage alternatives—not every bank should provide or trade mortgages and mortgage alternatives. As a matter of policy, no more than 40 percent (or another lower percentage) of banks should provide or trade mortgages or mortgage alternatives. There are substantial economies-of-scale, specialization, and knowledge-generation benefits to be gained by concentrating the sale/trading of mortgages and mortgage alternatives among a small segment of the banking industry.
- There should not be any government bailouts of failed banks. Financially distressed banks will be forced to restructure their obligations preferably without formal bankruptcy proceedings, by first converting financial instruments into equity in order of increasing seniority (i.e., preferred stock, then junior debt, and then senior debt).

- The government should not provide any third-party insurance for mortgages and mortgage alternatives originated by banks. In the best-case scenario, the governments should provide only second-loss insurance, wherein the banks/lenders take losses up to 75 percent of the asset value, and then the government will take on the remaining 25 percent.
- There should be uniformity and standardization of risk measures, with a system of introducing and adopting risk management innovations by individual banks.
- All banks must publicly disclose (on a real-time basis online) their holdings of mortgages and mortgage alternatives, and their cost basis for such assets.
- There should be uniformity and standardization of processes, instruments, permits, and licenses.
- Certification of mortgage officers.
- Portfolio limits for licensed financial institutions—mortgages and mortgage alternatives should account for less than a specific low percentage (e.g., 30 percent) of financial institutions' portfolios.
- Internet-based loan processing and quality control standards.
- Dynamic continuous real-time government auditing—irregular and impromptu auditing of banks.
- Limits on compensation of top-level and mid-level bank executives.
- Amendment of civil and criminal penalties for misconduct by banks, so that bank officers will bear some personal liability.
- Monitoring of job changes of senior and mid-level officers—certain positions must be subject to the approval of the central bank.
- Monitoring of the content and quality of training programs at financial institutions.
- Regulation of and limitations on compensation of top-level and mid-level bank officers:
  - Compensation must be approved by shareholders.
  - Compensation must be tied to changes in the quality of portfolios and charge-offs.
  - Compensation is subject to override by the central bank.
  - Absolute total annual compensation is capped by the central bank.
- All sales of mortgages and mortgage alternatives must be full-recourse sales or a minimum of 80 percent recourse sales.

Consumer Protection Agency

Consumer protection is a major element of mortgage markets in most countries due to the relative complexity and size of the average residential mortgage transaction. However, it seems that the consumer protection regulatory scheme in many countries remains deficient, as evidenced by the subprime crisis that occurred during 2007 to 2010 in the United States, United Kingdom, and various countries. One major commonality across countries has been that consumer protection statutes and enforcement have been disaggregated, so that there are often different consumer-protection government agencies for real estate, other personal property, other financial products, and so on, whereas these assets are often linked by different transactions or by one household. Hence, there is a need for substantial integration of consumer protection statutes and enforcement.

- There should be a national or multi-country consumer-protection agency; and integrated consumer protection statutes that will cover mortgages, mortgage alternatives, real estate auctions; loan origination; sales of financial products; use of credit reports; disclosure to consumers; unfair and deceptive practices; and real estate issues in addition to other consumer protection matters.
- See consumer protection statutes in New York State, California, and Texas, and the federal consumer protection statutes in the United States—but only as an example of issues and objectives, and not necessarily as statutes that should be copied verbatim.

Bankruptcy Statutes

Bankruptcy statutes are critical for the efficiency of the mortgage and mortgage-alternatives markets. In the United States and many developed countries, there have been conflicts between bankruptcy statutes and real estate statutes, particularly about the effects of bankruptcy stays and the perfection of security interests (Bernstein 2008; Painter 2006; Cherkis, King, and Collier 1992; Levitin 2009a; Levitin 2009b; Levitin 2010; Gelpern and Levitin 2009; Levitin and Goodman 2008; Levitin and Twomey 2011; Eggum, Porter, and Twomey 2008; Good and Hammond 2006). The major considerations are:

- Resolve conflicts among: (1) real estate foreclosure laws and title laws; (2) commercial law; and (3) bankruptcy statutes.
- There should be one unified Internet-based system of statutes for the perfection of security interests in personal property, intangibles, and real property.
- There should be short-form bankruptcy proceedings where the issues are not complicated, and there should be expedited court proceedings for prepackaged bankruptcy.

- There should be special proceedings for prepackaged bankruptcies.
- The special summary court proceedings for real estate foreclosures should also be available in bankruptcy court, such that persons who file for personal or corporate bankruptcy cannot avoid resolution of foreclosure claims.
- Bankruptcy statutes should permit mortgage modifications as part of expedited postfiling bankruptcy resolution processes. White (2009) studied data on more than 3.5 million subprime and alt-A mortgages (including about one-sixth of all foreclosures pending, and about 20 percent of the monthly total modifications in November 2008) and found that:
  - Most borrowers could not bear the residential mortgage debt burdens, that the excess mortgage debt is depressing home prices and consumer spending, and that the necessary deleveraging of homeowners is not occurring.
  - Modifications are not reducing principal debt, but rather, they are increasing it.
  - Servicers are incurring huge losses for investors by foreclosing. The average foreclosure loss on a first mortgage in November 2008 was $145,000 or about 55 percent of the average amount due. Loss severities increased steadily throughout 2007 and 2008 and were expected to worsen in 2009. In these circumstances, rational investors should accept mortgage principal reductions corresponding to home value declines of 20 percent or so, were it not for the various obstacles to servicers' restructuring of mortgage loans.
  - Voluntary mortgage modifications are not consistently reducing monthly payment burdens. As stated in the November 2008 report, only 49 percent of mortgage modifications reduced monthly payments below the initial payment, while 17 percent left the payment the same and 34 percent increased the monthly payment.
  - The variation among servicers in the number and quality of modifications is enormous. This variation suggests that not every servicer is doing the maximum possible to reach and work out terms with every defaulted borrower.
  - Fewer than half of modifications made in January 2008 were current in payments on November 25, 2008.
  - Many mortgage modifications are temporary (they were to last for less than 10 years). Thus, the totals reported by the industry include many loans that are being modified to include deferred payment shocks, negative amortization, or other nonamortizing features of the sort that caused the foreclosure crisis.

- Significant numbers of mortgage loans are seriously delinquent, but not in a modification program or in foreclosure. The foreclosure crisis is overwhelming the ability of servicers to either restructure or foreclose on all the delinquent loans.

Regulation of Mortgage Brokers

The federal governments of CIS/CEE countries and China should consider combining the roles of real estate broker, mortgage broker, and appraiser, and develop one comprehensive licensing program for all three functions—but to avoid conflicts of interest, such a professional cannot serve as an appraiser and real estate broker for the same property within any contiguous two-year period. The summary principles are:

- Mortgage brokers should have a strictly intermediary role—mortgage brokers cannot originate loans for their own accounts. The minimum services provided by mortgage brokers should be statutorily defined, for example, interview prospective borrowers, collect data, and match lenders and borrowers.
- There should be national or intercountry licensing of real estate brokers and mortgage brokers.
- There should be national minimum educational qualifications and continuing professional education.
- Licensing requirements should include two to three years of experience and formal written exam.
- Regulation of trade associations—there should be limitations, or an express ban, on rule making by real estate brokerage and/or mortgage brokerage trade associations.
- Mortgage brokers should be subject to certain aspects of bank regulations for loan origination and loan sales.
- There should be regional and national MLS systems (reduce or prohibit local MLS).
- There should be a public database of issued mortgage brokerage licenses and disciplinary actions against brokers.
- There should be minimum statutory standards for brokerage services rendered to consumers.
- There should be substantial monetary criminal penalties for professional misconduct and/or fraud.
- There should be clear national/regional (CIS/CEE/China) standards of liability and proof for fraud and misrepresentation. (See U.S. laws such as the Truth in Lending Act (TILA) and the New York Installment Sale Act.)

- There should be statutory caps on fees paid to mortgage brokers.
- The compensation of mortgage brokers should be a flat fee, rather than commission-based compensation. Mortgage broker commissions have introduced distorted and perverse incentives into the mortgage markets. The compensation of mortgage brokers must be linked to performance of mortgages or mortgage alternatives—a percentage of the flat fee should be paid at the closing and the remainder of the fees should be paid over the life of the mortgage-alternative product or loan/mortgage, and if the borrower defaults, then the remaining fee is forfeited.
- There should be a public database of current mortgage brokerage licenses and disciplinary actions against mortgage brokers.
- There should be minimum statutory standards for brokerage services rendered to consumers.
- There should be substantial monetary criminal penalties for professional misconduct and/or fraud by mortgage brokers. Such penalties should be assessed against individuals and groups of brokers and their supervisors, and deterrence should be a major objective. The thresholds for the cancellation of mortgage brokerage licenses should be set low enough to discourage misconduct.
- In the United States, misconduct by mortgage brokers has been concentrated among independent mortgage brokerage firms. It may be helpful to either limit the number of independent mortgage brokers firms, or allow mortgage brokers to operate only within licensed banks, licensed nonbank lenders, and insurance companies.
- There should be clear national or regional (CIS/CEE/China) standards of liability and proof for fraud and misrepresentation by mortgage brokers. This should also be reflected in consumer protection statutes.

Regulation of Real Estate Brokers

Although real estate brokers can influence many aspects of real estate transactions, their influence continues to be reduced by technological advances and the increasing penetration of broadband Internet in many countries, which allow prospective property purchasers to view videos and pictures of property and to conduct detailed market research at any time. There are several conflicts of interest inherent in current real estate brokerage industry practices, which have continued to distort prices, cause price-inflection, and create inefficiencies. The recommendations are:

- There should be national or regional (CIS/CEE/China) licensing of real estate brokers and mortgage brokers; minimum educational qualifications; and continuing professional education.

- Real estate brokers should have a strictly intermediary role and limited activities: interview consumers; collect information, show properties; and close transactions.
- Real estate brokers should be barred from advising consumers about purchase/sale agreements. The minimum services to be provided by brokers should be statutorily specified and should be strictly an intermediary role.
- Regulation of trade associations—there should be statutory limitations on rule making by real estate brokerage trade associations. In many countries, these trade associations exert undue and excessive quasi-regulatory influence on brokers, which often conflicts with government objectives and policies.
- Currently in most countries, real estate brokers coordinate and have excessive control over the property purchase process because they recommend and often recruit title companies, mortgage brokers, and lawyers for the sale/purchase process. Real estate brokers should be statutorily barred from recommending or recruiting these ancillary service providers, but should be required to direct consumers to government web sites where these ancillary service providers are listed.
- Real estate brokers should be subject to certain aspects of bank regulations for loan origination.
- There should be regional (CIS/CEE/China) and national multiple-listing systems (reduce or prohibit local MLS).
- There should be limitations/caps on brokerage commissions and compensation of real estate brokers.
- The compensation of real estate brokers should be a flat fee per property sold, rather than commission-based compensation—commissions have introduced distorted and perverse incentives into the mortgage markets.
- The compensation of real estate brokers must be linked to performance of any mortgages or mortgage alternatives—a percentage of the flat fee is paid at closing and the remainder is paid over the life of the loan/mortgage, and if the loan/mortgage defaults then the remaining fee is forfeited.
- A public database of existing real estate brokerage licenses and disciplinary actions against brokers should be created.
- There should be statutory minimum standards for brokerage services rendered to consumers.
- There should be substantial monetary criminal penalties for professional misconduct and/or fraud.
- Clear national/CIS standards of liability and proof for fraud and misrepresentation should be established. (See the U.S. TILA and the New York Retail Installment Sales Act.)

Regulation of Real Estate Appraisers and Mortgage Appraisers

Appraisers play an important role in real estate markets globally. The recommended principles are as follows.

There should be national or regional (CIS/CEE/China) regulation of appraisers. Many countries now have professional standards for appraisals (rules and regulations) although such rules are typically developed by private entities and/or trade associations—such rules should be developed and enforced by national governments.

There should be minimum education and experience and continuing education standards for appraisers, which must cover mortgage brokerage, real estate brokerage, mortgage alternatives, and the economic effects of mortgage products on real estate values (most appraisal curricula do not contain these elements).

There should be substantial criminal penalties for professional misconduct, fraud, or collusion by appraisers. Such penalties should include both monetary penalties and incarceration and suspension/revocation of appraisal licenses.

The current methods of compensation for real estate appraisers must be modified. At the present time, banks/lenders and investors and homeowners are the primary clients of appraisers—hence, there are substantial conflicts of interest because these clients can influence appraisal results by: (1) stopping payment before an appraisal is completed (appraisal fees are typically billed in stages); (2) by the actual or implied threat of cancelling all future repeat appraisal business; or (3) the actual or implied threat of not providing any loans for any properties that have been appraised by the appraiser. Appraisers have substantial incentives to inflate property prices, because their fees are often linked to the value of the subject property even though the amount of work they do for large and small properties is typically the same. Furthermore, most appraisal companies have less than four employees, and thus, cannot weather recessions and often do not spend many resources on marketing; and are substantially dependent on repeat appraisal business.

Private appraisers should not be compensated directly by their clients; rather, appraisers should be compensated either (1) by the government; (2) by a public-private trust that is funded from special taxes and fees paid by appraisal clients; or (3) through a government-sponsored and controlled trade association. Appraisers should not be compensated by any person who can benefit from the appraisal.

Furthermore, there should be a selection mechanism (implemented by the governments or by a government-sponsored and controlled trade association) to match appraisers with clients, such that at least the following rules will apply: (1) an appraiser cannot appraise a specific property more than twice in each contiguous five- to six-year period; (2) an appraiser can appraise only a limited number of properties for any one client in any two contiguous years; (3) a client cannot select an appraiser directly, but rather, the client will be presented with a choice of between three and six appraisers that will be selected either by the government or a government-controlled trade association based on a combination of qualifications/experience, auctions/bidding, and compliance record.

Home-equity mortgages—there should be statutes that require two separate appraisals by two unrelated external appraisers before any home-equity mortgage is approved. Such appraisers must provide sworn affidavits of complete independence from the owner/borrower; and the owner/borrower must also provide a similar affidavit sworn under penalty of perjury. There should be substantial penalties for violations of this statute.

Title Recording Systems and Land Ownership Systems

Title recording systems and landownership systems are obviously important for information purposes and for the perfection of security interests in assets. In most developed countries, there are often conflicts among title systems for various types of personal property and real property. The guidelines and principles are:

- There should be a government-operated, Internet-based national or regional (CIS/CEE/China) title system for both owned and leased real estate and personal property.
- The title system will also be used to perfect security interests or title in properties associated with mortgage alternatives.
- A title recording system that is similar to the Registration/Torrens System is likely to be more accurate but not necessarily the most efficient system.
- Long-term residential leases associated with mortgage alternatives, and commercial leases that exceed a specific threshold should also be recorded in title systems. (See Uniform Commercial Code, and state real estate statutes in the United States.)
- With regard to landownership systems, there are substantial differences between pure ownership systems (persons own interests in land directly, as in the United States) and leasing systems (the federal/state government owns all land, which it then leases to persons, typically for long periods). The appropriateness of either system will depend on the culture and government objectives in each country. However, countries that use leasing systems have had fewer problems in terms of price bubbles,

fraud, and other issues. Both types of landownership systems can be combined with one of the two main title recording systems (either the Recording System or the Torrens Registration system).

Leasing Statutes

There should be unified national or regional (CIS/CEE/China) leasing statutes for the leasing of both personal property and real property. Many mortgage alternatives introduced here involve forms of implicit leasing. These leasing statutes can be combined with mortgage statutes, and should be integrated into the systems/statutes for perfecting security interests in real property and personal property.

Penalty System for Banks and Nonbank Lenders

There should be a system of penalties for banks and nonbank lenders and their employees and agents in order to provide substantial incentives for the rapid development of the mortgage-alternatives market. The main principles are:

- Deterrence effect is more important than punitive effects.
- Penalty system should target top and mid-level employees. Penalties for individuals should focus on both total wealth and incarceration.
- Penalties for corporate entities should also focus on total wealth.
- Penalties should cover government investigators' monitoring costs, prosecutors' enforcement costs, and government administration costs.

Corporate Entities that Focus on Residential or Commercial Real Estate

Corporate entities that deal primarily in real estate often face different issues and risks than traditional companies. There should be special national or regional (CIS/CEE/China) statutes for corporate entities that will deal in primarily real estate. The U.S. REITs and REITs in many countries are not good examples because they have many inherent securities law, corporate governance, and constitutional law problems.

CREDIT RATINGS SYSTEMS

The corporate credit rating industry is critical in the development of mortgage markets. The two segments of the credit ratings industry (corporate credit ratings and individuals' credit reporting agencies) have been the subject of substantial dysfunctional and ineffective regulation in many countries. There are huge conflicts of interest in the corporate credit ratings sector because issuers and investment banks pay the credit rating agencies directly, and the credit rating agencies are not truly independent.

There should be more stringent regulations for credit ratings agencies (CRAs), which must be licensed by the government. These should include minimum quality standards and minimum training and experience standards (continuing professional education). Minimum education standards and certification for ratings analysts should also be established.

The CRAs must not be compensated directly by issuer-companies. Nwogugu (2011) develops some new compensation and incentive schemes for CRAs.

Creation of: (a) at least two government-controlled rating agencies—private entities owned by a consortium of CIS/CEE governments and the Chinese government; and (b) other rating agencies owned by anybody but licensed by the governments of the region (CIS/CEE/China).

Specific regulations prevent antitrust violations and conflicts of interest in the ratings agency industry—ratings shopping; duopoly, payment of fees (timing; amounts; source, etc.). For example, the U.S. treasury submitted proposed regulations for credit rating agencies to the U.S. Congress in July 2009, but these regulations do not solve the main conflict-of-interest problems inherent in corporate credit ratings; and are:

Conflicts of Interest

- *Bar firms from consulting with any company that they also rate.* Credit ratings agencies will face similar restrictions to other professional service providers, like accountants, and will be prohibited from providing consulting services to companies that contract for ratings.
- *Strengthen disclosure and management of conflicts of interest.* The legislation will prohibit or require the management and disclosure of conflicts arising from the way a rating agency is paid, its business relationships, affiliations, or other conflicts.
- *Disclose fees paid by an issuer along with each rating report.* Each rating report will disclose the fees paid by the issuer for a particular rating, as well as the total amount of fees paid by the issuer to the rating agency in the previous two years.
- *Look-back requirement to address the conflicts from a "revolving door."* If a rating agency employee is hired by an issuer and if the employee had worked on ratings for that issuer in the preceding year, the rating agency will be required to conduct a review of ratings for that issuer to determine if any conflicts of interest influenced the rating and adjust the rating as appropriate.

- *Designate a compliance officer.* Each rating agency will be required to designate a compliance officer who reports directly to the board or the senior officer of the firm with direct responsibility over compliance with internal controls and processes. The compliance officer will not be allowed to engage in any rating activities, marketing, sales, or setting of compensation, and will be required to submit a report annually to the SEC.

Transparency and Disclosure

- *Require disclosure of preliminary ratings to reduce "ratings shopping."* Currently, an issuer may attempt to "shop" among rating agencies by soliciting preliminary ratings from multiple agencies and then only paying for and disclosing the highest rating it received for its product. We would shed light on this practice by requiring an issuer to disclose all of the preliminary ratings it had received from different credit rating agencies so that investors will see how much shopping happened and whether there were discrepancies with the final rating.
- *Require different symbols to be used to distinguish the risks of structured products.* One of the challenges in the current crisis is that investors do not fully realize that the risks posed by structured products such as asset-backed securities are fundamentally different from those posed by corporate bonds, even with similar credit ratings. Our proposal requires rating agencies to use different symbols for structured finance products as an indication of these disparate risks.
- *Require qualitative and quantitative disclosure of the risks measured in a rating.* Agencies will be required to provide a much fuller picture of the risks in any rated security through the addition of qualitative and quantitative disclosure of the risks and performance variance inherent in any given security. Ratings cannot be a substitute for investor due diligence. Therefore, to facilitate investor analysis, we will require that each rating also include a clear report containing assessments of data reliability, the probability of default, the estimated severity of loss in the event of default, and the sensitivity of a rating to changes in assumptions. This report will present information in a way that makes it simple to compare this data across different securities and institutions. This additional information will increase market discipline by providing clearer estimates of the risks posed by different investments.

Strengthen SEC Authority and Supervision

- *Establish a dedicated office for supervision of rating agencies.* Our legislative proposal establishes a dedicated office within the SEC to strengthen supervision of rating agencies and to carry out the enhanced regulations required.

- *Mandatory registration.* Unlike the current voluntary system of registration, our proposal would make registration mandatory for all credit rating agencies. This will bring all ratings firms into a strengthened system of regulation.
- *SEC examination of internal controls and processes.* The SEC will require each rating agency to document its policies and procedures for the determination of ratings. The SEC will examine the internal controls, due diligence, and implementation of rating methodologies for all credit rating agencies to ensure compliance with their policies and public disclosures.

Reduce Reliance on Credit Rating Agencies

- *PWG review of regulatory use of ratings.* The Department of the Treasury will work with the SEC and the President's Working Group on Financial Markets to determine where references to ratings can be removed from regulations.
- *SEC recently requested public comment on whether to remove references to ratings in money market mutual fund regulation.* As part of a comprehensive set of money market fund reform proposals, the SEC requested public comment on whether to eliminate references to ratings in the regulation governing money market mutual funds, as a way to reduce reliance on ratings. The Department of the Treasury will work with the SEC to examine opportunities to reduce reliance and increase the resilience of the money market mutual fund industry.
- *Require GAO study on reducing reliance.* In addition to regulatory efforts to reduce reliance on credit ratings, this legislation would require the GAO to study and issue a report on the reliance on ratings in federal and state regulations.

Strongly Support SEC Actions on Credit Rating Agencies

- *Enable additional ratings on structured products.* Because structured products are often complex and require detailed information to assess, it can be difficult for a rating agency to provide "unsolicited ratings"—ratings on products it was not paid to rate. These ratings, while in existence previously, were ineffective because investors understood that these unsolicited ratings did not benefit from the same information as the fully contracted ratings. The SEC has proposed a rule that would require issuers to provide the same data they provide to one credit rating agency as the basis of a rating to all other credit rating agencies. This will allow other credit rating agencies to provide additional independent analysis to the market.

- *Require disclosure of full ratings history.* The SEC has proposed requiring nationally recognized statistical rating organizations ("NRSROs") to disclose, on a delayed basis, ratings history information for 100 percent of all issuer-paid credit ratings.
- *Strengthen regulation and oversight of credit rating agencies.* In response to the credit market turmoil, in February the SEC adopted several measures to increase the transparency of the rating agencies' methodologies, strengthen disclosure of ratings performance, prohibit certain practices that create conflicts of interest, and enhance recordkeeping and reporting obligations to assist the SEC in performing its regulatory and oversight functions. The SEC has allocated resources to establish a branch of examiners dedicated specifically to conducting examination oversight of rating agencies.

Some rating agencies have claimed that their ratings reports are a form of protected speech pursuant to constitutional laws, and therefore they cannot be held liable for any resulting damages incurred by the subject companies as a result of release of ratings reports. This issue remains a major problem in the regulation of CRAs. The resolution will depend on the constitutional laws of each country, unless countries decide to adopt a uniform approach to the issues, which is perhaps the most optimal solution. The potentially detrimental effects of adverse CRAs' ratings are often substantially outweighed by the benefits to the public. Given the conflicts of interest and inefficiencies in the credit ratings industry, making ratings protected speech will reduce rating agencies' incentives to provide accurate ratings, and since accuracy and timeliness of ratings are paramount, ratings will likely be better under a "no-protected-speech" regime or a variant. Rating agencies can purchase insurance for liability from issuing ratings, or provide "qualified ratings" or limited guarantees about the accuracy of their ratings.

The use of consumer credit reports should be eliminated in the loan origination process. Consumer credit scores (e.g., FICO, Experian) are substantially biased and distorted, and the reasons are as follows: (1) consumer credit scores do not consider true willingness to pay, as when the consumer is unemployed or underemployed, so that an unemployed married man (age 50, with a family of three) who owns an €800,000 home free and clear plus other assets but misses several credit card payments due to unemployment can be assigned a lower credit score than an 18-year-old teenager who earns minimum wage and works part time, has a few credit cards (whose average spending limit is €500), and has no assets; (2) consumer credit scores do not consider the relative liquidity of the consumer's assets; (3) consumer credit scores do not consider the relative-wealth effect where the individual's total wealth is often not known to, and is not considered by, the credit scoring company—for example, a millionaire whose sole credit card has a spending limit of €1,000, but who does not make timely credit-card bill payments or stops paying credit card bills due to a dispute with the lender will be assigned a low credit score, or a score that is lower than another person who has no or minimal assets; (4) the consumer credit scores are not calibrated by spending limits, thus a person who has six credit cards (each of which has a spending limit of €1,500), and spends less than €100 with each card in each month, and makes regular timely payments will be assigned a much higher credit score than another person that owns two cards (each of which has a spending limit of €60,000), and spends an average of €40,000 each month with each card, but makes late payments every month; and (5) consumer credit scores are not linked to earned recurring income, so that a person who has no income and six credit cards (average spending limit of €1,000) and makes timely and regular monthly credit card payments using gifts from relatives will have a better credit rating than another person who has three credit cards (average spending limit of €1,000), and cannot obtain funds from others, relies solely on his or her income, and makes late payments each month. Identity theft, unintentional reporting of false information, and delays in removing false information from credit reports remain major problems in consumer credit reporting, which can have adverse effects (e.g., dislike of mortgages and loans) in cultures/societies that are not used to such types of evaluation.

The subprime mortgage problems and the losses in the prime mortgage markets that occurred from 2007 to 2010 in the United States illustrate some of the problems inherent in reliance on consumer credit scores. Consumer credit scores typically cannot predict adverse systemic shocks that result in mass mortgage defaults (such as layoffs; mass pay cuts; reductions in availability of other consumer credit). Lenders typically use consumer credit scores only around the time of the origination of the loan—the borrower's circumstances can change rapidly and render the initial credit scores meaningless. Thus, lenders/banks should be encouraged not to rely heavily on consumer credit scores.

TAXATION

The taxation of mortgage alternatives is a critical element that can facilitate or hinder rapid growth of mortgage-alternatives markets. The major considerations are:

- The deduction of mortgage interest for tax purposes should be prohibited where feasible because it: (1) encourages excessive mortgage finance and inflation of appraisals; (2) causes overinvestment in real estate and misallocation of capital; (3) causes individuals to buy oversize and expensive houses; and (4) distorts the cost of homeownership relative to other investments. Elimination of deductibility of mortgage interest will help equalize (make individuals indifferent to) renting and homeownership, and thus reduce the often detrimental emotional/psychological attachment to homes, which breeds unfulfilled income/savings expectations and speculation.
- As explained here, there should be very high and graduated capital gains taxes (e.g., 95 percent in year 1, 90 percent in year 2) to prevent speculation and "flipping" of housing units during the first five years of ownership—subject to exemptions for special circumstances. The tax system should discourage the purchase of homes (single-family homes, condos/co-ops, and one- to four-family houses) for speculation.
- There should be a graduated sales tax (in addition to capital gains taxes) on the proceeds of sales of housing units. Such sales taxes should be significant (10 percent to 25 percent) for luxury homes and midprice homes in order to reduce speculation and bubbles.
- There should be a mortgage tax levied on all persons who obtain mortgages for the purchase of real estate. The proceeds of this mortgage tax will be used to finance government expenditures on monitoring mortgage markets.
- Property taxes should be based on the replacement cost rather than market values of properties.
- The tax systems should equalize the total cost of rental, and the total cost of ownership in order to prevent tax-based drift of otherwise unqualified persons into homeownership markets and mortgage markets.
- The proceeds of home-equity loans should be taxed substantially to: (1) prevent speculation, inflation, and excessive spending; (2) discourage the use of home equity as a savings mechanism; and (3) encourage investment in retirement products and pension plans. Such taxes may be waived for persons who immediately roll over all of such loan proceeds into fixed income retirement products within two months of obtaining the home-equity loan.
- The national governments should provide substantial tax incentives to banks, institutional investors, and nonbank lenders for: (1) the purchase or sale of 1-year, 2-year, and 3-year "strips" of traditional long-term mortgages and mortgage alternatives in secondary market transactions; and (2) the purchase or sale of traditional long-term mortgages and mortgage alternatives in secondary market transactions. These tax

incentives can be in the form of: (a) substantially reduced income taxes in interest income and capital gains earned from these products; (b) tax credits for achieving specific volumes of sales/purchases of mortgage alternatives and "strips" in secondary markets; (c) tax credits for the quality of mortgage alternatives and "strips" purchased in secondary market transactions; or (d) substantially reduced capital gains taxes for sales/purchases of mortgage alternatives. There should be regional (CIS/CEE/China) uniformity in the implementation of these tax incentives in order to encourage capital mobility and liquidity in mortgage-alternatives markets.

PENSION REFORM

Pensions should be a major factor in economic policy and planning for mortgage-alternatives markets. Pension systems should be reformed to prevent the overinvestment in housing and traditional mortgages (either whole loans or asset-backed securities [ABS]) that is now prevalent in most developing countries, which unfortunately, is encouraged by availability of mortgages and asset-backed securities. The main guidelines are:

- There should be limits on monetary investments in traditional mortgages, ABS, and mortgage alternatives by pension funds.
- Pension funds should not be permitted to provide mortgage insurance/guarantees or originate mortgages.
- The tax system (income tax; sales tax; property tax; capital gains tax) should make liquid investments (securities; interests; partnerships) more attractive than homeownership.
- Some of the mortgage alternative should include pension alternatives—for example, a lease with an option to buy where a portion of the lease payments is invested in an annuity, and if the lessee does not exercise the purchase option, then he or she gets the annuity as part of a pension plan.

ACCOUNTING AND TRANSPARENCY/DISCLOSURE

The general principles are:

- Follow IASB/IFRS standards as much as possible; appropriate areas for departure from IASB/IFRS are: (1) market value accounting, (2) leases, (3) pensions, (4) deferred taxes, and (5) intangibles.
- Ensure that disclosure standards facilitate transparency.

- There should be mandatory real-time online public disclosure of the holdings of traditional mortgages and mortgage alternatives (amount; property location; and terms of products; but not names of mortgagors/buyers) owned by financial institutions and nonbank entities whose assets exceed a minimum threshold.
- There should be a convergence of tax and book accounting standards so that there are minimal book-tax differences.
- There should be a regional (CIS/CEE/China) accounting standards organization that is sponsored, organized, and controlled by a consortium of the national governments of these countries. This organization will be staffed with both government officials and private industry executives and funded by the governments and special taxes. This organization will develop and monitor accounting standards.
- Private accounting rule-making entities (similar to FASB in the United States) should be prohibited. Accounting regulations are critical to the functioning of economies, and should not be delegated to private entities whose interests may conflict with those of the government or overall social welfare.

CENTRAL BANKS

The central banks of the CIS/CEE countries and China are obviously crucial for policy development and coordination, monitoring, and enforcement. Some recommended guidelines and principles are:

- There should be closer coordination among central banks of CIS/CEE countries and the Chinese central bank—in terms of disclosure standards; risk management, regulatory actions; collateral valuation standards; auditing standards.
- There should be no or minimal discount window lending to financial institutions for use in providing mortgages.
- There should not be any government bailouts for failed lenders and insurance companies.
- No direct purchases of traditional mortgages or mortgage alternatives by governments.
- Establish and enforce real-time "dynamic" capital requirements and mandatory real-time online public disclosure standards for mortgages and mortgage alternatives owned by banks and some nonbank entities.
- Establish and enforce minimum underwriting criteria for various classes of mortgages, mortgage alternatives and financial products—and implement severe criminal penalties for noncompliance.

- Central banks must extend their direct supervision to nonbank financial institutions (insurance companies, securities firms, credit-card companies, pension funds, trusts) and nonfinancial institutions that are licensed to provide loans/mortgages.
- Central banks should work toward ratings-free risk-management standards.
- Basel-III is flawed. Value-at-Risk (VaR) and related methods should not be used.
- There should be stringent limits on the sales of government securities to fund bank lending, bank liquidity, or short-term spending; or to boost consumer spending.
- The traditional central bank monetary policies are no longer effective (as illustrated by the events in the United States) and these outdated policies include: (1) open-market purchases/sales of government securities and debts of corporations, (2) changing benchmark interest rates, (3) discount-window policies, (4) "static" capital reserve requirements for financial institutions, (5) regulation of the interbank and "repo" markets, (6) quantitative easing, and (7) large medium-term and long-term interest rate and currency swaps. Most market participants have since learned how to circumvent these central bank policy tools. The effectiveness of these policy tools is heavily dependent on the availability and accuracy of market data, which in turn has been substantially distorted by the use of derivatives, program trading, and inability to fathom the psychological state of market participants.
- Penalties for noncompliance with regulations must include criminal penalties not only for financial institutions, but also their top-level and mid-level officers.
- The volume of traditional mortgages must be capped, and should not exceed a specific percentage (e.g., 30 percent) of total outstanding real estate financial products.

MORTGAGE INSURANCE

Mortgage insurance remains a major element of mortgage finance in most countries. In the United States, the provision of mortgage insurance by the government and FHA had disastrous consequences: (1) inflation of property prices; (2) substantial declines in the quality/accuracy of mortgage underwriting standards; (3) increase in sales of low-quality mortgages into the secondary mortgage markets; and (4) increases in loan defaults and strategic defaults. Some relevant considerations are:

- Governments should not provide any mortgage insurance. In the best-case scenario, governments should provide only catastrophic "back-up" mortgage insurance; that is, mortgage insurance only for losses that exceed 70 percent of the loan principal/interest, so that the lenders absorb the first loss, and the government takes only secondary/residual losses.
- Only banks and nonbank entities that are licensed to provide mortgages and mortgage alternatives should be permitted to provide mortgage insurance and/or guarantees for mortgages and/or mortgage-alternatives products. The volumes of mortgage insurance and guarantees that are provided by banks should be restricted.
- No more than 50 percent of insurance companies in each country should be licensed to deal in the insurance and/or reinsurance of mortgages and mortgage alternatives.
- Reinsurance statutes for mortgages and mortgage alternatives should require: (1) dynamic and sufficient capital reserves; (2) minimal concentration of risk (by product, geography, asset class, type of borrower/buyer); and (3) maximum reinsurance periods (two to four years), so that reinsurance risk rotates and stimulates liquidity of risk.
- There should be strict limitations on the activities and rule-making capacity of insurance industry associations—these trade associations should not be permitted to enact binding rules for their members for risk management. In the United States, the National Association of Insurance Commissioners (NAIC) and the International Swaps and Derivatives Association (ISDA) have exerted substantial influence on risk management of insurance companies in ways that may not always be beneficial or in line with government policies.

HOME-EQUITY MORTGAGES

The mortgage wealth illusion has been show to be highly detrimental to both households and social welfare. The availability of home-equity mortgages: (1) fosters collusion with appraisers and thus, appraisal fraud; (2) fosters excessive and unpredictable consumer spending; and (3) makes it more difficult for the central banks to implement and monitor monetary policies.

The general principles are:

- Discourage home-equity mortgages by appropriate taxation—for example, high taxes on proceeds of home-equity loans.
- Provide substantial tax incentives for households that roll over unencumbered home equity into retirement and savings products such as annuities through reverse mortgages and other instruments.

- Provide substantial tax incentives for households that roll over the proceeds of home-equity loans into retirement and savings products.
- Statutorily limit the amount of home-equity mortgages as a percent of the home value.

Mortgages should be issued only when the house is unencumbered or the balance of the first mortgage is below a certain percentage of the home value (e.g., 30 percent).

PRIMARY MORTGAGE MARKETS

The primary mortgage markets that now exist in the United States, CIS, CEE, China, Latin America, Japan, Australia, and western Europe are government-directed, government-subsidized and heavily regulated markets. Government intervention in mortgage markets remains a major problem that is often costly for taxpayers and often obscures the execution of government policies such as monetary policy and social policy—in terms of types of tax subsidies, capital infusions by governments, adverse and ineffective regulation, lax enforcement, and inefficient procedures (transactions; litigation; etc.).

In the United States, one major weakness in the mortgage markets is the interaction between the consumer and the mortgage broker. The guidelines for change are:

- There should be standardization of lending processes and mortgages and mortgage alternatives—in order to enhance liquidity in secondary markets.
- There should be transfer of knowledge and human capital among market participants—this is another major source of systemic risk and contagion in markets and should be regulated strictly.
- Dynamic risk scoring systems should be developed and implemented.
- Dynamic risk-based capital requirements should be developed and implemented.
- Value-at-Risk (VaR) or any of its variants should not be used.
- The government should encourage amortizing mortgages by taxation and by statutes.
- The volume of traditional mortgages must be capped, and should not exceed a specific percentage (e.g., 30 percent) of total outstanding real estate financial products.
- The risk-management systems should be ratings-free.

- There should be mandatory real-time public disclosure (Internet) of mortgage and mortgage-alternatives holdings of regulated entities (insurance companies, banks, pension funds; etc.), nonregulated private entities (e.g., finance companies), and government agencies. The disclosure will provide details of each mortgage or mortgage alternative (principal, interest, term, etc.) but not the names of the borrowers.
- There should be mandatory notarization of mortgage and mortgage-alternatives contracts.
- Government intervention should be limited to: (a) subsidizing interest rates for low-income families; and (b) setting limitations on the volume of ARMs—overall volume and lender-specific volume.
- Income verification is critical. No-verification mortgages should be limited to situations where borrower has substantial assets, or where the lender has resources to manage housing units as rental units (e.g., a lender that specializes in rent-to-own contracts and/or installment sales contracts).
- There should be special taxes to reduce speculation, such as the following types of taxes:
  - Time-based capital gains tax based on the timing of sale or refinancing of the property, with capital gains tax rates starting at 95 percent to 100 percent in the first year, and declining by a specific percentage each year. The only exemptions will be sellers who are moving to a different state located at least 200 miles away. The problem with ordinary graduated time-based capital gains tax is that the seller can defer taxes by doing a tax-free sale, and can do a cash-out refinance, which is the equivalent of a sale without capital gains tax.
  - Value-based capital gains tax that is based on the sale value of the property, where sales of high-valued properties will incur higher taxes than sales of properties with average values. For example, residential property priced at $10,000 to $100,000 will be taxed at 15 percent; residential property sold at $100,001 to $350,000 will be taxed at 35 percent; residential property sold at $350,001 to $600,000 will be taxed at 50 percent; and residential property sold above $600,001 will be taxed at 65 percent.

Consumer Data

The general recommendations are:

- Mandatory filing of annual income tax returns by all adults and corporate entities.
- Credit reports should not be the primary decision criteria—by statute.

- Generally, consumers should obtain mortgage-alternative products through banks where they have a banking history.
- There should be a system of "Alternative Collateral," which reduces reliance on credit scores:
  - Verification of other assets of borrowers.
  - Bank or other private entity can provide guarantee in exchange for fees.
  - There must be expedited/summary legal proceedings for seizing of consumers' collateral upon default (minimal evidentiary standards; low costs for completion; supported by government agencies).
  - The government or the funds mentioned above should not provide mortgage guarantees.
  - Consumer data—credit card bills; utility bills; pay stubs; and so on.
  - Banks/lenders should be able to access government database of consumers' pay/salary/income with the consumer's written permission, in order to verify income.
  - Banks/lenders can also request life insurance and/or renter's insurance for prospective borrowers who are more than 50 years old.
  - Debt-to-income ratios.
  - Debt-to-net-worth ratios.

Servicing of Mortgages and Mortgage Alternatives

Servicing is a critical element of the mortgage-alternatives markets. In most developed countries, servicing is outsourced by banks and nonbank financial companies to smaller companies that have regional operations. These servicing companies then handle defaults and often outsource property sales to real estate brokers and also outsource property management to third-party companies, thus incurring additional transaction costs. Obviously there can be substantial cost savings, knowledge effects, and economies of scale by building much larger servicing companies that have national or international operations, and combining traditional servicing operations with in-house brokerage and property management. The main issues are:

- The government-sponsored funds should provide traditional servicing (combined with property management) to banks/lenders.
- The national governments should encourage consolidation of servicing companies and property management companies in order to reduce costs.
- There should be adequate training for staff of servicing companies.
- There should be standardization of reporting, valuation, surveillance, and processes.

- Computerization and automation of processes and forms.
- Customer relationship management (CRM) system.
- Continuous improvement of origination and risk-management processes—with feedback loops to origination groups and IT groups.
- Risk-management surveillance—changes in consumer's status (income, job, etc.), regional economic trends; company-specific changes, changes in property values; and so on.

Limitation on the Types of Companies that Can Offer Mortgage Insurance or Guarantees

Not all banks and financial institutions should be licensed to offer mortgages and mortgage alternatives. The events in the United States, Japan, and western Europe have proved that it can be disastrous to permit all banks to provide mortgages and all types of credit products—this only magnifies systemic risk. Mortgages require specialized skills—in credit, technology, human/consumer psychology, accounting, risk management, and law. Most financial institutions truly do not have such skills, cannot develop such skills, and end up copying what other financial institutions have done. Loan syndication compounds these problems and the result is a domino effect whenever there is a small problem. As a matter of policy, less than 50 percent of financial institutions in the CIS region should be statutorily permitted to offer mortgages or mortgage alternatives.

Similarly, not all financial institutions (insurance companies, pension funds, trusts, etc.) should be statutorily allowed to provide mortgages and mortgage alternatives.

CREATION OF SECONDARY MORTGAGE-ALTERNATIVES MARKETS

The objective is to create an Internet-based regional (CIS/CEE/China) secondary market for mortgages and mortgage alternatives, and the issues/policies are:

- Creation of two to three Internet-based trading and reporting platforms for trading of mortgage alternatives, whole loans, guarantees, and mortgage insurance.
- The primary trading mechanisms will be assignments, partitioning, and auctions.
- Listings—members will post listings of assets that are for sale, and negotiate directly with sellers (Loopnet model).

- Ongoing individual auctions—members will bid on listed items (eBay model).
- Weekly Dutch auctions of consignments.
- No absolute auctions.
- Membership of secondary markets—members must comply with minimum capital, experience, and education requirements. Membership will be open to both institutions and qualified individuals that meet requirements (mostly experience and education requirements).
- Standardization of instruments (mortgages and mortgage alternatives) and methods (assignments, partitioning, and auctions).
- Risk-scoring systems.
- Dynamic risk-based capital requirements.
- No VaR or any of its variants.
- Ratings-free risk management systems.
- Mandatory public disclosure of mortgage holdings of regulated entities (insurance companies, banks, pension funds, etc.), nonregulated private entities (finance companies, etc.), and government agencies.
- Rules for the market and market members.
- Integration with private debt markets, and international debt markets.
- Elimination of, or substantial limits in, the use of consumer credit reports in loan origination and loan sales decisions.

STATUTORY BAN OF TRADITIONAL "WESTERN" SECURITIZATION

For the reasons stated in Chapter 11, there should be a statutory ban of traditional "Western" securitization of mortgages and mortgage alternatives. The events in the United States, Latin America, Australia, and western Europe have conclusively proved that securitization is not beneficial and increases systemic risk.

There should be limited and regulated syndication of mortgages and mortgage alternatives (e.g., whole loan trading). There should be severe criminal penalties for entities and individuals that attempt any form of securitization of mortgages or mortgage alternatives.

ALTERNATIVES TO FORECLOSURE

There are now alternatives to traditional foreclosures such as loan modifications, forbearance, pre-foreclosure sales, relocation to rental housing, and deeds-in-lieu. The more viable alternatives to foreclosure are:

- Deed-in-Lieu—This should be the primary alternative to foreclosure.
- Rent-transition market mortgages where: (1) on default without cure, there will be only a summary court proceeding with brief evidentiary requirements; and (2) the mortgagor will automatically become a tenant in the same property and pay an agreed-upon rent.
- Summary judicial proceedings that do not exceed 15 days; and have specific minimal evidentiary requirements.
- Nonjudicial foreclosures where the mortgage-alternatives contract contains a Power-of-Sale Clause.
- Financial products that contractually eliminate the need for foreclosure—the designing of these would be the best solution.
- Mortgage alternatives that implicitly eliminate the foreclosure option.

In addition to the above-mentioned alternatives, the elimination of borrowers' right-of-redemption after default without cure is absolutely necessary in order to reduce transaction costs and the cycle of defaults by unqualified borrowers (Clauretie and Herzog 1990; Essene and Apgar 2007; Miles 2005; Ambrose and Capone 1996; Scarberry 2009; Levitin 2010; Shiller 2009; Peterson 2009; Svenstrup and Willeman 2006; Struyk and Whiteley 2002; Palacin and Shelburne 2005; Institute for Real Estate, Construction and Housing 2006; Lea 2010; Ong 2005).

THE PRICE-DISCOVERY PROCESS AND VIABILITY OF MORTGAGE-ALTERNATIVES MARKETS

Perceived market liquidity has substantial effects on actual market liquidity and the functioning of both primary and secondary mortgage markets—this was amply demonstrated by the drastic decline in the liquidity of the U.S. ABS markets in 2007 to 2010. Perceived declines in liquidity tend to cause further reductions in liquidity and this effect is more pronounced in recessions (Institute for Real Estate, Construction and Housing 2006; Barisitz 2005; Ma 2009; Chen 2006; Berger, Hasen, and Zhou 2007; Deng, Zheng, and Ling 2005; Ben-Shahar, Leung, and Ong 2009; Duffie 2009; Duffie, Gârleanu, and Pedersen 2007).

Typical mortgage markets (and bond markets) are over-the-counter (OTC) markets, and prices are determined based on completed transactions, and hence demand and volume distort pricing. Standard economic theory suggests that in optimal markets, the laissez-faire interaction of supply and demand provides a sufficient forum for determination of true prices. These theories were effectively contradicted by the mark-to-market accounting debacle in the United States. These theories fail to incorporate other considerations or account for major phenomena such as the following: (1) in these "modern" markets, there are often substantial divergences among market values, present values of assets, "forward" values, and perceived values of assets, which results in arbitrage that is detrimental to social welfare; (2) accounting disclosures are tied to such market-based pricing, and disclosure of such pricing has significant information content and adverse psychological effects on investor perceptions; (3) such price discovery mechanisms expose the economy to the idiosyncrasies and whims of relatively few individual traders; (4) prices for long-term instruments are substantially distorted by temporary fluctuations that are not linked to the intrinsic value of assets; (5) such pricing mechanisms foster unnecessary and detrimental financial contagion; (6) the "matching" of orders does not indicate true demand and supply trends; (7) it is critical to decouple market price from intrinsic value, temporary euphoria, unrelated volatility, linkages to other markets (such as government bond and interest rate derivatives); and (8) the mere existence of substantial transaction costs and monitoring costs.

The "mark-to-market" accounting debacle that occurred in the United States during 2007 to 2009 was a primary cause of the banking crisis, the bankruptcy of Lehman Brothers, and the perceived insolvency of many financial institutions, which eventually resulted in financial contagion and ill-advised government bailouts. Hence, the entire mark-to-market scheme and debate in the United States has been part of a continuing mirage imposed on the public, which essentially permits banks to take large accounting losses to shield their earnings from corporate taxes while their executives are paid large bonuses for "failure"—other aspects of this continuing mirage include government bailouts and inadequate regulation of executive and mid-manager compensation at financial institutions. Mark-to-market accounting causes distress fire sales by financial institutions, which in turn decreases the market price of assets. Hence, there is a need for "blended" pricing systems that combine the "perceived reality" of mark-to-market accounting with intrinsic value and a long-term approach to asset valuation.

Other viable pricing systems for mortgages and mortgage alternatives are as follows.

The market price is not a "realized price" but the real-time average of prices of similar mortgage alternatives based on a set of government-approved pricing models used by banks. The prices are collected by the government through mandatory public disclosures of holdings and cost-basis of market participants. Hence, even if there is no trading volume, there can be dependable prices that reflect intrinsic values of assets.

The market price can be a real-time range of prices published online by the government, based on specific features of the subject mortgage alternative. Hence, the price of each mortgage alternative can be determined by looking at a chart that tabulates values based on the features of mortgage alternatives. This pricing system assumes that there is substantial standardization of mortgages and mortgage alternatives.

By statutes, the market prices for a mortgage alternative can be a forward price (mortgage alternatives do not trade in spot markets), and the minimum contract duration is at least one year. This forward market creates: (1) a time lag between intention and execution; (2) a time lag between money markets and mortgage-alternatives markets; (3) a time lag between occurrence of economic trends and reflection of such trends in economic data; (4) a time lag between rental markets and mortgage markets; (5) a time lag between mortgage markets and property-value markets; and (6) a time lag between savings markets (typically based on short-term rates) on one hand, and on the other hand, the mortgage-alternatives market.

The market price can be a weighted average of: (1) a real-time range of prices published online by the government, based on specific features of the subject mortgage alternative (this pricing system is based on substantial standardization of mortgages and mortgage alternatives); and (2) actual market prices realized in spot market transactions.

By using a realistic pricing system that reflects intrinsic value, and by requiring mandatory public disclosure of holdings of both mortgage alternatives and traditional mortgages and the associated cost-basis of financial institutions, a lot of uncertainty, speculation, transaction costs, price inflation, and detrimental arbitrage can be reduced or eliminated.

MONITORING ALTERNATIVES TO PRIMARY AND SECONDARY MORTGAGE-ALTERNATIVES MARKETS

The traditional primary and secondary mortgage markets are highly inefficient and have substantial information asymmetry that is detrimental to social welfare because it causes unnecessary speculation, inflation of prices and mortgage rates, and price volatility. In both developing countries and developed countries, in most instances, the mortgage broker is the public face of the "bank" and coordinates the mortgage application and loan processing, while a third-party servicing company handles postorigination payments processing—the actual lender is often removed from the borrower, and its processes are automated and online. Unfortunately, mortgage brokers are not subject to the same statutes and penalties as banks—and this has resulted in high volumes of mortgage fraud and low-quality loans. Hence, there is substantial need for more regulation of mortgage brokers.

An Open Secondary Mortgage Market has the following characteristics: (1) regulated by the national government or a consortium of national governments; (2) open to both individuals and private and public entities that meet the capital, experience, and regulatory requirements for membership; (3) is transparent to the public on a real-time basis (mandatory public disclosures of holdings of each member of the market); (4) Internet-based market; (5) has relatively low entry barriers (membership price are regulated by the government and are relatively low); (6) there are no limitations on the volume of trades among market participants; and (7) mortgages and mortgage alternatives are classified as securities, and mortgage and real estate laws are integrated into the securities law framework. Some of the feasible alternatives to open secondary mortgages and the mortgage-alternatives markets are:

- The purchase of mortgages and mortgage alternatives by government-sponsored and controlled private funds/entities.
- An interbank bulk-sale secondary market for mortgages and mortgage alternatives.
- A system of reinsurance of mortgages and mortgage alternatives.
- Traditional bulk loan syndication.
- Forward contracts for sales of individual assets or portfolios (mortgages and mortgage alternatives).
- Swaps of principal risk and/or interest rate risk for individual assets or portfolios (mortgages and mortgage alternatives).

However, some of these alternatives: (1) can or will reduce transparency in mortgage markets and debt markets; and (2) can substantially increase detrimental government intervention in markets, which is often expensive and a cause of government deficits (and thus, declining government credibility), reduction of social services, and reduction of major public projects. Thus, there must be regulations to define, control, and limit these alternatives to traditional secondary markets (mortgages and mortgage alternatives).

There should be "Connecting Bridges" between primary and secondary Mortgage markets. These bridges are now critical given the events of 2006 to 2010 and the global financial crisis. The subprime mess in the United States and the global financial crisis occurred because of a substantial "gap" between the primary bond/mortgage markets and the secondary mortgage/bond markets. This gap was:

- Temporal—Trading in the primary markets (whole loans; participations) was temporarily removed from the global 24/7 trading of CMBS/RMBS. Primary mortgage market products are typically long-term products (15 to 30 year mortgages), but the products in the secondary markets were mostly various combinations of tranched short-term (interest-only) and midterm (principal-only products and mortgage derivatives).

- Physical—While the primary mortgage markets in most countries (United States, United Kingdom) were local, the secondary mortgage markets were international (and foreign investors purchased substantial U.S. and European and Latin American ABS). The investors in primary mortgage markets were quite different from investors in the secondary mortgage markets.
- Psychological—The primary mortgage markets were psychologically detached from the secondary mortgages markets. Participants in either market did not have to hedge their products with products from the other market. Because each ABS contained many mortgages, it was often difficult and unnecessary for market participants to establish any direct relationships between both markets—they could only look at overall trends, which were colored by, and analyzed within, the context of other economic data released by governments. The primary mortgage market is driven by the raw emotions of families that want to fulfill their lifelong dreams of homeownership. On the other hand, the secondary market is driven by (1) the greed of profit-seeking banks and mortgage brokers who will churn low-quality loans for slim margins, (2) algorithm-driven trading systems, and (3) large institutional investors who like the "sophistication," the perceived focus of CMBS/RMBS, and the absence of operational burdens of traditional mortgages.
- Regulatory—The regulations that applied to the secondary mortgage markets (securities laws; private debt exchanges) were often different from the regulations for primary mortgage markets (state debtor-creditor statutes; Uniform Commercial Code).
- Social—Investors in primary mortgage markets (banks; small and medium investment funds) were quite different from investors in the secondary mortgage markets (Fannie Mae; Freddie Mac; large institutional investors).
- Technological—The secondary mortgage markets were perceived as much more technical and sophisticated and often involved the use of advanced math. In reality, many of the secondary market participants did not quite understand the ABS products and could not develop accurate models to value or hedge ABS products.

Apparently, in most developed countries (and some developing countries), during 1995 to 2007, there were not adequate or accurate feedback mechanisms from the secondary mortgage markets to the primary mortgage markets, which would have indicated the inherent problems in the overall mortgage markets.

The second major problem was that primary market participants adjusted their risk tolerances and underwriting standards to the risk tolerance of secondary market participants who were more interested in volume-based fees than in improving the quality of mortgages. Hence the quality of underwriting standards declined. These problems can be solved by: (1) tying compensation to loan quality and actual loan-losses; (2) setting absolute caps on compensation of market participants in the primary and secondary markets; and (3) limiting the annual volume of secondary market transactions that can be completed by any entity. In the United States, about five major banks controlled more than 80 percent of the ABS market, which was a negative factor during 2007 to 2010.

INCENTIVES FOR BANKS AND FINANCIAL INSTITUTIONS

One major objective should be to provide sufficient incentives for financial institutions to:

- Provide mortgage alternatives and mortgages.
- Effectively manage risk, beginning with the marketing and origination processes.
- Promptly identify and handle problem mortgage alternatives and loans.
- Collaborate with mortgage brokers and real estate brokers.
- Collaborate with property appraisers.
- Facilitate the implementation of central bank policies.
- Implement appropriate risk management systems and computerization.

Some types of incentives are:

- Tax incentives: reduction of tax rates, tax credits, and so on.
- Tax credits based on overall product quality.
- Tax credits based on combined product volume, product performance, volume of consumer complaints, and quality of interaction with mortgage brokers and real estate brokers.
- Tax credits for risk management partly based on default rates; default management; quality of reserves for associated savings/investment products; interest-rate risk management; credit risk; liquidity; and so on.
- Tax abatements.
- A points system where the bank will accumulate points (based on risk management, asset quality, etc.), which will be used for various purposes such as discount window loans and offsetting capital requirements.

INCENTIVES FOR BORROWERS/BUYERS TO USE MORTGAGE ALTERNATIVES

The objective is to provide sufficient incentives for buyer-borrowers to use mortgage alternatives. Types of incentives include:

- Tax incentives: reduction of tax rates, tax credits, and so on.
- Limited deductibility of interest paid for mortgage-alternatives product.
- Lower tax rates or no taxes for income from savings/investment products associated with mortgage alternatives.
- Tax credits based on the tenure of the mortgage-alternatives product.
- Tax credits based on combined product volume, product performance, volume of consumer complaints, and quality of interaction with mortgage brokers and real estate brokers.
- No deductibility of interest paid for traditional mortgages.
- High capital gains taxes (80 percent to 95 percent) for housing units that are owned for less than four years (exceptions may be granted in special cases, for example, relocation of primary residence to another town that is more than 200 miles away).
- Tax-free rollover of proceeds of mortgage-alternatives products into retirement plans, pension plans, and long-term annuity products.
- Tax credits for minimal or no use of third-party consumer credit reports, and standard asset-liability management techniques.

RISK-MANAGEMENT AND RISK-TRANSFER SYSTEMS

Designated lenders and financial institutions must be required to implement risk management systems for their portfolios of mortgage alternatives. The elements and guidelines are:

- Computerized asset appraisal processes and documentation.
- Regular (e.g., quarterly) internal appraisal reviews.
- Approved default risk models.
- Defined procedures for default management.
- In an environment of drastically reduced volumes of real estate foreclosures and auctions, the lender becomes a frequent participant in the property-values submarket.
- The government should implement incentive systems to reward quality and innovation in risk management and sharing of ideas.
- Government policies should facilitate the transferability of risk, for example, by insurance and reinsurance.

REFERENCES

Allen, J. 2009. Price movements in the Canadian residential mortgage market. Available at: www.bankofcanada.ca/en/res/wp/2009/wp09-13.pdf.

Allen & Overy. 2006. Financial institutions: Mergers & acquisitions in central and eastern Europe: Key legal issues and Allen & Overy's experience. August.

Ambrose, B., and R. Buttimer. 2009. The adjustable balance mortgage: Reducing the value of the put. Working paper, Pennsylvania State University, University Park. Available at: www.business.uconn.edu/finance/seminars/papers/Ambrose_Buttimer_New_Mortgage_UConn.pdf.

Ambrose, B. W., and C. A. Capone. 1996. Cost-benefit analysis of single-family foreclosure alternatives. *Journal of Real Estate Finance and Economics* 13 (2): 105–120.

Andersen, L., and R. Hilz-Ward. 2006. Improving the conditions for residential mortgages in Ukraine: An analysis of mortgage lending opportunities and selected interventions—A case study. *Housing Finance International* 21 (1): 3–13.

Bar-Gill, O. 2009. The law, economics and psychology of sub-prime mortgage contracts. *Cornell Law Review* 94: 1073–1093.

Barisitz, S. 2005. Banking in central and eastern Europe since the turn of the millennium: An overview of structural modernization in ten countries. Oesterreichische Nationalbank (Austria), Foreign Research Division.

Bedi, R. 2009. Laundering the proceeds of mortgage loan fraud. Working paper, Saw Centre for Financial Studies, National University of Singapore.

Ben-Shahar, D., C. Leung, and S. Ong. 2009. *Mortgage markets worldwide*. Hoboken, NJ: Wiley-Blackwell.

Berger, A. N., I. Hasen, and M. Zhou. 2007. Bank ownership and efficiency in China: What lies ahead in the world's largest nation? Bank of Finland Research Discussion Papers No. 16: 10.

Bernstein, D. 2008. Bankruptcy code modifications and mortgage markets. October. Available at: http://papers.ssrn.com/sol3/papers.cfm?abstract_id=1292336.

Black, R., K. Jaszczolt, and M. Lee. 2002. Solving the housing problem: Lessons from Poland and Hungary in creating a new housing finance system. USAID Warsaw, June 2002. Available at: www.ceemortgagefinance.org/pdfs/Comparative_Studies_Solving_the_Housing_Problem.pdf.

Bottelier, P. 2010. Beijing's new challenge: China's post-crisis housing bubble. *Carnegie Endowment for International Peace—Policy Outlook*. July.

Butler, S., P. Merstallinger, and A. Duber. 2002. Legal and financial aspects of the Slovenian mortgage banking system. Unpublished paper, Ministry of Finance—Housing Finance and Mortgage Reform Component, Ljubljana, Slovenia.

CAAMP. 2010a. Annual state of the residential mortgage market in Canada. Available at: www.caamp.org/meloncms/media/Fall%20Consumer%20Report%20WEB.pdf.

CAAMP. 2010b. Revisiting the Canadian mortgage market: Risk is small and contained. (January). Available at: www.caamp.org/meloncms/media/CAAMP%20%20Winter%20Report%20Black_2.pdf.

Canada Mortgage. Evolution of the mortgage market in Canada. Available at: www.canadamortgage.com/articles/learning.cfm?DocID=34&CFID=...&CFTOKEN=86657438.

Capitas Group International. 2008. Gulf cooperation council mortgage market analysis. Working paper. Available at: www.capitasgroupintl.com/whitepapers.html.

Capitas Group International. 2010a. Towards a regulatory framework for mortgage financing in KSA. Working paper. Available at: www.capitasgroupintl.com/whitepapers.html.

Capitas Group International. 2010b. Expanding the Saudi mortgage market: The path to home-ownership. Working paper. Available at: www.capitasgroupintl.com/whitepapers.html.

Chen, W. 2006. Legal implications of a rising China: WTO: Time's up for Chinese banks—China's banking reform and non-performing loan disposal. *Chinese Journal of International Law* 7: 239–242.

Cherkis, L., L. King, and W. Collier. 1992. *Real Estate Transactions and the Bankruptcy Code*. 5-18–5-19.

Chiquier, L. 2006. *Housing Finance in East Asia*. The World Bank. Available at: http://equatorprinciples.ifc.org/ifcext/economics.nsf/AttachmentsByTitle/ea_housing_finance/$FILE/Housing+Finance+East+Asia+report+Dec+2006-final.pdf.

Clauretie, T. M., and T. Herzog. 1990. The effect of state foreclosure laws on loan losses: Evidence from the mortgage insurance industry. *Journal of Risk and Insurance* 56 (3): 221–233.

Cooke, A. 2007. *Property title issues in Asia*. Republished by Real Estate IQ—A Division of IQPC Worldwide. Available at: www.iqpc.com/uploadedFiles/Topic/Real_Estate_IQ/Assets/5.pdf.

Courchane, M., and J. Giles. 2002. A comparison of U.S. and Canadian residential mortgage markets. Working Paper EWP0201, University of Victoria, Canada.

D'Anjou, M. 2009. The financial crisis has led to changes in the Canadian mortgage market: Should variable rate mortgages still be preferred? Desjardins Economic Studies. March 4.

DBRS. 2007. Residential mortgages and securitization in Canada: Overview of the mortgage market. (May). Available at: www.dbrs.com/research/211674/residential-mortgages-and-securitization-in-canada-overview-of-the-mortgage-market.pdf.

Deininger, K., and S. Jin. 2003. The impact of property rights on households' investment, risk coping, and policy preferences: Evidence from China. *Economic Development and Cultural Change* 51 (4): 851–882.

Deininger, K., and J. Songqing. 2002. Land rental markets as an alternative to government reallocation? Equity and efficiency considerations in the Chinese land tenure system. World Bank Policy Research Working Paper No. 2930 (November).

Deng, Y., D. Zheng, and C. Ling. 2005. An early assessment of residential mortgage performance in China. *Journal of Real Estate Finance and Economics* 31 (2): 117–136.

Deshpande, R. S. 2007. *Emerging issues in land policy*. INRM Policy Brief #16, Asian Development Bank. Available at: www.adb.org/Documents/Papers/INRM-PolicyBriefs/inrm16.pdf.

Duffie, D. 2009. *How Should We Regulate Derivative Markets? PEW Financial Reform Project*, Briefing Paper #5.

Duffie, D., N. Gârleanu, and L. H. Pedersen. 2007. Valuation in over-the-counter markets. *Review of Financial Studies* 20 (6): 1865–1900.

Dunning, W. 2009. *Annual state of the residential mortgage market in Canada*. Canadian Association of Accredited Mortgage Professionals. November.

Eggum, J. P., K. M. Porter, and T. Twomey. 2008. Saving homes in bankruptcy: Housing affordability and loan modification. *Utah Law Review*, 1123. Available at: http://ssrn.com/abstract=1349151.

Essene, R. S., and W. Apgar. 2007. Understanding mortgage market behavior: Creating good mortgage options for all Americans. Working paper, Harvard University. Available at: www.jchs.harvard.edu/publications/finance/mm07-1_mortgage_market_behavior.pdf.

European Central Bank. 2009. *Housing Finance in the Euro Area*. March.

Federal Reserve Bank of San Francisco. 2006. Postal savings in Japan and mortgage markets in the U.S. FRBSF Economic Letter Number 2006-03. March 3.

Freshfields Bruckhaus Deringer LLP. 2009. *Amendments to Russian Pledge Law*. January.

Gelpern, A., and A. J. Levitin. 2009. Rewriting Frankenstein contracts: The workout prohibition in residential mortgage-backed securities. *Southern California Law Review* 82: 1077–1152. Georgetown Public Law Research Paper No. 1323546; CLEA 2009 Annual Meeting Paper; Rutgers School of Law-Newark Research Papers No. 33. Available at: http://ssrn.com/abstract=1323546.

Good, S., and C. M. Hammond. 2006. Real estate auctions: Legal concerns for an increasingly preferred method of selling real property. *Real Property, Probate & Trust Journal* 40: 766–776.

Green, R., and S. Wachter. 2005. The American mortgage market in historical and international context. *Journal of Economic Perspective* 19 (4): 93–114.

Guseva, Y. 2009. Russian mortgage finance and legal reforms in times of financial crises: Transplanting American law models. *Columbia Journal of East European Law* 3 (10): 75–144.

Hong, F., and J. Chen. 2009. The relationship between home mortgage loan and real estate market in China: Evidence and insights from a regional perspective. Working paper.

Institute for Real Estate, Construction and Housing Vienna. 2006. HFA: A Housing Finance Agency for Central Eastern and South Eastern Europe feasibility study (Executive Summary).

Kiff, J. 2009. Boring but effective? Canadian residential mortgage markets. IMF working paper. Available at: www.imf.org/external/pubs/ft/wp/2009/wp09130.pdf.

Klesta, E. 2009. Experience in cross-border residential mortgage lending in the EU: Examples from Portugal and Greece. Working paper, Unión de Créditos Inmobiliarios.

Klyuev, V., and P. Mills. 2007. Is housing wealth an ATM? The relationship between household wealth, home equity withdrawal, and savings rates. *IMF Staff Papers* 54: 539–561.

Konishi, A. 2002. The GHLC reform and Japanese housing finance market. Third Workshop on Housing Finance in Transition Economies. Warsaw (December 5–6). Available at: www.oecd.org/dataoecd/33/12/1844710.pdf.

Kopeikin, A. B. 2010. *Housing reform in Russia: Affordable housing market making.* Institute for Urban Economics (Russia).

Kosareva, N., and R. Struyk. 1993. Housing privatization in the Russian Federation. *Housing Policy Debate* 4 (1): 81–100.

Kosareva, N., and A. Tumanov. 2008. Assessing housing affordability in Russia. *Problems of Economic Transition* 50 (10): 6–29.

Kramer, B. 2006. Residential securitization in Japan: The outlook for growth and performance. *Housing Finance International.* Available at: www.housingfinance.org/uploads/Publicationsmanager/0006_Jap.pdf.

Lea, M. 2010. Alternative forms of mortgage finance: What can we learn from other countries? (February). Available at: www.rohan.sdsu.edu/~realest/images/Harvard-Lea.pdf.

Levitin, A. J. 2009a. Bankruptcy markets: Making sense of claims trading. *Brooklyn Journal of Corporate, Financial & Commercial Law* 4: 64–74.

Levitin, A. J. 2009b. Resolving the foreclosure crisis: Modification of mortgages in bankruptcy. *Wisconsin Law Review* 2009: 565–575.

Levitin, A. J. 2010. Back to the future with Chapter 13: A response to Professor Scarberry. *Pepperdine Law Review* 37 (February): 1261; Georgetown Public Law Research Paper No. 10-05; Georgetown Law and Economics Research Paper No. 10-03. Available at: http://ssrn.com/abstract=1534912.

Levitin, A., and J. Goodman. 2008. The effect of bankruptcy strip-down on mortgage markets. Georgetown University Law Center Business, Economics and Regulatory Policy Working Paper Series, Research Paper No. 1087816; Public Law & Legal Theory Working Paper Series, Research Paper No. 1087816. Available at: http://works.bepress.com/adam_levitin/11.

Levitin, A., and T. Twomey. 2011. Mortgage servicing. *Yale Journal on Regulation* 28 (1): 24–25.

Londerville, J. 2005. Mortgage-backed securities in Canada: The size of the market and prospects for the future. *Briefings in Real Estate Finance* 4 (3): 199–207.

Ma, Y. 2009. A discussion on development of China's housing mortgage-backed securitization and American experiences. *Asian Social Sciences* 4 (4): 98–102.

Mashkina, O., P. Heliste, and R. Kosonen. 2007. The emerging mortgage market in Russia: An overview with local and foreign perspectives. Working paper, Helsinki School of Economics, Finland.

Mayer, C., K. Pence, and S. Sherlund. 2009. The rise in mortgage defaults. *Journal of Economic Perspectives* 23 (1): 27–50.

McGee, J. 2009. *Why didn't Canada's market go bust*? Federal Reserve Bank of Cleveland—Economic Commentary. December. Available at: www.clevelandfed.org/research/commentary/2009/0909.cfm.

Miles, D. 2005. Incentives, information and efficiency in the UK mortgage market. *Economic Journal* 115 (502): C82–C98.

Min, D. 2010a. Future of housing finance reform. November. Available at: www.americanprogress.org/issues/2010/11/housing_reform.html.

Min, D. 2010b. True north: The facts about the Canadian mortgage banking system. August. Available at: www.americanprogress.org/issues/2010/08/pdf/canadian_banking.pdf.

Mortgage Architects. 2007. *Comparing the Canadian and U.S. sub-prime and alternative mortgage markets: Why the U.S. sub-prime fallout is a U.S.-only phenomenon*. Available at: http://files.newswire.ca/40/MASubprime.pdf, accessed June 15, 2009.

Nemoto, N. 2005. *The battle over Japan's mortgage markets raises default risks*. Standard & Poor's—Global Fixed Income Research. September.

Nwogugu, M. 2011. *International risk regulation, mechanism design and constitutional economics of institutions*. (Book manuscript).

Ong, S. 2005. Mortgage markets in Asia. *Paper for presentation at the European Real Estate Society Conference, Dublin.*

Ozeki, K. 2007. Japan credit perspectives: Overview of Japan's residential mortgage market. Fixed Income Research, PIMCO. (March).

Painter, S. 2006. Subprime lending, suboptimal bankruptcy: A proposal to amend §§ 522(f)(1)(B) and 548(a)(1)(B) of the Bankruptcy Code to protect subprime mortgage borrowers and their unsecured creditors. *Loyola Chicago University Law Journal* 38: 81–91. Available at: www.luc.edu/law/activities/publications/lljdocs/vol38_no1/painter.pdf.

Palacin, J., and R. C. Shelburne. 2005. *The private housing market in eastern Europe and the CIS*. Discussion Paper Series, #2005-5. United Nations Economic Commission for Europe, Switzerland.

Peterson, C. L. 2009. Foreclosure, subprime mortgage lending, and the mortgage electronic registration system. *University of Cincinnati Law Review* 78 (4). Available at: http://ssrn.com/abstract=1469749.

Quigley, J., and R. Van Order. 1990. Efficiency in the mortgage market: The borrower's perspective. *AREUEA Journal* 18 (3): 237–252.

Rabenhorst, C., and N. Mihalache. 2006. Moldova: Guiding mortgage market development through legal reform. *Housing Finance International*, 26–33. Available at: www.housingfinance.org/pdfstorage/hfi/0703_Mol.pdf.

Radulovic, A. 2006. Housing finance and regional integration—former Yugoslav case: Could it work? *Housing Finance International* (September): 28–36. Available at: www.housingfinance.org/pdfstorage/hfi/0609_Yug.pdf.

Renaud, B. M. 2004. *Mortgage finance in emerging markets: Constraints and feasible development paths*. Available at: www.usc.edu/schools/business/FBE/seminars/papers/L_11-12-04_RENAUD-MortgFin.pdf.

Scarberry, M. S. 2009. A critique of congressional proposals to permit modification of home mortgages in Chapter 13. *Pepperdine Law Review* 37: 635. Available at: http://ssrn.com/abstract=1520794.

Segre, N. 2010. A comparison of home mortgage loan defaults and foreclosures in the US and in certain EU countries, including a discussion of governmental responses and some observations concerning contributing causes. European Real Estate Society, Milan (June).

Shiller, R. J. 2009. Policies to deal with the implosion in the mortgage market. *The B.E. Journal of Economic Analysis & Policy* 9 (3): Article 4.

Standard & Poor's. 2010. Canada's mortgage market: Some observations on the country's shallower housing downturn. September.

Struyk, R., and D. E. Whiteley. 2002. *Mortgage default insurance in the U.S.: Implications for Russia.* Washington, DC: Urban Institute. March.

Svenstrup, M., and S. Willeman. 2006. Reforming housing finance: Perspectives from Denmark. *Journal of Real Estate Research* 28 (2): 105–128.

Tang, B., S. Liu, and S. Wong. 2006. Housing mortgage and housing transaction in China: Bridging the missing links. *Housing Finance International* 20 (3): 30–38.

Tiwari, P., and Y. Moriizumi. 2003. Efficiency in housing finance: A comparative study of mortgage instruments in Japan. *International Journal of Housing Policy* 3 (3): 267–288.

Toronto Dominion Bank. 2010. Canadian mortgage market primer. June. Available at: www.td.com/economics/special/el0610_cdn_mort_market.pdf.

Traclet, V. 2005. Structure of the Canadian housing market and finance system. Background paper prepared for CGFS Working Group on Housing Finance in the Global Financial Market.

White, A. M. 2009. Deleveraging the American homeowner: The failure of 2008 voluntary mortgage modifications. *Connecticut Law Review* 41: 1107–1127.

CHAPTER 14

Asset-Liability Matching Is a Hindrance to Lending

In most developing countries, most banks do not provide mortgages or long-term loans (loans whose terms exceed three years) because of the perceived problems of asset-liability matching (ALM) (International Association of Insurance Supervisors 2006; Kaluszka and Kondratiuk-Janyska 2004; Kawaller and Koch 2006). ALM is a staple of undergraduate and graduate finance degree programs, and most commercial bank training programs in both developed countries and emerging markets countries. In developed and developing economies, the assets and liabilities of housing finance lenders are often mismatched, which creates perceived interest rate risk for the lenders, because an increase in market interest rates raises the cost of deposits without immediately raising the return on the then-existing mortgage assets. In ALM studies, bankers are erroneously trained to believe that the modified durations of assets and liabilities must be "matched" in order to reduce the bank's portfolio sensitivity to interest rates risk. The two main types of ALM are: (1) duration matching, and (2) cash-flow matching. Most of the discussion in this chapter pertains to both methods. Many authors have used conditional value-at-risk (CVaR) and traditional VaR for cash-flow matching. However, Nwogugu (2005) and other authors (Zenios 1995; Hardy and Wirch 2004) have shown that CVaR and related methods are wrong. Cash-flow matching is severely limited by the availability of bonds, which constantly changes. The objective of ALM is not really to reduce or eliminate risk, but to establish limits and restrictions for managing risk—and this is one of the main weaknesses of ALM in theory and practice.

The ALM problem may be fully solved only if: (a) banks lend only one-day loans that are very liquid; or (b) hedging of interest rate risk is done on a continuous time basis for 24 hours every day (which does not occur, and will probably be prohibitively expensive). Historically, there have been very few bank runs, and where there have been bank runs (or catastrophes or natural disasters), banks typically ration customers' cash withdrawals.

If there is ever a bank run, it is likely to create financial contagion, which in turn will cause other banks to want to sell assets/loans to meet liquidity needs—and all of such activity will erode liquidity in the secondary loan markets unless the government intervenes, which is unlikely given the sheer size of the bank loan markets in most countries. Thus, ALM does not add any value and is merely an illusion of risk management.

Interest rate risk accounts for a relatively small percentage of the risk that most financial institutions (such as pension funds, insurance companies, banks) face—such as catastrophe risk, policy-discontinuance risk (insurance policies are cancelled before the insurance company recovers its costs), basis risk, default risk, legal risk (e.g., documentation; compliance), price risk, accounting risk, changes in government regulations, inflation risk, actuarial risk, underwriting risk, liquidity risk, prepayment risk, call risk, and errors in mortality forecasts.

Furthermore, many financial institutions use inconsistent methods for calculating duration/modified duration (MD) and convexity: some calculations are based on book values while others are based on market values of assets and liabilities; some calculations do not make adjustments for the differences in basis risk in corporate bonds versus government bonds; and some financial institutions use effective duration for assets, and use MD for liabilities. According to the EDHEC (June 2010) survey of asset liability management in institutions, less than 50 percent of institutions understand the statistical/math techniques and strategies that are required for ALM.

ALM distorts incentives in lending and investment decision making. ALM overemphasizes interest rate risk, which is then reflected in loan documents, compensation of bankers/risk-managers, and propensity to lend. As mentioned, ALM introduces a time bias (i.e., lenders' preference for providing short-term loans, rather than long-term loans). ALM is conjectured to cause a risk-suppression bias where there is excessive focus on interest rate risk and not on other types of risk. ALM causes a Temporal Loan Management Segmentation Effect where the focus around the time of loan origination is on credit risk and recovery risk, and then after, the lenders' focus shifts to interest rate risk and ALM. In an ALM regime, the perceived success of many bank managers and insurance managers is evaluated within the context of interest rate risk management and cash-flow matching, to the detriment of management of other risks.

ERRORS IN THE FORMULAS FOR DURATION, MODIFIED DURATION (MD), AND CONVEXITY

The main problem with ALM is that the duration, MD, and convexity formulas are wrong. The duration/MD formulas have no relationship whatsoever to business cycles or economic fundamentals and have no relationship with the changing credit quality of the bond-issuer/borrower over time. This is a critical issue, because: (a) for fixed-income instruments, the value of each periodic coupon payment depends on the dynamic/evolving credit quality of the issuer and the state of the business cycle, and the investors' varying opportunity set at time of payment of each coupon; and (b) the certainty of each periodic coupon payment depends on economic fundamentals and ability to hedge inflation risk and interest rate risk—certainty here is from the investor's perspective, and inflation and interest rate risk both reduce the actual certainty because both risks can reduce real payments.

Apart from economic and behavioral issues associated with perceptions of time-values and risk, another major problem is that existing calculus formulas are wrong under existing differentiation rules, the derivative of the function $h(x) = a\,f(x) + b\,g(x)$ with respect to x is:

$$h'(x) = af'(x) + bg'(x)$$

That is:

$$\frac{d(af + bg)}{dx} = a\frac{df}{dx} + b\frac{dg}{dx}$$

The derivative of $h(x) = 1/f(x)$ is:

$$h'(x) = -\frac{f'(x)}{f(x)^2}$$

This inverse function rule is written as:

$$\frac{d(1/f)}{dx} = -\frac{1}{f^2}\frac{df}{dx}$$

$$D'[k^* f(x)] = k^* f(x) \text{ (constant multiple rule)}$$

The power rule is written as:

$$\text{If } y = ax^n, \text{ then } dy/dx = anx^{(n-1)} \text{(power rule)}$$

Another variant of the power rule (the general power rule) is:

$$D([g(x)]^r)/dx = r^*[g(x)]^{r-1*}d[g(x)]/dx$$

The standard time value of money (TVM) equation for duration/MD, net present value (NPV), and IRR/MIRR has the following form:

$NPV = \Sigma_{i=n}[\{x_i^* (1 + r)^{(-i)}]$. Applying the same constant multiple rule and power rule and the general power rule to the TVM equation, the differentiation result is:

$$\partial NPV/\partial r = \sum_{i=n}[\{x_i^* - i\}/(1+r)^{(i-1)}]$$

This result is inaccurate as can be confirmed by any simulation in which the discount rate (r) is changed by 1 percent intervals (or smaller intervals), and the resulting values of NPV are calculated—a 1 percent change in the interest rate r causes a much different change in NPV than is predicted by the power rule, and the general power rule, and the inverse function rule. If the inverse function rule is applied to differentiate the NPV/IRR TVM equation, the result is:

$$\partial NPV/\partial r = \sum_{i=n}[\{-i/(1+r)^{(i-1)}\}/\{(1+r)^{(i*2)}\}]$$
$$= \sum_{i=n}[\{-i/(1+r)^{(i-1)}\}*\{(1+r)^{(-i*2)}\}]$$

This result is wrong as can be confirmed by any simulation. Thus, contrary to Handforth (2004) and Liao, Tsai, and Chiang (2009), the formulas for duration, MD, and convexity are also inaccurate (even after adjustments for prepayment risk and default risk). Similarly, consider a simple equation $y = x^2$. Under the power rule, $dy/dx = 2x$, and Table 14.1 shows the various values of x, x^2, and $2x$, and the actual values of dy/dx. However, for each one-unit increase in x, y changes by more than $2x$.

Table 14.2 also shows the predicted and actual values of the differentiation of the equation $y = x^3 + 2x$. Here, applying the traditional calculus rules, $dy/dx = 3x^2 + 2$. However, for each one-unit increase in x, y changes by more than $3x^2 + 2$. The table assumes that the x in $3x^2 + 2$ refers to the magnitude of the change in x, and not to the initial or ending values of x (which is a liberal interpretation of the general power rule).

These summary simulations show that the power rule is inaccurate. The standard proof of the power rule is stated in Purcell and Varberg (1987, 103), and in Goldstein, Lay, and Schneider (1996), and is as follows:

Let $y = ax^n$; and assume that x_1 is the starting value, which changes to x_2; and $dx = x_2 - x_1 = b$;

$$dy = (a)\{(x_1 + b)^n - x_1^n\}$$

If both sides of the equation are divided by dx, then:

$$dy/dx = [(a)\{(x_1 + b)^n - x_1^n\}]/b = a[\{(x_1 + b)^n - x_1^n\}/b]$$

TABLE 14.1 First Derivative of X^2

		First Derivative of X^2	
X	x^2	Predicted ($2x$)	Actual
1.00	1.00		
2.00	4.00	2.00	3.00
3.00	9.00	2.00	5.00
4.00	16.00	2.00	7.00
5.00	25.00	2.00	9.00
6.00	36.00	2.00	11.00
7.00	49	2.00	13.00
8.00	64	2.00	15.00
9.00	81	2.00	17.00
10.00	100	2.00	19.00
11.00	121	2.00	21.00
12.00	144	2.00	23.00
13.00	169	2.00	25.00
14.00	196	2.00	27.00
15.00	225	2.00	29.00
16.00	256	2.00	31.00
26.00	676	20.00	42.00
146.00	21,316	240.00	172.00
1,346.00	1,811,716	2,400.00	1,492.00
2,546.00	6,482,116	2,400.00	3,892.00
3,746.00	14,032,516	2,400.00	6,292.00
12,546.00	157,402,116	17,600.00	16,292.00
812,546.00	660,231,002,116	1,600,000.00	825,092.00
1,912,546.00	3,657,832,202,116	2,200,000.00	2,725,092.00
3,912,546.00	15,308,016,202,116	4,000,000.00	5,825,092.00
13,912,546.00	193,558,936,202,116	20,000,000.00	17,825,092.00
26,912,546.00	724,285,132,202,116	26,000,000.00	40,825,092.00

The other issue in the standard power rule is the expansion of $(x_1 + b)^n$ with the binomial theorem—the binomial theorem states that:

$$(x_1 + b)^n = \sum_{k=n} [\{n!/(k!(n-k)!)\}b^{(n-k)}x_1^k]$$

As shown in Nwogugu (2011), the expansion of $(x_1 + b)^n$ with the binomial theorem differs substantially from the result derived by a manual expansion of terms. See Purcell and Varberg (1987, page 103), which explains the standard, generally accepted proof of the power rule. The Purcell and Varberg proof, and the Goldstein, Lay, and Schneider (1996) proof

TABLE 14.2 First Derivative of $X^2 + 2x$

		First Derivative of $x^3 + 2x$	
x	$x^3 + 2x$	Predicted Value ($3x^2 + 2$)	Actual Value
1.00	3.00		
2.00	12	5	9
3.00	33	5	21
4.00	72	5	39
5.00	135	5	63
6.00	228	5	93
7.00	357	5	129
8.00	528	5	171
9.00	747	5	219
10.00	1,020	5	273
11.00	1,353	5	333
12.00	1,752	5	399
13.00	2,223	5	471
14.00	2,772	5	549
15.00	3,405	5	633
16.00	4,128	5	723
26.00	17,628	302	1,350
146.00	3,112,428	43,202	25,790
1,346.00	2,438,572,428	4,320,002	2,029,550
2,546.00	16,503,472,428	4,320,002	11,720,750
3,746.00	52,565,812,428	4,320,002	30,051,950
12,546.00	1,974,766,972,428	232,320,002	218,431,950
812,546.00	536,468,059,846,972,000	1,920,000,000,002	670,582,606,350
1,912,546.00	6,995,772,346,831,970,000	3,630,000,000,002	5,872,094,806,350
3,912,546.00	59,893,317,559,532,000,000	12,000,000,000,002	26,448,772,606,350
13,912,546.00	2,692,897,603,623,030,000,000	300,000,000,000,002	263,300,428,606,350
26,912,546.00	19,492,356,937,505,600,000,000	507,000,000,000,002	1,292,266,102,606,350

focus on limits when b approaches zero, so their solution approximates reality only for very small values of b that are around zero.

But as $b \to 0$, if the binomial theorem is used for expansion of $(x_1 + b)^n$, then:

$$dy/dx = \lim_{b \to 0} a^*[x_1^n + nx_1^{(n-1)}b + \{n(n-1)/2\}x_1^{(n-2)}b^2 + \cdots\cdots$$

$$+ nx_1 b^{(n-1)} + b^n - x_1^n]/b$$

$$= \lim_{b \to 0} a^*\{b[nx_1^{(n-1)} + \{n(n-1)/2\}x_1^{(n-2)}b + \cdots\cdots + nxb^{(n-2)}$$

$$+ b^{(n-1)}]/b\}$$

$$dy/dx = \lim_{b \to 0} an\{x_1^{(n-1)}\}; \text{ which is the standard power rule}$$

However, Purcell and Varberg (1987, 103), and Goldstein, Lay, and Schneider (1996) fail to state that the power rule may approximate reality only for very small numbers around zero. Also, the standard power rule is problematic in at least two ways: (1) the x_1 in the differentiation result $\{anx_1^{(n-1)}\}$, can be interpreted to refer to the initial value of x (x_1) or to the final value of x (x_2), and not to the magnitude of the actual change in x—in fact, in Purcell and Varberg (1987, 103), it refers to the initial value of x; and (2) the standard power rule and the inverse function rule provide vastly different results for the differentiation of $y = ax^{-n}$, which is the standard component of "Time Value of Money" (TVM) equations—ideally, both rules should provide the same differentiation result; (3) in a different study, the author manually expanded $(x_1 + b)^n$, and the results were different from the expansion obtained by using the binomial theorem, and so there is the question of whether the binomial theorem is accurate.

The other errors inherent in the duration, MD, and convexity formulas are described as follows.

In the duration/MD formulas, the weights apply only to the numerator of each term in the time-value-of-money equation, and thus, are inaccurate as a measure of the estimated recovery period.

The duration/MD/convexity formulas do not account for the differences between short-term risk and long-term risk (assumes that risk is constant for the life of loan), or for reinvestment risk.

The duration/MD/convexity formulas do not account for sunk costs (such as due diligence costs; monitoring costs; transaction costs), which are significant in emerging markets, and affect both the recovery risk and sensitivity to interest rates.

As mentioned earlier, the power rule and the inverse function rule in differential calculus are wrong, and thus the formulas for duration, MD, and convexity are inaccurate. Since the convexity formula is a second derivative (calculus), it is inaccurate; furthermore, convexity is highly sensitive to changes in the maturity dates and stated coupon rates of fixed income instruments, all of which makes it a much less accurate measure.

The MD formula may be a correct measure of sensitivity to interest rates only if any change in interest rates is permanent for all loan terms, but if interest rates fluctuate along all segments of the yield curve, then such fluctuations that are within a certain range (*X* percent to *Y* percent) will not have any effect on medium-term or long-term loans, all else held constant.

The duration/MD/convexity formulas do not account for prepayment risk, and hence if the bond can be prepaid, the true duration is truncated (much less than the standard duration).

DEFAULT/BANKRUPTCY RISK AND ILLIQUIDITY

The duration/MD/convexity formulas completely omit the firm's default/bankruptcy risk, which changes over time (a financially distressed firm may not pay some coupons in the future). Since the default risk is inversely related to the probability of payment of coupons/principal, increasing default risk increases duration and recovery risk. That is, if the bond has high-default risk, the true duration is not truncated, as is postulated by standard finance theory, but is actually extended (much longer than the standard duration) because recovery of the principal amount takes much longer than usual and there is likely to be some loss of principal.

The duration/MD formulas do not account for the sensitivity of the borrower's operations/business to interest rates (separate from the borrower's credit quality), which affects the loan's sensitivity to interest rates.

The duration/MD/convexity formulas do not account for illiquidity and investors' holding periods in debt markets, and since most investors do not hold bonds to maturity, illiquidity is just as important as prepayment risk and interest rate risk; if an investor can sell the bond before maturity (and within the context of fluctuating interest rates), the true duration and MD are truncated (much less than the standard duration) (Babbel, Merrill, and Panning 1995; Beber, Brandt and Kavajecz 2007; Bhaduri, Meissner, and Youn 2007; Clauss 2010; Duffie, Gârleanu, and Pedersen 2007; Duffie 2009).

Discounting and Perceptions of Time

The duration/MD/convexity formulas overweight long-term cash flows and underweight short-term cash flows. The formulas weight the cash flows of the loan/bond with a number series (e.g., 0.5, 1, 1.5, 2, 2.5, 3, 3.5, . . . *n*), which supposedly reflects the timing of the cash flows (years, months, weeks, and days), but does not reflect the value of each time period or the risk of the periodic cash flows. Thus, for a 10-year bond with semiannual coupons, the implicit weighting system erroneously implies that cash flow #6 is six times less relevant than cash flow #1, which is inaccurate because the first differences of the numbers in the series do not correspond to the absolute differences in the time periods (i.e., for the 10-year semiannual bond mentioned, cash flow #10 is not 10 times as distant as cash flow #1, and cash flow #20 is not four times as distant as cash flow #5).

The transformation of the duration to the MD formula and to the price value of a basis point (PVBP) erroneously changes a measure that estimates the time for principal recovery to a measure that calculates the sensitivity to interest rates. This is because the timing of the cash flows does not correspond with changes in interest rates along the yield curve (PVBP may be accurate only if the change in interest rates is uniform across the yield curve). Furthermore, the weighting of the cash flows in the MD formula does not account for the effects of compounding of interest that is separate from the discounting of each cash flow, nor the supply/demand imbalance in debt markets and/or scarcity/oversupply of hedging instruments or reactions to specific government policies, which may distort market reactions to changes in interest rates. These factors can distort the price/interest rate relationships predicted by the PVBP formula.

The duration/MD/convexity formulas erroneously assume that all time periods have the same value to all investors. As explained in the foregoing paragraphs, time units have different values to different persons, in terms of both absolute value and relative values of time. Liu and Aaker (2007), LeBoeuf (2006), Leclerc, Schmitt, and Dube (1995), and Zauberman and Lynch (2005) have analyzed the effects of different valuation of time on discounting and vice versa. The value of time differs dramatically among individuals and companies because of the following: (a) perceptions of time in the long term versus short term—time may have more or less value in the short term compared to the long term; (b) opportunity costs of different units of time; (c) uncertainty tends to cause deferrals of decisions about consumption, leisure, and some elements of production (production not required for long-term needs); (d) the ability or inability to process information and/or hedge risks changes individuals' and groups' perceptions of time and time value; (e) uncertainty reduces the value of time, and this effect is amplified where there are no hedging instruments or hedging opportunities; the effect is not symmetrical in that decreases in uncertainty do not necessarily increase the value of time, because as uncertainty increases, the decision maker's focus changes to consumption; and (f) the value of time within groups is conjectured to be inversely related to the "volatility" of group consensus, the magnitude/quality of knowledge of group members, opportunity costs of group members (not opportunity costs of the group), and so on.

The key issue is that, to be accurate, the opportunity set must be defined with respect to perceptions of time and the value of time (Khwaja, Silverman, and Sloan 2007; Attema et al. 2010; Ortendahl and Fries 2005). Sandri et al. 2010) analyzed the disinvestment decision (project termination and liquidation of assets) within the context of entrepreneurial decision making, and they found that the standard NPV decision model was not the typical decision behavior. Sandri et al. found that most individual decision makers understand the value of waiting; their choices are weakly related to the disinvestment triggers derived from a formal optimal stopping benchmark consistent with real-options reasoning. Sandri et al. also observed a pronounced loss aversion in that most individuals hold on to a losing project for even longer than real-options reasoning would predict—this effect has been documented in many prior empirical studies. Kogut (1990) empirically studied search patterns of undergraduate students and found that individuals were making decisions based on the total return from searching, rather than simply the marginal return from another draw (from a known distribution of prices). Kogut's findings contradict standard economic theory, which predicts that individuals should continue to search until the expected gain of another search is less than the marginal search cost; and that once individuals have made a draw (or have selected an item from a known distribution) and then continued, they should never return to a selected price (or item) drawn earlier. These findings are critical and are proof that the NPV/IRR framework is substantially flawed. The NPV/IRR framework relies on cutoff points without regard to the following critical factors: (a) the psychological gains/losses from the search (the project); (b) the individual's/group's perception of the magnitude of the search costs (both the initial investment and intermittent investments); (c) the perceived value of sunk costs; and (d) the regret associated with sunk costs (which can affect project benefits—employee motivation, calculation of ROI, awards of employee incentives and performance bonuses, career concerns, the project termination decision, allocation of costs among departments, etc.). Poole (2000) analyzed and identified the effects of human perception of time on financial decision making. Gollier (2010) found that, contrary to Weitzman (1998), when future interest rates are uncertain, using the expected net present value implies a term structure of discount rates that is decreasing to the smallest possible interest rate; but on the contrary, using the expected net future value criteria implies an increasing term structure of discount rates up to the largest possible interest rate. Gollier showed that if the aggregate consumption path is optimized and made flexible to news about future interest rates, risk aversion and utility maximization are equivalent.

The duration/MD formula erroneously assumes that earlier cash flows are more relevant than later cash flows. In reality, later-period cash flows can be substantial and more valuable (per dollar) than early-period cash flows if: (1) the yield curve remains inverted for a long period of time; (2) the reinvestment in the early years are substantially less than both the reinvestment rates in later years and the discount rate; (3) macroeconomic conditions change, for example, there is rampant deflation, recessions; (4) prior reinvestment rates remain very low compared to the discount rate(s); (5) the decision maker's opportunity set is reduced substantially over time; (6) the firm's or the project's tax position, tax rates, and/or tax statutes change in future; and (7) there are changes in the intertemporal value of cash (versus nonliquid assets), which increases the utility of cash in future periods.

Framing Effects and Reinvestment Risk

Duration/MD erroneously predicts that long-term bonds are more sensitive to interest rates than short-term bonds—but this prediction can be wrong in any of the following circumstances: (a) the corporate issuer's business is much less sensitive to interest rates than that of other issuers; (b) the company has a reputable Treasury department such that its bonds are perceived by investors to be good hedges against inflation risk and interest rate risk; (c) the long-term bond is convertible into the issuer's equity and is secured by tangible assets, and the conversion value and conversion option of the bond dampens the bond's sensitivity to interest rates; (d) when interest rates rise, the issuer's credit quality increases, which more than offsets any resulting price declines; or (e) due to general illiquidity, and scarcity, the bond's price does not react to changes in interest rates.

However, a rise in interest rates that increases the lender's cost of deposits may become an issue only if the bank/lender does not provide sufficient long-term mortgages at the new higher interest rates. ALM is a reaction to framing effects; and some of the inherent biases and framing effects are as follows.

Depending on forward rates, and availability of forward contracts, and the state of the yield curve, a 30-year loan is not much different from a one-year loan that is rolled-over (to the same borrower and/or other borrowers) at the end of each year, or a one-month loan that is rolled over at the end of each month (to the same borrower and/or other borrowers). Thus, a 30-year fixed rate loan can be less sensitive to interest rates than a one-year loan, if some of the following conditions exist:

- The lender's holding period is less than one year; and/or the borrower can prepay the 30-year loan at any time; and the estimated time to prepayment is less than one year. In such cases, the shortened holding period truncates the standard duration and MD.
- The due diligence costs, transaction costs, hedging costs, and monitoring costs associated with the 30-year loan are significantly less than those of the one-year loan—the cumulative total of such costs incurred for the one-year loan (or a series of comparable one-year loans) often exceed the loan losses incurred by holding the 30-year loan, when interest rates rise. This situation may occur in many emerging markets.
- The business of the borrower of the 30-year loan is much less sensitive to interest rates than that of the borrower of the one-year loan. Thus, any loss from increases in interest rates that the lender incurs from holding the 30-year loan will be more than offset by increases in the credit quality of the borrower of the 30-year loan.
- The bank/lender can easily assign/sell one- to two-year "strips" of long-term loans (the 30-year loan) where such strips have the same or lower sensitivity to interest rates than a regular one-year loan.

In many emerging market debt markets, if there is no secondary loan market or if there is a thinly traded secondary loan market, then it is possible that the illiquidity of a one-year business loan precludes customer cash withdrawals just as much as the illiquidity of a 30-year mortgage. If the key issue is that the bank must have adequate cash to meet customer withdrawals (from retail deposit accounts), then the problem can be partly solved by originating enough performing long-term loans, by assigning one- to two-year strips of long-term loans, or by originating equivalent short-term loans.

Where there is sufficient liquidity across the yield curve, actual and perceived duration gap risk and ALM are likely to be much less significant because: (a) lenders/banks can easily sell long-term loans in order to meet customer withdrawals of short-term deposits); (b) changes in interest rates will be hedged more cheaply; (c) financial institutions can rebalance their loan portfolios more quickly and cheaply to reduce adverse effects; and (d) the increase in prices (or stability of prices) due to increased liquidity can more than offset any bond price declines due to increases in interest rates. Actual and perceived market liquidity can be a much more important valuation factor and interest rate risk factor than duration risk. This was illustrated from 2007 to 2009 in the U.S. ABS markets where liquidity for most short-term ABS declined substantially before the crisis affected the long-term ABS submarket.

Hence, for the average financial institution in developing countries, the perceived illiquidity and relatively high interest rate risk of mortgages is a framing effect (and perhaps an illusion) because: (1) many of the companies that issue short-term debt are more sensitive to interest rates than consumer mortgages are sensitive to interest rates; (2) in most developing countries (and some developed countries), short-term business loans are as illiquid as, or even more illiquid than traditional mortgages; (3) almost all debt markets are relatively illiquid OTC markets and have relatively few participants; (4) the relative illiquidity of debt markets (and its submarkets) vary drastically during recessions and expansions such that a mortgage that is deemed illiquid during an expansion may be more liquid than some government bonds and corporate loans during an economic recession; and (5) the illiquidity of mortgages is tempered by mortgage insurance (most corporate bonds and business loans do not have associated bond insurance) and embedded prepayment options.

In many circumstances, reinvestment risk can be a much more important valuation factor and interest rate risk factor than duration risk, particularly in developing countries where: (1) due diligence costs are substantial; (2) transaction costs and monitoring costs are substantial; (3) lenders have much less flexibility to reverse or amend their lending decisions—and litigation costs are significant; (4) secondary loan markets are small, illiquid, and limited; (5) skilled credit analysts are rare, and credit analysis processes are not completely automated; and (6) the borrowing rates for long-term loans are substantially higher than the banks' costs of customer deposits. In such circumstances, it will be probably much more profitable for lenders/banks to originate good long-term loans/mortgages (which have low reinvestment risks) rather than short-term loans.

Immediately after its origination, the MD for a 30-year, 102 percent LTV mortgage is based on its 30-year term. However, the MD of the underlying property is based on the estimated holding period of the property, which is typically shorter than the 30-year period. Thus, if the same bank owns the underlying property, it can record a lower MD in its ALM analysis.

Consider two 30-year loans held by a bank that are exactly the same except that one is interest-only and the other is an amortizing loan whose amortization period is equal to the loan term (thus, their effective interest rates are different). The use of the MD formula will predict that the amortizing loan has a much shorter duration than the interest-only loan but the opposite is the reality in many circumstances for the following reasons. For the first 7 to 10 years of the loan term, the borrower pays minimal principal repayments for the amortizing loan (most of the payments during this period are interest; and the amount of principal repayment during this period is inversely proportional to the stated interest rate). Both loans have the same default risk, and default risk is typically greatest during the first six years of loans, and if the borrower defaults within the first

13 years (i.e., if the lender has more than 20 percent to 35 percent of the original principal amount at risk), the lender will spend the same amount of resources to foreclose either of both loans and recover assets. More than 70 percent of mortgages are prepaid within 13 years, and less than 30 percent of all mortgages are held until maturity; and the typically higher interest rate for the interest-only loan compensates for the lack of amortization. The cumulative difference between the interest rates of the interest-only loan and the amortizing loan during the first 6 to 13 years of the loan term sometimes exceeds the repaid principal for the amortizing loan—and this cumulative difference is also subject to compounding based on the available reinvestment rates. Thus, the reality is that contrary to the MD and duration formulas, the interest-only loan sometimes has the same or shorter "recovery period" (duration) than an amortizing loan with similar terms.

Interest rates fluctuate daily (and hourly in some cases), so hedging ALM risk on a daily/weekly/monthly basis involves or can cause substantial regret; and the cumulative regret can complicate decision makers' human decision processes, and can make such individuals extremely risk-averse, extremely risk-sensitive, or extremely insensitive to risk over time, none of which are optimal states.

These foregoing framing effects show that the ALM analysis is inaccurate; the framing effects also illustrate the importance of providing liquidity in secondary mortgage and mortgage-alternatives markets, given the costs of hedging ALM risk. ALM is expensive to hedge (sometimes as much as the difference between short-term and long-term interest rates) in terms of information systems, human capital, psychological costs (e.g., regret), administrative costs, and costs of financial instruments, and most banks can fund their lending only with medium-term loans and long-term loans, so then there may not be any benefit to ALM. This is because: (1) most of the ALM hedges do not provide any incremental liquidity; (2) the hedges are very expensive; (3) the hedges may not capture the prepayment risk and the bank's holding period; (4) the ALM hedges typically do not capture credit risk, which affects loan/bond prices.

Choudhry (2007) has documented several major problems inherent in ALM analysis, some of which are as follows. In ALM analysis, the repricing intervals chosen for maturity-gap analysis are arbitrary. ALM models erroneously assume that: (1) cash flows and investors' internalized discount rates remain constant as interest rates change, and (2) the asset-liability mix remains constant and there is no growth of assets or liabilities over time. ALM analysis does not consider the time value of money. Some assets and liabilities have embedded prepayment options, which can distort scheduled cash flows. The MD analysis used in ALM may be accurate for only small changes in interest rates (below 50 bps) (Agca 2002).

EXISTING LIQUIDITY DERIVATIVES (SWAPS AND OPTIONS) ARE INACCURATE AND INEFFICIENT

Ranjan and Art (2008) discussed liquidity indices. Cherian, Mahanti, and Subrahmanyam (2009); Clauss (2010); Mahanti, Nashikkar, Subrahmanyam, Chacko, and Mallik (2008); Fleming (2003); Goyenko, Subrahmanyam, and Ukhova (2011); and Sarr and Lybek (2002) discussed various measures of liquidity. Anson (2010) introduced a framework for measuring liquidity risk for various types of asset classes. Ranjan, Meissner, and Youn (2008) and Golts and Kritzman (2010) discussed liquidity derivatives. Ranjan, Bhaduri, and Youn (2007) distinguished between two types of liquidity risk (asset risk and funding risk) and proposed the following five instruments for hedging liquidity risk:

1. *Bermuda-Style Return Put Option*: The option holder has the right to put (swap) the investment to the option seller in exchange for a predetermined strike price (similar to a regular put); the option holder also pays the option seller the return from the original investment.
2. *Withdrawal Option*: This instrument grants the holder the right to transfer the illiquid investment to the option seller at the market price. This instrument is similar to a regular put but without a fixed exercise price, and thus does not provide protection against declines in value, but only against perceived illiquidity—and does not isolate illiquidity accurately.
3. *Return Swaption:* This instrument grants the holder the right to enter into a "return swap," wherein the holder will swap his or her fund's periodic return for LIBOR rate payments.
4. *Liquidity Option*: This instrument is a "knock-in" barrier option where the barrier is a liquidity metric; for a bondholder who also holds this liquidity option, the option comes into existence only if the bond's liquidity declines below a stated barrier (e.g., trading volume falls below X for Y consecutive days), upon which the option holder will have the right to sell the bond to the option seller at the then-prevailing market price. The liquidity option does not provide protection against price declines.
5. *Return Swap:* This instrument is a swap wherein the holder will swap his or her fund's periodic return for LIBOR rate payments.

The five instruments introduced by Ranjan, Bhaduri, and Youn (2007) are problematic because:

1. The five instruments don't isolate liquidity risk—the structure and pricing of the liquidity swaps and options are affected by, and depend on,

liquidity, and vice versa, and are also affected by credit risk and pure investment risk of the investment. The gains/losses from the swaps/options cannot be solely attributed to liquidity risk. For example, in the *Return Swaption* and the *Return Swap*, receiving LIBOR while paying out the hedge fund returns does not hedge liquidity risk, particularly where LIBOR has low or no correlation to the hedge fund returns (even if LIBOR and the returns are correlated, the LIBOR payments still don't make the hedge fund interests sufficiently liquid in terms of transferability of ownership). Furthermore, when interest rates are low (lower than 3 percent), even after seven years the holder would have recouped less than 30 percent of his principal investment. With regard to the liquidity option (public markets) and the withdrawal option (private markets): (a) the holder's contingent right to sell the subject asset at the prevailing market price does not isolate or reduce liquidity risk effects—that is, the excess of the prevailing market price over the book value (and vice versa) is not solely attributable to liquidity risk and can be attributed to other factors such as availability of capital, and so on; (b) when liquidity has dropped below the stated benchmark, for most financial instruments, it is likely that the market price will have also declined substantially such that selling the asset at prevailing market prices will not capture the loss attributable to liquidity risk; (c) the option can have value (i.e., time value, volatility value) that is not related to liquidity risk; and (d) the option can have or lose value due to nonliquidity factors such as counterparty credit risk, time of year, legal/documentation risk, and so on.

2. In all five instruments, volatility remains a dominant element of the pricing model and hedging strategies. The prices are erroneously modeled as a continuous function of time. None of the pricing models includes any element of liquidity and thus there is a pricing gap between cause and effect. In most instances, volatility and the bid-ask spread are only secondary/minor indicators of liquidity. The bid-ask spread includes elements of sentiment, firm-specific trading/execution costs, and differences in knowledge, and is meaningful only for a specific trade or volume of asset; thus its usefulness as an indicator is limited. Taleb (2009), Mandelbrot (2008), Shilling, Sirmans, and Benjamin (1987), and Nwogugu (2003) have shown that the use of stochastic calculus and many assumptions in options pricing are inaccurate.
3. Most of the financial instruments do not provide protection for declines in market value that are caused by liquidity risk only.
4. The purchaser of the liquidity options and/or swaps will be exposed to counterparty credit risk, settlement risk, and legal risk. Thus, the five instruments increase systemic risk.

5. The five instruments do not reduce the harmful activities of arbitrageurs; and in fact they provide arbitrage opportunities—they create demand for LIBOR-based instruments, hedge fund indices, and equity index futures.
6. The five instruments do not address accounting rules and the resulting balance sheet effects. Liquidity risk is often analyzed with respect to, or because of, balance sheets. Accounting rules have substantial effects on the recording/classification of effects of liquidity risk—in the form of final valuations, reserves for losses, deferred recognition of gains/losses, classification of purpose of assets (as available-for-sale or held-to-maturity), and the classification of timing of assets (as short- or long-term assets). Hence, the use of these five instruments is likely to result in opportunities for manipulation of balance sheets.
7. The underlying and erroneous assumption is that trading volume is an accurate measure of liquidity—but trading volume represents only completed orders that may or may not reflect true market psychology or liquidity (i.e., some orders may have been completed under conditions of desperation or distress or overconfidence).
8. The five instruments do not distinguish among the effects of order sizes, percentage of completed orders, and the relative liquidity of similar financial assets (e.g., similar bonds or stocks).

Kritzman and Golts (2009) also introduced liquidity options, which have similar defects to those of the liquidity derivatives introduced by Ranjan, Bhaduri, and Youn (2007).

POSSIBLE SOLUTIONS TO THE PERCEIVED ALM PROBLEM

Within the context of financing real estate transactions, there are several solutions to these perceived ALM problems (Oviedo 2001; Reitano 1990). Interest rate risk can be hedged using capital market instruments, but they are expensive (sometimes as much as the difference between short- and long-term interest rates). The interest rate risk can be controlled by using adjustable-rate or floating-rate mortgages with interest rate caps. The lenders can issue long-term bonds to finance their mortgages. The government and the banking industry can provide secondary market liquidity (by establishing entities that will trade in loans/mortgages), which will drastically reduce or eliminate the need for ALM, because sufficient liquidity of long-term loans reduces the need to hedge interest rate risk. Lenders can invest in mortgage-alternative products that have much shorter "effective recovery periods" (durations) than traditional mortgages. Lenders can increase the percentage of total customer deposits that have restricted withdrawals (customers can withdraw such deposits only during specific withdrawal windows). Banks can borrow in short-term interbank markets using their long-term loans as collateral. Lenders/banks can sell portions of any long-term loan (e.g., 6-month, 1-year, 2-year, and 3-year strips) through assignment contracts—in order to shorten their weighted-average recovery periods.

A new market can be developed for time-liquidity units (TLUs), which can be OTC instruments or fixed-income instruments that are traded among investors and financial institutions, and are exchangeable for loan strips, bills, cash, and bonds. Each class of time-liquidity unit will be defined in terms of interest rate, face value, liquidity, and maturity.

Liquidity can be measured in various dimensions: (a) horizontally, by comparing liquidity of similar assets in one time period; (b) horizontally, by comparing the liquidity of the same asset during the same time interval in a day or week or month; (c) horizontally, by comparing liquidity of the different order sizes of the same financial asset; and (d) vertically, by comparing both matched/unmatched trading orders and trading volume over time.

The proposed TLUs will serve different functions in markets, including the following:

1. Enable investors to isolate and hedge against liquidity risk.
2. Enable investors to balance or eliminate fluctuations in perceived portfolio risk or portfolio value that is attributable to liquidity.
3. Reduce the adverse effects of temporary illiquidity on traditional accounting methods and mark-to-market valuations, and also reduce the effects of illiquidity on long-term performing assets. These adverse effects were a major cause of the demise and bankruptcy of Lehman Brothers and the financial distress and near-bankruptcy of Merrill Lynch (which was sold to Bank of America in dire circumstances).
4. Ensure more efficient price discovery because investors who exploit liquidity risk (especially in fixed income markets) and volatility risk in ways that reduce overall social welfare will be forced out of the market.
5. Facilitate regulatory enforcement—illegal arbitrage, insider trading, and so on can be substantially reduced and made more identifiable by the use of TLUs.

Each TLU will: (a) function with respect to only one identifiable financial asset (the "complementary asset"); (b) will always exist during its stated life, but will have attributable value only when the average "periodic liquidity" during a pre-specified period of time falls below a pre-established minimum benchmark liquidity and when the holder/beneficiary wants to sell the complementary asset (otherwise, the TLU's agreed-upon market value will be zero)—hereafter, the "existence contingency." Thus, TLUs will be used primarily for "available-for-sale" securities/instruments and not for financial instruments that are held for the long term (held-to-maturity securities/interests); and (c) be transferable/assignable only with the consent of the two parties.

CONSTITUTIONALITY OF CENTRAL BANK RESTRICTIONS ON DAILY CASH WITHDRAWALS BY CUSTOMERS

As mentioned in the preceding sections of this chapter, if a bank run occurs, there are likely to be bank runs on other banks, and the central bank will most probably not be able to intervene and provide liquidity to banks. Most banks' assets and liabilities are mismatched, so banks will have to ration/restrict daily cash withdrawals by customers. Such action can be challenged in court on constitutional grounds. However, there are four key issues:

1. In most countries, the central bank owns the currency, reserves the right to manage the currency without interference, and can replace the currency with other means of exchange.
2. The typical currency is a note (a debt obligation).
3. In countries that suffer from rampant corruption and/or have large "informal sub-economies," restricting cash transactions can substantially reduce corruption and increase transparency in the system.
4. In countries that suffer from excessive "street crime" (assault, robbery, muggings) and kidnappings, restricting customer cash withdrawals can substantially reduce crime.

Two scenarios will be analyzed: Type 1 situations where the central bank restricts the amount of daily cash withdrawals by customers without bank runs, but permits unlimited debit card transactions; and Type 2 situations where the central bank restricts the amount of daily cash withdrawals by customers because of bank runs, but permits unlimited debit card transactions.

For constitutional law analysis, the state action is the enactment of the central bank's cash restriction order.

Substantive Due Process

The central bank's cash restriction order does not constitute violations of substantive due process, particularly where the permitted amount of daily cash withdrawals is sufficient for the average customer. Bank runs impose substantial costs on banks, and can result in fire sales of banks' assets at depressed prices, which will also make it less likely that depositors will get their funds. Deposit insurance is costly to governments, which will have to pay out substantial amounts without the central bank's cash restriction order. Furthermore, the government's legitimate interest in promulgating efficient laws that protect depositors, reduce the cost of government, reduce corruption, and increase transparency in the economy far outweighs any gains from either implementing deposit insurance (which is often limited) or permitting unlimited cash withdrawals in any circumstance. Furthermore, debit card transactions are unlimited, increase transparency, reduce transaction costs and monitoring costs, and provide valuable audit trails.

Equal Protection

The central bank's cash restriction order does not constitute a violation of the Equal Protection Clause of the U.S. Constitution, where the central bank's cash restriction order does not discriminate between different classes of bank customers that have deposit accounts. Securities brokerage accounts are not comparable because they are subject to different regulations, and brokerage firms do not use cash and securities in customers' accounts to provide loans to third parties. The central bank's cash restriction order does not unfairly discriminate between lenders that provide different types of loans (e.g., mortgages, short-term debt, project finance debt). The central bank's cash restriction order does not unfairly discriminate between lenders that have the knowledge and infrastructure for risk management and lenders who do not have such knowledge. The central bank's cash restriction order does not unfairly discriminate between lenders who can afford to absorb the losses that arise from assets sales in bank runs and lenders who cannot afford such losses—any such discrimination will put some banks at a significant competitive disadvantage. Any discriminatory classifications that arise as a result of the central bank's cash restriction order are far outweighed by economic or regulatory purpose and enhance social welfare and/or the government's regulatory objectives. The central bank's cash restriction order is not overbroad, and is narrowly tailored to a class of persons (depositors) and to a class of entities (banks) deemed to be at risk. The government's interest in protecting depositors and ensuring effective capital markets far outweighs the following: (a) the significant economic losses that banks incur from bank runs, investigations of corruption, and actual illegal activities; and (b) the disincentive effects of deposit insurance on banks (reduces propensity to develop accurate underwriting and risk management standards; increases banks' misplaced reliance on ALM).

Right to Contract

The central bank's cash restriction order does not violate the depositors' or the bank's constitutionally guaranteed right to contract for the following reasons. First, the depositor and bank both have constitutionally guaranteed property interests in entering into contracts on their own terms—such property interests arise from state constitutional law, state contract law, state property law, expectations, and norms. Second, the cash restriction order does not contravene any prevalent government interest; the order is necessary to improve social welfare, protect depositors' and banks' economic interests, and provide necessary incentives to reduce crime and increase efficiency in banking transactions. The cash restriction order also prevents or reduces costly government intervention in the banking system—to stop illegal activity.

Takings

The central bank's cash restriction order does not constitute violations of the Takings Clause of the U.S. Constitution. Under the accepted interpretation of the constitutions of many common law countries, government regulation of private property constitutes a Taking if it does not substantially advance a legitimate government interest, and the regulation is not imposed with simultaneous payment of adequate compensation for the property owners for any resulting economic losses. In this instance, the cash restriction order substantially advances major government interests and public interests, and is necessary to prevent the potential collapse of banking systems and asset markets in the country, and possible contagion effects in other countries. The losses incurred by the depositor, which can be considered as uncompensated Takings, include the opportunity cost of use of the restricted funds in the bank account, but the alternative (fire sales of bank assets at depressed prices) will result in much worse outcomes. The monetary amount of the losses incurred by depositors is transferred to "public use" in the form of a more stable banking system, greater transparency, and reduced crime. Thus, any Taking can be construed as being for public use because the general public benefits and the stated Takings advances the government's interests to some extent.

CONCLUSION

Unfortunately, ALM is so ingrained in bankers and government regulators that it has compelled them to curtail vital investment in their national economies, thus severely limiting economic growth. In most developing countries, banks are funded primarily by short-term deposits, and the prospect of unexpected deposit outflows requires that the bank maintain liquid assets. Similarly, insurance companies have to make estimates of future possible payouts and ensure that there is sufficient cash flow—ALM encompasses cash-flow matching, which is more common among insurance companies and pension funds and pertains to future estimates of possible cash outflows. In most developing countries, government securities markets are relatively small, but business loans are relatively illiquid (no or minimal secondary markets), and hence banks limit themselves to providing only short-term business loans whose short-term maturities make them essentially self-liquidating. Traditional mortgages have long-term maturities and are perceived as relatively illiquid with high transaction/monitoring costs, which causes most banks and financial institutions not to provide mortgages (in addition to illiquidity, verification of the credit quality of each mortgage is difficult)—this perception is based in part on ALM principles and is the major limitation on lending in most developing countries.

REFERENCES

Agca, S. 2002. *The performance of alternative interest rate risk measures and immunization strategies under a Heath-Jarrow-Morton framework*. PhD Thesis, Virginia Polytechnic Institute and State University.

Anson, M. 2010. Measuring a premium for liquidity risk. *Journal of Private Equity* 13 (2): 6–16.

Attema, A., H. Bleichrodt, K. Rohde, and P. P. Wakker. 2010. Time-tradeoff sequences for analyzing discounting and time inconsistency. *Management Science* 56 (11): 2015–2030.

Babbel, D., C. Merrill, and W. Panning. 1995. Default risk and the effective duration of bonds. Policy Research Working Paper #1511, World Bank.

Beber, A., M. Brandt, and K. Kavajecz. 2007. Flight-to-quality or flight-to-liquidity? Evidence from the Euro-area bond market. *Review of Financial Studies* 22 (3): 925–957.

Bhaduri, R., G. Meissner, and J. Youn. 2007. Hedging liquidity risk. *Journal of Alternative Investments* 10 (3): 80–90. Available at: https://www.alphametrix.com/wp-content/uploads/2011/01/JAI-Winter-2007-Liquidity-Derivatives-by-Bhaduri-Meissner-Youn1.pdf.

Cherian, J., S. Mahanti, and M. Subrahmanyam. 2009. Trading agents and liquidity risk. *Journal of Investment Management Conference Series*. Spring.

Choudhry, M. 2007. *Bank asset and liability management: Strategy, trading, analysis*. Hoboken, NJ: John Wiley & Sons, 260–290.

Clauss, P. 2010. *Liquidity risk integration in portfolio choice: The bid efficient frontier*. January 20. Available at: http://ssrn.com/abstract=1505391.

Duffie, D. 2009. How should we regulate derivative markets? PEW Financial Reform Project, Briefing Paper #5.

Duffie, D., N. Gârleanu, and L. Pedersen. 2007. Valuation in over-the-counter markets. *Review of Financial Studies* 20 (6): 1865–1900.

EDHEC. 2010. *EDHEC survey of the asset and liability management practices of European pension funds*. June. Available at: www.edhec-risk.com/edhec_publications/all_publications/RISKReview.2010-06-30.4236/attachments/EDHEC-Risk_Survey_ALM_Pension_Funds.pdf.

Fleming, M. 2003. Measuring treasury market liquidity. *Federal Reserve Bank of New York–Economic Policy Review* 9 (3). Available at: www.ny.frb.org/research/epr/03v09n3/0309flem.pdf.

Goldstein, L., D. Lay, and D. Schneider. 1996. *Calculus and its applications*. Upper Saddle River: Prentice Hall.

Gollier, C. 2010. Expected net present value, expected net future value, and the Ramsey rule. *Journal of Environmental Economics and Management* 59: 142–148.

Golts, M., and M. Kritzman. 2010. Liquidity options. *Journal of Derivatives* 18 (1): 80–89.

Goyenko, R., A. Subrahmanyam, and A. Ukhova. 2011. The term structure of bond market liquidity and its implications for expected bond returns. *Journal of Financial and Quantitative Analysis* 46 (1): 111–139.

Handforth, F. 2004. Duration and convexity of mortgages in the context of real estate investment analysis. *Journal of Real Estate Portfolio Management* 10 (3): 187–192.

Hardy, M., and J. Wirch. 2004. The iterated CTE: A dynamic risk measure. *North American Actuarial Journal* 8 (4): 62–75.

International Association of Insurance Supervisors. 2006. *Standard on ALM*. October. Available at: www.iaisweb.org/__temp/Standard_on_Asset_Liability_management.pdf.

Kaluszka, M., and A. Kondratiuk-Janyska. 2004. On risk minimizing strategies for default-free bond portfolio immunization. *Applicationes Mathematicae* 31 (3): 259–272.

Kawaller, I., and T. Koch. 2006. Incorporating prepayment risk considerations when making hedging decisions. *Bank Asset/Liability Management* 22 (3): 1–7.

Khwaja, A., D. Silverman, and F. Sloan. 2007. Time preference, time discounting, and smoking decisions. *Journal of Health Economics* 26 (5): 927–949.

Kogut, C. A. 1990. Consumer search behavior and sunk costs. *Journal of Economic Behavior & Organization* 14 (3): 381–392.

LeBoeuf, R. 2006. Discount rates for time versus dates: The sensitivity of discounting to time-interval description. *Journal of Marketing Research* 43 (1): 59–72.

Leclerc, F., B. Schmitt, and L. Dube. 1995. Waiting time and decision making: Is time like money? *Journal of Consumer Research* 22 (1): 110–119.

Liao, S., M. Tsai, and S. Chiang. 2009. Analyzing yield, duration and convexity of mortgage loans under prepayment and default risks. *Journal of Housing Economics* 18 (2): 92–103.

Liu, W., and J. Aaker. 2007. Do you look to the future or focus on today? The impact of life experience on intertemporal choice. *Organizational Behavior and Human Decision Processes* 102 (2): 212–225.

Mahanti, S., A. Nashikkar, M. Subrahmanyam, G. Chacko, and G. Mallik. 2008. Latent liquidity: A new measure of liquidity, with an application to corporate bonds. *Journal of Financial Economics* 88 (2): 272–298.

Mandelbrot, B. 2008. "New Methods of Statistical Economics," revisited: Short versus long tails and Gaussian versus power-law distributions. *Complexity* 14 (3): 55–65.

Nwogugu, M. 2010/2011. *On regret theory and anomalies in polynomials and net present value.* (Book manuscript).

Nwogugu, M. 2005. Further critique of GARCH/ARMA/VAR/SV models. *Applied Mathematics & Computation* 182 (2): 1735–1748.

Nwogugu, M. 2003. Decision making under uncertainty: A critique of options pricing models. *Journal of Hedge Funds & Derivatives (Derivatives Use, Trading and Regulation)* 9 (2): 164–178.

Ortendahl, M., and J. F. Fries. 2005. Framing health messages based on anomalies in time. *Medical Science Monitor* 11 (8): 253–256.

Oviedo, R. A. 2001. A critique of the traditional graphs of duration-YTM: An alternative "average length" measure to replace duration in yield-curve analysis. Working paper, McGill University, Montreal, Canada.

Poole, B. 2000. On time: Contribution from the social sciences. *Financial Services Review* 9 (4): 375–387.

Purcell, E. J., and D. Varberg. 1987. *Calculus with analytic geometry.* 5th ed. Upper Saddle River, NJ: Prentice-Hall.

Ranjan, B., and C. Art. 2008. Liquidity buckets, liquidity indices, liquidity duration and their applications to hedge funds. *Alternative Investment Quarterly*, 15–20.

Ranjan, B., G. Meissner, and J. Youn. 2008. Hedging liquidity risk: Potential solutions for hedge funds. *CFA Digest* 38 (3): 5–6.

Reitano, R. 1990. Non-parallel yield curve shifts and durational leverage: Is there a lever between your yield curve and your surplus? *Journal of Portfolio Management* 16 (4): 62–67.

Sandri, S., C. Schade, O. Mußhoff, and M. Odening. 2010. Holding on for too long? An experimental study on inertia in entrepreneurs' and non-entrepreneurs' disinvestment choices. *Journal of Economic Behavior & Organization* 76 (1): 30–44.

Sarr, A., and T. Lybek. 2002. Measuring liquidity in financial markets. IMF Working Paper. Available at: www.imf.org/external/pubs/ft/wp/2002/wp02232.pdf.

Shilling, J., C. Sirmans, and J. Benjamin. 1987. On option-pricing models in real estate: A critique. *Real Estate Economics* 15 (1): 742–752.

Siegel, L., and B. Waring. 2004. TIPS, the dual duration, and the pension plan. *Financial Analysts Journal* 60 (5): 54–61.

Taleb, N. 2009. Finiteness of variance is irrelevant in the practice of quantitative finance. *Complexity* 14 (3): 66–76.

Zauberman, G., and J. Lynch. 2005. Resource slack and propensity to discount delayed investments of time versus money. *Journal of Experimental Psychology: General* 134 (1): 23–37.

Zenios, S. 1995. Asset/liability management under uncertainty for fixed-income securities. *Annals of Operations Research* 59 (1): 77–97.

CHAPTER 15

New Mortgage-Alternative Products for Primary Mortgage Markets in China and CIS/CEE Countries

There are often substantial differences between residential mortgages and commercial mortgages. In some countries both types of mortgages are originated and/or sold in different submarkets. In the secondary commercial mortgage markets, the dominant mechanisms are loan participations, and to a lesser extent, loan syndications. "Portfolio lenders" (in most countries, they are usually commercial banks, life insurance companies, pension funds, REITs, and savings and investment funds) hold commercial mortgages on their books while "conduit lenders" sell or securitize the commercial mortgages that they originate.

The main mortgage alternatives are installment sales contracts, rent-to-own programs, income mortgages, leasehold mortgages, full-recourse loans, and phased payment contracts (buyer pays down payment, and construction starts; then buyer pays remainder of purchase price over two to three years). These mortgage alternatives have substantial benefits (social, economic, and psychological) and should be developed into viable and liquid markets. Research and the events of 1990 to 2010 (in the United States, Japan, Mexico, Australia, China, and Europe) have confirmed that the traditional mortgage has produced savings, investment, and consumption patterns and household decision-making patterns that are grossly suboptimal and highly detrimental to social welfare. The reformulation of the mortgage market model is one feasible alternative, but that process may be costly in terms of time, resources, belief revisions, and political impact—it may be more effective to develop alternative household allocation/consumption models. For example, installment sales contracts significantly eliminate or reduce the many costs and negative psychological effects inherent in foreclosure processes, and thus can reduce the effective borrowing rate for consumers. A 15-year rent-to-own program can eliminate all of the negative social and psychological problems associated with consumer defaults and negative credit reports (default will not be reported to a credit rating agency or will have a much less severe credit impact than a mortgage default). An installment contract can eliminate the excessive spending and borrowing that is facilitated by home-equity loans. A full-recourse loan reduces strategic defaults and social/psychological problems inherent in the housing purchase and default decisions. An income-market loan eliminates inefficient foreclosure (because payments are adjusted to suit the borrower's income and macroeconomic conditions) and inefficient disclosure (banks do not recognize losses on loans prematurely because loan payments are adjusted to borrower income).

In the United States and in most developed countries, the term *alternative mortgages* typically refers to four types of mortgages: interest-only adjustable-rate mortgages (ARMs), option ARMs, limited- or no-documentation loans, and high loan-to-value ratio loans. LaCour-Little and Yang (2010) analyzed alternative-mortgage products (including interest-only and other deferred amortization structures) and developed a game theory model of contract choice given uncertain future income and house prices across different types of borrowers. LaCour-Little and Yang found that deferred amortization contracts are more likely to be selected in housing markets with greater expected price appreciation and by households with greater risk tolerance; and that such products necessarily have greater default risk, especially among lower-income households that are aggressive in housing consumption levels. Cocco (2010) also discussed endowment mortgages, which are popular in the United Kingdom (and links the mortgage to endowment policy that involves stock markets). Other researchers have also analyzed new mortgage products: Azevedo-Pereira, Newton, and Paxson (2003); Olszowy (2006); Renaud (2009); Cohn and Fischer (1975); Lea (2010); Ambrose and Buttimer (2009); Bar-Gill (2009); Rossi (2010). However, the results of LaCour-Little and Yang and the related articles discussed therein and Cocco completely omit the key issues such as: (1) who is best positioned to bear the debt burden and to hedge fluctuations in property values; (2) the public health consequences of alternative mortgages and traditional mortgages; (3) the nature of contracting and the intertwining of mortgage markets, savings markets, and property-values markets; (4) the inefficiencies and conflicts of interest in mortgage markets; (5) the prevalence of both irrational borrowers and borrowers whose attachments to their houses result in suboptimal decisions and allocations; (6) the competition between rental markets; and (7) the information effects and social/psychological costs of default penalties in rental markets (eviction) and property-values markets (foreclosures).

THE ADJUSTABLE BALANCE MORTGAGE

Ambrose and Buttimer (2009) proposed a new type of mortgage called the *adjustable balance mortgage*, which is inefficient and does not solve the "foreclosure incentive" problem. The adjustable balance mortgage is similar to a fixed-rate mortgage (FRM) because it has a fixed interest rate and is fully amortizing. At fixed, preset time intervals (e.g., monthly, quarterly, or semiannually), the value of the property/house is calculated based on changes to a local house price index. If the property value is lower than the originally scheduled mortgage balance for that date, then the mortgage balance will be reduced to equal the lower property value, and the monthly payment is reduced (recalculated based on this new lower property value). If the house retains its most recent value, then the mortgage balance and the monthly payments remain the same. If the property increases in value at the next reset date, the loan balance will be increased to equal the new property value, subject to the limitation that the loan balance cannot exceed the scheduled loan balance based on the original loan balance and scheduled amortization. Thus, borrowers must lose their initial equity in the property, plus any built-up equity, before the mortgage balance is reset. However, the mortgage principal balance is not increased if home prices rise above the original/initial loan balance, and hence, the lender does not fully share in increases in property value, but shares in declines in property value. The adjustable balance mortgage is simply the sum of a loan modification (that is built into the mortgage) plus a traditional fixed-rate amortizing mortgage. In the United States, the Obama administration's and the Bush administration's mortgage-modification programs have failed, and more than 40 percent of U.S. households that modified their mortgages between 2008 and 2011 subsequently defaulted and went into foreclosure proceedings. The U.S. Office of the Comptroller of the Currency reported that up to 37 percent of modified mortgages were 60 days into a second default within six months of the mortgage modification.

Some people believe that the U.S. federal loan-modification programs (U.S. Treasury, U.S. Federal Reserve Bank, and U.S. FDIC programs) have not been as successful as expected because they focus strictly on borrower payment-to-income ratios, and as a result do not eliminate or reduce the borrowers' incentive to default for long. Such arguments are misguided, because: (a) many of the government loan-modification programs do not consider the Selective Credit Fulfillment Bias; (b) the government loan-modification programs do not fully analyze the payment-to-income issues (e.g., the household income was not properly verified, household income is variable, there are new household expenditures that reduce the amounts available for mortgage payments, and/or the monthly mortgage payment is more than 30 percent of the household's gross monthly income); (c) participants in mortgage-modification programs choose strategic default for other reasons, for example, revenge, to intentionally frustrate lenders, to spend money on other items/products, due to perceived hopelessness of their situation, or because of their core beliefs about prospects of recovery of the housing market; (d) participants in mortgage-modification programs choose strategic default because the composition of their family has changed due to divorce, separation, death, or relocation, or because their children have graduated from college; (e) participants in mortgage-modification programs choose strategic default because they simply do not want to deal with the emotional burden of mortgage payments and associated expectations; and (f) participants in mortgage-modification programs choose strategic default because they estimate that their nonpayment of interest/principal/taxes during the 9- to 18-month foreclosure period exceeds any equity they may ever get from ownership. Figure 15.1 shows the mark-to-market loan-to-value ratios for some U.S. states.

Thus, contrary to Ambrose and Buttimer (2009), the adjustable balance mortgage does not reduce the borrower's incentive to default if the house value declines. The proposed adjustable balance mortgage completely misses the key issues, which are that: (a) mortgage default is driven primarily by changes in income and shocks in family circumstances (such as emergency health care and not changes in property values; (b) home buyers know that real estate markets have cycles and home prices usually rise after having declined; (c) the major cause of strategic default is not declining or "underwater" property values—but rather, prospects of future income, estimated probability of magnitude of increases in property values, changes in household preferences, and estimated timing of increases in property values (thus a homeowner who has sufficient income, but whose mortgage balance exceeds the property value may continue making mortgage payments if he or she estimates that there will be a timely recovery/increase in property values); and (d) strategic defaults constitute a small percentage of all mortgage defaults.

In many countries, the proposed adjustable balance mortgage will create substantial tax liabilities for the buyer-borrower. For example, in the United States, if the property index values decline and the lender adjusts the mortgage balance downward, the borrower will have to recognize a taxable gain on the extinguishment of debt. The lender's recognition of losses will immediately be reflected in its income statement and balance sheet, and thus, will most likely have a negative effect on its stock price.

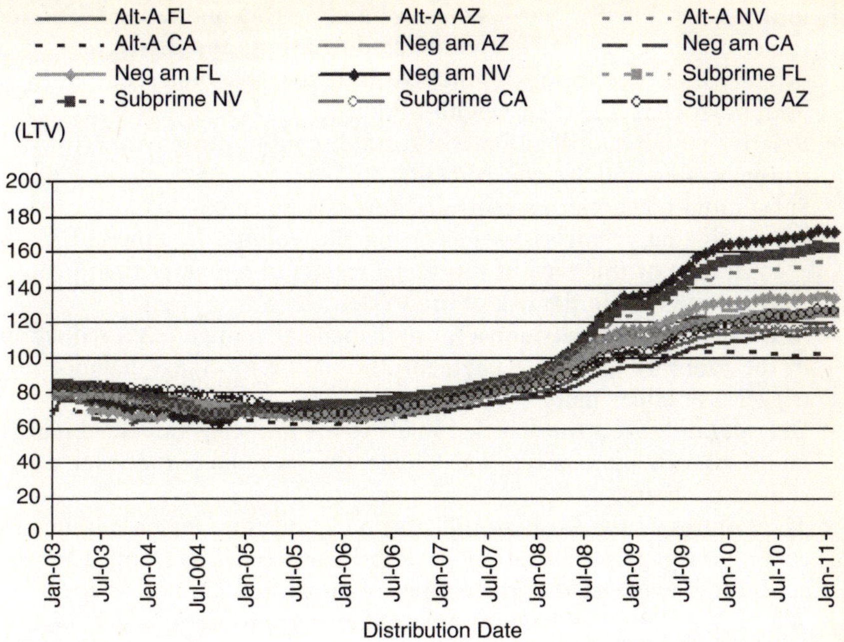

FIGURE 15.1 Mark-to-Market Loan-to-Value Ratios for Some U.S. States (Underwater Mortgages as of 2011)
LTV: Loan-to-value.
Source: Standard & Poor's, "Residential Mortgage Servicing Standards: A Cost-Benefit Analysis," 2011.
www.standardandpoors.com/ratings/articles/en/us/?assetID=1245301117714.

THE CONTINUOUS WORKOUT MORTGAGE, SHARED APPRECIATION MORTGAGES (SAMs), SHARED INCOME MORTGAGES (SIMs), AND SHARED EQUITY MORTGAGES (SEMs)

The continuous workout mortgage (Shiller 2009; Feldstein 2009), which was explained in detail in Shiller et al. (2011), is somewhat similar to the adjustable balance mortgage, and has the same problems as the adjustable balance mortgage (introduced by Ambrose and Buttimer 2009), traditional mortgages, and Islamic finance products. Some of these problems and weaknesses are described as:

- Improper combinations of savings/investment markets, property-values submarket, rental submarkets, and mortgage markets.
- Costly lack of flexibility as to location and asset and wealth rebalancing.

- Informational inefficiency—excessive and detrimental reliance on consumer credit scores and corporate credit ratings; and dissemination of defaults and foreclosures, which worsen the economic conditions of both borrowers and their neighborhoods.
- Relatively high coordination costs and discontinuous payoffs (for borrower, lender, and the government).
- Substantial renegotiation costs and foreclosure costs.
  - Additive aggregate risk—increasing the volume (number of loans/contracts) of this type of mortgage results in a greater than proportional increase in the risk of the lender.
- In most jurisdictions/countries, any beneficial change (e.g., reduction) in the monthly mortgage payment and/or the mortgage balance may trigger a taxable "gain."
- Default (and foreclosure) is tied solely to the property-values submarket and the mortgage market, and almost always reduces the value of the subject property.
- The failures of the Bush administration's and the Obama administration's mortgage modification programs between 2008 and 2011 are substantial evidence that these types of mortgages are not efficient.
- Where the mortgage balance is less than the property value, the borrower may still choose strategic default for any of the following reasons: (1) the borrower's expectations (about price appreciation, the economy, personal matters) are negative; (2) the borrower has to change the household's wealth or income allocations, that is, due to illness, losses in investments, disability, death, unforeseen circumstances, relocation.
- These mortgages cannot cure default risk and liquidity risk.
- As explained in the chapter on mortgages, these mortgages reduce two-sided matching in the marriage markets and the job market; and also dampen/reduce monetary transmission.
- These mortgages can cause substantial regret.

These same problems are inherent in shared appreciation mortgages, (SAMs), shared income mortgages (SIMs), and shared equity mortgages (SEMs), which were analyzed in Ebrahim, Shackleton, and Wojakowski (2009).

TRADITIONAL ALTERNATIVE MORTGAGES

The Mortgage Bankers Association (Lea 2010b) released a report that studied international alternative mortgages (the study analyzed the four main types of alternative mortgages—interest-only ARMs, option ARMs, limited or no-documentation loans, and high loan-to-value ratio loans. The study results showed that:

- Ninety-five percent of new loans made in the United States in 2009 were long-term fixed-rate products, which was much higher than data from various countries—such as 1 percent in Spain, 2 percent in Korea, 10 percent in Canada, 19 percent in the Netherlands, and 22 percent in Japan. Also, in 2009 variable-rate loans accounted for 5 percent of new loans made in the United States, while other countries had higher percentages—38 percent in Japan, 91 percent in Ireland, 92 percent in Australia and Korea, and 47 percent in the United Kingdom. According to a study by the European Mortgage Federation (EMF) on the efficiency of mortgage collateral, borrowers remain liable for mortgage deficiencies in Belgium, Germany, Greece, the Netherlands, Spain, France, Ireland, Portugal, and the United Kingdom.
- The popularity of the long-term FRMs and securitization in the United States (compared to other countries) is attributable to the existence of the government-backed secondary mortgage market institutions that lower the relative price of this type of mortgage.
- The U.S. ban of prepayment penalties on FRMs is very unusual. Of the countries sampled, most subjected FRMs to an early prepayment penalty except Denmark, Japan, and the United States. In Australia, Canada, Denmark, Germany, the Netherlands, and Switzerland, the prepayment penalties are designed to compensate the lender for lost interest over the remaining term of the fixed rate. Thus, mortgage rates in those countries do not include a significant prepayment option premium; other financing techniques, such as covered bonds, are more common.
- There are many problems inherent in the use of the FRM as the ideal consumer mortgage instrument for all borrowers. In effect, the cost of the prepayment option is socialized, with everyone paying a premium in the mortgage rate for the option. This contrasts with the European view that only borrowers who exercise the option for financial advantage should pay the cost.

Cheng (2010) and Chen, Huang, and Liang (2008) analyzed and described the reverse mortgage submarket in China. It is somewhat ironic that in the United States most reverse mortgages are made through Federal Housing Administration's Home Equity Conversion Mortgage Program. The growing number of senior citizens in the United States has increased the volume of reverse mortgages, which are typically issued only to persons aged more than 62 years, and more than 5 percent of borrowers are aged between 62 and 65 years. (See Reverse Market Insight at www.rminsight.net/.)

Most reverse mortgages require borrowers to pay monthly mortgage insurance premiums, which range from 0.5 percent to 1.5 percent of the loan balance.[1] Prospective borrowers are required to consult a reverse mortgage counselor who has been certified by the U.S. Department of Housing and Urban Development before they submit an application for a reverse mortgage. Traditional mortgages (Fei and Yongheng 2008, 2011; Yongheng 2010; Yongheng, Wu, and Gyourko 2010), alternative mortgages (Piskorski and Tchistyi 2010), and reverse mortgages have the same inherent problems as the adjustable balance mortgages, indexed mortgages, and Islamic finance products discussed in this chapter.

In the United Kingdom, "pension mortgages" have inherent problems such as: (a) the lump sum received from the pension balance may not be sufficient to pay off the mortgage balance; (b) the pension mortgage provides very low flexibility; (c) real estate is much less liquid than traditional pension account investments (such as stocks and bonds), and after payment of the mortgage balance, the homeowner may not have sufficient liquid assets for daily expenses at a time when they are past their prime earnings years; (d) pension mortgages are very expensive for the government, which typically has to contribute up to forty percent of the pension amount; (e) in most instances, the homeowner cannot prepay the pension mortgage until he or she reaches the minimum retirement age; and (f) if the homeowner becomes unemployed or dies, he or she may not be able to make enough contributions to the pension account and the property will be foreclosed.

INDEXED MORTGAGES

Many researchers have developed indexed mortgages where the monthly payment and/or interest rate and/or the principal balance are indexed to inflation and/or a wage index. Nejadmalayeri (2011), Erol and Patel (2005), and Buckley, Lipman, and Persaud (1993) analyzed indexed mortgages. Indexed mortgages have the same problems as the adjustable balance mortgage, traditional mortgages, and Islamic finance products, which are discussed herein. Some of these problems/weaknesses are as follows:

- Improper combinations of savings/investment markets, property-values submarket, rental submarkets, and mortgage markets.
- Costly lack of flexibility as to location and asset and wealth rebalancing.
- Informational inefficiency—excessive and detrimental reliance on consumer credit scores and corporate credit ratings, and dissemination of defaults and foreclosures, which worsen the economic conditions of both borrowers and their neighborhoods.
- Relatively high coordination costs and discontinuous payoffs (for borrower, lender, and the government).

- Substantial renegotiation costs and foreclosure costs.
- Additive aggregate risk—increasing the volume (number of loans/contracts) of this type of mortgage results in a greater than proportional increase in the risk of the lender.
- In most jurisdictions/countries, any beneficial change (e.g., reduction) in the monthly mortgage payment and/or the mortgage balance will most probably trigger a taxable "gain." Also, the government will lose substantial tax revenues due to mortgage modifications, which will have substantial effects on municipal governments that are heavily dependent on property taxes.
- Default (and foreclosure) is tied solely to the property-values submarket and the mortgage market, and almost always reduces the value of the subject property.
- The failures of the Bush administration's and the Obama administration's mortgage modification programs between 2008 and 2011 are substantial evidence that these types of mortgages are not efficient.
- Where the mortgage balance is less than the property value, the borrower may still choose strategic default for any of the following reasons: (1) the borrower's expectations (about price appreciation, the economy, personal matters) are negative; (2) the borrower has to change the household's wealth or income allocations, that is, due to illness, losses in other investments, disability, death, unforeseen circumstances, and relocation.
- These mortgages cannot cure default risk and liquidity risk; and the mortgages dampen monetary transmission.
- As explained in the chapter on mortgages, these mortgages reduce two-sided matching in the marriage markets and the job market.
- Many of the indices are not accurate.
- Indexed mortgages can cause substantial regret.

ISLAMIC FINANCE PRODUCTS

Islamic finance generally prohibits interest; gambling; uncertainty or ambiguity relating to the subject matter, terms, or conditions; unjust enrichment; dealings in pork, alcohol, arms and ammunition, or pornography; speculation; and exploitation or unfair trade practices. Islamic finance products, such as leasing (*Ijara*), safekeeping (*Wadiah*), profit-sharing (*Mudharabah*), cost-plus (*Murabahah*), and joint-venture (*Musharakah*); forward sale contract (*Salam*); contract of manufacture (*Istisna*); and fee-based funds management (*Wakalah* and *Sukuk*), have existed for many centuries, but these products have some of the same problems inherent in traditional "Western" mortgages, installment land contracts, and alternative mortgages, some of which are discussed in Anderson (2010), Farooq (2009), and Asutay (2008). Other problems associated with Islamic finance products are:

- Inefficient and improper combinations of savings markets, property-value submarkets, and leasing submarkets.
- In Islamic finance, the borrower's interest in the subject property and in the contract are often not defined or properly defined.
- Lack of flexibility—borrowers are tied to one property, one location, and one product.
- Limited liquidity of financial products.
- Adverse speculation—although Islamic finance products are better than traditional Western mortgages at reducing "normal" speculation, Islamic finance products facilitate "institutionalized speculation" and collusion where lenders and financial institutions (which typically buy and hold the title to the subject property for much of the loan term) have substantial incentives to prop up property values. Almost all Islamic finance transactions require that the lender assume asset-value risk (in addition to cash-flow risk, documentation risk, and credit risk) at inception of the transaction. This partly explains the collapse of the Dubai real estate markets in 2009 to 2010.
- The fundamental Islamic finance principle of sharing risk and reward in transactions often conflicts with the prohibition of interest, and with the determination of market values of assets and cash payments. That is, because Islamic financial products are overly dependent on the property-values submarket, the whole financial system is substantially exposed to shocks and conflicts of interest in appraisals. Furthermore, in Islamic finance, the sharing of risk and reward, and thus fairness, is often constrained by the following factors. Information asymmetry between the lender and the borrower affects the degree of fairness of allocation of risk and rewards—there are usually no standards, and sharing is often done on a deal-by-deal basis; semi-illiterate borrowers or borrowers who cannot negotiate well will accept suboptimal terms or less than their fair share of rewards. Altruism sometimes affects negotiations and outcomes in Islamic finance.
- In some Islamic finance jurisdictions, the remedies for default are often not well defined or enforced properly, and borrower-buyers forfeit their equity interests in the subject asset. For example, an Ijara buyer-borrower who stops making monthly payments may lose all of his or her interests in the subject property, which is not fair.
- The Islamic finance principle that each financial transaction must be linked to a "tangible, identifiable underlying asset" precludes the financing or use of otherwise valuable intangibles (such as contract rights).

- The costs of compliance for some products can be substantial.
- These products can cause substantial regret.

COOPERATIVE MORTGAGES

Ebrahim (2009), Besley, Coate, and Loury (1993, 1994), and Hart and Moore (1998) analyzed cooperative mortgages. Cooperative mortgages have the same problems as the adjustable balance mortgage, traditional mortgages, and Islamic finance products, which are discussed here; some of these problems are:

- Improper combinations of savings/investment markets, property-values submarket, rental submarkets, and mortgage markets.
- Costly lack of flexibility as to location and asset and wealth rebalancing.
- Informational inefficiency—excessive and detrimental reliance on consumer credit scores and corporate credit ratings, and dissemination of defaults and foreclosures, which worsen the economic conditions of both borrowers and their neighborhoods.
- Relatively high coordination costs and discontinuous payoffs.
- Substantial renegotiation costs and foreclosure costs.
- Additive aggregate risk—increasing the volume (number of loans/contracts) of this type of mortgage increases the risk of the lender.
- These products can cause substantial regret.

THE PRICING OF MORTGAGES AND BEHAVIORAL FINANCE—MOST MODELS ARE INACCURATE

Almost all researchers have used stochastic calculus and traditional options pricing models for the valuation of structured products and mortgages. The above-mentioned articles on participating mortgages, adjustable balance mortgages, and traditional mortgages all used options models and stochastic calculus to value the mortgages. However, most of these valuation models/approaches are inaccurate, and do not consider regret theory. An, Yongheng, and Clapp (2010) confirmed that mobility also plays a critical role in borrowers' choices to default, but most mortgage pricing models don't incorporate the mobility option accurately. Contrary to Breuer and Perst (2007), and as explained in Nwogugu (2005, 2006a, 2006b); Dvorak (2010); Weber et al. (2007); Mattos, Garcia, and Pennings (2008); and Kalayci and Basdas (2010), cumulative prospect theory (Nwogugu 2006a, 2006b; Raeva, Mittone, and Schwarzbach 2010) cannot be used in the design of structured products. Regret theory is a more accurate approach for financial engineering.

Baule and Tallau (2011) analyzed the pricing and performance of bonus certificates in the German market under several alternative models, with different assumptions about volatility behavior, and found significant overvaluation where the issuers make an excess return while the buyers pay too much (most of the valuations by issuers were based on options models and stochastic calculus). Henderson and Pearson (2011) analyzed the offering prices of 64 issues of a popular retail structured equity product and found that they were on average, almost 8 percent higher than estimates of the products' fair market values obtained using option pricing methods. They also concluded that issuing firms might introduce complexity in innovative securities to exploit uninformed investors. Rossetto and Van Bommel (2009) analyzed Endless Leverage Certificate (ELC) by using Monte Carlo analysis to value ELCs and found that due to limited liability, a typical ELC written on a typical Deutscher Aktien IndeX (DAX) stock can be worth 0.3 percent more than its intrinsic value (the difference between the value of the underlying and the financing level); in January 2007 the 5,129 ELCs issued on the 30 DAX stocks traded at an average premium of 0.67 percent over the intrinsic value, and the median bid-ask spread, expressed as a percentage of the underlying, was 0.18 percent. Rossetto and Van Bommel also found that upon knockout, investors received on average 3.2 percent less than the theoretical knockout value, which is consistent with discontinuous trading of the underlying.

Stoimenov and Wilkens (2005) compared the daily closing prices of a large variety of structured products with their theoretical values derived from the prices of options traded on the Eurex (European Exchange). Stoimenov and Wilkens found that for most products in the primary market, the issuing banks charged large implicit premiums. They also found that for the secondary market, the product life cycle was an important pricing parameter. Grünbichler and Wohlwend (2005) found that structured products in the Swiss market were mispriced in both the primary market (by issuing banks who typically relied on options models) and the secondary markets by traders and investors (who also relied on options models and stochastic calculus); and that the extent of misvaluation is appreciably greater in the primary market than in the secondary market. Benet, Giannetti, and Pissaris (2006) analyzed the pricing of reverse-exchangeable securities (RES) and found that there is a significant pricing bias in favor of the issuing financial institution, which can be attributed to credit enhancement (from observed positive correlation between the RES terminal payoff and issuer financial performance). Benet, Giannetti, and Pissaris also stated that market completeness and possible tax advantages may affect the demand for, and the rapid expansion of the RES submarket. Bergstresser (2009) analyzed the issuance and individual performance of more than one million issued structured notes and found that investors focus on the performance of structured notes, and issuers prefer to issue notes whose underlying risks are easier for them to hedge; most of the notes were sold at a significant premium, and the premium estimates over the entire period are close to the estimates in Henderson and Pearson (2011), which were based on a small sample of one type of note. Bergstresser also noted the significant variation of the premiums across time period, which had been declining significantly since 2005.

Carlin (2009) found substantial empirical evidence that the law of one price is violated in retail financial markets (i.e., there is significant price dispersion even when products are homogeneous); and despite the large number of firms in the market, prices remain above marginal cost and may rise as more firms enter the markets. Carlin attempted to show that such anomalies arise when firms add complexity to their price structures (which takes advantage of the financial illiteracy of consumers), which ultimately leads to price dispersion and failure of competition. Carlin hypothesized that professional advice (i.e., by securities brokers) can eliminate such information advantages, unless the firms increase aggregate complexity, decrease price dispersion across the industry, and/or implement incentive contracts for brokers, all of which have significant social welfare implications because retail securities markets are relatively large.

All of the existing literature on mortgage pricing is based on inaccuracies and common fallacies, some of which are as follows.

Many researchers erroneously believe that lenders price mortgage risk to cover their expected costs of doing business with each borrower (including some normal profit). Hence, most mortgage models express mortgage risk almost solely in terms of interest rates; but the reality is very different. Mortgage markets are highly competitive, and prospective borrowers often have very low switching costs. Lenders realize this, and respond in the following ways: (1) offering low interest rates that may not be related to standard estimates of property-specific risk or borrower-specific risk; (2) bundling mortgages with other financial services wherein the mortgage terms (interest rate, fees, etc.) may not reflect the standard risk postulated by economic models; (3) offering lower or higher interest rates in order to build brand equity or to attract new customer deposits. Hence, lenders' evaluation of mortgage risk often departs substantially from what standard economic models predict; the implication is that almost all empirical studies of mortgage pricing are inaccurate, and lenders can incur substantial losses from mortgages in many ways other than formal default. Some examples are: (1) underwater mortgages—the property values can decline to levels below the outstanding mortgage balance; (2) monitoring costs—lenders often incur substantial monitoring costs such as appraisals, administrative costs, and assessment of the value of mortgage insurance; (3) the combination of non-recourse clauses in the mortgage documents, volatile property values, and a substantial decline in the credit quality of the insurer that provides mortgage insurance; (4) a change in accounting rules pertaining to asset valuations (e.g., mark-to-market) or recognition of income; and (5) an increase in capital reserve requirements for some types of mortgages, which substantially reduces the bank's lending capacity and budgeted income and creates more administrative expenses.

Most empirical studies of mortgage markets completely omit the effect of accounting rules on mortgage pricing. This issue has become much more relevant in many countries during the past few years, particularly those that have enacted mark-to-market rules (Allen and Carletti 2008). Historical accounting and mark-to-market accounting represent two extreme positions that substantially distort values. Nwogugu (2009) introduced a new accounting method that reflects permanent changes in asset values while incorporating market values. Many banks have sustained mortgage losses but don't recognize such losses in their financial statements either because the borrower continues to make payments or because there is mortgage insurance (regardless of the credit quality of the insurer).

Contrary to most or all existing empirical studies, many lenders knowingly or unintentionally express or price credit (mortgage) risk in ways other than interest rates, such as: (1) events of default (the type, timing, magnitude, and severity of events of default can be based on various scales depending on the industry and company; (2) the length of cure periods; (3) the contractual terms for post-default redemption, (4) the conditions for prepayment and the prepayment penalties; and (5) conditions for mortgage insurance (insured events).

Most or all empirical studies and models of mortgage pricing completely omit the effects of mortgage insurance on lenders' setting of interest rates, and the effect of the credit quality of the third-party insurer on the value of the mortgage.

Magri and Pico (2011) analyzed mortgage pricing in Italy and found that Italian lenders have increasingly priced mortgage interest rates based on household credit risk. They found that for mortgages granted between 2000 and 2007, a 1 percent increase in the probability of default caused a 21 basis point rise in mortgage interest rates, which was lower than the 38 basis point premium Edelberg (2006) estimated for the United States at the end of the 1990s. The Magri and Pico results were based on formal default rates and omitted analysis of effects of mortgage insurance (and insurers' credit quality); thus, they reflect the errors found in most similar empirical studies that are discussed herein.

Liu and Skully (2008) analyzed the impact of securitization and structural changes of the Australian mortgage market on the mortgage-pricing behavior of banks, and found that banks reduced their mortgage interest rates in order to respond to increasing competition. Liu and Skully presented a simple model to explain the potential factors that may affect bank behavior in terms of cost effects and market structural changes. They found that lenders' yield spreads are significantly related to bank market share, existing and new loan concentration indexes, and securitization, all of which indicate that lower concentration and increased competition in the banking industry are significant causes of changes in lenders' spreads. Liu and Skully stated that their findings are consistent with both the securitization literature and price concentration studies.

DISTORTION OF ECONOMIC DATA AND NATIONAL ACCOUNTING

The production-side and lending-side "borrowing cycle" in the mortgage markets grossly inflates and distorts economic data (such as GDP/GNP, corporate profits, sales revenues). Consider the production of a housing unit's building materials. Suppliers borrow to finance production of components. Construction firms borrow for working capital and for equipment leasing and purchases. The developer in turn borrows to finance the project. By the time the housing unit is completed and sold by the developer, various parties have borrowed three to five times the production cost of the housing unit, and all the borrowed amounts are accounted for as sales revenues in

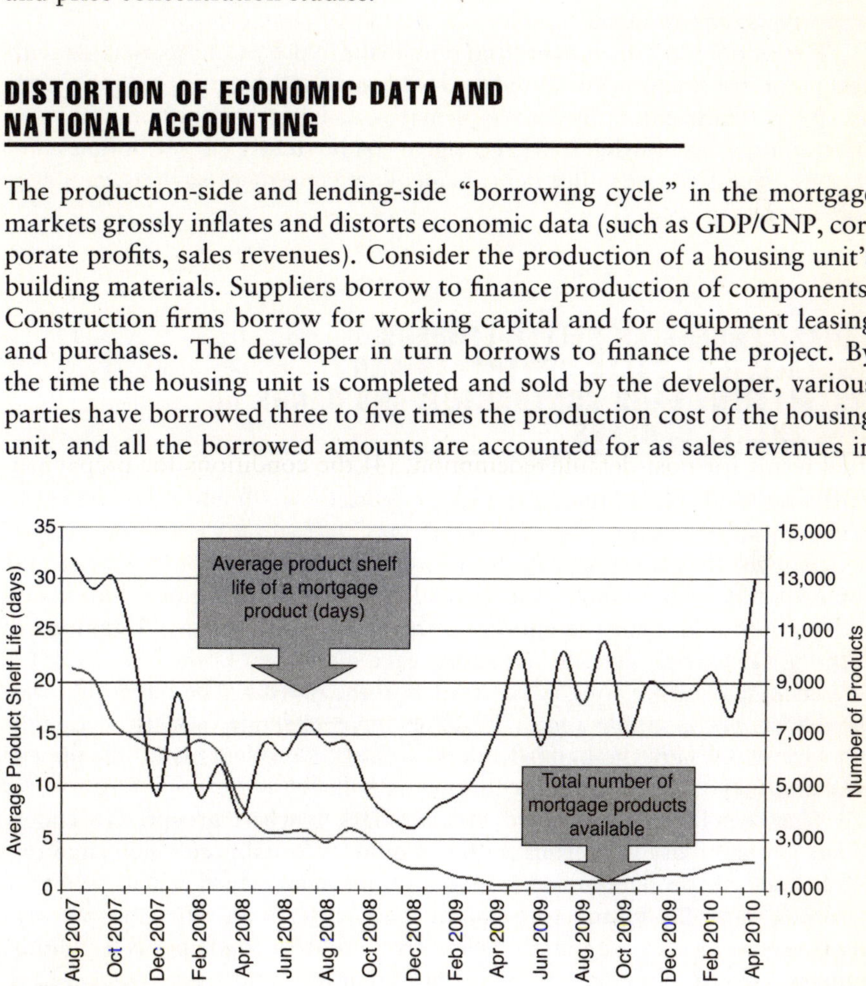

FIGURE 15.2 Average Product Shelf Life of Mortgages in the United Kingdom: April 2010
Source: Industry data.

various forms. On the lending side, the mortgage broker originates a loan, books profits, and immediately sells the loan to a bank, which may resell the loan to another bank or to a securitization program; and all the parties in the sale-chain will book profits and economic activity from what is essentially one loan. These unnecessary transaction costs and somewhat illusory economic activity can be reduced or eliminated by appropriate mortgage alternatives.

The problems and distortions associated with the use of consumer credit scores (such as FICO) can be eliminated or substantially reduced by the use of mortgage alternatives.

The emotional attachments and unrealistic expectations associated with traditional mortgages can be reduced and managed by using mortgage alternatives. These emotions are the primary cause of fraud and unwarranted price inflation in housing markets, which inadvertently causes bubbles and crashes, excessive consumer debt, inadequate retirement savings, and economic recessions.

BANKS/LENDERS AS SELLER-LENDERS (INSTALLMENT SALES CONTRACTS AND INSTALLMENT LAND CONTRACTS); AND BANKS AS REAL ESTATE BROKERS

Zhizhong (2009) and Freyfogle (1987) analyzed installment sales contracts. Zhizhong states in part, "Article 167 of our Contract Law is the sole and explicit one to stipulate especially the installment sale in our country's civil and commercial law. It finds the legal precedent to deal with the installment sale in our country and has the important theoretical and practical significance. Although the article uses the advance legal experience of other countries for reference, it is rather rough and still has some defects. The paper analyses the defects of the article and make some concrete suggestions to revise and improve it." Where the banks/lenders are also the sellers (as in installment land contracts), there can be the following benefits:

There can be interlender property submarkets where prospective lender-sellers can purchase properties that match their clients' preferences; and can effect noncash property swaps. Such an inter-lender market will probably be much more liquid and transparent than whole-loan mortgage markets because it will have much more "derivative"/indirect participants (e.g., individuals and households) than whole-loan markets; and banks/lenders have broader geographical coverage and access to prospective buyers/sellers than real estate brokers.

Most importantly, the inter-lender property submarket and some seller-lenders can disintermediate and almost completely eliminate real estate brokers if lenders have adequate geographical market coverage, Internet-based customer networks, and good relations with their customers (see Nwogugu 2007). The intermediation function of real estate brokers has often been questioned and found to be inefficient (Salter, Johnson, and Webb 2007; Nadel 2007; Nwogugu 2007). Couch, Mahalik, and Moore (2001) noted that the Gramm-Leach-Bliley Act of 1999 did not expressly mention but raised the issue of permitting banks to enter nontraditional business lines to provide real estate brokerage and real estate management services. However, in 2007 to 2008, the U.S. Congress introduced a bill named HR 111, which would have amended the Bank Holding Company Act of 1956 and the Revised Statutes of the United States to prohibit financial holding companies and national banks from engaging, directly or indirectly, in real estate brokerage or real estate management activities. Hughes et al. (1996) showed empirically that geographical expansion diversifies region-specific risk and reduces failures of financial institutions. Wheelock and Wilson (2009) found that during 1984 to 2006, many commercial banks benefited from increasing returns-to-scale, regardless of ownership structure and branch banking restrictions—Hughes, Loretta, and Moon (2001) and Feng and Apostolos (2010) found similar results. Wagner (2010); Klein and Seidenberg (2010); and Elsas, Hackethal, and Holzhäuser (2010) analyzed the diversification of banks. Beck, Demirguc-Kunt, and Levine (2006) found that more concentrated banking systems have a lower than normal probability of financial crises, possibly due to better diversification of risks within the large financial institutions. Banks/lenders are better positioned to serve as real estate brokers than ordinary persons and the traditional small company because: (1) banks/lenders have obvious information advantages (about prospective buyers' and sellers' financial condition and preferences) compared to individual real estate brokers; (2) banks can drastically reduce search costs and transaction costs (legal fees, appraisal fees, mortgage fees, etc.) for prospective buyers; (3) combining the lending and brokerage functions can substantially reduce or eliminate traditional brokers' substantial incentives to inflate property prices, facilitate "flipping" of properties, or to organize fraudulent transactions; (4) the fixed and variable costs incurred by traditional real estate brokers are already being incurred by banks, and will be eliminated if banks are also real estate brokers; (5) unlike traditional real estate brokers, banks can assess the customer's entire financial situation, make judgments based on comparative analysis (with data about other customers), and provide better advice about real estate and other financial decisions—this is critical because the "truth-telling gap" in the usual broker-client relationship (wherein the prospective property buyer and/or seller do not truthfully disclose their wealth and/or income and/or preferences to real estate brokers and mortgage brokers) has been a major cause of improper sale/purchase transactions, mortgage fraud and foreclosures; (6) the fears that broker-banks will limit credit to brokerage-customers of competing banks is somewhat unfounded because such banks can gain from selling other financial products and services; and (7) the possibility of banks that are also real estate brokers creating national or regional monopolies is low, because many customers have accounts at several banks; for real estate brokerages and many banking services, their switching costs are low, and many nonbank entities provide loans.

Brobeck and Woodall (2006) state in part,

> *Traditional real estate brokers perform a useful consumer service in facilitating the purchase and sale of houses and land. Moreover, they have established a "system" that is very convenient for home buyers and sellers. Unfortunately, these traditional brokers also act as a price-setting cartel that maximizes their opportunities to charge a "fixed" commission of either 6% or 7%, depending on the local real estate market. Furthermore, in order to increase the chances of the "double-dip"—one broker collecting the entire commission—they often do not adequately represent the interests of their clients in searching for buyers or houses, or in securing the best prices on these houses—highest for sellers, lowest for buyers. Traditional brokers harm consumers in three main ways. They try to charge a high, fixed price for their services, yet they often do not adequately represent the interests of their clients in searching completely for the best buyers or properties, or in negotiating the best price for sellers or buyers.*

Nwogugu (2008) explained some of the antitrust problems inherent in the operations of real estate brokers.

Where banks/lenders are also seller-lenders, banks can have almost full capital reserves; and banks will probably have much greater incentives to develop and implement better origination/underwriting standards; and property prices will more likely be stable and accurate because a lot of adverse speculation will have been removed from property markets. Large seller-lenders can achieve substantial cost savings and economies of scale in operations pertaining to property insurance; property taxes; brokerage commissions; transaction costs; monitoring and documentation costs; avoided foreclosure costs; and avoided loan renegotiation costs. A variant of the installment land contract can solve two problems: (1) property owners who have underwater mortgages can still sell their property (subject to the mortgage), and (2) households that cannot qualify for traditional mortgages can use installment sales contracts to purchase property.

The buyer-borrower's possible nonperformance can be insured by a third-party insurance company. It is banks/lenders that provide the mortgages that eventually cause shocks and bubbles, so banks/lenders should bear some of the first losses and the responsibility for hedging such shocks.

Where financial institutions are seller-lenders, the incidence of blighted neighborhoods will probably decline because many banks/lenders can afford to maintain vacant properties and pay real estate taxes (unlike individuals) and have the resources to market properties. Thus, tax revenues (which are the primary source of income for many municipal governments) will likely be more stable.

It is more efficient and less costly (socially, economically, and psychologically) to aggregate and place the debt burden inherent in the purchase of properties on a company that has specialized skills, than to shift and distribute the debt burden down to families/households who: (1) have other obligations, (2) do not have the skills to manage debt, (3) have distorted expectations, (4) often cannot separate business decisions from emotions and personal preferences, and (5) may have the wrong priorities when allocating household resources such as time, money, and relationships. Aggregation of debt burdens results in economies of scale and learning/knowledge effects—one bank that makes 100,000 distinct mortgages in a town can pay annual property taxes and property insurance premiums with the click of a button, can negotiate property taxes with the municipal government, can negotiate for discounts on property insurance premiums, or can self-insure its properties (which lowers the effective interest rates charged for mortgage alternatives). The alternative is to have 100,000 households worry about increases in property taxes and insurance rates, and with most not knowing how to negotiate or reduce property tax and insurance costs. The reality is that the cash savings of most households are sufficient for only two to six months of living expenses. For example, in New Jersey, since 1999, property taxes have been a major economic and political issue and substantial amounts of resources (human capital, money, municipal resources) have been needlessly spent on debates about the issue.

Furthermore, appraisal fraud and the many conflicts of interest inherent in the property appraisal process can be drastically reduced when the lender owns the underlying property. The potential shocks (e.g., declines in home values; illiquidity; natural disasters) inherent in the "savings" component of housing (home equity) and associated distortions in expectations can be reduced or eliminated by reducing the emotional attachment to housing units while encouraging more liquid savings vehicles.

The traditional installment sales contract (or contract-for-deed or installment land contract) has many inherent problems, some of which are discussed in Whitman (2009), Coogan (1981), Clemmer (2007), Moringiello (1996), Conway (1990), and Bormuth (1993). These problems include: (1) total or partial forfeiture by buyer-borrower due to nonpayment (in the United States and some countries, the installment land contract has been used to effectively defraud buyer-borrowers and deprive them of their interests in the property by forfeiture clauses); (2) constructive foreclosure or foreclosure imposed by courts due to nonpayment or nonperformance of the installment land contract; (3) buyer-borrower's limited right of redemption; (4) unjust enrichment of seller-lender; (5) unconscionability of installment sales contracts; (6) non-uniform treatment of installment land contracts in bankruptcy courts; (7) buyer-borrower's inability to obtain home-improvement loans/capital; and (8) inability to build home equity or equity that can be monetized.

Freyfogle (1987), Abshire (1965), and Coogan (1981) analyzed the issue of whether there is an implicit lease in the traditional installment land contract. Mixon (1970) analyzed installment sales contracts as a housing finance tool for low-income home purchasers. Milo (2004) discusses the issues of retention of title and national differences in European property law. Way (2009) analyzed various forms of informal homeownership methods such as lease-to-own, intestacy, seller-financed purchases, and installment land contracts, and recommended improvements to U.S. laws.

RENEGOTIATION AND SEQUENTIAL INVESTMENTS

Noldeke and Schmidt (1998) analyzed sequential investments and the option to own. Within the context of mortgage markets, (1) foreclosures and the subsequent auctions are forms of investment by the lender; and (2) the lender's monitoring costs and opportunity costs are also forms of investment.

Talley (1994) analyzed liquidated damages within the context of mechanism design. The mortgage-alternative products developed in this chapter are conclusive proof that most, if not all, of the results in Neeman and Pavlov (2009), Piskorski and Tchistyi (2010), Sundaresan and Anderson (1996), Sundaresan and Zapatero (1999), Rubinstein and Wolinsky (1992), Evans (2006), and Horwicz and Reiter (2006) are impractical and inaccurate (especially where home equity accounts for 60 to 80 percent of total household wealth in most developed countries). Agarwal et al. (2011) analyzed the effect of securitization on the renegotiation of residential mortgages and found that bank-held residential mortgages were about 30 percent more likely to be renegotiated than securitized mortgages, which implies that frictions introduced by securitization create substantial obstacles to effective renegotiation of residential loans. Fisher (2004) analyzed how the "equity of redemption" affects mortgage renegotiation and the value of mortgaged real estate, and found that a mortgagor may not be able to renegotiate his mortgage debt in order to delay repayment when faced with a reinvestment opportunity during the mortgage term; and that failure to optimally renegotiate the mortgage does not necessarily result in foreclosure but may result in underinvestment. Fisher argues that an additional period of time between default and foreclosure (known as a period of equitable redemption) may allow the mortgagor to accrue sufficient cash flow to not only avoid foreclosure but to mitigate underinvestment in nondefault states; and since this extra period of time may not be achievable *ex post* due to a hold-up problem, its inclusion *ex ante* may be welfare improving. The Fisher findings are wrong—as explained in prior chapters in this book; mortgagors often use the equitable redemption feature to unnecessarily delay repayment and frustrate lenders. The objectives and methods of Fisher (2004) and Agarwal et al. (2011) are misplaced because they imply that renegotiability of mortgages is a laudable objective or good characteristic of mortgages. On the contrary, renegotiation imposes substantial detrimental psychological and economic costs on:

- Households (e.g., depression; decrease of economic/social aspirations; intra-household arguments and disagreements; multiplier effects on co-workers).
- Neighborhoods (e.g., subsequent redlining; reduction of property values).
- Lenders' staff (depression; frustration; distorted performance measures; empathy that can lead to bad decisions; etc.).

Furthermore, contrary to generally accepted economic theory, renegotiation of mortgages is also costly to governments in the following ways:

- The reduction of principal or interest in renegotiations reduces lenders' incomes and thus reduces income taxes that would have been earned by the government.
- Renegotiation substantially reduces the values of the subject property and surrounding properties, which reduces property taxes, which is a major source of revenue for local governments.
- Renegotiation causes redlining (where lenders refuse to lend to residents of neighborhoods that have experienced substantial renegotiations of home mortgages) and neighborhood blight, which causes crime, homelessness, drug abuse, and unemployment, which increase the governments costs of providing social services and rehabilitating neighborhoods.
- Renegotiation compels banks/lenders to write down assets, which increases the banks' risk profile and their cost of capital, which compels governments to provide more capital to banks (rather than use such capital for other programs).

- Renegotiation also reduces the productivity of both borrowers and lenders' staff, which reduces overall output in the economy and thus, reduces government revenues.
- Government often has to spend money to provide incentives to encourage lenders and borrowers to participate in mortgage renegotiation programs. The recent failure of the Bush administration's (2008 to 2009) and the Obama administration's (2009 to 2011) mortgage modification programs[2] is evidence of problems inherent in renegotiation, and completely rebuts the findings of Clauretie and Jameson (1994), which concluded that mortgage renegotiation was uncommon and should not be included in mortgage pricing models, and that there was no direct evidence of the frequency of loan renegotiations, and that empirical tests using delinquency and foreclosure placement rates demonstrated that renegotiation was not more likely to occur in states with greater foreclosure costs or in conventional mortgages.

The costs of foreclosure are substantial and have been estimated at up to 40 percent of the pre-foreclosure value of the property. According to a 2008 report of the Joint Economic Committee of the U.S. Congress (Setzer 2008; Palmeri 2008) and Standard & Poor's reports (2008), the costs of foreclosure are:

- The homeowner incurs a typical loss of $7,200, which includes loss of equity in the property, moving expenses, and legal fees. This amount does not include the costs of reduced availability of personal and business credit. Typically, the default remains on the borrower's consumer credit reports for 7 to 10 years, during which the borrower cannot qualify for most loans.
- The neighbors who live near the foreclosed house incur at least $1,508 in losses from the decrease in the value of their own home. Some lenders redline neighborhoods that contain many defaulting borrowers.
- The local government loses an average of $19,227 per housing unit in reduced property taxes and fees (as home prices decrease). However, affected cities and towns can collect unpaid property taxes when the foreclosed property is sold or, if such taxes remain unpaid, the city/town will become the owners of the property through tax title.
- The lender incurs a loss of about $50,000 per housing unit (for an outstanding mortgage balance of $200,000 to $270,000). The Joint Economic Committee's list of pre- and post-foreclosure expenses incurred by the lender includes: (1) loss on property/loan property maintenance; (2) appraisal; (3) legal fees; (4) lost revenue; (5) insurance; (6) marketing; and (7) clean-up. S&P's report stated that 26 percent of the loan

amount was the average cost of foreclosure, and S&P's details of the lender's losses are as follows: (1) $40,000 is cash loss on the property for a typical loan of $210,000. The lender loses about 19 percent of the outstanding mortgage balance due to only the decline in the market value of the home; (2) property taxes (3 percent of loan amount); (3) maintaining hazard insurance; (4) legal fees (1 percent); (5) an appraisal; (6) lost revenue (an estimated 13.6 percent of the loan amount); (7) marketing fees (broker's commission—6 percent); and (8) home maintenance (3 percent of loan amount). In addition to these direct losses, bank regulations require that lenders provide cash capital reserves to cover potential losses from defaulted loans, which reduces amounts available for new loans, and thus reduces the lenders' revenues/profits.

The above-mentioned foreclosure costs do not include the psychological costs of foreclosure, which often results in substantially reduced productivity, and has adverse multiplier effects (on co-workers, customers, and household members). Thus, foreclosures and industry-specific recessions are symbiotic/complementary, and default/foreclosure may be a major cause of structural change in industries where many employees are homeowners.

According to LPS Applied Analytics,[3] in the United States and as of June 2011, about 4.2 million mortgage borrowers were either seriously delinquent or their mortgages had been referred to lawyers to pursue foreclosure auctions—about 66.66 percent and 33.333 percent of such borrowers had not made any mortgage payments at all for at least one year and two years, respectively. As of May 2011, the typical foreclosure process in the United States lasted for an average of 565 days (i.e., from their first missed payments to the final auction). In New York and Florida, the averages are 800 days and 807 days respectively.

The costs of default are also substantial and include some of the economic costs mentioned above, in addition to substantial psychological and social costs (i.e., depression, redlining by banks; loss of opportunities due to bad credit scores or credit ratings).

Given the substantial costs of default and foreclosure, pre-renegotiation default represents a major change in borrower commitment and/or borrower preferences, or the existence of a set of involuntary adverse conditions that affect the borrower (for which resolution is not guaranteed in the short term or long term) and/or a borrower's state of mind and set of beliefs that confirm a deep-rooted unwillingness to make payments due. Also, the average duration of property market crashes is 2.5 to 3.5 years. Thus, it is somewhat unrealistic to believe that in all or a majority of circumstances there will be substantial post-renegotiation commitment and/or performance by such defaulting borrower.

RECURSION OF MORTGAGES AND THE PERCEPTION OF DEFAULTS AS LOW-PROBABILITY EVENTS

Krainer and Marquis (2004) analyzed traditional mortgages as recursive contracts—this recursion characteristic of the traditional mortgage is perhaps one of its major weaknesses because it reduces or eliminates conditional adaptability; makes the mortgage contract unable to respond to changing conditions even where small adjustments can save substantial transaction costs and monitoring costs; and reduces the adverse psychological effects of mortgages. Conditional adaptability (Bergemann and Välimäki 2002) is a state where the magnitude of adaptability of the mortgage or financial instrument (i.e., to change its terms such as interest rate or timing of payments) depends on the state of other factors that may not be under the control of the holder of the financial instrument. Mortgages should not be viewed in isolation, but rather, as an element of, or within the context of, a constantly changing mix of household/investor wealth, preferences, horizons, knowledge, tax constraints, and obligations. Although recursion in this context implies some measure of predictability, recent history in the mortgage markets of United States, Europe, and Asia has shown that adaptability is more efficient and socially optimal than predictability.

For traditional mortgages, alternative mortgages, and participating mortgages (collectively, "mortgages"), borrower default has often been viewed as a low-probability event because of historically low formal default rates, and perhaps this is why finance professionals didn't bother about systemic risk (what happens when many borrowers default at the same time) and the adverse effects of most types of existing mortgages on monetary transmission. However, the subprime mortgage crisis in the United States and the global financial crisis have shown the importance of aggregate-risk analysis. Also, the default rates and default circumstances of floating-rate mortgages differ substantially from those of fixed-rate mortgages. "Quasi-default" is introduced here as an alternative measure of default and includes the following circumstances: (1) the number of borrowers who habitually make very late mortgage payments (as a percentage of total floating-rate or fixed-rate mortgagors); (2) the number of borrowers who don't pay the full amount of the scheduled periodic mortgage payments (as a percentage of total floating-rate or fixed-rate mortgagors); (3) the number of borrowers who borrow cash from relatives and friends in order to make their monthly mortgage payments (as a percentage of total floating-rate or fixed-rate mortgagors); (4) the number of borrowers who rent out sections of their properties legally or illegally in order to be able to make their mortgage payments (as a percentage of total floating-rate or fixed-rate mortgagors); (5) the number of cash-strapped borrowers who use their credit cards to make their periodic mortgage payments (as a percentage of total floating-rate or fixed-rate mortgagors); (6) the number of borrowers who use all or part of their government welfare benefits to pay mortgage obligations (as a percentage of total floating-rate or fixed-rate mortgagors); (7) the number of borrowers who substantially reduce their expenditures on household necessities such as food and health care, in order to make mortgage payments (as a percentage of total floating-rate or fixed-rate mortgagors); (8) the number of borrowers who restructure their mortgages while continuing to make payments (as a percentage of total floating-rate or fixed-rate mortgagors); (9) the number of borrowers who obtain second jobs in order to be able to pay their mortgage payments (as a percentage of total floating-rate or fixed-rate mortgagors)—this second-job phenomenon usually causes an *income concentration* effect wherein paying jobs tend to be concentrated among mortgagors, and unemployment increases and the rate of new business formation declines; and (10) the number of borrowers who lie about their income/assets in mortgage applications in order to obtain mortgages (as a percentage of total floating-rate or fixed-rate mortgagors). Thus, given the severe economic and social costs of default, by the time a borrower enters formal reportable default, there have been substantial changes in the borrower's financial condition and preferences that are very likely to make further continuance (e.g., loan modification) ineffective. The reality is that the quasi-default rate is often not reported or tracked; it is much greater than reported formal default, and causes substantial economic, social, and psychological harm. The subprime mortgage crisis could have been discovered in time and prevented if lenders, market participants, and government analysts had been tracking quasi-defaults.

Some banks that provide credit cards and mortgages are often able to see elements of quasi-defaults because they use databases to monitor and analyze consumer spending. Thus, when central banks lower benchmark interest rates and buy bonds to boost economic activity, these banks often refuse to provide new loans; this happened in the United States during 2009 and 2010 when bank lending did not increase substantially after the U.S. Federal Reserve invested capital in banks and lowered interest rates. This phenomenon is henceforth referred to as the "quasi-default gap" in expectations of central banks and financial institutions. However, the Quasi-Default Gap is not present in all countries, particularly not in highly controlled economies such as China. Yongheng, Morck, Wu, and Yeung (2011) found that the speed and efficacy of China's stimulus is attributable to strict government control over its banking system and corporate sector, which ensures enforcement of monetary and fiscal policies (unlike in the United States and western Europe). They also found that state-owned enterprises are fueling a real estate bubble and that China's seemingly highly effective macroeconomic stimulus package may have induced costly resource misallocation.

In many developed countries, the social costs of default remain substantial—individuals who have defaulted but otherwise can be productive cannot get new jobs or start new companies simply because of the default notations in their credit histories. The irony is that a substantial percentage of these defaults are caused by circumstances that are often beyond the control of the individual, such as death of a relative, serious illness, layoff or loss of a job, natural disasters, and emergency expenses. Default is treated as a cardinal sin, whereas default is merely the result of an involuntary or voluntary reallocation of household resources.

The Submarkets

The property-values submarket (Case and Shiller 1996) refers to a section of the real estate market that deals in only property prices (sales) and hedging of property prices. The rentals submarket refers only to that section of the real estate market that deals in rentals of property.

CHARACTERIZATION OF THE NEW MORTGAGE-ALTERNATIVE PRODUCTS

This section explains the key characteristics of some new mortgage-alternative products. The mortgage alternatives developed herein are different from the generally accepted definitions of alternative mortgages. The mortgage-alternatives are developed by using set theory, boundary-value conditions, and some elements of mechanism design; that is, the structure of the mortgage alternative is a set of specific characteristics (many of which have boundary values) within mortgage-characteristics spaces. This is in contrast to most empirical and theoretical studies of optimal design of debt contracts, wherein the structure of mortgages was not derived mathematically. The mortgage alternatives are summarily described as follows.

1. *Information neutrality.* The contract origination decision does not rely on consumer credit scores or corporate credit ratings, and the lender does not report post-origination defaults or late payments to credit bureaus. This reduces dissemination of adverse information that worsens the borrower's and neighborhood's economic condition, and also increases two-sided matching in job markets and marriage markets.

2. *Location neutrality.* This characteristic refers to two possible scenarios: (1) where the lender owns the subject property, the buyer-borrower can switch to other properties owned by the same lender for a fixed number of times during the loan term without incurring substantial transaction costs (e.g., without selling the property and then buying another property); or (2) where the borrower holds title to the subject property (as in a traditional mortgage), the borrower can sell the property subject to the existing mortgage and simultaneously use the sale proceeds to purchase another property, which will serve as the collateral for the original mortgage. This local-neutrality feature increases the buyer's mobility and reduces lock-in costs; it also increases two-sided matching in job markets and marriage markets. Lock-in costs refer to the often substantial economic and psychological costs incurred by the buyer's inability to sell the property and move to another property. Many have bad relationships with neighbors; live in houses that are too small, too big, or too far from jobs; and so on.
3. *Default neutrality.* The buyer's default and expectations are not tied to the foreclosure process or to a forfeiture clause, but rather are linked to the savings/investment market, the cash market, and the property-values submarket—in most developed countries and consumer credit systems and credit rating agencies, default or foreclosure tends to reduce matching in job markets and marriage markets.
4. *Wealth neutrality.* The buyer can use different types of permitted wealth to satisfy the loan obligation, and thus reduce the costs of illiquidity of assets and household portfolio rebalancing.
5. *Renegotiation-proofing.* On default, remedies are easily implementable without incurring substantial costs, and the necessity of renegotiation is substantially reduced or eliminated (the existence of the possibility of pre-default or post-default renegotiation of traditional mortgages provides incentives for default and exponentially increases default costs and resolution costs).
6. *Sequential nonredundancy.* Unlike traditional mortgages, on default, the steps/procedures in the stated remedies for default for this mortgage alternative are value-increasing and nonredundant because: (1) subsequent post-default changes in the condition of the buyer-borrower or seller-lender cannot or are highly unlikely to render the remedies suboptimal or redundant (i.e., foreclosures and the borrower's right of redemption can be redundant); and (2) any redundant steps/procedures in remedies can be avoided or eliminated. For traditional mortgages, the steps/procedures from initial default to foreclosure to the subsequent auctions are sequential and structured, and participants cannot skip any

subprocess in the sequence regardless of the magnitude of inefficiency of that subprocess.

7. *Cumulative nonseparability.* All or a stated percentage of the buyer-borrower's payments accrue to the buyer-borrower at any time and in any condition (i.e., default, prepayment, full payment, assignment) and are nonseparable (in traditional mortgages, separability occurs through forfeitures, foreclosures, and assignments). The buyer-borrower's payoff is a nonseparable function.
8. *Continuous payoffs.* The buyer-borrower's payoffs are continuous in time and space, and the payoffs are not materially interrupted by default, declines in property values, and changes in the buyer-borrower's income or preferences. The seller-lender's payoffs are also continuous in time and space because they are not materially changed by default, declines in property values, and changes in the seller-lender's income or preferences. On default, the seller-lender can profit from giving the buyer only a percentage of the buyer's imputed equity in the contract, and the seller-lender also avoids the losses, delays, and multiplier effects caused by foreclosures.
9. *Decreasing recursion.* The seller-lender's returns from this mortgage alternative are recursive in a decreasing manner over time (as time progresses, the payoff is increasingly not a function of all payments made by buyer and seller-lender), primarily because: (1) the probability of foreclosure is greatly reduced, (2) the mortgage alternative is wealth neutral, and (3) the implicit interest rates are reset.
10. *Decreasing opportunity cost.* The buyer-borrower's opportunity cost decreases as time progresses. The buyer's opportunity cost includes risk-adjusted returns from: (1) traditional mortgages—risks include inflation, reduced productivity, mortgage stress, transaction costs, lack of flexibility; (2) investments in securities—risks include inflation, transaction costs, market volatility; (3) interest on cash deposits; (4) rental; (5) all-purchase of the property; and (6) doing nothing. Similarly, the seller-lender's opportunity cost declines as time progresses primarily because foreclosure is precluded, and the lender can still profit if default occurs.
11. *Nonadditive aggregate risk.* This refers to two related qualities: (1) if this type of mortgage alternative is the majority of all outstanding mortgage alternatives and other types of mortgages in a country, social welfare can be maximized at relatively low costs and systemic risk will always be lower than under the regime of traditional mortgages (thus, aggregate rationality is different from individual rationality of one mortgage alternative or traditional mortgage); and (2) for any bank/lender that is active in a given region (only regions but not towns/villages/cities), increasing the volume (number of issued contracts/loans) of this type

of mortgage alternative results in a less than proportional increase in the risk profile of that lender, if all else is held constant (region refers to a group of states in a country). This can be attributed to several factors including: (1) the location neutrality reduces the probability of default as the number of borrowers in the region increases (they have more flexibility/choice and more incentives to make payments); (2) as the number of lender-owned properties in the region increases, information neutrality reduces the flow and dissemination of information/data that drastically reduces property values and thus, loan values; (3) default neutrality eliminates foreclosure (which exponentially increases the seller-lender's risk and losses); and (4) renegotiation-proofing eliminates the substantial economic and psychological costs of renegotiation, which increases the seller-lender's risk and losses; and thus, the number of loans increases. Most traditional Western mortgages, indexed mortgages, and the adjustable balance mortgage have exactly the opposite effect—increasing the volume of such mortgages results in a greater than proportional increase in the risk of the lender, all else held constant.

12. *Time-preference neutrality*. The buyer-borrower's time preference (short/long horizon) does not affect or has minimal effects on the buyer-borrower's refinance decision and default decision.
13. *Limited manipulation*. The market values and appraised values of the subject property are much less likely to be manipulated by any of the following observable or unobservable factors: (1) appraisal fraud and/or collusion between appraisers and other parties; (2) temporary price pressures such as the banks' fire sales of properties (at extremely low prices) in foreclosure auctions; (3) information aggregation—there typically will be less negative data/information (about default, foreclosures, properties, and borrowers) that can reduce property values; (4) flipping; (5) neighborhood blight and abandonment of properties due to tax liens, default, and so on; and (6) false disclosures by borrowers. This is partly because in the context of this mortgage alternative, the lender has substantial incentives to ensure accurate appraisals; there are no foreclosures and there are few opportunities for speculation; and the costs of appraisal errors and collusion for appraisal fraud are borne by the bank/lender.
14. *Preference matching*. The mortgage alternative substantially increases the matching of the true (and often unrevealed) preferences of the buyer-borrower and the seller-lender by providing them with alternatives and flexibility of terms. In most instances, the buyer-borrower's and the seller-lender's preferences are dynamic as time progresses, whereas the terms of traditional mortgages and alternative mortgages remain fixed based on conditions/preferences that existed at the time of

origination of the mortgages. Most mortgages and mortgage origination processes don't have accurate or efficient preference-elicitation mechanisms. Buyer-borrowers whose circumstances have changed don't have to live with unwanted or inappropriate mortgages, and lenders can avoid nonperforming illiquid mortgages, bankruptcies, and foreclosures. The reduced or lack of preference-revelation during the life of the traditional mortgage and the adjustable balance mortgage substantially decreases their efficiency.

15. *Participant substitutability.* The buyer-borrower and the seller-lender can be substituted simultaneously, sequentially, or randomly at relatively low costs, and with minimal or no ambiguity and at relatively lower risk (compared to traditional mortgages) without changing the initial buyer-borrower and seller-lender payoff functions. Participant substitutability (different from asset substitutability) expands the market for the underlying property, increases liquidity, facilitates noncash property swaps, and can help solve the matching problem in marriage markets and job markets.
16. *Low ambiguity.* There is relatively low ambiguity about foreclosure outcomes, default costs, and monitoring costs. In the mortgage markets, ambiguity usually arises from property prices, interest rates, types of third-party transactions in the subject neighborhood or subject city, ability to refinance, and the liquidity of similar properties.
17. *Transmission-positive consistency.* The mortgage alternative facilitates the transmission of monetary policy in a consistent manner over time. Such consistency increases the credibility of government monetary policies. For example, when the central bank increases benchmark interest rates and reserve requirements in order to control inflation and slow activity, the lender's interest income will increase because of the capped floating rate, and the lender will be compelled to reduce origination of new mortgages/loans. When the central bank buys government securities (and perhaps corporate bonds) or reduces the reserve requirement or reduces benchmark interest rates in order to increase money supply and boost economic activity, interest rates generally decline, the lender's interest income will decline because of the capped floating rate, and the lender will be compelled to originate more loans to generate income; the borrower will not have any meaningful incentive to refinance, and more capital can be channeled to finance the expansion of businesses. Also, because the lender owns the collateral (and not a mortgage asset) and hence is subject to reduced capital reserve requirements, the average bank/lender can provide more business loans. Such increase in money supply is much less likely to increase price levels because of reduced incidence of refinancing and inability to obtain home-equity loans.

18. *Reserve neutrality.* The changes in the borrower's condition and credit rating and any default have or are likely to have minimal effects on the lender's capital reserve requirements. Traditional Western mortgages tend to be "reserve negative" (declines/increases in the borrower's credit quality increase/reduce the lender's capital reserve requirements, and thus reduce lending capacity). Changes in reserve requirements often have adverse systemic effects on banks and the banking industry: (1) banks typically have to change the prices of their services; (2) changes in reserve requirements can affect many banks in very different ways, and thus it is not accurate monetary policy; (3) the changes in reserve requirements affect the perceived credit quality of banks—thus an increase in reserve requirements can reduce aggregate investment where bank credit quality is considered a major economic indicator; (4) changes in reserve requirements can create suboptimal incentives for banks—for banks to increase lending to less desirable industries/purposes (with attendant high transaction and monitoring costs), and simultaneously reduce lending to more desirable industries/purposes; (5) increasing reserve requirements can cause immediate liquidity problems for banks that have low reserves; (6) the typical reserve requirement applies to checking accounts and transaction accounts and not to savings accounts, CDs, and deposits by foreign entities, which are sometimes subject to much lower reserve requirements—but increasingly, savings accounts are used for transactions (just like checking accounts).
19. *Automation efficiency.* The mortgage alternative is more amenable to automation than comparable traditional mortgages and the adjustable balance mortgage. Payment of property taxes and property insurance bills for many properties in one city/region can be aggregated and automated, and the seller-lender can achieve economies of scale. Also, servicing costs are likely to be lower (than for traditional mortgages) because the seller-lender will be much less reliant on consumer credit scores; foreclosures and inefficient continuance by the buyer-borrower after defaults will also be precluded.
20. *Decreasing monotonicity.* There is decreasing monotonicity in the relationship between the principal balance (size) and inherent risk of this type of mortgage alternative, as time progresses. As the principal balance of this mortgage alternative increases, there is a less than proportional increase or decrease in the risk of the mortgage alternative. That is, for small and large mortgage alternatives ($x < y$), the corresponding risk measures, which are functions $f(x)$ and $f(y)$, do not have a constant relationship. Decreasing monotonicity of a function is different from "monotonically decreasing" functions.

21. *Self-insurance or no mortgage insurance.* For this mortgage alternative, there is no need for third-party mortgage insurance (and the lender can self-insure the mortgage alternative), because the lender holds title to the property (foreclosure/recovery costs are precluded), and the lender's participation increases liquidity in the property-values submarket. Third-party mortgage insurance has been and remains a major cause of adverse systemic risk in both developed and developing economies; and reinsurance does not eliminate but merely redistributes the risk in ways that also increase systemic risk. As was amply illustrated during the subprime mortgage crisis in the United States and the global financial crisis of 2007 to 2011, mortgage insurance provides substantial incentives to lenders and securitization sponsors to reduce their underwriting standards. For example, when one default of an insured mortgage occurs, the lender, servicer, insurer, and one to three reinsurers (and in some cases, state and federal government bank examiners) will spend substantial resources (staff, administrative expenses, etc.) to investigate the default (before workouts or insurance payout or foreclosure).
22. *Participation constraints.* (1) The buyer-borrower cannot participate in the property-values submarket (cannot obtain home-equity loans or hypothecate the contract or sell the property until he or she makes full payment for the obligation); (2) the seller-lender cannot pledge, encumber, or hypothecate the contract or the underlying property until there is default.
23. *Strategic complementarity* and *supermodularity.* The buyer-borrower's payoff function is complementary to the seller-lender's payoff function; that is, even on default or at expiration of the contract, the best strategy implemented by the buyer-borrower to maximize his or her payoff also increases the marginal returns of the seller-lender, and provides substantial incentives for the seller-lender to comply with the terms of the contract, and vice versa. The buyer-borrower's payoff function $f(.)$ and the seller-lender's payoff function $f(.)$ depend on actions/strategies of two or more types of participants z_i and z_j in the action space ($i = 1\ldots n$; $j = 1\ldots n$). Supermodularity and complementarity imply that $\partial^2 f/\partial z_i \partial z_j \geq 0$; for all $i \neq j$; where z_i and z_j are strategies of participants in the action space and each action is chosen from an interval z_i, $z_j \ \varepsilon \ [a,b]$.
24. *Non-nullity.* The mortgage-alternative contract almost ensures that the seller-lender, the buyer-borrower, and the government (and in some cases, the immediate neighborhood of the subject property) will always have non-negative payoffs in all circumstances.
25. *Asset-liability balance.* The mortgage alternative reduces or does not cause or eliminate perceived asset-liability mismatch and liquidity gaps

in one of the following ways: (1) the effective duration and effective modified duration of the asset are relatively short, because the lender holds full or partial title, and/or can easily sell the collateral and/or its interest in the contract before maturity/expiration of the loan/contract (unlike a traditional mortgage, which is typically illiquid); (2) the mortgage alternative has an implicit or stated capped floating-rate interest that is pegged to short-term rates; and (3) the implicit interest rate and periodic payment amount for the mortgage alternative are indexed to inflation and to a wages index, respectively. As described in this book, the perceived asset-liability mismatch results in development of elaborate, costly, and often redundant risk management systems.

26. *Regret-positivity.* The mortgage alternative reduces regret by both the buyer-borrower and the seller-lender, primarily because: (1) there is more matching of their unrevealed preferences; (2) foreclosure is eliminated; and (3) tenure neutrality and location neutrality increase two-sided horizontal matching by both the seller-lender (matching with other lenders) and the buyer-borrower (matching with other buyer-borrowers). Vertical matching refers to matching between seller-lenders and the buyer-borrowers. Regret-neutral refers to a state where the mortgage alternative has no effect on ex-post regret of the seller-lender or buyer-borrower.
27. *Bankruptcy efficiency.* This mortgage alternative maximizes the seller-lender's and buyer-borrower's payoffs if the buyer-borrower declares bankruptcy or if an involuntary bankruptcy petition is filed against the buyer-borrower. This is typically achieved by partitioning the contract interests such that there is no fraudulent conveyance or taxable gain. Thus, the borrower's bankruptcy will have minimal effects on the value of this mortgage alternative to the buyer-borrower and seller-lender. Mortgagees sometimes file for bankruptcy as a way to avoid or delay foreclosure—the bankruptcy filing may also have the same effect.

THE NEW MORTGAGE-ALTERNATIVE PRODUCTS

Type-A Installment Sales Contracts

In this type of installment sales contract, the seller retains title to the property until the loan is paid off, and the buyer retains an increasing ownership interest in only the installment sales contract (but not in the underlying property); the seller-lender cannot use the underlying property as collateral for another loan. The buyer has full lessee rights to the property and can sublease the property. The buyer will make monthly payments to the seller-lender (property insurance and property taxes are included in the monthly payments). Any down payments by the buyer will reduce the buyer's monthly payments. The buyer and seller can assign/sell their interest in the installment sales contract to third parties (but buyer-borrower can assign its interest only with written permission from the seller-lender). The buyer will have the option to elect to have the seller invest a portion of the buyer's monthly payments in an annuity contract or bonds. If any party defaults on the installment sales contract, or if the installment sales contract is canceled at any time, then the seller-lender will pay the buyer one of the following chosen by the buyer-borrower: (1) a 20- to 40-year annuity contract issued by the seller-lender (or another entity with equivalent corporate credit rating), whose present value will be *X* percent (where *X* percent is never less than zero, but is greater than 50 percent and may exceed 100 percent, if the property value increases above a pre-agreed percentage at the end of the loan term, or at default, or at prepayment) of the buyer-borrower's built-in equity in the installment sales contract (the amount of implicit loan principal repaid); or (2) a one-time cash payment (or payment of cash equivalents like Treasury bills) by the seller-lender, which will be equal to *Y* percent (where *Y* percent is greater than 50 percent and may exceed 100 percent, if the property value increases above a pre-agreed percentage at time of prepayment or default or expiration of the loan) of the amount of loan principal repaid by buyer-borrower; or (3) a pre-agreed percentage share of proceeds of sale of the property, based on the buyer's payments and equity in the installment sales contract. In some jurisdictions, the exchange of the buyer-borrower's interest in the contract for an annuity or cash will be deemed a tax-free exchange. There is no "default" but when a borrower/lessee stops making payments, it is merely a "change of allocations." The implicit interest rate is indexed to inflation, and the periodic payment amount is indexed to an index of wages. The implicit interest rate is a capped floating rate (which is capped at 20 to 350 basis points above the then-prevailing fixed lending/mortgage rate), and thus, eliminates inefficient costly refinancing and speculation associated with traditional mortgages. The implicit interest rate for the installment sale contract declines as the buyer makes more monthly payments on time; and vice versa, with annual or semiannual resets (credit quality considerations are asset specific and consider the selective credit fulfillment bias).

This proposed mortgage alternative has 27 characteristics described earlier: (1) information neutrality; (2) location neutrality; (3) default neutrality; (4) wealth neutrality; (5) renegotiation-proofing; (6) sequential nonredundancy; (7) cumulative nonseparability; (8) continuous payoffs; (9) decreasing recursion; (10) decreasing opportunity cost; (11) nonadditive aggregate risk; (12) time-preference neutrality; (13) limited manipulation;

(14) preference matching; (15) participant substitutability; (16) low ambiguity; (17) transmission-positive consistency; (18) reserve neutrality; (19) automation efficiency; (20) decreasing monotonicity; (21) self-insurance or no mortgage insurance; (22) participation constraints; (23) strategic complementarity and supermodularity; (24) non-nullity; (25) asset-liability balance; (26) regret-positivity; and (27) bankruptcy efficiency.

For the installment sales contracts described in this chapter, some common objectives and success factors are as follows:

- Standardization of installment sales contracts (see New York Retail Installment Sales Act)—in terms of forms, disclosure, filings, disclosure to consumers, and so on.
- There should be mandatory public disclosure of installment sales contracts for affected properties (recorded in government Internet databases like mortgages).
- There should be substantial criminal penalties for offending sellers.
- There should be tax incentives for buyer-borrowers and seller-lenders to use installment sales contracts.
- The installment sales contracts should be integrated into the federal/national commercial law (i.e., Uniform Commercial Code) regulatory framework.

The Defeasance Investment Contract

The buyer contractually enrolls in a 20- to 40-year voluntary investment program wherein each month: (1) the buyer spends a fixed minimum amount to purchase fixed income securities (bonds, convertible securities, and ordinary preferred stock) that have an aggregate face value equal to 65 percent to 85 percent of the monthly carrying cost of buying a property (mortgage P&I payments, property insurance, taxes, maintenance), and the buyer will be able to choose from a broad menu of such securities; or (2) the buyer makes a cash payment that is roughly equal to the monthly carrying cost of buying a property (mortgage P&I payments, property insurance, taxes, maintenance), and the seller will invest a portion of the buyer's monthly cash payments in an annuity contract. The buyer retains an increasing ownership interest in the installment contract (and the seller-lender holds full title until contract expiration); or retains an increasing ownership interest in the installment contract *and* in the underlying property until the loan is paid off (the buyer's interest is only an unrecordable contingent reversion interest that exists on full payment of loan amount and/or the sale of the property). As part of the investment program, the buyer will be granted full lessee (and subleasing) rights in the subject property. The seller-lender will have limited right of inspection of the property (the lender is the seller, and a qualified nonbank institutional investor (QII) can act as the lender/seller but cannot borrow from another lender for the specific transaction—the possibility of substitution of lenders and QIIs can provide liquidity in and expands the market). There will be statutes that define the minimum requirements for QIIs (assets, staff, computer systems, experience, etc.).

If the buyer defaults or if the contract is canceled, and the portfolio gains do not exceed the omitted required monthly investments, and if the buyer does not cure the default within four to six months, (1) the buyer gets only a pro-rated portion of the portfolio and the annuity contract, and loses the lessee rights without any court proceedings; or (2) a 20- to 30-year annuity contract (issued by the seller-lender or another company with the same or greater corporate credit rating) whose present value will be equal to *Y* percent (where *Y* percent does not exceed 80 percent) of the buyer-borrower's equity in the installment sales contract (i.e., percentage of the amount of loan principal repaid); or (3) a one-time fixed cash payment equal to *B* percent (where *B* percent does not exceed 80 percent) of the amount of implicit-loan principal repaid by the buyer-borrower (the scheduled cash payment will typically increase as the buyer-borrower makes more monthly payments).

If the buyer prepays or successfully makes all the required minimum monthly investments, then the buyer will choose one of several alternatives, which are described as: (1) if the buyer elects to take the property, then the buyer gets full ownership interest in the property, plus the excess of the portfolio balance, if any, over the cumulative total scheduled payments of a 104 percent loan-to-value (LTV) traditional mortgage (i.e., the future value); or (2) if the buyer elects to take the portfolio, then the buyer will get only a portion of the portfolio whose value is equal to the excess of the portfolio balance over the cumulative interest payments for a traditional 100 percent LTV mortgage that has the same term and implied interest rate; and (3) the buyer will get the full title to the property and the annuity contract. The lender/seller can request a down payment, which will reduce the amount of the required minimum monthly investment. The buyer does not pay for property insurance, maintenance, or property taxes. The buyer and seller can both sell/assign their interests in the defeasance investment contract. In some jurisdictions, the exchange of the buyer-borrower's interest in the contract, for an annuity or a portion of a portfolio or cash will be deemed a tax-free exchange. There is no "actionable default" but when a buyer stops making payments, it is merely a "change of allocations." The implicit interest rate is indexed to inflation, and the periodic payment amount is indexed to an index of wages. The implicit interest rate for the defeasance investment contract declines as the buyer makes more monthly payments on time, and vice versa, with annual resets—credit considerations are asset-specific.

The implicit interest rate is a capped floating rate, and thus eliminates losses incurred from inefficient and costly refinancing associated with traditional mortgages. The rationales for this product are: (1) the lender/seller is better positioned to hedge against price fluctuations and to manage debt than the buyer; (2) the transaction is perceived by the buyer as an investment, rather than mortgage debt; (3) economies of scale and operating efficiencies can be achieved by aggregating the costs of property insurance, property taxes, and property maintenance (co-ops and condominiums); (4) the buyer's skills in security analysis can be a benefit, and can be used to reduce the cost of homeownership; (5) the transaction fosters savings/investment habits and reduces speculation in both housing and securities markets; (6) with regard to traditional risk measures, the property is much more liquid than a 20- to 30-year mortgage, and thus, the asset (contract) has a much shorter duration or recovery period than a 20- to 30-year traditional mortgage; (7) the contract substantially reduces credit risk and adverse foreclosure costs; (8) the default remedies in the rental markets have less negative effects on social welfare than the default remedies in the mortgage markets or housing-values submarkets; and (9) in some jurisdictions, the buyer's balance sheet will not show any debt, but will show only an interest in a contract and a corresponding entry in the equity accounts.

This proposed mortgage alternative has the following 27 characteristics, most of which were defined earlier:

1. *Information neutrality.*
2. *Location neutrality.*
3. *Default neutrality.*
4. *Tenure neutrality.*
5. *Renegotiation-proofing.*
6. *Sequential nonredundancy.*
7. *Cumulative nonseparability.*
8. *Continuous payoffs.*
9. *Decreasing recursion.*
10. *Decreasing opportunity cost.*
11. *Nonadditive aggregate risk.* This refers to two related qualities: (1) if this type of mortgage alternative is the "majority" of all outstanding mortgage alternatives, social welfare can be maximized at relatively low costs (thus, aggregate rationality is different from "individual rationality" of one mortgage alternative or traditional mortgage); and (2) for any bank/lender that is active in a given region, increasing the volume (number of issued contracts/loans) of this type of mortgage alternative in that region results in a decrease or a less-than-proportional increase

in the risk of that lender, if all else is held constant ("region" refers to a collection of states in a country, but not a city or smaller areas). This can be attributed to several factors such as: (1) the location neutrality reduces the probability of default as the number of borrowers in the region increases (borrowers have more flexibility/choice and incentives to make loan payments); (2) as the number of lender-owned properties in the region increases, information neutrality reduces the flow and dissemination of negative information/data that drastically reduces property values and thus, loan values, and this reduces the lender's risk; (3) default neutrality completely eliminates costly foreclosure (which exponentially increases the seller-lender's risk) and the costly monitoring costs associated with default; and (4) renegotiation-proof-ness eliminates the substantial costs of renegotiation, which increases the seller-lender's risk. Most traditional Western mortgages, indexed mortgages, and the adjustable balance mortgage have exactly the opposite effect—increasing the volume of such mortgages in a region results in a greater than (and sometimes exponential) proportional increase in the risk of the lender, all else held constant.

12. *Time-preference neutrality*. The buyer-borrower's time preference (short/long horizon) does not affect, or has minimal effects on the buyer-borrower's refinance decision, default decision, and post-default choice of remedies.
13. *Limited manipulation.*
14. *Preference matching*. The mortgage alternative substantially increases the matching of the true (and often unrevealed) preferences of the buyer-borrower and the seller-lender. Buyers whose circumstances have changed do not have to live with unwanted and/or inappropriate mortgages; and lenders avoid nonperforming illiquid mortgages and foreclosures. The reduced or lack of preference-revelation during the life of the traditional mortgage and the adjustable balance mortgage substantially decreases their efficiency.
15. *Participant substitutability.*
16. *Low ambiguity.*
17. *Transmission-positive consistency*. The mortgage alternative facilitates the transmission of monetary policy in a consistent manner over time. Such consistency increases the credibility of government monetary policies.
18. *Reserve neutrality*. The changes in the borrower's condition and credit rating and any default have or are very likely to have minimal effects on the lender's capital reserve requirements. Traditional Western mortgages tend to be reserve negative (declines in the borrower's credit quality increase the lender's capital reserve requirements).

19. *Automation efficiency.* The mortgage alternative is more amenable to automation than comparable traditional mortgages, the adjustable balance mortgage, and participating mortgages. Payment of property taxes and property insurance bills for many properties in one city/region can be aggregated and automated, and the seller-lender can achieve economies of scale. Also, servicing costs are likely to be lower (than for traditional mortgages) because the seller-lender will be much less reliant on consumer credit scores; foreclosures and inefficient-continuance by the buyer-borrower after defaults will also be precluded.
20. *Decreasing monotonicity.*
21. *Self-insurance or no mortgage insurance.*
22. *Participation constraints.*
23. *Strategic complementarity* and *supermodularity.*
24. *Non-nullity.*
25. *Asset-liability balance.* The mortgage alternative reduces or does not cause or eliminate perceived asset-liability mismatch and liquidity gaps in one of the following ways: (1) the effective duration of the asset is relatively short, because the lender can easily sell the collateral and/or its interest in the contract (unlike a traditional mortgage, which is relatively very illiquid); (2) the mortgage alternative has an implicit or stated capped floating-rate interest that is pegged to short-term rates; (3) the implicit interest rate and periodic payment amount for the mortgage alternative are indexed to inflation and to a wage index, respectively (wage indices respond to changes in interest rates and aggregate business activity). As described in this book, the perceived asset-liability mismatch results in development of elaborate and often redundant risk management systems.
26. *Regret-positivity.*
27. *Bankruptcy efficiency.*

The Lender Annuity Contract

The buyer contracts to purchase a 20- to 40-year annuity contract, and the purchase contract grants the buyer the full lessee (and subleasing) rights to the property for the same term (the 20- to 40-year annuity contract will start on the date that the buyer defaults or pays for the annuity contract in full). The seller-lender will have limited right of inspection of the property. The face value of the annuity contract is the estimated value of the property on the closing date. Hence, the buyer's single monthly payment will consist of interest, principal repayment, property taxes, and property insurance. The buyer also pays for maintenance and capital expenditures. The seller-lender will buy the property on or before the closing day; and cannot use the property as collateral for another loan. Any down payment by the buyer will decrease the buyer's scheduled monthly payments. If the buyer defaults on the monthly payments and does not cure the default within four to six months, the lender will issue to the buyer only a pre-agreed pro-rata portion of the annuity contract; the buyer will lose the lessee rights and will be evicted through summary court eviction proceedings or a nonjudicial contractual eviction. If the buyer prepays all required payments, or pays all the monthly payments until the end of the term of the contract, then the seller-lender will pay to buyer (at buyer's option):

- The 20- to 40-year annuity contract (which will be issued by the seller-lender or another company that has the same credit rating) and then the buyer will start paying regular market rent.
- Full ownership interest in the property plus a pre-agreed portion (generally not to exceed 50 percent) of the 20- to 40-year annuity contract.

The implicit interest rate for the annuity contract is a capped floating rate that also declines as the buyer makes more monthly payments on time; and vice versa, with annual resets (and thus, the contract considers changes in credit quality and the *Selective Credit Fulfillment Bias*). The implicit interest rate is capped at 100 to 300 basis points above the then-prevailing fixed mortgage rates, and is reset annually or semiannually, and thus, moots the inefficient and costly refinancing associated with traditional and alternative mortgages. The implicit interest rate is indexed to inflation, and the periodic payment amount is indexed to an index of wages. In some jurisdictions, the exchange of the buyer-borrower's interest in the contract for an annuity and/or the underlying property will be deemed a tax-free exchange. There is no "actionable default" but when a borrower/lessee stops making payments, it is merely a "change of allocations." The rationales for this product are: (1) the lender/seller is better positioned to hedge against price fluctuations and to manage debt than the buyer; (2) the transaction is perceived as an investment, rather than mortgage debt, and thus fosters a savings/investment habit; (3) economies of scale and operating efficiencies can be achieved by aggregating the costs of property insurance, property taxes, and property maintenance (co-ops and condominiums); (4) the property is much more liquid than a 20- to 30-year mortgage, and thus, the asset (contract) has a much shorter "effective recovery period" (similar to "Duration") than a 20- to 30-year traditional mortgage; (5) the contract substantially reduces credit risk and adverse Foreclosure costs; (6) the default remedies in the rental markets have less negative effects on social welfare than the default remedies in the mortgage markets or housing-values submarkets; and (7) in some jurisdictions, the buyer's balance sheet will not show any debt, but will show only an ownership interest in an annuity contract and a corresponding entry in the equity accounts. Technically, the product is a "Dynamic Credit-Sensitive Reversible Frame" and the conceptual equivalent of the following two transactions: (1) buying the property with a mortgage and paying off the mortgage, and (2) immediately after paying off the mortgage, entering into a reverse mortgage that pays a fixed monthly payment over 20 to 40 years.

This proposed mortgage alternative has the following characteristics: (1) information neutrality; (2) tenure neutrality; (3) location neutrality; (4) default neutrality—the buyer's default is not tied to the foreclosure process, but rather is tied to both the savings/investment market and the property-values submarket; (5) wealth neutrality; (6) renegotiation-proofing; (7) sequential nonredundancy; (8) cumulative nonseparability; (9) decreasingly recursive payoffs; (10) decreasing opportunity cost; (11) nonadditive aggregate risk; (12) limited manipulation; (13) continuous payoffs; (14) preference matching; (15) low ambiguity; (16) participant substitutability; (17) transmission-positive consistency; (18) reserve neutrality; (19) automation efficiency; (20) decreasing monotonicity; (21) self-insurance or no mortgage insurance; (22) participation constraints; (23) strategic complementarity and supermodularity; (24) non-nullity; (25) asset-liability balance; (26) regret-positivity; and (27) bankruptcy efficiency.

The Structured Bond Mortgage

The buyer obtains a mortgage that requires monthly payments and whose monthly interest rate is calculated based on reference benchmarks, such as 2X LIBOR minus *Y* percent subject to a cap of *C* percent; or 2X T-bill minus *Y* percent subject to a cap of *C* percent, or 3X LIBOR minus *V* percent subject to cap of *C* percent (hence, the monthly or quarterly interest rate cannot exceed *C* percent). The implicit interest rate is indexed to inflation, and the periodic payment amount is indexed to an index of wages. The buyer does not have any present ownership interest in the property but has only a future conditional reversion interest in the property—the lender holds title to the property. During the mortgage term, the buyer will have full lessee interests in the property and can sublease the property. The buyer will pay for only maintenance and capital expenditures. The seller-lender will have limited right of inspection of the property. The buyer will not pay any principal repayment, property insurance, or property taxes. At the end of the mortgage term or if the buyer defaults, the buyer will get either: (1) only a predetermined percentage of any capital appreciation if the property is sold (where the property value is determined in whole or in part based on a local/regional property index), or (2) an annuity whose present value at that time is pre-agreed and increases as the buyer makes more payments. Also, if the buyer defaults and does not cure the default, there will be summary court proceedings for eviction or a nonjudicial eviction. In some jurisdictions, the exchange of the buyer-borrower's interest in the contract for an annuity or cash or a percentage of capital appreciation will be deemed a tax-free exchange. This type of mortgage can provide valuable hedging for the lender.

This proposed mortgage alternative has the following characteristics: (1) information neutrality; (2) location neutrality (the borrower can sell the property subject to the existing mortgage and simultaneously use the sale proceeds to purchase another property, which will serve as the collateral for the original mortgage); (3) default neutrality; (4) wealth neutrality; (5) interest negativity—the buyer-borrower's interest in the property is a future contingent interest, which does not exist until the buyer either defaults, or the lender-seller defaults, or the contract term expires (the "interest positive" state applies when the buyer-borrower's ownership interest is a present on-contingent interest); (6) renegotiation-proofing; (7) sequential nonredundancy (8) decreasing recursion; (9) time-preference neutrality; (10) limited manipulation; (11) continuous payoffs; (12) preference matching; (13) low ambiguity; (14) participant substitutability; (15) transmission-positive consistency; (16) reserve neutrality; (17) automation efficiency; (18) decreasing monotonicity; (19) self-insurance or no mortgage insurance; (20) participation constraints; (21) strategic complementarity and supermodularity; (22) non-nullity; (23) asset-liability balance; (24) regret-positivity; and (25) bankruptcy efficiency.

The State Investment Contract

The federal government is the seller of the housing unit or property, and presumably builds the housing units or property. Many developers charge developer's fees of 6 to 10 percent of total construction costs in addition to profits from home sales (net profits of 15 to 50 percent). Rather than grant tax credits and other tax concessions to private real estate developers who have substantial incentives to inflate construction costs and housing prices, it is often much cheaper and more efficient for the government to build the housing units, and subsidize tenants while encouraging savings/investment. For the 20- to 40-year term of the contract, each month, the buyer must choose one of the following (1) purchase a minimum volume of long-term or medium-term government bonds that are hedged against currency risk and inflation risk; or (2) make monthly cash payments to the government, and a portion of the buyer's monthly payments will be credited towards a national social security program or national pension program for the benefit of the buyer, which matures when the buyer-lessee reaches a specified age, or after a pre-agreed time period. Any initial down payment by the buyer reduces the required monthly securities purchase or cash payment. In exchange, the buyer gets full lessee rights (including sublease rights) in the property for the contract term. The seller-lender will have very limited right of inspection of the property. A portion of the buyer's monthly payments or investment is credited toward a national social security program or national pension program or national health insurance program for adults. The seller-lender pays for property insurance or property taxes (which are implicitly included in the monthly required bond purchases or cash payments), but the buyer pays for maintenance and capital expenditures. If the buyer defaults and does not cure the default during the cure period (four to six months), the buyer gets only a pro-rata share of the government bond portfolio (e.g., approximately 65 percent to 85 percent of the buyer's imputed equity in the contract). If the buyer prepays or makes all regular payments, then at the end of the contract, the buyer will get either: (a) the full fee-simple ownership interest in the property *plus* a percentage (Y percent < 50 percent) of the government bond portfolio; (b) only the government savings/investment/pension account (X percent $= 100$ percent), plus continued use of the property in exchange for monthly rent; or (c) only a fixed cash payment (Z percent $= 65$ percent to 85 percent of the buyer's imputed equity in the contract) plus continued use of the property in exchange for monthly rent. For each choice, Y percent and X percent can exceed 100 percent if the property value has increased above a prespecified percentage threshold. Buyers can sell/assign their interest in the state investment contract, only with the government's permission. The government can assign its interest in the investment contract but only to AAA-rated institutional investors. In some jurisdictions, the exchange of the buyer-borrower's interest in the contract for an annuity or cash or an investment portfolio will be deemed a tax-free exchange. There is no "default" but when a borrower/lessee stops making payments, it is merely a "change of allocations." The implicit interest rate is indexed to inflation, and the periodic payment amount is indexed to an index of wages. The state investment contract will be integrated into the federal/national securities law framework. The investment contract is not recorded like mortgages, and the buyer-lessor does not have title to the property unless he or she pays all the required payments and, in addition, elects to get full fee-simple ownership in the property.

This proposed mortgage alternative has: (1) tenure neutrality—the buyer-lessee can choose from temporary leasing to permanent leasing to full ownership but all or some of his or her "shadow interest" in the contract is converted into a savings program (a tenure negative state implies exposure to uncertainty in the property values submarket and/or the rental submarket);

(2) location neutrality; (3) default neutrality; (4) wealth neutrality; (5) renegotiation-proofing; (6) sequential nonredundancy; (7) cumulative non-separability; (8) decreasing recursion; (9) decreasing opportunity cost; (10) nonadditive aggregate risk; (11) time-preference neutrality; (12) limited manipulation; (13) continuous payoffs; (14) preference matching; (15) low ambiguity; (16) participant substitutability; (17) transmission-positive consistency; (18) reserve neutrality; (19) automation efficiency; (20) decreasing monotonicity; (21) self-insurance or no mortgage insurance; (22) participation constraints; (23) strategic complementarity and supermodularity; (24) non-nullity; (25) asset-liability balance; (26) regret-positivity; and (27) bankruptcy efficiency.

Lease with Forward Contract

The buyer: (1) pays a down payment (which can be zero); (2) leases the property for the term of the contract (20 to 40 years); and (3) enters into a forward contract with the seller, where the seller delivers the property free and clear to the buyer at the end of the contract for a delivery price of $1. The seller-lender pays property insurance and property taxes and has limited rights of inspection. Hence, the contract is a frame, and the monthly lease payments will include elements of the principal repayment, interest, property taxes, and insurance costs. The buyer-borrower assumes responsibility for premises liability. The buyer has an ownership interest in only the contract but not in the underlying property. If the buyer defaults on the lease payments and does not cure the default within four to six months, then the buyer will be evicted with summary court proceedings or a nonjudicial eviction and will get only the sum of: (1) a cash payment equal to pro-rata equity interest in the contract (based on the down payment and monthly payments), plus (2) a cash payment equal to pro-rata percentage of the appreciation in the value of the property, if any.

At expiration of the contract or if the buyer prepays the full purchase price, then the buyer gets the property. The rationales are that: (1) the lender/seller is better positioned to hedge against price fluctuations than the buyer; (2) the transaction is perceived by the buyer as more of an investment, rather than mortgage debt; (3) economies of scale and operating efficiencies can be achieved by aggregating the costs of property insurance, property taxes, and property maintenance (co-ops and condominiums); (4) the transaction reduces speculation in property markets; (5) the property is much more liquid than a 20- to 30-year mortgage, and thus, the asset (contract) has a much shorter duration or recovery period than a 20- to 30-year traditional mortgage; (6) the contract substantially reduces credit risk and adverse foreclosure costs; (7) the default remedies in the rental markets have less negative effects on social welfare than the default remedies in the mortgage markets or housing-values markets; and (8) in some jurisdictions, the buyer's balance sheet will not show any debt, but will show only an interest in a contract and a corresponding entry in the equity accounts; and similarly, the lender's balance sheet will record a forward contract.

This proposed mortgage alternative has the following characteristics: (1) information neutrality; (2) tenure neutrality—the buyer-lessee can choose from temporary leasing to permanent leasing to full ownership but all or some of his or her "shadow interest" in the contract is converted into a savings program (a tenure-negative state implies exposure to uncertainty in the property-values submarket or the rental submarket); (3) location neutrality; (4) default neutrality; (5) wealth neutrality; (6) renegotiation-proofing; (7) sequential nonredundancy; (8) cumulative nonseparability; (9) decreasing recursion; (10) decreasing opportunity cost; (11) nonadditive aggregate risk; (12) limited manipulation; (13) continuous payoffs; (14) preference matching; (15) low ambiguity; (16) participant substitutability; (17) transmission-positive consistency; (18) reserve neutrality; (19) automation efficiency; (20) decreasing monotonicity; (21) self-insurance or no mortgage insurance; (22) participation constraints; (23) strategic complementarity and supermodularity; (24) non-nullity; (25) asset-liability balance; (26) regret-positivity; and (27) bankruptcy efficiency.

Lease with Option to Buy (LWOB)

The buyer/investor will enter into a long-term (e.g., 7 to 15 years) lease contract with the seller/lessor. All or a portion of the buyer's monthly rent payment will be allocated toward: (a) the down payment for an installment sales land contract; (b) an ownership interest in the property; or (c) an interest in the LWOB contract. The buyer will have an option to purchase the property, beginning from the date of the LWOB contract, at declining purchase prices (declining strike prices) that are reset every month; prices are based on the rent payments made by the buyer/lessee and the initial stated value of the property during a stated period of time (e.g., 7 to 30 years) (the strike prices will be roughly equal to the amortized principal balance of an equivalent fully amortizing fixed-rate mortgage). The buyer/lessee will not pay for property taxes and property insurance (which can be implicitly included in the monthly payments), but may be required to pay for maintenance. The buyer has an interest in the LWOB contract and a contingent unrecordable ownership interest in the underlying property, which is based on the amount that is credited toward equity in the LWOB contract. The seller retains title in the property until the entire purchase price is paid. If the buyer exercises the purchase option, a portion of the cumulative rent may be applied to the payment of the purchase price. The buyer can assign/sell the contract; and the seller can also assign its interest in the contract to third parties. The buyer has no interest in the underlying property until the purchase option is exercised and the purchase price is paid in full—until then, the buyer/lessee only has an interest in the LWOB contract. If the buyer defaults or if the contract is canceled before he or she exercises the option, the seller-lender will pay the buyer only a 10- to 20-year annuity that will have a present value equal to a percentage of the buyer's imputed equity in the contract. The buyer can either confirm his or her intent to buy the property at inception of the contract, or the buyer's intent is not expressed until the buyer exercises the purchase option—the differences have substantial accounting and tax implications. Also the buyer/lessee may not pay property taxes and property insurance, or the buyer/lessor may implicitly pay property taxes and property insurance. The implicit interest rate is indexed to inflation, and the periodic payment amount is indexed to an index of wages. The implicit interest rate is a capped floating rate that declines as the buyer makes more payments on time. The lender is the seller, and a qualified institutional investor (QII) can act as the lender/seller but cannot borrow from another lender for the specific transaction—the substitution of lenders and qualified institutional investors can provide liquidity in and expand the housing market.

This mortgage alternative has the following characteristics: (1) information neutrality; (2) tenure neutrality; (3) location neutrality; (4) default negativity—the buyer's default is not tied to the foreclosure process, but rather is tied to the rental submarket; (5) wealth neutrality; (6) renegotiation-proofing; (7) sequential nonredundancy; (8) time-preference neutrality; (9) limited manipulation; (10) nonadditive aggregate risk; (11) time-preference neutrality; (12) limited manipulation; (13) continuous payoffs; (14) preference matching; (15) low ambiguity; (16) participant-substitutability; (17) transmission-positive consistency; (18) reserve neutrality; (19) automation efficiency; (20) decreasing monotonicity; (21) self-insurance or no mortgage insurance; (22) participation constraints; (23) strategic complementarity and supermodularity; (24) non-nullity; (25) regret-positivity; and (26) bankruptcy efficiency. Some elements and important considerations are:

- Standardization of LWOB contracts (see New York Installment Sales Act)—forms, disclosure, filings, disclosure to consumers, and so on.
- Mandatory public disclosure of LWOB contracts for affected properties (recorded in Internet databases like mortgages).
- Substantial criminal penalties for offending sellers.
- Tax incentives for buyers and sellers.

Income-Market Loan Contracts

Each month, the borrower pays the lower of: (1) the standard P&I/interest payment for an amortizing loan, or (2) a fixed percentage of the borrower's monthly income that by law shall not exceed 33 percent (e.g., 25 percent or 30 percent) of his or her after-tax income; but the difference between the standard P&I/interest payment and the income-based payment is added to and increases the mortgage principal. Alternative 2 can also be a monthly payment that is indexed to a *city index* that is constructed from the city or regional unemployment rate, average household income, number of foreclosures, and average property value. Thus, the borrower's monthly payment will decline as unemployment and number of foreclosures increase, and will increase as average monthly income and average property values increase. Both types of payment are indexed to inflation rates and to a wage index. If the average value or per-square-meter value of the property type (e.g., residential, retail, office) in the metropolitan statistical area (MSA) declines by X percent for two consecutive years, then the principal balance of the loan will be automatically reduced by X percent at the end of the year. Although the loan term may be fixed at inception, by contract, the loan term can be extended depending on the total payments made by the borrower as a percentage of the total standard scheduled minimum P&I payments. The term of the installment sales contract will also be indexed to the city index (that is, constructed from the city or regional unemployment rate, average household income, number of foreclosures, and average property value) such that the loan term will increase as unemployment and the number of foreclosures increase, and the loan term will decrease as average household monthly income and the average property value increase, but there will be a minimum loan term. The borrower will not have title to the property until the borrower pays the entire purchase price; that is, the borrower will have only an equity interest in the installment sales contract, but not in the underlying property. Any reductions of the monthly payment or the principal balance of the loan will also be matched with a simultaneous reduction of the buyer-borrower's equity in the property, so that the buyer-borrower does not recognize any taxable gain. The mortgage interest is not tax deductible. Any missed loan payments will be added to the loan principal. Thus, this financial product is automatically adjusted to suit the borrower's income, changes in an index of property values and market conditions, and does not trigger foreclosures or write-downs in lenders' balance sheets. The title to the property will remain in the seller-lender's name until the buyer's equity in the mortgage contract exceeds 65 percent of the original value of the property, after which the title will be shared by the seller-lender and the buyer, and when the buyer has made full payment, he or she will get full title to the property. If the buyer defaults and does not cure the default (does not make a specific number of periodic payments), then: (1) there will be either a summary court proceeding for eviction or a nonjudicial eviction if title has not been transferred to the buyer, or (2) a deed-in-lieu of foreclosure, if partial title has been transferred to the buyer-borrower. On "default" the lender will pay the buyer one of the following at the buyer-borrower's option: (1) a one-time cash payment equal to 65 percent to 85 percent of the buyer's imputed equity in the contract, plus a predetermined percentage of any capital appreciation if the property is sold; or (2) a 10- to 20-year annuity whose present value at that time is pre-agreed (e.g., 65 percent to 85 percent of the buyer's imputed equity in the loan contract) and increases as the buyer makes more payments. In some jurisdictions, the exchange of the buyer-borrower's interest in the contract for an annuity or cash or share of future sales proceeds will be deemed a tax-free exchange. The implicit interest rate is indexed to inflation, and the periodic payment amount is indexed to an index of wages. The implicit interest rate for the loan contract is a capped floating rate that declines as the buyer makes more monthly payments on time; and vice versa, with annual or semiannual resets.

This mortgage alternative has the following characteristics: (1) information neutrality; (2) location neutrality; (3) wealth neutrality; (4) renegotiation-proofing; (5) sequential nonredundancy; (6) cumulative nonseparability; (7) decreasing recursion; (8) nonadditive aggregate risk; (9) time-preference neutrality; (10) continuous payoffs; (11) preference matching; (12) limited manipulation; (13) low ambiguity; (14) participant substitutability; (15) transmission-positive consistency; (16) reserve neutrality; (17) automation efficiency; (18) decreasing monotonicity; (19) self-insurance or no mortgage insurance; (20) participation constraints; (21) non-nullity; (22) asset-liability balance; and (23) regret-positivity.

Some considerations are:

- Standardization of income-market loan contracts.
- Consumer protection statutes.
- Special expedited court proceedings for income-market loan disputes.
- Mandatory public disclosure of income-market loan properties (recorded in government Internet databases like mortgages).
- Tax incentives for lenders.
- Tax incentives for borrowers.

Registered Revolving Consumer Capital Pools (RRCCP)

A registered group of individuals forms a capital pool and contributes cash to the pool each month; and each month or quarter, the capital pool provides cash for one or more members to purchase a property or housing unit. The group will typically register the RRCCP in a national Internet-based register. Members of the group must contractually commit to members for a minimum number of years. Group members may assign their RRCCP obligations to third parties in exchange for specified consideration and with consent of the RRCCP. Group members may also terminate their RRCCP obligations by payment of acceptable consideration to the RRCCP, or by forfeiture of the property purchased with funds from the RRCCP. The RRCCP retains title to the purchased property, and leases the property to the buyer/member until the member completes a prespecified minimum tenure in, and minimum payments to, the RRCCP. If the member defaults and does not cure such default, the RRCCP will cancel his or her membership and issue a 10- to 20-year annuity to the person—this annuity will have a present value that is a fraction of the member's at-risk capital (the amount of cash that the member has contributed since he or she received his or her last payout from the RRCCP). Similar capital pools already exist in many countries, but the pools are small and have limited geographical spread. In these contracts, the buyer/member sometimes retains a partial ownership interest in the property, and a default/breach by the buyer-seller will probably result in lengthy court foreclosure proceedings (six months to two years). By changing the structure of these capital pools, registering them, expanding their geographic coverage, and enacting appropriate consumer protection statutes, these capital pools can become effective financing mechanisms. The rationales are: (1) the RRCCPs are framed as co-investments with other people who have similar interests, and so RRCCPs will likely create much less stress than mortgages; (2) there is an element of altruism inherent in the RRCCPs because some members will believe that members are helping themselves by investing in the RRCCP; (3) there is an element of perceived fairness in investment in the RRCCP because there is no stated "interest rate" or loan covenants, and there are no opportunities for members to consciously or subconsciously judge the lenders' approval processes; (4) the RRCCP membership-rights can be transferred/sold.

The RRCCP governance documents can also include the following rules: (a) the RRCCP will distribute cash (D) to each holder of a membership unit at least once every X months ($X < 18$ months); (b) each member will have no more than \$$Y$ at risk at any time; that is, a member's maximum loss is \$$Y$; (c) the number of members is unlimited or limited; (d) members can "reinvest" all or a part of their periodic distribution into the RRCCP in exchange for a larger future distribution; (e) the administrative expenses of the RRCCP will be paid by all members; (f) each holder of a membership unit will contribute a fixed amount (J) to the RRCCP each month, and one person can own several membership units; (g) the cumulative contributions of a holder of a membership unit in any one cycle (ΣJ) must be equal to or less than the cash distribution paid to that holder for that cycle ($D > \Sigma J$) after adjusting for the time value of money, in order to maintain an incentive to participate. Some relevant objectives are:

- There should be standardization of RRCCPs' structure and members' rights.
- There should be consumer protection statutes.
- There should be special expedited court proceedings for RRCCP disputes.
- Mandatory public disclosure of RRCCP properties (recorded in government Internet databases like mortgages).
- There should be tax incentives for RRCCPs and their members.
- There should be effective disclosure statutes for RRCPs.

This proposed mortgage alternative has the following characteristics: (1) information neutrality; (2) location neutrality; (3) default neutrality—the buyer's default is not tied to the foreclosure process, but rather is tied to both the savings/investment market and the property-values submarket; (4) renegotiation-proofing; (5) continuous payoffs; (6) participant substitutability; (7) limited manipulation; (8) preference matching; (9) low ambiguity; (10) transmission-positive consistency; (11) decreasing monotonicity; (12) self-insurance or no mortgage insurance; (13) participation constraints; and (14) strategic complementarity and supermodularity.

Leasehold Mortgages with Leasehold-in-Lieu

The buyer purchases only a long-term (20 to 50 years) leasehold interest in the property, which is financed with a leasehold mortgage. The leasehold interest grants the buyer only the right to use and sublease the property, but not a fee-simple ownership interest in the property. The buyer may be required to pay property taxes and property insurance expenses. If the buyer-mortgagor defaults without subsequent cure of default, the mortgagee will evict the buyer from the property without any court proceedings or through a statutory expedited court procedure. There must be statutory cure periods for such mortgages. The implicit interest rate for the loan contract is a capped floating rate, which declines as the buyer makes more monthly payments on time; and vice versa, with annual resets (this precludes costly and inefficient refinancing). The leasehold mortgage closes the often wide divergences between "rental submarkets" (based on rents only) and "property-value submarkets" (based on fee-simple interests in housing units). In the United States, during 1999 to 2007, these submarket divergences/gaps led to inflation of house prices based on low interest rates where home prices had no realistic relationship to market rents. The advantage of the leasehold mortgage is that borrower "defaults" have much less negative effects on title systems, liquidity, and property values, compared to what happens with traditional mortgages. Under the leasehold mortgage regime, upon borrower default, the fee-simple ownership does not change, there is no expensive foreclosure, and the fee-simple interest in the property can still be sold subject to the leasehold mortgage. Some sellers sell their housing units only because of short-term issues, but can afford to pay the property taxes and insurance and maintenance for long periods, whereas the incomes of some prospective buyers are very volatile. The needs of these types of buyers and sellers can be matched using leasehold mortgages. These types of sellers can expand the housing and mortgage markets. The leasehold mortgage may also provide some tax advantages in jurisdictions where mortgage interest is deductible for income tax purposes.

This proposed mortgage alternative has the following characteristics: (1) information neutrality; (2) location neutrality; (3) wealth neutrality; (4) renegotiation-proofing; (5) sequential nonredundancy; (6) cumulative nonseparability; (7) decreasing recursion; (8) nonadditive aggregate risk; (9) limited manipulation; (10) continuous payoffs; (11) preference matching; (12) participant substitutability; (13) automation efficiency; (14) decreasing monotonicity; (15) participation constraints; (16) strategic complementarity and supermodularity; (17) asset-liability balance; (18) regret-positivity; from (19) bankruptcy efficiency.

Lease with Reversion Mortgage (LWRM)

The buyer buys only: (1) a reversion interest in the property (the right to own the property after the reversion term, which may be 20 to 40 years, and the right to a percentage of the proceeds of any sale of the property before the expiration of the reversion period), and (2) the right to lease or sublease the property for a fixed rent for the reversion term. The reversion mortgage is secured by the reversion interest. Hence, the buyer pays a monthly rent and a monthly P&I payment. The implicit interest rate for the loan contract is a capped floating rate that declines as the buyer makes more monthly payments on time; and vice versa, with annual resets (in order to preclude inefficient and costly refinancing). If the buyer defaults on the lease payments without subsequent cure, he can be evicted by the seller or the mortgagee without any court proceedings via an expedited statutory procedure. If the buyer defaults on the reversion mortgage without cure, then the buyer will get only a portion of the scheduled percentage reversion interest on sale of the property and there is no foreclosure. In some jurisdictions, the exchange of the buyer-borrower's interest in the contract for a reversion interest or annuity or cash will be deemed a tax-free exchange. The implicit interest rate is a capped floating rate; is indexed to inflation; and the periodic payment amount is indexed to an index of wages. The implicit interest rate is reduced as the borrower makes more payments on time, and vice versa. The advantage of the LWRM is that buyer-borrower defaults have much less negative effects on title systems, liquidity, and property values, compared to what happens with traditional mortgages. Under the LWRM regime, upon borrower default, the fee-simple ownership does not change, there is no expensive foreclosure, the mortgagee must record the LWRM, and the fee-simple interest in the property can still be sold subject to the LWRM.

This proposed mortgage alternative has the following characteristics: (1) information neutrality; (2) tenure neutrality; (3) location neutrality; (4) wealth neutrality; (5) renegotiation-proofing; (6) sequential nonredundancy; (7) cumulative nonseparability; (8) decreasing recursion; (9) decreasing opportunity cost; (10) nonadditive aggregate risk; (11) limited manipulation; (12) continuous payoffs; (13) preference matching; (14) low ambiguity; (15) participant substitutability; (16) transmission-positive consistency; (17) automation efficiency; (18) decreasing monotonicity; (19) self-insurance or no mortgage insurance); (20) participation constraints; (21) strategic complementarity and supermodularity; and (22) non-nullity.

The Deferred Growth Contract

There are three to six "evaluation periods," each of which last three to five years. The buyer-borrower makes a down payment of 20 percent to 30 percent of the property value, but does make any other payment during the evaluation period. At the end of each evaluation period, the property will be appraised by an independent appraiser paid by an escrow agent, and if the property price appreciation exceeds the sum of all P&I payments with compounding during the same period, then the borrower will not make any payments, and if not, the deficiency is added to the mortgage balance. If the buyer-borrower cancels the contract, the seller-lender will pay him or her only an annuity whose present value is equal to his or her equity in the contract. At the end of the mortgage term, the borrower gets only a 15- to 25-year annuity with a present value that is equal to the excess of the market value of the property over the future value of all the P&I payments. The seller retains title to the property until the loan is paid off, and the buyer retains an increasing ownership interest in only the contract (but not in the underlying property) until the loan is canceled or the contract expires. The subject property can be one of many in a region (or a country), but the lender will typically present several properties for the buyer to choose from, and the buyer can switch properties for a fixed number of times owned by the seller-lender during the life of the loan without selling/buying property. The buyer has full lessee rights. The buyer and seller can assign/sell their interest in the contract to third parties. In some jurisdictions, the exchange of the buyer-borrower's interest in the contract for an annuity or cash will be deemed a tax-free exchange. The implicit interest rate is indexed to inflation, and the periodic payment amount is indexed to an index of wages. The implicit interest rate for the contract is a capped floating rate that declines as the buyer makes more payments on time; and vice versa, with annual resets (replaces inefficient costly refinancing associated with traditional mortgages).

This mortgage alternative has the following characteristics: (1) information neutrality; (2) tenure neutrality; (3) location neutrality; (4) default neutrality—the buyer's default is not tied to the foreclosure process, but rather is tied to the savings/investment market; (5) wealth neutrality; (6) renegotiation-proofing; (7) sequential nonredundancy; (8) cumulative nonseparability; (9) decreasing recursion; (10) decreasing opportunity cost; (11) nonadditive aggregate risk; (12) time-preference neutrality; (13) limited manipulation; (14) continuous payoffs; (15) preference matching; (16) low ambiguity; (17) participant substitutability; (18) transmission-positive consistency; (19) reserve neutrality; (20) automation efficiency; (21) decreasing monotonicity; (22) self-insurance or no mortgage insurance; (23) participation constraints; (24) strategic complementarity and supermodularity; (25) non-nullity; (26) asset-liability balance; (27) regret-positivity; and (28) bankruptcy efficiency.

The Best-Path Investment Contract

This mortgage alternative has the following characteristics: (1) information neutrality; (2) tenure neutrality; (3) location neutrality; (4) default neutrality—the buyer's default is not tied to the foreclosure process, but rather is tied to both the savings/investment market and the property-values submarket; (5) wealth neutrality; (6) renegotiation-proofing—see explanation earlier; (7) sequential nonredundancy; (8) cumulative nonseparability; (9) decreasing recursion; (10) decreasing opportunity cost; (11) nonadditive aggregate rationality; (12) time-preference neutrality; (13) limited manipulation; (14) continuous payoffs; (15) preference matching; (16) low ambiguity; (17) participant substitutability; (18) transmission-positive consistency; (19) reserve neutrality; (20) automation efficiency; (21) decreasing monotonicity; (22) self-insurance or no mortgage insurance; (23) participation constraints; (24) strategic complementarity and supermodularity; (25) non-nullity; (26) asset-liability balance; (27) regret positivity; and (28) bankruptcy efficiency.

The buyer purchases a property (with specific features) with a long-term installment sales contract (loan) from the seller. The conveyance is not recorded until the loan is paid in full. The seller-lender retains title to the property until the loan is paid in full; but the buyer retains an increasing ownership interest in only the installment sales contract (but not in the underlying property) until the loan is paid off. At inception of the contract, the buyer will open an investment account with the lender; and each month, the buyer will invest an amount equal to the greater of the following, subject to a maximum cap: (1) the average monthly rent for that type of property in the same town/city; (2) the monthly P&I payment for an equivalent full-amortization installment sales contract loan; or (3) the average income-return from specific bond mutual funds. If the buyer-borrower defaults on the investment contract or cancels the investment contract at any time, then the seller/sponsor will pay the buyer, at buyer's option, only either: (1) an equity interest in the subject property (e.g., tenancy-in-common, joint tenancy, or joint venture) based on the buyer's monthly payments and equity in the investment contract; (2) the total return from the equity index, plus principal; (3) the total return from a hypothetical investment in a money-market index or convertible bond index; or (4) a cash payment that will be based on the buyer's prior investment. When three unrelated borrower-buyers default in three different contracts, and they all have a common lender, the lender can exchange its interests in one installment sales contract for interests of two defaulters in two contracts and essentially "consolidate" the three defaulters at one property, and the other two properties will become free and clear without expensive foreclosures and auctions. This "exchange-of-interests" feature can be made a mandatory term in installment sales contracts and may be suited to buyer-borrowers that are small families or single individuals or retirees. In some jurisdictions, the exchange of the buyer-borrower's interest in the contract for an annuity or interest in property will be deemed a tax-free exchange. The implicit interest rate is indexed to inflation, and the periodic payment amount is indexed to an index of wages. The implicit interest rate in the investment contract is approximately equal to or greater than the interest rate on a similar installment sales contract, and is a capped floating rate, which declines as the buyer makes more payments on time; and vice versa, with annual or semiannual resets of the implicit interest rate (and thus, precludes inefficient costly refinancing associated with traditional fixed-rate and floating-rate mortgages).

The buyer will have full lessee rights while making monthly loan payments, and may or may not pay for property insurance and property taxes. The buyer and seller can assign/sell their interest in the investment contract to third parties.

The Convertible Lease-Option Contract

This proposed mortgage alternative has the following characteristics: (1) information neutrality; (2) tenure neutrality; (3) location neutrality; (4) default neutrality—the buyer's default is not tied to the foreclosure process, but rather is tied to both the savings/investment market and the property-values submarket; (5) wealth neutrality; (6) renegotiation-proofing—see explanation earlier; (7) sequential nonredundancy; (8) cumulative nonseparability; (9) decreasing recursion; (10) nonadditive aggregate rationality; (11) time-preference neutrality; (12) limited manipulation; (13) continuous payoffs; (14) preference matching; (15) low ambiguity; (16) participant substitutability; (17) transmission-positive consistency; (18) reserve neutrality; (19) automation efficiency; (20) decreasing monotonicity; (21) self-insurance or no mortgage insurance; (22) participation constraints; (23) strategic complementarity and supermodularity; (24) non-nullity; (25) asset-liability balance; (26) regret positivity; and (27) bankruptcy efficiency.

The buyer purchases a property (with specific features) with a long-term installment sales contract (loan) from the seller. The conveyance is not recorded until the loan is paid in full. The seller-lender retains title to the property until the loan is paid in full; but the buyer retains an increasing ownership interest in only the installment sales contract (not in the underlying property) until the loan is paid off. The subject property can be one of many that are owned by the lender in a region (or a country)—but the lender will typically present several properties for the buyer to choose from, and the buyer can switch properties for a fixed number of times during the life of the loan without selling/buying property. The buyer has full lessee rights while making monthly loan payments, and may or may not pay for property insurance and property taxes. The contract will contain summary eviction and/or nonjudicial eviction clauses as remedies for any nonpayment by the borrower-lessee that is not cured. The buyer and seller can assign/sell their interest in the installment sales contract to third parties. The buyer will have the option to elect to have the seller invest a portion of the buyer's monthly payments (*Y* percent) in one or more equity market indices. If the buyer-borrower defaults on the installment sales contract, or if the property is sold at any time (i.e., if the buyer cancels the installment sales loan contract), then the buyer will get at his or her option, only: (1) an equity interest in a selected housing unit or property (e.g., tenancy-in-common, joint tenancy, or joint venture) based on the buyer's monthly payments and equity in the installment sales contract; (2) the total return from the equity index or several equity indices, plus principal; or (3) the total return from a hypothetical investment in a money-market index or convertible bond index. The buyer-borrower also has the "look-back conversion option" to convert the installment sales contract into a lease agreement (effective from inception of the installment sales contract or from another agreed-on date)—on exercise of such conversion option, the buyer will get only a cash payment or stock index units calculated by assuming that the lender invested a fixed portion (*X* percent) of the buyer's monthly payments in a stock index or several stock indices and/or currency indices. *Y* percent and *X* percent will usually be different, and the greater the difference between *Y* percent and *X* percent, the greater the tenure neutrality of the installment sales contract. The lender can assign its interest in the installment contract to a third party. Thus, when three unrelated borrower-buyers default and they all have a common lender, the lender can assign its interests in one installment sales contract to two of the defaulters and essentially consolidate the defaulters at one property, and the other two properties will become free-and-clear without expensive foreclosures and auctions. This "exchange-of-interests" feature can be made a mandatory term in installment sales contracts; and may be suited to buyer-borrowers that are small families or individuals or retirees. The lender buys the subject property either before doing a transaction with the buyer-borrower or at the closing of the transaction. The implicit interest rate is a capped floating rate (which declines when interest rates fall), and thus, precludes inefficient costly refinancing associated with traditional fixed-rate and floating-rate mortgages. Also, the loan is not based on traditional consumer credit scoring, but rather is partly based on the buyer's assets, income, and payment history for the loan—hence, the lender will reduce the implicit interest rate for the loan if the buyer maintains a satisfactory payment history. The implicit interest rate for the installment sales contract declines as the buyer makes more monthly payments and makes more payments on time; and vice versa, with annual or biannual resets of the implicit interest rate.

The Combination Investment Contract

This proposed mortgage alternative has the following characteristics: (1) information neutrality; (2) tenure neutrality; (3) location neutrality; (4) default neutrality—the buyer's default is not tied to the foreclosure process, but rather is tied to both the savings/investment market and the property-values submarket; (5) wealth neutrality; (6) renegotiation-proofing; (7) sequential nonredundancy; (8) cumulative nonseparablility; (9) decreasing recursion; (10) decreasing opportunity cost; (11) nonadditive aggregate rationality; (12) time-preference neutrality; (13) limited manipulation; (14) continuous payoffs; (15) preference matching; (16) low ambiguity; (17) participant substitutability; (18) transmission-positive consistency; (19) reserve neutrality; (20) automation efficiency; (21) decreasing monotonicity;

(22) self-insurance or no mortgage insurance; (23) participation constraints; (24) strategic complementarity and supermodularity; (25) non-nullity; (26) asset-liability balance; and (27) regret-positivity.

The buyer signs an investment contract pursuant to which the buyer must make a fixed monthly investment payment to the sponsor/lender for a specific term (loan term). The investment contract grants the buyer the use of the property (residential unit or commercial property) during the term of the investment; and at the end of the term, the ownership of the property will revert to the buyer for a fee of $1. The lender buys the subject property either before doing a transaction with the buyer-borrower or at the closing of the transaction. The conveyance to the buyer is not recorded until the buyer makes all the required investment payments. The seller-lender retains title to the property until the all investment payments are paid in full. The buyer retains an increasing ownership interest in only the investment contract (but not in the underlying property) until the loan is paid off. The subject property can be one of many that is owned by the lender in a region (or a country)—but the lender will typically present several properties for the buyer to choose from, and the buyer can switch properties for a fixed number of times during the investment term without selling/buying property. The buyer has full lessee rights while making monthly investment payments, and does not pay for property insurance and property taxes. The investment contract will contain summary eviction and/or nonjudicial eviction clauses as remedies for any nonpayment by the borrower-lessee that is not cured. The buyer and seller can assign/sell their interest in the investment contract to third parties. The buyer has the option to "combine" his or her other free-and-clear assets (such as annuities, securities; other real estate; retirement accounts; pension payments) with the equity that he or she has in the investment contract, and transfer all such assets to the seller-lender, in exchange for any of the following: (1) stock index units for one index or several indices; (2) shares of specified ETFs (the seller-lender may change the specified ETFs every calendar quarter; (3) the subject property; or (4) a basket of government bonds. There will be an agreed-upon procedure for valuing the assets before the exchange. The implicit interest rate in the investment contract is similar to an equivalent installment sales contract and is a capped floating rate (which is capped at B percent, where B is 20 to 350 basis points above the then prevailing fixed mortgage rate), and thus precludes inefficient costly refinancing and speculation associated with traditional fixed-rate and floating-rate mortgages. Also, the investment contract is not based on traditional consumer credit scoring, but rather, is partly based on the buyer's assets, income, and payment history for the implicit loan—hence, the lender will reduce the implicit interest rate for the loan if the buyer maintains a satisfactory payment history (the implicit interest rate for the investment contract declines as the buyer makes more payments on time; and vice versa, with annual or biannual resets of the implicit interest rate). The combination investment contract is essentially a framing effect, where the buyer-borrower's and seller-lender's expectations are tied to equity markets, debt markets, and property-values markets; adverse speculation and the costs of default are substantially minimized.

The Annuity Upfront Contract

The buyer purchases a 20- to 40-year annuity contract, which grants the buyer the lessee rights to the property for the same term (the 20- to 40-year annuity contract will start on the date that buyer pays for the annuity contract in full). The seller-lender will have very limited right of inspection of the property. The purchase price must be paid with cash or other marketable assets or by an exchange of real estate, and not with the proceeds of any debt. The buyer does not pay directly for property insurance or property taxes (which are built into the annuity contract) but pays for maintenance and capital expenditures. The implicit interest rate for the annuity contract declines as the buyer makes more monthly payments and makes more payments on time; and vice versa, with annual resets (and thus changes in credit quality are asset-specific; and the contract considers the selective credit fulfillment bias). The implicit interest rate is a capped floating rate (which is capped at 20 to 300 basis points above the then prevailing fixed mortgage rates, and is reset annually or semiannually), and thus affects only the monthly cash payout to the buyer. The rationales for this product are: (1) the lender/seller is better positioned to hedge against price fluctuations and to manage debt than the buyer; (2) the transaction is perceived as an investment or asset-swap, rather than mortgage debt, and thus fosters a savings/investment habit; (3) economies of scale and operating efficiencies can be achieved by aggregating the costs of property insurance, property taxes, and property maintenance (co-ops and condominiums); (4) the contract substantially reduces credit risk and adverse foreclosure costs; (5) the transaction enables households to rebalance their portfolios without substantial exposure to housing markets; and (6) the buyer's balance sheet will not show any debt, but will show only an ownership interest in an annuity contract and a corresponding entry in the equity accounts. The annuity upfront contract is a frame, and is the sum of: (a) the present value of a series of monthly property payments (property insurance, property taxes, and mortgage payment); (b) the present value of an annuity that makes variable monthly payments; (c) the difference in current value and the terminal value of the underlying subject property; and (d) the difference between the current value of any property exchanged for the subject property, and the future value of that exchanged property.

This proposed mortgage alternative has the following characteristics: (1) information neutrality; (2) tenure neutrality; (3) location neutrality; (4) default neutrality—the buyer's default is not tied to the foreclosure process, but rather is tied to both the savings/investment market and the property-values submarket; (5) wealth neutrality; (6) renegotiation-proofing; (7) sequential nonredundancy; (8) cumulative nonseparability; (9) decreasing recursion; (10) decreasing opportunity cost; (11) nonadditive aggregate risk; (12) time-preference neutrality; (13) limited manipulation; (14) continuous payoffs; (15) preference matching; (16) low ambiguity; (17) substitutability; (18) participant substitutability; (19) transmission-positive consistency; (20) automation efficiency; (21) decreasing monotonicity; (22) self-insurance or no mortgage insurance; (23) participation constraints; (24) strategic complementarity and supermodularity; (25) non-nullity; (26) asset-liability balance; and (27) regret-positivity.

The Combined Services Contract

The buyer-borrower makes a down payment of 0 to 20 percent of the property value, but does not make any other loan payment during the contract term; the buyer-borrower (and his/her spouse) must: (1) maintain all bank accounts at the lender's offices; these bank accounts will be primarily savings accounts linked to debit cards, and will have an interest rate that is about 50 to 65 percent of the prevailing deposit account interest rates (the bank accounts will be subject to lower capital reserve requirements for nontransaction accounts); (2) conduct all financial services transactions through the lender; and (3) maintain all securities accounts and pension/retirement accounts at the lender's offices. The buyer-borrower and his/her spouse must have a minimum amount of retirement assets and verifiable annual income and securities. Thus, the buyer-borrower will not make any P&I payments, and will not pay for property insurance or property taxes. The combination of the following will more than offset the lender's perceived loss of P&I payments: (1) fees that the lender will earn from financial services transactions (i.e., brokerage fees, transaction fees, pension account management fees); (2) the reduced deposit interest rate; (3) the lower capital reserve requirement for non-transaction bank accounts will enable the bank to provide more loans and earn interest income; and (5) the resulting greater amount of deposits enables the bank to borrow more from the central bank discount window, and to increase its loan volume and interest income. Thus, the buyer-borrower builds imputed equity in the loan contract, but does not have any interest in the underlying property until the end of the loan term or cancelation of the contract or default, upon which the seller-lender will pay him or her only a 15- to 25-year annuity, whose present value is equal to the buyer-borrower's equity in the contract. The buyer-borrower can choose to prepay the loan (outstanding loan balance), at which time, the restriction on banking services will be terminated (i.e., the borrower can conduct financial services transactions anywhere). At the end of the loan term, or if the borrower prepays the loan, the buyer-borrower gets full title to the property. The seller retains title to the property until the loan is paid off, and the buyer retains an increasing ownership interest in only the contract (but not in the underlying property) until the loan is canceled or the contract expires. The buyer has full lessee rights and sublease rights. The buyer can assign/sell their interest in the contract to third parties only with the lender's permission. In some jurisdictions, the exchange of the buyer-borrower's interest in the contract for an annuity or interest in the underlying property will be deemed a tax-free exchange. The implicit interest rate is indexed to inflation, and the periodic payment amount is indexed to an index of wages. The implicit interest rate for the contract is a capped floating rate that declines as the buyer makes more imputed payments on time (i.e., as the buyer complies with the contract terms); and vice versa, with annual resets (replaces inefficient costly refinancing associated with traditional mortgages).

This mortgage alternative has the following characteristics: (1) information neutrality; (2) tenure neutrality; (3) location neutrality; (4) default neutrality—the buyer's default is not tied to the foreclosure process, but rather is tied to the savings/investment market; (5) wealth neutrality; 6) renegotiation-proofing; (7) sequential nonredundancy; (8) cumulative nonseparability; (9) decreasing recursion; (10) decreasing opportunity cost; (11) nonadditive aggregate risk; (12) time-preference neutrality; (13) limited manipulation; (14) continuous payoffs; (15) preference matching; (16) low ambiguity; (17) participant substitutability; (18) transmission-positive consistency; (19) reserve neutrality; (20) automation efficiency; (21) decreasing monotonicity; (22) self-insurance or no mortgage insurance; (23) participation constraints; (24) strategic complementarity and supermodularity; (25) non-nullity; (26) asset-liability balance; (27) regret-positivity; and (28) bankruptcy efficiency.

The Zero-Payment Market-Value Contract

The buyer-borrower makes a down payment of 10 to 20 percent of the property value, but does not make any other payment during the term of the contract. The property value at inception of the contract is pegged to a local/regional property price index. The lender holds title to the property until the borrower pays the outstanding balance or until the loan term expires. The lender's/mortgagee's usual return is the future value of the P&I

payments (with different compounding rates). However, the lender is often undercompensated by the usual interest rates (due to the costs of foreclosure and relative illiquidity of mortgages). Many borrowers don't hold mortgages until expiration, but rather sell the property. The borrowers who hold mortgages until expiration almost always obtain home-equity loans or reverse mortgages. Hence, a lender almost always has some interest in the property at all times. There will be annual or biannual "evaluation periods" when the property value is calculated based on the property index. At the end of each evaluation period, the property's value will be determined by reference to a local/regional property index, and if the property price appreciation during the evaluation period exceeds the sum of all loan payments (P&I, plus property tax and insurance payments), with compounding during the same period, then the borrower will not make any payments; if not, the deficiency is added to the "shadow mortgage balance." Thus, the borrower can prepay the loan at the end of each evaluation period by paying the shadow mortgage balance, which will typically be calculated as the future value of the initial mortgage balance plus all loan payments (P&I, plus property tax and insurance payments). At loan expiration or if the borrower cancels the loan or defaults, then: (1) the lender will issue a 15- to 25-year annuity to the borrower that has a present value equal to the excess, if any, of the market value added (MVA) of the property (measured with the property index) over the future value of the monthly loan payments (FVL) (P&I, plus property insurance and property tax payments), if any; or (2) the lender will make a one-time cash payment to the borrower that will be the excess, if any, of the MVA over the FVL. If the MVA is lower than the FVL, then the borrower will not get anything and either will be evicted through summary court proceedings or nonjudicial eviction or will become a regular tenant. The implicit interest rate will be a capped floating rate, which will be higher than the regular rate in order to compensate the lender for not receiving current cash payments. The lender will record the imputed interest payments as income.

This mortgage alternative has the following characteristics: (1) information neutrality; (2) tenure neutrality; (3) location neutrality; (4) default neutrality—the buyer's default is not tied to the foreclosure process, but rather is tied to the savings/investment market; (5) wealth neutrality; (6) renegotiation-proofing; (7) sequential nonredundancy; (8) cumulative nonseparability; (9) decreasing recursion; (10) decreasing opportunity cost; (11) nonadditive aggregate risk; (12) time-preference neutrality; (13) limited manipulation; (14) continuous payoffs; (15) preference matching; (16) low ambiguity; (17) participant substitutability; (18) transmission-positive consistency; (19) reserve neutrality; (20) automation efficiency; (21) decreasing monotonicity; (22) self-insurance or no mortgage insurance;

(23) participation constraints; (24) strategic complementarity and supermodularity; (25) non-nullity; (26) asset-liability balance; (27) regret-positivity; and (28) bankruptcy efficiency.

CONCLUSION

Despite the enactment of new statutes and other large-scale government interventions in many countries, the global financial crisis, the subprime mortgage crisis, and the numerous documented problems inherent in traditional mortgages (that are now prevalent in Europe, North and South America, Africa, and Asia) have shown that the adverse social, economic, and psychological costs of mortgages/foreclosures continue to increase with the growth of the Internet, automation, and cross-border trade/transactions. All the existing alternative-mortgage products have not solved these problems, and some products actually amplify the problems.

Although they have always been inefficient, traditional mortgages were sometimes erroneously justified by the instant gratification culture in many societies, and the perceived need to prevent or reduce crime and jealousy by enabling mortgage-financed homeownership. However, crime control and investigation methods have vastly improved during the past decade.

There is a substantial need for new mortgage alternatives that address the many dimensions and consequences of financing the purchase of real property—ranging from ineffective government policies (monetary and fiscal policies) to public health problems; behavioral biases of individuals and groups; emotional attachment to houses; association of perceived housing wealth with permanence of wealth; harmful speculation; inadequate household savings; inefficient household allocations and consumption; inaccurate property values; fraud and misconduct; mismatch of lifecycle needs of households; management of default; and so on. The mortgage alternatives introduced here address many of these issues, and more importantly, can help reduce or eliminate the psychological effects of property transactions, which are often not identified or managed properly.

NOTES

1. See the National Reverse Mortgage Lenders Association (U.S.).
2. In the U.S. Treasury-sponsored "HopeNow initiative," lenders were expected to stop adjustable-rate mortgages from increasing to higher rates at the first reset of the mortgage. The "Hope For Homeowners" program was enacted by the U.S. Congress in July of 2008, and its intent was to have lenders write off a substantial portion of the principal balance of mortgages for financially distressed

households. The Obama administration's "Making Home Affordable Program" of 2009 (which includes the "Home Affordable Modification Program") was created by the Financial Stability Act of 2009 and provided financial incentives to servicers/lenders to renegotiate loans and reduce the stated interest rate for a significant period of time. These government-sponsored mortgage modification programs implemented between 2007 and 2011 were aimed at the approximately 7 million U.S. households that were delinquent on their mortgages and the 11 million households that had underwater mortgages.

3. See Les Christie, "Foreclosure limbo: staying without paying," CNNMoney, June 12, 2011, http://money.cnn.com/2011/06/09/real_estate/foreclosure_squatter/index.htm.

REFERENCES

Abshire, P. 1965. Contracts un-conscionable installment sales contract: *Williams v Walker-Thomas Furniture Co.*, Civil No. 18,604, U.S. App. D.C. *American Business Law Journal* 3 (3): 348–349.

Agarwal, S., G. Amromin, I. Ben-David, S. Chomsisengphet, and D. D. Evanoff. 2011. The role of securitization in mortgage renegotiation. Federal Reserve Bank of Chicago Working Paper No. 2011-02. (March). Available at: http://ssrn.com/abstract=1739915.

Allen, F., and E. Carletti. 2008. Mark-to-market accounting and liquidity pricing. *Journal of Accounting and Economics* 45: 358–378.

Ambrose, B., and R. Buttimer. 2009. The adjustable balance mortgage: Reducing the value of the put. *Real Estate Economics*, forthcoming. Available at: www.business.uconn.edu/finance/seminars/papers/Ambrose_Buttimer_New_Mortgage_UConn.pdf.

An, X., D. Yongheng, and J. Clapp. 2010. Omitted mobility characteristics and property market dynamics: Application to mortgage termination. *Journal of Real Estate Finance and Economics* 41 (3): 245–271.

Anderson, S. 2010. Recent developments: Forthcoming changes in the Shari'ah compliance regime for Islamic finance. *Yale Journal of International Law* 35: 237–337.

Asutay, M. (2008). Islamic banking and finance: Social failure. *New Horizon* 169: 1–3. www.islamic-banking.com/resources/7/NewHorizon%20Previouse%20Issues/NewHorizon_OctDec08.pdf.

Azevedo-Pereira, A., D. P. Newton, and D. A. Paxson. 2003. Fixed-rate endowment mortgage and mortgage indemnity valuation. *Journal of Real Estate Finance & Economics* 26 (2–3): 197–221.

Bar-Gill, O. 2009. The law, economics and psychology of sub-prime mortgage contracts. *Cornell Law Review* 94: 1073–1093.

Baule, R., and C. Tallau. 2011. The pricing of path-dependent structured financial retail products: The case of bonus certificates. *Journal of Derivatives* 18 (4): 54–71.

Beck, T., Demirguc-Kunt, A., and Levine, R. 2006. Bank supervision and corruption in lending. *Journal of Monetary Economics*, 53 (8): 2131–2163.

Benet, A., A. Giannetti, and S. Pissaris. 2006. Gains from structured product markets: The case of reverse-exchangeable securities (RES). *Journal of Banking & Finance* 30: 111–132.

Bergemann, D., and J. Välimäki. 2002. Information acquisition and efficient mechanism design. *Econometrica* 70: 1007–1033.

Bergstresser, D. 2009. The retail market for structured notes: Issuance patterns and performance, 1995–2008. Working paper, Harvard Business School, Boston.

Bernard, C., and P. P. Boyle. 2011. A natural hedge for equity indexed annuities. *Annals of Actuarial Science*, forthcoming.

Besley, T., Coate, S., and G. Loury. 1993. The economics of rotating savings and credit associations. *American Economic Review* 83: 792–810.

Besley, T., S. Coate, and G. Loury. 1994. Rotating savings and credit associations, credit markets and efficiency. *Review of Economic Studies* 61: 701–719.

Bormuth, M. C. 1993. The Wyoming installment land contract: A mortgage in sheep's clothing—Or what you see isn't what you get—*Metropolitan Mortgage & (and) Securities Co. v. Belgarde. Land & Water Law Review* 28: 309–314.

Breuer, W., and A. Perst. 2007. Retail banking and behavioral financial engineering: The case of structured products. *Journal of Banking & Finance* 31 (3): 827–844.

Brobeck, S., and P. Woodall. 2006. How the real estate cartel harms consumers and how consumers can protect themselves. Consumer Federation of America. Available at: www.consumerfed.org/elements/www.consumerfed.org/file/housing/Real_Estate_Cartel_Study061906.pdf.

Buckley, R., B. Lipman, and T. Persaud. 1993. Mortgage design under inflation and real wage uncertainty: The use of a dual index instrument. *World Development* 21 (3): 455–464.

Carlin, B. I. 2009. Strategic price complexity in retail financial markets. *Journal of Financial Economics* 3 (91): 278–287.

Case, K., and R. Shiller. 1996. Mortgage default risk and real estate prices: The use of index based futures and options in real estate. *Journal of Housing Research* 7 (2): 243–250.

Chen, J., Z. Huang, and J. Liang. 2008. Innovation of finance: The application of reverse mortgage in China. *International Seminar on Business and Information Management* 1: 359–363.

Cheng, Y. 2010. China reverse mortgages. Available at: www.chinalegalchange.com.

Clauretie, T., and M. Jameson. Residential loan renegotiation: Theory and evidence. *Journal of Real Estate Research* 10 (2): 153–163.

Clemmer, S. 2007. Texas's attempt to mitigate the risks of contracts for deed—Too much for sellers—Too little for buyers. *St. Mary's Law Journal* 38 (3): 755–808.

Cocco, J. F. 2010. *Understanding the trade-offs of alternative mortgage products*. (May). Working paper, London Business School, UK. Available at: https://www.ifk-cfs.de/fileadmin/downloads/events/conferences/COCCO09092010.pdf.

Cohn, R., and S. Fischer. 1975. Alternative mortgage designs. Available at: www.bos.frb.org/ economic/conf/conf14/conf14d.pdf.

Conway, T. 1990. "Equitable adjustment" in real estate contract foreclosures: Victory for the contract vendee or death of installment land contract financing? *South Dakota Law Review* 35: 402–412.

Coogan, P. F. 1981. Is there a difference between a long-term lease and an installment sale of personal property? *NYU Law Review* 56: 1036–1046.

Couch, K., R. Mahalik, and R. Moore. 2001. Banks as real estate brokers—Letting free enterprise work. Southwest Economy—Federal Reserve Bank of Dallas. Available at: www.dallasfed.org/eyi/money/0108.html.

Dvorak, T. 2010. Financial literacy and the design of retirement plans. *Journal of Social Economics* 39 (6): 645–652.

Ebrahim, M. S. 2009. Can an Islamic model of housing finance cooperative elevate the economic status of the underprivileged? *Journal of Economic Behavior & Organization* 72 (3): 864–883.

Ebrahim, M. S., M. B. Shackleton, and R. M. Wojakowski. 2009. Participating mortgages and the efficiency of financial intermediation. *Journal of Banking & Finance* 35 (11): 3042–3054.

Edelberg, W. 2006. Risk-based pricing of interest rates for consumer loans. *Journal of Monetary Economics* 53 (8): 2283–2298.

Elsas, R., A. Hackethal, and M. Holzhäuser. 2010. The anatomy of bank diversification. *Journal of Banking & Finance* 34 (6): 1274–1287.

Erol, I., and K. Patel. 2005. Default risk of wage-indexed payment mortgage in Turkey. *Journal of Housing Economics* 14 (3): 271–293.

Evans, R. 2006. Mechanism design with renegotiation and costly messages. (March). Available at: www.econ.cam.ac.uk/faculty/evans/papers/costly-message/costly_messages.pdf.

Farooq, O. M. 2009. Comment on: Masudul Alam Choudhury, Islamic critique and alternative to financial engineering issues. *JKAU: Islamic Economics* 22 (2): 259–266. www.kau.edu.sa/Files/320/Researches/57081_27354.pdf.

Fei, P., and D. Yongheng. 2011. Housing finance in China. In *China's housing reform and outcomes*, ed. Joyce Y. Man. Cambridge, MA: Lincoln Institute of Land Policy.

Fei, P., and D. Yongheng. 2008. Emerging mortgage markets in China. In *Mortgage markets worldwide*, ed. D. Ben-Shahar, C. Leung, and S. E. Ong. Hoboken, NJ: Wiley-Blackwell.

Feldstein, M. 2009. How to save an "underwater" mortgage. *Wall Street Journal*, August 7.

Feng, G., and S. Apostolos. 2010. Efficiency, technical change, and returns to scale in large US banks: Panel data evidence from an output distance function satisfying theoretical regularity. *Journal of Banking & Finance* 34 (1): 127–138.

Ferrell, A., J. E. Bethel, and G. Hu. 2008. Legal and economic issues in litigation arising from the 2007–2008 credit crisis. Harvard Law and Economics Discussion Paper No. 612; ch. 5 in *Prudent lending restored: Securitization after the mortgage meltdown*, ed. Y. Fuchita, R. Herring, and Robert Litan, 163–235. Washington, DC: Brookings Institution Press; Harvard Law and Economics Discussion Paper No. 612; Harvard Law School Program on Risk Regulation Research Paper No. 08-5. Available at: http://ssrn.com/abstract=1096582.

Fisher, L. 2004. Renegotiation in the common law mortgage and the impact of equitable redemption. MIT Center for Real Estate, Massachusetts Institute of Technology, Cambridge, MA. http://web.mit.edu/cre/research/papers/wp87fisher.pdf.

Freyfogle, E. 1987. The installment land contract as lease: Habitability protections and the low-income purchaser. *New York University Law Review* 62: 293–310.

Grünbichler, A., and H. Wohlwend. 2005. The valuation of structured products: Empirical findings for the Swiss market. *Financial Markets and Portfolio Management* 19 (4): 361–380.

Hart, O., and J. Moore. 1998. Cooperatives vs. outside ownership. Working Paper 6421, National Bureau of Economic Research, Cambridge, MA.

Henderson, B. J., and N. D. Pearson. 2011. The dark side of financial innovation: A case study of the pricing of a retail financial product. *Journal of Financial Economics* 100 (2): 227–247.

Horwicz, L., and S. Reiter. 2006. *Design of Mechanisms*. Cambridge, UK: Cambridge University Press.

Hughes, J. P., W. Lang, L. J. Mester, and C. Moon. 1996. Efficient banking under interstate branching. *Journal of Money, Credit & Banking* 28 (4): 1045–1071.

Hughes, J. P., J. M. Loretta, and C. Moon. 2001. Are scale economies in banking elusive or illusive? Evidence obtained by incorporating capital structure and risk-taking into models of bank production. *Journal of Banking & Finance* 25 (12): 2169–2208.

Kalayci, E., and U. Basdas. 2010. Does the prospect theory also hold for power traders? Empirical evidence from a Swiss energy company. *Review of Financial Economics* 19 (1): 38–45.

Klein, P. G., and M. R. Saidenberg. 2010. Organizational structure and the diversification discount: Evidence from commercial banking. *Journal of Industrial Economics* 58 (1): 127–155.

Krainer, J., and M. H. Marquis. 2004. Mortgages as recursive contracts. Working paper, Federal Reserve Bank of San Francisco.

LaCour-Little, M., and J. Yang. 2010. Pay me now or pay me later: Alternative mortgage products and the mortgage crisis. *Real Estate Economics* 38 (4): 687–732.

Lea, M. 2010a. *Alternative forms of mortgage finance: What can we learn from other countries?* Paper prepared for the Harvard Joint Center for Housing Studies National Symposium "Moving Forward: The Future of Consumer Credit and Mortgage Finance"; Harvard Business School, February 18, 2010; revised April 14, 2010. Available at: www-rohan.sdsu.edu/~realest/images/Harvard-Lea.pdf.

Lea, M. 2010b. *International comparison of mortgage product offerings*. Research Institute for Housing America (RIHA) and Mortgage Banker's Association (U.S.). Available at: www.housingamerica.org/RIHA/RIHA/Publications/74023_10122_Research_RIHA_Lea_Report.pdf.

Liu, B., and M. Skully. 2008. The impact of securitisation and structural changes of the Australian mortgage markets on bank pricing behaviour. *International Journal of Banking, Accounting and Finance* 1 (2): 149–167.

Magri, S., and R. Pico. 2011. The rise of risk-based pricing of mortgage interest rates in Italy. *Journal of Banking & Finance* 35 (5): 1277–1290.

Mattos, F., P. Garcia, and J. Pennings. 2008. Probability weighting and loss aversion in futures hedging. *Journal of Financial Markets* 11 (4): 433–452.

Milo, M. J. 2004. Retention of title in European business transactions. *Washburn Law Journal* 43: 1231–1241.

Mixon, J. 1970. Installment land contracts: A study of low income transactions, with proposals for reform and a new program to provide home ownership in the inner city. *Housing Law Review* 7: 523–619.

Moringiello, J. M. 1996. A mortgage by any other name: A plea for the uniform treatment of installment land contracts and mortgages under the bankruptcy code. *Dickinson Law Review* 100, no. 4 (January): 733–743.

Setzer, G. 2008. Foreclosures cost lenders, homeowners, the community big bucks. Mortgage News Daily, June 2. Available at: www.mortgagenewsdaily.com/622008_Foreclosure_Costs.asp.

Nadel, M. S. 2007. A critical assessment of the traditional residential real estate broker commission rate structure (Abridged). *Cornell Real Estate Review* 5: 26–30. www.realestate.cornell.edu/crer/images/uploads/article/abridged_RateStructure_Nadel.pdf.

Neeman, Z., and G. Pavlov. 2009. Renegotiation-proof mechanism design. Available at: http://economics.uwo.ca/faculty/pavlov/workingpapers/renegotiation.pdf.

Nejadmalayeri, A. 2011. Wages, inflation, and mortgage design. *Journal of Economics and Business* 63 (5): 503–516.

Noldeke, G., and K. M. Schmidt. 1998. Sequential investments and options to own. *The RAND Journal of Economics* 29 (4): 633–653.

Nwogugu, M. 2005. Towards multifactor models of decision making and risk: Critique of prospect theory and related approaches, part one. *Journal of Risk Finance* 6 (2): 150–162.

Nwogugu, M. 2006a. A further critique of cumulative prospect theory and related approaches. *Applied Mathematics & Computation* 179 (2): 451–465.

Nwogugu, M. 2006b. Regret minimization, willingness-to-accept-losses and framing. *Applied Mathematics & Computation* 179 (2): 440–450.

Nwogugu, M. 2007. Issues in disintermediation in the real estate brokerage industry. *Applied Mathematics & Computation* 186 (2): 1054–1064.

Nwogugu, M. 2008. Some antitrust problems and related economic issues in real estate brokerage, professional licensing for real estate websites and rent-control/rent-stabilization. *Corporate Ownership & Control* 6 (1): 398–403.

Nwogugu, M. 2009. *Goodwill/Intangibles Rules, Earnings Management and Competition*. http://ssrn.com/abstract=1068123.

Olszowy, A. 2006. Alternative mortgages: Managed risk or gamble? *Federal Reserve Bank of Boston—Communities & Banking*, 3–5.

Palmeri, C. 2008. The painful cost of foreclosure. *Business Week*, May 8. www.businessweek.com/the_thread/hotproperty/archives/2008/05/the_painful_cost_of_foreclosure.html.

Piskorski, T., and A. Tchistyi. 2010. Optimal mortgage design. *Review of Financial Studies* 23 (8): 3098–3140.

Raeva, D., L. Mittone, and J. Schwarzbach. 2010. Regret now, take it now: On the role of experienced regret on intertemporal choice. *Journal of Economic Psychology* 31 (4): 634–642.

Renaud, B. M. 2009. Mortgage finance in emerging markets: Constraints and feasible development paths. In *Mortgage Markets Worldwide*, ed. D. Ben-Shahar, C. Leung, and S. Ong. Hoboken, NJ: Wiley-Blackwell.

Rossetto, S., and J. Van Bommel. 2009. Endless leverage certificates. *Journal of Banking & Finance* 33 (8): 1543–1553.

Rossi, C. 2010. *Anatomy of risk management practices in the mortgage industry: Lessons for the future*. Research Institute for Housing America (RIHA). (May) Available at: www.housingamerica.org/RIHA/RIHA/Publications/72939_9946_Research_RIHA_Rossi_Report.pdf.

Rubinstein, A., and A. Wolinsky. 1992. Renegotiation-proof implementation and time preferences. *American Economic Review* 82: 600–614.

Salter, S., K. Johnson, and J. Webb. 2007. Theory of the real estate brokerage firm: A portfolio approach. *Journal of Real Estate Portfolio Management* 13 (2): 129–135.

Shiller, R. 2009. Policies to deal with the implosion in the mortgage market. *The Berkeley Electronic (B.E.) Journal of Economic Analysis and Public Policy* 9 (3), Article 4. Available at: www.bepress.com/bejeap/vol9/iss3/art4.

Shiller, R., R. Wojakowski, M. S. Ebrahim, and M. Shackleton. 2011. Continuous workout mortgages. Cowles Foundation Discussion Paper No. 1794, Yale University. Available at: http://cowles.econ.yale.edu/P/cd/d17b/d1794.pdf.

Standard & Poor's. 2011. Residential mortgage servicing standards: A cost-benefit analysis. www.standardandpoors.com/ratings/articles/en/us/?assetid=124530111714.

Stoimenov, P. A., and S. Wilkens. 2005. Are structured products "fairly" priced? An analysis of the German market for equity-linked instruments. *Journal of Banking & Finance* 29: 2971–2993.

Sundaresan, S., and R. Anderson. 1996. Design and valuation of debt contracts. *Review of Financial Studies* 9 (1): 37–68.

Sundaresan, S., and F. Zapatero. 1999. Valuation, optimal asset allocation and retirement incentives of pension plans. *Review of Financial Studies* 12 (4): 835–872.

Talley, E. L. 1994. Note: Contract renegotiation, mechanism design, and the liquidated damages rule. *Stanford Law Review* 46: 1195–1205.

Wagner, W. 2010. Diversification at financial institutions and systemic crises. *Journal of Financial Intermediation* 19 (3): 373–386.

Way, H. K. 2009. Informal homeownership in the United States and the law. *St. Louis University Public Law Review* 29 (1): 113–123.

Weber, B., A. Aholt, C. Neuhaus, P. Trautner, C. Elger, and T. Teichert. 2007. Neural evidence for reference-dependence in real-market-transactions. *NeuroImage* 35 (1): 441–447.

Wheelock, D., and P. Wilson. 2009. Are U.S. banks too large? Working Paper 2009-054-A, Federal Reserve Bank of St. Louis Research Division.

Whitman, D. 2009. Installment land contracts: Pitfalls and cautions. Working paper. Available at: http://files.ali-aba.org/thumbs/datastorage/skoob/articles/BKAC0903_Tab10-Whitman_thumb.pdf.

Yongheng, D. 2010. State of the commercial real estate market in China. *PREA Quarterly* (Winter).

Yongheng, D., R. Morck, J. Wu, and B. Yeung. 2011. Monetary and fiscal stimuli, ownership structure and China's housing market. Working paper, March. Available at: http://ssrn.com/abstract=1775363.

Yongheng, D., J. Wu, and J. Gyourko. 2010. Just how risky are China's housing markets? VOX, July 28. Available at: www.voxeu.org/index.php?q=node/5353.

Zhizhong, W. 2009. On the defects of the stipulation relevant to installment sale in China contract law. *Wuhan University Journal (Philosophy & Social Sciences)* 3.

CHAPTER 16

Conclusion

The principles introduced here can be applied to many countries. U.S. laws are similar to those of commonwealth countries, and many countries have recently enacted statutes/regulations that are similar to, or based on, U.S. commercial laws, securities laws, and constitutional laws. This "transplanting" of statutes creates systemic risk when statutes are inefficient, costly, or disruptive.

The foregoing constitutional torts and their economic effects render many economic models inaccurate and moot (Persson and Tabellini 2004; Myerson 2000; Wadhwa, Belton, Chang, Mackie, and Marrese 2010; Blume, Müller, Voigt, and Wolf 2009; Conant 2008; Beaulier 2009; Bhattarai 2010; Brunet 2007; Backhaus 2001; Blankart and Koester 2007). Many types of economic models are based on specific assumptions about mortgage choice, housing choice, reasons for strategic default and foreclosure, lender's recourse and risk management procedures, government responses to systemic risk, and so on. However, the background and nature of these decisions/choices (within the context of constitutional torts) were not made clear in most empirical studies.

Subprime mortgages, elements of some mortgage statutes, foreclosure, real estate investment trusts (REITs), asset securitization, and anti-deficiency judgment statute laws are unconstitutional, create rights of action for constitutional tort claims, and affect market psychology and the behavior of market participants. Under U.S. laws, the two main forms of real estate title systems (recording and Registration/Torrens) are unconstitutional. Such unconstitutionality has significant economic ramifications for property owners, title insurance companies, governments, regulators, and lawyers, and has not been sufficiently addressed in the literature. The validity of title systems significantly affects housing tenure, housing choice, property values, rates of strategic defaults, propensity to renegotiate mortgages/leases, and the cost of title insurance. Thus, the propensity to sell, the propensity to buy, holdouts, shirking, contract performance, adverse selection, risk aversion, willingness to accept losses, and agency problems in real estate markets are influenced by legal factors. These factors have not been reflected in most housing-demand and housing-price forecasting models. The aforementioned unconstitutionality of elements of mortgages, land titles, REITs, and foreclosure process compounds the errors in underlying assumptions of most economic models that are used to forecast elements of the real estate, mortgage, and REIT markets. Ghent, Kudlyak, and Slivinski (2009); Hendershott and Weicher (2002); and Blume, Müller, Voigt, and Wolf (2009) explain how some of the assumptions are wrong.

Within the context of banking and financial services, preemption and federalism are closely related concepts. In countries that have nonhomogenous populations, there can be optimal amounts of federalism, but in most instances, limited federalism of the type that exists in the United States can be costly, and was one of the major causes of the subprime crisis of 2007 to 2010, and the failure of the U.S. government's bailout programs. The inability of many central banks worldwide to effect lasting change in their respective economies during the global financial crises of 2007 to 2010 can be partly attributed to a combination of federalism and the fragmentation of banking processes in the mortgage sector. Clearly, although many countries have copied the U.S. Constitution (e.g., Brazil), the U.S. Constitution lags woefully behind the constitutions of many U.S. states, which have been amended/updated to suit modern transactions and ways of life. But unfortunately, such changes remain restricted to each individual state. Both the U.S. Constitution and the state constitutions are somewhat limited in scope given the increasing complexity of daily life and transactions. Most national and state constitutions use "traditional" tests of unconstitutionality, which often do not consider the risks inherent in transactions, assets, agreements, and relationships (the analysis of constitutionality above was based on "traditional" tests of unconstitutionality; the same results will be obtained in the proposed risk-based tests described here instead). Hence, in constitutional law analysis, there is a substantial need to revise the definitions of property interests and develop and implement risk-based tests for unconstitutionality of statutes or government relationships. It is quite clear that the past and current regulatory regimes for risk management (as it pertains to mortgages, foreclosure processes, and title systems) in both developed countries and developing countries did not and do not incorporate constitutional analysis.

The REIT as used in the United States and the associated federal laws are unconstitutional—they constitute violations of the Contract Clause, the Equal Protection Clause, the Interstate Commerce Clause, and the Free Speech Clause. New laws are required to define rights and obligations of all parties involved in the formation and operation of REITs. Since most

REIT statutes in other countries are based on and similar to U.S. REITs, it is likely that these foreign REIT statutes are also unconstitutional (especially in common law countries). The unconstitutionality of REITs may result in the decline or collapse of REIT stock markets where such status is acknowledged by the government or by market participants—so far this has not been the case. The possible responses by governments to general acknowledgement of the unconstitutionality of REITs include: (1) redrafting REIT statutes; (2) enacting emergency legislation that will automatically convert REITs to common trusts or ordinary limited liability companies (e.g., C corporations or LLCs in the United States); and (3) dissolving REITs and liquidating their assets (a less likely alternative).

REFERENCES

Backhaus, J. 2001. Economic principles of constitutions: An economic analysis of constitutional law. Indpendent Institute Working Paper #40. Available at: http://www.independent.org/pdf/working_papers/40_economic.pdf.

Beaulier, S. 2009. Book review: The Constitution and economic regulation: Objective theory and critical commentary. *Law & Politics Book Review* 19 (5): 324–325.

Bhattarai, K. 2010. Constitution and economic models for the Federal Republic of Nepal. *Economic Journal of Nepal* 33 (1): 1–15.

Blankart, C., and G. Koester. 2007. The economic analysis of constitutions: Fatalism versus vitalism. *Economic Journal Watch* 4 (2): 169–183.

Blume, L., J. Müller, S. Voigt, and C. Wolf. 2009. The economic effects of constitutions: Replicating—and extending—Persson and Tabellini. *Public Choice* 139: 197–225.

Brunet, F. 2007. The European economic constitution: An analysis of the constitutional treaty. Working paper prepared for the First Annual Research Conference of the European Union Centre of Excellence. Available at: http://euce.dal.ca/Files/Paper_first_confer/ferranbrunet.pdf.

Conant, M. 2008. *The Constitution and economic regulation: Objective theory and critical commentary*. Piscataway, NJ: Transaction Publishers.

Ghent, A. C., M. Kudlyak, and S. Slivinski. 2009. Deterring default: Why some state laws decrease the probability of mortgage foreclosures. Richmond Fed Economic Brief, Federal Reserve Bank of Richmond. EB09-09. Available at: http://www.richmondfed.org/publications/research/economic_brief/2009/pdf/eb_09-09.pdf.

Hendershott, P., and J. C. Weicher. 2002. Forecasting housing markets: Lessons learned. *Real Estate Economics* 30 (1): 1–11.

Myerson, R. 2000. Review: Economic analysis of constitutions. *University of Chicago Law Review* 67 (3): 925–940.

Persson, T., and G. Tabellini. 2004. Constitution and economic policy. *Journal of Economic Perspectives* 18 (1): 75–98.

Wadhwa, P., T. Belton, J. Chang, D. Mackie, and M. Marrese. 2010. European rates strategy: The European stabilization mechanism. J. P. Morgan. Available at: https://mm.jpmorgan.com/stp/t/c.do?i=E0271-555&u=a_p*d_414788.pdf*h_ajfko049.

Wilks, S. 2009. The impact of the recession on competition policy: Amending the economic constitution? *International Journal of Economics & Business* 16 (3): 269–288.

About the Author

Michael C. I. Nwogugu is a management consultant based in New Jersey, United States. Mr. Nwogugu is also affiliated with an energy- and waste-management company, and a start-up Internet/entertainment company. Mr. Nwogugu has been a cofounder and chairman of several new ventures (now dormant) in technology/Internet and health-care sectors. Mr. Nwogugu has also worked in real estate (portfolio management and management consulting). Mr. Nwogugu has been an article reviewer for the *European Journal of Operations Research* and the *American Statistician*. Mr. Nwogugu has written and published articles on real estate, Constitutional Economics, Mechanism Design, Law & Economics, Corporate Governance and Risk Finance, in internationally referred journals such as *Managerial Auditing Journal; International Company and Commercial Law Review; Journal of Hedge Funds & Derivatives; Applied Mathematics and Computation; Journal of International Banking Law & Regulation; Computer and Telecommunications Law Review*; *Journal of Risk Finance; Corporate Control & Ownership; International Journal of Mathematics, Game Theory and Algebra*; and *Chaos and Complexity Letters*. Mr. Nwogugu earned a BSc (Architecture) degree from University of Nigeria (Nigeria), a BA (Architecture) degree from the City University of New York (New York, New York, United States), and an MBA degree from Columbia University (New York, United States). Mr. Nwogugu also attended Suffolk University Law School (Boston, Massachusetts, United States). Mr. Nwogugu is a Certified Management Accountant (IMA) and was a Certified Public Accountant (U.S.).

Index